The Mists of Rāmañña

Published with the support of the School of Hawaiian, Asian, and Pacific Studies, University of Hawai‘i

The Mists of Rāmañña

The Legend That Was Lower Burma

Michael A. Aung-Thwin

University of Hawai'i Press
Honolulu

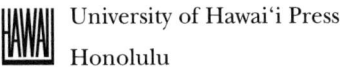

Printed in the United States of America
10 09 08 07 06 05 6 5 4 3 2 1

Library of Congress Cataloging-in-Publication Data

Aung-Thwin, Michael.
The mists of Rāmañña : the legend that was lower Burma / Michael A. Aung-Thwin.
p. cm.
Includes bibliographical references and index.
ISBN 0-8248-2886-0 (hardcover : alk. paper)
1. Burma—History—To 1824. 2. Burma—Historiography. 3. Legends—Burma. I. Title.
DS529.2.A86 2005
959.1—dc22

2004029695

University of Hawai'i Press books are printed on acid-free paper and meet the guidelines for permanence and durability of the Council on Library Resources.

Designed by University of Hawai'i Press production staff

Printed by The Maple-Vail Book Manufacturing Group

To my father, a Mon

Contents

Preface and Acknowledgments ix

1 Introduction 1

2 The Pyū Millennium 13

3 Rāmaññadesa, an Imagined Polity 43

4 Thatôn (Sudhuim), an Imagined Center 79

5 The Conquest of Thatôn, an Imagined Event 104

6 The Conquest of Thatôn as Allegory 119

7 The Mon Paradigm and the Origins of the Burma Script 154

8 The Place of Written Burmese and Mon in Burma's Early History 179

9 The Mon Paradigm and the Evolution of the Pagán Temple 201

10 The Mon Paradigm and the Kyanzittha Legend 236

11 The Mon Paradigm and the Myth of the "Downtrodden Talaing" 261

12 Colonial Officials and Colonial Scholars: The Institutionalization of the Mon Paradigm 281

13 Without the Mon Paradigm 299

Notes 323
Bibliography 403
Index 425

Preface and Acknowledgments

In October 1999 the Royal Netherlands Academy of Sciences, in cooperation with the International Institute of Asian Studies and the Research School of Asian, African and Amerindian Studies, sponsored a colloquium on "Coastal Burma in the Age of Commerce" in Amsterdam. Invited to present a paper, I submitted "Lower Burma and Bago in the History of Burma," an essay subsequently published in 2002 in *The Maritime Frontier of Burma: Exploring Political, Cultural and Commercial Interaction in the Indian Ocean World, 1200–1800.*

When I began the paper, I accepted the conventional wisdom of what I subsequently called the "Mon Paradigm." This thesis, which has been in place for well over a hundred years, asserts that Mon Lower Burma civilized Burman Upper Burma during the most important era of its history, the "classical" period when the kingdom of Pagán emerged to found the "golden age" of Burmese culture. (By Burmese, here and throughout the book, I mean the cultural group, while I use Burman to refer to the ethnolinguistic group.) But as I began my research, I soon realized that the existing primary evidence simply did not support the conventional view, and more recent scientific data only confirmed my initial reaction. This led me to reexamine the Mon Paradigm more thoroughly, and my early, tentative results became a small part of my article for the Amsterdam colloquium. Later I developed that part into a more detailed paper called "The Legend That Was Lower Burma" that I delivered at a conference on "Text and Context in Southeast Asia," held at Yangôn in December 2001.

Professionally and personally I had wanted to test my challenge of this sacrosanct thesis before my Burmese colleagues, many of Mon background, who knew the indigenous languages and had an intimate knowledge of the country's history. The participants included some of the best Burma scholars from the country and abroad, along with many other Southeast Asian specialists from Europe, Asia, and North America. The paper intrigued the

Burma scholarly community, inspiring the Burma Historical Commission to initiate a project designed specifically to investigate my thesis further.

As of this writing I have not heard from the Commission regarding its findings, but I would be very surprised if it discovered anything substantially new to contradict my study because the evidence supporting it has been available for some time and is, quite frankly, overwhelming. Indeed, the problem is not the evidence per se but its interpretation. For the past 125 years, analysis of early Burma has almost always occurred within the framework of the Mon Paradigm, invariably producing the same conclusions.

In this long process of disentangling more than a century of convention, I have incurred many debts of gratitude. First, I wish to acknowledge the role played by the creators of the Amsterdam colloquium, particularly Jos Gommans and Jacques Leder. Without their invitation, I would probably be working on something else entirely, and the Mon Paradigm might have been perpetuated for several more generations. In the same spirit, I would like to thank Daw Ni Ni Myint, historian of Burma and, at the time, director of the Universities Historical Research Centre, which hosted the Burma conference, for giving me the opportunity to present my thesis in what (to me) was a most challenging academic environment.

I also owe many thanks to my former student Sun Laichen, now assistant professor at the University of California at Fullerton, for translating a crucial Chinese document and providing me with his expertise regarding Chinese sources on Burma in general. In regard to Chinese sources, I also thank Geoff Wade from the University of Hong Kong, currently spending some time at the National University of Singapore. My longtime mentor and supporter Kris Lehman, of the University of Illinois, was, as he has always been, unstinting in his valuable feedback. Professor U Saw Tun of Northern Illinois University also answered questions regarding obscure or difficult Burmese meanings that only a very few experts like him can elucidate. Another such expert, John Okell, taught me Old Burmese at London University's School of Oriental and African Studies and continues to help whenever I ask. Professor Victor Lieberman, a Burma colleague from the University of Michigan, generously sent me important unpublished sources from his private collection which helped confirm my conclusions and pushed my analysis that much farther; he also provided me with his usual gracious and helpful comments. John Whitmore, a friend and mentor for more than twenty years since he chaired my dissertation committee, who always has time for his students, offered thoughtful constructive criticism that invariably placed the study in a broader Southeast Asia framework. I also benefited appreciably from discussions with Burma scholars U Myint Aung, U Nyein Lwin, Elizabeth Moore, Bob Hudson, and Pamela Gutman, who have done, or are currently doing exciting new work on the period before Pagán. To Ken Breazeale, historian of Thailand with the East-West Center here in Honolulu, I owe much with regard to information on Thai sources and other subjects that proved to be very helpful. I also wish to thank Professor Lily Handlin of Harvard University, noted American historian-turned-Pagán-art historian (having seen the light), for many things including her tough, close reading of the manuscript. To the staff at both Hamilton and Sinclair Libraries, University of Hawai'i, who obtained whatever I wanted via Interlibrary Loan, and particularly to Yati Barnard, Southeast Asia Librarian, for her tireless help, I owe much as well. Finally, I wish to express my appreciation to all my formal and informal graduate students at the University of Hawai'i and elsewhere (including my son, now a historian of colonial Burma with the National University of Singapore), all of whom listened politely and patiently to the "Mists of Rāmañña" whenever I managed to corral them instead of running away in terror.

I am not certain what my father, Moses Aung-Thwin, would have thought of all this, being Mon himself. But the little I know of him leads me to believe that he would have welcomed an iconoclastic study of this kind. And so it is to his memory that I dedicate this book.

1 Introduction

IN 1479, when King Dhammazedi of the kingdom of Pegu declared on his Kalyani Inscriptions[1] that the legendary Suvaṇṇabhūmi of Buddhist tradition was the Mon kingdom of Rāmaññadesa in Lower Burma,[2] he inadvertently created a twentieth-century historiographic issue that I have called the "legend that was Lower Burma,"[3] still with us today. Suvaṇṇabhūmi, "the land of gold," was, of course, the region to which the two most famous Buddhist missionaries, Soṇa and Uttara, were said to have gone from the Third Buddhist Council of Aśoka in the third century BC to propagate the faith, an event long celebrated as the introduction of Buddhism to Southeast Asia. This council was perceived by Theravāda Buddhists as the most orthodox of Buddhist councils, so the version of the scriptures the missionaries carried with them to Suvaṇṇabhūmi, and therefore also to Rāmaññadesa, was also considered the most orthodox. By thus linking Lower Burma with the sacred geography, sacred genealogy, and sacred chronology of Aśoka's Buddhist India, King Dhammazedi, in one stroke, gave Rāmaññadesa an antiquity, orthodoxy, and legitimacy it never had. Then for nearly four hundred years Dhammazedi's attempt to link Aśokan Buddhist India with Lower Burma and the legendary foundations of his own kingdom was all but forgotten in the historiography of the country.[4]

Two and a half centuries later, between 1712 and 1720, a private individual named U Kala wrote the most comprehensive chronicle of Burma's monarchy that has survived, the *Mahayazawingyi*. In it he recounted for the first time the most complete version of the now- famous story about the conquest of Thatôn by King Aniruddha of Pagán in 1057. It begins with Shin Arahan, the celebrated monk who was said to have come to Pagán in the mid-eleventh century and converted the king to the orthodox version of Theravāda Buddhism. Desiring to promote the religion, Aniruddha asked Shin Arahan how to proceed. Shin Arahan told the king that if he wished to establish the faith in Pagán—which at the time was said to be rampant with the Aris, a heterodox sect—he must have possession of the orthodox texts. To get them, the king should request a copy from the Mon King Manuha of Thatôn in Lower Burma, as he possessed many sets of the "pure" *Tipiṭakas.*

When Aniruddha approached Manuha with this request, he was rudely refused, so Aniruddha attacked and conquered Thatôn, taking back to Pagán not only the *Tipiṭakas,* on thirty-two white elephants, but also King Manuha, the royal family, and the country's entire population of 30,000, among whom were myriad artisans and craftsmen, learned clergy, and other people of letters. Upon his return to Pagán, Aniruddha placed the texts in the specially constructed Pitaka Taik (library), a building that still stands today.[5] Thereafter, the "true" religion shone radiant in his kingdom, and, lamented one late Mon chronicle, Pagán flourished "like unto a heavenly city."[6]

In the nineteenth century, over two hundred years after U Kala's account was written, Dhammazedi's fifteenth-century claim that ancient Suvaṇṇabhūmi was Rāmaññadesa and U Kala's eighteenth-century account of the conquest of Thatôn—two temporally, causally, and textually *unrelated* narratives—were combined for the first time by colonial scholarship and synthesized into a new theory: that the Mon Theravāda Buddhist culture of Lower Burma "civilized" Burman Upper Burma. This is the thesis that I call the Mon Paradigm.[7]

The historiographic and pedagogic implications of the Mon Paradigm are enormous. Because Pagán is considered to have been the "golden age" of Burma's culture and therefore also the foundations upon which the country's subsequent culture was built, the Mon Paradigm implies that the Mon people and the culture of Lower Burma were the ultimate origins not only of Pagán civilization, but also of Burma's culture in general. To the Mon of Lower Burma have been attributed Pagán's orthodox Buddhism of the Mahāvihāra school; its indigenous elements of the conceptual system (including even the Cult of the 37 Nats); its ideologies of leadership, legitimacy, and authority as reflected in the idealized organization at court;[8] its pantheon of patron-saints, including Upagupta, Maitreya, and Gavaṁpati; its writing system (hence, that of the entire country); its fine arts and crafts; its unique temple architecture; the immediate source for its literature; and even its irrigation technology.[9] All these, in turn, were said to have been implemented during a "Mon period" in the history of Pagán under the champion of Mon culture, King Kyanzittha, who almost single-handedly accomplished this "civilizing" process.[10]

As noted in the Preface, I accepted the Mon Paradigm when I began research on the role of Lower Burma in the Bay of Bengal. I had no intention of challenging the conventional view, and was, in fact, trying to *prove,* not *disprove,* the existence of Rāmañña. I had no inkling at the time that my research would lead me in the opposite direction. Yet the more data I gathered on Lower Burma before and during the Pagán period, the more I realized that something was amiss. There was just no primary evidence—that is, authentically dated contemporary and original material—to support the belief that a civilization—as defined both in the popular sense of the term and more strictly as urbanization—existed in Lower Burma during the first millennium AD.

Even more unsettling, I had not yet begun to look at any *new* evidence, only the old data that have been around for many years, much of it originally uncovered by the scholars of the Mon Paradigm. In fact, this entire book could have been written without the most recent evidence, the bulk of which is relevant mainly to the Pyū, whom I discuss in Chapter Two. In other words, the viability of the Mon Paradigm does not hinge on dramatic new evidence that I recently uncovered but on *old data* that scholars have long known about. This, then, is *not* an indictment of evidence but of methodology: of the way data have been assessed and used to conform to a preconceived theory.

Throughout the twentieth century, respected scholars of Burma, not a few of whom were of Mon cultural background or otherwise intimately connected to it, continued to perpetuate and expand the Paradigm.[11] It became the basis for virtually all scholarship on Pagán and early Burma, and has succeeded in dominating the study of early Burma for over a century. Its thesis also struck a responsive chord with other twentieth-century scholars of early Southeast Asia. In part this was because it involved the Mon people, who by then had become sentimental favorites. Colonial perception held the Mon to have been the oppressed victims of later-arriving, less civilized Khmer, T'ai, and Burmese speakers. These newcomers were thought to have conquered or otherwise integrated the Mon, absorbed their culture, and ignominiously ended their presumed great achievements at places such as Dvāravatī, which at that time had just been discovered. In the Mon-Burman situation especially, colonial scholars saw a replication of the Greek and Roman experience, in which the conquered had given their culture to the conquerors.

To be sure, there was at least one detractor among the few Mon specialists of the time. This was Pierre Dupont, an archaeologist and art historian whose research focused on Dvāravatī. He had serious doubts about at least one component of the Mon Paradigm: the alleged antiquity of Mon civilization in Lower Burma. Over half a century ago he suggested that the Mon of fifteenth-century Burma had probably recast their past "in a form that would bestow the dignity of age on their newly purified faith."[12] In part, his view was shaped by his research on Dvāravatī, whose Mon culture, he thought, preceded that of Lower Burma. But his assertion was more than academic self-interest. Dupont was not a Burma specialist, and as a result he was unencumbered by its intellectual baggage or the ethnic nationalism of the era. He could, therefore, assess the situation more objectively. Dupont had actually hit the nail on the head, but did not pursue his thoughts much further, for, as a nonspecialist of Burma, he did not have the language tool (Old Burmese) to do so and had other priorities in any case. Also, he was apparently reluctant to contradict those who did know Old Burmese, specialists in the field who were, by then, totally convinced of the correctness of their theory.

Thus, the Mon Paradigm continued unquestioned. Eventually, it became so dominant and pervasive, both as an intellectual idea and in the number of prominent scholars of early Burma who subscribed to it, that it not only fed upon itself, but consumed virtually everything else in its path in order to perpetuate itself.[13] Conflicting information was interpreted to fit, not to reexamine it, so that pertinent data were analyzed only within its framework of "truth." The following rationalization is representative of the kind of reaction by advocates of the Mon Paradigm when faced with evidence that contradicted it. "When we consider how important the Mons must have been in the civilising of the Mranmā, it is surprising how rarely they are mentioned in Old Burmese."[14] And such statements were used to *prove* not *disprove* its case. Even fictitious individuals and places (like Makuta and Rakṣapura), about which I will have much to say, emerged virtually from thin air to sustain the thesis.

The Mon Paradigm continued unabated despite the fact that throughout these same years new archaeological data suggested that another culture, an ethnolinguistic group of Tibeto-Burman speakers popularly known as the Pyū had been present earlier and found throughout much of the country for an entire millennium. They had been centered in Upper Burma, with settlements also in Lower Burma.[15] But the influence of the Mon Paradigm was so pervasive and dominant that scholars acknowledged this information in only the most perfunctory manner and continued as if the Pyū evidence had little or no bearing on their concerns. Part of the reason was probably their assumption that since Lower Burma "belonged" to the Mon, who were thought to have arrived earlier than the Pyū and subsequently overlapped with them, the Pyū (and later, Burmese speakers) must have been confined to Upper Burma. This produced an imaginary, ahistorical image (and map) of Burma as a land of discreet and absolute ethnic divisions that unfortunately became the basis for much scholarship (see Figure 1).[16]

By 1983, another non-Burma scholar, the late Paul Wheatley, renowned historical geographer of East and Southeast Asia, again raised doubts about

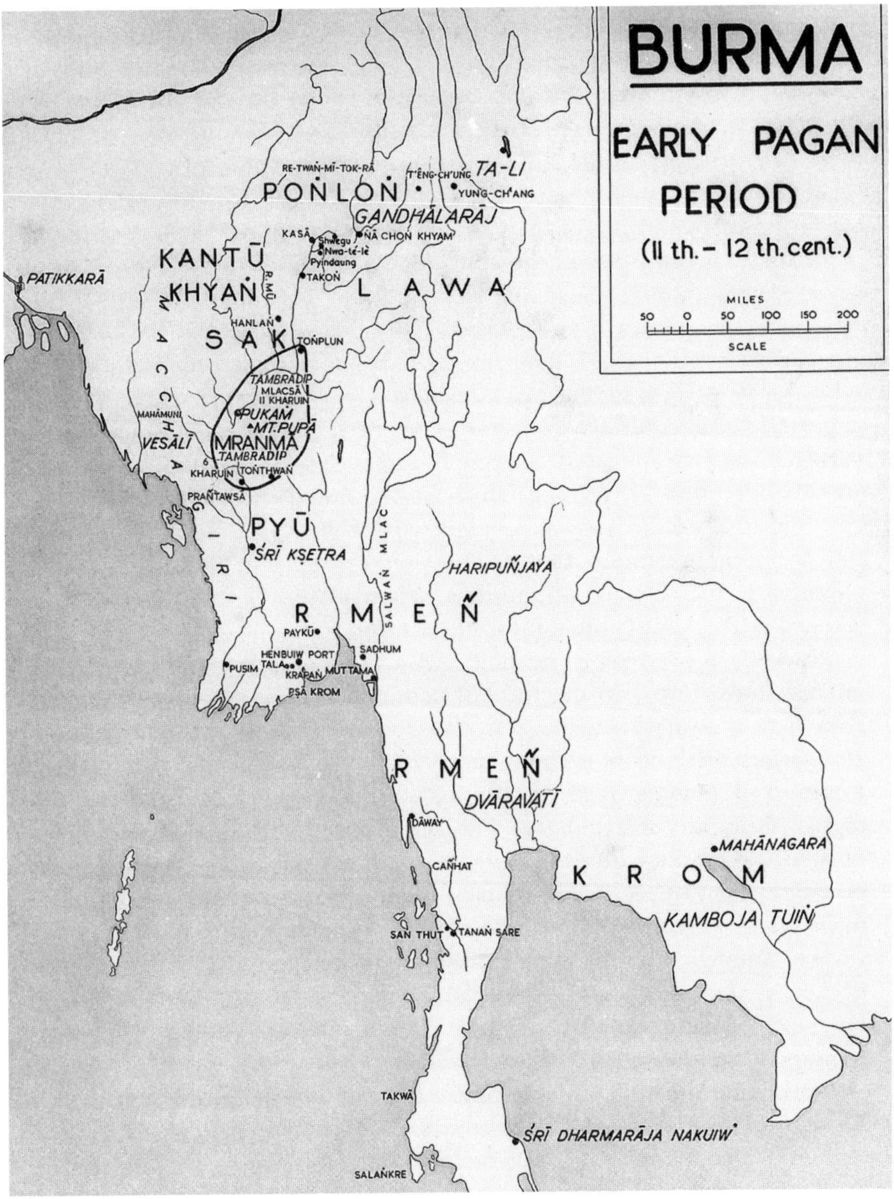

FIGURE 1: Conjectural Map of Ethnic Groups. *Source:* G. H. Luce, *Old Burma-Early Pagan* (New York, 1970).

the antiquity of Mon civilization in Lower Burma. After noting Dupont's observations of nearly thirty years before, he wrote that according to later traditions of both the Burmese and the Thai, and of the Mon themselves, "the hearth of Môn culture was situated in Lower Burma, particularly in the neighborhood of the cities of Thatôn and Pegu." But, he reasoned, had there been such a civilization, there should have been a rich harvest of related Buddhist materials and Mon remains at these avowed centers datable to the first centuries of the Christian era. Yet, he noted, "the opposite is the case." It is a paradox, he concluded, "which in the present state of knowledge cannot be resolved."[17]

But as this study will show, it was a "paradox" not because of "the present state of knowledge," but because the data already available at the time Wheatley wrote had never been considered *independently* of the Mon Paradigm. The issue could have been resolved then and there, but non-Burma scholars like Wheatley and Dupont found it difficult to push the subject any further when Burma specialists had accepted the Mon Paradigm so enthusiastically and more or less ignored or were unaware of what non-Burma specialists outside the country were saying. This lack of thoughtful attention to the research of outside scholars meant the unquestioned persistence of the Mon Paradigm for many more years.[18]

Indeed, as I have seen nothing in Burma scholarship either inside or outside the country during the last century that has contested the Mon Paradigm, it is very likely that it would have continued for at least another generation. The bulk of even the most recent research on early Burma continues to perpetuate it, demonstrating to me at least, that the Mon Paradigm is still alive and well and quite sacrosanct.[19] It has been difficult to challenge methodologically, not least because it has been entrenched for over a century, its arguments densely woven together, and its foundations buried in labyrinthine, subtle, and well-hidden tautologies extremely laborious to untangle. But it has been difficult to challenge conceptually as well, because several disciplines—from archaeology, history, and art history to epigraphy, paleography, and linguistics, not only of Burma but of other regions of Southeast Asia—have based their own works on it, giving the *impression* that the Mon Paradigm has a broad, interdisciplinary consensus. No matter what the data say, one always has to account for the presence of an early Rāmaññadesa in Lower Burma first.

The institutional barrier in Burma studies has not been easy to breach either, for a personalized, patron-client colonial and postcolonial academic structure has made it extremely difficult for those who might want to contest the conventional view. One has to be at a distance from that academic setting—that is, to be located outside Burma and England, physically as well as intellectually—in order to successfully challenge the Mon Paradigm without reproach; indeed, rewarded for doing so. But once these kinds of often "silent obstacles" had been overcome, all it really took to dispel the Mon Paradigm was a harder, closer look at the data already available, most of it the product of those very same scholars who had perpetrated the fiction in the first place. The positive reactions to my work that are beginning to come from both Burma and overseas scholars encourage me that the established ideology may at last be starting to crumble.[20]

Approach to the Problem

My initial approach to the discrepancy between evidence and conclusion was to offer alternate explanations for the evidence. But because I remained within the Mon Paradigm's theoretical framework, I arrived at the same results. The antiquity of Mon Rāmaññadesa—the ultimate basis for the Mon Paradigm—had *automatically* made every coin, votive tablet, Buddha statue, inscription, potsherd, or settlement site found in Lower Burma to be Mon and earlier. That has led to numerous other tautologies which accepted only the conclusions and evidence conforming to the cherished premise. Those that were contradictory were rationalized as "improbable," "unreliable," or as Luce remarked, "surprising." In other words, *premise and proof had become synonymous.*

It is, of course, understandable for a school of thought not to question its own premise. But that has also meant that those subscribing to the Mon Paradigm never asked some very basic questions. The situation is similar to the old myth that the Nanchao kingdom of Yunnan was T'ai.[21] This assertion remained unchallenged for many years simply because no one asked the most basic question that would have immediately helped resolve the issue: what language did the people of Nanchao speak? It turns out to be Lolo from the Tibeto-Burman, rather than T'ai from the Austro-T'ai family. No one asked those kinds of questions of the Mon Paradigm either, questions that would have challenged it at the outset.

So I decided to ask them, albeit over a century later. First, if a Mon kingdom in Lower Burma called Rāmaññadesa existed from before the first century of the Christian millennium onward—as the historiography has it—then why are the Rmeñ (Mon), as a distinct ethnolinguistic group, not mentioned in the country's original, contemporary sources until 1,100 years later? Second, why does the first evidence of a Lower Burma kingdom appear only 1,300 years later? And third, why does Rāmaññadesa and its putative center, Thatôn (Sadhuim), not materialize in original and contemporary domestic epigraphic sources until 1,400 years later? New evidence was not needed to ask these questions.

I therefore adopted a strategy of reexamining the evidence as if the

Mon Paradigm did not exist at all, that is, *independently* of those premises and assumptions, and hence outside its framework of analysis. To do this, I had to reassess the original evidence not only for evidentiary reliability, but, more important, to also remove it from the subtle influences of the nineteenth- and twentieth-century sociopolitical framework in which past and current generations of Burma scholars have worked.[22]

Specifically, I had to reexamine the primary sources in the original language, or in translation when I could not read the language. In terms of epigraphic material, I had to reread every Old Burmese and Old Mon inscription of the period, taking care to distinguish editorial interpolations that have sustained the Mon Paradigm from the original text itself.[23] I analyzed most of these inscriptions in their published versions, but on several occasions had to scrutinize the actual rubbing or photograph of the rubbing, particularly when I needed to reread crucial words in their original or near-original state. With manuscript material, I used the published versions also used by the Mon Paradigm, for the most part. I looked at the originals on microfilm in those cases where I needed to reassess them afresh for the same kinds of reasons that I needed to investigate their stone counterparts more closely. Only as a secondary effort have I reconsidered the factual basis of the evidence, because it became clear almost immediately that the evidence itself was not the main problem. With regard to archaeological data, I deliberately went back to the raw data and reports, rather than using the interpretive conclusions, for these invariably assumed the validity of the Mon Paradigm.

Essentially, then, I studied the same archaeological, epigraphic, chronicle, and, to a lesser extent, art historical, and numismatic evidence used by the Mon Paradigm, along with whatever new information carbon-14 and thermoluminescence dating provided. To reiterate, the crucial difference in my approach was not so much reassessing the *credibility* of the evidence as it was reexamining it *outside the analytical framework* of the Mon Paradigm. This meant, ultimately, *not assuming* a chronological or cultural relationship between the data found in Lower Burma and Mon speakers—the fundamental flaw of the Mon Paradigm.

Results of the Approach

Once I used the above approach, an entirely new picture with several different options sprang up almost immediately. Perhaps most important, I found that neither the Old Mon inscriptions nor the earliest Mon texts of Burma supported the Mon Paradigm. Indeed, as we shall see throughout this book, the history of the Mon in Lower Burma, as told by the Mon themselves, is *not* consistent with the Mon Paradigm, but with the archaeological, art historical, epigraphic, chronicle, and Chinese sources.

Thus there is no evidence to support: a) the presence of a Mon (or any other) kingdom in Lower Burma prior to the rise and development of Pagán, b) the conquest of Thatôn by Aniruddha, or c) the "civilizing" of Upper Burma by Lower Burma. In fact, the primary evidence suggests just the reverse: it was the kingdom of Pagán that was responsible for the demographic, cultural, and infrastructural development of Lower Burma, providing it with the wherewithal that turned a sparsely populated "frontier region" into an independent polity for the first time only in the late thirteenth century. In short, it was Upper Burma that was responsible for the civilizing of Lower Burma.

Accordingly, Chapter Two describes the Upper Burma Pyū culture of the first millennium that was responsible for the subsequent rise of the Pagán kingdom by perhaps the ninth century. The chapter summarizes the current academic situation in Burma studies regarding this Pyū culture and its implications for the question of state formation in the country. By now it is quite clear that Tibeto-Burman language speakers dominated the general geographic region of Upper Burma known to its historians as the "heartland" for approximately the two centuries prior to, and for most of the first millennium AD. It is with this group that Burmese speakers made first contact and from whom they borrowed their Indic culture. There is no primary evidence of another polity or kingdom led by Austro-Asiatic, Mon language speakers in Lower Burma or anywhere else in the country during that same period of time.

Chapter Three examines the etymology and historicity of the entity and concept of Rāmaññadesa, the "Realm of the Rman," employing contemporary and near-contemporary indigenous and external sources. Not a single contemporary external record mentions any polity in Lower Burma prior to the late thirteenth century, and not a single indigenous epigraphic source mentions it prior to the fifteenth.

That led, in Chapter Four, to the reexamination of the etymology and historicity also of Thatôn, the alleged center of the alleged Rāmaññadesa. As one might expect, Thatôn does not appear in original epigraphic sources either until the latter half of the fifteenth century; indeed, it appears in the same inscriptions in which Rāmaññadesa is also first recalled. As for the site alleged to have been ancient Thatôn, there is no scientific evidence of its eleventh-century existence or of its occupation at the time by Mon speakers, or that it is even the same site claimed to be the Thatôn of legend.

If there is no evidence of a Mon kingdom until the very late thirteenth century at the earliest, and no mention of "its" capital until the fifteenth century, then the historicity of its conquest by Aniruddha in 1057 becomes highly problematic. Chapter Five, therefore, searches for the first mention of the conquest story in epigraphy, while Chapter Six considers the same issue in the chronicles. While the conquest does not appear in epigraphy at all, a short and convoluted version of it first appears not in Burmese, but in Northern Thai chronicles written in the sixteenth century. Indeed, as stated above, it was not until the early eighteenth century that an extended, "full-blown" version appears in Burmese chronicles for the first time in the *Mahayazawingyi* of U Kala. Why did the story appear only then? What function did it serve? If the story were not historical, what other purposes might it have served, and why at that specific time? I attempt to answer these questions, albeit superficially, in Chapter Six, for the context in which these chronicles were written is still not well understood and the subject by itself would require a monograph.[24]

Without the conquest of Thatôn, of course, the consequences attributed to it can no longer stand *prima facie*. But in order to dispel the Mon Paradigm thoroughly and completely, I show that the primary evidence does not support that claim in any case. One of the most important consequences of the alleged conquest involves the origins of the Pagán writing system, long attributed to the Mon of Rāmaññadesa via Dvāravatī. But the theory proposed by the Mon Paradigm for the advent of that script is simply impossible, while paleographically and linguistically, it remains to be demonstrated, let alone proved. Tentatively, I hold that the Old Burmese (Pagán) script was adopted from the Pyū, who in turn had earlier borrowed theirs from a South Indian script. And it is from that Pagán Old Burmese script that written Old Mon, Arakanese (which is practically Old Burmese), and the main Shan scripts of Burma were subsequently derived. I address the issues and problems inherent in all this in Chapter Seven, but ultimately leave the topic open for linguists to resolve.

In order to prove the contention made in Chapter Seven, original, dated epigraphy must show that written Old Burmese in the Pagán script preceded written Old Mon in the same script, the two being virtually identical in Burma. Chapter Eight demonstrates that is the case; Old Burmese inscriptions in the Pagán script were indeed present well before the first dated evidence of written Old Mon in the country, possibly by as much as a hundred years. Therefore, the former could not have come from the latter; rather, the reverse is more likely.

In Chapter Nine I address another important ancillary conclusion claimed by the Mon Paradigm: that the style of what became one of Pagán's most ubiquitous religious architectural forms, the hollow temple (or *gu*), was Mon. There is no evidence to demonstrate that the typical Pagán period *gu*, with its distinct engineering feature (a true vault), was a Mon contribution. Neither the style nor this engineering feature on which the integrity of the style rests can be found in any other Pagán-period Mon site anywhere in Southeast Asia. The conclusion also assumes a very problematic link between artistic style and ethnicity. Once again, the evidence shows that the situation was likely to have been the reverse of what the Mon Paradigm asserts. It is likely that the kingdom of Pagán was the source for the most prevalent religious architectural form of Lower Burma, that is, the *stupa*, and that the genuine Pagán *gu*, along with its engineering knowledge, disappears in Burma's history shortly after the decline of Pagán.

One of the most intriguing problems in the historiography of Pagán is the modern legend of King Kyanzittha. Created by G. H. Luce, it is very much a bulwark of the Mon Paradigm. The king was said to have been responsible for the establishment of Mon culture, from which arises the alleged and celebrated "Mon period" at Pagán. The king was also given the credit for introducing Sinhalese Theravāda Buddhist orthodoxy to the kingdom, so that he, not Aniruddha (as the traditional view has it), was said to have been the one who really reformed the *sangha* and the religion. Upon closer scrutiny, it turns out that the modern legend of Kyanzittha and the consequences attributed to his reign cannot be supported, even by the same evidence used to sustain it. Chapter Ten deals with this issue.

These chapters address the three most crucial components alleged by the Mon Paradigm: the antiquity of Rāmaññadesa, the mechanism by which the latter's culture was transported to Pagán, and the "civilizing" of Burman Upper Burma by Mon Lower Burma. But the Mon Paradigm's influence was not limited to the study of early Burma. It went well beyond that to shape the historiography of the "early modern" as well as the colonial and postcolonial periods. Chapter Eleven is, therefore, concerned with one of the most important issues in Burma studies shaped by the Mon Paradigm: the notion of the "downtrodden Talaing," an alleged derogatory Burmese term for the Mon people. This phenomenon was said to have originated with King Alaungpaya and his reunification of Burma in the mid-eighteenth century. The chapter describes how this belief became embedded in the Mon Paradigm, and how it subsequently developed into the primary organizing principle of Burma's entire precolonial and much of its postcolonial historiography. Most revealing, the notion of the "downtrodden Talaing" can be found initially *only in the English-language scholarship of the colonial period;* it exists nowhere in the indigenous literature of the time, Burmese or Mon. Only with subsequent colonial persistence did the idea of a downtrodden Talaing class become part of twentieth-century Burma Mon mythology.

These chapters virtually beg the question of how, when, and by whom, the Mon Paradigm was begun. Who were the scholars and officials responsible? What were the pressing issues of the time that may have motivated them and shaped their ideas? Although this topic, the subject of Chapter Twelve, surely requires an entire book by itself, I nevertheless attempt to provide a general chronological and topical narrative of people and ideas. I describe the way in which the Mon Paradigm, entangling itself in the political issues of the day and missionary concerns surrounding ethnicity, emerged and developed during the early colonial era, and how the Paradigm subsequently became institutionalized as historical "truth" in the official and unofficial canon of Burma Studies. Thus, the intimate relationship between the colonial scholar and the colonial official is very much a part of the story of the Mon Paradigm and Burma's historiography.

In the final chapter, I offer an alternative scenario, suggesting what Burma and early Southeast Asian history might look like *without the Mon Paradigm*. This discussion is woven around several well-known, more general topics: a) the formation of the state, b) "Indianization," c) the rise of "classical" Pagán, d) the "crisis of the thirteenth century," and the "decline" of the "classical" states, e) the actual role of historic Rāmaññadesa in the "long sixteenth century," and f) the implications of all the above for the understanding, organizing, and periodizing of Burma's history today.

Still, I wonder whether Southeast Asian scholars can genuinely accept the alternatives. Can we shed our modern, postindustrial, market biases that trade and commerce were the major causes for state formation in much of (especially Mainland) Southeast Asia, and consider instead that agriculture and the agrarian interior may have given birth to the states in question? Can we imagine the "Indic" development of Pagán, and that of other early Mainland Southeast Asian states, without the dominating influence attributed to the Theravāda Buddhist Mon culture of Lower Burma that early, so ingrained in the epistemology of the field? Indeed, can we accept just the opposite, that Upper Burma may actually have "civilized" Lower Burma in terms of its religious and conceptual systems, its script, its literature, its art and architecture, its physical and administrative infrastructure, perhaps even its codified law and legal system, with all the attendant consequences for other adjacent areas of Southeast Asia? Can we envision a late Mon Lower Burma that actually "belonged" to the "early modern" period rather than to the earlier "classical" era? And, finally, can we perceive a precolonial and postcolonial Burma in which ethnic conflict is not *the* dominating and determining factor? All this would require a paradigm shift, which is exactly what I am asking Southeast Asian scholars to consider.

2 The Pyū Millennium

THE PEOPLE and culture that inhabited "Burma" during the pre-Pagán millennium have conventionally been called the Pyū, a designation begun in the early twentieth century, probably by C. O. Blagden. For the sake of convenience, he used the term to represent the fourth (and at that time unknown) language found on the quad-lingual so-called Myazedi Inscriptions of ca. 1112 AD, which he was in the process of deciphering, an enormous, daunting, and pioneering task.[1] From that focused purpose, the term Pyū has come to represent today the people, culture, and period that spanned the time between the second century BC and the early ninth century AD and laid the foundations for the kingdom of Pagán.[2]

A different and genuinely indigenous scheme for periodizing Burma's history could have been adopted, similar to the one used by the late Burmese chronicles. They had organized Burma's history on the basis of what they considered the most important criterion, namely, Buddha-prophesied cities and their dynasties, and hence, the Śrī Kṣetra Dynasty, the Pagán Dynasty, the Inwa (Ava) Dynasty, and so on. This would have avoided the use of reified ethnicity as the basis for the analysis and organization of Burma's history—a hallmark of colonial scholarship—so that the current chapter might have been named "The Pre-Pagán Millennium" or the "Early Urban Period" instead, more neutral categories of chronology and periodization.

Yet if the Mon Paradigm is to be dismantled thoroughly and convincingly, its own criterion for analyzing the evidence—reified ethnicity—within its own organizing principles of history must be addressed and not simply dismissed or ignored, so that the issue does not become merely a case of unsupported assertion or denial. My use of the Mon Paradigm's methodology of reified ethnicity does not constitute an endorsement or acceptance; it is only a method to dissect the Mon Paradigm on its own terms. Therefore, I have retained and used reified ethnicity as a category of analysis and a periodization scheme, but only when discussing the Mon

Paradigm's own perspective, to show that even using this system, the millennium of cultural development that laid the foundations for the genesis at Pagán was still not based on the Mon but on the Pyū. In other words, whether defined as a reified ethnic group or a culture, the Mon had little or nothing to do with the rise and development of Pagán.

Identifying the Pyū

Let us begin with the word "Pyū." Where did it come from and whom did it represent? The English orthographic rendering comes from the Cantonese pronunciation of the Chinese character romanized as P'iao,[3] which meant "rebel" in early Tsin Dynasty texts (265–420 AD) and "cavalry" in later T'ang and subsequent texts.[4] In about the ninth century the Chinese used the word P'iao to refer to a culture and people thought to have been living in what is now Burma.

Yet according to other Chinese sources, the P'iao did not refer to themselves as such, but as *t'u-lo-chu,* while the Javanese were also said (by the same Chinese sources) to have used the same ethnonym, calling them *t'u-li-ch'u.*[5] The term seems to have been the same as that found in contemporary Arabic accounts (one dated to 880 AD) regarding the people apparently of that area whom they called T.rsul.[6] This word was finally anglicized in the twentieth century by modern scholars as Tircul, and is now understood as the name by which we think the Pyū referred to themselves.

But in truth there have been no serious or scholarly attempts to decipher the term Tircul either. Chen Yi-Sein, a Burma scholar of Chinese descent, mentioned in passing that it might be a reference to the Telugu people of Southeast India, but provided little explanation, analysis, or evidence for that assertion.[7] Certainly, the gaze towards South India is understandable, for much of the material and epigraphic evidence found in Burma during the earlier part of the Pyū period shows important influences stemming from that region, especially before the seventh century AD. Those from Nagarjunakonda are most obvious in the early architecture and iconography of the Pyū,[8] while that of Vanavasi in present day Goa on the west coast of South India is recognizable in the writing system.[9] However, what Chen apparently did not consider was that Tircul (or *t'u-lo-chu*) was an ethnonym. If the word were a reference to the Telegu people, it could not have been a reference to the P'iao people also, for the latter were, all scholars feel, Tibeto-Burman, not Dravidian speakers. Besides, without linguistic evidence, no necessary connection can be established between a particular group of people and cultural remains, even if found in the same area inhabited by that group. Telegu influence on the art and architecture of Burma at that time does not mean that its general population, or even the people who produced these remains, must have been Telegu speakers also.

What is even more puzzling is that neither the Pyū themselves (in eleven centuries of civilization and approximately 25 of their inscriptions), nor their closest cousins, the Burmese speakers (in twenty-one centuries and over 1160 of their inscriptions) ever used this alleged ethnonym Tircul. The Chinese texts mentioned above and an Old Mon inscription of King Kyanzittha of Pagán assigned to 1102 are the only occasions that I know of when the word thought to be Tircul is mentioned.[10] As for the word Pyū, it does not appear in Old Burmese until the early thirteenth century, although there is no unequivocal linguistic evidence (let alone analysis) to prove that it was a reference to the word P'iao of the Chinese.[11] Thus, while the word Tircul (or its original Chinese, *t'u-lo-chu*) seems to have been the name used by the people the Chinese called the P'iao, there is no necessary link between the thirteenth-century Old Burmese word Pyū and the ninth-century P'iao of the Chinese. Although reasonable to assume, it is conjecture nevertheless, based on a thirteenth-century phonetic resemblance. The connection between the two, in short, is based on modern assumptions of what the ancient pronunciations of both the Cantonese and Old Burmese words might have been. All this leaves open the door for future research on the etymology of the word and the identity of the P'iao and/or Pyū people in Burma.

Since what they were called by others is not the focus of this study and cannot be resolved here in any case, I shall reluctantly perpetuate the convention (again, like Blagden, for the sake of convenience) and refer to these people of the pre-Pagán millennium also as Pyū, or when applicable as Tircul. Regardless of the name we give them, a Tibeto-Burman-speaking people inhabited the same areas that were almost immediately thereafter occupied by Burmese speakers, adopted Indic culture during the first millennium AD, and laid the foundations for the kingdom of Pagán in innumerable ways.

Origins and Development of the Pyū Polity

For the past century Burma scholars have been conducting research on the Pyū people and culture. Most of the questions have focused on the probable origins of these people, the language they spoke, the important features of their culture, and the chronology, size, structure, and scale of their polity. Most scholars knowledgeable about this culture agree more or less that they were of "northern" origins, that they spoke a Tibeto-Burman language, that their dominant belief system at the height of their cultural growth was Theravāda Buddhism with other Indic elements incorporated in it, that they already lived in large, urbanized settlements in the plains of the Irrawaddy valley as early as the second century BC, and that they lasted, at least as a polity or various polities and as a culture, until the mid- to late ninth century AD. There are, however, references to the Pyū as individuals in late Pagán and early Ava inscriptions, to be documented below.[12]

Most of the information on the Pyū language, certain aspects of their conceptual system, external glimpses of their kingdom, and particulars about their art and architecture had been gathered prior to the Second World War. However, much of the important, detailed analyses and concrete evidence concerning their physical environment, iconography, writing system, cities, and the general time frame in which they inhabited the country (which in part has been based on radiocarbon results) has emerged since the War. Indeed, it has only been about two years of this writing that some of the most important radiocarbon dates and other data concerning "their" material remains have appeared. Our current knowledge of the Pyū, then, is the result of a relatively long and irregular process of investigation—as the citations in this chapter will reveal.[13] What follows is a synthesis of approximately a century of research and scholarship on this culture, whatever name it is given, particularly as it pertains to the focus of this book.

We can assert with practically no equivocation that between the second century BC and the late ninth century AD, much of the country known currently as Myanmar was dominated, or at least occupied, by people conventionally known as the Pyū. Its heartland was the plains areas carved out by the confluence of the Irrawaddy and Chindwin rivers, a Y- shaped configuration located in the Dry Zone of Upper Burma that has been inhabited since the Paleolithic Age. At the height of Pyū culture, this nucleus where most of the culture's material and human resources lay was bounded on the south by Śrī Kṣetra (Old Prome), on the north by Halin, and on the east by the Kyauksé valley. Its periphery extended to parts of coastal Lower Burma and Arakan as well. Thus the Pyū culture seems to have occupied an area that was, by and large, virtually the same as that controlled by the precolonial Burmese state, and in certain cases it extended into the territory claimed by colonial and modern Burma.[14]

As we can tell at a glance by examining Figure 2, conspicuously missing is a Mon polity or kingdom or even a recognizable community of Mon speakers in any part of the territory during that same millennium, especially one contiguous to the Pyū state or kingdom, as claimed by the Mon Paradigm.[15] That is not to say that no Mon speakers were living here and there in Lower Burma, but rather that the *only* archaeological, epigraphic, and historical evidence we have of a state, polity, or kingdom, in both

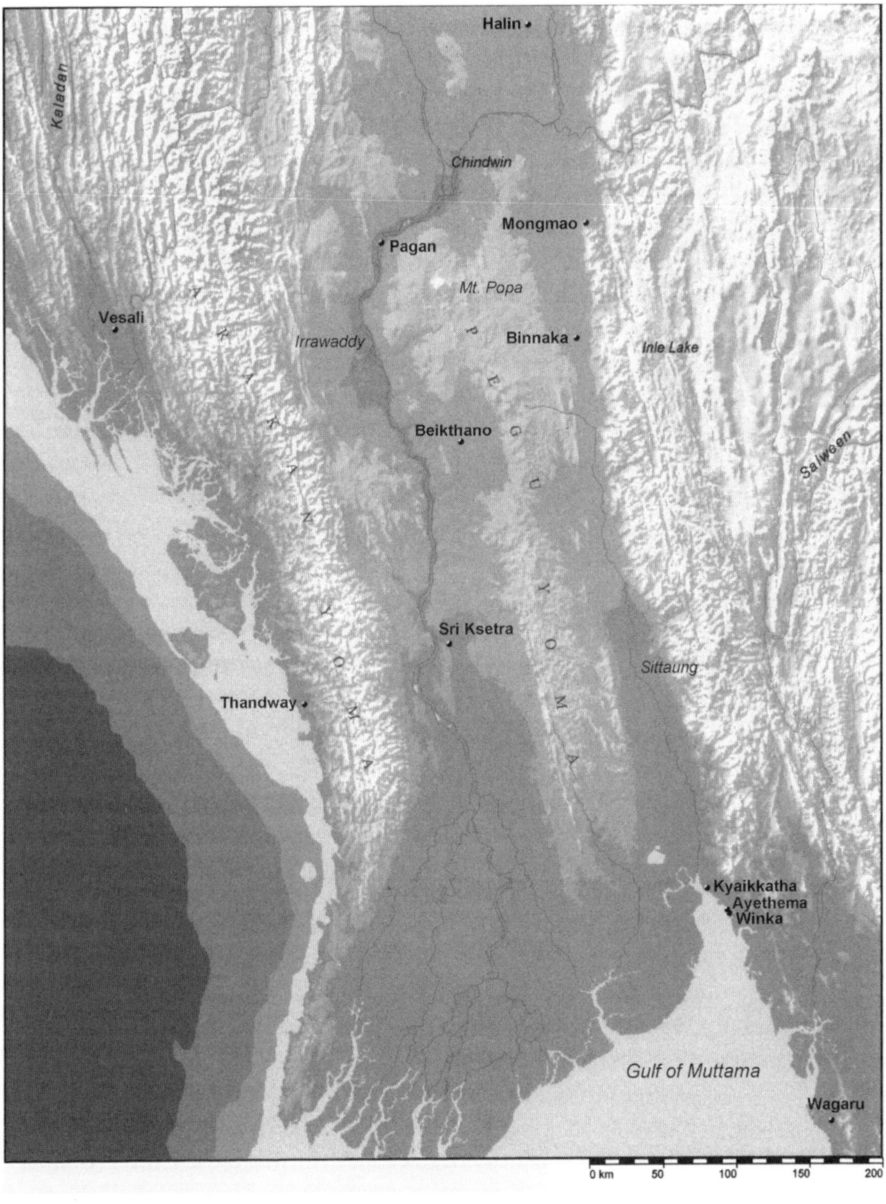

FIGURE 2: Pyū Period Urban Sites

Upper and Lower Burma during the first millennium AD is the one belonging to the Tibeto-Burman speaking culture we now call the Pyū.

The archaeological evidence we currently possess shows that the Pyū lived not only in much of the same general geographical space that their immediate successors, the Burmese speakers, later occupied but even in some of the same towns and cities.[16] These walled cities of the Pyū—at least five large ones and numerous smaller ones—at one time or another were located adjacent to and seemed to have controlled the three most important irrigated regions of precolonial Burma: the Mu valley north of the confluence of the Chindwin and Irrawaddy, the Kyauksé plains on its southeast, and the Minbu region south and west of the former two.[17] All three regions are endowed with rich soil and watered by perennial rivers and streams. What provided the economic mainstay of the kingdom of Pagán[18] was the same productive agricultural area inhabited by the Pyū and later by Burmese speakers. Evidence of Pyū culture, like that of Pagán, extends beyond this core region to the coasts of Lower Burma[19] and Arakan, where one of its inscriptions and two of its coins have been found.[20] Their artifacts reached as far east as Oc-eo around present day Ho Chih Minh city.[21] Indeed, Taw Sein Ko, without providing the source, stated that the Arakanese continued to use the term Pyū for "Burma" until the twelfth century.[22]

Arguably the most important feature found in the Pyū period that may not have been present previously in the same area was urbanization, and hence, according to some of the best scholars on this issue, also state formation.[23] The oldest urban site so far discovered and scientifically excavated is called Beikthano Myo by modern scholars, the Burmese rendering of "Viṣṇu City."[24] Probably the first capital of a culturally and perhaps even politically uniform kingdom in "Burma," it is a large settlement measuring approximately nine square kilometers (nearly 300 hectares) which has been radiocarbon dated, after calibration, to a period between 180 BC and 610 AD.[25] It lies on the east bank of one of the Dry Zone's three most productive irrigated regions, Minbu, with direct land access to the well-watered Kyauksé plains to its northeast, where two other apparently contemporaneous Pyū cities have also been found.

These are Mongmao (or Maingmaw) and Binnaka,[26] virtually identical in numerous ways, located in or near the Kyauksé valley, which later (if not earlier) was the major rice-producing area of Burma until Lower Burma was developed by the British in the late nineteenth and early twentieth centuries. At Binnaka, in addition to many brick structures whose floor plans are the same as those found at Beikthano and other Pyū sites, many artifacts have been recovered that are recognizable as being part of Pyū culture. This includes what are probably pre-Buddhist funerary practices of secondary burial, where remains of ash and bone are deposited in urns.

Artifacts of gold, such as necklaces, precious stone images of elephants, turtles, and lions (or perhaps they are tigers), distinctive Pyū pottery, terracotta tablets with writing that strongly resembles the Pyū script, and various kinds of acid-etched onyx beads identical to those found at Beikthano, along with others made of amber and jade, have been recovered. Apparently Binnaka continued to be occupied until about the nineteenth century, for artifacts of that period as well as the intervening periods have been found there.[27] There is even a palm-leaf *sittan* (record) of Binnaka that survives, suggesting that the city was part of the last precolonial monarchy's administrative domain.[28]

Mongmao, unearthed in 1979, is also located in the Kyauksé plains. The city is circular in shape, similar to Beikthano and another later, more famous Pyū city, Śrī Kṣetra. At one and a half miles in diameter, enclosing 222 hectares, Mongmao is one of the largest ancient cities on the entire Kyauksé plains. It has two inner enclosure walls, the outer of which is square while the inner one is circular. The plan of a circle within a square suggests a *zata,* a zodiac sign which represents a view of the heavens from the perspective of the sun,[29] the manner in which nineteenth-century Mandalay was also conceptualized.[30] At almost dead center, Mongmao also has what is thought to be a nineteenth-century temple called the Nandawya Paya (royal palace pagoda), which was probably built upon the ruins of an ancient one. The city is bisected by a canal, thought to be contemporary to the city, although no scientific dating has yet confirmed that.

Mongmao has been tentatively dated to the first millennium BC, based on its Pyū artifacts. It has also yielded distinctive silver coins identical to those found at Beikthano and Binnaka, stone molds for casting silver and gold ornamental flowers, a gold armlet in association with a silver bowl that had Pyū writing on it, pottery with rouletted patterns common to this period, along with acid-etched onyx elephant-shaped beads, the former found inside funerary urns virtually identical to those found at Beikthano and Binnaka. If the funerary urns at Beikthano represent a pre-Buddhist period, as Stargardt has argued,[31] then both Binnaka and Mongmao may have been contemporary with the former, as indeed other Burmese archaeologists have suggested.

The next or perhaps contemporaneous "capital" or preeminent center of the general period was most likely Halin, not Śrī Kṣetra, as claimed by the Mon Paradigm for reasons that bolstered its claim to an early Mon kingdom in Lower Burma. Misreading the ninth-century narrative of the *Man Shu,* which he himself translated, Luce identified two *kingdoms* mentioned in it as Pyū centers,[32] placing one, Mi-no, in central Burma. Mi-no he identified as Halin, and the other, Mi-ch'ên, as either Pegu or a site near it, which he said was inhabited by Mon people. This identification "proved" to Luce that a Mon center existed in Lower Burma in the ninth century, for it was made to be contemporary with Mi-no (alias Halin).

Yet the *Man Shu* never said that Mi-no and Mi-ch'ên were P'iao cities or that they were necessarily located in what is now Burma. The relevant chapter in the *Man Shu* states only that they bordered "on the Southern Man;"[33] that is, the people of the Nanchao kingdom in western Yunnan. Thus the cities could have been anywhere in Mainland Southeast Asia. Since the paragraph regarding Mi-no and Mi-ch'ên immediately precedes that on the P'iao kingdom, it is possible that they were contiguous to the latter, but that is about all we can speculate.

The *Man Shu* does mention a raid in 835 AD of these two *kingdoms* (not cities!) by the Man forces. The text describes their location as "both . . . bordering on the sea," thus clearly removing Halin from the picture (contrary to Luce's identification of it), for Halin is located in the heart of the Dry Zone, approximately a dozen miles southeast of Shwebo, in the Mu valley. The *Man Shu* also states that they call their princes and chiefs *Shou,* . . ." perhaps a reference to the word *chao,* used as an honorific by T'ai speakers, whose habitat, significantly, stretched into today's Assam. The *Man Shu* then records that "the kingdoms have no cities with inner or outer walls, . . ." which virtually precludes the Pyū of Burma as candidates, for they lived behind walled cities. As for "the Mi-ch'ên king [he] lives in a wooden stockade on the margin of the sea, in the water. The four feet of the house consist of stone lions. . . . The common people live in 'lofts.' . . . At each end of their 'lofts' they set drums. After drinking liquor they beat the drums. . . ." This description reminds one of many communities in Southeast Asia that used "frog drums" and lived in long houses well off the ground.

The *Man Shu* goes on to state that the kingdoms "are 60 day-stages southwest of Yung-ch'ang city of the Man," which might place Mi-ch'ên somewhere on the western coasts of Burma, perhaps in what is now Arakan, where evidence of two kingdoms contemporary with the Pyū exist in their centers, Vesali and Dhanyawaddy. However, they were both walled cities. Then, "in the ninth year of Ta-ho (835 AD) (the Man) destroyed their kingdoms and looted their gold and silver. . . . They captured two or three thousand of their clansmen, and banished them to wash the gold of the Li-shui."[34] In short, whoever these people were and wherever their kingdoms might have been located, none of the above information even remotely resembles the archaeological evidence we have on the Pyū people and their culture.

In the very next paragraph of the *Man Shu,* in a *separate section* labeled "P'iao kingdom" that is distinctly marked off from those labeled "Mi-no kingdom and Mi-ch'ên kingdom" is indeed the narrative about the P'iao. Clearly, then, the information about the kingdom of the P'iao is entirely different from the other two, textually as well as historically. Apparently Luce had confused the entry regarding Mi-no and Mi-ch'ên with that on the P'iao that followed immediately after.

The section on the "P'iao kingdom" begins by stating that it is 75 day-stages south of Yung-ch'ang city of the Man (not "60 day-stages southwest" of it, as noted for Mi-no and Mi-ch'ên), placing it 15 days-march farther south, perhaps around Śrī Kṣetra. It also states that "the people of the kingdom use a silver coinage. They use green bricks to make the walls surrounding their city. It is one day-stage to walk around it. . . . The common people all live within the city wall. There are twelve gates. In front of the gate of the palace where the king of (this) kingdom dwells, there is a great image seated in the open air, over a hundred feet high, and white as snow. . . . They reverence the Law of the Buddha. . . . In the 6th year of Ta-ho (832 AD), Man rebels looted and plundered P'iao kingdom. They took prisoner over three thousand of their people. They banished them into servitude . . . and told them to fend for themselves."[35]

Not only are the dates different (832 and 835), none of the Mi-no and Mi-ch'ên information in the *Man Shu* fits that on the Pyū. Moreover, the data on the P'iao accord with much of the archaeological evidence we have on the Pyū, down to their silver coinage, Buddhist beliefs, size of the city walls, and even (in the case of Śrī Kṣetra and perhaps Halin as well) the twelve gates. But since the last sentences used for the P'iao and the Mi-no/Mi'chen kingdoms are nearly identical—they speak of their looting, of taking "three thousand" of their people, and their banishment into servitude—Luce must have thought that these two narratives were referring to the same event and people.

Yet the translation of the *Man Shu* is Luce's own after all, so he should have known in detail what was in it. It appears, therefore, that he was more concerned with making sure that Mi-no was Halin and Mi-ch'ên was in Lower Burma than he was in accurately representing what the text actually had to say. Identifying Mi-no as Halin had little or nothing to do with the information in the Chinese text or the archaeological evidence. Rather, its purpose was to place the *other* kingdom mentioned with it, Mi-ch'ên, in the same chronological and historical context in order to sustain the Mon Paradigm that the Mon were in Lower Burma in the ninth century.

Both the archaeological and epigraphic evidence suggest that Halin actually emerged earlier, overlapped in time with, and may have lasted longer (as a Pyū city) than Śrī Kṣetra. (As cities under the domination of Burmese speakers, of course, both lasted well into the precolonial period.) The published radiocarbon analysis of what were once Halin's wooden gates yield an early date of 70 AD,[36] demonstrating that it preceded Śrī Kṣetra by nearly six centuries. These early dates for Halin also suggest that the city was contemporary with Otein Taung, (pottery hill), a settlement located in the urban complex of Pagán near the Sulamani temple, where recent radiocarbon dating reveals a period of occupation between 650 and 980 AD.[37] The early radiocarbon dates for Halin are also supported by the recovery of an earlier version of the Brāhmī script (Mauryan and Guptan) than that found at Śrī Kṣetra, whose inscriptions show a later version of that same script.[38]

Moreover, a set of unpublished radiocarbon dates recently rediscovered by Bob Hudson in the files of the New Zealand laboratory where the original analysis on Halin's organic remains was conducted, extends its period of activity to approximately 870 AD.[39] That is over three decades beyond the conventional date given for its demise, wrongly dated to 835 AD in any case.[40] Indeed, if Halin's occupation was continuous, it may have lasted for eight centuries. These and the earlier radiocarbon dates show that Halin also overlapped in time with Beikthano, the oldest city so far discovered, and therefore presumably with Binnaka and Mongmao as well, since they were likely contemporaries of Beikthano. The data show continuous urban settlement in the most important centers of the Dry Zone of Burma between the second century BC (Beikthano) and the founding of Pagán.

Halin is also located in the Dry Zone of Upper Burma about a dozen miles southeast of present day Shwebo; it is the largest, northernmost city of this culture so far discovered. Importantly, it is also close to bronze sites that have been recently discovered.[41] The city appears to be the farthest inland among the major cities of this period, located north of the confluence of the Irrawaddy and the Chindwin rivers, where it controlled the vast, rich agricultural area drained by the perennial Mu River and myriad other streams. Subsequently, if not during Pyū times, it became the largest irrigated region of precolonial Upper Burma.[42] The Halin area is also known for its salt production, a highly prized commodity in the ninth century.

The selection of Halin's location was obviously designed to control these natural economic resources, a strategy that also explains the locations of Binnaka and Mongmao, both of which lay adjacent to or in the fertile Kyauksé plains. Beikthano, which lay across the Irrawaddy from Minbu, the third richest agricultural area in the Dry Zone, also had direct access to Kyauksé. Contrary to the claim made by the Mon Paradigm that the Kyauksé valley was first inhabited by the Mon,[43] a topic to be addressed in Chapter Ten, the best evidence we have today shows that it and the other productive areas had already been occupied by the Pyū for nearly a millennia before dominance by Burmese speakers, and well before Mon speakers first appeared in the epigraphic record of Upper Burma.

The excavated city of Halin is rectangular but with curved corners, its walls approximately two miles long on the north-south axis and one mile on the east-west.[44] It is nearly twice the size of Beikthano, at 664 hectares.[45] It has four main gates at the cardinal points, presumably with two intermediate ones on either side of each main one, again totaling twelve, the same as recounted by the Chinese for one of the Pyū cities. This number and configuration has symbolic Hindu-Buddhist cosmological implications, a feature also found in subsequent major Burmese capitals such as Pagán and even nineteenth-century Mandalay.[46]

Like the entrances of Beikthano and perhaps Śrī Kṣetra, Halin's curve inward, as if to enhance the movement of fast-wheeled vehicles in and out. The southeastern gateway yielded forty human skeletal remains, perhaps signs of a non-Buddhist practice that may have preceded Buddhism (later known as *myosade*), where live humans were allegedly crushed underneath the gates at the time of construction to produce a "green spirit" (the *nat sein* of modern times) to protect the entrance from supernatural forces beyond the power of human sentries.[47] This practice was probably eliminated by the time Buddhism appeared at Halin, so that the skeletons may represent "old" Halin on which was built the current excavated Buddhist city.

Traces of a moat exist on all sides except the south, where it was probably not needed, as land was dammed there to create reservoirs. As the land slopes north to south, water from the north must have flowed into the moat, filling it first, then into the walled area to irrigate the fields, finally exiting on the south and replenishing the reservoir. It is a pattern also found at Mongmao and Beikthano and at two ancient cities in Burma in what is now Arakan (Dhannyawaddy and Vesali),[48] not to mention old Sukhodaya in Thailand that emerged a millennium and a half later.[49]

The brick structures found at Halin were square or rectangular with interior spaces and projections on one side in some cases, characteristic of the predominant style of *gu* (hollow temples) built at Pagán later, a topic to be discussed in Chapter Nine. Earthen funerary urns were also found buried within and outside these structures. Another structure, dubbed the "assembly hall," is similar to one at Beikthano that once had eighty-four wooden pillars to support a superstructure. The one excavated at Halin has post holes in four parallel rows, with signs that the posts had all burned down.

Halin yielded many characteristically Pyū artifacts, including a small stone slab inscribed in what has been called the Pyū language. Each of the two Pyū lines is followed by a few characters in the old Brāhmī script, a tradition later called *nissaya* that continued with Burmese and Pali. The purpose of the inscription was to record the death of one "Honorable Ru-ba."

Another inscription, with eight lines of Pyū but no interlinear Brāhmī, was discovered in the early twentieth century. It records the name of a high personage, possibly a queen or princess, by the name of Śrī Jatrajiku.[50]

The excavations at Halin also produced silver coins with the usual distinctive Pyū designs of *srivatsa* (an auspicious symbol), *bhadrapitha* (throne), rising sun, conch, and *trisula* (trident) in various combinations on each side; gold, onyx, and terracotta beads; stucco and terracotta objects with designs identical or similar to those at other sites; clay burial urns such as those found at Beikthano; iron swords, spearheads, axe heads, arrow heads, sockets for doors, and caltrops, again identical or similar to those found at Beikthano; and three bronze mirrors with long tenons for handles. There were also fine gold objects, such as rings, beads, and pendants. A stone (agate) seal, probably used as an inset to a ring, was also found inscribed with the word *daya-danam* in "South Indian characters" of the fifth century. That another such piece and a Pyū coin were found at Oc-eo in Vietnam, with the identical name in Pali, suggests that this was either a Halin product with wider distribution, or it was a rather common fashion found elsewhere in Southeast Asia and brought to Halin.[51] Either way, it shows contact between India, Upper Burma, and Lower Vietnam during this time. Also found at Halin and other major Pyū sites, including some on the coasts were well-burned, large, distinctively "fingermarked" bricks of mostly uniform size used to build religious and secular structures.[52]

By the seventh or eighth century Śrī Kṣetra had probably superceded Halin as capital or paramount city of the Pyū kingdom.[53] It is dated to the early part of the eighth century by the Burmese chronicles, and to between the fifth and ninth centuries by archaeology, epigraphy, paleography, and art history. The beginning portions of perhaps the earliest extant Burmese chronicle, the *Zatatawpon Yazawin,* gives the following information about Śrī Kṣetra: ". . . in *Sakarāj* 101 [739 AD], on the 11th waxing day of the month of Tagu, replete with the seven requisites beginning with the moat, having established the golden city of Śrī Kṣetra together with the golden palace, Thagya [Sakrā] lifted Dwattabaung and placed him on the throne."[54]

An eighth-century date for Śrī Kṣetra is a bit later than some of the archaeological, epigraphic, and art historical evidence suggests, so there may have been more than one period when it was present and/or dominant. Much like the First and Second Ava periods in Burmese history, where the same site served two successive dynasties, hundreds of years apart, what little we have on Śrī Kṣetra seems to suggest that there were at least a "first" and "second" Śrī Kṣetra period and dynasty, if not a third.[55] Archaeologists have noticed several levels of habitation at Śrī Kṣetra, and the earliest Burmese chronicles recall certain dates and people forgotten by later ones, while epigraphy mentions other "dynasties" forgotten by both. The religious art also suggests several distinct occupations, with earlier influences stemming from Southeast India sites such as Nagarjunakonda and Amarāvatī and later influences from southwest India, such as Vanavasi, while ninth-century influences include those from the kingdom of Nanchao. Thus the totality of the evidence does not support a single occupational period for Śrī Kṣetra, with its size, wealth, influence, power, and so on, remaining unchanged throughout, and its development linear and continuously progressive. Rather, the pattern appears to have been more a "punctuated equilibrium."[56]

In any case, Śrī Kṣetra has yielded the most extensive remains of Theravāda, or Pali, Buddhism and is the largest of the urbanized areas, with a circumference of about 8½ miles, or about 1,400 hectares of occupied area.[57] Also, as shown above, the ninth-century *Man Shu* stated that a city that is presumably Śrī Kṣetra "is one day-stage to walk round it."[58] It is circular in shape, with twelve gates and a pagoda at each of the four corners.[59] It also has inward curving gateways, such as those found at Halin and Beikthano. In the center of the city was what most scholars think represented the rectangular palace site, 1,700 by 1,125 feet, symbolizing both a *mandala,* and a *zata* (horoscope), reminiscent of Mongmao.

The *Man Shu* states that the walls of the Pyū capital in the ninth century (either Halin or Śrī Kṣetra), were covered with green, probably glazed bricks.[60] Such bricks have been found in some of the oldest *stupas* in Pagán, such as the tenth-century Ngakywènadaung,[61] and also in the exterior decoration of Pagán temples such as the thirteenth-century Sulamani and the interior floors of others, such as the twelfth-century Dhammayangyi.

We should realize that even these well-known sites, except perhaps for Beikthano, have not been excavated with the degree of thoroughness that most archaeologists normally desire. This means that some of the important Pyū cities, especially Mongmao and Binnaka could yield much more data than they have so far, enhancing the current picture of a fairly uniform culture widely dispersed over the length and much of the breadth of the country during the first millennium AD. Indeed, there are many smaller sites in the Dry Zone which have not seen extensive or any excavation in which Pyū artifacts have been discovered. Such sites have, until recently, rarely appeared in the published literature of the field. They include Wati (an urban area west of Mongmao),[62] Ayadawkye Ywa in the Mu valley, west of Halin, south of a recently discovered bronze site called Nyaunggan, and several others in Myin Mu township, which controls the mouth of the Mu River on the Irrawaddy.[63]

This Pyū domain was more or less elliptically shaped, comprised of the flat plains that surround the confluence of the Irrawaddy and Chindwin river valleys. It was longer than it was wide, stretching from Śrī Kṣetra in the south to Halin in the north, Binnaka and Mongmao to the east, and probably Ayadawkye Ywa to the west. Indeed, the *Chiu-t'ang-shu,* an account not given to exaggeration when discussing Southeast Asian "barbarians," states that the P'iao kingdom extended 3,000 *li* from east to west and 3,500 *li* from north to south, approximately 1,000 and 1,250 miles respectively. The *Hsin-t'ang-shu* has it even bigger. Both texts contend that to the east of the P'iao kingdom was Chen-la kingdom (Cambodia), to the west Eastern India, on the south the ocean, and to the north So-lo city, a Nanchao fort. Southwest [southeast?] is To-ho-lo (Dvāravatī), and northeast was Yang-chü-mieh, capital of Nanchao.[64] (As we can see, nothing is mentioned on the south of the P'iao but the ocean, where Mon Rāmaññadesa is claimed to have been!) The *Chiu-t'ang shu* also states that there are nine dependencies of the P'iao: the *Hsin-t'ang-shu* actually names them. The Chinese sources also list the tribes bordering on the P'iao and eighteen "dependent kingdoms" by name, including Java and Champa, and mentions 32 out of 298 districts of the P'iao kingdom.[65]

As urban dwellers foreshadowing the rise of the "classical" states, the Pyū were not alone in Southeast Asia. They were contemporaries of those living in Funan and (perhaps) Champa in what is now Cambodia and Vietnam, Dvāravatī in modern-day Thailand, Tambralinga and Takuapa on the Malay Peninsula near the Isthmus of Kra, and Śrī Vijaya, which was probably centered at Palembang in southeast Sumatra.[66] There were also several polities in central and east Java that were contemporaries or near-contemporaries of the Pyū that mentioned them by their ethnonym, *t'u-li-ch'u,* as shown above. Thus, throughout Southeast Asia, as in Burma, foundations were being laid during this period for the rise of Southeast Asia's "classical" states, the "golden age" of at least Mainland Southeast Asian history and arguably the most important in Burma's premodern (and some would say modern) sociopolitical and cultural history. As a consequence of this particular role in Burma's history, in an earlier work I called this Pyū period "the formative age" in Burma's history.[67] It was this earlier Pyū culture of Burma, not the much later-arriving Mon in the country, that provided the crucial political, ideological, economic, and cultural foundations of the rise of Pagán.

The Material Foundations of the Pyū

To the Pyū—as to their successors, the Burmese speakers centered at Pagán—whereas wet-rice agriculture was vital, trade was only important. A T'ang Dynasty source described it thus: "the land is suitable for pulse, rice, and the millet-like grains. Sugarcane grows as thick as a man's shin. There is no hemp or wheat."[68] Rice, perhaps of the Japonica variety, which in Burma has been found earlier than Indica, was apparently the mainstay of the Pyū state.[69] Not surprisingly, therefore, evidence of irrigation tanks and canals abounds at Pyū urban sites. It has even been argued that the techniques of building dams, canals, and weirs found in nineteenth-century Upper Burma can be attributed to the Pyū of Beikthano.[70] However, some of the canal-building techniques may have been created at a later age, perhaps during the Pagán period, when they became the prevailing and preferred method of irrigation.[71] And although not demonstrated unequivocally with scientific evidence, some of the irrigation techniques found at the Pyū sites, such as bunding, could well have been contemporaneous to the sites, for the irrigation works were deliberately built in close conjunction with the design and placement of Pyū cities relative to the landform and water resources. Also, as shown above, some of the oldest and most important Pyū sites, such as Mongmao and Binnaka, were located right in what later became the heart of Pagán's irrigated agriculture system—the well-watered Kyauksé plain—so it is unlikely that the Pyū placed their cities there without any intention of utilizing these bounties of nature. Indeed, the Pyū may well have been responsible for first irrigating Kyauksé.

As the Pyū heartland was in Upper Burma where most of its population, material resources, and largest cities lay, it was, for many centuries, the Pyū who began one of the most important and dominant themes in Burma's history, what I have elsewhere called "Dry Zone paramountcy."[72] Virtually all the centers of power, culture, and resources, both human and material, in Burma's urban history of approximately 2,100 years were centered in the Dry Zone of Upper Burma. There were only two brief exceptions, totaling approximately 218 nonconsecutive years, when the country's political center moved to the coast. Yet, these short exceptions have been made to appear as the rule by some,[73] well out of proportion to what the evidence actually shows.[74]

This Pyū pattern of Dry Zone Paramountcy was subsequently perpetuated by the Burmese speakers. As noted above, one important fact we often forget is that the area occupied by the Pyū was not only the same general Dry Zone area in which the Burmese speakers later settled, but the Burmese speakers settled in some of the same valleys, and even in some of the same towns and cities. Of course, the Dry Zone is also the same general region where the stone and metal cultures of Burma's prehistory are found.[75] Following the Pyū decline in the late ninth century, Halin and Śrī Kṣetra remained important political, economic, and demographic centers for virtually all subsequent kingdoms. Even when the focus of power shifted to Pegu, once in the mid-sixteenth century and again in the early eighteenth, Śrī Kṣetra, locally called Prañ by then, continued to be a strategic prize, for it controlled the land passes to Arakan and its resources.[76] As a whole, then, the Dry Zone of Upper Burma was very much the nucleus for the kingdom of Pagán and nearly all subsequent Burmese dynasties for approximately 2,000 years, hence the term the "heartland of Burma."

But Dry Zone Paramountcy created its own problems, illustrated by a concept geographers call "constancy of place."[77] It provides societies with certain advantages as well as disadvantages. The Dry Zone nourished its human inhabitants with the best soils of Burma, watered by perennial rivers that flowed from higher and wetter areas, along with seasonal floods. This resulted in predictable and regular yields that helped shape the stable nature of the social and political systems. At the same time, however, constancy of place also creates certain problems that beset these societies time and again. And because they are invariably addressed in similar ways, it produces oscillations of long duration from which it was difficult to break free. The Burmese speakers shared with the Pyū perspectives on the world shaped by the same physical environment.

In addition to agriculture, the Pyū may also have participated in the regional and international trade of Southeast Asia, in part suggested by a distinctive coinage presumably used in commerce and not simply created for symbolic reasons as earlier scholars have assumed.[78] In most Pyū cities as well as in many of the small villages with Pyū artifacts, distinctive Pyū silver coins have been discovered. A copper coin with *devanāgarī* writing, thought to have been prevalent in Nepal and denoting a five-*pice* denomination, was found at Binnaka. In 1971 a hoard of some 500 of these "Pyū coins" were found at an ancient city called Kyaikkatha on the Lower Burma coasts on the Gulf of Martaban, while others have been found at Tavoy. Another hoard of about 36 coins was found in the area that later became Pegu.[79] The *Hsin-t'ang-shu,* a Chinese text of the time, stated that the P'iao "take gold and silver to make it into coin. It is like a half moon in appearance, called *dengchietue* [*dinga,* an Indic term] and *zudantuo*."[80] This is perhaps the first evidence of commercial coinage in the country, but after the Pyū period *indigeneous* coins for whatever purpose disappear until the nineteenth century with King Mindon's attempts at modernization.

Such numismatic evidence has often been construed as evidence for the presence of an early Mon state in Lower Burma. Robert Wicks attributes one particular type to be of Pegu provenance, dated stylistically to the fifth century AD.[81] And although he wrote that the coin was of "Pegu provenance," *not* "Mon provenance," nevertheless, the section where this is discussed appears under the subheading "The Mon of Thaton and Pegu." It suggests, then, that these alleged fifth-century Pegu coins belonged to the Mon, with the inference that some kind of Mon state or society there at the time had minted them.

Even if these coins are correctly assigned to the fifth century on stylistic grounds, their mere presence at a place that did not become the city of Pegu until 800 years later, and only subsequent to that was proved to be inhabited by Mon speakers, need not in any way suggest their presence there also during the fifth century. Pegu, itself, does not appear as a place name until 1266 AD in an Old Burmese inscription, a topic to be fully discussed in Chapter Three. Moreover, no Old Mon language is inscribed on these coins so no link between Mon culture and the artifact has been established. Like most scholars of Southeast Asia, Wicks assigned Lower Burma finds, particularly those from "traditional Mon centers" such as Pegu and Thatôn to the Mon, thereby creating an unsubstantiated link between geography, chronology, ethnicity, and the artifact. To be sure, when Wicks was writing, no one had yet challenged the Mon Paradigm, so it was not an issue that he needed to address.

That some trade with far-off places occurred is evident as early as Beikthano. What resembles Red Polished Ware, supposedly a hallmark of northwest India has been found there, along with carnelian and onyx beads similar to those of Hastinapura and Brahmapuri of second century AD India and other parts of Southeast Asia, such as the Tambon Caves in the Philippines. Many sprinkler vessels reminiscent of Roman ware, perhaps produced in South India at Arikamedu, have also been unearthed.[83] And what appears to be a kind of rouletted blackware found in western Java and other parts of Southeast Asia has also been discovered at Beikthano and the other Pyū cities.[84]

Like most others in Southeast Asia at the time, the Pyū culture also conducted trade and diplomatic relations with China. In 800 and 801–802 AD, Śrī Kṣetra sent a formal embassy, along with a group of about thirty-five musicians, to the T'ang capital, where their instruments and songs, all on Buddhist themes, were recorded in fairly good detail.[85] These musicians were said to have been wearing "K'un-lun dress," which Luce summarily concluded was Mon.[86] Yet most modern scholars, particularly Wheatley, do not identify K'un-lun with the Mon but with people of various ethnic backgrounds who lived in Island and Coastal Southeast Asia.[87] The *Hsin-t'ang-shu* goes on to state that the embassy itself came from "the city of Sri" but it did not say that the musicians accompanying them were P'iao, so any group of musicians living or working at Śrī Kṣetra could have been part of the troupe. Indeed, the Chinese source adds that the P'iao music was all in the *fan* (Sanskrit) dialect.[88] Although no original evidence has yet been found of musical instruments attributed to Śrī Kṣetra itself, five bronze figurines of musicians that belonged to the Śrī Kṣetra period were discovered just outside the city walls during the excavation season of 1966–1967, near the Payamā *stupa*. That they were culturally Pyū, of course, is impossible to tell, especially as their dress resembles that of South India or Ceylon, and they are playing instruments clearly recognizable as belonging to that region of South Asia.[89]

This kind of cultural and economic relationship with other regions of Asia was obviously facilitated by towns and cities located on the Lower Burma coasts on the Gulf of Muttama, such as Winga, Hsindat-Myindat, Sanpannagon, and Mudon,[90] that possessed Pyū artifacts. Although there is insufficient evidence to state unequivocally that the Pyū kingdom also had military and administrative control over these coastal cities and towns, their distinctive cultural artifacts, particularly "fingermarked" bricks, and others with Buddhist and Brahmanic symbols, are found all over the country.[91]

Indic Influences and Pyū Culture

It was upon these indigenous material and physical environmental foundations that were laid the intellectual influences from outside, most notably India. Important aspects of Buddhist, Brahmanic, and Hindu doctrines, themes, motifs, and principles represented in religious structures, iconography, and written texts have been found among Pyū remains. Most of these have been discovered at seventh-century AD Śrī Kṣetra, the city that yielded perhaps the most evidence in terms of Indic culture. According to Stargardt, however, evidence of Buddhism among the Pyū may have appeared even earlier, at Beikthano, probably around the early part of the fourth century AD.[92] If correct, I would contend, it did so at Halin, Mongmao, and Binnaka also, as they were probably contemporaries of the former.

By the Beikthano period, the Pyū were placing the remains of their cremated dead in pottery and stone urns and burying them in or near certain isolated *stupas,* a practice that is consistent with early Buddhist practices of interning the remains of holy personages in *stupas.* Stargardt thinks that this practice at Beikthano may have been the result of an "interaction" between the pre-Buddhist Pyū funerary practices and a later age, when Buddhist influences became part of the Pyū conceptual system.[93] Although Pyū culture exhibited signs of a pre-Indic, pan-Southeast Asian megalithic culture and belief system—especially in its funerary rituals and other rites dealing with fertility, the sun, seasons, and monsoons[94]—by about the fourth century AD, Buddhism, and the Brahmanic context in which it was created and carried, had already become the dominant conceptual system of the Pyū.

At Beikthano also, what appears to be a Buddhist monastery, a large *stupa,* and a smaller shrine have been excavated. They probably date post fourth century.[95] The distinctive design and floor plans of the monastery[96] is in many important respects reproduced at Pagán in the thirteenth-century Sômingyi Monastery. Some evidence of Ceylonese contact with the Pyū can also be discerned this early, particularly in the Anurādhapura style "moonstones" (half-circle, carved stone thresholds on monastery and temple doorways) discovered at both Beikthano and Halin.[97] However, such architectural features also point to links with Nagarjunakonda in South India.[98] At Mongmao, a brick structure nearly identical to another thought to be a large *stupa* at Beikthano was also excavated. These architectural styles, ground plans, even the brick size and construction techniques of these buildings point to South India's Andhradesa, particularly Amarāvatī and Nagarjunakonda.[99]

By perhaps the seventh century, at Śrī Kṣetra, tall cylindrical *stupas* were built—the Bawbawgyi, Payagyi, and Payamā—whose prototypes point to the (conjectured) great *stupas* at Beikthano and Mongmao, where unfortunately only the foundations remain. Śrī Kṣetra also produced hollow temples, such as the Bèbè, Lémyethna, and the East Zegu, that were, along with several others, prototypes for the later hollow temples *(gu)* of Pagán.[100] The Yahanda Gu at Śrī Kṣetra has a vaulted roof, characteristic of hundreds of *gu* built at Pagán. If this vaulted roof at Śrī Kṣetra was contemporary to the building and not a later repair, then the Pyū may have been the ones who passed on that very important engineering technique to the Burmese speakers at Pagán, a topic to be discussed more fully in Chapter Nine.

The solid *stupas* of Śrī Kṣetra were, in turn, the prototypes for Pagán's, such as the Shwézigôn, Shwéhsandaw, and Mingalazedi, and ultimately, the Shwédagôn in modern Yangôn. Indeed, the earliest reliably dated solid *stupas* in Burma are found first in the interior of Upper Burma among the Pyū—in the Bawbawgyi, Payagyi, and Payamā—and only eight centuries later in Lower Burma. Even the Shwédagôn Pagoda, whose legend takes it back to the Lord Buddha's time, cannot be proved by epigraphy to be earlier than the fourteenth or fifteenth century AD when its inscriptions were erected. This important issue will be discussed in Chapter Three.

In terms of iconography, Buddha statues with *bhumispasa mudra* (earth-touching posture) were very much a part of Śrī Kṣetra's art, a favorite pose that continues to be portrayed even today. Along with Theravāda Buddhist iconography, what is thought to be Mahayanist statuary was also discovered. A four-armed bronze Bodhisattva Avalokiteśvara was found near the Bawbawgyi *stupa,* identified, of course, by the Mahayanist Buddha Amitābha on his elaborate headdress.[101] Pyū iconography also revealed evidence of tantric and other forms of Mahāyāna Buddhism. Avalokiteśvara, Tārā, Mānuṣi, Jambhala, Lokanātha, and Hayagrīva, all prominent in Mahāyāna Buddhism, were very much part of the Pyū, and later the Pagán scene.[102]

Brahmanism was also well represented in iconography at Śrī Kṣetra. The standing figures of Viṣṇu and his consort, Lakṣmī, are found together in bold relief on a sandstone slab. Other manifestations of Viṣṇu were found, one with four arms, standing on his vehicle, Garuḍa, while another has him reclining on the serpent Ananta, a motif also found at eleventh-century Pagán in the Nat-hlaung-gyaung. On three lotus flowers that emerge from the navel of this reclining Viṣṇu are members of the Hindu Trinity: Brahmā, Viṣṇu, and Śiva.[103]

In Lower Burma as well, archaeologists have uncovered "two reliefs of the four-armed Vishnu sleeping on the Ananta serpent, with the Hindu Trinity, Brahma, Vishnu, and Shiva growing from his navel. Also . . . the great . . . four-armed Shiva, with his vehicle the bull Nandi, crushing the buffalo-demon, his spouse Parvati seated against his thigh."[104] These came from the Thatôn area, and there are, or were, a good many other Brahmanic sculptures found elsewhere in Lower Burma. In the Kawgun Cave, some thirty miles above Moulmein, "low down on the west wall," is another such figure of Vishnu with a partially read inscription in South Indian script, saying Śrī Parameśvara-pāda. It has been dated paleographically to the sixth or seventh-century AD.[105]

This reverence for Viṣṇu[106] continued into at least eleventh-century King Kyanzittha's reign at Pagán, where he traced his mythical genealogy not only to historical Śrī Kṣetra but also to Viṣṇu. Indeed, King Kyanzittha's first inscription regarding this theme was erected at Śrī Kṣetra, at the time still a prominent city under the Pagán kingdom.[107] The Brahminism of the Pyū period, particularly at Śrī Kṣetra, was said to be of the Vengi-Pallava tradition, to which Pyū sculpture has been linked, stylistically dated to the first half of the fifth century AD. Other "Hindu" or Brahmanic images also point to the Andhra region.[108]

At a particular time in its history, or perhaps together with Brahmanism, Theravāda Buddhism made its impact on the ideology among the Pyū. Pali inscriptions bearing the Theravāda Canon have been discovered among Pyū ruins, one inscription taken from the *Abhidhamma* and others from the *Maṅgala Sutta, Ratna Sutta,* and the *Mora Sutta.*[109] In 1926, in a relic chamber of a ruined pagoda at or near Śrī Kṣetra, a gold manuscript consisting of twenty thin gold plates incised in Pyū script[110] of the fifth century (seventh century according to Charles Duroiselle)[111] but expressed in the Pali language was found. It revealed eight extracts from a wide range of Pali texts, including the *Abhidhamma* and the *Vinaya.*[112] That alone should confirm the presence of Theravāda Buddhism there at that time. The "*ye dhamma hetuprabhava*" formula (he who sees the *dharma,* sees me; he who sees me, sees the *dharma*), said to be distinctly Theravāda Buddhist, is also found on dozens of votive tablets of the same period, another two gold plates, and other stone inscriptions.[113]

But note the kind of reasoning given by the Mon Paradigm to rationalize its assumptions that these early Pali influences were "more or less concurrent influences in the Mon country from an early period." This is best illustrated by a direct quote from Duroiselle: "As Prome is on the Irrawaddy, the presumption is that the Pali Canon was introduced there by way of the river route, not by some difficult overland track; and consequently that it was known in the Mon region round the mouths of the river before it reached Prome."[114] Of course, a river route from Lower Burma to Prome does not necessarily imply an *earlier* Mon connection; this is a self-fulfilling argument indeed.

Another Pali inscription, said to be in South Indian characters of the seventh to the eighth centuries, has also been found about forty miles northeast of what later became Pegu. It contains part of an excerpt from the *Vinaya Mahāvagga,* very similar to the gold leaf Pali manuscript noted above,[115] and suggests the scope of this prevailing religious and literary influence over the Lower Burma region as well. In Tadagale, a few miles north of modern Yangôn, a bronze standing Buddha was found, said to be in Gupta style and dated to the fifth century AD.[116] At the same place a clay votive tablet was discovered inscribed with what some scholars call a "Pyū/Pali" script, said to be of the seventh century AD,[117] and another votive tablet with a fragmentary Pali inscription in tenth-century writing.[118] At the Botahtaung Pagoda, also in Yangôn, a Pali inscription with a Buddhist formula, thought to be of the seventh century AD, was found in the relic chamber exposed as a result of bombing during World War II.[119]

Much of this Theravāda Buddhism was probably derived from the Andhra region, where it thrived during the fifth and sixth centuries AD, when perhaps Halin, then Śrī Kṣetra, or perhaps both simultaneously, were the exemplary centers in Burma. Such a model, in which one center lay in the agrarian interior and one on, or with easy access to, the commercial coast, was, of course, typical of the ancient world. This South Indian school of Theravāda Buddhism has been associated with Buddhaghosa, in contrast to the Ceylonese Theravāda, which is associated with Soṇa and Uttara and the North Indian Sanskrit school with Upagupta.[120] The issue is more complicated in practice, but the point I am trying to make here is that two of the three traditions, those of Buddhagosa and Upagupta, can be found in Pyū culture prior to the mid-eleventh century presumed Mon-Burman contact.[121]

A Hīnayāna sect appeared to have been present at Śrī Kṣetra also, the Sarvāstivāda. This group wrote the Buddhist Canon in Sanskrit rather than in Pali, and one of their strongholds lies in northeastern India in the Magadha region.[122] They differed little with the Theravāda as both belonged to the broader Hīnayāna and followed the same *Vinaya.* One important belief found in the Sarvāstivāda is the ideology of Maitreya, the future Buddha, who will descend to earth after the allotted 5,000 years have elapsed to preach the ultimate sermon so that all humans hearing it will attain *nirvana.*[123] Among other pieces of evidence, Maitreya is found in Pyū culture by a bronze statuette with an inscription identifying him.[124] The concept of Maitreya was central to Burmese Buddhism as well as its political ideology for millennia, and was known at least during the Śrī Kṣetra period.[125] And long after Śrī Kṣetra had declined as the premier center of the Pyū, a terracotta votive tablet with a Pyū inscription was found in the relic chamber of the eleventh-century Shwéhsandaw at Pagán. The prayer was precisely for that boon—to be reborn when Maitreya returns to earth to preach the ultimate sermon.[126] At Pagán, of course, nearly every donation ended with that same request; indeed it is still the main wish of devotees today.[127]

During the early twentieth century, a silver cylindrical reliquary was discovered at Śrī Kṣetra on which was embossed the names and figures of the last four Theravāda Buddhas of this present *kalpa* (age).[128] Each Buddha, seated in *bhumispasa mudra* is identified by name in both Pali and Pyū. From the center of the reliquary rises a banyan tree, today often regarded as a symbol of the yet-to-arrive Maitreya. This kind of reliquary was clearly a miniature of their larger counterparts, the hollow *gu* (temple), in which were placed the same four Buddhas in the same cardinal directions, with the unopened lotus bud on top, representing the future Buddha.[129] Such symbolism became ubiquitous subsequently, at Pagán especially.

In other words, various forms of Buddhism existed in Upper and Lower Burma, including what was considered "orthodox," long before the Mons allegedly brought orthodoxy to the Burmese speakers after Aniruddha's conquest of Thatôn in 1057 AD and certainly before the first presumed Burman-Mon contact, for that did not occur until the late eleventh and early twelfth centuries. Indeed, not a single, *dated,* original Old Mon language inscription has been found on a single piece of art historical and archaeological material from Lower Burma during the Pyū period prior to the rise of Pagán.[130]

The only belief system about which we have little or no record this early in contemporary sources is *nat* worship, an indigenous supernaturalism centered on and perhaps incorporated by the Cult of the 37 Nats. Although many aspects of this latter cult actually reside within the conceptual framework of the Brahmanic, Hindu, and particularly Buddhist contexts, it has also been assumed to have been an earlier, distinct Mon contribution, particularly by H. L. Shorto, the late, distinguished scholar of Mon. Yet all the sources he cited for that argument are fifteenth century and later.[131] Indeed, the cult itself may be fairly late, as no original evidence for it as such exists in the Pagán inscriptions.[132]

In addition to religious beliefs per se, the conceptions of state and king during the Buddhist period of the Pyū seemed to have been centered on Indic ideologies as well. They instituted a monarchy based on royal families that used the Indic names of Varman and Vikrama.[133] Their major cities were created to symbolize heaven on earth, revealing Hindu-Buddhist cosmological concerns of time and space that were expressed in the twelve gates found in several Pyū cities. Each of the twelve gates represented a sign of the zodiac, suggesting that the city was sacred space and time on earth. Typically, this heaven on earth was Tāvatiṁsa, the favorite of several Buddhist heavens throughout Burma's history, ruled by the high Brahmanic deity Indra and his thirty-two lords, a motif and design that is most clearly illustrated by the nineteenth-century royal palace at Mandalay.[134] The belief that Indra (Sakrā in the Pali tradition and Thagya in the Burmese) oversaw the creation of Śrī Kṣetra can be found in an eleventh-century Pagán inscription[135] as well as the Burmese chronicles. In the latter, Sakrā, standing at the center of the future city, envisioned a circle drawn by a rope dragged around by a Nāga.[136]

The Burmese dating system of what Buddhist scholars call the Lesser Era *(Cūḷasakarāj)*, that starts on Friday, 20 March 638 AD when the month of Vesakha begins, is apparently derived from the North Indian, not the Ceylonese or South Indian traditions.[137] The Pyū had been using this era several hundred years prior to the first appearance of the Burmese speakers and their subsequent contact with the Mon.[138] Indeed, in Burma Studies, it is called the "Pyū Era."[139]

And finally, Indic culture can be found in the Pyū writing system, whose connections to the Pagán script, in which Old Burmese, Old Mon, Arakanese, and much later, Shan, were written, will be more fully discussed in Chapters Seven and Eight. Suffice to say here that, as is true virtually everywhere else in Hindu-Buddhist Southeast Asia during this period except Sinicized Vietnam, the Pyū writing system was also borrowed from India.[140] Brāhmī scripts of both North and South India—the former, of the period of Aśoka's edicts, and the latter, of the Tamil Sangam literature, both dated approximately to the third and second centuries BC—as well as later northeastern Indian scripts of the Gupta era and South Indian Kannada of the same era are found at Pyū sites.[141] The script which ultimately became Pyū itself seemed to have developed during the early Halin period and is thought by some, although not others, to be most closely related to Southwest India's Kadamba, a topic to be fully discussed in Chapter Seven.

The fact that inscriptions at Halin and Śrī Kṣetra included interlinear Brāhmī of the South Indian variety suggests that although the Pyū were beginning to experiment with their own script, they were still not confident enough with their language to leave out Brāhmī entirely from the writing system, whereas earlier, at Beikthano, Brāhmī stood alone.[142] By the time the royal funerary urn inscriptions of Śrī Kṣetra were written perhaps in the seventh and early eighth centuries AD, the Pyū language was being written in the Pyū script without any interlinear Brāhmī.[143] And by the time the two gold plates from Maung Kan's field, the silver casket, and the gold-leafed manuscript mentioned above were written, the Pyū script was willing to tackle even the Pali language.[144] This, indeed, is indicative of a turning point in the development of the Pyū script, for it had finally gained the confidence and ability to write Pali, the status language, the language of the Buddha, the language most capable at the time of the highest forms of expression. The names of each of the four Buddhas of this *kalpa* (age) represented on the silver reliquary—Gotama, Koṇāgamana, Kakusandha, and Kassapa—are written not in Pali but the Pyū language, as are each of the Buddha's four disciples,[145] while at the bottom are the names, probably of the donors, Śrī Brabhuvarman and Śrī Prabhudevī.

Thus, the best evidence available suggests that sometime between the second and the sixth centuries AD, the Pyū had been experimenting with a script, and although linguists seem to agree that all scripts of India ultimately stem from Brāhmī, Pyū's immediate precursor appears to have been western South India's Kadamba alphabet of Vanavasi[146] a script also used during the fifth to sixth centuries AD in North Kannada, near Goa.[147] The dates of the latter script as well as the place from where it came correspond well with the chronology of and source of influence for Beikthano and Halin.[148] By the Pagán period, and probably earlier, the Pyū people had already addressed some of the problems of adapting Tibeto-Burman tones to an Indo-European alphabet and vowel system that did not need to mark tones. The Pyū face of the Myazedi Inscriptions shows a wide range of these tones being used,[149] possibly eight,[150] a process very likely adopted by the writers of Old Burmese, as we shall see in Chapter Seven.

The Decline of Pyū Civilization

After approximately a millennium of existence and influence by the Pyū and their culture in the areas now considered the heartland of precolonial Burma, the *Man Shu* stated that the kingdom of Nanchao "looted and plundered the P'iao kingdom. They took prisoner over three thousand of their people . . . [and] banished them into servitude at Chê-tung, and told them to fend for themselves. At present their children and grandchildren are still there, subsisting on fish, insects, etc. . . . Such is the end of their people."[151] The same account preserved in the T'ang History is somewhat different, its translator, Parker, writing that "in the year 832 the Nan-chao monarch kidnapped 3,000 *Burmans* and colonised his newly acquired eastern dominions with them" [my emphasis].[152] This suggests, of course, that the Burmese speakers were already present in Pyū society, although one wonders whether the term "Burmans" was actually in the original.[153]

Whatever the case may be, a political vacuum had been created as a result of the raid, and into it moved the Burmese speakers. They were either already present in Pyū society or, as one scholar contends, were part of the Nanchao forces who galloped down the passes but chose to remain in Burma for reasons bordering on modern sentiments regarding political "freedom."[154] However, archaeological, epigraphic, and early chronicle evidence suggests, instead, an indigenous, historical continuity between Pyū and the Burmese speakers irrespective of the Nanchao raid. Certainly there is nothing in the narrative of the *Man Shu* to suggest that the Pyū kingdom as a whole was destroyed—it was only "looted and plundered"—or that the Pyū as a people and culture disappeared totally because 3,000 of them may have been taken away as labor. The size of the Pyū kingdom and its many walled cities throughout the land not only indicates a population many times the number said to have been taken, but one that was not concentrated in any single city in a single locality. There is also radiocarbon evidence, noted above, from nearly four decades after the Nanchao raid, of continued human activity until at least 870 AD at Halin, said to be the city looted. Śrī Kṣetra also continued to be an important city well into the Ava period (1364–1527) and beyond, while the settlement at Pagán continued unaffected by the alleged crisis, to subsequently become the next capital of Burma for four more centuries.[155] Indeed, several Pyū-language inscriptions were discovered centuries after the Nanchao raid of 832: one at Pagán in the reliquary of Aniruddha's Shwéhsandaw Pagoda and therefore thought to be mid-eleventh century, another near the front (east) gate of Pagán with an unknown date, the third, of course, the famous fourth face of the so-called Myazedi Inscriptions of 1112 AD, and the fourth in Lower Burma.[156] The Pyū as a people also continued to be mentioned in several Old Burmese inscriptions of the early thirteenth and the second half of the fourteenth centuries. In the inscriptions of Pagán and Ava, a Pyū concubine, a Pyū carpenter, a Pyū village, Pyū rice lands totaling some 234 acres, Pyū toddy palms, a Pyū mound, a Pyū "female husband" (spouse?), and a Pyū firewood dealer are mentioned.[157]

This suggests that the Nanchao raid may have affected only one Pyū city, perhaps the capital, and not the kingdom or polity as a whole. Thus, although the Nanchao raiders may have precipitated a change in the political situation by weakening the established leadership, thereby providing the Burmese speakers an opportunity to take charge, the Pyū people or their culture did not disappear entirely. Indeed, Pyū culture was preserved in Pagán institutions and culture. Virtually the entire Indic culture of

Pagán—the writing system, the measurement of time, the most important religious beliefs, the best of its engineering techniques for building temples, its conceptions of statecraft, the most enduring symbols relating to the capital city; and even some of the underlying principles found in dance and music—is recognizable in the parent culture of the Pyū.

And because this Indic culture can be documented among the Burmese speakers only after they had settled in the plains of the Irrawaddy River valley—certainly there is no evidence of Indic culture among the proto-Burmese speakers (the Lolo) when they still lived where most scholars think was their original western Yunnan homeland[158]—over one and a half centuries before their first assumed contact with the Mon in the late eleventh century AD at the earliest, it is most likely that the Burmese speakers derived it from the Pyū, not from the Mon or the proto-Burmese.[159]

Following the Nanchao raid, sometime between the mid-ninth and early eleventh-centuries, the walled city of Pagán was built. This is dated in a horoscope of the city to precisely 849 AD by one of the earliest Burmese chronicles,[160] while the most recent radiocarbon results taken from a charred teak fragment of the palace within the walled city provides a calibrated date (with 95.4 percent probability), at the earliest end of the spectrum, of 980 AD.[161] The foundations of the main wall, which we might expect to have been built earlier instead of later than the palace,[162] yielded a calibrated date of 1020 AD at its earliest spectrum. But fill from what is thought to have been an abandoned latrine between the walled area and the moat produced a calibrated radiocarbon date, again at earliest, of 990 AD.[163]

It is true, of course, that these radiocarbon dates include a late spectrum as well, so that the plateau between early and late dates is a large one, even though the 95.4 percent probability of the calibrated dates is very close in most cases to the uncalibrated ones dated "BP" (before present, that is, 1950). But there is ample epigraphic evidence for the later years at Pagán and the late end of the spectrum of the carbon dates, that is, the twelfth and thirteenth centuries. My focus, therefore, is on the less well-known early period, to see if there is any scientific basis for some of the earliest traditional accounts regarding the origins of the Pagán Dynasty as exemplified by its fortified capital and palace.

Clearly there is, and it deserves serious consideration. The dates given for the palace and latrine are close to those recorded in the *Zatatawpon Yazawin* and belong to the decade during which an epigraphically confirmed king of Pagán reigned[164] and a late copy of a royal inscription in Burmese dated to 984 AD exists.[165] The inscription was presumably erected during the reign of Aniruddha's grandfather (Saw Rahan, 956–1001), who was followed by his father (Kyaung Phyu, 1001–1021), then by Aniruddha himself, who ascended the throne in 1044 AD. Thus, even the 1020 AD radiocarbon date for the foundations of the city walls falls within the reigns of these three historical individuals, when a monarchy of Burmese-speaking kings had already been established at Pagán, and shortly after Pyū dominance had waned in the Dry Zone.

The scientific evidence, therefore, tends to support chronicle and other traditional accounts, not only that Pyū and Burman cultures were contemporaneous or nearly so,[166] but that Pyū culture immediately preceded and overlapped in time and space with Burman culture in the kingdom of Pagán. It suggests that the Burmese speakers had absorbed whatever population and culture remained of the Pyū after the Nanchao raid. And because the city of Pagán became the capital of a kingdom under the leadership of Burmese speakers almost immediately after Pyū domination ceased, it means the Burmese speakers followed right on the heels of the Pyū, leaving no occasion for a putative "Mon period" to have preceded the "rise" of the kingdom of Pagán, as implied by the Mon Paradigm. The Pyū were clearly the immediate predecessors of the Burmese speakers—historically, socially, economically, politically, geographically, infrastructurally, and artistically. It was they who gave their culture to the Burmese speakers, not the Mon, who did not even appear on the scene until two hundred years later.

Not surprisingly, therefore, the Burmese chronicles recalled the Pyū to have been the founders of the Pagán dynasty. This sentiment is reflected in the tradition of Pyuminhti (Umbrella of the Pyū King),[167] probably an etymon, the linguistic form from which another form is historically derived whereby the essential meaning of a word is seen in its origins.[168] Even more telling, the first several kings of the Pagán Dynasty, as recorded in Burmese chronicles, follow the patronymic system found in the culture of Nanchao and other Tibeto-Burman speakers such as the Pyū, where the last portion of the predecessor's name was used as the first portion of his successor's.[169] Most significant, this connection made between the Burmese speakers and the Pyū by the Burmese chronicles occurred well before modern, twentieth-century research pointed in the same direction, which suggests that such traditions of an earlier relationship may have been well founded.

All the above evidence suggests that a fairly widespread, relatively uniform (or at least similar) culture existed over much of the country before and during most of the first millennium. It displayed characteristic Upper Burma (Pyū) cultural features, none of which can be identified as having belonged to Dvāravatī, the only known Mon cultural center thought to have existed during the same period of time. And even if one can show that some Mon artifacts may have come from Dvāravatī into the Pyū region, it can hardly be considered evidence to support the kinds of claims made by the Mon Paradigm. Such evidence should come as no surprise in any case, since the Pyū were actively linked by trade and diplomacy to a wider region of Southeast Asia.

Conclusion

Despite this rather clear continuity that exists between the Pyū and Burman environment, culture, and history, the Mon Paradigm nevertheless claimed that the reason for the growth and development of the kingdom of Pagán was a Lower Burma Mon contribution to virtually every aspect of the culture of the Burmese speakers at Pagán. This notion implies at least a *tabula rasa* between the "end" of the Pyū and the "beginning" of the Burmese speakers, a conclusion also not supported by the evidence.

At the same time, however, although there is continuity between Pyū and Burman culture, it does not mean that the kingdom of Pagán cannot, or should not, be regarded as an apt marker for important qualitative and quantitative change. Change itself is not at issue, but whether that change was a movement from Mon to Burman or from Pyū to Burman culture. In terms of the cultural group who was now in the leadership position of the central plains, and in terms of the more evolved structure of state and society—in short, in terms of the composition of leadership, the scale of the kingdom, and the structure of state and society—Pagán was indeed a changed entity.

Certainly the size of the exemplary center had changed. Pagán was a relatively small (approximately 140 hectares) walled city compared with the much larger (664–1,400 hectares), cities of the Pyū.[170] The large size of the earlier cities suggests that much of the population resided within the walls, as corroborated by the *Man Shu*.[171] It is there that the remains of their important secular and religious structures (palaces, temples, mausoleums), as well as their sources of food (irrigated fields) can be found.[172] In contrast, in the kingdom of Pagán, the majority of the population could not have lived inside the small area enclosed by the capital's walls. Instead, the evidence shows that the vast majority of its people—the crown service groups *(kywan-tō)*, the *purā kywan* attached to the *saṅgha*, and the nonattached *asañ*—lived outside the city walls, and by Pagán's zenith in the late twelfth and early thirteenth centuries, as far away as 100 miles from the capital city itself. Indeed, the bulk of the kingdom's most vital agricultural resources where most of these people were located—the irrigated regions of Kyauksé, Minbu, and the Mu Valley—were not protected, as in Pyū times, behind the capital's defensive walls. It is true that Pagán had regional fortifications, but nevertheless these were situated quite a distance from the center.

This new configuration suggests, among other things,[173] that both quantitative and qualitative changes had taken place following the Pyū period. Economic growth meant concomitant demographic growth (or vice versa), perhaps ultimately triggered by the ability to harvest three crops annually of the new, greater-yielding *padi* of the Indica variety. This would have been enhanced by the building of new or the refurbishing of old irrigation works,[174] along with an influx of much-needed labor from surrounding areas attracted by this growth. Thus, Pagán seemed to have been a much wealthier, more hierarchic, administratively larger, more powerful, more stable, more centralized, and more secure state than the Pyū state had been. Otherwise, the Pyū configuration of the state, with the majority of the population and rice lands located inside the walls of much bigger, well-defended cities rather than spread far outside them, would most likely have remained intact.

The new state was wealthy and stable enough to patronize the Buddhist church, provide scholarships for students, pay artisans and architects to build nearly 3,000 religious edifices, including hundreds of monasteries, dozens of libraries, and other infrastructural projects such as dams, canals, reservoirs, and wells, on a scale that was not evident before. The majority of the religious buildings were also located outside the city walls. The state and society were further able to provide economic and other incentives for international visiting scholars to this exemplary center, and to maintain these programs with endowments of productive rice lands and hereditary labor or service of that labor for hundreds of years.[175] The kingdom of Pagán was also strong enough to expand its territory to nearly the country's modern size and enjoyed a stature within the "international Buddhist community" in the twelfth and thirteenth centuries of being the foremost center of Theravāda Buddhism in the region, one which pilgrims, monks, and scholars from distant lands eagerly visited.[176]

In light of the above, then, the following question needs to be asked. To what extent was this qualitative and quantitative change a result of Mon influence, as claimed? The answer is, not much, if any. By the time the conquest of Lower Burma had occurred, between 1055 and 1057, the genesis of Burmese rule was already nearly a century old, the walled fortifications of their exemplary center had already been built for a quarter century, and Aniruddha, thought to be the one who initiated first contact with the Mon of Lower Burma, had already been on the throne for thirteen years. He had already consolidated the northern, eastern, and western flanks of the country, leaving the southern portion, Lower Burma, for last.

It is during this final phase of unification that Burmese speakers first came in contact with Mon speakers, as the earliest evidence of Mon culture in Pagán appears only in the King Kyanzittha's reign (1084–1112). By then, state and society at Pagán already possessed much, if not most, of its important institutions: a hierarchic, predominantly agrarian society ruled by a central, hereditary monarchy that probably controlled the kingdom by means of a widespread administrative structure and certainly by a conceptual system based on Buddhist ideas of kingship and state. Mon culture appeared in Upper Burma only much later and therefore could not have played the kind of role in the development of the kingdom of Pagán that the Mon Paradigm claims.

Indeed, it was just the reverse: the culture of Pagán provided the most important Indic and non-Indic factors in the development of the Lower Burma Mon state, which emerged for the first time in the country only in the very late thirteenth century, as will be demonstrated in subsequent chapters. It was Pagán that provided the wherewithal for the origins and development of a much later Thatôn and Rāmaññadesa, having already acquired—from at least two centuries of integration with the Pyū—the necessary political, economic, religious, literary, social, and artistic ingredients to do so.

Yet the Mon Paradigm dies hard. When Winga, a Lower Burma site, was discovered in the 1980s near Thatôn, it was automatically assumed to have been Mon since it was in Lower Burma and close to Thatôn, despite the fact that the two artifacts from Winga submitted to TL dating produced very late dates of 1499 and 1662 A.D.[177] Despite such scientific evidence contradicting the Mon Paradigm, Winga became yet another brick in the house laid by the Mon Paradigm, and is considered by Burma scholars today to have been part of the legendary Suvaṇṇabhūmi of Buddhist literature, an ancient Eldorado claimed by fifteenth century King Dhammazedi to have been the "realm of the Rmañ" since the early Christian era.

3 Rāmaññadesa, an Imagined Polity

IN THE PREVIOUS chapter we saw how widespread the Pyū kingdom was in the Dry Zone of Burma, centered at various sites in different periods, controlling the plains of the Irrawaddy and Chindwin River valleys especially between the second century BC and the mid-ninth century AD. Perhaps its political hegemony, or at least influence, but certainly its culture extended even to the maritime regions of what is now the northern part of the Gulf of Muttama, precisely the area where the Mon kingdom of Rāmaññadesa was supposed to have been thriving. If the Pyū kingdom was the prevailing polity in Burma during the first millennium AD, and was immediately followed by the Burmese kingdom of Pagán, which subsequently also occupied that same territory, and later Lower Burma, what happens to the Mon Paradigm's claim that Rāmaññadesa was present and dominant in the same regions during the same time?

This chapter addresses that problem. It analyzes and describes original contemporary and near-contemporary data to show that the presence of a Mon Theravāda Buddhist polity called Rāmaññadesa (or anything else) in Lower Burma prior to the expansion of Pagán into that region cannot be substantiated. This suggests that the doubts Dupont and Wheatley had about the antiquity of a Mon polity in that place during the first millennium were prescient and justified. Wheatley, particularly, was quite disappointed, writing that the "external sources relating to Lower Burma in the days before the Burmese conquest are exiguous, obscure and unreliable,"[1] so that as far as he was able to ascertain, "there is no evidence other than that of the chronicles for the existence of a Mon state, subsuming and transcending individual chieftainships, in the delta lands of Lower Burma in early times."[2] Since his study focused on the development of urbanism in Southeast Asia, rather than on the specific claims being made by the Mon Paradigm regarding a kingdom of Rāmaññadesa and its role in the development of Pagán, he ended this part of his enquiry by writing that because Lower Burma settlements lacked "'cities with walls and suburbs' . . ." [that is, urbanism, and to him, by extension, state formation] "[it] is of no direct concern to us at the moment."[3] For us, however, the absence of urban forms in Lower Burma during the first millennium AD is precisely the issue.

Rmeñ, Rman, Man, and Mon

In attempting to discover the origins of the putative political entity called Rāmaññadesa, it is instructive to first examine the etymology of the term itself. The modern word *mon* is the current orthography of the ethnonym *Rmeñ,* which later, in Burma, became *Rman,*[4] thence *Man* (dropping the "r"). The term *Man* was still used as recently as the late nineteenth century.[5] Indeed, I have not seen the term *mon* as such in original and contemporary epigraphs of Burma before the fourteenth century; it is always *rmeñ.*

Christian Bauer writes that the "ethnic name of the Mon people occurs for the first time [in Burma], in Old Mon, . . . in Kyanzittha's New Palace Inscription of AD 1102 as *rmeñ,*" confirmed by his source, Luce.[6] Bauer adds that the ethnonym is found earlier "in three Pre-Angkor (Old Khmer) inscriptions . . . and in two Old Javanese inscriptions . . . "[7] as *ramañ, rmmañ, rāmaṇyacampādīñ* in the former, and *ṛmĕn* and *rĕmĕn* in the latter.[8] The former three are said to be found in sixth- to tenth-century Old Khmer language inscriptions, while *ṛmĕn* and *rĕmĕn* can be found in Javanese language inscriptions, the former dated to the eleventh century.[9] If these inscriptions are original and their chronology is correct, then clearly the ethnonym was already known and used elsewhere in Southeast Asia well before the term *rmeñ* appeared in Pagán. Although that may seem to verify the early presence, or at least knowledge, of the Rmeñ people where these inscriptions are found, they say nothing about a Rmeñ Theravāda Buddhist polity—or kingdom, state, or "imagined community"—in Lower Burma called Rāmaññadesa prior to the rise and decline of Pagán.

In the 1102 inscription of Pagán mentioned above, thought by all Burma scholars to have been erected during the last decade of King Kyanzittha's reign,[10] these Rmeñ are described as participating in an important state ritual of integration, the construction of the King's palace, singing their own songs, along with the Tircul (presumably the Pyū) singing theirs, and the Mirmā (Mranmā), theirs. Note that both Mranmā and Tircul are also ethnonyms, so that they too are addressed by their ethnonyms by people who did not necessarily belong to the same ethnocultural group. That was apparently the preferred, customary way of the culture writing the inscription for identifying people at the time, rather than using names given to them by outsiders, such as the Chinese using P'iao for the Tircul and Mien for the Mranmā, and, of course, since colonial times the English term Burman for the Mranmā.

The context and manner in which these three groups (really four, but the name of the last is illegible on the inscription) were described suggests further that the terms *rmeñ, mranmā,* and *tircul* were, at the time, also perceived to have been distinct cultures. That is to say, Rmeñ songs were being distinguished from Mirmā and Tircul songs, so that these terms were being used as adjectives for their respective cultures. There were such things, then, as Rmeñ, Tircul, and Mirmā songs, not just Rmeñ, Tircul, and Mranmā people. Although all were participants in what appears to have been a unifying state ritual, the inscription was nevertheless a statement about cultural differences, at least in terms of their music.

The inscription does not say what the relative numbers were among these three groups (although Luce managed to count 126 Rmeñ).[11] Yet from what we know of Pagán's development and history, by the time the inscription was erected, presumably the Tircul,[12] the oldest group among the three, might have been the smallest in number, having over 3,000 of them deported to Yunnan by the Nanchao troops in the ninth century when their kingdom was looted and plundered, and the rest were presumably integrated with the next people to dominate the scene, the Mranmā. The Rmeñ may or may not have been a larger group than the Tircul by the twelfth century, since the Rmeñ were newly arrived in Upper Burma, while the Mranmā probably were.

That the Rmeñ were first mentioned in Upper Burma only by 1102 or thereabouts suggests that they were relative latecomers in the process of state development in Burma, arriving a good 500 years after evidence of urban settlement at or near what is now the city of Pagán and at least 100 years after the establishment of the city walls themselves. Certainly, the first mention of the Rmeñ people appears in the original sources of Upper Burma well after Pagán had already consolidated its power over and unified much of the major river valleys. Thus, although the Rmeñ as a cultural group was apparently known much earlier in Cambodian and Javanese sources, their presence in Upper Burma cannot be verified in contemporary and original epigraphs until the early twelfth century, too late to be of much consequence in state development there in the manner claimed by the Mon Paradigm.[13]

Apart from their late presence in Upper Burma, how the word *rmeñ* later became *mon* is also important to this investigation. Once again, we turn to Bauer, who writes that the modern reflex *mon* is "the result of the simplification of the initial and the shift of OM [Old Mon] final palatals /c,-n/ to spoken Mon (SM) final dentals /-t, -n/ in certain contexts."[14] But when precisely or even approximately that sort of "simplification" might have occurred in history would be difficult to say, especially since spelling in written Mon (which would be needed to show this change) apparently lags behind the spoken language.[15] In terms of the modern written form *mon,* Burma Mon scholars think that that derivation actually comes "through the medieval *rman.*"[16] What this suggests is that the term *mon* is not derived directly from the Old Mon *rmeñ* but via an intermediate "medieval" phase *rman,* from there to *man,* and finally to *mon.*

Even more important to our investigation, this sequence is also pertinent to the development of the word Rāmañña. Blagden feels that like the term *mon,* the term *rāmañña* is also derived from the Middle Mon *rman* in a distinct and later development, *rman* being derived from the Old Mon *rmeñ.* He suggests that it "is the ultimate native original from which, at some time or other in the Middle Ages [by which he most surely meant the post-Pagán period], scholars invented the form *rāmañña* by a deliberate process of word coining in order to create a form which would fit into a Pali context."[17] This is made clear on the Kalyani Inscriptions, where the Pali *rāmañña* is always represented by the Mon *"rah rman,"* meaning "the Mon country."[18] Bauer appears to concur with Blagden on this sort of process elsewhere when he shows how the T'ai word *raman* also does not derive from Old Mon or Khmer, as suggested by Nai Pan Hla, a Burma Mon scholar,[19] but from Pali. The conclusion that Pali word coining is intimately involved in the development of the word *rāmañña* (at least in Burma) is critically important, for both *rman* and *rāmañña* appear late in the epigraphy of Burma,[20] not until the fifteenth-century Kalyani Inscriptions of King Dhammazedi. Blagden seems to be saying that the word *rāmañña* did not emerge until after the word *rman* appeared. He then goes further by suggesting that *mon* and *rāmañña* are "one and the same word, the latter being merely a scholarly form artificially coined for use in a Pali context and based upon an older phase of the former, which was the genuine native ethnic name" (i.e., *rmeñ*).[21] This means *rāmañña* (again, at least in Burma) was originally not a place name, as most scholars assume, but a Pali rendition for the ethnonym *rmeñ,*[22] although I leave all this for the linguists to determine more precisely.

What we do know for certain is that the term *rmeñ* itself, in Burma at least, does not appear before the twelfth century. This suggests, following Blagden, that the earliest possible date, even theoretically, for the term *rāmañña* to have emerged in Burma is the early twelfth century, still over 200 years after Pagán's founding and half a century after Pagán's conquest of Lower Burma.

Blagden's conclusion that the words *rman* and *rāmañña* appear rather late was obviously the reason for the following response from Luce. He wrote that "one may safely postulate, *though it does not occur,* an alternative Old Mon form *rman,* from which the Pali name for the country of the Mons, Rāmaññadesa, found in the Kalyani inscription (1476 AD) has been formed" [my emphasis].[23] Normally careful about the chronology of words, Luce had to postulate in this case an earlier Old Mon version of *rman*—even though, according to his own words, "it does not occur"—for otherwise, Aniruddha would not have had a Rāmaññadesa to conquer in 1057! If the putative "kingdom of Rāmaññadesa" preceded the kingdom of Pagán, as the Mon Paradigm would have it, then the word *rman* that precedes and leads to the development of the term *rāmañña* (in the Burma evidence) must be also older than *rāmañña*'s first mention in the country's epigraphy, which Luce had to acknowledge did not occur until the third quarter of the fifteenth century.[24] To deal with this inconvenient absence, Luce had to conjecture that an earlier Old Mon version of *rman* must have existed.

Rāmaññadesa in Contemporary Epigraphic Sources

The evidence of domestic contemporary epigraphy bears out the linguistic analyses of both Bauer and Blagden to a certain extent. There is not a single primary source anywhere in the country, in any language, contemporary to the entire first millennium AD, that mentions the word Rāmaññadesa. None of the approximately dozen long Old Mon inscriptions of King Kyanzittha, some dated to the very late eleventh century, that referred to Pagán, Śrī Kṣetra, Bodh Gaya in India, as well as other sacred sites in Lower Burma, ever once mention Rāmaññadesa. Neither is its putative center Sudhammapura (Thatôn) mentioned, even though several of the inscription stones were found in the area that later became Thatôn.[25] Subsequently, an Old Burmese inscription of 1196–1198 of King Narapatisithu extols the far-flung boundaries of the Pagán kingdom. Even if this is an exaggeration, it mentions Tenasserim, but it does not mention Rāmaññadesa.[26]

Indeed, no Old Burmese inscription of the Pagán period (ninth to the fourteenth centuries) at any time refers to the region of Lower Burma as Rāmaññadesa. Rather, it was always called Ussā, Ussā Pegu, or Ussā Prañ (kingdom or country of Ussā), a term derived from Ussāla in South India (presumably Orissa) and still used to refer to the Pegu region today.[27] Lower Burma is also called "Tanluiṅ Prañ," (city, country, kingdom, or capital, of the Tanluiṅ) in an Old Burmese inscription dated to 1105 and 1107 AD.[28] At the time however, the word *tanluiṅ*, the presumed precursor of modern *talaing*, was a general reference to the people in Lower Burma,[29] and not, as commonly believed, a reference to the Mon specifically, an issue to be discussed in greater detail in Chapter Eleven. The point here is that although the "Tanluiṅ Prañ" of the 1105/1107 Old Burmese inscription was certainly a reference to Lower Burma, whether it was also a reference to the Rmeñ people exclusively is by no means clear. Whatever the historical connections between the Tanluiṅ and the Rmeñ people and culture, no Old Mon or Old Burmese inscription of Pagán mentions Rāmaññadesa during Pagán's 400-year history. And by the time the word appears in the Mon language, it is already in mid-fifteenth-century Middle Mon, not Old Mon.

Similarly, none of the 217 extant Old Burmese inscriptions[30] erected during what is known in indigenous historiography as the First Inwa Dynasty (1364–1527) mentions Rāmaññadesa either. When Mingaung I, one of this dynasty's strongest, most able kings, identified his realm in 1400, he claimed to rule Tanluiṅ Prañ, not Rāmaññadesa. And of approximately 29 ethnolinguistic groups mentioned in Ava inscriptions, the Rmeñ are not mentioned once; the Tanluiṅ, however, are.[31] Even at the height of the Lower Burma "Mon" Dynasty centered at Pegu, a 1457 inscription of Ava refers to the king of that kingdom as the "Tanluiṅ king," not the Rmeñ or Rman king.[32] By the zenith of the Ava period, an inscription of 1446 still refers to Lower Burma as Ussā Paikū (Ussā Pegu).[33] Another inscription in the same year calls this region "the kingdom of Hanthawaddy ruled by his majesty, great King Yazadhiyat" rather than the kingdom of Rāmaññadesa ruled by the "great *Rman* king Yazadhiyat."[34] What this evidence suggests—and we shall see it repeatedly—is that the term and the concept of Rāmaññadesa is a later, Lower Burma invention. It was never part of the earlier, (admittedly exogenous) vocabulary of Pagán and Ava.

Not until the Kalyani Inscriptions of King Dhammazedi in 1479 was Rāmaññadesa, as an idealized ancient kingdom of the Mon, first mentioned in the original epigraphy of Burma, nearly two hundred years after the Pagán kingdom had already declined and 1400 years after Rāmaññadesa was claimed to have first emerged.[35] Appropriately, throughout Dhammazedi's Kalyani Inscriptions, the word he uses for the Mon people is also the then-current *rman,* not the older *rmeñ,* or the future *man* and *mon.*[36] His usage not only confirms the evolution of the term in Burma from *rmeñ* to *rman* to *man* to *mon,* as Blagden had suggested, but also the relatively late appearance of those terms in the epigraphy of Burma. It further shows that the word *tanluiṅ* was not an exclusive reference to the *rmeñ* at the time, at least not from the perspective of this Mon king. By 1482, even after King Dhammazedi had publicly named the imagined "precursor" of his kingdom Rāmaññadesa in his Kalyani Inscriptions, Upper Burma did not recognize that contention and continued to refer to Lower Burma as the "[d]ownstream region, throughout Ussā Paikū."[37]

Rāmañña (or Rāmaññadesa) *as a reference to a place in Lower Burma* cannot be found in contemporary *external* epigraphy either. Although a Khmer inscription of the tenth century did mention a "Rāmaṇya," it did not identify the place; its context, moreover, suggests it might have been in Khorat.[38] Nor do the earliest T'ai language inscriptions refer to a Rāmaññadesa in Lower Burma.[39] Of them, the Rāma Gāṁhèṅ Inscription of 1292 is the first T'ai-language source to mention a city or center in Lower Burma at all. It calls Pegu by its formal Pali name of Haṅśābati (Haṁsavatī), which only later became the center of the Mon.[40]

Similarly, no relevant contemporary or near-contemporary epigraphy from South India mentions any Rāmaññadesa in Lower Burma. The inscription of Rājendra Coḷa I of South India, erected on the Rājarajeśvara temple in Tanjore, celebrates the 1025 raid of Śrī Vijaya and parts of Island Southeast Asia via Tenasserim (which the inscription calls Mâppapâḷam),[41] near or where Rāmaññadesa was supposed to have been located. The inscription lists thirteen places but does not mention Rāmañña or Rāmaññadesa.

In Śrī Laṅka, the Devanagala Rock Inscription of Parākramabāhu I, erected in 1165 to commemorate a raid on Lower Burma, does mention an Aramaṇa, said to be the Sanskrit form of the Pali Rāmañña. However, this interpretation is contested, not only linguistically but in terms of location, as one renowned scholar has convincingly argued that the Aramaṇa of that particular inscription is a reference to South India, not Lower Burma.[42] His opinion is confirmed by the Kiri-Vehera Slab Inscription, undated but assigned by the editor to between 1191 and 1196. It recalls an Aramaṇa within the context of a raid on the "Pandyan country" in a "war against the rulers of Coda, Pandya. . . ." So do the Slab Inscriptions of Nissanka-Malla and the inscription of the "North-Gate of the Citadel," both dated to the same time as the Kiri-Vehera, where Aramaṇa was again clearly a reference to South India, not Lower Burma.[43]

Despite the fact that on these occasions when Aramaṇa is mentioned as references to South India, nonetheless when the undated Poḷonnaruva Slab Inscription of the Velaikkaras, assigned to the period between 1137 and 1153 by the editor, mentioned an Aramaṇa,[44] Burma scholars immediately concluded that it was Lower Burma.[45] The event has even become a minor myth in early Burma's history.[46] A Sinhalese prose work called the *Butsarana,* attributed to the twelfth-century recounts an Aramaṇa as well,[47] although it cannot be shown that Lower Burma was meant. Even if the records where Aramaṇa is not clearly a reference to South India were, for purposes of argument, assumed to be references to Lower Burma, they still belong to a period between a hundred and nearly two hundred years later than Aniruddha's and Kyanzittha's expansion into Lower Burma in the mid-eleventh-century. They are too late to support the claim that Rāmaññadesa was a Theravāda Mon state in Lower Burma earlier than Pagán that contributed to its "civilizing" process.

Lower Burma in Other Contemporary Sources

Contemporary, external accounts of Lower Burma by travelers from several different regions of the world provide no support for the presence of a kingdom or polity called Rāmaññadesa either.

Arabic Accounts

Several Arabic sources that deal with Southeast Asia appear, at first glance, to be pertinent to this issue. Wheatley has written that their trading ships penetrated the seas of Southeast Asia early in the seventh century and continued for the next thousand years. But, he warns, although these are one of the richest sources for the study of early Southeast Asia, they must be used with caution, not least because most were written secondhand. Only Abu Dulaf and Ibn Battutah described places they had visited personally, and even so there is some doubt that they visited Southeast Asia. Ibn Battutah's account, especially, would be too late (mid fourteenth-century) to be a factor in this discussion. Even one Mas'ūdī's claim to have visited Southeast Asia, Wheatley cautioned, is likely to be invalid. And the rest obtained some of their information from sailors and merchants in the ports of the Persian Gulf, but most often copied "directly and extensively" from earlier accounts, reproducing earlier mistakes in the process.[48] There are other problems of language, transliteration, lore, and the like.

In Gabriel Ferrand's collection of Arab, Persian, and Turkish texts,[49] a place called Rahma was said to have been mentioned. In one of these, a record of Ibn Khordazbeh (mid ninth century), states: "They say that the king of Rahma . . . [here G. E. Harvey, assuming that the place was a reference to Rāmaññadesa and without providing any analysis or argument, parenthetically adds "Lower Burma"] has fifty thousand elephants."[50] The source continues to say that ". . . his country produces cloth made of velvety cotton, and aloe wood of the sort called *hindi*." Another Middle Eastern source by Sulaymān, also said to have been a mid-ninth-century record, adds that in the provinces belonging to this king of Rahma " . . . are found cloths so fine and light that it can pass through a signet ring. It is of cotton." Then it states that ". . . the same country produces the rhinoceros," a subject of amazement to the observer, who concludes that ". . . he is found in other parts of *Ind*" [my emphasis].[51] Finally, a third source, by Ibn al Fakih, states that "In Ind lies a realm called Rahma, bordering on the sea. Its ruler is a woman."[52]

From the explicit statements that Rahma was in "Ind" and also from its best-known products, such as elephants and especially the high-quality cotton, prized throughout Asia for millennia, Rahma was obviously a reference to a place in India, where, indeed, many places are named after the god

Rāma.[53] It is possible, however, that this Rahma could also have been in Arakan, where the first of only two women sovereigns in Burma's history has been recorded,[54] and where the earliest kings according to Arakanese chronicles reigned in their city called Rāmawati.[55] But there is no evidence that Lower Burma ever had the kind of reputation for its fine cotton products that was being described here, certainly not in the ninth century or, for that matter, any other period in its history. And finally, Rahma as it appears in these ninth-century sources, could not have been a reference to the Mon word Rāmañña in Burma in any case, since as we have seen, the term *rman* must first precede the Pali word coining that produced Rāmañña, and *rman* did not appear in original sources in Burma until the fifteenth-century Kalyani Inscriptions. How could these ninth-century Arabic sources have been referring to a place with a term that appeared in Burma only six hundred years later?

Sinhalese Chronicles

Rāmañña is also not found in the earliest of the Sinhalese chronicles, the *Dīpavaṃsa,* thought to have been written in the fourth century AD,[56] nor in the *Mahāvaṃsa,* its enhanced and enlarged sequel, said to have been written in the sixth century AD.[57] It is only in their much later, thirteenth-century successor, the *Cūḷavaṃsa,* that Rāmañña is first mentioned,[58] a fact rather persuasive of its lateness. Even more intriguing, the first part of the *Cūḷavaṃsa* was thought to have been written by a monk named Dhammakitti from Burma who had been invited over to Ceylon during the reign of Parākramabāhu II (1236–1271).[59] This means Rāmañña as a place name in the Sinhalese chronicles did not appear earlier than Dhammakitti, even if later rewriting may have inserted the name in the earlier sections of the *Cūḷavaṃsa.* This is assuming, of course, that the word was a reference to Lower Burma in the first place. In other words, by the time the name appears in the *Cūḷavaṃsa,* it is too late to support the Mon Paradigm's claims.

Indeed, one could argue that because the *Cūḷavaṃsa* was completed only after 1815 and the reign of the last Śrī Laṅkan king, Rāmañña could have been added retrospectively at any time to any part of the text after the thirteenth century.[60] All we know for certain is that the latest version of the extant manuscript, which had to be after 1815, from which the published version is derived, contained the word. By that time the notion that Rāmañña was Lower Burma was well known in the literature of both Śrī Laṅka and Burma.

Thus, Rāmaññadesa is mentioned neither in the earliest extant copy of the Sinhalese chronicle, the *Dīpavaṃsa,* nor in its subsequent addition, the *Mahāvaṃsa,* where it should have been had it existed earlier. It is found for the first time only in the *Cūḷavaṃsa,* which was not compiled until the mid- to late thirteenth century, and then by a monk not from Śrī Laṅka but from Burma.

Chinese Sources

Of the several chronologically relevant references to what is now Burma in the Chinese sources, none, as far as I know, mentions an independent kingdom or polity in Lower Burma before the very late thirteenth century, especially one that produced cotton cloths so fine as described by the Arabs. One of the earliest Chinese accounts alleged to include a reference to Burma is the *Fu-nan tu-su ji* (An account of the customs of Fu-nan), a third-century work cited in *juan* 787 of the *Tai-ping Yu-lan,* an encyclopaedia of the tenth century.[61] In it is described a place called Lin-yang, which has been translated by modern editors as "Rammanya." However, there are serious difficulties if this "Rammanya" were meant to represent the *Rāmaññadesa* of the Mon Paradigm. Note that I am *not* disputing the rendering of the Chinese term Lin-yang as "Rammanya" at this time, but whether this Lin-yang can be placed anywhere in a maritime setting, especially on the coasts of Lower Burma.

First, and apart from the fact that "Lin-yang" itself is the *modern Mandarin pronunciation* of the original term from which is derived "Rammanya"[62] (obviously swayed by modern scholarship on Burma), the actual passages in the text, as translated for me,[63] suggest an entirely *different geographic setting and location* for this city, *whether or not the original Chinese term is equivalent to "Rammanya."* The text states, in part, that "to the southwest of Fu-nan, there is the country of Lin-yang. It is 7,000 *li* from Fu-nan. The [people of that] place follow the Buddhist teachings, and there are several thousand Buddhist monks." A second, short reference from the same encyclopedia adds that "the land is flat and extensive, and the population numbers more than 100,000 families. The men and women act benevolently and perform acts of merit and they all serve the Buddha."[64] A third entry on Lin-yang has the following: *"There are no sea routes connecting it with any outside land"* [my emphasis].[65] This statement is supported by an extract taken from another work, dated to the first half of the sixth century, which states that one can travel to Lin-yang by horse or cart, but *there is no water transport* [my emphasis]. Then it adds: ". . . the country of Lin-yang is 2,000 *li* [not 7,000 *li* as reported above] overland from the country of Jin-chen. . . . The whole country worships the Buddha. . . . The waters at this place flow erratically, but discharge into the Heng River, . . ." the modern Chinese reference to the Ganges.[66]

Thus even if the *linguistic* connection between the two words is correct, the Chinese description of Lin-yang suggests it was some other place that was *not on the coast,* for it was said to have been located on a "flat, extensive land" without any "water transport" or "sea routes connecting it." *Prima facie,* therefore, it is not describing Lower Burma, which is a submergence coast with many sea routes to and from it. Indeed, because of the geographic description, both Luce and Chen Yi-Sein placed Lin-yang in Upper Burma, the latter suggesting that it was a reference to Beikthano Myo, one of the "Pyū cites,[67] which exacerbates the difficulties in ways too numerous to consider here. Moreover, neither the *Chia Tan,* the *Chiu-t'ang-shu,* nor the *Hsin T'ang-Shu* mentions a Lin-yang anywhere in Burma, despite the fact that the first describes the routes to and from Burma, the second, its boundaries and "garrison cities," and the third, its "eighteen dependent kingdoms."[68]

Another difficulty is the disparate and contradictory distances and directions given in the Chinese accounts about Funan. If Lin-yang were 7,000 *li* (approximately 2,300 miles) "southwest" of what was thought to have been Funan, it should have been located somewhere in Sumatra, which is clearly not the case if the geographic description given is correct. If "southwest" were a mistake for "northwest," then Lin-yang should be located somewhere on the east coasts of India. That would make some sense if the "Heng River" is indeed an old reference to the Ganges River. If, however, Lin-yang were 2,000 *li* (approximately 630 miles) "overland" from the "country of Jin-chen," as recorded in the sixth-century text, and assuming Jin-chen is somewhere in the Gulf of Thailand,[69] it would also place Lin-yang somewhere in the very far north of Burma and certainly not where Rāmaññadesa was claimed to have been. In the end, Lin-yang's identification with any place in Burma, particularly its maritime areas, cannot be proved or even suggested with the evidence at hand.

When one turns to the records of the Chinese Buddhist pilgrims, the results are the same: there is no record of an independent kingdom located in Lower Burma between the first and the very late thirteenth century AD. Neither Hsüan-tsang nor I-tsing (I-Ching), two of the best-known Chinese Buddhist pilgrims who described Buddhist centers in Southeast Asia during the seventh century, ever once mentioned a Rāmaññadesa anywhere. Yet they included in their reports virtually every other existing Buddhist kingdom, large and small, in Southeast Asia of the seventh century. I-tsing particularly, who not only personally traveled in Southeast Asia in 671 AD, but also included in his report the biographies of sixty other Buddhist monks, most of whom had also traveled the sea route to India,[70] did not once mention a Rāmaññadesa in Lower Burma. He wrote: "Thence northeast, beside the great sea in a valley of the mountains, is the kingdom of Shih-li-ch'a-talo (Crisksetra). Further, to the southeast, in a corner of the great sea is the kingdom of Chia-mo-lang-chia (Kamalanka). Further, to the east, is the kingdom of To-lo-po-ti."[71] Similarly, Hsüan-tsang's record, the *Ta-T'ang Hsi*

Yu Chi, states: "Thence [from Samatata] northeastwards is the kingdom of Shih-li-ch'a-ta-lo (Sri Kshetra). Next, to the southeast, in a recess of the ocean, is the kingdom of Chia-mo-lang-chia (Kamalanka).[72] Next, to the east is the kingdom of To-lo-po-ti (Dvāravatī). . . ."[73] There is no Rāmaññadesa mentioned between Śrī Kṣetra and Kamalanka or Dvāravatī, precisely the area of Lower Burma where it was supposed to have been during this time!

In addition, Luce's rendition of Paul Pelliot's translation has the following crucial difference regarding Hsüan-tsang's statement: "Southward from this the country *borders the sea;* it is the kingdom of Shih-li-ch'a-ta-lo (Criksetra)" [my emphasis]. In other words, the extent of Śrī Kṣetra's influence or power was described as having extended right down to the Gulf of Muttama where no Rāmaññadesa was mentioned. All this is further confirmed in a recent study by Tatsuo Hoshino. He looked at all relevant Chinese sources focused on the Central Mekong Valley in the seventh and eighth centuries. None mentioned any kingdom or polity named Rāmañña or anything else between the Pyū in Burma and the Mon at Dvāravatī.[74]

Similarly, the *Man Shu,* "Book of the Southern Barbarians," records activities in what is now Burma during the ninth century. It describes the entire Irrawaddy River valley down to the Lower Burma coast as being inhabited and dominated by the Kingdom of the P'iao.[75] No mention whatever is made of any other kingdom or people inhabiting what is now Lower Burma. When the Pyū visited the T'ang capital with a musical troupe, again no mention was made of Rmeñ people or culture. The music, wrote Governor Su Kiyu who recorded the occasion in his "Geography" was all in Sanskrit.[76] As some of these musicians wore what the Chinese termed Kun-lun dress, Luce concluded decades ago, without explanation, that this term was a reference to the Rmeñ of Lower Burma.[77] It is a very doubtful interpretation and speculatively self-fulfilling. It is certainly not supported by arguably the most scholarly historical geography of early Southeast Asia, that by Wheatley, nor, for that matter, by any other scholar of early Southeast Asia. The term Kun-lun, Wheatley shows convincingly, was a reference to people of Island Southeast Asia or those who lived on the coasts of Southeast Asia in general. The Kun-lun, he wrote, were "really a succession of peoples ranging from Malays around the coasts of the Peninsula to Chams along the shores of Indo-China. . . ."[78]

There is also no evidence that the Chinese rendition of the word Kun-lun is in any linguistic way, phonetically or otherwise, related to the word *rmeñ* or *mon.* Historically a connection in Burma between Kun-lun and Rmeñ—hence also Rāmaññadesa—would have been anachronistic in any case, as the Rmeñ appeared only much later. Indeed, no other Chinese source dealing with Southeast Asia that I am aware of has linked the term *rmeñ* with the term (or people called) Kun-lun.[79]

It was in the context of associating Kun-lun with Rmeñ that Luce made the assertion regarding the *Man Shu*'s reference to Mi-ch'ên (discussed in Chapter Two), which he conjectured was a reference to Pegu, and by implication, the Mon.[80] As we have seen, the text itself contained nothing to make such an inference. It stated only that the people of Mi-ch'ên had short black faces, called their princes and chiefs *Shou,* and that their kingdoms had no cities with inner or outer walls.[81] Needless to say, the *Man Shu* never mentioned the ethnolinguistic identity of Mi-ch'ên's inhabitants either; they certainly were not called Kun-lun.[82] Even if Mi-ch'ên were Pegu, Luce mistakenly concluded that simply because Pegu in the fourteenth century was inhabited by Mon speakers, they also must have inhabited it in the ninth, thereby assuming a static, ahistorical link between location and reified ethnicity.

Sung records on Burma also do not mention a Rmeñ or any other kingdom in Lower Burma. Indeed, Chau-Ju-Kua, who includes P'u-kan (Pagán) in his account of the Sung period, lists some twenty-one "countries" in South and Southeast Asia along with another eight "countries in the sea," but makes no mention of a Rāmaññadesa or any polity in Lower Burma. Nor did the Chinese traveler Chou-Ta-Kuan, who visited Angkor in the thirteenth century, recall any local memory of a kingdom in Lower Burma named Rāmaññadesa.[83]

Similarly, of the official Chinese sources that had information on Burma—the *Shih-chi* (Historical records), *San-kuo-chih* (Annals of the Three Kingdoms), *Hsin T'ang-Shu* (New History of the T'ang dynasty), *Yüan-shih* (History of the Yüan or Mongol dynasty), and *Ming-shih* (History of the Ming dynasty) along with other treatises such as *Ling-wai-tai-ta* (Reply to enquiries on the region beyond the South Ranges), and *T'ien-hsia-chun-kuo-li-ping-shu* (The topography of the Chinese empire)—none mentions a Rāmaññadesa or any other kingdom in Lower Burma that was independent of, or different from, Pagán.[84]

Neither do the Chinese records mention any embassy sent to or from any independent Lower Burma polity prior to the very late thirteenth-century and the decline of Pagán,[85] that is, not until 1298, when for the first time, a Yüan source records one. The *Zhi-yuan Zhengmian Lu* (Records of the expeditions against Mian during the reign of the Zhi-yuan) states: "In the 2nd year (1298), Yunnan province sent Guan-zhu-si-jia as envoy to the kingdom of Deng-long" [which the translator notes is the word Talaing]. Its king dispatched his mother's brothers, Wu-la-he and Wu-du-lu-xin-he, to accompany Guan-zhu-si-jia back to the court."[86] Another translation of the same work has this additional important word: a "*new* Teng-lung kingdom" [my emphasis].[87] Thus, that a "new Teng-lung [Talaing] kingdom" in Lower Burma seeking autonomous recognition from China emerged for the first time only in the very late thirteenth century is consistent with all the evidence already presented.

Rāmaññadesa in Late Southeast Asian Sources

The earliest Mon texts themselves do not trace the origins of their own state in Lower Burma to events prior to the very late twelfth and early thirteenth century either, apart from their legitimation links to the Buddha. Nor do the late chronicles of Southeast Asia. The most important of these, although too late to be considered contemporary evidence for the existence of Rāmaññadesa in Lower Burma during the first millennium AD, nevertheless had some revelations on Rāmaññadesa that are important. A Rāmaññanagara is mentioned in one of the earliest Pali chronicles of Northern Thailand, the *Cāmadevīvaṃsa,* written perhaps in the fifteenth century. Even then, this Rāmaññanagara is likely to have been a place in the kingdom of Haripuñjaya itself, not in Lower Burma.[88] The *Jinakālamāli,* another Northern Thai chronicle written in Pali in the sixteenth century by a monk who lived in Chiang Mai, also mentions a "Rammaṇa Country," spelled differently from the one in Lower Burma, as one can see, but exactly the same way as the one thought to be in Khorat, within Thailand itself.[89] Besides, by the time the *Jinakālamāli* was written, over two hundred years had passed since the end of the Pagán Dynasty and a half century since the Kalyani Inscriptions had publicly proclaimed ancient Rāmaññadesa to have been in Lower Burma. Even if the *Jinakālamāli*'s references were to Lower Burma, they are too late to be considered contemporary proof of Rāmaññadesa's earlier existence.

Similarly, neither of the two earliest Burmese chronicles, the *Zatatawpon Yazawin* and the *Yazawingyaw,* mentions Rāmaññadesa. Certain sections of the first were probably written during the late thirteenth century, with much added later, while the second was written around 1520, by Shin Thilawuntha of Ava. Another text attributed to the Ava period (1364–1527), called the *Kungya Po Yaza Mu Haung* by Wun Zin Min Yaza, minister to at least two successive kings of the First Ava Dynasty (1364–1527)—Mingyi Swasawke (1368–1401) and Mingaung I (1400–1423)[90]—also fails to mention Rāmaññadesa, although it does recall Thatôn in the context of a religious reform. Indeed, even the most comprehensive history of Burma's monarchy to have survived, U Kala's *Mahayazawingyi,* written between 1712 and 1720, does not mention Rāmaññadesa, only Thatôn.[91] Thatôn is, however, described quite explicitly as "the country of the Talaing people" in the *Zimme Yazawin* by Sithu Gamani Thingyan, the earliest extant copy of which dates to 1762.[92] Of the local records called *sittan* and *thamaing* that survive, even the *Dagon Hsan-daw-shin thamaing* (History of the Hsan-daw-shin or Shwédagôn Pagoda at Yangôn) does not refer to its own locality as Rāmaññadesa. Only in a late copy of an undated but clearly late text dealing with the "geography of the country" is it stated that of the various provinces *(taing)* in the kingdom, Bassein, Pegu, and Martaban comprise Rāmañña *taing*.[93]

The *Chiang Mai Chronicle* of Thailand, which Hans Penth states was written during the reign of King Tilok in the late fifteenth century,[94] mentions a Rāmaññadesa-Haṁsavatī "of the Mon Country," another explicit statement about its ethnolinguistic makeup and location. The statements are made in the context of King Mangrai of Chiang Mai contemplating a conquest of that region in the 1280s.[95] Again, even if this passage in the *Chiang Mai Chronicle* was actually recorded at the time of Mangrai's rule and preserved until the text was subsequently written in either the fifteenth or nineteenth century, it is still too late to be considered contemporary evidence that supports the presence of Rāmaññadesa in Lower Burma prior to the mid-eleventh century. Interestingly though, the story of Mangrai and Wareru, the ruler of Haṁsavatī, whom Mangrai was about to attack, reads very much like the Aniruddha and Manuha story—a trope to be discussed more fully in Chapter Six. In both, a universal Pali model of kingship and his *dhammavijaya* (righteous conquest) is being invoked.[96]

The chronicle goes on to state that Mangrai even traveled to "Phukam-Ava" in 1290–1291 with a similar intention of subjugating it, as he did Haṁsavatī.[97] But neither the kingdom nor city of Ava was founded until 1364, so this chronicle, or perhaps this particular section of it, had to have been composed after that date. It is also interesting that Mangrai is said to have asked for artisans and craftsmen ("goldsmiths, bronzesmiths, ironsmiths") from the king of Phukam-Ava, whom he then settled in his own kingdom. This is perhaps a reference to the probable flight of skilled artisans from declining Pagán, as they sought more lucrative employment in developing Chiang Mai, much like Indian and Southeast Asian craftsmen of nearby declining kingdoms had sought employment in developing Pagán earlier. What is telling about the Northern Thai chronicles' references to Rāmañña is that none mentions this kingdom until it is more or less coterminous with accounts of events and people of the very late thirteenth century, exactly the time when domestic and external epigraphy, and Chinese and Śrī Laṅkan sources also mention it.

Even the Southern Thai chronicle of Nakhon Sri Thammarat,[98] a polity that lay just across the mountains on the southeastern side of the Tenasserim Peninsula so that the fringes of Rāmaññadesa, had it been there, would have been its neighbor, not only fails to mention it, but attributes the founding of its own city to King Narapatisithu of Pagán who reigned in the late twelfth and early thirteenth centuries[99] and included Tenasserim in his domain. In fact, the title *baña* placed in front of the title Narapatirajaraja by these chronicles of Nakhon Sri Thammarat is Mon and may reflect a local honor bestowed upon him by them. The king is also prominent in the origins stories of the Lower Burma Mon in their later chronicles, the earliest extant copy of which dates to the second quarter of the sixteenth century.[100] Unfortunately, it is unclear when the chronicle of Nakhon Sri Thammarat was actually written, but dates ranging from the mid-sixteenth, seventeenth, and eighteenth centuries have been considered.[101] Finally, in *The Royal Chronicles of Ayuthaya* neither Rāmaññadesa as a kingdom nor Thatôn as a city in Lower Burma is mentioned.[102]

The Development of Lower Burma: The Contemporary Epigraphic Evidence

Contemporary epigraphic evidence from Lower Burma shows that the earliest urban sites in Lower Burma after the decline of the Pyū in the ninth century were most likely created and settled by Old Burmese speakers well before Old Mon speakers appeared on the scene. No polity, not even a rudimentary state structure based on urbanization, existed in the region until well after the Kingdom of Pagán had conquered and established an infrastructure there. One can find no archaeological or epigraphic evidence of a major center in Lower Burma comparable to, and earlier than, Pagán. In addition, the evidence we do have contradicts the Mon Paradigm in a most profound way.

Thirty-six putative "place names" in Lower Burma had been identified and published in English by Luce and the Mon Paradigm scholars by the late 1960s, most dated by original inscriptions between the eleventh and fifteenth centuries AD, a time period that covers the Pagán and much of the Ava and Pegu periods.[103] Because these names have been presented as if they were *all* genuine urban sites—and they are not—I have rearranged them according to what the evidence actually has to say about them: that is, I have listed them according to whether they were urban, natural geographic entities, or sacred or mythical in nature (see Table 1). In the process I have removed Suvaṇṇabhūmi altogether from the list of names, for it does not belong in Lower Burma, as will be demonstrated below. To the remaining thirty-five place names, I have added four more urban sites:

Table 1: Urban, Sacred/Mythical, and Natural Sites in Lower Burma: Eleventh to Fifteenth Centuries AD

Site	Type	Initial Language	Date	Reign
Bassein	Urban	Old Burmese	1264	Narathihapade
Bassein River	Natural	Middle Mon	1479	Dhammazedi
Bilin	Urban	Old Burmese	1266	Narathihapade
Botahtaung	Sacred/Mythical	Burmese		
Danubyu	Urban	Old Burmese	1400	Anoratha IV
Hlaing River	Natural	Middle Mon	1479	Dhammazedi
Hmawbi	Urban	Old Burmese	1400	Anoratha IV
Irrawaddy River	Natural	Old Burmese	1442	Narapati I
Kanbè	Urban	Old Burmese?	1198	Narapatisithu
Kawliya	Urban	Middle Mon	1479	Dhammazedi
Kelatha Mount	Sacred/Mythical	Old Mon	1098	Kyanzittha
Khabin	Urban	Old Burmese	1198	Narapatisithu
Kun-gyan-gôn	Natural	Middle Mon	1479	Dhammazedi
Kyaik Ba	Sacred/Mythical	Old Mon		
Kyaik Maraw	Sacred/Mythical	Middle Mon	1455	Shin Saw Bu
Kyaik Talan	Sacred/Mythical	Old Mon	1098	Kyanzittha
Kyaik Tè	Sacred/Mythical	Old Mon	1098	Kyanzittha
Letkhaik	Urban	Old Burmese	1191	Narapatisithu
Martaban	Urban	Old Burmese	1176	Narapatisithu
Maunglaw	Urban	Pali	1077–1084	Saw Lu
Mergui	Urban	Old Burmese	1044–1077	Aniruddha
Moulmein	Urban	Old Burmese	1266	Narathihapade
Myaungmya	Urban	Old Burmese	1400	Anoratha IV
Pa-an/Du'wop	Urban	Old Mon?	14th century	Unnamed Queen
Palè Ridge	Natural	Middle Mon	1479	Dhammazedi
Pegu	Urban	Old Burmese	1266	Narathihapade
Rakṣpura	Sacred/Mythical	Pali		Rajadhiraja?
Rangoon	Urban	Pyū/Old Burmese	1113/1198	Narapatisithu
Salween River	Natural	Old Burmese	1196	Narapatisithu
Sittang	Urban	Middle Mon	1479	Dhammazedi
Syriam	Urban	Old Burmese	1400	Anoratha IV
Tavoy	Urban	Old Burmese	1196–1198	Narapatisithu
Thandôk	Urban	Old Burmese	1196–1198	Narapatisithu
Tharawady	Urban	Old Burmese	1400	Anoratha IV
Thatôn	Urban	Burmese/Pali	1479	Dhammazedi
Twanté	Urban	Old Burmese	1198	Narapatisithu
Wanet Stream	Natural	Middle Mon?	1479	Dhammazedi
Winga	Urban	Middle Mon	1479	Dhammazedi
Zingyaik	Urban	Middle Mon	1479	Dhammazedi
Zôkthôk	Urban	Middle Mon?		

Tavoy, Thandôk, Maunglaw, and Mergui, not included in Luce's list, but all confirmed by dated epigraphy to have existed between 1044 and 1196–1198.[104] I have also separated Rakṣapura from Thatôn, an erroneous link as we shall see in Chapter Four, and have placed the former in the mythic realm and the latter as an urban site.

That makes a total of forty names of sites, real and imagined, seven of which refer to natural places (rivers, streams, ridges, and mounds) and seven to sacred or mythological places. The rest (twenty-six) are genuine urban settlements. Of these, all but five of the twenty *earliest* ones are recorded in Old Burmese and written in the Pagán script. Except for five dated to 1400, the remainder date between the eleventh and thirteenth centuries. Only much *later,* in most cases, several *centuries* later, did thirteen of these twenty Old Burmese urban sites *reappear* in Middle Mon of the fifteenth century. *Most revealing, not a single inscription written in the Mon language relating to an urban site in Lower Burma predates any written in Old Burmese.* Clearly, Lower Burma was settled and urbanized by Burmese speakers well before Mon speakers appeared on the scene centuries later.

Indeed, the names of towns we now think of as "quintessentially" Mon—such as Pegu, Bassein, and Martaban—were first found written in Old Burmese as Paykū, Pusiṁ, and Muttama respectively, to be rewritten only centuries later as Bago, Kusim, and Mattma in fifteenth-century Middle Mon.[105] Pegu is a classic example of this process. The Mon version of Pegu, written (and therefore presumably pronounced) Bago, is found for the first time spelled as Bago in King Dhammazedi's fifteenth-century Mucalinda Inscription.[106] It appears much earlier, in 1266, in Old Burmese as Paykū. This means the pronunciation of Pegu as Bago is a *later* Mon adaptation of the *earlier* Old Burmese, and did not appear as such until 200 years later.[107] Similarly, Bassein (pronounced Pathein in Burmese) is spelled in the Old Burmese original as Pusiṁ, and appears (at latest) in 1264, while its Middle Mon counterpart reappears only by the fifteenth century as Kusim.[108] As for Muttama, it likely appeared as early as 1176 AD in Old Burmese,[109] whereas its Middle Mon equivalent surfaces as Mattma only by 1493, nearly three hundred years later.[110]

This pattern is also true for most of the other Lower Burma place names.[111] Letkhaik appears as early as 1191 in Old Burmese, to reappear in Middle Mon as Kakkhret only by 1497. Tavoy (Old Burmese Taway, Tawai) appears as early as 1196–1198 AD, and only later reappears in Old Mon as Dawāy.[112] Old Burmese Malalaṁ Kruṅ-Wa (Maulamyaing or Moulmein) becomes Middle Mon Mat Lam-Luim in 1479 and Mahlamluim in 1527. Old Burmese Takun becomes Middle Mon Dagôn, which, in the eighteenth century, becomes Yangôn.[113] Old Burmese Tala (across from Takun and dated to 1198) also does not appear in Middle Mon as Dala until 1479. Old Burmese Sanlyaṅ (Syriam) first appears around 1400, then subsequently as Sreñ in Middle Mon in 1479. Old Burmese Roṅmla (Myaungmya), dated to 1400, surfaces as Middle Mon Roṅ Mra by 1442. Old Burmese Krapaṅ (Khăbin) of 1198 is later written in Middle Mon as Krabaṅ, although the precise date is uncertain. Old Burmese Mopī (Hmawbi) appears in 1400, to become Middle Mon Muh Bī in 1479. Old Burmese Tanu-Phlū (Danubyu) also appears in 1400, to become Middle Mon Dhanu-Plu by 1479. Even the Salween River, which empties into the heart of what we normally think of as "Mon land" appears first in Old Burmese as Salwaṅ in 1196 and again in 1292 as Sanlwaṅ; it is not mentioned at all in the Mon epigraphy of the period under discussion.[114] (See Figure 3 for the locations of these Old Burmese place names.)

To be sure, five names among the forty were thought to have been recorded in Old Mon.[115] Of them, however, only one, Du'wop, is an urban site, said to be near, or at present-day Pa-an.[116] Moreover, the inscription on which it appears, at the Kawgun Cave, is not dated, so we cannot know to which century the Old Mon language on the stone belongs. For according to the best Mon scholars, written Old Mon in Burma using the Pagán script covered a period from approximately the eleventh to the mid-fifteenth century, as we shall see. However, there is a clue to the date in the contents of the inscription, which reads: "This image of the Buddha *(kyāk),* it was I, queen of Martaban (?), dwelling in the town of Du'wop, who carved it and made this holy Buddha."[117] Because Mattma (i.e., "Martaban") is mentioned, it is possible that Du'wop existed at that same time Martaban did, which would make the earliest date 1176, although Luce dates Martaban to 1326.[118] Du-wop may have existed in 1292 if the Rāma Gāṁheṅ inscription's identification of Martaban with the T'ai "Moan..n" is correct,[119] in which case Du'wop could not have emerged earlier than 1292.[120] Moreover, Burmese history knows of no queen in Lower Burma as sovereign until Shin Saw Bu, who reigned during the fifteenth century. Whatever date one takes as valid, the presence of Du'wop as a Lower Burma urban site (even if recorded in Old Mon) cannot be construed as evidence for the presence of Rāmaññadesa prior to Pagan's growth and development. Of the other four Old Mon names, Kyāk Bār, Kyāk Talaṅ, and Prāsāt Mahādhāt Satih are sacred sites in the region, while Kelāsa-Parvvata is the "Silver Mountain of Viṣṇu" to which King Kyanzittha was tracing his genealogy. None, therefore, is the name of a city, town, or village, that is, part of a state infrastructure.

The first of these, Kyāk Bār, simply means "two pagodas"[121] and is not evidence of a state infrastructure. The second, Kyāk Talaṅ, is also not an urban settlement, but nevertheless poses some problems. Presumed to

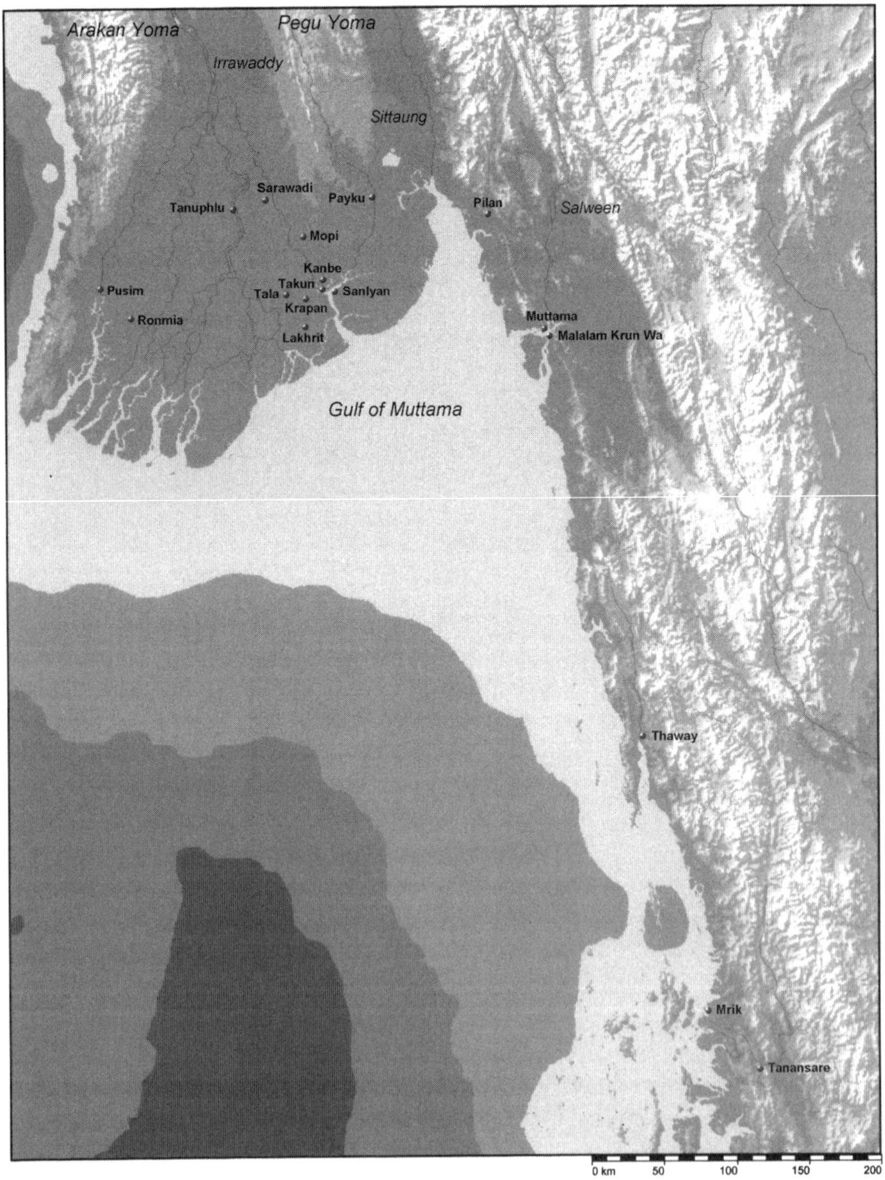

FIGURE 3: Old Burmese Place Names in Lower Burma

have been at or near the modern town of Ayetthèma north of Thatôn, it is a temple that was repaired by King Kyanzittha,[122] a ritual many Burmese Buddhist kings performed to serve, among other religious purposes, as a public declaration of their hegemony and authority over the area in which the temple stands. That the holy site itself was contemporary to King Kyanzittha's reign or earlier seems reasonable enough, but that fact in itself neither suggests the existence of a polity or state there, nor is it evidence of the region's primary linguistic or cultural affiliation. Although the word *kyāk* (a reference to holy objects) is Mon, it is, after all, the language in which the inscription itself is written, so of course one would expect Mon words in it. But that does not prove that the inhabitants of the region where it was erected were mainly Mon speakers, any more than the Sanskrit inscriptions of Aśoka in Dravidian areas imply that the inhabitants were speakers of Indo-Aryan languages. It certainly does not prove the prior presence of an independent Mon polity or state in that locality.

Also, the provenance of this inscription is unknown. Blagden was given a rubbing and photograph of its bottom half from a broken stone which was then located at the Phayre Museum. He wrote that "the original location of this record is unknown to me.... It seems probable that this pagoda was somewhere in the Mon country of Lower Burma, but in the absence of information as to the place where the inscription was found I am unable to say anything positive about it."[123] Only later in 1938 did Pe Maung Tin, in an article in the *Journal of the Burma Research Society*, make an attempt to identify its original place as Thatôn,[124] by which time the Mon Paradigm was firmly in place and most likely influenced his decision. All that the inscription actually had to say about the place, Kyāk Talaṅ, according to Blagden's translation, is that Kyanzittha, "who is lord of the city of Arimaddanapūr... [illegible] this pagoda of Kyāk Talaṅ, which was in ruins, in order that it might become a name of renown (and) a (place of refuge?) of all the world and all mankind for a long time, (he) caused workmen to build (and) encase (it) afresh firmly and fairly, bigger than before,... (and) had (it) dedicated...."[125] Kyāk Talaṅ, then, is not a name of an urban area that might have belonged to a state substructure, but a sacred site whose ethnolinguistic and political origins are not clear, although its people could have been Mon speakers.

The third name written in Old Mon, Kelāsa-Parvvata, is actually the Mount Kailaśa of Hindu-Buddhist mythology, the "silver mountain," the abode of Viṣṇu, who is to be reincarnated as King Kyanzittha.[126] The king was actually tracing his mythical genealogy to the dispensation of Buddha Kassapa when, as king of Patna, and then later as King Rāma of Oude, he was showing his prowess. Thereafter, stated King Kyanzittha, during the time of Śākyamuni Buddha, he (Kyanzittha) was the sage Bisnū, "who had supernatural power (and) glory, who possessed the five transcendental faculties, who dwelt upon a silver (mountain?) named Kelāsaparwwata."[127] This statement is the only "evidence" for Luce's contention that "Mt. Kelasa north of Thatôn"[128] was an actual Old Mon site. Clearly, it belongs to the realm of mythology and legitimation, not toponymy. That Luce even attempted to claim it as an actual geographic and historical place in the eleventh century demonstrates the lengths to which he had to go in order to make his case.

The fourth name written in Old Mon is found on a duplicate inscription of the above, *in situ,* and refers to the king's repair of a temple called Prāsāt Mahādhāt Satih (the *Prasada* of the Great Relic), which is presumed to be the Kyaik Tè Pagoda, now a famous shrine in the area. Again, nothing is said about its cultural or political context, although by the time the name of the temple changed from the Pali (Prāsāt Mahādhāt Satih) to become Kyaik Tè, a Mon word, Mon speakers were likely already living there. But we do not know when this change occurred; at the time of King Kyanzittha's inscription, it was called Prāsāt Mahādhāt Satih, so that its Mon name of Kyaik Tè was probably adopted later.[129]

In short, the three sacred sites and the mythical silver mountain of Viṣṇu are neither urban sites that might have suggested a state infrastructure in Lower Burma, nor records produced by an autonomous polity. Rather they are sacred places, actual or mythical, whose names appear only when their temples were repaired by an Upper Burma king celebrating his conquest of the area and legitimating his rule. Their existence, then, says little or nothing about an earlier, independent Rāmaññdesa; rather, it indicates the opposite: Upper Burma's hegemony over Lower Burma. Their content also says nothing about an autonomous Mon polity or state; rather, they recall what is known in Burmese history as the "Kyanzittha Legend," a legitimating prophecy attributed to the Buddha, which declares that Viṣṇu will be reborn as Kyanzittha in Pagán.[130] As Blagden aptly put it, these epigraphs, "though in the Mon language and found in various parts of Burma, nearly all emanated from the Burmese headquarters at Pagán and were in substance Burmese records; they really throw more light on Burmese than on Mon conditions."[131] My point exactly.

Finally, and most revealing, among these forty names, approximately five *urban sites* were recorded *exclusively* in Middle Mon of the fifteenth century, that is, *without an older* Old Burmese or Old Mon counterpart, suggesting that these were *new* settlements developed only after the fifteenth century.[132] And that is precisely the case with Suwaṇṇabhuṁ, Rāmaññadesa, and Sudhuim (Thatôn), all of which are written in Middle Mon and not found until King Dhammazedi's Kalyani Inscriptions of 1479. They have *no earlier* Old Mon or Old Burmese equivalents.

Even *prima facie,* then, because *all urban sites* in Lower Burma dated by original epigraphy were first recorded in Old Burmese preceding any recorded in Middle Mon by several centuries, the urbanization of Lower Burma, after the Pyū era, was begun by *Burmese speakers* well before Mon speakers subsequently became the dominant power in the same region. Equally important, none of these urban sites, in any language, can be dated prior to the conquest of and expansion into Lower Burma by Kings Aniruddha and Kyanzittha in the mid-eleventh century, with the possible exceptions of several iron age and Pyū sites.[133] Not until the Pagán kingdom conquered and "pacified" Lower Burma in the eleventh century did the process of state development in the region begin. After their reigns, Lower Burma saw increasing settlement by Burmese speakers from the Pagán kingdom, particularly under King Narapatisithu, whose inscription of 1196–1198 identified the limits of his kingdom, including urban sites in the province of Tenasserim (as Tanaṅsare) southeast of Mergui, the southernmost reach of Pagán's hegemony.[134]

This is not particularly surprising, since under Narapatisithu, the kingdom of Pagán produced the most wealth and exhibited the strongest military and political power in the four hundred years of its existence.[135] By the late twelfth and thirteenth centuries, when the majority of these urban sites first appeared in epigraphy, religious donations by individuals from Pagán were being made in places as far south as Tala, Taguṁ (Yangôn) Taway, Mergui, and Tenasserim.[136] Thus, by then, most of Lower Burma must have been under the administrative and political control of the Pagán kingdom, becoming its main outlet to the sea and to other places in South and Southeast Asia, its towns and cities taking the role of provincial capitals where royal appointees acted as *in situ* governors presumably supported by garrisoned troops. (See Figure 4 for urban sites during the Pagán kingdom.)

That the kingdom of Pagán actually reached this far is probably the reason a Chinese source stated that if one wanted to go to the kingdom of the Coḷas in South India, the route was via Pagán. In a similar vein, Taranatha, the Tibetan monk-historian who wrote later, but from earlier sources, stated that "Pukham" was situated on the ocean.[137] Since one could *not* go to South India via the *city* of Pagán, and because it was certainly *not on the ocean,* both the Chinese and the Tibetan were obviously referring to the *kingdom* itself. That means both sources considered Lower Burma and its maritime coast to have been very much a part of the kingdom of Pagán, from which place one could, indeed, go to South India.

It seems then, that prior to the conquest, pacification, and settlement

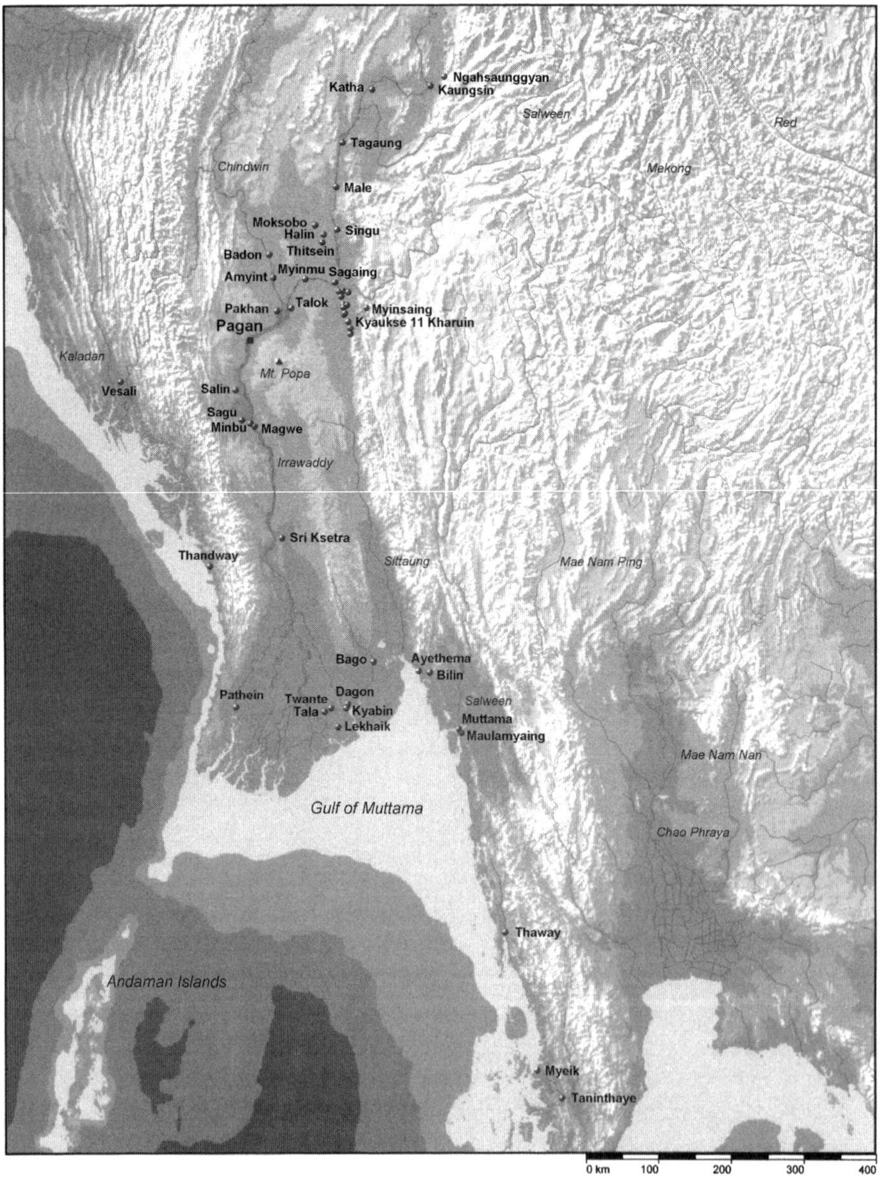

FIGURE 4: Urban Sites during the Pagán Period

of Lower Burma by the kingdom of Pagán, much of it was probably a swampy, frontier area, sparsely inhabited, with only a few coastal towns and villages, remnants of the earlier Pyū state, and with little or no cultivated hinterland.[138] Indeed, during the first millennium much of that hinterland supposed to have been Rāmaññadesa may well have been under the ocean,[139] especially its putative center, Thatôn, for it was located in an area that geographers call a submergence coast where the sea comes right up to the land creating a seascape with many fjords. And although that kind of natural environment may have been ideal for a maritime kingdom, one still needs evidence of its existence during the first millennium, as claimed. Certainly the hinterland around Thatôn and the Irrawaddy Delta, the area where the Mon Paradigm placed the towns and cities of what it considered "Rāmaññadesa,"[140] had not yet been created by the silt from the Sittaung and Irrawaddy rivers to have supported an urban area of the size and scope claimed. Lower Burma, in other words, did not yet possess the geographic, demographic, economic, political, and cultural wherewithal to have supported any kingdom or polity, much less to have been the source of civilization for another in Upper Burma the size, scope, and scale of Pagán. This is the most reasonable picture of eleventh-century Lower Burma that we can reconstruct from the available evidence. In reality, then, it was the kingdom of Pagán that developed Lower Burma, so that the origins of *historic* Rāmaññadesa can be attributed to Upper Burma's prior development and subsequent expansion south, rather than a mythical Rāmaññadesa that "civilized" the kingdom of Pagán.

One thing is clear: most, if not all, of the above data was available and well known to the Mon Paradigm scholars. In fact, it was they who discovered and compiled it in the first place. Furthermore, the information had also been published in English and long available to those who could not read Old Burmese or Middle Mon. This means it was really the theory itself —the conviction that Rāmaññadesa was earlier than Pagán—that blinded scholars to their own evidence. For well over a century now the dominating influence of the Mon Paradigm in Burma Studies has prevented even obviously contradictory data from effectively challenging it.

King Dhammazedi and the "Legend that was Lower Burma"

Where did this "imagined polity" of Rāmaññadesa come from? As stated in Chapter One, it all began with King Dhammazedi of Pegu, the center of the first Mon kingdom in Burma. Known formally as Rāmādhipati, Dhammazedi, who reigned between 1472–1492, had become king at Pegu after having fled Ava with one of his predecessors, Queen Shin Saw Bu.

Between 1476 and 1479, Dhammazedi erected ten stones written in Mon and Pali called the Kalyani Inscriptions[141] that celebrate his reform of the *saṅgha* in the Mahāvihāra tradition of Ceylon, considered the most orthodox among Theravāda Buddhists of the time. The stones still stand today at the Kalyani Sima (ordination hall) just west of Pegu city, and were translated into English over half a century ago by different scholars.[142]

Two of the most authoritative translations were made by Blagden and Taw Sein Ko. The former attempted to reconstruct those parts of the stones that contained the Mon text (seven out of ten stones); most of which had already broken into pieces by the time he saw them. As a result, he had to depend heavily on Taw Sein Ko's translation of the Pali text, taken from the other three stones that were better preserved, since both texts conveyed the same message. Blagden, who Bauer contends had never been to Burma (if so, in my opinion, it was to his advantage in this particular case),[143] nevertheless worked closely with Robert Halliday, an American missionary resident there and sometimes called the "father of Mon studies in Burma." Halliday had just finished compiling his Mon dictionary and had read some portions of the Mon text on the inscriptions with a Mon monk, U Thilawuntha by name, who had recalled reading the same in a palm-leaf manuscript dealing with a history of *sima* (ordination halls) in Lower Burma. It turned out that the manuscript included some of the broken portions of the stone where the Mon text had once been legible, as well as some other, weathered sections. Not verbatim, the manuscript was still considered very valuable and so was used to reconstruct some of the missing parts in Blagen's translation. Thus, although important sections of the Mon segment of the Kalyani Inscriptions dealing with Aniruddha are flaked off, the Pali section is largely intact. Adding the manuscript just mentioned, the two reconstructed a reasonably reliable reading of what King Dhammazedi had to say in Mon.

The inscriptions were meant to commemorate, record, and legitimate the king's purification of the *saṅgha* and the religion according to the procedures followed by the Mahāvihāra tradition of Śrī Laṅka. It is in them that one finds the entity called Rāmaññadesa for the first time in the country,[144] intimately connected to Suvaṇṇabhūmi, the legendary "Land of Gold," the "Eldorado of the East," as Wheatley put it. As both the mythologies of Rāmaññadesa and Suvaṇṇabhūmi are closely intertwined in Burma, and both are believed to represent the whole region of Lower Burma, they must be examined together.

Dhammazedi began the link between Suvaṇṇabhūmi and Lower Burma by recounting the celebrated mission of two of the most famous monks in Theravāda Buddhism, Soṇa and Uttara, who were attributed with taking to Suvaṇṇabhūmi the version of the scriptures which had been recited at the

Third Buddhist Council of King Aśoka.[145] However, Suvaṇṇabhūmi in the original account of Soṇa and Uttara's mission probably referred to a place in India, certainly not Mainland Southeast Asia.[146] In fact, the story of their mission comes straight from the *Dīpavaṃsa,* according to Wheatley, its *loci classici.*[147] This original story was subsequently embellished and expanded in the *Mahāvaṃsa,* which had apparently added the following information. In Suvaṇṇabhūmi, it noted, there was a "fearsome female demon [who] would came forth out of the sea . . . to devour (the child [of the royal family]) and vanish again." The two *theras* happened to arrive at a time when a prince was born. At first, the people thought that the monks were friends of the demon, but later they drove away the demon and erected a bulwark around the country by reciting a *sutta.* Sixty thousand people embraced the new faith, while 3,500 young men and 1,500 girls of noble family entered the Order. "Thenceforth," stated the Ceylonese chronicle, "when a prince was born in the royal palace the kings gave to such the name Soṇuttara,"[148] obviously after Soṇa and Uttara.

Dhammazedi took this story from the *Mahāvaṃsa* and inscribed it almost verbatim on his Kalyani Inscriptions. His narrative begins by stating that the capital of Suvaṇṇabhūmi

> was situated on the seashore; and an ogress who lived in the sea [was in the habit of] coming up [and devouring] every child of the king that was [born in the king's palace. On the very night of the arrival of the two Theras,] a child of the king was born (and) the ogress, saying [that a child had been born in] the king's [palace], came up out of the sea together with a retinue of five hundred. . . . Then . . . (not?) desiring to allow the ogres to return again (later on?), throughout the extent of the [country] our lords the two Theras set guards; and to all the people, [who had assembled together], (they) preached the law of the Brahmajalasutta, and delighted them all. . . . At that time sixty thousand people attained to the comprehension of [the Law] . . . thousand five hundred came out (and) became monks. . . . Thenceforward, *in the Mon country* all young children, that were (born?) [on the anniversary day of that event, were named Soṇuttara.] . . . In order to prevent the savage demons (servants) (of Varuna?), (from seizing) them, men had to inscribe [on palm leaves figures of the creatures with?] heads of ogres (and) bodies of lions [created by the supernatural power of the Theras?] and put them on (their heads?). . . . From the time that our two lords came (and) established the religion *in the Mon country* . . . it shone *in the Mon country* for a very long while [my emphases].[149]

In one stroke, by inserting the phrase "in the Mon country" at several strategic places in the narrative,[150] Dhammazedi had transferred the Suvaṇṇabhūmi of Aśokan Buddhist India[151] to Lower Burma. Even the number of converts (60,000) was retained. Then he placed the capital of Suvaṇṇabhūmi on the seashore, which enhanced its local authenticity, as Thatôn is now located approximately seventeen miles inland from the coast. Following that, he made the chronological connection between Lower Burma and Suvaṇṇabhūmi even more explicit.

> (At the conclusion of this Council), Moggaliputtatissamahāthera reflected that in the future (the religion would be established in neighboring foreign countries, and sent such Theras as Majjhantikathera with the injunction: 'Do you establish the religion) in those neighboring foreign countries.' (Of these Theras, he sent) our lord Soṇathera and Uttarathera to establish the religion *in the Mon country, (which was also called Suvaṇṇabhūmi)* [my emphasis].[152]

Then followed other attempts to historically and geographically "localize" the story. Dhammazedi stated that when the two Theras arrived, "a king called Sīrimāsoka ruled over the country of Suvaṇṇabhūmi. His capital was situated to the northwest of the Kelāsapow Pagoda. . . . This town is called, to this day, Goḷamattikanagara. . . ." The "duplicate" Pali text on one of the stones then added: "The Mons who came thereafter called it Tuik Gala" (Taikkala), an actual town in the area,[153] currently some thirty miles from Thatôn, at the foot of the Kelāsa hills near a village named Ayetthèma, probably a Pyū site.[154]

Not only had Dhammazedi taken the Soṇa and Uttara story from the *Dīpavaṃsa/Mahāvaṃsa* and redirected their mission to Lower Burma, but he had also inserted familiar geographical features and the actual names of towns and mountain ranges of his day. Then by crafting a name derived from Aśoka, Sīrimāsoka, he created a king of an alleged Thatôn dynasty who had ruled over Suvaṇṇabhūmi. This person then appears in later Mon chronicles in which this dynasty is a mere list of names.[155] But neither Sīrimāsoka nor Manohor (the last of this legendary dynasty and the Manuha of the later chronicles) can be found in any Mon source prior to Dhammazedi's inscriptions.

Probably for the first time in Burma's history, then, Lower Burma was identified as Suvaṇṇabhūmi. Indeed, I have nowhere found either the term Suvaṇṇabhūmi or the link to Lower Burma earlier than Dhammazedi's Kalyani Inscriptions.[156] Thereafter, all references in *modern* Burma scholarship to Suvaṇṇabhūmi as Lower Burma cite Dhammazedi's inscriptions as proof.[157] Four hundred years later, this story of Suvaṇṇabhūmi, Sīrimāsoka, and Manohor would also persuade modern western scholars that it was indeed historical.

A few years after his Kalyani Inscriptions were erected, Dhammazedi made another important link on his Shwédagôn Pagoda Inscriptions. Perhaps for the first time also, he tied this sacred site directly to a relic of the Buddha. The stones are inscribed in Pali, Mon, and Burmese, and include the legend of Tapussa and Bhallika. These two men are said to have been merchant brothers, who, in the Buddhist literature of India and Ceylon, are considered the first lay disciples of the Buddha and who had obtained eight handfuls of Buddha's hair to enshrine in a temple.[158] In the *Thergāthā Commentary,* they are brothers; in the *Aṅguttara Commentary* they are not only brothers but also receive the eight handfuls of Buddha's hair; and in the *Vinaya Piṭaka* itself, they are not brothers, but friends, and Tapussa is a merchant from Ukkala in Orissa.[159] Of course, Ukkala is also the name for the Pegu region of Lower Burma. The two men are also found in different forms in texts that describe the various dispensations of the Buddha, but although they take different forms, they represent the same two individuals.[160] They are, in other words, standard characters found in many different "plays."

The pertinent part of the Shwédagôn Pagoda Inscriptions that linked the temple with the Buddha states:

> Later on . . . because in this Mon country the religion had not been (firmly) established, people knew not (the caitya of?) the hair relics and they could not venerate (and) worship (it). . . . Because [of that] on the land of the caitya such things as trees, jungle creepers, grass and rubbish had sprung up, (and had become?) a forest (concealing it?), people were not aware of its site. From the year of the exalted Buddha's achieving *parinirvāna* two hundred and six years had elapsed, (when) our lords the two arhats named Soṇathera and Uttarathera came (and) established the religion in the country of Suwaṇṇabhum. When the religion had been established (and) when they were monks, . . . then King Sīrimāsoka said to the two arhats, 'O my lords, the gem of the Law and the gem of the Order are we able to venerate (and) worship, (but) the gem of the Buddha, (though) we desire to venerate (and) worship (it), we cannot. A relic of the exalted Buddha, that we may set our minds (at rest upon), a gem of the Buddha that we can venerate (and) worship (it), we cannot. A relic of the Buddha that we can venerate, worship (and) adore, let my lords provide for us!' . . . Then our lords the two Mahātheras showed to King Sīrimāsoka the caitya of the hair relics of the exalted Buddha that Tapussa and Bhallika had enshrined on the top of the Tambagutta hill, which the forest bushes had covered (and) concealed, and people did not know (its) site. Then King Sīrimāsoka had the forest bushes cleared away and also caused the caitya and the *prāsāda* (which was also?) the *cetīyaġhara* to be built up and offered (them). From that time also all the people who dwelt in this Mon country in due course kept coming

> and worshipping (it). . . . Thereafter, at the time when her Majesty [Shin Saw Bu] . . . and her son named Rāmādhipatī . . . [Dhammazedi] were rulers, (they made) many offerings.[161]

Dhammazedi had done several things here. First, he had taken a prominent theme out of Aśokan India—the "rediscovery" of the original pagodas and the Buddha's relics (buried earlier by King Ajatasattu,[162] in the search for which Soṇa and Uttara played a leading role)—and had applied it to the Shwédagôn Pagoda and Lower Burma. By so doing, he had placed the origins of the most holy shrine in his kingdom, the Shwédagôn Pagoda in Yangôn, to the Buddha's time,[163] hence, the original name of the Shwédagôn, San Daw Shin or "Temple of the Holy Hair relic." Dhammazedi had been a high-ranking former monk who was trained at the city of Pagán, which had retained its prestige as a place of religious scholarship, and he had lived in the Kingdom of Ava. Therefore, Dhammazedi knew the original Buddhist texts well and understood their significance, particularly the desirability of having the Buddha's bodily relics placed within the most famous temple in his own kingdom.

Second, the Shwédagôn Pagoda Inscriptions state that Tapussa and Bhallika hailed from a place called Pokkharavatī, in the kingdom (or city) called Asītañjana, both in India. The temple in India in which the two brothers enshrined the Buddha's hair was also called Asītañjana. However, the unflaked section of the Burmese face of the Shwédagôn Inscriptions shows that Dhammazedi added one more place name immediately preceding the two places in India: namely, "the Rāmañña region."[164] By inserting this phrase just before Pokkharavatī and Asītañjana, he had linked, once again, the sacred history, geography, and chronology of Buddha's India with the Yangôn area of Lower Burma. This was more than just a linking of the founding of the Shwédagôn with the Buddha's time; Dhammazedi was also suggesting that Bhallika and Tapussa had visited Lower Burma personally.

Third, he had fused Aśoka and his namesake, the legendary Mon king, Sīrimāsoka, by having the latter talk to Soṇa and Uttara as if they were contemporaries of each other and close acquaintances, further cementing the link between the Suvaṇṇabhūmi of Aśokan India and "the Mon country." But more subtly, he wove their narrative into that of Tapussa and Bhallika as well, even though these figures were actually quite distant, even mythically, in time and place, and not found together in the Buddhist texts with Aśoka and Soṇa and Uttara.

Dhammazedi had thus taken people and events separated by several centuries within the South Asian religious tradition—Bhallika and Tapussa were from the Buddha's time and Soṇa and Uttara from Aśoka's time—and collapsed them into one time and place in Lower Burma. This *conflation* of time, events, individuals, and places, what some call "messianic time," I will return to when I deal with the chronicles particularly.

Rāmaññadesa was therefore given a nonlinear, ahistorical, "contemporaneity" with the Buddha and Aśoka, an antiquity and a stature that it never had historically. Suvaṇṇabhūmi, Soṇa and Uttara, Sīrimāsoka, Bhallika and Tapussa, the Shwédagôn Pagoda, and Rāmaññadesa were all linked together, so that the sacred history, the sacred genealogy, the sacred chronology, and the sacred geography of Buddhist India became part of Lower Burma's, and subsequently, also part of its historiography. All these linkages reappeared in the eighteenth-century Mon "chronicle" called the *Slapat Rājawaṅ Datow Smin Roṅ*,[165] on which much Burma Mon scholarship is based.

One question remains: why did Dhammazedi not choose Pegu, his own capital, rather than Thatôn, to be the center of Suvaṇṇabhūmi? Would it not have been in his interests to link his own capital city with all these sacred traditions? I think the answer may lie in the value that age commanded, that is, in the purity and legitimacy of the past, rather than the corrupt present or the uncertain future.

In practical terms as well, the tradition Dhammazedi was inventing, or reformulating, had to at least be older than Ava's, and preferably older than Pagán's. Pegu was relatively new, having been established as Lower Burma's first Mon capital in the late thirteenth century during the reign of Binnya U. Moreover, Ava still loomed large in Upper Burma during that time—indeed, it reached its zenith in the fifteenth century—and Pagán's decline, which was very much a factor in the rise of the Magadu Dynasty to which Dhammazedi was heir, was also relatively recent. Both were therefore probably in the collective memory of the culture.

Although Pegu was the capital of the first autonomous Mon state in Lower Burma, finally independent of Upper Burma's hegemony, Dhammazedi knew it could not be made into the center of the first Theravāda Buddhist state in the land contemporary to Aśoka's reign or the Buddha's time. But he could make his capital the center of an "unfinished renaissance," one that was resurrecting the "pure" Sinhalese tradition believed to have been brought earlier to Thatôn, by his reordination of the clergy in the *upasampadā* procedures of Ceylon. And the coming of Soṇa and Uttara to establish the orthodox religion in Suvaṇṇabhūmi which Dhammazedi deftly turned into Lower Burma was exactly what was needed in this newly independent Mon state to show the population that their current autonomy and glory lay in a remoter past than Pegu's, a past to which Dhammazedi had linked via Thatôn in the sacred language of Pali and then to their own, Lower Burma *lingua franca*, Middle Mon. His reign was indeed a time of religious, political, and ethnocultural euphoria, when Pegu and a Mon-led Lower Burma had achieved the kinds of religious and political heights heretofore unknown to them in Burma.

But that Thatôn religious tradition, Dhammazedi claimed, had been corrupted by the time he ascended the throne, which was the reason for his purification of the *saṅgha.* The one to blame for this decline was the (mythical) king of Thatôn, Manuha, who had allowed the religion to decay and therefore deserved to have his city fall into ruin. Dhammazedi was now reconnecting his *saṅgha*'s lineage to that of the Buddha via the Third Buddhist Council by sending his own monks to Śrī Laṅka to be reordained where this lineage was preserved in the Mahāvihāra tradition. Manuha, thus, became a scapegoat par excellence, a function later scholars would embellish even more by linking him to a totally unrelated narrative in the late Burmese chronicles regarding the conquest of Thatôn.

What is also interesting in the historiography of this development is that Dhammazedi's linking of Suvaṇṇabhūmi and Lower Burma was not unequivocally and universally accepted by his immediate successors, either in Burma or elsewhere. Neither the Sinhalese nor the Thai sources concurred with that link. The Sinhalese chronicles referred to Lower Burma as Rāmañña, and sometimes Aramaṇa,[166] but not Suvaṇṇabhūmi; the Rāma Gāṁhèṅ Inscription of 1292 claimed that Sukhodaya had a "Surbarnnabhum" under its own hegemony, thought to have been located within Thailand itself.[167] The Javanese had their own Suvaṇṇabhūmi as well.[168] Even within Burma, the name was not considered to have been a reference to Lower Burma: some of the earliest sections of the *Zambudipa Okhsaung Kyan,* that were probably recorded in the early seventeenth-century, associates Suvaṇṇabhūmi with the Shan provinces.[169] Thus King Bayinnaung, whose new Toungoo Dynasty replaced Dhammazedi's and who made Lower Burma the center of his capital in the mid-sixteenth century was reported to have said that because he felt Chiang Mai was Suvaṇṇabhūmi, no prisoners of war were to be taken from that city.[170] (However, the *Chiang Mai Chronicle* itself never claimed to have been Suvaṇṇabhūmi.)[171] By the early eighteenth century, U Kala in his *Mahayazawingyi* actually seemed unsure of where this Suvaṇṇabhūmi was supposed to have been and had the following to say: "it is said that this place called Suvaṇṇabhūmi is Thatôn Pyi . . ."[172] Only in the mid-nineteenth century did the *Sāsanavaṃsa* (History of the religion), written by a cleric under King Mindon, finally consider Suvaṇṇabhūmi to have been located in Lower Burma. But he thought of it as one of three "Rāmañña countries," the other two being "Haṁsavatī and Muttima" (that is, Pegu and Muttama).[173] By that time, as we shall see, colonial scholarship had already concluded that Suvaṇṇabhūmi was Lower Burma.

Another interesting feature of this tradition was that originally only Lower Burma acknowledged it. Suvaṇṇabhūmi is not mentioned in any inscription of Pagán or Ava, and when it is mentioned later in the standard, "secular" Burmese chronicles written in Upper Burma, it is at first only with reference to Lower Burma.[174] Even U Kala's eighteenth-century account of the story of Soṇa and Uttara and Suvaṇṇabhūmi is found not in his narrative about Burma but in that about Aśoka's life, which suggests that he took the story from the Sinhalese chronicles. And when he does mention the two *theras* and their mission to Suvaṇṇabhūmi after Aśoka's Third Council was over, as shown above, he was still unsure where it was located. Considering that by his time the tradition that Suvaṇṇabhūmi was Lower Burma had been around, at least in Lower Burma, for nearly three hundred years, U Kala's uncertainty about whether Suvaṇṇabhūmi was really supposed to have been in Lower Burma shows how late this tradition was finally incorporated into the conceptual system of Upper Burma. It was only in the nineteenth-century Upper Burma text, the *Sāsanavaṃsa,* that the Soṇa and Uttara story was first mentioned, and even then, only in the context of the history of the establishment of Therāvada Buddhism in Lower Burma.[175] For its establishment in Upper Burma, credit is given instead to the Elder Dhammarakkhita, also a major figure at the Third Buddhist Council,[176] who had been sent from there to establish the religion in Upper Burma.

There were therefore two different narratives regarding the arrival of Theravāda Buddhist orthodoxy, one for Lower Burma and one for Upper Burma, both traced back to the all important Aśoka's Third Council. Only since the annexation of Burma by the British,[177] when Lower Burma and Yangôn became the political and demographic center of the country as a whole, with the corresponding rise in stature of the Shwédagôn Pagoda as a "national shrine," that the link to orthodoxy via Soṇa and Uttara also seems to have gained "national" rather than only regional preeminence. Prior to that, it was very largely a Lower Burma tradition.

When the Kalyani Inscriptions were discovered in the nineteenth century and their full contents published toward the last decade of that century and the beginning of the next, they had the effect of confirming the historicity of the Soṇa and Uttara story, and therefore also the historicity of Lower Burma as Suvaṇṇabhūmi.[178] What later Burma scholars did not realize, of course, was that the narrative in the Kalyani Inscriptions was the same one Dhammazedi intentionally created in the first place.

Eventually, Dhammazedi's association of Lower Burma, Suvaṇṇabhūmi, and Rāmaññadesa became common knowledge in twentieth-century Burma's colonial historiography. Luce's inset map in volume 2 of his *Old Burma-Early Pagán* representing the maritime provinces in Lower Burma is titled "Rāmañña Desa," while elsewhere he explicitly wrote that this region was "the ancient Suvaṇṇabhūmi."[179] Similarly, other Burma scholars throughout the twentieth century asserted that Lower Burma was indeed Suvaṇṇabhūmi,[180] this, despite the fact that for many years, the best modern scholarship has contradicted the notion as highly unlikely. The late Wheatley, in the most exhaustive scholarly research on this topic, with detailed and extended analyses of contemporary or near-contemporary Greek, Arabic, Chinese, and Indian sources, concluded more than forty years ago that Suvaṇṇabhūmi, when not referring to India, meant Southeast Asia collectively, and more specifically, archipelago Southeast Asia, not the Mainland.[181] Senarat Paranavitana has also shown that Lower Burma was not known to the Sinhalese as Suvaṇṇabhūmi either.[182] Similarly, the distinguished Pali scholar, Malalasekera added to the discussion by writing that "there were two places of the same name, one originally in India itself and the other in Further India."[183] So it was with many of the classical place names given to important locations in Southeast Asia—Śrī Kṣetra, Sunāparanta, Tambadīpa, Haṁsavatī, Ayodhyā, Kamboja, Champa—whose original counterparts lay in India. Other scholars, like J. F. Fleet, did not consider Suvaṇṇabhūmi to have been in Southeast Asia at all, placing it in Bengal instead,[184] which was known to have had regular trade with Bharukaccha (Broach, in Northwest India), Benares, Mithilā, Sāvatthi, and Pāṭaliputra, all great Buddhist cities in India. Suvaṇṇabhūmi, as shown above, is also used by other Southeast Asian polities in Thailand and Java as representing their own kingdoms. Thus only in Burma Studies is Lower Burma Suvaṇṇabhūmi, its scholars either unfamiliar with, or stubbornly resisting the scholarship of the past half century done on the subject.

Conclusion

When the primary evidence concerning Lower Burma is examined independently of the Mon Paradigm's assumptions, ancient Rāmaññadesa indeed turns out to be an "imagined polity." Created by King Dhammazedi in the late fifteenth century, it was meant to legitimate his newly reformed religion and its sacred relics by linking their lineages to the Buddha and Aśokan Buddhist India.

And because the Kalyani Inscriptions of Dhammazedi traced the origins of Rāmaññadesa to the last centuries BC, while the earliest western-language travelers' accounts on Lower Burma showed Mon people inhabiting the region, the idea of an ancient Rāmaññadesa seemed plausible to later nineteenth and twentieth-century writers, who concluded that the Mon "must have" been living in that same area since ancient times. This analysis, of course, ignored both the language in which the Lower Burma place names were first written and the chronology of the evidence, so that it became a self-serving, synchronous approach, not much different from the way Dhammazedi had conflated time to link the sacred sites in his kingdom and the activities of his reign with Aśokan Buddhist India. That kind of ahistorical methodology—as if the society being reconstructed operated in "messianic time" rather than the narrative being a legitimation strategy devised by contemporary leaders—badly distorted Lower Burma's actual history.

Acceptance of the antiquity of Rāmaññadesa as historical, especially by nineteenth and twentieth-century colonial scholars and officials, in turn had a profound effect on the way the Mon came to view their own history in Burma, which had serious repercussions on their nationalistic sentiments, activities, claims, and publications,[185] a topic to be discussed more fully in Chapter Twelve. Suffice it to say here that by the late twentieth and early twenty-first centuries, the academic idea of an ancient Rāmaññadesa had become *commensurate with its desired political consequences.* One of these desired political consequences was to weaken central power, hence that of the majority ethnic group as well. This was accomplished by establishing "local autonomy" and empowering minority groups on the "periphery," a not-so-subtle *cause celebre* current among many academics in the field of Southeast Asian studies. And if Mon Rāmaññadesa were to be acknowledged as having existed prior to, and having "civilized" Burman Upper Burma—which represents the "center" and the major ethnic group par excellence—at least in the *academic* realm, the *political* cause of periphery empowerment could be legitimated and much better served. Whether or not it was inadvertent, the academic perpetuation of the Mon Paradigm nevertheless produced a picture that political activists desperately *wanted to see,* rather than one actually determined by the evidence; part of the reason the thesis remained unchallenged for so long.

Ironically, however, during the late fifteenth century the notion of an ancient Rāmaññadesa was meant to serve the *center's* religious and political interests,[186] the so-called "Great Tradition." It was not meant to serve the interests of "the folk" on the periphery, the so-called "Little Tradition." The story Dhammazedi used to recreate the antiquity of Rāmaññadesa—concerning Suvaṇṇabhūmi, Bhallika and Tapussa, Soṇa and Uttara, the demoness, and the Shwédagôn—were all part of the Great, not the Little, Tradition. Yet today, the notion of the "antiquity of Rāmaññadesa" is being promoted as part of the Little Tradition—a "local" idea, a "contested narrative" whose "voice" needs to be heard—when in fact, the notion originated with Pegu, the *center* of Lower Burma. The picture is even more complicated today since these ideas now belong to *both* the center and the periphery, whose configuration itself has also changed: Pegu is no longer the center but has become part of the "periphery."

Finally, since the antiquity of Rāmaññadesa is a myth, early Burma and Southeast Asia scholarship that has been based on its presumed historicity, especially works written or published most recently,[187] must be reevaluated within the framework of a "Mon-less" Lower Burma. Such a scenario also affects the current understanding of the "preclassical" period, the making of the "classical" period, and the circumstances around which the "post-classical" or "early modern" period emerged in Mainland Southeast Asia, topics to be discussed in Chapter Thirteen.

4 Thatôn (Sudhuim), an Imagined Center

SINCE NO KINGDOM or polity independent of Pagán can be found in Lower Burma until, at earliest, the late thirteenth century, this obviously raises serious questions about the existence of its center as well. To be sure, as nucleus of the larger entity, a center can and often does precede it, so conceivably Thatôn could have existed prior to and independent of the evidence for the larger polity. That there was no Rāmaññadesa at the time does not necessarily mean there was no Thatôn also.[1] What, then, is the evidence regarding Thatôn itself?

Before dealing with the primary evidence, we should consider several things regarding Thatôn. First, the formal Pali name by which Thatôn was known, Sudhamma and variations thereof can suggest a variety of different origins and functions. An early Buddhist text, the *Buddhavaṃsa,* records four different Sudhammas, all in India. It is the city in which the Sobhita Buddha was born; it is also his father's name; it is the park in which the Sobhita Buddha was born; and it is a park in Sudhammavati City where Sujāta Buddha held his first assembly of monks.[2] It was also a name for "Indra's Hall."[3] Although revealing as to the religious symbolism of Sudhamma, none of this tells us much about the historical place in Lower Burma now called Thatôn.

Second, in its domestic context the word Thatôn has a rather revealing etymology. According to Blagden, Thatôn is only the Burmanized form of the place name [Sudhuim], the oldest form of it "I have not, as yet, succeeded in tracing [it] . . . in its Mon form,"[4] he wrote. He then made a startling remark: "the probability . . . is that it is not really a Mon word at all, . . . [that] the common vernacular name is really derived from the scholarly one [Sudhammavati or Sudhammanagara . . . and derived] from Pali, not from Sanskrit."[5] Had it been derived from Sanskrit, he wrote, the name would have been . . . *Sadhaw,* just as the Sanskrit word *dharma* has resulted in the Mon . . . *dhaw.* Therefore, "the actual founders of the town were Buddhists of the Pali-using school, who gave it that name [Sudhuim] and no other, in which case the foundation is probably not as old as legendary history makes out. Or else it may have had a much older native name which has now been forgotten, and after the introduction of Pali Buddhism into the Mon country it may have been renamed by its now current, scholarly appellation. But I know of no evidence to show that the place ever had any other name than its present one. . . ."[6]

This conjecture is rather astounding: the name of the quintessential city of Mon origins in Burma is not even Mon and ultimately derives from Pali! Indeed, Halliday does not include the word in his dictionary while Shorto includes it with a query, and *categorizes it as Middle, not Old Mon.*[7] That it is written in Middle Mon is consistent with the evidence regarding the chronology of other place names in Lower Burma located near Thatôn, where all *dated,* urban place names written in Mon occur after the mid-fifteenth century.

Blagden's analysis suggests, furthermore, that the vernacular form Thatôn came only *after* its former Pali name was coined, so that the "vernacular name is really derived from the scholarly one."[8] It was not, as in many other place names in Southeast Asia, a local one that was only subsequently honored with Sanskrit and Pali suffixes. Thus, it is neither like Muttamanagara, clearly taken from the native Muttama to which was attached the Sanskrit *nagara,* nor like Haṁsavatī, a totally unconnected scholarly name for the local name Pegu.

But as this chapter is less a search for the etymology of the word and more for the *city* of Thatôn as a historical center of the Mon prior to the development of Pagán, we will not pursue the present topic further, except to reiterate that the origins of the word lay in its formal Pali name Sudhamma and its variations, which must have preceded its local form, Sudhuim, which did not appear in original domestic epigraphy until the last quarter of the fifteenth century, and whose local pronunciation (Thatôn) is Burmese, not Mon.

Thatôn in Archaeology

The archaeological issues concerning the city of Thatôn center on its identity, chronology, and ethnicity. There is an excavated urban site within today's Thatôn that archaeologists have assumed to be the Thatôn in question.[9] Although not unreasonable, there is no scientific, epigraphic, or other literary evidence that this particular site was the Thatôn of Burma's legend and history. And without such evidence, what stands there today could have been *any old city.* Indeed, the debate, such as it is, is reminiscent of the "search for Troy" in classical western archaeology, where at one time nearly every new site discovered near the Bosporus was considered to be

Troy. Most certainly, the name Thatôn was given to the site not because of archaeological or epigraphic evidence contemporary to or found at the site, but because of local tradition and the prevailing assumptions of the Mon Paradigm.

At this site virtually all that might point to a polity of sorts is a partially excavated structure that might be a palace and approximately half of the rectangular city walls. But these walls are built on a plan that is, according to the late, distinguished archaeologist of Burma, U Aung Thaw, "like the more modern cities of Amarapura and Mandalay."[10] I am not implying here that Thatôn was necessarily as recent as Amarapura or Mandalay, but rather that its chronology prior to the fifteenth century is highly uncertain. The following quote, from the *Burma Gazetteer: Thaton District,* contains one of the earliest reports on the site.

> The ground plan of the outer rampart is a square or oblong within which is an open space of about 150 feet, and then a second but lower wall, rampart, or moat. The east and west inner walls are each 7,700 feet long while those on the north and south are about 4,000 feet each, enclosing a space of about 700 acres. The angles, however, are not exact right angles. The centre of the city is the fortified royal citadel measuring from the north to south 1,080 feet, and east to west 1,150 feet. This was for the defence of the palace, the 'throne room' being, as is now the case at the Burmese capital, nearly the centre point of the city. There are two gates or spaces for entrance in the northern and southern faces of the rampart, but it is impossible to say how many on the eastern and western. Of the citadel no remains exist save those of a small pagoda at one corner, the shape of which is not discernible. The walls are of earth and in some places much worn away, but some places appear to have been faced with rough stones."[11]

The remains of Thatôn, therefore, do not resemble the cities of the preclassical period in Southeast Asia to which it was said to belong—such as Dhanyawaddy and Vesāli in Arakan, Śrī Kṣetra, Mongmao, Beikthano, Wati, and numerous other Pyū cities in central Burma, early Sukhodaya in Thailand and Angkor Borei in Cambodia. All or most of these cities have more or less rounded corners or circular designs in general, sometimes with two or more concentric moats and walls surrounding them. Instead, in its largely rectangular plan Thatôn resembles the cities that arose after Pagán.[12]

And even if a case can be made that the site under discussion is older, the evidence points to its belonging to the Pyū culture of Upper Burma, for distinctively Pyū fingermarked bricks have been used at Thatôn and nearby sites such as Kyaikkatha, Sanpannagon, and Tavoy. Beads and pottery similar to those at Beikthano have also been found.[13] Indeed, I would not be surprised if the origins of the name Sudhamanagara actually went back to the Pyū rather than the Mon, an issue addressed below.

Chronologically the site also poses some problems. The excavations, conducted between 1975 and 1977, did not produce any radiocarbon or other scientific dates, and by now much of the site has probably been contaminated.[14] Until excavations of uncontaminated sections are conducted properly, there is no way to know whether the site is post fifteenth century, as the etymology of its name suggests, or belongs to an earlier period. Certainly there is no evidence that this particular site was the city said to have been conquered by Aniruddha in 1057—even assuming that event was historical, which is now in doubt as we shall see in the next two chapters.

Even if uncontaminated material can be found and successfully dated prior to Pagán, that the city was "Mon" will still be conjectural, for any presumed relationship between the Mon and any particular site would be difficult to document without linguistic evidence. To be sure, ample Indic and presumably local cultural remains excavated at or near this site suggest settled occupation at an early period. Bas reliefs, laterite statues, ablution stones, grooved laterite drains, laterite finials, animal figures of lions, tigers, and elephants, altar stands, a whole terraced *stupa* made of laterite, and even a laterite wall presumably of a fort with sculptured panels have been unearthed in the general vicinity.[15] There is also evidence of bronze Buddha images, Śiva, Pārvatī, Nandi, Viṣṇu, *dvārapālas* (guardian deities), terracotta plaques, along with evidence of Theravāda Buddhist texts such as the *Vessantara* and other popular *Jātakas* as well as other items related to this school of thought.[16]

Yet even though not a single one of these remains has been dated scientifically or by epigraphy, a necessary connection between the remains and Mon speakers has always been assumed because of the Mon Paradigm. But even supposing that a stylistic case can be made that artifacts found at the site called Thatôn "look like" those of Dvāravatī or Haripuñjaya—the only Mon standards available during the general period in question—there still is no evidence that Mon speakers inhabited the site *at the same time.* In fact, as noted in earlier chapters, Winga, a site celebrated as Mon and said to have been contemporary with or earlier than the mythical Rāmaññadesa, cannot be dated by epigraphy earlier than 1479,[17] a date confirmed by TL results. That Thatôn was *later* inhabited by Mon speakers, of course, is not being disputed.

No archaeological, epigraphic, or other scientific evidence demonstrates that the excavated site called Thatôn is the Thatôn of legend, that it is older than Pagán, or that it was inhabited by Mon speakers during the first millennium. Instead, because the Mon Paradigm asserted that Thatôn was already the center of a highly developed Theravāda Buddhist kingdom inhabited by Mon speakers prior to the rise and development of the Pagán kingdom, researchers *automatically* assumed that everything found there had to have been Mon. Premise, once again, had become proof.

Sudhuim in Domestic Epigraphy

The only kind of evidence that can unequivocally determine whether a certain ethnolinguistic group produced a particular artifact, built and occupied a particular place, or was present during a particular period of time is securely dated epigraphy found at the site written in the language known to have been spoken by that same group. In this case, one needs at least one original, *in situ* epigraph written in Old Mon, unambiguously dated to sometime *prior* to the mid-eleventh century and preferably corroborated by radiocarbon or other scientifically derived chronology. But not one of the six original stone inscriptions in the Old Mon language written in the Pagán script, found at or near Thatôn itself, or any of the eight more found in all of Lower Burma, erected prior to the late fifteenth-century Kalyani Inscriptions, ever once mentioned Sudhuim.[18] Nor is the word found in any original Old Burmese inscription of Pagán from among the approximately 700 stones that remain from several centuries of Upper Burma rule of most of the country.[19]

Yet, as noted in Chapter Three, under King Narapatisithu's reign (1173–1210) the urban sites of Tenasserim, Tavoy, and Muttama were under Pagán control,[20] while earlier, during Aniruddha and Kyanzittha's reigns, evidence documents Pagán's conquests into at least two places beyond Mergui. Since all these towns were located much farther south than the site alleged to have been ancient Thatôn, it, too, should have been mentioned, as it lay directly on the land route to Tenasserim. Subsequently, in the twelfth and thirteenth centuries, kings and queens of Pagán made donations in Takun, Tala, Pegu, and Mergui, but not at Thatôn.[21]

When Mingaung I, a contemporary of King Yazadarit of Pegu, listed some Lower Burma cities that he claimed to control or contest, such as Tala and Takun in the Delta, not once did he mention Thatôn.[22] When Queen Shin Saw Bu, the second of only two women sovereigns of Burma, set up several donative inscriptions in Lower Burma, one of the legible ones records the building of a temple at or near Muttama, just south of Thatôn, but fails to mention that city at all.[23] At the height of the Ava period, another able king, Narapati I, would claim on an inscription of 1448 that he controlled centers in western and Lower Burma such as Arakan, Sittwe (also in Arakan), Bassein, and Myaungmya in the Delta. Again, Thatôn was not on the list.[24] In short, even during the period when Pegu had emerged as the center of Mon power in Lower Burma, Thatôn was still not mentioned in either Mon or Burmese epigraphy.

Thatôn finally appears, as Sudhuim, *for the first time* in original domestic Middle Mon epigraphy in 1479, on King Dhammazedi's Kalyani Inscriptions,[25] where it was connected to the famous Manuha of the chronicles whose formal title is given as Sūriyakumā. Later in the same inscriptions, the city appears again among a long list of *sima* (ordination halls) said to have existed throughout Dhammazedi's kingdom during his reign. It was called the Gavaṁpati *sima* of Sudhuim.[26]

A decade later, in 1486, Sudhuim appears again as Sudhammapura in three Mon inscriptions.[27] In them, the famous Buddhist *arahant* Gavaṁpati is said to have been reborn as a disciple of the Buddha, who goes to Sudhuim to preach Buddhism where Sīrimāsoka, said to have been a kinsman of his in a former existence, ruled. Thereupon, Sīrimāsoka requested that the Buddha himself visit the city, which he did, making Sudhuim a "Buddha-visited-city," an honor of utmost importance to Theravāda Buddhists.

This data led Shorto, the eminent Mon scholar, to conclude, in a seminal article called "The Gavampati Tradition of Burma,"[28] that Gavaṁpati was the patron of the Mon and the tutelary deity of Thatôn.[29] That in itself creates no problems. However, Shorto then projected this "Gavaṁpati tradition" that he himself had constructed backward to eleventh-century Pagán. He reasoned that because Gavaṁpati is mentioned in an eleventh-century Old Mon inscription of King Kyanzittha in a context of city-building, the Gavaṁpati tradition, and by implication the city of Thatôn, must have existed in the eleventh century as well.[30]

Yet the inscription that Shorto cited as evidence has only the following to say on the subject:

> Thereupon the Lord Buddha spake . . . to the Lord Ānan thus: " Ānan, hereafter a sage named Bisnū, great in supernatural power, great in glory, possessing the five transcendental faculties, together with my son Gawaṁpati, and King In, and Bissukarmmadewaput, and Katakarmmanāgarāja, shall build a city called Sisīt [Śrī Kṣetra]. After that, the sage Bisnū . . . departing from thence, shall go up to Brahmalok; (and) departing from Brahmalok, shall come to be in the city of Arimaddanapūr, (and) shall bear the name of King Śrī Tribhuwanādityadhammarāja, (and) shall uphold my religion."
>
> At that time the Lord Gawaṁpati, hearing the explanation of the Lord Buddha . . . questioned (him) thus: " . . . did my lord truly say that hereafter a sage named Bisnū together with me should build the city of Sisīt?" "Truly, Gawaṁpati, thus (it is). . . . Therefore, Gawaṁpati, go thou to King In, (and) speak thou thus: '. . . the Sage named Bisnū, who is great in supernatural power (and) glory, together with me shall build the city of Sisīt. . . . After the

> sage Bisnū has built the city of Sisīt, he shall depart from thence (and) in the city of Arimaddanapūr he shall become King [Kyanzittha].'"[31]

Neither the Mon people, nor Thatôn, nor Gavaṁpati's relations with either, is mentioned or implied. Only two cities are recalled: Śrī Kṣetra and Arimaddanapūr (Pagán)—and those in an archaeologically and historically correct sequence—so that the important links being made are between Gavaṁpati and Śrī Kṣetra on the one hand, and King Kyanzittha and Pagán on the other. Thatôn was never a part of Kyanzittha's legitimation scheme. Thus the earliest evidence we have regarding the Gavaṁpati tradition is found in and concerned with *Upper, not Lower Burma,* and is concerned with the "establishment" of Śrī Kṣetra and Pagán, the "quintessential" capitals of the Pyū and Burmese speakers respectively, *not with Thatôn* and Mon speakers.

The earliest epigraphic evidence, suggests, therefore, that Gavaṁpati is far more likely to have originally been the patron of the Pyū and Burmese speakers than of the Mon, and more likely the tutelary deity of Śrī Kṣetra and Pagán, not Thatôn. Had Thatôn and the Mon been as important in the eleventh century, either symbolically or historically as Shorto claimed, and if King Kyanzittha—said to be the patron par excellence of Mon language and culture—was indeed celebrating the genealogy of great Buddhist cities of Burma such as Śrī Kṣetra and Pagán, why were Thatôn and the Mon never mentioned?

In the Kalyani Inscriptions Sīrimāsoka, Gavaṁpati's kinsman, was said to have been the reigning king at Thatôn when Soṇa and Uttara arrived nearby with the Holy Scriptures. This is well after the Buddha's *parinibbānna,*[32] not during his lifetime, as the 1486 inscription used by Shorto states. On another occasion during the Buddha's lifetime, Gavaṁpati is again present, operating as liaison between the reigns of Sīrimāsoka at the beginning of the dynasty and Sūriyakumā at the end when Lower Burma was said to have been Suvaṇṇabhūmi, representing respectively, the beginning and end of Thatôn's dynastic list. In yet another existence, Gavaṁpati is hatched from one of two eggs found in the vicinity of Zingyaik hill in Lower Burma as Candakummā; from the other egg is hatched Sūriyakumā[33]—the infamous Manuha—the two representing the Moon and Sun respectively. So this story "makes" Gavaṁpati also a contemporary of Sūriyakumā. In King Dhammazedi's time, Gavaṁpati was a Mahāthera who preached at Thatôn, and in the eighteenth century, he was reborn as Wimala, one of two brothers who founded Pegu. In the context of reincarnation (or more precisely, avatarship), Gavaṁpati's mythology is, of course, indifferent to historical chronology; he is present everywhere at any time, as different beings performing different functions.

This conflation of time, events, places, and individuals was an ahistorical scheme used by Kyanzittha and later Dhammazedi for legitimation purposes. It was also, unfortunately, one to which Shorto succumbed. He had conflated time, events, places, and individuals by placing the Gavaṁpati "tradition of the Mon" in King Kyanzittha's eleventh-century Pagán when his sources for that tradition were clearly fifteenth-century Pegu and later. This was the result, essentially, of a *modern synchronous* approach to history within the context of an assumed Lower Burma antiquity. Apparently the use of "messianic time" is not a characteristic only of "traditional" societies.

Although one may concede that part of Shorto's argument can be supported by the texts of the 1486 inscriptions, as well as an eighteenth-century manuscript that he translated called "Gavampati,"[34] neither Gavaṁpati's role as tutelary deity of Thatôn nor as patron of the Mon can be found in the eleventh-century inscription of King Kyanzittha he cited. That information can be found only in the fifteenth and eighteenth-century texts noted, information that was then anachronistically projected backwards.

Exciting and thought provoking though his thesis may be, Shorto's mistake lay in accepting the Mon Paradigm's assumption that everything Mon and Lower Burma was earlier and everything Burman and Upper Burma was later.[35] In circular fashion, this projection backwards of what was actually a much later Mon tradition not only helped cement the notion of an earlier Thatôn in Lower Burma—and therefore a Mon civilization also—but made it appear as if Pagán had borrowed components of its belief system from the Mon of Lower Burma when it was clearly the other way around. In fact, because the Gavaṁpati tradition appears in the original evidence at Pagán in the eleventh century, four hundred years earlier than it does in Lower Burma, the traditions surrounding Gavaṁpati most likely went from Upper to Lower Burma, a pattern consistent with all the other evidence we have on the chronology and direction of state development in the country.

The Rakṣapura Issue

Because the overwhelming body of evidence fails to mention Sudhuim earlier than Dhammazedi's Kalyani Inscriptions, Luce was obviously compelled to find a *substitute* for it in "original" epigraphy, preferably one dated prior to Aniruddha's alleged conquest. This resulted in a most bizarre thesis, one that I call here the Rakṣapura Issue.

In the 1930s the archaeological service found two inscriptions at Thatôn written in Pali and Mon that are now known as the Trāp and Paṇḍit Inscriptions. They were not found *in situ;* that is, they were not permanently attached to the place where they are now located—the Shwézayan temple compound at Thatôn—and therefore, their provenance is unknown. Also, it is not entirely clear who erected them. Most serious, we do not know when these inscriptions were erected; there is no legible date on either.

Despite this, Luce dated them anyway, to "c. 1050," so that they just barely preceded Aniruddha's alleged conquest of Thatôn by seven years. As he put it: "they [the inscriptions] must precede, and very shortly precede, Aniruddha's capture of the city."[36] He then took an isolated word from the two inscriptions—Rakṣapura (city of demons)—with no coherent narrative attached to it, and concluded that this Rakṣapura was really a reference to Thatôn. And presto! not only was the existence of Thatôn "confirmed" in original, eleventh-century Old Mon epigraphy, but the inscriptions conveniently "preceded" the alleged conquest of Thatôn by seven years. The entire analysis was patently self-fulfilling.

No reasoning was provided for these assertions, particularly how the term Rakṣapura might have been connected historically, linguistically, or palaeographically to the words Thatôn or Sudhuim. Luce then contradicted himself almost immediately by stating that these *rakṣas* (demons) were actually Malayan "Vikings."[37] It is not clear to me how one arrives at Thatôn and the Mon from Rakṣapura and the Malays; it was never explained. Besides, if we were to pursue the logic of Luce's own argument, Rakṣapura should have been a Malay, not a Mon city, and its king, a Malay, not a Mon. Apart from this illogic, the fact remains that Thatôn (Sudhuim) is not mentioned on the Trap and Paṇḍit Inscriptions in any way, shape, or form![38]

To be sure, there are numerous late Mon chronicles and legendary accounts that link *rakṣa* stories to Muttama and Thatôn, as we have seen in Dhammazedi's use of the *Dīpavaṃsa* story regarding the ogress.[39] But this sort of tale is hardly evidence of Thatôn's eleventh-century historical existence or that the city was called Rakṣapura. Besides, such stories of demons are not unique to the Mon—they are also found among the Arakanese and Burmese—and were obviously an allegory of Buddhism's ability to conquer metaphorical demonhood, a literary device for validating conversion to the "true faith." In many of these stories, those not yet converted to Buddhism have usually been described as ogres or uncivilized people who worshiped "false gods" or professed "false doctrines" (such as the Aris of Pagán) until they saw the light.

The stories may also have been allegories of chaotic events of the late thirteenth and early fourteenth centuries in coastal Southeast Asia. Both the Javanese kingdom of Majapahit and a resurgent Śrī Vijaya in a new Malacca[40] had become important; along with the rise of Ayudhyā and its interests regarding the Malay Peninsula.[41] The Javanese influence particularly had gained momentum not only in the Straits of Malacca but in the northern parts of the Malay Peninsular near the Isthmus of Kra and into Tenasserim. That they may have come in contact with Yazadarit's authority in Tenasserim during that time, when it was under Pegu's control or influence, is attested by one of the earliest Mon chronicles, which mentions "Java *Kalas*" (literally "Java Indians") wreaking havoc in the region around the same time.[42]

In other words, had these accounts been historical, the term Rakṣapura was most likely a reference to some *other city*, in the sense that Yazadarit drove these *rakṣas* or "demons" out of his kingdom back to Rakṣapura where they belonged. If not the Javanese, the *rakṣa* may have been references to the Malays, or T'ais from Ayudhyā, with whom Yazadarit's dynasty had obvious contact. The reference also could have been to the inhabitants of nearby Ogre Island (Bilu Kyun in Burmese) in the Gulf of Muttama near Thatôn.[43]

Besides, these stories about demons actually convey exactly the *opposite* meaning to the one Luce wanted to suggest. If allegorical, the *rakṣas* represent barbarism prior to the civilizing influence of Buddhism, and if historical, they represent the kingdom's enemies, so that Rakṣapura had to be a name given to some *other*, demonized place. How, therefore, can one assign the term to Thatôn, when the *rakṣas* were either (allegorically) its antagonistic elements or (historically) its actual *enemies?* Common sense alone suggests that no Buddhist king would have called his own beloved, holy, and Buddha-prophesied city the "City of Demons" anyway. After all, the Pali term for Thatôn, Sudhamma, stemmed from revered, not disparaged, Buddhist traditions.

One can hardly consider this kind of illogical argument as proof for the existence and chronology of Thatôn. Indeed, to have based such an important component of the Mon Paradigm—the identification and date of the center of Rāmaññadesa—on such flimsy data and analysis, on a single term whose meaning was just the opposite of the attributed, desired purpose, reveals a consistent pattern of forcing data into a preconceived mold no matter how illogical or weak.

Thatôn in External Sources

None of the contemporary or near-contemporary epigraphy from South Asia mentions Thatôn or its Pali equivalents. The 1025 inscription of Rājendra Coḷa I of South India that celebrated his raid against Śrī Vijaya and other parts of Southeast Asia did not mention Thatôn, although thirteen other urban areas were included as his raid went along the Tenasserim coast, south of where Thatôn was supposed to have been located.[44] Had the city been a vibrant and powerful Theravāda Buddhist center in the vicinity, why was it not even mentioned? More than a century later, in 1165, the Devanagala Rock Inscription that Parākramabāhu I had erected to commemorate a raid conducted in precisely the area of Lower Burma alleged to be Rāmaññadesa did not mention Thatôn, even though Kusumīya, the Pali term for Pusim or Bassein, was included as one of the Lower Burma delta towns raided.[45]

Some of the best, sometimes the only, evidence we have for early Southeast Asia are the Chinese sources: not a single official one mentioned Thatôn. Even more compelling—because Thatôn was alleged to have been a great Buddhist center—not a single Chinese Buddhist pilgrim among the dozens who visited Southeast Asia and India mentioned Thatôn either. Neither Hsüan-tsang nor I-tsing (I-Ching), two of the most prolific, included the city in their accounts, although they described in often precise detail, virtually every other Buddhist center in Southeast Asia in the seventh century.[46]

In short, not a single pertinent contemporary or near-contemporary source—internal or external, in Burmese, Mon, Pali, Tamil, Sinhalese, or Chinese—during the entire first millennium and well into the fifteenth century mentions the city. Is this not reason enough to reexamine the theory that a pre-Pagán Thatôn existed in Lower Burma and that it was the center of a flourishing Mon Theravāda Buddhist kingdom called Rāmaññadesa, for which no evidence exists either?

Thatôn in Fifteenth- and Sixteenth-Century Sources

The search for Thatôn next led me to later domestic literary sources. Several did mention what could be construed as Sudhuim, but since none of these texts is original and contemporary, and their earliest extant copies date to the late eighteenth century, none can be considered a source able to verify the existence of Thatôn earlier than the period in which they were created, and even that assumes that their copiers were faithful to the originals. But these sources are important, nevertheless, for showing how late the mythology of Thatôn appears, how *unimportant* it was to the Burma Mon earlier, and how it is more closely linked to the Mon of Thailand than to those of Lower Burma.

As noted in earlier chapters, the *Zambu Kungya Po Yaza Mu Haung* was reportedly written during the First Ava Dynasty (1364–1527) by Wun Zin Min Yaza, an advisor to three successive Ava kings. Although the work itself was said to have been written during Mingaung I's reign (1401–1423),[47] the only extant palm-leaf copy that I have found (on microfilm) is dated to 1825.[48] It is too late to be considered an original, contemporary source, but it does have the markings of an early Ava source and contains information found in only one other Ava chronicle, the *Zatatawpon Yazawin,* to be discussed more fully in Chapter Six. The *Zambu* is one of the earliest to mention Thatôn, but in the context of Aniruddha's religious reform rather than a conquest. This raises numerous questions about the historical and religious circumstances in which the *Zambu* and other Burma chronicles were written, issues well beyond the scope of this book.

Close to the *Zambu* in time is the *Cāmadevīvaṃsa,* a Northern Thai chronicle which Thai scholars claim was written sometime between 1410 and 1417 by a monk named Bodhiraṃsi.[49] It is a "history" of the kingdom of Haripuñjaya, perhaps a Mon polity, located in what is now Thailand. It also mentions a Sudhamma, that in context may refer to Lower Burma.[50] It states:

> At that time [the early tenth century] the people of Haripuñjaya suffered from a widespread cholera epidemic. Many died of the disease. Those who lived in houses with a cholera victim contracted the disease in such increasing numbers that none of them survived. At last, even those people who touched an object in a cholera-infected house became inflicted with the disease and died.
>
> The people suffering with cholera were abandoned; those who survived destroyed their houses and fled for safety. Therefore, the remaining population of Haripuñjaya, in order to save their own lives, fled to a city named Sudhamma and settled there. The city of Haripuñjaya consequently fell into decline, . . . and was abandoned . . . altogether.
>
> The king of Pukam, observing the masses of weak and starving people, was moved to pity and out of his compassion restored the city of Sudhamma for them to occupy.
>
> Unable to bear their suffering any longer, the people of Haripuñjaya left Sudhamma . . . and went to Haṁsavatī . . . where they continued to live. At that time the king of Haṁsavatī, seeing the (needs of the) people of Haripuñjaya, out of his compassion and sense of justice . . . gave them many necessities, including clothing, jewelry, paddy, rice, various salty and sour foods, and dwelling places.
>
> The inhabitants of Haripuñjaya and of Haṁsavatī [note: *not* Sudhamma!] came to know and love each other. Even their languages were the same. Because no difference was found in their speech, they were able to understand each other easily. After six years, the cholera epidemic subsided. When the disease was brought under control, those who wanted to return to Haripuñjaya departed and dwelt again in the city.
>
> Those who did not want to return or who were too old or who had married the sons or daughters [of the local people] remained at Haṁsavatī. . . . With the return of so many of its former inhabitants, Haripuñjaya was restored

to its former glory. The people of Haṁsavatī, who still loved their friends and relatives in Haripuñjaya often visited them, bearing many letters.[51]

There are several intriguing pieces of information in this quote. "The king of Pukam" suggests that this Sudhamma might have been in Burma, although a Sudhamma within the kingdom of Haripuñjaya is also mentioned.[52] Chronologically as well, it is possible that someone from the Pagán Dynasty was involved, since the recent radiocarbon tests which date the foundations of Pagán's city walls to the late tenth century and the *Cāmadevīvaṃsa*'s reference to the epidemic during the reign of one Kamala, around 921 AD are close enough to consider seriously. Moreover, Sudhamma's *restoration* by the king of Pukam suggests the city's prior existence, although how much earlier is difficult to tell, as is the ethnolinguistic group inhabiting it at the time.

The problems, however, are more serious. First, although the language of Haṁsavatī's inhabitants was said to have been the same as that of the refugees from Haripuñjaya (assumed to be Mon), nothing is said of the language of Sudhamma, the city at issue, so there is no proof that the language of its inhabitants, presumably Mon, was the same as that of Haripuñjaya. Indeed, that the narrative moves from Sudhamma to Haṁsavatī without any explanation, especially when "the king of Pukam" was said to be so compassionate, suggests either some confusion or a combination of two different stories.

Second, the narrative that included Sudhamma in this text may have been a later addition to an older section,[53] since the alleged epidemic, directly related to the narrative on Sudhamma, has been dated by George Coedes to the first half of the eleventh century.[54] Although Coedes does not tell us why he chose that particular date, I suspect it is because it fits the timing of Aniruddha's alleged conquest of Thatôn. Without a Mon Thatôn at that time, to which the refugees from Haripuñjaya could flee, the historicity of the epidemic itself would have come under question, as indeed it has more recently among Thai scholars, but for different reasons.[55] It is entirely possible that this epidemic occurred earlier in the tenth century, as implied by the *Cāmadevīvaṃsa*'s dating of it, and that might explain an early migration of Mon speakers into Lower Burma. But that in itself is not evidence of a Theravāda Buddhist Mon *kingdom* there prior to the decline of Pagán in the late thirteenth century. Besides, the first time Pagán—as Pukaṁ, the same word used by Thais even today to refer to the city and kingdom—is mentioned in external epigraphy is in the Pô-Nagar Cham Inscription of 1050.[56]

Moreover, because the *Cāmadevīvaṃsa* states that the people who had fled to Sudhamma subsequently moved to Haṁsavatī (Pegu), it suggests that Thatôn and Pegu were contemporaries or nearly so. Yet the first mention of Pegu in regional epigraphy by its formal, Pali name of Haṁsavatī is in Rāma Gāṁheṅ's Inscription of 1292[57]; Burmese epigraphic evidence notes Pegu earlier, in 1266.[58] If Pegu and Thatôn were generally contemporaneous, and if this link were not made later for purposes of unifying the origins of the Lower Burma Mon state, then the earliest that Suddhama might have existed as a city or town in Lower Burma is the late thirteenth century, exactly the same period when Rāmaññadesa also emerged in history.

The issue, therefore, is a problem of text-event contemporaneity. Even the original *Cāmadevīvaṃsa,* which has not survived as such, was not written until well after the decline of Pagán, while the date of the earliest extant copies from which the published version of 1920 is derived is not given by the translators of this edition. But considering the number of years that palm-leaf manuscripts can survive, it is unlikely that even the earliest extant copies are earlier than the eighteenth or nineteenth century. The *Cāmadevīvaṃsa,* in short, is too late and problematic a source on which to base the historicity of Thatôn.

About a century later, if the dating is correct, another Northern Thai chronicle, the *Jinakālamālī* was said to have been written. It is dated variously between 1517/1518 and 1528, and attributed to Ratanapañña Thera,[59] a monk living in Chiang Mai, a major center in early Thai history. Although Sudhamma is mentioned here as well, and in the context of a cholera epidemic as in the *Cāmadevīvaṃsa,* the *Jinakālamālī* dates the episode to 657 AD,[60] placing the event during the height of the Pyū period at Śrī Kṣetra, nearly 400 years before the city walls of Pagán were even built. Its account of the epidemic—assuming that it was the same one—is a bit different.

> During his reign [one Kambala of Haripuñjaya who is perhaps the Kamala of the *Cāmadevīvaṃsa*], an epidemic of cholera raged for six years. And the citizens, not being able to survive there, all fled to the city of Sudhammanagara. Next, being harassed by the king of Puṇṇagāma, all the Haripuñjaya citizens living in the city of Sudhammanagara left for the city of Haṁsavatī. When the epidemic of cholera had subsided, all of them returned to Haripuñjaya.[61]

There are several interesting pieces of information in this account as well. Because the Sudhammanagara in question is placed in the seventh century, it may have been a reference to Śrī Kṣetra, which also flourished at that time in Burma. This is linguistically possible, for Shorto has argued that the name Sudhammanagara could have been an etymon for Śrī Kṣetra, that is, the linguistic form from which another form is historically derived, so that the essential meaning of a word is seen in its origins.[62] Moreover, this Sudhammanagara was mentioned in connection with a king of Puṇṇagāma, which modern scholars have assumed is a reference to Pagán,[63] but it is *not.* Puṇṇagāma probably means the "city of the hermit" (or brahmin, although wrongly spelled) the name by which Śrī Kṣetra, not Pagán, was most commonly known,[64] and therefore consistent with the date and etymon. Pugarāma, not Puṇṇagāma, is the term for Pagán, and it is used only after the fifteenth century and largely during the eighteenth century.[65]

All this implies that Pyū Śrī Kṣetra in Central Burma may have been the Sudhammanagara mentioned in the *Jinakālamālī,* and therefore was not a reference to Thatôn of Lower Burma. This would suggest that the Sudhamma tradition originally might have been Pyū, and only later, via the Burmese speakers, became part of the Lower Burma tradition: Thatôn, after all, is the Burmese pronunciation of Sudhuim. Indeed, as we shall see below, late Mon texts also trace Thatôn's founding to two brothers who went there as hermits and hence the term Puṇṇagāma, the "hermit city," for which, as noted, Śrī Kṣetra is best known. Once again, it suggests movement of culture, in this case origin myths, from north to south.

In the final analysis, like the *Cāmadevīvaṃsa,* the *Jinakālamālī* was also written too late to prove that Sudhammanagara, if in Burma, was a contemporary of either Śrī Kṣetra or Pagán. But the text has many other problems, which will be discussed in Chapter Six, when I deal with the alleged conquest of Thatôn by Aniruddha.

Around the same time the *Nidāna Árambhakathā,* a Mon genealogy of kings, was said to have been compiled. Shorto wrote that the manuscript from which the published version is derived had a Pali colophon that suggests the main part, originally entitled "Rāmaññ'-uppatti-dīpaka,"[66] was composed by a monk after the end of Dhammazedi's line in 1538. But because later authors have added to it, the story actually goes up to at least 1661 and the reign of Pyi Min of the Second Ava Dynasty. Apparently the last page of the manuscript was missing, for Shorto did not provide the date of the extant copy that he used, a copy which can be found at the National Library in Bangkok and from which the published version of 1912 was taken.

The *Nidāna* opens with a very brief account of the history of Thatôn, omitting all mention of the "first" dynasty, as recorded in the *Uppanna Sudhammawatī-rājāwaṁsa-kathā,*[67] and enters into detail with the reign of King Manuha. The *Nidāna* is said by Shorto to have mentioned Thatôn in the context of Aniruddha's alleged conquest in 1057. If 1538 is in fact the original date when these earlier parts of the *Nidāna* were written, this then, is so far the earliest, nonepigraphic Mon text to mention Thatôn.

However, there are some problems here as well. First, Shorto concluded that the history of Thatôn in the *Nidāna* "is almost entirely legendary."[68] Second, by the time it was first written, over half a century had elapsed since the Kalyani Inscriptions were erected in which Thatôn was first mentioned. That means the *Nidāna* cannot be considered an independent source that proves the pre-Pagán existence of Thatôn. Moreover, before the mid-sixteenth century, the Mon Dynasty of Pegu, of which Dhammazedi was a part, was conquered by the Toungoo rulers, who established their capital at Pegu. From there they reunified Burma once more, particularly under Kings Tabinshwehti (1531–1550) and Bayinnaung (1551–1581). When the *Nidāna* gets to this part of the story, around 1540 and particularly Tabinshwehti's reign, the events are very precisely recorded in months and often days,[69] suggesting that the author may have lived around that time.

Third, the published text in which the *Nidāna* appears[70] was compiled and published only in 1910 or 1912, and its original provenance is unknown or at least has not been established to be earlier than the *Nidāna*'s alleged compilation (1538), if correct. The same is true of the "Rāmaññ'-uppatti-dīpaka," the original title Shorto said was the main part of the *Nidāna*.[71]

Finally, some parts of the late sections, or the latest version, of the *Nidāna* must have been compiled in the nineteenth century, for one of the miscellaneous traditions included in it is the story of Prince Asah's fight with the Indian, a story found in the *Lik Smin Asah,* a Mon romance not composed until 1825, to be discussed below.[72] The *Nidāna* also includes the story of Wimala and Samala, the legendary founders of Pegu, two brothers whose ancestors were said to have come from India to live as hermits at Thatôn, and who subsequently founded that dynasty. Because the names of the brothers are said to be found in the dynastic lists of the Vijayanagara Dynasty of South India (fourteenth–seventeenth centuries AD),[73] at least according to Phayre, *prima facie,* this version of the Thatôn/Pegu origins stories must also be late. That the story of Samala and Wimala is not mentioned in Dhammazedi's inscriptions regarding the origins of Pegu, his exemplary center, suggests that it might be a post-Dhammazedi legend added subsequently.

Shortly after the *Nidāna* was written, the *Yazadarit Ayedawpon* was composed by Bannya Dala, a Mon minister in the court of King Bayinnaung. The work was said to have been written in Burmese, although there is some controversy as to whether it was actually a translation of an earlier Mon work into Burmese or composed in Burmese from the start. In it, Thatôn receives about a sentence, which is also all but legendary. But unlike the *Nidāna,* the *Yazadarit Ayedawpon* has no known subsequent additions. As a result, it does not contain the later Price Asah, or the Samala and Wimala stories, confirming its editor's opinion that it was probably written during Bayinnaung's reign, well before the destruction of Pegu in 1599, only after which the Samala and Wimala story appears for the first time in Mon texts.[75]

The *Yazadarit* begins with the usual prophecies and stories about the arrival of the historical Buddha to Lower Burma. Like Dhammazedi's Kalyani Inscriptions, links are made to the ancient Buddhist city in north India, Kapilavastu, rather than to the much later Hindu kingdom of Vijayanagara in South India. As a result, links are also made to Tapussa and Bhallika, the famous merchant brothers of Buddha's India who were said to have enshrined eight strands of the Buddha's hair (or eight handfuls) in the Shwédagôn, rather than to Samala and Wimala.

Tapussa and Bhallika were said by the *Yazadarit* to have come from a place called Ukkalapa, Lower Burma's counterpart to Ussāla (or Orissa), after which both Pegu district and a municipality in north Yangôn is today named. After they had enshrined the Buddha's hair, the author absentmindedly has the brothers returning to Rajāgṛha in India, rather than to Lower Burma, the place they were said to have come from earlier in the text.[76] That Tapussa and Ballikha, rather than Samala and Wimala, were the focus of attention shows that this text followed Dhammazedi's lead in the Kalyani Inscriptions as to the origins of Mon civilization in Lower Burma with Suvaṇṇabhūmi and Thatôn and not the other, later version in which Hindu Vijayanagara was prominent.

The narrative in the *Yazadarit* differs from the *Nidāna* in yet another way.[77] It is more concerned with the local scene. That is, it is far more focused on the Muttama and Pegu regions of Lower Burma, where the first Mon Buddhist kingdom arose under Magadu, and with linking the founder of Pegu, not to Samala and Wimala as did later Mon texts, but to a Buddha prophesy about Muttama. This stated that an ogre *(rakṣa)* named Sumani, living in the Muttama region, would become in time "lord of the white elephant." As prophesied by the Buddha, a succession of kings ensued. But no names or dates are given. The next paragraph jumps from the Buddha's time to King Narapatisithu of Pagán (1173–1210), who, the *Yazadarit* states, descended to Lower Burma in the twelfth century via his royal barge, called the *cakra,* on which he was touring the country. This is a local variation of the *cakravartin's* disk-spinning that conquers the world. It was only after Narapatisithu's tour that he founded the city called Motamo (Muttama). Leaving a *myosa* (lit. "town eater" or governor) there to govern it, Narapatisithu subsequently returned to Pagán.[78]

The ogre transformed its state of existence to that of a human at a place called Takowan and was named Magadu, who was, by all accounts, a historical figure. Then, after a series of human and supernatural events that closely linked Magadu's rise as founder of the first Mon dynasty in Burma with Sukhodaya and the T'ai—he was said to have eloped with the daughter of the king of Sukhodaya—he returned to his birth place.[79] From there he engineered a marriage alliance with the governor of Muttama appointed by Narapatisithu, eventually taking the city and adopting the regnal name of Waru, the Wareru of Burmese history, in 1281 AD. Subsequently he was said to have compiled a civil code *(dhammathat),* later called the *Waru Dhammathat,* popularly known as the *Wagaru Dhammathat.*[80] Detailed accounts of Magadu (Wagaru) that follow include a march on Tala (west of Yangôn) by Pagán's forces, led, it said correctly, by Yazathingyan,[81] one of the famous so-called Shan Brothers. This event is independently confirmed by at least one contemporary Old Burmese inscription of Pagán,[82] but it is unlikely that the author of the *Yazadarit* would have known of it or had access to it because he lived over 300 years later in a distant place. Pagán's march on Lower Burma gave Magadu the opportunity to take Pegu, at the time ruled by one Taraphya, after which Magadu put a minister in place who had been selected by the king of Sukhodaya.

Ultimately, the Buddha's prophecy regarding Wagaru's title of the "lord of the white elephant" comes true, as one is given to him by Sukhodaya's king, legitimating his rule as a *cakravartin.* Also during Wagaru's reign first mention is made of the contact between Muttama and Śrī Laṅkan Buddhism.[83] Wagaru reportedly died in 1294; according to this account, he was killed while in the toilet by the sons of Taraphya, whom he had earlier overthrown. His death precipitated a struggle for the throne by his younger brothers, sons, and several others with the T'ai title Saw. Intrigues that directly involved troops from Sukhodaya and Chiang Mai and victories over and subsequent truces with the latter are all part of the story. Names of kings, queens, princes, and princesses are given, along with their exploits, until finally Pegu rises in ascendancy with Binnya U, and Muttama becomes a vassal city. Only when Binnya U died in about 1385 did Yazadarit emerge, in whose name the book was written. From then until the end of the book, where his horoscope is given, the history is consumed with the drama between Ava's Mingaung I and Yazadarit, the former often overshadowing the latter.

Thus the "secular" history of Lower Burma even from the Burma Mon perspective in the *Yazadarit* actually begins with Burmese King Narapatisithu of Pagán and Magadu of Muttama. This is consistent with the general time frame and the way in which Lower Burma actually developed, particularly if only the contemporary archaeological, epigraphic, and Chinese records are used. This was also the time—the late twelfth and early thirteenth centuries—when most of the first towns and cities in Lower Burma began to appear in original epigraphs. That Magadu and his rise to power are linked to the T'ai polity of Sukhodaya rather than to South India is also supported by several contemporary T'ai inscriptions.[84] The *Yazadarit,* in other words, is focused on the local, thirteenth-century origins of Pegu, whose historical links are to Pagán, Muttama, Sukhodaya, and Magadu, rather than to the origin stories that appeared much later, and whose links are to Vijayanagara and Wimala and Samala.

Thus the rise of the first Mon dynasty in Lower Burma as told by the earliest Mon history to have survived—especially one devoid of later interpolations—is more about Muttama than it is about Thatôn, more about Sukhodaya and Pagán than about Śrī Laṅka and Vijayanagara. It is more about the region of which it was actually a part, a perspective that corresponds well with the best evidence we have. This rather straightforward historical nature of the work is not surprising, as the author was an experienced minister in the court of Bayinnaung, knowledgeable in warfare and administration, and known for his scholarship.[85]

Thatôn and Pegu in the Most Recent Domestic Sources

Finally, we come to the most recent texts that describe the origins of the first putative capitals of the Mon in Lower Burma, Thatôn and Pegu, for by now they are inexorably linked. All originals of these texts postdate Dhammazedi's and Bayinnaung's dynasties by several centuries, including the later sections of the *Nidāna,* and as such are not contemporary evidence for the early presence of Thatôn or Pegu. They are discussed here for their importance in showing how recent some of the myths about Thatôn really are, and how *insignificant* the city was in the past, even to the Mon themselves.

We begin with U Kala's *Mahayazawingyi* whose section on Thatôn appears to be a summary of Mon legends concerning the founding of that city by two "Indian brothers,"[86] stories that are also contained in the seventeenth-century portions of the *Nidāna,* as shown above. The late eighteenth-century Burmese chronicle, the *Myanma Yazawinthit* (New history of Myanma or the Myanma people), which often quotes U Kala's work verbatim, also links Thatôn's origins to two Indian brothers who are probably Samala and Wimala of the Mon texts.[87] Although from the time of U Kala's chronicle onward, Burmese sources more or less assume that Thatôn was the capital of the Mon in Lower Burma, in the Mon chronicles themselves, Thatôn's role in the history of the Mon people is still obscure and rarely mentioned.

Nearly contemporary with Twinthin's *Yazawinthit* is the late eighteenth-century *Slapat Rājawaṅ Datow Smin Roṅ* (History of kings). Sometimes hailed as the most important "chronicle" of the Mon, it was compiled by a monk probably a few decades after U Kala wrote his *Mahayazawingyi*.[88] The title was actually given to the work by Père W. Schmidt, who first published it in German in 1906. C. O. Blagden subsequently began an English translation of Schmidt's work, but apparently never completed it, and that manuscript eventually passed on to Robert Halliday, an American missionary. Using both Schmidt's and Blagden's works, along with what he considered to be the best of the Mon manuscript versions, Halliday published his own English translation of it in the *Journal of the Burma Research Society* in 1923.[89]

The manuscript that Schmidt used is quite problematic. It was first sent to Blagden in 1892 by an H. L. Eales, who was an official engaged in the census of Burma of 1891. Eales, in turn, had obtained it from Maung Dut, "a Talaing" who was employed by the British Government as a revenue officer. The latter had acquired it from a Maung Meik of Saingdi, a village near Pegu, who said he had gotten it from his great-grandfather, one Bala Theikti, who had brought it back to Burma after a campaign against Thailand during Bodawpaya's reign. That original from Thailand was then said to have been given to a monk of Kokainggyi, but the son of Bala Theikti was said to have made a copy of it prior to the donation. The manuscript Blagden got from Eales was that son's copy, the original having been lost.[90] Thus, apart from the circuitous route this most celebrated "history" of the Mon in Burma has taken, the manuscript was not even an indigenous Burma work but was taken from Thailand where it had been written by unknown hands.

In any case, the *Slapat* lists the standard seventeen generations of the "kings of Pegu," beginning with Samala and Wimala, who were said to have received the city of Pegu from Indra, while Thatôn's role in the development of Pegu and Lower Burma Mon civilization is conspicuously absent. The list ends with King Tissaraja, who is described as a "heretic turned to wrong-doing" who destroyed Buddha images and forbade worship of the Buddha. But a devout maiden refused to be swayed from the worship of the true religion, until finally victory was hers with the help of the Buddha. After that, Buddhism becomes dominant once again in the region with the "next" (actually former), Wareru (Magadu) Dynasty of Martaban.

The steadfast Buddhist maiden sounds as if Shin Saw Bu (1453–1472) were her model, while Tissaraja's age of heresy was probably an allusion to the period when the great Hindu Empire of Vijayanagara (fourteenth to seventeenth centuries) transgressed beyond its natural border, the Bay of Bengal, and exerted its influence over Lower Burma,[91] either directly, via Arakan, or both. The "dark age" that was said to have preceded Wareru's Dynasty may well have been the sixteenth and early seventeenth centuries—which actually followed Shin Saw Bu's dynasty in Lower Burma—when Pegu was burnt to the ground by Arakanese forces in 1599. Thereafter, eye-witnesses described Lower Burma as a depopulated wasteland without any central authority, ruled by individual warlords, the most famous of whom was the Portuguese adventurer Filipe de Brito y Nicote, also mentioned in the *Slapat* as a major character.[92] The memory of such devastation probably inspired the eighteenth-century author with an appropriate Buddhist "dark age" metaphor. To him, a Buddhist monk, periods of disorder were invariably followed by periods of order, so that in his work, the period of order was linked to Wareru's late thirteenth-century dynasty. Thus, the *Slapat*'s author seems to have projected backwards what was really a much later, and historical, period of "darkness" onto an unknown earlier time of darkness that preceded Wareru's period of order with the rise of Muttama.

It seems likely that the legend of Samala and Wimala as founders of Pegu entered Lower Burma only in the sixteenth and seventeenth centuries. Not only are the brothers said to be traceable to the lists of Chalukya kings and those of Vijayanagara,[93] their legend is not mentioned in Shin Saw Bu's or Dhammazedi's inscriptions or the *Yazadarit*. Their tale cannot be found in the earlier Buddhist texts either, unlike Tapussa and Bhallika, Soṇa and Uttara, and the ogress of Suvaṇṇabhūmi who devoured royal children. So it appears to be a post-Dhammazedi origins creation that emerged only after the fall of Pegu in 1599 with the rise of a new dynasty several decades later.[94] With a new dynasty came a new origins myth, this one accurately revealing influences from South India, possibly via the Arakanese, who were, in fact, the ones to destroy the old dynasty. (The Hindu artifacts found in Lower Burma noted in previous chapters may actually have belonged to this period rather than the first millennium AD.) Not coincidentally, the Wimala and Samala myth also appears only in those portions of the *Nidāna* that were added towards the mid-seventeenth century; and as noted, they may also be the "Indian brothers" in U Kala's and Twinthin's eighteenth-century stories about Thatôn.[95]

In contrast, the origin myths of the Mon in Dhammazedi's inscriptions go back mainly to the stories found in the Sinhalese chronicles and the Pali Buddhist texts of Śrī Laṅka. In Dhammazedi's account, the great Buddhist kings such as Aśoka, Parākramabāhu I, and Aniruddha are all important, while Soṇa and Uttara, Bhallika and Tapussa, and Sīrimāsoka are also central figures. Between Dhammazedi's reign and the destruction of Pegu the *Yazadarit Ayedawpon* appeared, which, after making a brief and perfunctory link to the Buddha, maintained its focus on the actual historical events, individuals, and places important to the region. All the other stories and characters in the *Slapat* that followed the *Ayedawpon* clearly belong to the period *after* Pegu was destroyed and Lower Burma had turned into a wilderness.

The next important Mon text, the *Lik Smin Asah,* written in 1825, retains the story of Wimala and Samala, but in altered form. Here, one of the brothers' offspring, Prince Asah, eventually fights against the Vijayanagara empire,[96] which leads me to believe that the story was perhaps an allegory about the conflicting external influences that shaped Mon culture in Lower Burma.[97] The story of the two brothers and their descendants in the *Lik Smin Asah,* is, therefore, one of the latest layers in the strata of Mon texts. At the bottom are the earlier Buddhist layers created by Dhammazedi, and in between them are the more secular historical strata by Bannya Dala and his *Yazadarit.* I have no doubt that others are in the process of being developed today that will stand on top of the *Lik Smin Asah.*

Sir Arthur Phayre's account regarding the origins of Thatôn and Pegu drew largely on these *later* (post-Dhammazedi) Lower Burma Mon sources. He traces Thatôn's origins in the story of the two sons[98] of King Thiha (Lion) of Karanaka in Southeast India, who had come to dwell as hermits in "the savage land" of Lower Burma, founding the city of Thatôn.[99] Supporting what we now know of the actual history of that area, Phayre writes: "Of the early history of Thathun, only vague tradition remains, though a list of fifty-nine kings, for the most part fabulous, who are said to have reigned there, is found in the Talaing chronicles."[100] Subsequently, according to Phayre, another set of brothers (but clearly not, for they are Wimala and Samala again), said to be sons of the reigning king of Thatôn, leave it to found Pegu.[101] The elder of the two brothers, Samala, becomes the second king of the Mon at Pegu, succeeding one whose name was taken from a list of exemplary kings found in the *Cūḷavaṃsa.*[102] Samala reigns for twelve years, the exact number that kings of ancient South India were theoretically expected to rule before relinquishing the throne and committing suicide.[103] Subsequently, he is killed by his younger brother, Wimala, who takes over; although in another version, Wimala dies at the age of seven and is reborn in India as Gavaṁpati.[104] Since the origins of Thatôn and Pegu had been inexorably combined by the time of the manuscript Phayre used, the story of the two brothers had also been combined so that one is reborn as Gavaṁpati, while the other is reborn as Sūriyakumā, our infamous Manuha.[105]

In sum, because the narrative concerning the origins of Pegu and Thatôn is a multilayered text derived from different periods of Lower Burma's history, in which time, place, events, and individuals had been conflated for purposes of legitimacy, it often seems contradictory, redundant, anachronistic, and confusing. The concept of reincarnation allowed the simultaneous presence of multiple personalities and locations, as well as anachronistic, ahistorical, and redundant scenarios. Everything now fits everywhere, much in the same way Dhammazedi, in his inscriptions, collapsed Buddhist India's chronologies, geographies, and genealogies into Lower Burma's, and Shorto, in his interpretation of the Gavaṁpati tradition, did much the same thing. Some of these conflated texts are then conflated even further by the time they appear in the twentieth century.

Conclusion

Traditions in Burma are seldom discarded entirely; they are retained and added to. All the different origins stories of Thatôn and Pegu finally become part of the Lower Burma Mon tradition, resulting in a prevailing (even if confusing), multilayered product. This tradition, in turn, was incorporated into the broader Burmese narratives, so that the result was an *integrative,* not a *contested* narrative.[106] Had they been contested stories, the final product—that is, the topmost layer representing the latest addition—would likely have expunged rather than included the earlier, especially contradictory material. Instead, the nineteenth-century Burmese texts representing the "winners" in the struggle for power in precolonial Burma did not delete, but retained the legends and history of the Mon people, as well as those of the Arakanese and Shan, as shown by U Kala's, Twinthin's, and the *Hmannan*'s treatment of these people and the accounts of themselves. Lower Burma's Mon narrative was even incorporated into the mid-nineteenth-century Pali chronicle, the *Sāsanavaṃsa,* written in Upper Burma and meant to represent Upper, not Lower Burma orthodoxy.[107] By the mid- to late nineteenth century, the earlier Lower Burma stories dealing with Soṇa and Uttara, Bhallika and Tapussa, and the later ones concerning Wimala and Samala[108] had become part of a larger, kingdom-wide narrative, even if initially they had belonged and were meaningful only to the Mon of Lower Burma.

In this process of narrative integration, certain stock characters or markers played crucial roles. Most of these links in Burma's indigenous history begin with a set of two brothers,[109] or sometimes male friends, who act as founders of sacred cities or religious sites, at the beginning of which an actual historical "conjuncture" in Fernand Braudel's sense, seems to have occurred. Bridging the needed gaps further are Buddhist deities such as Gavaṁpati who act as liaisons between past and present, old and new, indigenous and foreign, interior and coast, change and continuity.

What is striking in these stratified origins narratives is that Thatôn is almost an *afterthought.* It is not even mentioned in any original domestic source until the erection of King Dhammazedi's inscriptions. Even when it does appear in original epigraphy, it is not in a context of celebration but of embarrassment, for the religion introduced to Thatôn by the Buddha, restored by Gavaṁpati, and renewed by Soṇa and Uttara had been permitted to decay by its king, Sūriyakumā (our Manuha), who was hatched, of course, from "the other" (bad) egg.[110]

Only in 1486 did someone—perhaps Dhammazedi, we do not know—erect three more inscriptions that provided Thatôn with a more sanitized record and genealogy in the person of Gavaṁpati (hatched from the "good egg") and Sīrimāsoka, both of whom were responsible for the personal visit to Thatôn by the Buddha. Thus it was only after Dhammazedi's first indictment of Thatôn with Manohor in his Kalyani Inscriptions that an attempt was made a decade later to rectify and perhaps rescue the situation by providing the city with a better record. But it was too late, for Thatôn had already been derided publicly at the "national" level.

The Mon chronicles that appeared after Dhammazedi's inscriptions ignored the 1486 attempt to give it a bit more credibility. Thatôn is barely mentioned in the *Nidāna* or the *Yazadarit Ayedawpon,* while the first center of Mon culture in Lower Burma is not Thatôn but Martaban and Pegu. And in the eighteenth-century texts, the "Gavampati" and *Slapat,* Thatôn was not mentioned, nor did it play even a minor role in the history of the Mon in Lower Burma. Robert Halliday wrote in 1913 that of the three great Mon capitals—Thatôn, Martaban, and Pegu—only the last "lives in the memory of the bulk of present-day Talaings as the great city of their kings."[111]

But that sentiment was not shared by colonial scholars, as became apparent in the first few decades of the twentieth century when the idea of Thatôn as a "national tragedy" became an issue in Burma's historiography. Only then was Thatôn transformed into both the Camelot of the Burma Mon and the ultimate symbol of their defeat, their Alamo. This new sentiment was a late, external perspective, the direct result of colonial scholarship on the Mon.

Similarly, none of the Burma Mon texts looked east to what many colonial and other modern scholars have considered to be the homeland of the Mon: Dvāravatī. Rather, their gaze was west to South Asia: Śrī Laṅka earlier, and later, South India's empire of Vijayanagara and the Talingas. Thus, while modern western officials and scholars were nostalgically looking towards Dvāravatī *on behalf of the Burma Mon;* the Burma Mon themselves were gazing in the opposite direction, towards South Asia.

In fact, not a single Mon inscription of Burma, from the eleventh-century stones of King Kyanzittha's to those of the fifteenth century belonging to King Dhammazedi and later, attributes the origins of the Burma Mon, either as allegory or history, to Dvāravatī or Haripuñjaya; neither place is even mentioned. This suggests that as early as the Pagán Dynasty the Mon of Burma had apparently already forgotten from whence they came, until colonial scholarship rediscovered that history and told them.[112]

But colonial scholarship also turned ethnicity into an issue of major political, social, and economic importance and divisiveness, so that the cultural differences between Mon and Burman that had rarely been that important an issue in the course of their everyday lives, now became a central adversarial theme in the historiography of Thatôn. The Thatôn tradition, once of little importance to the Mon, had now become a *cause celebre* of their nationalism, endorsed and encouraged by their colonial masters.

That, in turn, shaped the interpretation of the multilayered and integrative narrative of Mon Lower Burma, so that the new, modern Thatôn focus became the only "orthodox" one. Heretofore, as long as religious legitimation was the primary issue of concern in society—and it had been—and both Burman and Mon sought legitimation in the same religious tradition—and they did—the cultural narrative was inclusive rather than exclusive, integrative rather than contested. But in the twentieth century ethnicity became a contested political, and hence economic and social, issue at a national level. That took both Mon and Burman out of their previous more localized historical context and placed them in a much broader, international modern, adversarial one. It was only then that the inclusive narrative turned into a nationally contested one. But this was the modern world reinterpreting the local narrative to fit its own purposes.

Once ethnic nationalism and nationhood became the most important issues, reified ethnicity, the foundations on which the majority of today's modern nations are built in the first place, reared its head. In this political, and also historiographic, struggle, the alleged conquest of Thatôn by King Aniruddha became a central theme, the topic of the next two chapters.

5 The Conquest of Thatôn, an Imagined Event

SINCE THERE is no contemporary evidence for the existence of a Mon polity in Lower Burma named Rāmaññadesa, and none for a center named Thatôn until the fifteenth-century, clearly, the story of Aniruddha's conquest of that city in 1057 is problematic, as are the consequences said to have affected the development of Pagán's culture. This chapter will investigate the story of Aniruddha's conquest by examining the extant epigraphy, and Chapter Six will examine it as the tale appears in chronicles and other literary sources.

One could protest that since there is no evidence for either a Rāmaññadesa or Thatôn as early as Aniruddha's reign, the conquest story must be a myth as well, and therefore superfluous. However, one must remember that the Mon Paradigm claims about Rāmaññadesa and Thatôn have only now been shown to be erroneous. And since my analysis purposefully moves from the general to the specific, the order in which the Aniruddha story appears in it naturally follows that of Rāmaññadesa and Thatôn. If it therefore seems like a foregone conclusion, it is only because my analysis in the previous two chapters has made it so. Besides, it is important to demonstrate by evidence, not simply by inference, that the Aniruddha story does not hold water historically.

The Aniruddha Story

Aniruddha's alleged conquest of Thatôn has been described briefly in Chapter One. As far as I can tell, this complete version of the Aniruddha story does not go back to any one particular *Ur* source, but has had several variations in different sources. It also appears to have experienced a nonlinear pattern of development with some sources having "informed" it retroactively. But before examining the chronicles, let us first look at the stones.

EVIDENCE FROM CONTEMPORARY EPIGRAPHIC SOURCES

Leaving aside for a moment the symbolic attributes and allegories projected onto Aniruddha by posterity—of a *cakkavattī* (world conqueror) in command of thirty-two white elephants achieving a *dhammavijaya* (righteous victory) as a *dhammarāja* (righteous king) searching for the "holy grail" as it were—the following is an assessment of all the epigraphic evidence available regarding the historicity of this story.

Of more than 600 original extant inscriptions belonging to the Pagán period in both Upper and Lower Burma, Aniruddha's conquest of Thatôn is not mentioned in a single one.[1] Had such a momentous event taken place—the conquest of what would have been one of the most important kingdoms or polities in the region—with the kinds of religious, cultural, political, and military ramifications it was said to have had, then surely Aniruddha himself, if not his contemporaries or successors would have mentioned it in at least one inscription among hundreds that were struck, many of which record events of far less importance.

But there is a caveat. One Burmese inscription, with a date of 1067 AD, raises some interesting problems. It records the building of a temple by a king named "Manuho of Thatôn." In it, this Manuho requests King Aniruddha for lands to be dedicated to his temple. When I first came upon this inscription early in my research, it nearly put an end to this book right then and there. For here is a king named Manuho of Thatôn, living in Pagán under the aegis of King Aniruddha ten years after the date given to the alleged raid, just as the later chronicles reported.

But because the proponents of the Mon Paradigm themselves rejected this stone as a late record, concluding that it was written in "coarse" and "late cursive" Burmese, "hardly earlier than the sixteenth century,"[2] I had second thoughts. Why would the proponents of the Mon Paradigm dismiss this stone as late, based on a paleography that was certainly not foolproof, when it would have convincingly made their case? Their conclusion was at first puzzling, and it became clear only as I pursued the subject further.

I came to realize that the Mon Paradigm *needed* the 1067 Inscription to be a later record because otherwise crucial information contained in the Trāp and Paṇḍit Inscriptions mentioned in Chapter Four would have to be rejected. In other words, if the 1067 stone were accepted as original and struck contemporaneously to the date which appears on it, it would have raised serious questions about the "king" allegedly found on the Trāp and Paṇḍit Inscriptions, and hence about the entire Mon Paradigm. Both scenarios could not be accepted as valid; and the Trāp and Paṇḍit Inscriptions were much more crucial to the Paradigm than the 1067 stone.

Specifically, Luce had gone through an elaborate argument to "demonstrate" that a word reconstructed as "Makuta" on the Trāp and Paṇḍit Inscriptions was an archaic form of the name Manuha, which he said had evolved into Manoha and Manohari[3] on the fifteenth-century Kalyani Inscriptions, to finally become the garbled version of the chronicles in Manuha. As he was concerned with evidence being contemporary, while mistrusting the chronicles on virtually every occasion (except when it served his purpose as in this case), he had to have a contemporary eleventh-century epigraphic version of Manuha. This he "found" in "Makuta," which proved to him that the Aniruddha conquest story in the chronicles was historical, for it was "confirmed" by epigraphy.

However, if the 1067 Inscription were accepted as an authentic, eleventh-century stone, then "Makuta" could not have been an archaic form of Manuha—for the difference in time between the two inscriptions would have been only seventeen years. Without a preconquest "Makuta" in epigraphy to "confirm" the conquest story, its historicity would have come under question, since it would no longer be found in epigraphy, but only in the chronicles.[4] That in turn would have further undermined the entire Mon Paradigm, for the mechanism by which Mon culture supposedly came to Upper Burma was Aniruddha's conquest of Thatôn, an event found only in the chronicles.[5] Ultimately, the issue rests on whether any evidence exists in the epigraphic record, particularly in the Trāp and Paṇḍit Inscriptions, of the man who would be King "Makuta."

It all began with a lecture in January 1950, when Luce read a paper entitled "Mons of the Pagán Dynasty" at the Rangoon University Students Union Hall at a seminar convened by the All Ramannya Mon Association.[6] It was there that he publicly articulated the myth of King Makuta by identifying an illegible word on the Trāp Inscription, and a partly legible fragment *(maka)* on the Paṇḍit Inscription, as "Makuta." These, he claimed, were references to Manuha, the king thought to have ruled Thatôn when Aniruddha conquered it. That was what compelled him to date the stones to "c. 1050," saying they "must precede, and very shortly precede, Aniruddha's . . . " conquest of Thatôn in 1057.[7]

There are several serious problems with this interpretation. First, the dates on the two stones were illegible when they were first discovered in the 1930s, and, of course, they have not improved with time.[8] The stones were written partly in Old Mon and partly in Pali, but since the Old Mon language in Burma remained basically unchanged from the eleventh to the fifteenth centuries, while its script remained the same for an even longer period of time,[9] there is no certainty that the language and script on the stones are necessarily eleventh-century Old Mon rather than, say, fifteenth-century Old Mon.[10]

Second, and more directly pertinent, Luce's identification of "Makuta" is not supported by the Trāp and Paṇḍit Inscriptions at all. In fact, no such word exists on either stone. The words "Makuta" and "Makata" that were parenthetically inserted by the editors in the latest published volume of these inscriptions were not legible when the stones were first discovered.[11] The editors did place both "Makuta" and the *ta* of "Makata" (since the *maka* is legible) in parentheses,[12] acknowledging that the reading is conjectural. But since Luce had already "identified" the illegible words as "Makuta" and "Makata" over twenty years earlier—an interpretation with which its editors were obviously familiar—even their speculation, no matter how well qualified by these parentheses was *not independent* of the Mon Paradigm. One wonders what words they would have chosen to place in the parentheses had Luce's interpretation not already influenced the issue.

What is clear if one reads the Trāp and Paṇḍit Inscriptions independently of the Mon Paradigm assumptions is that the legible evidence suggests something else entirely. The Trāp Inscription states, in the Pali section, that "[illegible] rājānama Rājādhirājā, . . ." that is, "the name of the king is Rājādhirājā." (Luce had placed "Makuta," in the illegible portion in front of this phrase, that is, inside my brackets). Similarly, the Paṇḍit Inscription has the following: "Maka [illegible] rājānama Rājādhirājā. . . ."[13] Now, unless one were hoping for another, earlier king, what better evidence can there be than this, that the king mentioned in the inscriptions was Rājādhirājā, the formal title of Yazadarit, one of the most celebrated monarchs of the Pegu Dynasty? He was one of the most militarily powerful and effective monarchs to have ruled Pegu during the last quarter of the fourteenth and the first of the fifteenth centuries. For thirty-five long years he held sway over the area where the Trāp and Paṇḍit Inscriptions were originally found.[14] His reign also falls well within the period that Shorto allots to the Old Mon language and script in Burma, where noticeable changes did not emerge until the middle of the fifteenth century.[15] Thus these stones probably belonged not to the eleventh but to the late fourteenth and early fifteenth centuries. In other words, the above phrase—which is, in any case, in Pali not Old Mon—should be read as it actually appears: "the name of the king is Rājādhirājā," nothing more. The evidence as it stands shows only the name Rājādhirājā repeated several times throughout both inscriptions, not "Makuta."

Moreover, Shorto affirms that Mon kings bore at least three names: "the Sanskrit regnal name, usually found only in inscriptions; the name, or names, by which they were generally known, which might or might not be identical with that which they bore before their accession; and the Pali name used in the genealogies."[16] Since the Trap and Paṇḍit records are written on stone—even if technically not in Sanskrit at least in its equal in Burma, Pali—Rājādhirājā must have been the regnal name of the king because "Makuta," being a common name, would have been inappropriate for this medium.

There is, therefore, no good paleographic, linguistic, historical, or cultural reason to go searching for another king unless one *wanted* to find a name phonetically closer to the Manuha of the Aniruddha story in order to "prove" he, and therefore also Thatôn, existed prior to Aniruddha's alleged conquest. The illegible section on the Trāp Inscription where Luce inserted "Makuta" and on the Paṇḍit, where the editors placed *(ta)* after a legible *maka* shows how contrived the word "Makuta" really is. Since the entire word in the Trāp Inscription is illegible, and only the *maka* is legible on the Paṇḍit, and presuming that both referred to the same word and that both were references to a king, the word should be "Makata" anyway, not "Makuta." By replacing the legible *ka* of *maka* with a conjectural *Ku,* one is clearly looking for a vowel on the second syllable phonetically closer to the *nu* of Manuha. The consonant *k* of *ku* is also quite different from the *n* of *nu* in the written Pali. This is taking liberties that go well beyond what the evidence actually shows, and demonstrates the dominating influence of the Mon Paradigm on the analysis of existing evidence.

If I were looking for a Mon king whose name would best fit the legible portions on the inscription, I would have thought that the words *maka* (and the conjectural *ta* or *tu*) would have pointed in the direction of Makatu (pronounced and romanized as Magadu, the founder of the Lower Burma Mon dynasty at Martaban in the late thirteenth century) or his younger brother who succeeded him, named Makata.[17] Both names are much closer to the legible portion of the evidence *(maka)* than any of Luce's conjectures, and both brothers were considered by Mon histories to have been the founders of the Martaban Dynasty, which became the Pegu (Mon) Dynasty of Lower Burma,[18] inherited by Yazadarit and Dhammazedi. Magadu himself was said to have been born at or near the Thatôn region.[19] Thus Magadu and especially Makata make far better paleographic candidates for the legible word *maka* than a fictitious Makuta. At least the original, legible portion of the word *maka,* even if read in the way Luce had read the inscription, far better supports Makatu than it does Manuha or "Makuta."

In short, the Trāp and Paṇḍit Inscriptions were *assigned* a date of 1050 to deliberately and explicitly support the story of Aniruddha's conquest of Thatôn, from which other conclusions "logically" and predictably followed. The Mon language on the inscriptions automatically became eleventh-century Old Mon, and Rājādhirājā was reinterpreted as Manuha via "Makuta" via "Makata" via *maka.* Since the word Rakṣapura was found on the same inscription, it "became" Thatôn, as was shown in Chapter Four. What had been dependent variables had become independent variables, and they in turn became the basis for interpreting other dependent variables so that more "evidence" fell into place. Even undated temples at Pagán now possessed dates assigned to them on the basis of Aniruddha's alleged conquest of Thatôn, a topic discussed more fully in Chapter Nine.[20]

Whatever the final verdict, the evidence seems compelling with regard to the following. The phrase "the name of the king is Rājādhirājā" seems irrefutable and exists for everyone to see. That makes him the only candidate supported by the evidence as it stands, *not* as it is *reinterpreted* to fit an *a priori* belief. "Makuta" was an imaginary ruler of an imaginary Rāmaññadesa centered at an imaginary Thatôn, the conquest of which was just as imaginary.

None of this should be construed to suggest deliberate intellectual dishonesty or the manipulation of data. Rather it is that all scholars must weigh evidence and make decisions. But the reasons for acceptance or rejection must be scrutinized by those who come later, to reject or accept, in whole or in part, the earlier decisions. Such decisions, however, have almost everything, ultimately, to do with one's assumptions. So it was with the Mon Paradigm: the assumptions underlying it favored the Trāp and Paṇḍit Pali-Mon Inscriptions over the Burmese inscription of 1067.

Where does all this, then, place the 1067 Inscription? Upon closer scrutiny, it appears not to have been a contemporary and original source, but for reasons different than those given by the Mon Paradigm, such as late orthography and syntax. In my opinion, the orthography seems old enough, although there are some peculiar, non-Pagán usages in it. For example, the word Sudhuim is not spelled in its oldest form, as it appears on the fifteenth-century Kalyani Inscriptions, but as Sahtuim, a relatively late way of pronunciation and spelling. Moreover, Aniruddha's name is spelled Anorahta, also a later form, found at the earliest in 1316 in original epigraphy, and more or less spelled that way in chronicles thereafter.[21] The syntax resembles that of other Old Burmese inscriptions of the same general period—although a respected scholar of Burmese language seems to think that the syntax is also late[22]—but Burmese syntax has not changed fundamentally since Pagán days.

In addition, the abbreviated version of the word for "at" *(nhuik)* is used in this inscription. Rather than spelling out the word itself, its symbol is used, just as "e.g." or "i.e." are used in English in place of "for example" and "that is." This abbreviation is a late development in the Burmese language, rarely found in Pagán (and most likely, also Ava), inscriptions. The Sanskrit *s* rather than its Pali equivalent *th* (also pronounced as a *th* in spoken Burmese) is used in this inscription to spell common words such as *"saṅghika,"* "dock," "bodily relic," and "Thursday," not ordinarily found transcribed that way.[23] Words such as *taññ* (to erect), *saññ* (as identifier of subject), *bhurā* (Buddha, temple, monk, holy objects) also do not appear the way they were normally written in Pagán times. The way Manuho is written, spelled, and presumably pronounced is not the way one usually finds it elsewhere.[24] And, as the Mon Paradigm concludes, the script is cursive and not basically the square form one finds in Pagán letters. To be sure, the latter is not enough to disqualify it as Pagán writing, as squareness is often the consequence of writing on stone with straight-edged chisels, and may not have anything to do with the evolution of the script itself. But coupled with the factors already mentioned, there is reasonable doubt that this inscription is contemporary to the period to which it is dated.

There are other puzzles in terms of subject matter. The "author" of the stone, "King Manuho," gave himself the grandiose titles assumed by Pagán kings,[25] rather than the earliest Sanskrit title found so far associated with "him" in the Kalyani Inscriptions: namely, Sūriyakumā.[26] "He" makes other peculiar claims, for example, that he is lord of thirty-one (rather than the normal thirty-two) white elephants, and while still allegedly a prisoner of another king and in another kingdom. "He" describes beating a magic drum with the hand bone of a lion, a phrase which reminds one of the *Nidāna Árambhakathā* and the *Lik Smin Asah,* mid-sixteenth and nineteenth-century Mon texts respectively.[27] This Manuho then states that heavy rains[28] and an earthquake had destroyed some temples and exposed previously enshrined bodily relics of the Buddha, which he then rededicated. It was only after recording all this that the date 1067 AD appears on the stone, the kind of format one usually finds on stones inscribed subsequent to the events described on them. Otherwise, the date normally appears in the first sentence.

In other words, the information about Manuho and Thatôn seems to have been narrated by someone else much later. Indeed, the reverse of the stone has a date of 1268 inscribed on it, over two hundred years after the alleged event, although my analysis of that face suggests that its date is authentic and has nothing to do with the text on the obverse with which we are currently concerned.[29] The latter seems to have been inscribed even much later than 1268 when the story of Manuha had long become part of the country's tradition.

If, as the Mon Paradigm proponents suggest, this inscription is hardly older than the sixteenth century,[30] we know that by that time the story of Manuha of Thatôn was already well known, not only in Burma but in the two Northern Thai Pali chronicles mentioned in Chapter Four. In fact, there is a Bodawpaya recast of this stone made in 1785, well after U Kala's chronicle had been written.[31] The minister in charge of these recasts, Twinthintaik Wun Mahasithu includes the Manuha story in his own chronicle in ways that are even more interesting. It appears, therefore, that the story of Aniruddha and Manuha on the "1067" inscription is a late one, probably taken from the chronicles, so that the 1067 "original" was likely a recast stone. In the end, even the late recast has nothing explicit to say about any conquest of Thatôn; it is only because we already know the story that we are able to make such an *a posteriori* connection.

With the exception of this single, puzzling and clearly late inscription, no other stone inscription struck during nearly four centuries of the Pagán period, by elite or commoner, victor or vanquished, ever mentioned Aniruddha's conquest of Thatôn. That means the event, especially the version that has come down to us, either did not occur at all, or was conflated with another event in which Aniruddha reformed the religion, along with his expansion into Lower Burma (both of which likely occurred close in time to each other) by later writers, either inadvertently or for their own reasons.

However, casting doubt upon the historicity of the conquest of Thatôn per se does not mean that Aniruddha did not march upon, conquer, and establish Pagán's authority and hegemony in Lower Burma in the mid-eleventh century. Indeed, if one studies his known activities carefully, it is clear that his unification of what was then Burma was well planned and deliberate. After first building forty-three forts along the Irrawaddy north to Bhamo and the China border—clearly a military priority—he secured his western and eastern passages: Arakan on the west, and the Inlé Lake region on the east. Once this immediate periphery was secured militarily, he developed anew or rebuilt and repaired the Kyauksé valley irrigation works. That was what provided his kingdom with the economic and demographic wherewithal to expand into Lower Burma in the first place.

All this he accomplished during the first thirteen years of his reign, only after which he marched on Lower Burma and, in some cases, established for the first time, major port cities and towns there, while securing and developing those that may have existed already.[32] Thus an inscription of Pagán, dated to about thirty years after Aniruddha's march south (although it may have been erected later) mentions how the king, "showing great strength," took "the . . . region of Ussā Paikū," as Lower Burma was known then, and is still known today.[33] That march south must have been early in 1056, or even earlier, initially taking Śrī Kṣetra, then moving down to the modern Yangôn area of Twanté and Khabin, several miles west of which Aniruddha subsequently built several pagodas and many small forts strategically located to control the coastal movements of commerce.

Another inscription, possibly a recast, records a donation Aniruddha made while on this Lower Burma campaign. It describes his battle with the *Gywan* (thought by Luce to be Cambodians),[34] presumably somewhere on the Tenasserim Peninsula, apparently the consequences of his thrust into an area where the Khmers may have been moving.[35] It is also interesting that the first mention of Pagán (as Pukaṁ) in external epigraphy is found on two Cham inscriptions of Phanrang, dated to before 1050, suggesting there was knowledge of Pagán's expansion even in what is now southern Cambodia and Vietnam.[36]

That Aniruddha's campaigns reached the Tenasserim Peninsular, as far south as Mergui, today one of the last major towns near the southern boundary of Burma is attested by the discovery there of his special votive tablets.[37] Had Thatôn existed at the time of Aniruddha's march south, its conquest should have been mentioned because it would have been right on the path to Mergui. But it was not, and of nearly twenty-eight votive tablets attributed specifically to Aniruddha, not a single one was recovered from Thatôn.[38]

This is important, for he left them wherever he went, as they were markers of the state's reach into the periphery, statements indicating the extent of its power, many signed by him, or identifiable as his by its style.[39] Many were written in the Sanskrit language and *devanāgarī* script. There are a few attributed to him personally that were written in the Pagán script,[40] an important issue that will be addressed in Chapter Seven.[41] An inscription on one of these tablets found at Mergui bears the name of Saw Lu, Aniruddha's son and presumed heir apparent, who was said to have accompanied the king on this campaign.[42] Perhaps he was later stationed there for political reasons, as his competitor for the throne, King Kyanzittha, was already in ascendancy at the time. Kyanzittha continued Aniruddha's conquests in Lower Burma, establishing the authority of Pagán at other strategic places. Two inscribed tablets belonging to two governors he appointed and stationed at Tavoy, north of Mergui, have been found. They expressed their subordinate position to their lord, King Kyanzittha.[43]

If, using only original, contemporary epigraphy, one constructs a linguistic map of Lower Burma from the eleventh to the end of the thirteenth century, it would show a wide swath of Burmese speakers generally following the Irrawaddy River valley, and from there hugging the coast of Tenasserim all the way to Mergui, the southernmost point of the Pagán kingdom. And this map would not show any linguistic interruption by any polity, state, or kingdom in which Mon was the *lingua franca.*

An interesting phenomenon that helps confirm this untrammeled expansion south by Burmese speakers during the Pagán period is Tavoy's dialect, which had preserved Pagán Old Burmese spelling (and presumably pronunciation), well into the twentieth century.[44] This suggests that the Pagán Old Burmese dialect spoken at Tavoy had become isolated from mainstream (by then Ava) Burmese spoken in the rest of the country sometime after Pagán's settlement of Lower Burma between the eleventh and thirteenth centuries. The kind of event of the magnitude to affect such isolation would have been the migration of a large number of people who spoke a different language into the area between Martaban and Pegu, north of Tavoy: that is, the Mon. The subsequent establishment of a kingdom led by these Mon speakers in the late thirteenth century that remained viable for the next two and half centuries ensured the fossilization of Pagán Old Burmese in Tavoy.

There is ample contemporary and subsequent evidence, and little or no disagreement among Burma historians, that Aniruddha did expand into Lower Burma and consolidated his kingdom in the mid-eleventh century, perhaps between 1055 and 1056. He returned to Pagán by 1058 at the latest, since he dedicated a temple that year there. But such expansion into Lower Burma does not necessarily suggest the conquered areas were already inhabited by Mon speakers, particularly as there are no original, *dated* records in Old Mon originating from that locality prior to Aniruddha's conquest.[45] That is ultimately the only sure indication that a certain place may have been inhabited by a particular ethnolinguistic group. Although I do not dispute Pagán's expansion into Lower Burma, or even the possible presence there of Mon speakers, there is nevertheless no contemporary evidence to support that presence, and certainly none to suggest a conquest of a "Mon" Thatôn, even if it existed.

Evidence from Fourteenth- and Fifteenth-Century Inscriptions

Not a single Ava period (1364–1527) inscription out of approximately 217 stones that have survived mentions Aniruddha's conquest of Thatôn either.[46] My search, therefore, took me to other original epigraphic sources in Lower Burma that may have mentioned the event. Most scholars point to the Kalyani Inscriptions as containing the ultimate proof of Aniruddha's conquest of Thatôn. But scrutiny of their content suggests no such thing.

In both the Pali and Mon versions of the Kalyani Inscriptions, Aniruddha is mentioned only very briefly, and in a context that had nothing to do with military activities. The Mon version is laconic: "A thousand six hundred and one years from the attainment of Parinirvāṇa by the exalted Buddha, in the year [419] of the common Era, . . . [illegible here, but Blagden, using the Pali version inserts the following in the illegible Mon section] King Anuruddha established the religion in Pukām, . . ." which Blagden said at the time was conjectural. That is the full extent of the information regarding King Aniruddha in the Kalyani Inscriptions, and yet proponents of the Mon Paradigm have used this scanty sentence to prove his conquest of Thatôn and all the consequences attributed to it.

Similarly, the Pali narrative, which Blagden estimates could not have fit in the space where the Mon text is illegible had it been written in Mon, has only a little more to say: "King Anuruddha, the lord of Arimaddanapura, took a community of monks together with the *Tipiṭaka* and established the religion in Arimaddanapura, otherwise called Pugāma."[47] That is it! Where the monks and texts come from that Aniruddha took with him is not disclosed.[48]

The information on Sudhuim (Thatôn) and King Manohor in the Kalyani Inscriptions is equally brief. More important, it is *not linked* to the Aniruddha narrative. Instead, Manohor is part of a story concerning the arrival and decay of Theravāda Buddhism in various places in the Buddhist world, Thatôn being just one of them. The Mon version has only this to say: a king named "Sūriyakumā, who bore the name of King Manohor, . . . ruled the city of Sudhuim." The Pali version, used for the illegible part, states that "during the reign of Manoharī, who was also known by his princely name of Sūriyakumāra, the power of the kingdom became very weak." That is it! There is nothing here regarding a conquest by anyone, implied or explicit.

As for the date of Sudhuim's weakness, the translator adds the following conjectural sentence: "[This happened] a thousand six hundred years from the attainment of Parinirvāṇa by the exalted Buddha [1056–1057] (and) when the religion (had been) established (in) the Mon country a thousand (three hundred and sixty-four years?)."[49] The translator's footnote for the conjectural sentence states rather matter-of-factly: "The passage in parentheses has been added conjecturally by subtracting 236 from 1600, *there being no equivalent in the Pali for this whole sentence*" [my emphasis].[50] This portion of the translation, therefore, is not part of the original evidence. Rather, it is a twentieth-century conjectural reconstruction used to date another conjectural reconstruction—the alleged conquest—which by that time was well known and considered historical truth.

That is the extent of the "epigraphic evidence" most often quoted by Burma historians as decisive proof for the conquest of Thatôn by King Aniruddha. Luce even footnotes the same edition and pages of the *Epigraphia Birmanica* I have used here, stating with assurance that: "For the capture of Thatôn, the clearest statement comes in the Pali/Mon Kalyani inscriptions of Pegu (1479 A.D.). . . ."[51] Either he did not read the passages himself or he believed in the conquest so completely that he failed to see what the evidence was actually saying. But Luce was not the only one who stated that the Kalyani Inscriptions mentioned the conquest of Thatôn. In the late eighteenth century, one of Bodawpaya's famous ministers, Twinthintaik Wun Mahasithu also did so, as we shall see in Chapter Six.

What has happened, then, is that two *unrelated narratives* regarding two *unrelated events* and two *unrelated individuals* found in the Kalyani Inscriptions—establishing the religion in Pagán by Aniruddha and the weakening of Thatôn during Manohor's reign—were linked by eighteenth-century chronicles to construe that a conquest had taken place at that particular time. This chronicle interpretation was then accepted by nineteenth-century colonial scholarship without any critical analysis.

Indeed, if one scrutinizes the very small section of the Mon-language narrative on the Kalyani Inscriptions that deals with Aniruddha—it occupies only one sentence out of over approximately 1,400 lines of text—it is clear that Aniruddha's function is to serve as a model Buddhist king.[52] His reform is mentioned together with that of another Pagán king, Narapatisithu in the late twelfth century, who also followed the Mahāvihāra tradition,[53] and that of Parākramabāhu I of Śrī Laṅka. They were said to have kept the religion pure and reformed the *saṅgha* according to the "orthodox" brand of Śrī Laṅkan Theravāda Buddhism that Dhammazedi was at the time also attempting to do.

Thus if one reads the narrative in its actual, historical context, these three kings were mentioned to provide models of legitimacy for Dhammazedi's own reform and to demonstrate his Sinhalese orthodoxy by linking him to them. The valid chapters created by such reforms, Dhammazedi notes, declined in Lower Burma as sectarianism developed and the Orders grew farther and farther away from their original purity. Since that impure form was what he ultimately came to inherit, during his reign he performs a *sāsana* reform and purifies the *saṅgha* once more in the Mahāvihāra tradition. Dhammazedi was legitimating his own reign by showing that he was following in the footsteps of the great Buddhist kings, beginning with King Aśoka, who kept the religion "pure" by reforming it. Aniruddha's place in the Kalyani Inscriptions had nothing to do with any conquest of Thatôn but with his reform that Dhammazedi was emulating.

And because the main purpose of the Kalyani Inscriptions was to legitimate Dhammazedi's reform, the narrative about Thatôn—which belonged in any case to the Manuha section of the narrative, not Aniruddha's—was meant to illustrate what happens when kings allowed the religion to decay. In that context, Manuha is, to be sure, also part of the overall theme, for he is the model of, and represents the antagonist par excellence. Dhammazedi was not concerned (in the Kalyani Inscriptions) with the secular activities of kings, but with their role (and his) as exemplary models in the history of the religion. That explains why there was precious little about these kings except what they did to perpetuate, or allow the decay of, the orthodox version of Theravāda Buddhism. That is not to say, however, that Dhammazedi's goals were all religious; he also had other concerns.

There were economic, political, and ideological reasons Dhammazedi may have preferred the Mahāvihāra's reordination tradition, for it followed certain unique procedures favorable to the state.[54] It likely differed, for example, from the North Indian tradition of Upagupta or the South Indian tradition associated with Buddhaghosa,[55] both of which had been present in Burma during the millennium before Pagán even emerged.

Economically, adherence to the Mahāvihāra tradition of Śrī Laṅka for *sāsana* reform allowed the use of its unique procedures surrounding the *upasampadā* ordination, which ultimately enabled the state to control or contain the flight of wealth from the taxable state sector to the tax-exempt religious sector. The Sinhalese procedures provided the Burmese state with a religiously sanctioned, nonviolent mechanism to control the flow of state wealth to the tax-exempt church, which neither the North nor South Indian traditions apparently had.

Politically, the king's carefully selected order of five monks (the minimum number needed for a valid chapter) who were to lead the reform were first sent to Śrī Laṅka to be reordained. According to the rules of the Mahāvihāra, one's rank was determined by the order in which one was ordained, or in this case reordained, which meant the king's chosen group would return with higher ranks than those of the monks who remained in Burma, *regardless of their previous rank.* In effect, he was rearranging the existing religious hierarchy in his favor, making his chapter the supreme heads of the church in the land.[56]

Ideologically, Dhammazedi had to counterbalance the influence of the South Indian tradition led by Buddhaghosa, who is often claimed by the Mon as a native of Thatôn,[57] particularly after having spent many years in Ava which may have adhered more closely to the Mahāvihāra tradition. And *sāsana* reform in the Mahāvihāra tradition resolved the issue. Indeed, Taw Sein Ko, who translated the Pali section of the Kalyani Inscriptions was puzzled by "the absolute silence of this epigraph regarding the celebrated Buddhist divine Buddhaghosa . . . " and questioned the "historical accuracy of the account relating to the mission of Buddhaghosa to Thatôn."[58] In fact, Dhammazedi probably left Buddhaghosa out deliberately.

But it was even more than that. Dhammazedi was also attempting to be "modern." The "global" momentum had been swinging in favor of the Sinhalese version of Theravāda Buddhism since perhaps the mid-eleventh century and the influence of the great Buddhist kings Vijayabāhu I, Parākramabāhu I, Aniruddha, and Narapatisithu. By Dhammazedi's time it had become the prevailing, mainstream, and "politically correct" ideology, while South India by that time was actually no longer Buddhist, but staunchly Hindu. Yet Lower Burma appears to have been clinging to that "outmoded" South Indian tradition of Buddhaghosa, a situation which Dhammazedi wanted to change. He wanted to bring his kingdom into the "modern" world. With a wider "global" vision, he desired to reform his realm to fit the more "enlightened" philosophies of the Buddhist world, so that it could be part of that new "international order" and the new "international community." It would have been extremely difficult for the conservative forces in Lower Burma to resist this reformation initiated with the might, power, prestige, and resources of the state behind it, led by an ex-monk who was well trained in, and knowledgeable about the Doctrine.

To transform Lower Burma's previous attachment to the South Indian Buddhist tradition and adopt the Śrī Laṅkan one, history had to be publicly rewritten. Dhammazedi did this by attaching the most prestigious lineage of the two Aśokan missionaries from the Third Buddhist Council, Soṇa and Uttara, to an alleged "earlier" Thatôn tradition, to which Pegu's could then be linked by the reordination process, and from there to Aśoka and ultimately the Buddha himself. In effect, Dhammazedi was suggesting that the Buddhaghosa school had corrupted the Soṇa and Uttara school. The definitive, legal source for this rewritten history was Dhammazedi's Kalyani Inscriptions. The evidence suggests that while Upper Burma had long adopted various Theravāda and Mahāyāna traditions from India and Śrī Laṅka, it was only in the mid-fifteenth century that Lower Burma, as an independent polity and state, first adopted the Sinhalese tradition and hence the need for an "invented tradition" of Lower Burma's antiquity.

Conclusion

The Kalyani Inscriptions of King Dhammazedi that supposedly offer proof of the conquest of Thatôn had nothing whatever to say about any Shin Arahan and his conversion of Aniruddha, nothing about the latter's request from any Manuha for the *Tipiṭakas,* nothing about the rebuff by that Manuha, nothing about the conquest of Thatôn, nothing about transporting thirty sets of the *Tipiṭakas* on thirty-two white elephants, along with 30,000 people and their king, to Pagán. In no way does the text of the Kalyani Inscriptions, even as conjecturally reconstructed, demonstrate that the conquest of Thatôn by Aniruddha ever occurred. It alludes only to Aniruddha's reform of the religion in the Mahāvihāra tradition of Śrī Laṅka, and then in a separate section that introduces another topic—the decline of orthodox Buddhism in Thatôn—it recalls the story of Manohor. Neither story is linked to the other either narratively or contextually in the Kalyani Inscriptions. Rather, they were *connected for us* by later chronicles from which the Mon Paradigm, an even later construction begun in the colonial period, subsequently obtained its thesis.

Not only did Dhammazedi's inscriptions make no claims of a conquest of Thatôn, no implied (certainly no explicit) relationship was intended or demonstrated to have existed between Aniruddha and the mysterious Sūriyakumā, alias Manohor of Thatôn. That was *read into* the narrative by others coming later. Aniruddha's reform of decaying orthodox Buddhism was something later chroniclers and modern scholars *wanted to see* in the context of their respective worlds, both political and academic—a sentiment clearly not shared by Aniruddha's contemporaries themselves—so that the story would be *commensurate with its desired consequences.* For the chroniclers, the "event" was momentous mainly for its religious consequences, while for modern scholars, it was important both politically and ideologically. One early twentieth-century scholar puts it as Aniruddha's "grand religious reformation."[59] I have little doubt that the importance of the conversion of Charlemagne and/or the Protestant Reformation in European history was in the minds of twentieth-century Burma scholars when they encountered the Aniruddha story in the chronicles.

6 The Conquest of Thatôn as Allegory

HAVING ESTABLISHED the absence of epigraphy to verify the historicity of Thatôn's conquest by Aniruddha, I now turn to the chronicles, for ultimately the story belongs to them. But since there is no epigraphic evidence for either the event or the place, when, how, and why did the story become part of Burma's chronicle tradition? The questions of when and how are relatively straightforward and answerable, but the question of why is necessarily interpretative and far more problematic.

One of the difficulties in assessing the chronicles of Mainland Southeast Asia lies with our own proclivities to separate, and then see irreconcilable distinctions between history and allegory, empiricism and symbolism, "religious" and "secular," linear and cyclic conceptions of time, ahistoricism and historicism, and diachronic and synchronous approaches to understanding the world. The sources generally fall into two categories: accounts written in Pali and those written in the vernacular, although these are by no means mutually exclusive and easy to separate. In some cases the Pali seems to have incorporated local history from the vernacular, often the only written version of that history we have. But the reverse is also true: myths, legends, and history begun by the Pali chronicles—that is, by the center—have become myths, legends, and history of the folk and periphery.

In other cases "secular" histories have incorporated legitimation criteria and mechanisms from religious histories—such as links to the Buddha or Aśoka—and integrated these with the actual history of kings, known as *rājavaṃsa* in the Pali tradition and *yazawin* in Burmese. And, if one is searching for a linear, historically progressive narrative in the more western and modern (though not postmodern) sense of the term, the largely allegorical, synchronous, and cyclic nature of these chronicles creates not a few problems.[1]

Although it is tempting to regard the process as strictly linear and evolutionary, in fact, most chronicles of Burma and Mainland Southeast Asia have been added to by later authors at one time or another. That means information contained in a recently recopied version of an "older" chronicle, say, "A," often has late information taken from chronicle "B" written closer in time to the recopy date. Thus, although "A" may be technically older, the information taken from "B" and placed later in "A," may not be. Simply because the author who wrote "A" lived earlier than the author of "B," it does not mean that "A's" account of a particular event is any earlier than that of "B"; indeed, it may be a much later interpolation. These kinds of nonlinear processes ultimately resulted in the version of the Aniruddha story that has come down to us today.

Yet in order to dispel the Mon Paradigm, it is necessary to use its own, western framework of analysis first, to demonstrate that it has no evidentiary basis. Only after that can the case be made that this approach, in any case, is largely irrelevant to the concerns of the societies that produced the chronicles. Otherwise we would still leave the "history" of the Mon Paradigm intact. I shall therefore begin by making the separations and distinctions decried above, but then attempt to understand the chronicles on their own terms, something the Mon Paradigm never did.

In trying to separate historical "facts" from myths and legends with etiological significance—however modern and discipline-centric the process may be—we find that the "religious" histories written in Pali often took a different path, with a different trajectory and focus all their own, for their concerns were different. They not only deviate from what are the main foci of modern, westernized historians—such as sequence of rule, political boundaries, origins of kingdoms, alliances, and so on—but they also often gloss over what might have been the "secular" concerns of the society in which they were written. In other words, while the more "secular" *rājavaṃsa* give priority to dates, kings, battles, and royal genealogy, these kinds of foci are often only *incidental* to authors writing the history of Buddhism, its relics, or its temples. The perspectives and priorities of the world of Pali literature are, therefore, different from those belonging to the world of vernacular literature, even if they are products of the same society.

We find, for example, that events in Pali chronicles surrounding kings and queens were often garbled and quite "anachronistic," and at other times historically "impossible," especially when time is conflated. But that is because they were never intended to be the framework on which to hang empirical historical "truths." Rather, they were included because they touched upon the sacred: the relics, the prophesied cities, the auspicious events. Yet because these Pali chronicles are sometimes the earliest surviving nonepigraphic sources in Burma, they are still important for finding the kinds of "historical" evidence we seek. And in other ways as well, they often shed light on what had been obscure.

Finally, these Pali chronicles of Mainland Southeast Asia owe many of their broader themes and some actual stories to the *Dīpavaṃsa, Mahāvaṃsa,* and the *Cūḷavaṃsa,* the earliest extant Pali chronicles that deal with the history of Theravāda Buddhism. But the Southeast Asian chroniclers clearly went well beyond what was taken from the Sinhalese sources, as we saw in the case of King Dhammazedi. In such instances, the "orthodox" Buddhist literature of Śrī Laṅka provided only a broad framework while its contents were nearly all Southeast Asian; a process that has been called "localization" in the field.

The Regional Pali, Burmese, and Mon Sources

With these kinds of issues in mind, let us take a look at some of the Burma and regional chronicles pertinent to the Aniruddha conquest story.

Zatatawpon Yazawin

A fact quite revealing in itself, the Aniruddha conquest story is *not* found in what may be the earliest extant chronicle of Burma written in Burmese called the *Zatatawpon Yazawin* (Chronicle of royal horoscopes).[2] The earliest portions of this text appear to have been written sometime in the late thirteenth or early fourteenth centuries. Although its original author is unknown, and later hands have clearly added information that takes it into the nineteenth century, internal evidence suggests that the original author was writing towards the end of the Pagán Dynasty and just before the beginning of the First Ava Dynasty in 1364. In part, this is suggested by a phrase which states that "the royal son of Tayôk Pye Min, Thihathuya, rules *the current kingdom* [or capital]"[3] [my emphasis], which was probably still Pagán or its immediate, brief successor, Pinya.[4] Both father and son were historical figures, confirmed by epigraphy, who reigned during the last decades of the thirteenth century. The author mentions by name Disāpramok, the famous minister of Tayôk Pye, who journeyed to Peking to convince Kublai Khan not to invade Pagán and left an inscription in 1285 AD describing that journey.[5] As far as I know, the *Zatatawpon* is one of only two chronicles[6] that mention this minister, and thus is another indication that the author may have lived close to the time when the minister was still famous. Thereafter, Disāpramok disappears from historiography until twentieth-century scholars read his inscription and resurrected him as an important figure.

The published text of the *Zatatawpon* that I use was taken from two extant manuscripts. What the editor considered the better copy was published "as is," while the other was used to help correct discrepancies, clarify, add to, and in other ways, enhance the first. These additions were placed in parentheses. The text has been divided into five sections by the editor.

The first section of the published text deals with the beginning of the world system, its eras, and the many dispensations of the Buddha. The second starts with the first king of the world, Mahāsamata, and Prince Siddhattha, who becomes the historical Buddha, and continues to Aśoka's reign and the beginning of Burmese history. A history of the Śrī Laṅkan kings is included in this section, which uses the standard Buddhist texts, such as the *Mahāvaṃsa* and the *Dīpavaṃsa,* along with others such as the *Buddhavaṃsa.*

Section three concerns the legendary and historical origins of "Burma," beginning with the Tagaung Dynasty, still considered by the Burmese to be the origins of its culture and people. In fact, the author begins this section by saying, "in this our country of the Myanmā, . . ." revealing an early identification of the state with the major cultural group, the Myanmā.[7] A genealogy of kings is provided, including their kinship ties to their predecessors. In the Burma section, all the kings of the Śrī Kṣetra, Pagán, Pinya, Sagaing, and Ava Dynasties are included, ending with heir apparent Narawara in 1671,[8] an obvious indication that these sections had been added later. The kings' dates of accession, their days of birth in numerals, their years as heir, their regnal years, and their age at and date of death are all given. In terms of regnal years, the *Zatatawpon* is the most accurate of all Burmese chronicles, particularly with regard to the best-known Pagán and Ava kings, many of whose dates have been corroborated by epigraphy. This again indicates that the original author must have been a contemporary of Thihathu, one of the famous Three Brothers, as he suggested.

After each dynastic list an explanatory section is provided, clarifying or qualifying certain information in the same sort of way we would use footnotes. A few are out of place, which suggests later interpolations. In these "notes" sections, the author would add what he considered additional important information, such as the size of each city, the number of gates it had, and so on. In one case the author states that the "great kingdom of Pugaṁ called Arimaddanā was founded in *Sakaraja* 23 [661 AD.]" by King Samuddayaza, with the famous nineteen villages as his base of strength;[9] these villages are very much a part of the legend and history of the origins of Pagán.[10] Interestingly, the date the author gives for the founding of Pagán is within twenty years of the earliest radiocarbon dates recently procured from the urban settlement area just a few hundred yards outside the gates of Pagán.[11] The author apparently also had access to earlier records now lost to us, as he calls this section *"yazawin mhat chyet akyin"* (Summary and notes of chronicles).[12]

Section four has the horoscopes, as diagrams and numerals, of thirty-six select kings of the Pagán, Sagaing, and Ava Dynasties, along with those of some other minor kings, beginning with Sôkkaté (Aniruddha's predecessor) and ending with the birth year (1607) of Min Yè Yandameik, who belonged to the Second Ava Dynasty. Also commanding horoscopes were the founding of major cities, palaces, exemplary temples, and important events, such as the first time the Mongols sent an embassy to Pagán. Since the horoscopes of later kings, such as Thibaw of the last dynasty, and temples built in the Kônbaung period were included towards the end of the text, it is again obvious that later hands have added to the original.

Section five has various statistical charts and data such as "the great Buddhist cities of Jambudīpa," "the 16 great countries," "the 19 great capitals," along with what appears to be actual administrative information, such as those cities in Burma (probably under the First Ava Dynasty) that were required to supply fighting men, the towns and villages belonging to the "Northern Horse" that had to supply various numbers of cavalrymen, lists of governors of certain cities, the royal tax from various regions, and so on.

In the section on the kings of Pagán, Aniruddha is given one short sentence of three phrases,[13] and the conquest of Thatôn is not mentioned. In fact, Aniruddha is not a hero in this text, the author actually invoking a "massacre of the infants" allegory in the king's unsuccessful search for the prophesied future King Kyanzittha when the latter's birth was announced. Information from manuscript "B" added in parentheses states that the author does not think the story has credibility, and although it is found in the ancient texts, it should nevertheless be considered carefully as it is only what the people have said.[14] In contrast to the single sentence given Aniruddha, the *Zatatawpon* gives Kyanzittha two full paragraphs out of a total six for the entire Pagán period. Clearly, the legend of Aniruddha had not yet begun by the late thirteenth century.

ZAMBU KUNGYA

The next relevant extant text to consider is the *Zambu Kungya Po Yaza Mu Haung* by Wun Zin Min Yaza, minister to at least two successive kings of the First Ava Dynasty (1364–1527): Mingyi Swasawkè (1368–1401) and Mingaung I (1400–1423).[15] It may be the oldest text to mention the Aniruddha story, but it tells it in a very different way. In it the rough outlines of the history of Śrī Kṣetra, Pagán, and Pinya are first described. Then the eighteenth-century version of the *Zambu,* which is more complete, says the following about Shin Arahan and the Aniruddha story.

> Nine years after Anawrahta's reign, a high monk came, named the lord arahat, Dwe Arahan, and the king honored him greatly. He was much devoted to the Religion and therefore conveyed the Lord Buddha's tooth relic from China to Ceylon for worship. The Religion flourished greatly. In the year 416 [AD. 1054]

> the King, ministers, officers, people, and monks of Thahton carried the three Pitakas of the scriptures upon thirty-three white elephants to Pagan Arimaddana and brought [took] them there.[16]

Thus, in what is clearly a late copy of the earliest known domestic version of what became the Aniruddha story, *the account is actually the reverse* of the conventional one, where no conquest is mentioned or implied. Instead, it is the people of Thatôn who go to Pagán with the texts. The story is similar, and relatively close in time, to the narrative provided in the Kalyani Inscriptions, where Aniruddha is said to have taken back with him to Pagán a community of monks to establish the religion there. Although the original palm-leaf manuscript of the *Zambu* appears not to have survived except as a late 1825 copy, its early parts have been incorporated into a late eighteenth-century text called the *Maniyadanabon,* from which the above quote is taken. I shall discuss the *Maniyadanabon* in greater detail below.

YAZAWINKYAW

About a hundred years later, a chronicle called the *Yazawinkyaw* appeared. Its earliest parts were apparently written in 1502[17] by the famous monk Shin Thilawuntha.[18] What is most interesting about his work in terms of the Mon Paradigm is that it did not *mention Aniruddha at all,*[19] the bulk of it focusing on the kings of India and Śrī Laṅka. This chronicle is, for the most part, a Burmese version of, and taken from, the *Mahāvaṃsa,* a text we know was present in Ava at the time. It was mentioned by title in an original inscription that lists the names of 295 manuscripts donated to a library in 1442, at the zenith of the First Ava Dynasty during which Thilawuntha played a very important part.[20] Only the last sections of the *Yazawinkyaw,* perhaps less than 10 percent, are concerned with Burma.

In the historical literature of Burma, then, at least in the *rājavaṃsa* tradition up to the fall of Ava, the story of the conquest of Thatôn has not yet appeared. Aniruddha is either not mentioned at all *(Yazawinkyaw)* or given only the briefest of descriptions *(Zambu* and *Zatatawpon).* We must suspect, therefore, that the legend of Aniruddha began later and may have become inexorably linked to another legend regarding the conquest of Thatôn found elsewhere.[21]

JINAKĀLAMĀLĪ

Aniruddha, said to be one of the greatest kings in early Burma's history, is extolled at length, along with his conquest story, in a chronicle that appeared well after his reign, from a much later, relatively distant, and culturally different polity. The *Jinakālamālī,* whose title in English is given as

"The Sheaf of Garlands of the Epochs of the Conqueror," appears about a decade or two after Thilawuntha's *Yazawinkyaw*. It was originally written in Pali by a Ratanapañña Thera of Chiang Mai, and is dated to 2071 BE (1527 AD) by modern scholars[22] or to the date at the end of the manuscript itself, 1516/1517.[23] At best, the text was written almost five hundred years after the alleged conquest of Thatôn and several centuries after Aniruddha's and Kyanzittha's expansion into Lower Burma.

The manuscript from which the published English translation is derived has gone through many revisions. The earliest extant version is the "Ayudhayā" copy, an eighteenth-century palm-leaf manuscript written in a later Cambodian script during the Ayudhayā period prior to 1788. That is, it was written *after* at least two conquests of Ayudhayā by the Burmese in the mid-sixteenth century and perhaps after the last conquest in the mid-eighteenth century. The *Jinakālamālī* went through at least a dozen versions, translated and retranslated from Cambodian to Thai to Pali to French to Thai to Cambodian and back again to Pali.[24] We also do not know what alphabet was first used to write the original version, Thai or Sinhalese. No original has been found, and only the one palm-leaf copy has survived. The chronicle was also revised at least four times during the Chakri Dynasty alone, whose last "revision," during Mongkut's reign, did not follow the original "Ayudhayā copy" verbatim.[25] Thus even early Thai nationalism could have been a component in the final Pali version of 1962.[26] By the time it comes down to us in the English translation of 1968 by N. A. Jayawickrama, the journey the chronicle has taken and the array of sources it has incorporated make it a rather broad compendium of knowledge of several different ages and places, rather than that of a singular time and place.[27]

There are six major sections in the *Jinakālamālī*, three of which are taken from Sinhalese and other standard Buddhist texts. These deal with the various dispensations of the Buddha, the Recitals, and Buddhism in Śrī Laṅka. The fourth section contains the legendary account of the founding of Haripuñjaya and Queen Cāmadevī. The fifth section deals with the kingdom of Chiang Mai; it features Mangrai until his death (Rāma Gāṁhèṅ is just barely mentioned), after which follows a period of unrest. The last section concentrates on King Tilok's accomplishments, even though his great-grandson, known as "Phra Muang Keo" in the text, is considered the greatest king in Mangrai's line according to the author, who, of course, wrote during that reign. Nonetheless, the religious activities during Tilok's reign seemed to have been more important to the author, for basically the *Jinakālamālī* is the account of the arrival of Sīhala orthodoxy—particularly the *upasampadā* tradition of the Mahāvihāra school—and its spread in Thailand from the end of the fourteenth into the middle of the fifteenth century This is about the same time that Dhammazedi's kingdom was going through the same process with the same school in Lower Burma.

Thus, although relatively distant in time and place from activities in Lower Burma, the *Jinakālamālī* is important here because it is the first chronicle of Southeast Asia that I know of to actually mention a conquest by an Aniruddha of a kingdom held by one Manohāra. But the story is hardly central to the thrust of the work; instead, it is a digression and only a small part of a much larger and broader Theravāda Buddhist, Mainland Southeast Asian, Chiang Mai legitimation theme. It may, therefore, have been a later addition. Aniruddha's role as a great Buddhist king[28] is far more important than the conquest story, especially as he plays a major part in the bringing of orthodox Buddhism to Thailand. He is given the credit for bringing to Mainland Southeast Asia what the author considers one of its most holy relics, the Emerald Buddha,[29] a central motif around which many other important events, including the Aniruddha conquest story, revolve.

The Jewel Image, as the Emerald Buddha is called in the text, was said to have been sculpted miraculously after the *parinibbānna* of the Buddha in Pāṭaliputra, Aśoka's capital, an activity in which a host of important deities and super elders were involved. Then came the Kali Yuga, the age of chaos, when the image was taken to the Island of Laṅka by "the people" for safekeeping. Finally, around 656 AD, approximately 1,200 years after the Buddha's *parinibbānna,* the great Buddhist centers of Mainland Southeast Asia enter the picture. At that time Aniruddha of Arimaddana is said to have gone to Śrī Laṅka with the intention of procuring the Holy Scriptures, and in the process he also obtains the Jewel Image, bringing it to Southeast Asia for the first time. Here, it is clear and significant that Aniruddha attempts to obtain the "holy grail" as it were, not from Lower Burma but from Śrī Laṅka.

His request for the original scriptures is refused, although the king of Śrī Laṅka offers to make a copy for him. Aniruddha, however, tells the king that "your writing . . . does not meet with my approval. I myself will write it down."[30] So he personally copies them, then places part of them on one ship and part on another with the Jewel Image, and returns to Pagán. On the way "a fierce gale" sends one ship to Mahānagara (thirteenth-century Angkor Thom) and the other to Pagán. Soon thereafter, Aniruddha seeks the ship that landed in Angkor. At first, the king of Angkor refuses, but after witnessing Aniruddha's miraculous powers, decides to give the *Tipiṭakas* to him. Aniruddha returns to Pagán with the scriptures, but forgets the Jewel Image, leaving it behind in Mahānagara.[31] In this sequence, the Aniruddha-versus-Manuha trope is recalled once again.

The narrative then goes through a variety of other personalities and events, both in Śrī Laṅka and Mainland Southeast Asia, until one King Ādicca, the lord of the city of Ayojjha, invades Mahānagara and captures the Jewel Image, taking it back with him to his capital and enshrining it there. "The King and the citizens there paid homage to the Jewel Image for a long time," said the *Jinakālamālī*.[32] Thereafter, the Jewel Image goes from one city to another via different conquering kings, all within Thailand and possibly Cambodia, providing legitimacy to those cities that manage to house the Image.[33]

Finally, the story leads to an emperor of the "Rammaṇa Country" and a different relic, called the Black-Stone Image. This emperor had taken a sacred black stone and made five Buddha images, depositing one at Mahānagara, one at Lava, one at Sudhamma and, said the *Jinakālamālī*, "retained two of them *here itself in the Rammaṇa Country* . . ." [my emphasis].[34]

The last phrase, "here itself in the Rammaṇa Country," is revealing and interesting, for it places the writer (or the original source of this phrase) in the Chiang Mai Valley cultural region, since the text was written there, or at least, from that perspective. However, since the *Jinakālamālī* also remarked that the inhabitants of the "Rammaṇa Country" speak "their own language,"[35] it sounds as if the language was not that of the author (presumably T'ai) but another, most probably Mon, the most viable candidate for that time and place.

Moreover, throughout the narrative "Rammaṇa" is not spelled "Rāmañña," and such distinctions were surely known to scholars of Pali obsessed with these kinds of details. Although the difference in spelling could simply be the result of the numerous versions the original text has gone through, why did subsequent authors not correct it as they were known to do often? It also does not explain the narrative's sense that these were two distinct places, especially since Sudhamma, normally thought of as the center of the Lower Burma Rāmañña, was already named as a separate place from Rammaṇa in the narrative, one of the five places to receive the Black Stone Image. And if the date given to the original *Jinakālamālī* is correct (early sixteenth century), by then, both the Mon kingdom of Rāmañña and the city of Sudhamma in Lower Burma were already known as such; they had been around and called that since 1479. So if the Rammaṇa and Sudhamma of the *Jinakālamālī* were the same as the Lower Burma Rāmañña and Sudhamma, why was that connection (and correction) not made by the author?

Knowing that the *Jinakālamālī* incorporated much information from the earlier, possibly fifteenth-century *Cāmadevīvaṃsa* (which is the main text we have for Haripuñjaya), and taking the *Jinakālamālī* narrative as it stands, it is tempting to think of the phrase "here itself in the Rammaṇa Country" as a reference to Haripuñjaya, a Mon kingdom that indeed preceded Chiang Mai in the same valley and probably laid the foundations for it.

What all this suggests is that Haripuñjaya was once probably also referred to as Rammaṇa ("the Mon Country").[36] Later, when the Mon speakers from Haripuñjaya fled the so-called cholera epidemic to Lower Burma, they naturally gave the generic name of their old home to this new place—a common enough practice in world history—which was only subsequently adapted to Pali to become Rāmañña. This situation is about the only one that is able to explain all the variables: two different polities in time and place, whose names though spelt differently meant the same thing, whose people spoke the same language, and whose history seems to be in the correct chronological sequence.

Finally the line of kings in the "Rammaṇa Country" descends to one Manohāra, and with him the story switches to Lower Burma and Rāmañña, where the *Jinakālamālī* story about Aniruddha's conquest of Thatôn appears.

> And it so happened that at that time a king named Anuruddha was reigning in the city of Arimaddana. He possessed supernatural power and had the ability to go through the sky. And he, indeed, sent an envoy to King Manohāra in order to obtain one black-stone image. But on account of his devotion to the Buddha, Manohāra did not give it. King Anuruddha becoming enraged with King Manohāra invaded the Rammaṇa Country with a large armed force, engaged Manohāra in battle, and capturing Manohāra alive returned to the city of Arimaddana. Manohāra too, whilst he was living in the city of Arimaddana had a colossal recumbent image made and honoured it continually. It was there, in that city of Arimaddana that Manohāra passed away. The King, the overlord of Mahānagara, coming to hear of King Anuruddha's devotion to the Buddha, gifted to him the black-stone image which he had been honouring. On hearing this, King Anuruddha had the people bring this black-stone image from Mahānagara and honoured it.[37]

One of the most intriguing features of this narrative is that it mentions for the first time three crucial details: the conquest of Manohāra's city; his capture, exile, and death in Arimaddana (Pagán); and his building of a colossal recumbent image there. Heretofore, no other source, epigraphic or chronicle, domestic or external, contained these three details in the same narrative.

Immediately following the conquest story, the *Jinakālamālī* switches to the founding of Haripuñjaya by Queen Cāmadevī, who came from Lava bringing with her a black-stone image. This event is said to have taken place

1,200 years after the Buddha's *parinibbānna* (about 656 AD).[38] Although Cāmadevī's place in the narrative does not fit well historically with Aniruddha and his conquest of Lower Burma, it does correspond in time to Śrī Kṣetra. Therefore, Shorto's suggestion that Sudharma-nagara may be an etymon for some of the titles of Śrī Kṣetra's kings[39] has some merit, and suggests that the Sudhamma in the *Jinakālamālī* may not be a reference to Thatôn at all—which, as we have seen, is very late historically—but to Śrī Kṣetra and the Pyū instead. On the other hand, the narrative also places Aniruddha's quest for the holy scriptures from Śrī Laṅka and Aniruddha's capture of Manohāra all at the same time, as it does Aniruddha's confrontation with a king of thirteenth-century Mahānagara. Everything seems to have been happening at the same time and every major figure and every important place seems to have coexisted.

Thus, making Cāmadevī and Aniruddha contemporaries of each other even though historically separated by about four hundred years, while placing the great Buddhist cities and kingdoms of Southeast Asia and the major events that transpired among them in the same general epoch, must have been deliberate. Even if some of these individuals and many of these kingdoms overlapped historically, the author of the *Jinakālamālī* appeared to be making the point that they all coexisted within a new "good" age, the one that succeeded the "bad" one, the Kali Yuga, when the Jewel Image was originally taken from Aśoka's India to Śrī Laṅka for safekeeping. And in these kingdoms that belonged to this post-Kali Yuga—Laṅka, Lava, Mahānagara, Rammaṇa, Rāmañña, Sudhamma, and Arimaddana—the rulers who preserved and honored the most important holy relics also preserved and perpetuated the religion, the ultimate test of legitimacy for state and leader. To those kings and queens were ascribed the highest accolades, while those who did not, met their just fate.

King Ādicca's conquest of Angkor and the transfer of the Jewel Image to Ayudhayā where it was enshrined as its palladium of state is one such example. Another is Aniruddha's conquest of Thatôn which demonstrated that a weak ruler like Manohāra who does not uphold the religion invariably loses to a strong one who does, while the symbol of power of the vanquished (in this case, the Buddhist scriptures) is also removed and taken by the victor. The Aniruddha story was therefore an *illustration* of such Buddhist principles. Similarly, that Aniruddha could frighten the king of Mahānagara with his magical powers to give up the rest of the Buddhist scriptures that went astray, was not a statement about their historical contemporaneity, but meant to symbolize the quintessential results of such a meeting between a powerful and a weak Buddhist king. Indeed, that may be the reason Manohāra's formal title in the Kalyani Inscriptions is Sūriyakumāra, the same as that of a historical thirteenth-century Cambodian king[40] during whose reign Angkor's decline accelerated. The name was given to Manohāra for what it represents (like Judas) rather than to identify the actual individual involved.

But there appears to be some historical facts underneath these allegorical statements. The story of Cāmadevī, "daughter of the Universal Monarch," who marries a provincial lord and with her husband subsequently establishes the kingdom of Haripuñjaya[41] is virtually the same one also found in the earliest Mon histories, where Magadu (Wareru) eloped with a daughter of Rāma Gāṁhèṅ[42] to establish their kingdom of Muttama. Such shared stories among distinct cultures such as (in this case) the T'ai and Mon, suggest that historical links between Sukhodaya and Muttama probably existed. As one historian of Thailand astutely remarked: "The texts of the Sukhothai inscriptions often appear to be a forerunner of the *Jinakālamālī*."[43] It also demonstrates that the author was concerned with the relationship between primary sources and history. Nevertheless, what we have in the *Jinakālamālī* is mainly a standard "plot" with representative characters and events, some clearly historical, but being used whenever and wherever the occasion seems to warrant them. The actual local histories of Burma, Thailand, and Cambodia during this early period had been integrated with universalizing Buddhist themes.

Ultimately, what holds these disparate components together in the *Jinakālamālī* is the concept of "messianic time," when the past and future come together in the present. And it resembles what we today might call a "synchronous approach" to history and society, exactly what Dhammazedi had done in his Kalyani Inscriptions when he conflated time and place with events and individuals.

Yet it is that very *conflation* of time, of allegory and history, and of different genealogies and geographies that appears to be bothersome to some of us westernized historians. Our concern with "proper" categories of analysis does not permit us to mix apples and oranges, so that events, stories, and individuals that "belong" to one period of time and place cannot be used in another. For the author of the *Jinakālamālī* however, that combination was precisely what made his narrative meaningful to both him and his audience. It was a mechanism (his "methodology" in today's jargon) needed to expound what he considered to be universal, religious truths, his ultimate concern.

Remarkably (or perhaps not so remarkably), underneath all this collapsing of time, places, events, stories, genealogies, and individuals, there does lie an *actual historical* period in Mainland Southeast Asia that would be recognized easily and legitimately identified as a unit by today's historians of Southeast Asia. It also stretched from about the seventh to the early sixteenth centuries, the same period of time in which most of the *Jinakāla-*

mālī's historical and mythical figures, places, and events are paramount. The period includes: the arrival of orthodox Theravāda Buddhism from Śrī Laṅka; the zenith and decline of the Pyū in the central Irrawaddy valley and that of the Mon at Dvāravatī in the central plains of Thailand; possibly Cāmadevī's founding of Haripuñjaya; the rise, expansion, and decline of Angkor; the emergence, development, and decline of Pagán and of Ava; the emergence, development, and decline of the most important T'ai polities, such as Lan Na, Sukhodaya, and Ayuthaya; and the establishment and the decay of Rāmaññadesa, the first Mon polity in Lower Burma. This historical period indeed witnessed the birth and decay of the "golden age" of Mainland Southeast Asia and its achievements in religion, literature, and the arts.[44] To the author of the *Jinakālamālī,* this exemplary period must have seemed just like the post-Kali Yuga.

It also includes some of the most important historical figures in the region and the events in which they participated or created: the Varmans and Vikramas, founders of Pyu Śrī Kṣetra; Cāmadevī, founder of Haripuñjaya; Vijayabāhu I and Parakramabahu I, great Buddhist kings of Śrī Laṅka who reestablished Theravāda Buddhism in their kingdom; Aniruddha, Kyanzittha, and Narapatisithu of Pagán, unifiers and consolidators of that kingdom; Sūryavarman I, and Jayavarman II and VII of Angkor, to whom is attributed much of its greatness; Rāma Gāṁhèṅ and Mangrai of Sukhodaya, responsible for that kingdom's development and expansion; Magadu of Martaban, founder of the first Mon polity in Lower Burma; and Rajadarit, Dhammazedi and Shin Saw Bu of Pegu, who established Rāmaññadesa begun by Magadu.

Thus the symbolic components found in the *Jinakālamālī* are not without some empirical foundations; messianic time, not without some linear basis; and exemplary individuals, not without some historical reality. Its author simply chose to celebrate the period's kings and queens, kingdoms and cities, and auspicious and powerful events largely with allegory rather than with history. It is not that he was entirely unconcerned with history as we understand it, but that to him, it was only *incidental* to his priority—religious truth.

However, no cycle is complete until its decay and the rebirth of a new one. In fact, the *Jinakālamālī* was written after the actual decline not only of the "classical age," when most of these ideal kingdoms and figures had long vanished, but also after some of their successors had emerged and declined. The author was writing at the beginning of the third such cycle of birth and decay, and saw in hindsight the all-important Law of Impermanence at work. Probably one of the more powerful events to have occurred within his own lifetime was the sack of Ava in 1527, the year before he completed the *Jinakālamālī.* That dramatic event was surely considered auspiciously didactic enough to reaffirm the author's belief that even a great Buddhist kingdom like Ava was subject to the Law of Impermanence when no great reformer king such as Aniruddha existed to extend it or no holy relic such as the Jewel Image existed to protect it. How much more careful must we of Chiang Mai be, to ensure that such events do not happen here. The *Jinakālamālī* was, indeed, one of several "Epochs of the Conqueror."

Allegorical or historical, provided the date of 1527 or 1528 for the original text is correct and the account of Aniruddha and Manohāra were part of that original text, the *Jinakālamālī* is the *first* record of Aniruddha's alleged conquest of Manohāra that I know of which includes the capture of a king named Manohāra, his building of a colossal recumbent image in Pagán, and his exile and death there. No earlier source that I have found so far has all three components in the same narrative. Indeed, it is the story still told today to tourists by guides in Pagán.[45]

This makes the *Jinakālamālī* extremely important, for it suggests that this may have been one of the earliest sources from which subsequent versions stem. However, because the Aniruddha and Manohāra story was also meant to be a didactic Buddhist principle, applicable to different times, places, individuals, and events, we cannot subject the story to certain standards of historicity. But that was precisely how the Mon Paradigm approached all chronicles; as if their narratives were meant to represent a strict, western concept of "historical truth" woven around a linear, progressive sequence of actual historical events. The test of their worth was whether the information in the chronicles was empirically verifiable or not. At least two generations of scholarship on early Burma have been based on that principle.

But by doing this, the Mon Paradigm took the *Jinakālamālī* and other chronicles of Burma out of their broader, Buddhist and Mainland Southeast Asia context, removing the didactic, symbolic, and allegoric intent. It then judged their narratives as if they were meant to be empirical, dealing only with "real" historical events. Rather than viewing the Aniruddha conquest story as a Buddhist allegory of the cyclic, impermanent nature of things—therefore requiring a continuous series of reforms by kings like him—it was analyzed for its empirical, historical value in a western, scientific sense. Under these criteria, of course, the story cannot pass the Mon Paradigm's litmus test and so was dismissed as "false" rather than "true historiography," the actual terms used by Luce.[46]

At the same time, however, to dispel the Mon Paradigm properly, I have had to work within it and use its evidence, categories of analysis, and criteria of historical "truth." Simply declaring the allegorical and symbolic as more important in these chronicles would still leave the Mon Paradigm's "history" intact. What I wanted to do first was to show how its history, using its own evidence, categories, and criteria, does not even have an empirical basis, and only then demonstrate that the chronicles can also be read as an allegory of certain Buddhist principles.

NIDĀNA ÁRAMBHAKATHĀ

Around the same time that the *Jinakālamālī* was written, the *Nidāna Árambhakathā,* a Mon genealogy of kings, was also said to have been composed, discussed briefly in Chapter Four. Like most Mon texts discussed here, the contents include more than what the title suggests. It has miscellaneous anecdotal material, origins legends, and different traditions and enters into detail only with the reign of King "Manuhaw," when the conquest of Thatôn by Aniruddha is mentioned. However, this account does *not* have the crucial details found in the *Jinakālamālī;* it says only that Manuha was taken captive to Pagán.[47] If 1538 is in fact the original date of those parts of the *Nidāna* containing the Aniruddha story, then this would be the earliest text written in Mon to mention it.

However, there are some problems. First, the *Nidāna* is only part of a larger work called the "Rāmaññ'-uppatti-dīpaka," whose original provenance is unclear, or at least has not been established as earlier than those parts of the *Nidāna* that contain the Aniruddha story. And as was shown in Chapter Four, some parts of the *Nidāna* must have been compiled at earliest in the seventeenth century, when de Brito was prominent in Lower Burma, and it may have been him with whom the "Indian" in this story has been confused.[48] Finally, because most palm-leaf manuscripts do not last more than a 100 to 150 years, the original *Nidāna* was probably recopied at least two times before it became the basis for the published version, by which time the full-blown narrative of the Aniruddha conquest story first found in U Kala's *Mahayazawingyi* written around 1720 was already well known.

YAZADARIT AYEDAWPON

The *Yazadarit Ayedawpon,*[49] said to have been written around the same time when the original parts of the *Nidāna* were composed—that is, during King Bayinnaung's reign (1551–1581)—is the next Mon text relevant to the conquest story. It belongs to a different genre, being technically a *pon* (story, memoir). Although the term is usually glossed as "biography," *pon* are not too different in content from *yazawin.* Apart from the *Nidāna,* whose provenance is ambiguous, the *Yazadarit Ayedawpon* is likely to be the earliest *extant* copy of a text regarding the history of the Mon in Lower Burma.

In the published edition I use here, the editor claims that a Mon source with the same title existed earlier, which Bannya Dala, its author, then translated into Burmese.[50] He was a renowned Mon minister who served King Bayinnaung and his predecessor. Most powerful during the period between 1518 and 1572, he was a chief advisor to the king, a writer-scholar, and a general who often took the battlefield personally. He was in charge of building the new Pegu Palace and was an eyewitness to many events, both in the field and at court. He died around 1572, after being assigned to a remote outpost in what is now Thailand, apparently having fallen out of favor with the king.[51]

In contrast to this version is Nai Pan Hla's translation of the same work. The preface to his edition states that there was no Mon palm-leaf manuscript called the *Yazadarit Ayedawpon* for Bannya Dala to have translated in the first place.[52] Instead, he writes that there is a two-part Mon text called the *Thaton-Hanthawaddy Chronicle.* The first part is called *Uppanna Suvannbhummi arambhakatha Sudhammavati Siharajadhiraja vamsa kyan,*[53] where the Thatôn Chronicle is found. This, he claims, Bannya Dala skipped and instead started with King Magadu of Hanthawaddy and ended with Yazadarit, which is why he (Nai Pan Hla) gave his work the title *Yazadarit Ayedawpon Kyan.*[54] Either way, the narrative is still a history of the origins and development of Pegu, not Thatôn, which Nai Pan Hla seems to lament.

At the same time, Nai Pan Hla himself does not provide any further information regarding the *Thaton-Hanthawaddy Chronicle,* particularly whether its original (none is mentioned) precedes the original *Yazadarit Ayedawpon,* who wrote it, or its date.[55] The title of the first part *(Uppanna . . .),* which Nai Pan Hla claims Bannya Dala skipped, sounds very much like an elaborated version of the first of two volumes published at Pak Lat only in 1910 and 1912. Since the presumed antiquity of these manuscripts has not been established, in effect Nai Pan Hla is saying that the sixteenth-century Mon minister Bannya Dala skipped the Thatôn section of a manuscript that was constructed only in the twentieth century, or at best, whose existence prior to the sixteenth century has yet to be demonstrated.

In contrast, the editors of the recently published *Mahayazawinthit* (New great chronicle of kings) feel that the *Mon Yazawin* (Mon chronicle) was actually the text that Bannya Dala translated into Burmese, but that he gave it the title *Yazadarit Ayedawpon.* In this they more or less agree with Tet Htoot and the editors of the *Yazadarit Ayedawpon* that I am using here.[56] The contents of the *Yazadarit* seem to confirm this view, since the work is less about the king whose name appears on the title than it is a history of the Mon beginning with Wareru; Yazadarit himself does not appear until towards the middle of the text. This, in turn, suggests that the *Mon Yazawin* is older than the *Ayedawpon* although the extant copy of the latter precedes that of the former.[57]

In any case, there are, according to Nai Pan Hla, nine versions of the

Ayedawpon, all in Burmese. Four are said to be palm-leaf manuscripts, one is probably a paper copy, and four are printed or other kinds of compilations. All four palm-leaf manuscripts are copies, the earliest of them is conjecturally dated to 1757.[58]

Our main concern here is this: the *Yazadarit Ayedawpon,* one of the earliest *extant* copies regarding the history of the Mon in Burma, which may have been taken from an earlier Mon source and written by a Mon, *does not mention* Aniruddha's conquest of Thatôn. Instead, it begins the history of the Mon in Burma with Wareru and Martaban. However, it does have an odd and short, out-of-place paragraph in the middle of Yazadarit's story which states that Aniruddha came searching for the royal relics at Dagôn (not Thatôn), but since there was no prophecy for that event, he could not obtain them and returned to Pagán.[59] The next paragraph jumps back to Yazadarit and the fourteenth century. Clearly, this is a late insertion taken from the eighteenth-century *Slapat Rājawaṅ Datow Smin Roṅ,* to be discussed in greater detail below. Thus the *Yazadarit,* probably the second oldest extant Burma Mon text, does not mention the conquest of Thatôn.

"GAVAṀPATI"

The next major Mon-language text to appear is a palm-leaf manuscript called "Gavaṁpati." Although Shorto does not state this in his unpublished translated manuscript, he does write elsewhere that the earliest extant copy of this text may date to 1710,[60] which would make it the third oldest extant copy of a Burma Mon "history" of themselves, assuming the *Nidāna*'s sixteenth-century date is correct. But the date Shorto gives the "Gavaṁpati" seems to be at odds with some of its contents. Internal evidence suggests that at least parts of it may have been inserted later, for it freely uses English terms such as "Tavoy," "Martaban," and "Rangoon" (unless these were Shorto's translations of the indigenous terms).[61] If the terms are original, they most likely would belong to the period following the First Anglo-Burmese War of 1824–1826, for even Capt. George Baker's account of Burma in 1759 still used the indigenous "Tavay" for Tavoy, suggesting that the "Gavaṁpati"(or these parts) may have been written after that time.[62] The "Gavaṁpati" also refers to Tavoy as "the boundary of the Mon country . . . [and] because the Buddha sat down there [cross-legged] the place was first called Th(a)way (which means cross-legged), which became corrupted and it is now called Daway or Tavoy."[63] The word "now" is what reveals in part its lateness, for Tavoy is an English term, while Taway is Old Burmese and goes back to the Pagán period. Even though parts of the "Gavaṁpati" are this late, it still does not contain the Aniruddha story, which means the conquest of Thatôn had not yet emerged as a *cause celebre* amongst the Mon.

MAHAYAZAWINGYI

Then comes a major development: U Kala's *Mahayazawingyi,* written sometime between 1712 and 1720.[64] It is the first chronicle of Burma with the most comprehensive and complete version of Aniruddha's conquest of Thatôn.[65] As noted in Chapter One, he deals with Shin Arahan, King Manuha, the unorthodox Ari monks, the request from King Manuha for the "orthodox" scriptures, the attack on Thatôn, the deportation of the royal family and population of Thatôn, the transporting of thirty sets of the *Tipiṭakas* on thirty-two white elephants, and, of course, the story of Manuha in exile and his building of a colossal Buddha image.[66] But it is still unclear how U Kala acquired this fully developed story.

The preface in the published version of U Kala's chronicle, edited by Saya Pwa, generally accepted as the most authoritative, provides a fairly detailed genealogy of the author. He was said to be of the "rich person" *(thuthe)* class, related to Shan chiefs *(sawbwa)* on his mother's side and to *myosa* (literally "town eaters"), or regional administrative officers of the crown, on his father's side. His ancestors were said to have gone back to King Bayinnaung's reign, to the Monyin Sawbwa, whose descendants kept their fiefs and served the crown, including during Bayinnaung's conquest of Ayudhyā in 1563 and his heir apparent's victory over Chiang Mai. Some were appointed *myosa* over Lower Burma cities such as Wagaru (presumably named after our now famous founder of Martaban). U Kala's mother, Mani Awga, whose father was a court minister, married a rich man of Sinkaing. With this pedigree, it is possible that U Kala had access to family documents at court that went back to King Bayinnaung's reign (1551–1581) when the *Yazadarit Ayedawpon* was written. U Kala certainly knew and wrote about Yazadarit, as his chronicle contained the equivalent of over a hundred published pages on Yazadarit's reign alone,[67] more space than he gives to many other famous Burmese kings. It is obvious he had access to this and other sources from Lower Burma, which was, by then, probably a Mon area.

U Kala may also have had access to sources such as the *Jinakālamālī,*[68] perhaps brought back from the conquest of Chiang Mai and pieced together the rest from several similar sources. One of these could have been the *Nidāna,* if its original main part, the "Rāmaññ'-uppatti-dīpaka," was indeed written in 1538 and, as Shorto claimed, contains the conquest story. But I know of no text in Burma, original or copy, where the Aniruddha conquest account is as complete as U Kala's.

At the same time we must be careful about focusing only on the dates of original compilations. Although an earlier dated source, such as the *Jinakālamālī* may have contributed some components to U Kala's reconstruction during the *Jinakālamālī*'s rewriting in the late eighteenth century, it could have easily incorporated what U Kala had written since the first version. This would make it appear that since the *Jinakālamālī* is an earlier text, everything in it, including the Aniruddha story, must have been earlier as well, resulting in a false chronology. Unless we are certain not only of the dates when these manuscripts were first written but also what components those originals contained, our analysis is very uncertain because it is based largely on extant copies.

The editor of the *Mahayazawingyi* also states that U Kala used over seventy texts, including the "Thatôn Chronicle," the "Mon Chronicle," the "Ayudhyā Chronicle," and the "Chiang Mai Chronicle."[69] Yet none of the earliest extant copies of these chronicles we have today contains the conquest story. Although it is possible that the original "Thatôn Chronicle," presumably written in Mon, may have been older than U Kala's work, the earliest extant copy we have is in Burmese, said to have been copied verbatim from a Mon chronicle only around 1789;[70] and it does not mention the conquest story. Neither does the "Mon Chronicle," which, as we have seen, is likely to have been what Bannya Dala translated, later naming it the *Yazadarit Ayedawpon*. The standard "Ayudhyā Chronicle"[71] also does not mention the conquest story. If the *Chiang Mai Chronicle* that U Kala was said to have used is a reference to the standard one familiar to Southeast Asian historians; it too does not mention Aniruddha's conquest of Thatôn.[72] Nor does the Burmese history of Chiang Mai called the *Zimme Yazawin,* whose earliest extant copy is later than U Kala's work in any case.[73] And certainly U Kala could not have gotten his conquest story from the Kalyani Inscriptions since they had nothing to say about it.

The evidence we have suggests that the conquest of Thatôn in its most comprehensive version that has come down to us could *not* have been written with what U Kala was said to have used. That means he must have had other sources not mentioned by the editor, either now lost to us or about which we know nothing. However, as U Kala's work is by far the most complete of all chronicles written in Burma, there is no reason that the same cannot be true of the conquest story as well. Nonetheless, until there is a better and fuller grasp of the historical as well as literary context in which U Kala wrote, we may never know why it was with U Kala's chronicle that the story of the conquest of Thatôn finally attains this comprehensive character. What little we know is this.

U Kala was said to have written his history during the reign of King Taninganwe (1714–1733) of the Second Ava Dynasty, which was known for its resurrection of agrarian Upper Burma as the seat of the entire country after about seventy years of commercial Lower Burma dominance by Pegu. So it is conceivable that the euphoria of returning the capital to the traditional heartland and the desire to reunify the country from there once again was on U Kala's mind when he wrote his history, for during those later years of the Second Ava Dynasty, Ava had begun to lose its grip on Lower Burma. Reunification, a process that must begin with reconquering Lower Burma once Upper Burma's human and agrarian resources had been secured, was partially successfully under Kings Anaukpetlun (1605–1628) and Thalun (1629–1648). But this occurred at the beginning of the dynasty when Lower Burma was a depopulated and anarchic region controlled by individual warlords like the Portuguese adventurer de Brito. By the time of King Taninganwe's reign, when U Kala wrote, Lower Burma was no longer under Ava's control; indeed, Ava would soon be taken by Pegu. Perhaps the "conquest of Thatôn" by Aniruddha in the eleventh century as told by the *Jinakālamālī* and the conquest of all of Western Mainland Southeast Asia by King Bayinnaung in the sixteenth century, revived memories of the glorious past when Upper Burma was perceived to be the "center of the universe." Yet the general tone of U Kala's chronicle is not bombastic, it was rather matter-of-fact and relatively subdued, so it is difficult to attribute such sentiments to him.

It is possible that U Kala's perspective may have been shaped by something else: the religious reforms begun by the earlier kings of the Second Ava Dynasty, known for restoring the Mahāvihāra tradition of Śrī Laṅka. The reign of King Thalun particularly was one of the high points of these religious reforms,[74] as attested by his great work of merit, the Rājamanicūḷa Pagoda popularly known as the Kaungmhudaw ("royal good deed"), clearly an attempt to duplicate the ancient Sinhalese bulbous-style *dagaba* of Anurādhapura.[75] These "new" (really old) religious patterns of the past may have inspired U Kala to write about Aniruddha and Shin Arahan as promulgators of a grand religious reformation, for which, along with various other administrative and political reforms,[76] the Second Ava Dynasty was also well known.

U Kala's treatment of Shin Arahan in this regard provides some insight. It did not say that the monk was from Thatôn; instead, Arahan was endowed with an immaculate conception. At Indra's instigation, one of the *nats* in Tāvatiṁsa was reborn in the womb of a Brahmin's wife, and when the child came of age, he became a monk who grew to be famous in all of Jambudīpa, meaning here the civilized Buddhist world or Burma. Saying the religion has not yet been established at Pagán, Shin Arahan went there to do just that.[77]

The story is reminiscent of King Aśoka's conversion by the famous monk Nigrodha found in the *Mahāvaṃsa* and the *Dīpavaṃsa*.[78] Because religious reforms in the Śrī Laṅka tradition inevitably includes the stories found in its chronicle tradition as well, the latter may have been the inspiration for the Aniruddha and Arahan story; perhaps even for U Kala's writing of the *Mahayazawingyi* in the first place. So far not found earlier in

Burma, the story of Aniruddha and Shin Arahan was clearly the Burmese equivalent of the Aśoka and Nigrodha tale rediscovered by the religious reforms of the Second Ava Dynasty. Whatever the case may be, U Kala's place in the historiography of Burma certainly needs some fresh and original research.

SLAPAT RĀJAWAṄ

The next major source relevant to the topic to appear in Burma is the *Slapat Rājawaṅ Datow Smin Roṅ* (History of kings), written in Mon. The first forty-eight pages of the published and translated work establishes the standard links to the Buddha during the first *kalpa* (age) when he was King Mahāsamatta.[79] In a nonlinear manner, "interrupted" by many different subjects, events, and individuals, the narrative moves geographically between Buddha's India and Yangôn until it finally reaches King Aśoka's period of time and his subsequent ascent to *devaloka* (abode of the gods) whereupon Burma comes into the picture more prominently. Nothing is said of the conquest of Thatôn itself, although similar, perhaps representative events, are mentioned, reminiscent of the *Jinakālamālī*.

Thus, for example, the *Slapat* states that "in the time of King Tatabong [Dwattabaung, the founder of the First Śrī Kṣetra Dynasty] that monarch came marching down from Tharakhettara [Śrī Kṣetra] with a great army. Having a design to carry away the hair relics, when they began to dig a great storm arose and they were unable to carry out their purpose. He offered a golden umbrella (with) emerald handle and diamond cover, and digging into the southeast set it up there. Then he returned to his own city."

The same story, with a different king, is next described: "In the time of Mancesu [a king meant to be prior to Aniruddha and subsequent to Dwattabaung, although it sounds like Minshinsaw, Alaungsithu's son, who is later than Aniruddha], that monarch came marching down with intent to carry away the relics, and being unable to accomplish his object, he formed a precious emerald into the likeness of an altar, and having buried it on the western side as an offering to the relics of the exalted Buddha, he went up to his own city."

Finally, Aniruddha appears on the scene. "That king came marching down from Pagán with the design of digging up the relics. As soon as the diggers touched earth, and there were twenty men digging the relic chamber, a very severe storm arose, and the whole army of King Anoaratha scattered and fled. King Anoaratha having made gold and silver umbrellas offered them to the relics of the Buddha. Having buried precious gems of other lands to the north-east, he returned to his own place."[80] The "precious gems of other lands" may have been a reference to the Jewel Image he had obtained from Śrī Laṅka, the bone of much contention on Mainland

Southeast Asia, which suggests that this author may have had the *Jinakālamālī* among his sources as well. A briefer version of this story about Aniruddha in the *Slapat* had also been stuck awkwardly into the *Yazadarit Ayedawpon* in the middle of Yazadarit's reign. In any case, the unsuccessful attempts by Upper Burma kings to retrieve the "holy grail," as it were, remain a consistent theme in Mon stories, as does the destruction of the books, according to Shorto, "a favourite myth of the Mon historians."[81]

Note that neither Aniruddha nor the other two kings came down to Thatôn, but to Dagôn (modern Yangôn), where the Shwédagôn Pagoda is located, and all failed to obtain anything: no scriptures, no king, no Mon population, no thirty-two white elephants. There is also nothing about Aniruddha's conversion by Shin Arahan, or Aniruddha's request for the *Tipiṭakas* from Manuha—there is, in fact, no Manuha at all—or the refusal of that request, or Aniruddha's consequent attack of the city, or even the establishment of Theravāda Buddhism in Pagán thereafter.

Surely if Thatôn had been perceived to be a great center of Mon Theravāda Buddhism in Lower Burma, which had contributed to the growth of Buddhism in Upper Burma, and surely if such an important event as the conquest of Thatôn had actually occurred, it would have been mentioned by the author of a most important Mon "history of kings." That he does not is particularly puzzling because the author is said to have had many Mon sources in his possession. Yet the first part of this chronicle has nothing whatever of Suvaṇṇabhūmi or Thatôn, where they "should" have been.

It is true that the *Slapat* was written by a monk whose main interest was the history of the Shwédagôn Pagoda and the kings (and queen) who patronized it, and so the history of secular rulers per se would have been *only incidental* to the main thrust of the work. In the introduction and at the end, this religious purpose comes out very clearly. As the author put it, this "history of kings" was meant to demonstrate the Law of Impermanence, that their power and might, their wealth and grandeur, could not achieve "mastery over Death."[82]

Thus, Shin Saw Bu, the famous woman sovereign of Pegu, is a major figure and mentioned at length in the *Slapat,* particularly for her generosity to the Shwédagôn Pagoda.[83] So is Dhammazedi, who is given a great deal of space in the work for his contributions to the religion and the Shwédagôn, whereas Yazadarit, one of the most famous and powerful kings of Pegu according to both the Burmese chronicles and modern historiography, was not. In fact, in the "Gavaṁpati," he is actually called a demon *(rakṣa)*.[84] This neglect of such an important figure as Yazadarit leads me to believe that perhaps the Shwédagôn Pagoda, the centerpiece around which the events and personalities in the *Slapat* pivot, may not have been built yet even by Yazadarit's reign, for had it been, surely the latter would have donated to it.

The kinds of political events about which secular authors were concerned were simply not as important to the author of the *Slapat,* which may account for his omission of Aniruddha's conquest of Thatôn. But that does not explain why the monk included other battles between other kings in Burma, especially during the last decades of the eighteenth century when he dealt with Alaungpaya, De Brito, and others who were clearly not, to him at least, exemplary leaders nor major contributors to the Shwédagôn.

What has become clear is that the idea of a "Mon Lower Burma" may not have been as monolithic as colonial historians have made it out to be, for even at this late date, its literature of legitimation (of which the conquest of Thatôn was crucial), was still being written by different people in different places with different perspectives. That unified narrative would have to wait until 1910 and 1912.

MANIYADANABON

In the last decades of the eighteenth century, during the reign of King Singu, the immediate predecessor to King Bodawpaya, a monk by the name of Shin Sandalinka wrote the *Maniyadanabon.* The title can be translated roughly as "the book of precious jeweled precedents," and the bulk of the work is concerned with what the translator calls "submissions," or exemplary advice, from the chief minister to the king. It was probably modeled upon the Indian classic, *Milindapañha.* Sandalinka's work focused on the First Ava period and Mingaung I, using material from the *Zambu Kungya,* but he also added submissions from later periods by famous ministers, including Bannya Dala, author of the *Yazadarit Ayedawpon.* For the translated version of the *Maniyadanaboni,* Euan Bagshawe used a manuscript that was put into print in 1871 at the court in Mandalay after King Mindon set up a press there. Bagshawe wrote that the *Maniyadanabon* was one of the first of four Burmese texts selected for machine reproduction, which shows the priority it commanded.[85]

The most detailed and valuable first part of this text, as far as this current study is concerned, consists of information that included the *Zambu* and Min Yaza's earlier submissions, along with other historical notes that Sandalinka used, especially concerning Mingaung I's reign. After that, the translator writes, the quality declines.[86] The first part even includes submissions to Yazadarit of Pegu from a monk of Ava. Bagshawe notes that he carried the translation only up to "the death of King Mingaung, where Minyaza himself disappears from the scene."[87] Thus although the *Maniyadanabon* was written in 1781, the first section is very likely a good preservation of the late fourteenth-/early fifteenth-century *Zambu,* parts of which can still be found in the palm-leaf copy of 1825.[88]

At the end of the *Maniyadanabon,* where Burmese authors of the time usually wrote their names and the date of completion, Sandalinka noted that the work was compiled "from the various books of chronicles" in the year 1143 of the Burmese era (1781 AD).[89] By that time, U Kala's work had been around for over half a century, and Sandalinka, being the recipient of a high royal title under the king's patronage, would have had access to it and other court archives that survived the conquest of Ava in 1752. Nevertheless, Sandalinka's work, instead of creating something new, or continuing the "new" tradition of U Kala's account of the Aniruddha conquest, may have preserved an older, perhaps more accurate version of the story as found in the *Zambu,* in which a company of monks take the scriptures of Pagán to Thatôn rather than the other way around. This is also what the Kalyani Inscriptions suggest.

Myanma Yazawinthit

About the same time that Sandalinka wrote his text, another major Burmese chronicle was written, although the exact date is uncertain. The title of the published version of the first volume is *Myanma Yazawinthit* (New history of the Myanma [people or country]). It was written by Twinthintaikwun Mahasithu, a highly educated and cultured minister under King Bodawpaya. Twinthin was a well-known monk and teacher before he was made minister, and as a young man in his twenties, he lived through King Alaungpaya's reunification of the country. Knowledgeable in language and literature, poetry, religion, and history, he was a versatile scholar, and along with another minister was subsequently placed in charge of making an inventory of all original religious donations on stone and, in some cases, of recasting them anew. Hence he had access to and was familiar with the information, style of writing, orthography, and so on, contained in them.

In his chronicle Twinthin also accepts the story of Shin Arahan's immaculate conception found earlier in U Kala's work, but Twinthin has Shin Arahan reborn as the son of a Brahmin *at Thatôn,* who, upon reaching the right age, became a monk.[90] Since U Kala said nothing about Shin Arahan being born at Thatôn, it appears that Twinthin had added that information, for it is not found in the *Maniyadanabon* either, whose author was his contemporary.

Why it was important to link Shin Arahan with the city of Thatôn becomes clear only when we consider the story from the perspective of Bodawpaya's reign. The king, like Aniruddha, Dhammazedi, and Thalun before him, considered himself a reformer of the religion and espoused the Sinhalese tradition as orthodox. That means he would have wanted to identify his *saṅgha* with Thatôn's, since Dhammazedi had earlier made it the custodian of the orthodox version of the scriptures that stemmed from Aśoka's Third Council originally brought to Burma by Soṇa and Uttara.[91]

The link that Twinthin established between Shin Arahan and Thatôn would also provide the correct sort of genealogical relationship between Bodawpaya's *saṅgha* and Aniruddha's that Bodawpaya, and virtually all other kings subsequent to Pagán and prior to Mindon's reign, desired. Indeed, Shin Arahan's immaculate conception did not enhance his image as much as his birth at Thatôn did, particularly as one of the members of the orthodox Order.

Twinthin was also familiar with the Kalyani Inscriptions and cites them explicitly with regard to the Aniruddha story. "It is said in the Kalayni Inscription," he wrote, "that when Aniruddha attacked [*lup kram*] Thatôn, it was weak from hunger. . . ."[92] But as I have already shown, the Kalyani Inscriptions say no such thing, even if the Pali version does say that the city was "weak from hunger" and that the religion had become impure. Like Luce a couple of hundred years later, Twinthin had associated Aniruddha's reform and Thatôn's decay with a conquest, but he was taking his information from U Kala's chronicle, which he had in front of him. Twinthin had therefore projected Aniruddha's conquest of Thatôn from U Kala onto the Kalyani Inscriptions, not so much, it seems, as deliberate falsification, but probably because by then, like Luce, he already considered it to be common knowledge and historical. But by doing so, he, again like Luce, inadvertently provided false credibility to the story by remarking that it was confirmed in the Kalyani Inscriptions when it was not.[93]

Twinthin's manuscript has another puzzle in it: the number of elephants on which the *Tipiṭakas* were said to have been carried to Pagán has grown to thirty-three.[94] The only other source that has thirty-three instead of the conventional thirty two elephants is the *Zambu* which had been incorporated into the *Maniyadanabon,* virtually a contemporary of Twinthin's chronicle. One wonders to what extent Twinthin modeled himself upon famous ministers of old, particularly Min Yaza, who wrote the *Zambu.* But then the latter work has the Aniruddha story reversed from Twinthin's and U Kala's versions, both of whom had embellished the story even further with their reference to the Kalyani Inscriptions.

There were other "mentalities" working on Twinthin. He seems to have been the first chronicler in Burmese history to name his work after the people or country rather than after various kings. *Myanma Yazawin* means the "history of the Myanma people [or country]," as opposed to the conventional *Maha Yazawin,* meaning "history of kings," a distinction that has not been noticed by modern Burma historians for nearly a century now. If the complete title, *Myanma Yazawinthit* given to the first volume of the published version of Twinthin's chronicle accurately represents the title he gave his manuscript, then it is the first indigenous history written in Burma whose title was focused on the people, country, or state of Myanma, rather than on the genealogy of its kings.[95] It would reveal that Twinthin was thinking in inchoately modern "national" terms, in which "history" was seen as an account of the people, state, polity, or kingdom, and based primarily on the majority group, rather than just its monarchs. It is a conception not found readily (if at all) among his predecessors whose organizational schemes reflected their worlds: a chronology of royalty and their major accomplishments. That same kind of focus on kings and accomplishments also led Thai and Sinhalese Buddhist historians to treat Aniruddha and Bayinnaung as *cakkavattī,* universal monarchs, rather than as kings who were leaders of *national* groups.[96]

Similarly, whereas the organization of U Kala's chronicle follows a strict chronology of every king, his offspring and mates, and what they did for the state and religion, without any other divisions into "periods" of history, Twinthin's was one of perhaps only two others to organize history into different periods based on the rise and fall of specific dynasties.[97] Moreover, the names he gives to these dynasties are not personal ones, such as "the Alaungpaya Dynasty" (an appellation created for the Kônbaung Dynasty by western historians),[98] but the names of the centers from which they ruled; hence the Pagán Dynasty, the First Ava Dynasty, the Toungoo Dynasty, and so on. The religious reason for this is the thought that these cities had received the all-important Buddha prophecy, usually an honor bestowed *ex post facto.*[99] However, organizing history into periods ruled by different centers of power in Burma was quite consistent with his shift in the title of his work from *mahayagawin* to *myanmayazawin.*

Thus although Twinthin broke with his predecessors by subtly changing the conceptualization of *Yazawin,* he nonetheless included the same information contained in the others, revealing that he had similar priorities in terms of *content.* This comes out clearly in his summary of U Kala's account of the Aniruddha conquest.[100] A thorough study of Burmese chronicles is much needed.

Hmannan Mahayazawindawgyi

The next major chronicle to appear is the *Hmannan Mahayazawindawgyi.* Conventionally translated as the "Glass Palace Chronicle," it should really be called the "Chronicle of the Palace of Mirrors," for it was written in the Palace of Mirrors, one building of the palace complex, by a team of scholars.[101] Written in 1829, the compilers used a variety of sources, probably more than U Kala had used, but depended heavily on his work nonetheless. In the *Hmannan,* Shin Arahan's birth at Thatôn, an assertion begun by Twinthin, has been preserved, after which, the *Hmannan* quotes U Kala's account of Shin Arahan's immaculate conception and the subsequent attack of Thatôn almost verbatim.[102] Thus the *Hmannan* is simply preserving a tradition already well established by previous writers. When its authors disputed earlier accounts, most were of an extremely esoteric nature; there was little substantive critical analysis of sources concerning issues we might consider historically important. As was true with the *Slapat*, this tells us what the *Hmannan*'s overall purpose was: legitimation according to religious criteria. With regard to the Aniruddha story, it has gone from nothing in the *Yazawinkyaw* to approximately forty-four printed pages in the *Hmannan*.[103] Aniruddha's legend had indeed grown by 1829.

SĀSANAVAṂSA

In 1861 Paññāsāmi, a monk and tutor of King Mindon, who Mabel Bode called a "high ecclesiastic" and adherent of the traditional *Sīhala saṅgha*,[104] wrote the *Sāsanavaṃsa* [Chronicle of the religion]. It consisted of ten chapters, each one recounting the history of the religion in different parts of Asia. The third chapter deals with Suvaṇṇabhūmi, a place by then domestically accepted as the maritime provinces of Lower Burma, even though only a little more than a hundred years ago, U Kala had wondered where it was. The major supernatural figures found in the *Yazadarit* are mentioned, but a more detailed explanation is given for the genealogy of one of them, Gavaṁpati.[105]

In the *Sāsanavaṃsa* version, he was said to have been a prince in the city of Mithila in the "Middle Country" (that is, India), a reincarnation of a boy born of an egg (among two eggs), the result of a union between a "knower of charms" and a female serpent. His "brother," from the other egg, became a ruler named Sīharājā in the city of Sudhammapura (Thatôn) that Sakra had built for him. Clearly, there are some differences between the various Lower Burma Mon versions of Gavaṁpati and the Upper Burma version. But the important fact is that the *Sāsanavaṃsa*, an Upper Burma product, mentioned and incorporated the Lower Burma Mon versions at all, a point to which I shall return. The author then added parenthetically (and erroneously): "in the stone inscription, however, he [Sīharājā] is called by the name of Sirimāsoka."[106] Even as legend, Sirimāsoka is not Sīharājā; rather, he is the latter's successor, while the "stone inscription" to which Paññasāmī refers is either one of the three Mon inscriptions of 1486 or the Kalyani Inscriptions, both of which mention Sirimāsoka.[107]

Gavaṁpati, wishing to see and convert his mother, the serpent, now reborn as a human in a country "inhabited by hunters and fishermen," flew to Rāmaññadesa. When he arrived together with his brother, he preached the Doctrine to the inhabitants. It was then that Gavaṁpati decided to ask the Buddha to come to Rāmañña to preach the Gospel, and the Buddha, with many "hundred monks came by air to Sudhammapura in the Rāmañña country."[108] Exactly eight years after the *parinirvāṇa* of the Buddha, said the author, Gavaṁpati established the religion at Sudhammapura in the Rāmañña country.

According to the *Sāsanavaṃsa,* then, it is Gavaṁpati and the Buddha himself who introduce the religion to Suvaṇṇabhūmi for the first time, while its second establishment, 235 years later, is attributed to Soṇa and Uttara. The Aniruddha story follows, but it is exactly the *reverse* of the conventional one: "the king named Anuruddha of the town of Arimaddana [Pagán] brought an Order of monks from there [Pagán] together with the Piṭakas;"[109] so that the third reform of the religion in Suvaṇṇabhūmi is attributed to him. However, later in the text the author reverses himself and describes the conquest story in the conventional manner, without providing an explanation.[110]

What can we make of the *Sāsanavaṃsa,* which includes two apparently contradictory accounts of the Aniruddha story? First, the text sounds as if it combines different sources without attempting to rectify some of their discrepancies. The story of Aniruddha taking the scriptures to Lower Burma sounds like an extrapolation of the *Mahāvaṃsa* story where Vijayabāhu I requests and receives from Aniruddha a chapter of monks and the proper texts in the eleventh century, since Aniruddha would have had to first take them to Lower Burma before they continued to Śrī Laṅka. The story of the conquest, of course, is the conventional version found in the major chronicles.

Second, one must remember that in the nineteenth century, under the patronage of King Mindon of Mandalay, most Southeast Asian Theravāda Buddhists probably perceived the Burmese kingdom as the premier place where orthodox Theravāda Buddhism had been preserved. There it was patronized by a devout monarch who appears to have been more concerned with his accomplishments regarding Buddhism than anything else, despite British historiography to the contrary.[111] The Fifth Sāsana Council, held from 1868 to 1871 in Mandalay, the first since the Fourth Council, convened by Parākramabāhu I in 1165, was clearly the most prestigious event in the world of Theravāda Buddhism, and it legitimated king and state in a way that was surely envied by the "international community" of Theravāda Buddhists of the day. No Buddhist king had convened a council for seven hundred years, so that this was indeed an accomplishment of the highest order. The king was following in the footsteps of King Aśoka no less, thereby obtaining the title of "Convener of the Fifth Council" one he treasured beyond all others.[112] The *Tipiṭakas* were "purified" during these three years by a great assembly of learned monks from all over the Theravāda Buddhist world and inscribed on 729 marble slabs, each housed in individual shrines, all part of the Kuthodawgyi ("great royal merit") Pagoda that stands today at the foot of Mandalay Hill.[113] These were, one might say, the "King Mindon Version" of the Scriptures.

In contrast, Śrī Laṅka by the mid-nineteenth century no longer enjoyed the prestige of being the foremost Theravāda Buddhist country. It was under colonial rule and had been now for several centuries. Lower Burma was also by then under British rule so the religion could not have been considered orthodox there any longer either, especially without a king or a head of the *saṅgha*. Upper Burma, however, was still free and had a king and a head of the church, the Thathanabaing, as he was called in the nineteenth century.

Thus the "purity" and orthodoxy of Sinhalese Theravāda Buddhism may have come into question in Burma's highest ecclesiastical circles by that time, while Mandalay in the mid-nineteenth century was probably perceived to contain the most orthodox Theravāda Buddhism in the world.[114] There was every reason, then, for Paññasāmī, in the religious context of the mid-nineteenth century, to resist the conventional notion that Aniruddha had brought the true religion to Upper Burma from what by then was British-colonized Thatôn.

Third, because Upper Burma by that time had already claimed the orthodoxy of their texts by direct links to the Third Buddhist Council, the historical and secular details concerning such events as Aniruddha's conquest were "mere technicalities" that made little or no difference to devout Buddhists such as the author of the *Sāsanavaṃsa,* especially when compared with what he considered were the really important events: the religious reforms themselves. Even if such glossing over of historical events makes westernized historians uncomfortable, to Paññasāmī and others like the author of the *Slapat,* these historical problems were only incidental to the important issue. And that, in the nineteenth century, was that the kingdom of Mandalay, along with its king, its *saṅgha,* and its devotees, although hemmed in on all sides by nonbelievers or unorthodoxy, was perceived to be the only center left that defended and preserved the purest form of Theravāda Buddhism.

In sum, the precolonial chronicles contain three basic versions of the Aniruddha story: a) he took the scriptures to Thatôn (the *Sāsanavaṃsa*), b) they were brought from Thatôn by the people there (the *Zambu*), and c) he conquered Thatôn and forcibly took the scriptures back to Pagán (the *Jinakālamālī* and its successors). Of these, the last has come down to us in Southeast Asian historiography as the orthodox version. And yet it is *not* the version first found in the indigenous Burmese-Mon tradition but had come from *outside* it—from the Pali Buddhist tradition, where the relationship of Aniruddha and Manuha is more an allegory of Buddhist principles than a historical one, and from the colonial scholarship of the nineteenth and twentieth centuries that had decided to preserve that Pali Buddhist tradition.

PAK LAT MON CHRONICLES

Finally, in 1910 and 1912 came the first Mon chronicles to contain the conquest story. They were published at Pak Lat, a Mon center in Thailand.[115] The provenance and chronology of the manuscripts used for these two published volumes are uncertain and still have not been analyzed in any depth by a Burma Mon scholar that I am aware of. They are, therefore, difficult to assess. But what we do know is this.

The first volume, titled *Sudhammawati-rājāvaṁsa; Siharājādhirājā-vaṁsa (Sudhammawatī; Gawampatī; Rājādhirāj)*,[116] contains three parts, as the title indicates: a short history of Thatôn (the part that Nai Pan Hla claimed Bannya Dala skipped), a section on the "*Gawampatī*" story,[117] and a third section called "Yazadarit," a history of Martaban and Pegu from Wareru to Bannya Thau (Shin Saw Bu) of Pegu (essentially, the *Yazadarit Ayedawpon.*) The second volume, titled *Nidāna Rāmādhipati-kathā*[118] and published in 1912, apparently contains a brief account of Thatôn, particularly its siege and conquest by Aniruddha, the founding of Pegu, and a brief account of the legendary "first dynasty." This is followed by a brief history of Martaban under Wareru, his successors up to Bannya Thau of Pegu, which again, is probably taken from the *Yazadarit Ayedawpon.* The second volume is, therefore, more or less the same as the first, with additional parts such as the account of the "first dynasty," added to it. Halliday states that the sketches in the second volume "differ a good deal from those of the other volume though agreeing with them in the main."[119] Nonetheless, as one can see the three segments in each volume present rather clearly Mon myth and history: the first two parts are what westernized historians might call legendary, whereas the third section, beginning with Wareru, is what we might consider "real" history.

There are other difficulties with these two volumes, not the least being their "cut-and-paste" job of reconstruction. In addition, the second volume is said to be particularly difficult to read as it includes many words not contained in James M. Haswell's Mon "dictionary" of 1874 and whose meanings were not known to many literate Mon people in Burma at the time (1913).[120] That might, at first glance, suggest the text can be dated to earlier than 1874.[121] But that view was challenged by W. G. Cooper, who argued that most of the unknown words were actually miscopied ones.[122] It is certainly a subject that needs a competent Burma Mon scholar to untangle properly.

It is in the first, 1910 volume that the conquest of Thatôn by Aniruddha and the Mon Paradigm finally makes the "front page" in a Mon text. It reads:

> Now the king of Arimaddanapura [Pagán] mustered his army and rode his horse . . . and came to the city of Thaton in the land of Thudammawadi. He compassed it round about and beleaguered it for three months straitly. And those within could get neither food nor drink, and they were exceedingly famished, and so great was their hunger that they ate one another; and many perished thereby. . . . Then the folk could no longer abide such sufferings; and on the morning of Monday the eleventh waxing of Nayon, the moon being in the mansion of Visakha, in the year 42, king Manuha rendered himself. And the king of Arimaddanapura, having possession of king Manuha, took away the saintly monks, who were full of learning and piety; he took away the monks who knew the Three Scriptures and the Four Books of Divination, . . . he took them all to the land of Arimaddana. He chained king Manuha with golden chains and led him captive. From that time henceforth Thaton was desolate, but Pagan that is called Arimaddana flourished like unto a heavenly city.[123]

Whereas neither the *Yazadarit Ayedawpon* of the sixteenth century,[124] the "Gavaṁpati" and *Slapat* of the eighteenth, nor the early nineteenth-century *Lik Smin Asah*[125] once mentioned Aniruddha's conquest of Thatôn, this first volume published in 1910 did, and then in a very emotive style. What this means is that *the first time Aniruddha's conquest of Thatôn appears in its full-blown version in a Mon text is the twentieth century!* This is a very late realization of the story, myth or not, but one consistent with their late view of Thatôn as an exemplary center.

Conclusion

The story of the conquest of Thatôn by King Aniruddha in 1057 apparently does not go back to any single source, although it appears that the *Jinakālamālī* is the first to mention three crucial components of the story: the actual conquest of Manohāra (no city was mentioned), his exile in Pagán where he died, and his building of a colossal recumbent image of the Buddha in Pagán. Although the *Nidāna Árambhakathā,* written about the same time, is said to have made a brief statement about the conquest, that section cannot be securely dated and it does not have the details that the *Jinakālamālī* has. Subsequently, the story was embellished, added to, and enhanced by U Kala's full-blown version, the one most familiar to scholars today.

It did not seem to matter to modern historians that some of the later texts that mentioned the Anriuddha conquest were found in late palm-leaf copies that had gone through numerous versions, most of unknown provenance, and all with obvious late additions. Neither did the fact that many of these texts had integrated allegory with history, which colonial and postcolonial scholars advocating the Mon Paradigm made little or no genuine attempt to understand in any case. The only textual exegesis they conducted was to search for "empirical truth," so that the narratives in these texts were taken at face value and placed in a historical "true or false" framework of analysis while the rest was more or less discarded. The approach was essentially self-serving, allowing one to verify what one wanted to verify, and reject what one wanted to reject. Thus it was with the story of Aniruddha's conquest: colonial historians never once considered it to have been anything but historical, while virtually everything else that stood in its way was rejected as "false historiography."[126]

What they missed, and to me one of the most interesting aspects about the story of Aniruddha's conquest of Thatôn and Manuha, is the fact that it is not found in the earliest of either the Burman or Mon traditions where one would have thought it began, but in a broader Pali Theravāda Buddhist tradition of at least four Theravāda Buddhist countries—Burma, Śrī Laṅka, Cambodia, and Thailand—who all shared a chronicle tradition based on Śrī Laṅka's *Mahāvaṃsa*. Thus its meaning clearly lies in that tradition.

Yet it was removed from that broader culture and placed in what was thought to be a distinctly Burma tradition. This was done by later indigenous chroniclers and modern historians, probably one of the more important mistakes they made, for the text cannot be taken out of its Buddhist context. The "Aniruddha tradition" was not meant to be an exclusively Burma story; it belonged to all the Theravāda Buddhist countries of Mainland Southeast Asia that traced their orthodoxy to the Śrī Laṅkan chronicle tradition,[127] much like the story of King Arthur that belonged not only to the Britons but also to their rivals, the Anglo-Saxons and Picts, and later to the French and Germans as well.

As in Europe, at the time these Pali chronicles were written about Aniruddha, there were no nations in the modern sense, with irrevocable boundaries within which lived citizens clearly conscious of their identity as Burmans, Thais, or Cambodians. Aniruddha, as a great Theravāda Buddhist king, belonged to everyone in that tradition. That is one of the main reasons the earlier Northern Thai and the later mainstream Thai chronicles recount Aniruddha (and also Bayinnaung) as ideal Buddhist kings, *cakka-*

vattīs,[128] not Burman kings who reigned in a country called Burma with a distinct Burman identity. Aniruddha ruled from a great Buddhist city called Arimaddanapūra, which was not, at the time, the capital of a Burman nation, although inhabited mainly by Burmese speakers, but an exemplary Buddhist center, a microcosm of Tāvatiṁsa, the most cherished of Theravāda Buddhist heavens.

In the same way, the Kalyani Inscriptions depicted Aniruddha, Aśoka, and Parākramabāhu I—and of course King Dhammazedi who erected the stones—as quintessential models of righteous Buddhist kings, and *not national* monarchs. These kings were intimately involved in keeping the religion pure (because it inevitably decays according to the Law of Impermanence) until Maitreya returns in 5,000 years to preach the *dhammacarka,* the ultimate sermon, that will save all who are fortunate enough to be reborn as humans in his dispensation.

Dhammavijaya, "righteous victory," in the name of the religion, in which the reformer king searches for and obtains the most orthodox versions of the Holy Scriptures and relics, is very much a crucial part of that reformist theme. That was the reason Aniruddha's trip to Śrī Laṅka is necessary, where he successfully obtains the *Tipiṭakas* and the Jewel Image. That is probably also the reason the *Jinakālamālī* states that he obtained the scriptures originally from Śrī Laṅka (at the time considered the most orthodox land) rather than from Thatôn (which was probably just recently founded and therefore deserved no such recognition), particularly since Śrī Laṅka itself had obtained the orthodoxy of its scriptures from Aśoka's Third Buddhist Council.

It is for these reasons that Dhammazedi mentioned Aniruddha at all in his inscriptions, for he was a reformer king whose example Dhammazedi was following. There is no mention in his Kalyani Inscriptions of a conquest of Thatôn, as Twinthin and later scholars alleged,[129] not only because it did not occur, but because there was no reason to mention it. For Dhammazedi, Thatôn was part of the Manuha, not the Aniruddha story, to illustrate what happened when Buddhist kings allowed the religion to decay. Only in that context is Manuha part of the overall theme: he is a model that represents the antagonist par excellence succumbing to the protagonist Aniruddhas of Buddhist history.

There is another component here that should not be missed. Because the *Jinakālamālī* has Aniruddha obtaining his pure scriptures from Śrī Laṅka and not from Thatôn, it suggests that its author, Ratanapañña, a monk writing in Chiang Mai, did not recognize Dhammazedi's claims in his various inscriptions that Soṇa and Uttara came directly from Aśoka's Third Buddhist Council with the orthodox texts to Thatôn. Or perhaps Ratanapañña did not know about those claims at all, although they were made over half a century before he wrote the *Jinakālamālī*.

Yet by the time both the *Jinakālamālī* and Dhammazedi's Kalyani Inscriptions were written, although both showed concerns of a broader Theravāda Buddhist Śrī Laṅkan orthodoxy, they also revealed some parochialism. For even though Dhammazedi was saying, in effect, but quite explicitly as well, that he was, like the great reformer kings of the past, he also needed to link his local legitimacy with Aśoka's Third Council somehow. So he used the story in the *Dīpavaṃsa* of the mission of Soṇa and Uttara, deftly switching the location in his Kalyani and Shwédagôn Pagoda Inscriptions and placing it in Lower Burma.

Thus at the very least, the historiography concerning the arrival of Theravāda Buddhism in the region should be emancipated from the bondage of its own mythology, so that one now has the option of *not* viewing the story of Soṇa and Uttara's journey to Southeast Asia in the Śrī Laṅkan sources as historical. This was difficult to do heretofore, as their alleged conversion of a Mon kingdom in Lower Burma to Theravāda Buddhism somehow had to be accommodated.

In the case of the *Jinakālamālī,* of course, the localizing focus was Chiang Mai, even if its history was placed in a broader Theravāda Buddhist orthodoxy. One can now also take a fresh look, in either an empirical or allegorical sense, at other narratives in the Pali chronicles concerned with the great Buddhist heroes and heroines of Southeast Asia, such as Aniruddha and Cāmadevi, and kingdoms, such as Sudhamma and Haripuñjaya, without being concerned that the presence of Rāmaññadesa in Lower Burma might contradict it.

Indeed, the entire relationship amongst the Burmese, Sinhalese, and Northern Thai chronicles, especially those originally written in Pali needs reassessment outside the Mon Paradigm. How are the *Mahāvaṃsa*'s stories about Aniruddha, Vijayabāhu, and the relics; the *Jinakālamālī*'s account of a conquest of a Sudhamma and its king Manohāra; and the Burmese narrative of Aniruddha's purification of Pagán with monks from Thatôn, *textually* related? And why was U Kala's description of the Thatôn conquest the first and most comprehensive one? Was there an *Ur* text that I have missed, or did he put together the story for the first time from a variety of texts which in the context of the reformist policies of his period favored such an interpretation? Certainly the Mon chronicles are part of this issue and need to be studied in much greater detail, but they must be analyzed outside the framework of the Mon Paradigm as well. Of particular concern are the *Pak Lat Chronicles.* They were used as if they were much earlier, but they are actually part of early twentieth-century Mon nationalism and need to be assessed in that modern context by scholars competent in the Mon language.

Beginning with U Kala, the story of Aniruddha's conquest of Thatôn was removed from the larger Theravāda Buddhist orthodoxy and its broader application region-wide to become, instead, an integral and exclusive part of Burma's *national* history. That may explain why there is no contemporary evidence for it: it was part of a *later* legitimation and localization (or parochialization) process that continues today.

7 The Mon Paradigm and the Origins of the Burma Script

SINCE THE CONQUEST of Thatôn is not mentioned anywhere in the original epigraphy of Burma, and does not appear in the chronicles until, at best, the sixteenth century, the consequences that have been attributed to it—the heart of the Mon Paradigm—are all now open to question. These include the notion that the Mon of Lower Burma provided the kingdom of Pagán with its writing system, literature, religion, art, and architecture, along with components of its conceptual system and other cultural and technological achievements. Further analysis of most of these subjects I will leave to scholars in the appropriate disciplines, but in this chapter I shall address one of the most important claims: that as a direct result of Aniruddha's conquest of Thatôn, Pagán—and hence Burma—received its writing system from the Mon of Lower Burma, who in turn had obtained it from Dvāravatī.[1]

But since the conquest of Thatôn is no longer defensible, why does the issue of the script need to be addressed at all? The reason is the same as that in the previous two chapters: if the Mon Paradigm is to be convincingly dispelled, it is not enough simply to show that the Thatôn conquest is not historically viable, the thesis regarding the script still needs to be disproved and a more viable option offered, for if the Burma script did not come from the Mon of Dvāravatī via Thatôn, scholars will still want to know from where it came.

This chapter will attempt to trace the possible origins and development of the Burma script, while describing how the topic evolved within Burma Studies. I will demonstrate that no contemporary epigraphic or historical evidence exists to support the contention that the Pagán (hence) Burma script was derived directly or indirectly from Dvāravatī via Thatôn and will discuss the major scholars and their particular involvement in the topic. The conclusion reached here again reverses the Mon Paradigm: that Burma's Old Mon script derived from the Old Burmese script.

The Major Issues

The origins of the Burma script itself is still an unresolved issue, and since I am neither a linguist nor a paleographer, my main purpose here is not to resolve problems directly related to linguistics or paleography—although the latter is an integral part of epigraphy and so will be an important feature here—but to raise some historical and evidentiary questions that have a direct bearing on the subject.

There are some points on which all agree. First, the script used for both Old Burmese and Old Mon during the Pagán period, what I call the Burma or Pagán script, is "practically identical" except for two letters.[2] Second, the ultimate source for this script is South India. And third, the Burma script was apparently not derived *directly* from South India but through an intermediary. And herein lies the heart of the controversy. Who was the intermediary—the Pyū of Burma or the Mon of Dvāravatī?[3]

More specifically, is the Burma script a version of the Mon Dvāravatī script that is said to be based on the Old Tamil Pallava script of Kāñcipuram in Southeast India,[4] or is it taken from the Pyū script, which is itself derived either from the Kadamba of Vanavasi in Southwest India or the scripts of Andhra in Southeast India?[5] Since the conjectured sixth- to eighth-century Mon Dvāravatī script of Old Siam is considered to be "very different from the fourth to seventh-century Pyū script of Halin and Śrī Kṣetra,"[6] while the Burmese and Mon scripts of eleventh-century Pagán are "nearly identical,"[7] only one is likely to be the source for the Burma script, not both.

In addition to demonstrating the source paleographically, we must also show how and when transmission of the script occurred. To be historically tenable, the transmission should be chronologically sound, and there must be ample opportunity for such cultural borrowing to have taken place. For its part, the paleographic evidence should graphically exhibit at least an affinity between the source and the final product, based on actual, dated examples, not just on a conjectural reconstruction, despite the fact, as de la Vallée Poussin so aptly remarked, paleography is "une petite science conjecturale."

We need to be cautious, therefore, with paleography, for although it may suggest a probable relationship of scripts, it can be quite misleading if it is not corroborated by authentic dates derived from the same records under scrutiny. This is especially true when dealing with scripts that changed very little over long periods of time, such as the Pyū, Burmese, and Burma Mon scripts.[8] Although this is a complicated issue that perhaps only philologists and paleographers should address, I can, as a historian, still assess whether either of the two origins scenarios has any merit in terms of epigraphic and other historical evidence.

It is important to realize from the outset that there has never been a formal scholarly debate on the origins of the Burma script that has been published in English. Nonetheless, the published literature has generally fallen into two schools of thought, which are more the result of individual studies than any concerted attempt on the part of those involved to make their own positions distinct from those of others. In that sense the debate is somewhat artificial, since it is something I have reconstructed from the existing literature. But that does not mean the actual scholarship and the differences in opinion are any less genuine or valuable. It should come as no surprise that one school reflects the Mon Paradigm and its position that the Burma script came from the Mon of Dvāravatī, while the second, which originally consisted of only one scholar, suggests that the Pyū culture was the likely source for the Burma script.

The Mon Connection

There are three possible, theoretical sources for a Mon connection: Thatôn, Dvāravatī, and Haripuñjaya.

Thatôn

Although Forchhammer may have been the first to suggest in a general way that the Pagán script probably had Lower Burma Mon origins, it was Duroiselle who first made a scholarly and systematic case for it. In the first issue of *Epigraphia Birmanica* published in 1919, Duroiselle noticed the similarity of the Burmese and Mon alphabets and wrote that they were nearly identical except for two letters. This led him to conclude that "one of the two nations borrowed its alphabet from the other."[9] One can immediately see a problem of analysis, for both cultures could have borrowed the script from a third party rather than from each other. In fact, Blagden briefly hinted that this was a possibility, that the Pyū might have been the source, but he never pursued the issue. Given the state of knowledge regarding the Pyū in 1919, as well as the intellectual trend supporting the view that the Burmans borrowed virtually everything from the Mon, Duroiselle's analysis and conclusions, in hindsight, are neither surprising nor extraordinary.

Duroiselle then speculated that the historical event, the mechanism for this borrowing, was the conquest of Thatôn by Aniruddha, and herein lay the most egregious flaw. He wrote: "All evidence tends to show that the Burmese received their alphabet from the Mons about AD 1057. It is in that year that Anorata, king of Pagán, swooped down upon the deltaic provinces of Burma, that is, Rāmaññadesa, the Talaing country, and after a siege of three months, entered Thatôn, the capital." As proof, Duroiselle offered the following: "No inscription whatsoever in Burmese or Pali has yet been found at Pagán antedating Anorata, . . ." and "it is from that time that writing was adapted to common use by the adoption of a foreign alphabet to represent Burmese sounds. . . ."[10] So once again the foundations of the analysis returns to the catch-all cause—the conquest of Thatôn—the keystone of the Mon Paradigm.

Yet, just two years later, Duroiselle published a valuable reference called *A List of Inscriptions found in Burma* in which he enumerated approximately nineteen Burmese and Pali inscriptions that predated Aniruddha's reign.[11] Although he could have qualified what he had written earlier in 1919—that "no inscription whatsoever in Burmese or Pali has yet been found at Pagán antedating Anorata . . . "—he did not. Instead, he obfuscated his original position further by stating that the "principal alphabets" of Burma (including Pyū, Mon, Burmese, and Shan) were based on the Old Telegu-Canarese alphabets of South India.[12] But, he continued, whereas the Pyū script was influenced *directly* by the Kadamba script of Vanavasi in North Canara, as was the Mon script by the Pallavas of Kāñcipura, the Burmese and Shan scripts were derived *indirectly* from Mon.[13]

The statement about the Burmese and Shan scripts was not only unnecessary and speculative—without any paleographic support or historical explanation as to how that might have occurred—it also appears to be a contradiction. On the one hand, he had said the "principal alphabets" of Burma, including Mon, were based on the old Telegu-Canarese alphabets, but on the other, that they came (although indirectly) from the Pallava of Kāñcipura via the Mon. However, these two scripts—Old Telegu-Canarese of Vanavasi, by which Duroiselle later meant Kadamba,[14] and the Pallava of Kāñcipura—were quite different, particularly if we are dealing with the Pallava script, which was nearly 300 years later in time and almost as many miles apart geographically in South India.[15]

And since the Śrī Kṣetra Pyū and Mon Dvāravatī scripts are "very different," as Luce noted—suggesting that the comparison was indeed being made with the later Pallava script—while the Burmese and Mon scripts of Pagán are "nearly identical," about which all agree, how do the "very different" parent scripts end up producing "nearly identical" offspring? Perhaps it is linguistically possible, but it was never explained or demonstrated by either Luce or Duroiselle.

Duroiselle's "direct" and "indirect" influences are at the heart of the obfuscation, not least because he allowed only *one* "indirect" influence, that of the Mon, thereby, steering research away from another perfectly viable option that should have been considered as well: namely, the Pyū. Indeed, Duroiselle's *Epigraphia Birmanica*—founded most probably for scholarly purposes although I would not doubt some political influences working on the whole process—became the mechanism for maintaining that research direction in which the Mon were the focus of attention. In a word, both the analysis and conclusion regarding the origins of the Burma script had once again assumed the historicity and antiquity of Rāmaññadesa and the viability of the conquest of Thatôn.

One could argue that Duroiselle's position in 1919 (or in 1921) was not entirely unreasonable since in part it may have resulted from the lack of good data on the Pyū alternative. Yet in the late nineteenth century U Tun Nyein had discovered the Maung Kan gold plates with Pyū writing on them, while Louis Finot had by 1912 published his thoughts on that script as having been derived from southwest India.[16] And it was through the labors of Duroiselle himself,[17] as director of the Burma Archaeological Survey, that much additional information on the Pyū emerged, while their language had been deciphered by Blagden nearly a decade earlier.[18] Admittedly, during Duroiselle's time, there were no radiocarbon dates or modern excavations that pushed the Pyū urban culture back to the second century BC. But nearly all the evidence for the Pyū writing system was already available. The real problem was that no one considered even the possibility of a connection between the Pyū and Pagán scripts because the Mon Paradigm was so intellectually overwhelming and entrenched.[19]

Ultimately though, the problem was inherent from the start: it lay in the tautological nature of Duroiselle's initial assumption. In 1919 he wrote: "If it is considered that the Talaing and Burmese characters at that time [the Pagán period] were identical, *and that the greater antiquity of Talaing civilisation is accepted on every hand,* I think the rational conclusion is that the Burmese borrowed their alphabet from the Talaings . . ." [my emphasis].[20] Here is the ultimate basis for his thesis: the belief in the "greater antiquity of Talaing civilisation on every hand." That *premise,* as is demonstrated throughout this book, had become *proof.*

Even *prima facie,* Duroiselle's thesis that the Burmese borrowed its alphabet from the Mon after 1057 cannot stand scrutiny. Are we to believe that for nearly 150 years after the founding of a capital city whose kingdom was to rule the country for another five hundred years that the Burmese speakers still had not adopted a writing system for their vernacular? And this even after as long a period of contact with, and absorption of, the culture of the literate Pyū people and long after the alphabets of North and South India had arrived and had been in use in the society?[21] Are we to believe that only after the Burmese speakers had conquered some Mon refugees presumably living here and there in Lower Burma, that they immediately and suddenly waxed eloquent in hundreds of Old Burmese inscriptions?

Duroiselle's argument also implies that Aniruddha's grandfather, Saw Rahan, his father, Kyaung Phyu Min, and Aniruddha himself were all illiterate in Burmese. If this were so, how did they communicate with the obviously Burmese-speaking majority in order to administer their large and rapidly growing kingdom for the century and a half *prior* to 1057? How were royal orders issued, tax records maintained, people registered, laws implemented, and rituals of state conducted? Certainly not verbally, or in Sanskrit and Pali, the language of the elite clergy.

Beyond the domestic requirements for literacy, how did the Pagán kingdom communicate officially with other states, such as Sung China, to which it sent an embassy in 1004 AD,[22] half a century before allegedly knowing how to write in their own language? Did the ambassador go to the Sung capital without any written communiqué so that diplomatic relations with foreign states, even one as important as China, were also conducted verbally? This is not likely, especially as we have evidence that the Sung replied in writing, so that perhaps we can assume that the Pagán court even had knowledge of, or access to translating written Chinese.[23] Missions were sent to India as well, one in 1035 and two in 1079 and 1086 (or a decade later), to repair the famous Mahābodhi temple at Bodhgayā, a topic to be discussed in Chapter Eight.[24] Thus neither *prima facie* nor external evidence from both China and India supports Duroiselle's thesis that Pagán society was illiterate until after 1057 and the alleged conquest of Thatôn.

Even Old Mon evidence conveniently assigned to Thatôn does not support his thesis. Of the approximately ten Old Mon inscriptions found at or near Thatôn, most are undated, so we do not know to which century, between the eleventh and fifteenth, the language belongs, because, as stated above, the Old Mon writing system in Burma did not change perceptibly during that time.[25] In addition, only six of the ten stones can be said to have been found *in situ,* which means the provenance of the rest is unknown and cannot be attributed to Thatôn (which as we saw in Chapter Four never existed anyway). Nevertheless the data from all these inscriptions—two of the most important being the Trāp and Paṇḍit Inscriptions, whose provenance and chronology are also unknown—have been used to argue that an earlier Thatôn version of the Old Mon script existed. Two others, the Kyaik Talan and Kyaik Tè Inscriptions of 1098, were actually erected by King Kyanzittha,[26] which makes them Pagán, not Thatôn records.

Perhaps most important, all Old Mon inscriptions found at Thatôn *were written in the already developed Pagán script:* they were not the latter's linguistic precursors. Indeed, there is no such thing as a "Thatôn script" distinct from the Pagán script in the written Old Mon of Burma: they are one and the same. But the Mon Paradigm needed a distinct Thatôn script and an earlier Thatôn kingdom in order to make its case that a previous independent cultural and political entity had existed. Without these assumptions, Thatôn's role in Burma's history is reversed: it becomes the entity that received "civilization," including the script, from Pagán. That is very likely the reason Luce contrived the date of 1050 for the Trāp and Paṇḍit Inscriptions, because it meant they would precede Aniruddha's alleged conquest of 1057. This contention simply cannot be confirmed by original epigraphy.

Dvāravatī

Unlike Duroiselle and his colleagues who were the first generation of pioneers, the next generation of scholars *did* have much of the data we now have on the Pyū, with the exception of the most recent excavations and the TL and radiocarbon results of their remains. By then, there was ample, even if imperfect, information on the Pyū. The most renowned spokesperson of the second generation was Luce, who had the benefit of the more recent data (he died in 1979), making his assertions more culpable than those of the previous generation.

One of the second generation's "new" discoveries was the Mon kingdom of Dvāravatī, which was introduced to the field of Burma Studies around 1924 by Luce, who based his work on Pelliot and other French historians.[27] That only reinforced the Mon thesis begun by the first generation. Yet I cannot help but feel that had Luce lived ten more years, he might finally have changed his mind about the debt owed the Mons by the Burmans. His latest research, best reflected by his posthumous work, *Phases of Pre-Pagán Burma,* seems to have been heading that way.

Luce reconfirmed Duroiselle's 1921 claims that the Burma script was derived from the Mon, but went one step farther by specifying that it was derived from the kingdom of Dvāravatī.[28] Yet he did not explain how and when that might have occurred, nor did he provide any convincing linguistic evidence for that assertion. That is, he did not illustrate even paleographically how the two scripts might have been related. Consequently, there is no analytical or evidentiary basis on which to examine his theory, since he merely asserted his conclusion and then left it for future generations to *disprove.*

In an article published in 1961[29] Luce *had* devised a chart which he labeled "Stages of Old Mon Orthography" that provides a glimpse at the factors he likely considered in reaching his conclusion.[30] In the chart Old Mon words were grouped into four chronological and geopolitical categories covering six to seven hundred years and representing the "distinct kingdoms" of Dvāravatī, Thatôn, Pagán, and Haripuñjaya. Each word was given a period to occupy, and a "journey" of the orthography of approximately thirty-five Old Mon words from eighth-century Dvāravatī to a presumed mid-eleventh-century Thatôn kingdom, to twelfth-century Pagán, arriving at last at thirteenth-century Haripuñjaya.[31]

Besides being purely conjectural, this journey has some very serious problems. There is an obvious confusion between language and script, the two so inexorably intertwined that the journey allegedly taken by the Old Mon *language* was held to be synonymous with that allegedly taken by the script. In fact, these took two entirely different (even if conjectural) paths, as we shall see. That is to say, although the chart is a collection of Old Mon words—and therefore an analysis of *language*—the title of the chart, "Stages of Old Mon Orthography," clearly states he was thinking about the *script* as well.

Second, the existence of Thatôn in the eleventh-century has been shown to be mythical, so its place on this chart and the data assigned to it are also spurious. Neither the city nor the data actually existed at the time, so the Old Mon orthography attributed to Thatôn actually belongs to Pagán. To reiterate, there is no such thing as a "Thatôn" Old Mon script that is distinct from the Pagán script. The earliest dated Old Mon inscriptions found at Thatôn are those of King Kyanzittha in 1098, not the Trāp and Paṇḍit Inscriptions. All linguistic data derived from a conjectural eleventh-century Thatôn, said to represent a distinct, second "stage" of Old Mon orthography, actually belongs to the Old Mon language and script of eleventh-century Pagán.

A third problem with this journey is the conjectural dating of both Dvāravatī and its script. Although there is some evidence in the Chinese sources that supports the existence of what is thought to have been a political (or at least a cultural) entity called Dvāravatī in the seventh century, the dates assigned to the script still conform to a predetermined conclusion, as none of the Dvāravatī (Lopburi) inscriptions is dated.[32] And if, like the Pyū and Pagán Old Mon scripts, the Dvāravatī script also did not change for a long period of time[33] (as indeed suggested by the virtually unchanging orthography),[34] there is no assurance from paleography alone that the script on the Lopburi pillar is in fact seventh or eighth century rather than, say, thirteenth century. The only reason we know, for example, that the Pyū script on the Myazedi Inscription is twelfth century is that it is dated; the script itself is virtually identical to that of seventh-century Śrī Kṣetra.[35] The same, perhaps, can be said of the Lopburi script, especially as no dates appear on the stone.

It comes as no surprise, therefore, that Luce's comparison of the Old Mon orthography of Dvāravatī, Thatôn, Pagán, and Haripuñjaya words shows few differences. He wrote that "nearly all [the words from Dvāravatī] are common to the 11th century Burma Mon." And that "the spellings . . .

are almost identical."[36] Such similarity, however, does not imply that the Dvāravatī and Pagán *scripts* must also be related, or that the former had to be the progenitor of the latter. Without confirmed dates at both ends (of the *writing system*), there is no way to determine which preceded which.

To complicate the matter, the seventh-century date assigned to the Lopburi script also may have been determined, in part, to coincide with the period when historians think Dvāravatī flourished. And the historians, in turn, had based *their* periodization of Dvāravatī on the chronology provided by the paleographers.[37] The Chinese evidence for the entity we think was Dvāravatī[38] somewhat alleviates the issue of its existence around that time, but the dates assigned to "its" script would still remain unproven.

That the script may be relatively late is suggested by its dissimilarity to the earlier Pallava-Grantha script that was carried by Indians to Southeast Asia in the fourth century AD and used widely. According to Nilakanta Sastri, the Pallava-Grantha script at the time was "little differentiated from the ancestor of modern Telugu-Kannada"[39] (that is, Kadamba, the source for the Pyū script). And because the Pallava script of Mon Dvāravatī is said to be "very different" from the Kadamba, and hence the Pyū, script, Dvāravatī must have only later adopted the changed Pallava script called Vatteluttu (round hand) which first appeared only during or after the eighth century. Although Shorto thinks the Dvāravatī script belongs to the seventh century AD (since it fits its "history"), Guillon, following Diffloth,[40] dates it to the eighth century probably because of its Vatteluttu look. At the *earliest,* then, the Lopburi script could be seventh century, but it is not at all certain how late it was still being used.

The point is that although this "backward reckoning" method may have been used successfully by Indo-European linguists dealing with the Indo-Aryan languages of India, it can create many problems of circularity when there is no secure dating of Old Mon orthography. Indeed, the absence of dates regarding Old Mon epigraphy is a serious problem in general. According to one recent source, of a total of twenty-five Mon inscriptions so far recovered in what is now Thailand, only one of them is securely dated, to 1504.[41] This means that with that single exception, too late to be of any consequence to the present topic, the dates assigned to all Mon inscriptions in Thailand are conjectural.

Apart from the problems inherent in the journey of Old Mon orthography, the theory that the Pagán script came from Dvāravatī also fails to answer some basic historical questions. *How* and *when* that might have occurred has never been explained. I know of no record, primary or secondary, in the history of Southeast Asia that mentions at any time a migration of Mon people from *Dvāravatī* to Lower Burma which might have effected that alleged borrowing.

In fact, any putative Mon migration from Dvāravatī appears to be contradicted by Diffloth's study of Nyah Kur, the direct linguistic descendant of Dvāravatī Old Mon, which is still found in what is now central Thailand.[42] Its continued presence until today in a region that was thought to have been part of the kingdom of Dvāravatī suggests that Nyah Kur speakers did not migrate anywhere, but remained more or less in the same area where they retained their language over the intervening centuries. Indeed, according to present-day Nyah Kur speakers, they "have always been in the area where they are now. . . ."[43] Even if we assume that some of these people might have migrated elsewhere, there is no evidence, to date, of Nyah Kur's presence in Burma, the issue at hand. Indeed, a chronological map of Old Mon inscriptions on Mainland Southeast Asia drawn by Diffloth reveals no movement to the west of the Salween until the eleventh century. On the contrary, Diffloth's study shows that Dvāravatī Old Mon moved in exactly the *opposite direction.* From what is thought to have been the heartland of Dvāravatī in the central plain of Thailand, Old Mon went north and east to Chanasa (Canāśapura or Śrī Canāśa), on the Khorat Plateau and from there to Vientiane. The Vientiane inscriptions are dated, paleograpically at least, to the tenth and eleventh centuries AD.[44] The rest of the Old Mon inscriptions of Thailand have been assigned to the twelfth and thirteenth centuries and later, well after the *dated* eleventh century Old Mon inscriptions of King Kyanzittha, and therefore suggest a process that was just the opposite, as we shall see below.[45]

Moreover, the chronology implied by the relationship between Dvāravatī and Pagan is quite problematic. The earliest date given to the Dvāravatī script is the sixth century, while the latest sample is found in the ninth.[46] There is thus some 250 years between the disappearance of the Dvāravatī script and the appearance of the first Old Mon inscriptions of Kyanzittha in 1093 and 1098. (Nearly all other inscriptions found in Lower Burma prior to Kyanzittha's Old Mon inscriptions are either in the Kadamba script used by the Pyū to write Pali or Pyū, or in Devanagiri, which has linguistic links to Bengal or Nepal, and most of these are inscriptions on votive tablets.)[47] It is highly questionable, therefore, that a script that had already vanished in the Mon homeland by the ninth century could reappear completely intact in a culturally and geographically distant place after an interval of nearly 250 years![48] Knowledge of writing is not held in suspended animation to be revived in its pristine form ten generations later. The argument for the Dvāravatī origins of the Pagán script suggests that the Mon who were thought to have migrated to Burma from Dvāravatī simultaneously developed collective amnesia regarding their writing system as soon as they crossed over to Burma, and just as suddenly and simultaneously their remote descendants regained their collective memory after 250 years in order to hand the script in its original form over to the Pagán kings when they came marching down to conquer Lower Burma in the mid-eleventh century.

That illogic aside, there is not a single Old Mon language inscription *written in the Dvāravatī* (Lopburi) script that has yet been found in Burma.[49] Had this script been the progenitor of the Pagán script and somehow gone over to Burma prior to the first appearance of written Old Mon in the Pagán script, where is it? Surely, there should be some evidence of it, especially in the nearly 1,200 years that the Mon Paradigm claims the Mon spent in Lower Burma prior to Pagán's conquest of the region

To be sure, the script found on a single undated votive tablet in the Yangon Botahtaung Pagoda relic chamber is said, by Guillon, a Mon specialist, to be in the same "type of script" as that found on the Lopburi pillar,[50] thought to represent the quintessential Dvāravatī script. That might suggest, although Guillon himself does not claim this, that the Dvāravatī script can indeed be found in Lower Burma, and that literate Mon speakers were living there at the time. However, the Botahtaung text is *not in Old Mon* but in Pali, a different language altogether representing no particular linguistic, ethnic, or cultural group in Southeast Asia. Thus it cannot be used to suggest that the Dvāravatī Mon had migrated to, or were living in Lower Burma. In addition, it is only a *single* tablet not shown to have been found *in situ,* and therefore could have been carried there by anyone. Also, it could have been written by someone in Yangôn who knew how to write in that same script, or the tablet may have come directly from South India, the ultimate source of the script. There is no necessary "source-and-recipient" relationship between the script on the Botahtaung and the Lopburi pillar just because they happen to be in the same South Indian script.[51] To suggest *a priori* that the script must have taken that route once again privileges the Mon Paradigm's assumed chronology. If anything, the tablet speaks to the presence in Lower Burma of Tamils knowledgeable in Pali.

Furthermore, because the South Indian writing on the Botahtaung tablet and the Lopburi Pillar is in cursive style,[52] it is probably derived from the eight-century Vatteluttu script.[53] Because this cursive style is said to have appeared only by the eighth century in South India, it probably reached Lower Burma first (if one followed the traditional routes from South India to Mainland Southeast Asia), and only subsequently arrived at Lopburi. The Lopburi script, then, could well have been the *later* of the two to adopt the change that began in South India.

Another reason Dvāravatī was not likely to have been the source for the Pagán script is the fact that all dated Old Mon language inscriptions found in Burma are written in the *already developed* Pagán script; there are no examples in the country of Old Mon having been written in an earlier, less-developed stage in that script. This suggests that the Old Mon script of Burma may actually have been derived domestically (from Old Burmese, as we shall see below), or at least owed nothing to the Dvāravatī script.

Perhaps the most serious problem with the Dvāravatī thesis is that the bulk of the written data that has informed the understanding of the Old Mon language of Dvāravatī was *not* taken from Dvāravatī but from Pagán.[54] We are told that the main reason for this is that the Old Mon inscriptions of Dvāravatī number only a few (two, if only the stones are counted, more if each epigraph is counted separately),[55] and as of this writing only seven legible, relatively short, Old Mon inscriptions can be found at Haripuñjaya.[56] It is on the earlier group of inscriptions—fewer than ten at best—written in Dvāravatī Old Mon, per se—along with some domestic silver coins (and/or other inscribed metals) thought to have belonged to Dvāravatī itself[57]—that the entity known as Dvāravatī and its language has been based.[58]

In contrast, if we include those that King Kyanzittha erected in Lower Burma and elsewhere, there are approximately a dozen, very long Old Mon inscriptions that have survived, the linguistic data of which far exceeds those of Dvāravatī and Haripuñjaya.[59] Because of the quantity and quality of data found in Burma, then, *Pagán Old Mon is the basis for most of our information on understanding the Old Mon language itself,* and the Pagán script, the basis for accessing that information. Diffloth writes that "the Thatôn Old Mon and the Kyanzittha Old Mon inscriptions are our main source of information on the structure of the Old Mon language,"[60] which means—since the "Thatôn Old Mon" of Diffloth is actually Pagán Old Mon—that Pagán Old Mon is the standard by which to study Old Mon in general.

Understandably, Old Mon scholars may not have had much choice in the matter, given the limited number of Old Mon sources. But that does not change the fact that most of our knowledge of Old Mon structure has been taken from eleventh-century Pagán data, not Dvāravatī. What this means is that data was removed out of its context from one historically, culturally, and geographically different and distant place (Pagán), ascribed to another historically, culturally, and geographically different and distant place (Dvāravatī), and then anachronistically used to conclude that the latter was the origins of the former.

As if to underscore the point that no evidence exists linking the Dvāravatī to the Pagán script, neither Luce nor the other advocates of the Mon Paradigm have shown paleographically *how* the Mon script of Dvāravatī may have evolved into the Burma script of Pagán. Not even a conjecturally reconstructed chart has been published to demonstrate that the thirty-three consonants and fourteen vowels[61] of the Burma script—excluding tone markers that the Mon language did not use—were derived from the consonants, vowels, and nonexistent tone markers of the Dvāravatī writing system. Even if similarities can be shown to exist in their respective consonant-vowel systems—they are "nearly identical" during the Pagán period in any case—it is because both scripts ultimately come from the Sanskrit alphabet. It is not proof that Dvāravatī was the progenitor.

But one could still argue that some relationship must have existed between the Mon speakers of Thailand and twelfth-century Pagán, for after all, there were Old Mon language inscriptions and speakers in Pagán. True as that may be, it does not necessarily mean that Dvāravatī was the source of either. And that it was not helps explain the differences that are known to exist between Dvāravatī Old Mon and Pagán Old Mon,[62] between the Lopburi script in which Dvāravatī Old Mon was written and the Pagán script in which Kyanzittha Old Mon inscriptions were written, and the two-century gap between the latter two. None of these puzzles had been explained by the Mon Paradigm.

If, then, the people who spoke the Dvāravatī Old Mon language and wrote in the Lopburi script did not move anywhere in particular while the rest of the Old Mon speakers moved eastward, then how and approximately when did the Old Mon language itself get to Burma? What little evidence we have suggests that the Old Mon speakers who eventually made it to Prome and Pagán in the late eleventh and early twelfth centuries were probably the descendants of a splinter group who had separated from the original Dvāravatī population much earlier. Part of this separation may have been triggered by the movement of T'ai speakers southward, splitting the existing Mon population into east and west segments. Or perhaps the tenth-century Khmer move northwestward pushed Old Mon speakers into Lower Burma by the eleventh. Perhaps both happened. Whatever the answer may be, it is clear that Dvāravatī was not the source of the Pagan script.

Haripuñjaya

If not Dvāravatī, could the Old Mon script have come from Haripuñjaya? Here as well, there are problems of historicity and provenance. The only historical account in Southeast Asian history that actually speaks of a Mon migration to what may have been Lower Burma is the so-called cholera epidemic. The problem is dating the event; those given by the Northern T'ai chronicles are centuries too early to be of relevance here, while Coedes assigns it to the mid-eleventh century. But we should remember that Coedes's date is not only conjectural, but meant to coincide with Aniruddha's alleged conquest of Thatôn and therefore very much a part of the analytical framework of the Mon Paradigm. There is one other event suggested by an Old Burmese inscription which might have found Old Mon speakers in Lower Burma: an alleged battle between the forces of Pagán and Angkor around 1056 AD somewhere in Lower Burma. Old Mon speakers may have been among the levies of Khmer troops from the earlier conquest of the Thailand Rāmaṇya mentioned in Khmer inscriptions.[63]

However, most Mon scholars knowledgeable about the Haripuñjaya script contend that the Old Mon script went exactly the other direction, from Pagán to Haripuñjaya.[64] As one scholar put it: "There is evidence to the effect that the people of Haripuñjaya brought the Mon and the Burmese [i.e., Pagán] alphabet to their city and adapted it in northern Thailand. It survives to the present day."[65] Even the Northern T'ai chronicles, doubtful though the dates are, state that after the epidemic, some of the refugees returned to Haripuñjaya, probably taking the script back with them. Luce himself agrees that the script of the Haripuñjaya inscriptions "clearly derives in the main from that of eleventh- to twelfth-century Burma."[66] Diffloth confirms at least the late period of the Haripuñjaya inscriptions, noting that most of the well-known ones date to the thirteenth century.[67]

What all this evidence suggests is that the Old Mon script went from Pagán, to Thatôn, and from there to Haripuñjaya, and *chronologically in that sequence as well.* This means that the direction in which the script moved had nothing to do with the history of the Old Mon script at Dvāravatī itself.[68] Rather, it appears that Dvāravatī has been an inadvertent "red herring" all along and was never part of the picture regarding the Pagán Old Mon script in the first place.

My tentative explanation for the differences in the history of the Old Mon script of Burma and that of Dvāravatī is quite simple: *they were taken from two different writing systems that appeared in Southeast Asia at two different times.* The first, representing the Old Mon script of Pagán, was derived from Old Burmese via an earlier Pyū script from perhaps the fourth century, as is discussed below, while the second, Dvāravatī's, probably came from South India's Pallava script, later superceded by the Vatteluttu of the eighth century. With the decline of Dvāravatī in the ninth century, its script also disappeared in that place, but found its way towards the northeast to Chanasa and Vientiane, while its language continues as Nyah Kur to the present.

The Pyū Connection

Since the Mon connection regarding the origins of the Pagán script is not analytically, historically, or paleographically viable, what alternatives are left? These cannot simply be theoretical possibilities, but must exist within the context of Burma's known history.

SOUTHWEST OR SOUTHEAST INDIA?

The only option that meets the historical requirement seems to be the Pyū connection. I should make clear that my argument is less an attempt to trace the origins of the Pyū script per se than it is to trace the Pagán script from the Pyū. I withhold judgment on whether the old Finot thesis that the Pyū script came from Kadamba is correct or the more recent Falk thesis that it came from Andhra.[69] Rather, the focus here is the Pyū *connection* to the Pagán script.

This Pyū connection, in contrast to the Mon, has not had much exposure in English. It is largely the work of one lone Burmese scholar, who, during the generation in which the Mon Paradigm became entrenched and institutionalized, wondered about the thesis that the Burma script was derived from the Mon of Thatôn only after 1057 via Dvāravatī.[70] That person was U Tha Myat, a modest individual writing mostly in Burmese. As a result, he was, for the most part, ignored by western scholars.[71] In several short but detailed paleographic studies on the evolution of the Pyū script via its Indic predecessors, which he based on data taken from original Pyū epigraphy and published works on Indic scripts, Tha Myat showed how the Pyū script evolved from Kadamba, a script belonging to Southwestern India, and went from there to Śrī Kṣetra Pyū, to Myazedi Pyū, to the Burma script found on the Pagán inscriptions, and finally to the palm-leaf manuscripts of Burma.[72]

To be sure, there had been important groundwork done prior to U Tha Myat's work. In 1897 two gold plates were found at Maung Kan village near Prome. They were said to have been inscribed in the Pyū script expressing the Pali language and were first edited by U Tun Nyein, the government translator.[73] Then in 1912 Finot published an article in *Journal Asiatique* regarding a Pali stone inscription written in Pyū script discovered at the Bawbawgyi *stupa*, Śrī Kṣetra, and, for perhaps the first time, the script was recognized as having clear affinities to Kannada's Kadamba.[74] By the late 1920s Duroiselle had discovered the Khin Ba mound treasure trove, which included a gold-leaf manuscript of twenty leaves written in Pyū in the Pali language.[75] In the 1930s Duroiselle also recognized that the script used at Kyôntu near Pegu was what he called Telugu-Kanara, "closely resembling the Kadamba type."[76] And of course, we cannot forget the pioneering work done by Blagden, who deciphered the Pyū script that had been "dead" for nearly eight centuries. In other words, whereas most early Burma scholars recognized that the Pyū script came from Kadamba[77] before U Tha Myat's publications, none suggested that the Pyū script might have been the source for the Pagán and hence the Burma script. That was U Tha Myat's contribution. But it ran directly counter to the dominant thesis of the time: the Mon Paradigm.

Halin, Śri Kṣetra, and Pagán

At Beikthano, the earliest radiocarbon-dated Pyū site so far excavated, an inscription in Brāhmī datable to the second century AD has been found, apparently written in the Pali language with the phrase *Samgha siri.*[78] We are not told which form of Brāhmī it is, although it is probably the evolved Brāhmī of South India. Stargardt suggests the closet antecedent may be the letters used by the southern Ikṣvāku Dynasty, whose inscriptions are most common in Nagarjunakonda. And since the letters seem to have incorporated what she called a "chronological mixture of styles," the latest, from the fourth century, this sample probably belongs to that period.[79] This also suggests that during that period the Pyū had not quite fully developed their own script and were still using Indic ones to express complex religious sentiments.

But the main epigraphic basis for U Tha Myat's work were the Pyū inscriptions proper, which at the time he conducted his research numbered approximately twenty-five separate ones.[80] By Pyū "inscription" is meant the writing system used to write the Pyū and sometimes Pali languages, which later became popularly known as the Pyū script.[81] The earliest Pyū language inscriptions per se were probably found at Halin. Although Halin itself first appears about the first century AD according to radiocarbon results, its script dates to approximately the fourth century AD.[82] It is much earlier than the seventh century, to which Luce had dated it, for reasons bolstering the Mon Paradigm.[83] In fact, Halin writing predates by at least two hundred years the best paleographically dated evidence of Old Mon writing at Dvāravatī,[84] which is assigned at the earliest to the sixth century for the Nakhon Pathom and the eighth century for the Lopburi inscriptions.[85] Indeed, Stargardt feels that the earliest Pali text written in an Andhra script so far discovered in all of South and Southeast Asia is to be found in Pyū culture.[86]

In what U Tha Myat considers to be fourth-century Pyū, three lines of writing appear found on a funerary stone that records the builder to be one "glorious" Tubahi [who is?] "glorious" Dawintinmrin's son, [who is?] grandson of one Nagukanaw."[87] These do not appear to be names of royalty but perhaps belonged to people of some stature nevertheless. Another stone inscription found at Halin during the 1960s contains royal titles beginning with *Śrī Trivigrama.* It has seven lines of Pyū and seven lines of "interlineal" Brāhmī, suggesting that the Brāhmī may have been the parent script, still present and functioning.[88] Another small stone slab has eight short lines of Pyū with no Brāhmī, on which one can make out *Mahādevi Śrī Jatra.* As mentioned in Chapter Two, a fourth stone fragment has seven Pyū letters saying *Śrī Jatrādevī.*[89] U Tha Myat dates the letters of the stone with the *Mahādevi Śrī Jatra* on it to the fourth and fifth centuries AD.[90]

These inscriptions suggest that by the middle of the Halin period, the Pyū culture had developed its own writing system, probably taken from one of the Brāhmī evolutions. It probably received the script directly from the ancestor of Telegu-Kannada or Pallava-Grantha around 300 AD, when the first inscriptions in Southeast Asia with this script appeared,[91] whereas, as noted above, the cursive Pallava script on the Lopburi pillars may have developed only in the eighth century and if so, must have been a *subsequent* import from South India when the Pallavas emerged as a major force in South and Southeast Asia from the sixth century onward.[92] This means that even if at one time in India the ancestor of Telegu-Kannada was much the same as Pallava-Grantha, by the time the Lopburi inscriptions appeared in the seventh or eighth centuries, the early similarities were all but gone. That is probably the reason that Luce noticed such differences between the Pyū and the Dvāravatī scripts.

It is true that the largest number of Pyū inscriptions are found at seventh century Śrī Kṣetra and not Halin, most of them thought to have been inscribed between the sixth and eighth centuries AD or earlier.[93] Of them, the most celebrated is the gold manuscript noted above, whose contents are extracts from the *Abhidhamma* and *Vinaya Piṭaka*.[94] Votive tablets with similar extracts from the *Abhidhamma* in Pyū script have also been found there, along with ordinary statements made by donors regarding their good deeds.[95] In another find at Śrī Kṣetra, the four Theravāda Buddhas of this *kalpa* were mentioned by name on a silver cylindrical reliquary. Finally, Pyū was inscribed on royal funerary urns, all of them with dates, three belonging to the seventh century and one to the early eighth.[96]

The Pyū/Pali script has also been found in Lower Burma, at Tadagale,[97] Yangôn, which Luce assigns to around the seventh century,[98] and at Kyôntu, about twenty miles northeast of modern Pegu. Writing in what appears to be Kadamba script on bricks that had distinctive Pyū mason marks similar to those found at Old Prome and Pagán has also been found in Lower Burma.[99] A terracotta votive tablet written in the same Pyū script has been uncovered among the artifacts of the relic chamber of the Pagán Shwéhsandaw temple attributed to King Aniruddha.[100] One of the latest and most useful of Pyū texts, of course, are the already much discussed Myazedi Inscriptions of 1112–1113. Inscriptions in Pyū script have also appeared in Thandway (Sandaway) on the coasts of the Bay of Bengal in southern Arakan,[101] while the latest are at Pagán, said to belong to the thirteenth century. All this adds to the already large corpus of architectural, art historical, numismatic, and archaeological evidence that suggests it was the Pyū, not the Mon, whose culture dominated in Burma during the centuries preceding the rise of the Pagán kingdom and most likely contributed to the writing system of Pagán.[102]

U Tha Myat is also the only one of his generation who made an attempt to graphically demonstrate the evolution of the Burma script from known samples, something neither Duroiselle nor Luce did. Duroiselle tended to assert his views without explanation or documentation, except of the most general sort, while Luce accepted Duroiselle's conclusions without much comment, except to add Dvāravatī as the source of the Pagán script. As far as I can tell, U Tha Myat was not trained as a linguist, but neither was Luce. Besides, since U Tha Myat's study of comparative Indic, Pyū, and Burmese paleography is the only one of its kind, the result of a lifetime of devoted study, the data he left behind are rare and useful.

More specifically, U Tha Myat's *Mon-Myanma Akkhaya Thamaing* (History of the Mon-Burmese alphabet) graphically demonstrates the evolutionary path taken by all the vowels, consonants, and numerals of Pyū leading up to the Burma script. For the most part his material is taken from actual dated epigraphy.[103] He begins with Brāhmī, then proceeds in sequence through Kusana, Gupta, Grantha, Kadamba, Maung Kan Pyū (sixth-century Śrī Kṣetra),[104] Khinba Pyū (seventh- to eighth-century Śrī Kṣetra), Myazedi Pyū (twelfth-century Pagán), the Burma script (Burmese and Mon) on the inscriptions of Pagán, to conclude with the script on palm-leaf manuscripts. On the whole U Tha Myat's evolutionary scheme seems correct, and in virtually every case the immediate predecessor to the Burmese letters is quite clearly Pyū, not Dvāravatī Mon.[105]

There are a few minor puzzles in his evolutionary scheme after Śrī Kṣetra, especially if it implies a direct, linear development between Myazedi Pyū and the Pagán Burma script, for as we shall see below many Old Burmese inscriptions *preceded* the Myazedi Inscriptions, so that Myazedi Pyū cannot have been the immediate predecessor of Pagán Burmese. This suggests that even U Tha Myat may have been influenced by the Mon Paradigm's claim that the Myazedi Inscriptions were the first evidence of written Burmese, an erroneous conclusion that has led to many mistakes. As we shall see in Chapter Eight, the Mon Paradigm scholars could not entertain the possibility that the Old Burmese script on the Myazedi Inscription (and hence the Burma script) could have come from Pyū without destroying their main premise, so that their intellectual options were hindered by their own thesis.

I am suggesting, and the paleography shows, that the Burma (Pagán) script was most likely derived from Śrī Kṣetra Pyū much earlier than the time suggested by U Tha Myat,[106] that is, well before the twelfth-century Myazedi script. The development of the consonant *ka* in his chart, for example, has two additional conjectural stages between the *ka* of sixth-century Maung Kan Śrī Kṣetra Pyū and the Pagán *ka*,[107] but they are not based on actual epigraphy. The examples of other vowels and consonants in his evolutionary chart had been taken from actual epigraphy and pose no detectable problems. We also notice immediately that the consonant *kha* of the Pagán script appears to be a direct descendant of the *kha* of sixth-century (Maung Kan) Pyū rather than of its later stages (eighth-century Śrī Kṣetra and twelfth-century Myazedi Pyū) which are a bit different, at least as shown on U Tha Myat's graph. This suggests an earlier and direct borrowing from sixth-century Śrī Kṣetra.[108] In fact, in some cases, such as the *ga* and *gha,* and also the *ja,* the closest ancestor is Kadamba, which skips even the Śrī Kṣetra phase, while the *nga* is closest to the ultimate source: Brāhmī. Although I have no explanation for the apparent direct link of the *nga* consonant to Brāhmī (other than its simplicity limiting any significant changes), the Burma script apparently borrowed from the Pyū script much earlier than the twelfth century, perhaps after the decline of Śrī Kṣetra as political and cultural center. This explains part of the apparent differences between the Pyū script on the Myazedi Inscription and the other three languages written with the Burma script, although Robert Shaffer, a Tibeto-Burman linguist, has long held that Myazedi Pyū was not as different from the other three scripts as had been made out to be.[109]

Still, it would help if some evidence of the Burma script prior to the tenth and eleventh-century Old Burmese inscriptions could be found, for U Tha Myat's paleography and my contention would be on much more solid ground if we could verify the "missing links" of the *ka* consonant. The answer may actually reside with the Old Burmese inscriptions we already possess, particularly those that have been rejected as "impossible" by the Mon Paradigm, especially an early (1035 AD) inscription erected at Bodhgayā, India, a subject to be discussed in Chapter Eight.

There are also linguistic affinities between Pyū and Burmese that have had an effect on the Burma script—as both belong to the Tibeto-Burman family—but are not found in Mon and Burmese or Pyū and Mon. We can see how the Pyū and Burmese scripts adapted tones[110] to a "toneless" Sanskrit alphabet, not a reason for much concern among those speaking nontonal Mon.[111] Blagden noticed a "wide range of tones," nearly eight markers,[112] a number which may have been necessary since the Pyū (at least according to Luce) used two scripts,[113] one perhaps for writing toneless Pali and the other for tonal Pyū, one arriving earlier and the other evolving later.

Moreover, Pyū vocabulary, even according to Luce, is far closer to Burmese than to any other single language *in Burma of the time,*[114] particularly when contrasted to Mon. Not only are there similarities of cultural terms, which is expected given their long history together, but also of kinship and social terms, implying a much closer ethnolinguistic connection. Indeed,

Blagden so much as said that the Myazedi Inscriptions revealed the "former existence of a [Pyū] nation and language which have apparently been completely absorbed by the Burmese . . . ."[115] In the entire glossary provided by him and gleaned from the Myazedi Inscriptions, there is only *one word* in Pyū that may have had a connection to a probable Mon word—the word for "gold"—hardly a term that suggests close sociocultural or ethnolinguistic ties.

In contrast, many important words in both Pyū and Burmese are identical, such as "son," "wife," the numerals one, three, and eight, "grandchild," "to die," "to give," "to do," "myself," "year," "city," "likeness," "this," "was," "violence," "to be named (or) called," "that," "this," "shape," and the possessive affix. Or the words are nearly identical, such as "to pour," "dedication," "to donate," "oppress," "my," "to make," "to be sick." Also similar are particles following verbs and numerals, particles used to connect numerals with nouns or used after words in "the genitive relation," verbal affixes, and plural affixes.[116] Even the structure for making verbs negative is common to Pyū and Burmese.[117] Especially noteworthy are the above mentioned kinship terms such as "son" and "grandchild," or near-kinship ones such as "wife," as well as a most important political and administrative word—"city," "capital," "kingdom,"—in Old Burmese *prañ* and in Pyū *pri:,* still used today as "country" or "nation." Their affinity to each other suggests a closeness between the Pyū and Burman peoples well beyond geographic propinquity or casual historical interaction. It is a relationship not found between any other two major cultural groups at the time in Burma.

It is true that there are also affinities between Mon and Burmese vocabulary.[118] But to suggest, as some have, that kinship terms such as the Burmese word for "widow" *(kmay)* came from Mon[119] is unproven and quite absurd, for one of the last things to be borrowed from another culture are kinship terms. Besides, are we to believe that Burmese had no widows before they met the Mon? Or perhaps the Mon word for "widow" was intrinsically so much better than the Burmese that an entire ethnolinguistic population simultaneously changed its word for it and did it so thoroughly that not a trace of its vestige survives?

The relevance here is not the mere fact of borrowing, but a question of *when* and *which way* these words may have gone. So far, no one has demonstrated that any borrowing occurred between Burmese and Mon speakers during the Pagán period, but only subsequently, when, after the development of a Mon state in Lower Burma in the late thirteenth century, Burman-Mon contact was regular and constant for nearly 700 years. Nor has it yet been proved that certain words that are common to both necessarily came from the Mon rather than from the Burmese. The assumption that these loanwords *traveled only one way,* in this case from Mon to Burmese, and did so early, once again privileged the Mon and bolstered the Mon Paradigm.

Linguists tell us that there may be several different ways for words to become loanwords or appear connected. Blagden put it well when he wrote that if there arose a question of a particular Burmese word alleged to be connected to, say, a Chinese word, then it could be that (a) the word in Burmese may have come from Chinese, or (b) the word in Chinese may have come from Burmese, or (c) the word may have been borrowed from some third source, such as Sanskrit, or (d) it may have been derived from the original stock of the family to which both languages belong (Sino-Tibetan), or (e) the word may not be related at all, but coincidentally sound similar.[120]

As Mon and Burmese come from different language families, "d" can be eliminated, but there are four other ways in which loanwords, if that is what they are in the first place, may have been derived, not the least of which is that they may coincidentally sound similar.[121] Other than option "a" and "b," which is most probably what happened once the two cultures met, option "c" (borrowing from a third source) is also relevant. And even if one can show with linguistic principles that Mon loanwords are present in Burmese today, it cannot in any way even suggest that the origins of the *Burma script* used in the eleventh century also came from the Mon or that the borrowing occurred in the Pagán, rather than much later in the Ava and Pegu periods. The assumption of an earlier Mon civilization in Lower Burma, once again, has been the basis for such conclusions.

One of the difficulties in attempting to decipher approximately when the Pyū script was adopted by Burmese speakers is the archaism of the Pyū script. Most of the letters of the Pyū alphabet, whether taken from the Maung Kan gold plates of the sixth century, or those of eighth-century Śrī Kṣetra, or even the early twelfth-century Myazedi Inscriptions of Prince Rājakumār, are virtually identical.[122] As Luce himself put it well, over seven centuries the Pyū script changed but little,[123] even if the language itself may have.[124] That is precisely the reason one finds a sixth or eighth-century script on the early twelfth-century Myazedi Inscription. Although this raises concerns about the ability of paleography to determine the age of certain, unchanging scripts with any precision—in part because its methodology consciously seeks change and its conclusions are based on it—it is also paleography on which we must depend, even if in conjunction with other historical evidence.

Not only did the Pyū script not change over approximately seven centuries, but by the time of the Myazedi Inscriptions it was considered archaic when compared with the Indic script from which it originally came. Blagden noticed that twelfth-century Myazedi Pyū used forms that were obsolete in South India, some having fallen out of usage by the fourth century AD.[125] This suggests that the Pyū must have adopted the Kadamba or Andhra script before those features became obsolete. This is also about the same time that the earliest Halin Pyū writing appears.[126] Thus the unchanging character of the Pyū script, and its archaism particularly, may allow us to date the period of its inception even better.

On the other hand, any definition of archaism depends on the user's viewpoint. Even though the parent South Indian script may have gone through some changes—such that vestiges of it found in Pyū were no longer used in India and were therefore considered "obsolete" or "archaic"—the Pyū script in Burma itself had not changed. In other words, even if for a South Indian, certain features of the Pyū script appeared archaic, for a Pyū, it was current. And since it was still current to the Pyū, they kept using it for several more centuries, making it appear, as Luce put it, "archaic from the start."[127]

That, however, does not explain why the Pyū script did not change thereafter. And this is where history again comes in. The probable explanation lies in the common history of the Pyū and Burmans *after* Śrī Kṣetra's decline, which may have occurred after Sīhavikrama's death in 718.[128] By about 800 AD, the Pyū kingdom seems to have come under Nanchao domination,[129] the Chinese sources stating that "through its military strength and territorial proximity Nanchao has always held the Pyū kingdom in control," to the extent the leader of Nanchao took the title of "P'iao shin" (lord of the P'iao).[130] Perhaps because of Pyū resistance, their kingdom was said to have been "looted and plundered" by Nanchao in the first half of the ninth century,[131] shortly after which the Burmese speakers emerged in the historical records as leaders of Upper Burma, subsequently inhabiting the same general settlement areas that the Pyū had once occupied. Whether or not the Burmese speakers were part of the "advance guard" of the Nanchao kingdom, as some Burma scholars assert[132] is not clear. Equally possible is the option that the Burmese speakers were already in the plains of the Irrawaddy, integrated with the Pyū, as suggested by their close sociolinguistic ties. That there were also special linguistic and cultural ties between the Yi (Lolo) people—one of the ethnic groups said to have been part of the Nanchao kingdom—with the Pyū and Burmese also seems reasonable enough.[133]

In any case, as the new leaders of a state attempting to integrate numerous ethnic groups and their languages and cultures into one entity, the Burmans would naturally have made their language the *lingua franca* and their script the standard for the kingdom. When the Pyū lost their place to the Burmese speakers as leaders of state and society, it would have further accelerated the decline of the Pyū language, especially for public use. Once the spoken language was no longer used widely, the same fate would befall the written one, which, not surprisingly, all but disappeared in the epigraphic record as the script of state.[134] The Pyū language and script had become moribund and thus "frozen in time," which explains why the script hardly changed after eighth-century Śrī Kṣetra and why it was virtually the same when it was finally written again on the twelfth-century Myazedi Inscriptions.

From the mid-ninth to the mid-tenth century the power of the Burmese speakers was consolidated. They established themselves at the walled city of Pagán around the late tenth or early eleventh centuries, as confirmed by radiocarbon analysis and epigraphy, a period in which at least two verifiable kings, Saw Rahan and Kyaung Phyu Min, Aniruddha's grandfather and father reigned, if not ruled.[135] However, the early ninth century was not the end of the Pyū people, their culture, or even their writing system, for they continued to live in Burmese society at Pagán and even Ava for several more centuries, very likely contributing their skills in gold, wood, and silver crafts to the Burmans.[136] Their language and script continued to be used, albeit on a very irregular basis, as, for example, the terracotta votive tablet with six lines in Pyū script found in the relic chamber of the Shwéhsandaw Pagoda attests.[137] Of course the Pyū script and language on the Myazedi Inscriptions also testifies to their presence, or at least to someone with knowledge of both, in the early twelfth century, while another Pyū inscription is assigned to the late thirteenth century.[138] And, as noted in Chapter Two, there are epigraphic references in Old Burmese during the Pagán and Ava periods to Pyū as individuals and groups living there.[139]

Thus there were present at Pagán people who could still write in the old language, just as there are those today who can read and write Old Burmese (or Latin and Old English). The "archaism" of classical Latin or Old English compared with modern English no more suggests the absence of a paleographic relationship between them than those between Pyū and the other three scripts on the Myazedi Inscriptions simply because they might look different to the untrained eye. But it was more than that: the role that the Pyū script played on the royal Myazedi Inscriptions—that of a "classical ancestor" providing the prestige of tradition to the text and its context—is perhaps similar to the use of classical Latin today in commemorative inscriptions in English-speaking societies. One thing is certain: no evidence of a comparable relationship between the Old Mon writing system of Dvāravatī as a "classical ancestor" and the other languages of Burma can be found in the epigraphic record. Indeed, the Pyū-Burman cultural integration occurred probably two centuries *before* first proven contact between Burmese and Mon speakers, for only with Pagán's expansion into Lower Burma in the mid- to late eleventh century is there any epigraphic evidence to even suggest the latter encounter. It was only then that the Burma script, already functioning in Upper Burma, could have been given to the Mon of Lower Burma for the first time, which in large part explains why Old Mon writing cannot be found earlier than the late eleventh century anywhere in the country.

In sum, not only is there paleographic evidence that the Pyū gave their script to the Burmese speakers, resulting in the Burma script, but it is supported by their probable history together, revealed by their affinity in language, their patronymic linkage system, their arts and crafts, their architecture, their shared Indic conceptual system, their cosmological urban designs, their irrigation technology, and their settlement locations, all discussed in Chapter Two.

Conclusion

The Mon Paradigm's case regarding the Burma script has hinged on the *same assumptions* from which it began: that Mon civilization in Lower Burma was older than Burman civilization in Upper Burma in every instance and that the mechanism by which this putative earlier civilization was transferred was the alleged conquest of Thatôn by Aniruddha. Perhaps it may have been the lack of scientific data on the Pyū culture that kept earlier scholars from considering the Pyū option more seriously, although as we have seen, most of the relevant discoveries had been made by the late 1930s. Certainly, Mon Paradigm proponents never appeared to consider that the *reverse* could have occurred: that the Old Mon writing system might actually have been borrowed from the Old Burmese of Pagán. Neither the written Mon evidence, its analysis, and its documented history, nor the written Burmese evidence, its analysis, and its documented history has led, as it should have, to the conclusion that the Burmese borrowed its writing system from Mon. Rather it was as Duroiselle stated in 1919, "the greater antiquity of Talaing civilisation [had been] accepted on every hand."

The century-old thesis that the Old Mon writing system was responsible for the Burma script is simply no longer viable. There is no historical record of Mon immigration from Dvāravatī to Lower Burma, no evidence of written Mon in the Dvāravatī script in Burma, no proven or demonstrated paleographic relationship between the Old Mon writing system of Dvāravatī and that of Pagán, and no dated Old Mon inscriptions other than those in the Burma (Pagán) script in the entire country.

In contrast, there *is* paleographic evidence of the link between the Pyū script of both Halin and Śrī Kṣetra and the Pagán script, close cultural and linguistic ties between Pyū and Burmese speakers at least two to three centuries prior to the latter's first contact with Mon speakers, and several centuries of political and historical contact and integration between Pyū and Burman. Therefore, the Burma script most likely evolved from the Pyū, and the direction taken by the Burma script was probably much like that of early civilization itself in Burma: north to south, interior to the coasts, and hence Pyū to Burman and Burman to Mon, not the reverse.

8 The Place of Written Burmese and Mon in Burma's Early History

IF THE PAGÁN SCRIPT was not derived from the Dvāravatī script, but indirectly from the earlier scripts of either Vanavasi or Andhra via the Pyū, there should be evidence in the epigraphic record that Old Burmese writing preceded Old Mon writing in Burma. And indeed, this is what the evidence actually shows. However, since it runs directly counter to the Mon Paradigm's claims that written Old Mon preceded and was the source for written Old Burmese, the issue has become thoroughly obfuscated in Pagán-period minutiae. This chapter, therefore, attempts to plow through that obfuscation and clarify the place of written Old Burmese and Old Mon in Burma's history.

The Myazedi Issue

In 1886–1887 two nearly duplicate multilingual stone pillars of the Myinkaba Kubyaukgyi temple,[1] popularly known as the Myazedi Inscriptions, were discovered at Myinkaba village near Pagán by Forchhammer, the director of archaeology. The stones, conventionally dated to approximately 1112–1113 AD,[2] were inscribed on four sides, all apparently written in the same script, but each representing a different language, and all more or less conveying the same message. For the first and only time in Burma's history, Pyū, Pali, Burmese, and Mon were recorded (presumably simultaneously), capturing an extremely important moment in Burma's history: the crystallization of Burmese culture in the synthesis called the kingdom of Pagán, a polity which in turn laid the critical foundations for what was to become modern Burma. Yet precisely *how* that moment was reached, the issue being addressed in this book, is a matter of dispute.

The heart of the Myazedi Issue concerns the relative chronology of written Burmese versus written Mon in Burma. Whereas it is agreed by nearly all that King Kyanzittha's Old Mon inscription of 1093 found at Prome is the first, *dated* evidence of written Old Mon in the country,[3] the first evidence for written Burmese is said to have been the Myazedi Inscriptions of c. 1112–1113.[4] However, the latter conclusion was reached before having conducted any linguistic analysis on the comparative chronologies of written Old Burmese and Old Mon in Burma based on original and securely dated inscriptions, and as a result is totally arbitrary and self-serving.[5] It is one of the most egregious myths in Burma Studies still held to be true by scholars of Southeast Asia today. By that single assertion—that the Burmese found on the Myazedi is the first evidence of its written form—the Mon Paradigm scholars "established" that written Old Mon was older than written Old Burmese without having to prove it. Thus whenever Old Burmese inscriptions were found dated *prior* to 1112–1113—and the Mon Paradigm scholars knew of several, as I will show—they were automatically declared unreliable and impossible. From the start, then, Old Burmese never had a chance of being examined outside the Mon Paradigm's theoretical prejudices.

Consequently, all analyses of Burmese orthography presumed that the version on the Myazedi was the oldest form, the one from which all others were ultimately derived. Not only did this make orthography the ultimate litmus test for deciding chronology (and therefore the evolutionary scheme for Burmese), but the Burmese script on the Myazedi also became the standard by which all other written Burmese at Pagán was measured. All this, not coincidentally, made it consistent with the underlying assumption of the Mon Paradigm that Mon civilization preceded Burman in every case. Once again, premise had become proof.

The Myazedi Inscriptions state that the king mentioned on them, Śrī Tribhuvanāditya Dhammarāja—*assumed* to be Kyanzittha—was king 1,628 years after the Buddha's *parinibbānna*.[6] This should correspond to 1084 AD, if the Burmese tradition of 544 BC is used for calculating the date of the *parinibbānna*. But if another calculating era, such as that used in Thailand was intended, or if the date was meant to represent a yet-to-be-completed year, then the reign of this king must be changed accordingly and calculated with 543 BC (hence, to 1083 AD). Since the inscriptions also state that the king had ruled for twenty-eight years, it means the original of the two Myazedi stones had to have been inscribed thereafter, dating the Myazedi to 1111, *not* 1112, as conventionally given. The second stone with its newer-looking script could, of course have been inscribed much later than either date, an issue not yet discussed in Burma Studies. The inscriptions were thought to have been the product of Prince Rājakumār, the king's son by the chief queen, Trilokawataṁsakādewī, both of whom are mentioned on the stones.

In any case, the assumption that the Old Burmese script on the Myazedi is its oldest sample subsequently became the analytical framework for developing an evolutionary scheme of written Burmese at Pagán. In this scenario, Old Mon was automatically assumed to be the starting point, followed by Old Burmese, which then went through its prescribed transformations. The scheme envisioned a three-phase evolution that went from "Archaic" to "Standard Old" to "Modern" Burmese. The differences between Archaic and Standard Old Burmese—the pertinent comparison here—were determined largely by the internal inconsistencies of spelling in Archaic Burmese, which was considered "haphazard and diverse."[7] The language was thought to have become standardized only by the mid-twelfth century. Yet this "standardization" is based on a *single* inscription of Princess (or Queen) Ajāwlat ("Queen's Burmese," as it were), erected in 1165, that showed extraordinary consistency of spelling and other refinements.

Thus Ba Shin, then an assistant as well as colleague of Luce, wrote that the Archaic Burmese script found earliest on votive tablets "is cursive and the orthography archaic and uncertain."[8] He continued that "these . . . writings are good examples . . . [that] illustrate the experimental stage in the gradual development of . . . writing a language before it is standardised."[9]

In addition to the tautology—that Archaic Burmese showed archaism because it was archaic—the argument is fraught with other serious problems, not the least of which is that inconsistency of spelling alone is hardly a foolproof indicator of an inevitable, early stage in the development of a writing system, particularly Old Burmese. Even within Old Mon itself, Luce admits that "Rājakumār's spellings are much the same as his father's [Kyanzittha], but not quite so correct and careful. . . . This carelessness becomes *increasingly* conspicuous in the Mon inscriptions of the reign of the grandson (Alaungsithu) . . ." [my emphasis],[10] thereby demonstrating that as time passed, spelling did not necessarily become *more* consistent but sometimes even *less*. Shorto confirmed and extended this point by noting that the "extraordinary variations in spelling . . . [were] at an extreme in classical Old Mon,"[11] by which he meant Kyanzittha's Old Mon.[12]

In Old Burmese also, we regularly find inscriptions of Pagán after 1165 and the so-called "standardization" of Burmese (itself a problematic concept) continuing to display the "inconsistent" qualities of "prestandardization."[13] What I am saying is that "primitive" orthography does not always precede the mid-twelfth-century marker for standardization, nor does "advanced" orthography succeed it, since we often find stones with poor Burmese orthography inscribed *after* the ones with good (Queen's) Burmese.[14] There are also many cases of inconsistent spelling in inscriptions *that are contemporaneous* to each other, and in some instances, inconsistencies within the same inscription.

To provide just one example, in the Nyaungyangyi Daughter's inscription of *Sakarāj* 604 (1242 AD), the penmanship ("stonemanship" if you will) and orthography is so beautifully precise and consistent that the scribe (or the stone mason whom she hired for the actual inscribing) must have had a standard set of metal punches—Pagán's equivalent to the typewriter, I suppose. All consonants, vowels, and medials are virtually the same size and shape (in length, width, girth, diameter, and height) throughout the inscription.[15] So are the long-vowel markers of certain consonants, which suggests that the scribe must have had an additional set for making them.

Yet the texts of many *later* inscriptions showed much poorer penmanship as well as internal inconsistencies in orthography and calligraphy, suggesting not only that the scribe may have been inscribing "freehand," that is, without a complete set of standard punches, but was also less educated and hence the inconsistent orthography and sloppy calligraphy (and therefore, also less well paid for the work). This evidence calls attention to factors such as individual competence, education, training, technology, and economics, not simply linguistic or paleographic evolution.

Because scribes with different levels of education, penmanship, and literary competence were hired to inscribe stones, wide discrepancies in spelling can be found in both contemporary inscriptions and those distant in time. I suspect that scribes renowned for the quality of their work were also more expensive, and hence their clientele was limited to those who could afford them. As a consequence, the best Burmese can be found usually on those inscriptions issued by royalty or the elite classes.[16] High-quality Burmese orthography was not necessarily the result of its advanced stage, or poorer-quality orthography, of its primitive stage, any more than "good" novels or compositions of today must succeed "poor" novels and compositions of yesterday.

It appears to me, therefore, that a more westernized conceptualization of the relationship between linear time and progress in human society was interjected into the analysis of the development of the Old Burmese script, so that what were really socioeconomic and technological circumstances had become "evidence" for a preconceived linear and progressive evolutionary scheme.

In the final analysis the flawed evolutionary scheme devised for written Burmese by the Mon Paradigm, did not, in any case, address the issue of whether the Old Mon writing system preceded that of Old Burmese because the evolutionary analysis was confined to Old Burmese. It did not compare it with Old Mon because Old Mon was *already assumed* to be earlier. To the best of my knowledge, not a single linguistic examination of the relative ages of these two writing systems—based on original, contemporary, and datable sources and *independent* of the Mon Paradigm's assumptions—has been published in English.

To be sure, Luce produced several comparative language charts,[17] but they were based almost entirely on vocabulary and had little to say about the relative chronology of the *writing systems* except by inference.[18] Similarly, Duroiselle's work in the *Epigraphia Birmanica* very ably demonstrated the probable way in which Old Burmese orthography developed, using the original words found on the Myazedi, but that process was confined to written Burmese only; it was not compared with written Old Mon, the issue at hand. In addition, the study was limited to the information found in the Myazedi Inscriptions and based on the assumption that the stones represent the first example of written Burmese.

Thus what has been offered until now is a contrived evolutionary sequence in which Old Mon was *already determined* to have preceded Archaic Burmese, Archaic Burmese (which was "characterized" by inconsistent spelling) was said to precede Standard Old Burmese (which was determined, erroneously, by *consistent* spelling). After that Standard Old Burmese "gained ground during the period of transition," another invented phase based on the above assumptions, until the reign of King Narapatisithu (1174–1211), "when Burmese became the main language of the inscriptions of Pagán."[19] Although a historian, I cannot help but wonder what linguists would think of a scheme that used the orthography of one written language and its putative "evolution" as the ultimate (sometimes *only*) test for the comparative ages of the writing systems of *two different languages?*

Old Burmese in Domestic Lithic Epigraphy

What does the epigraphic evidence have to say regarding the Mon Paradigm's contention that the Burmese on the Myazedi Inscriptions was its earliest written example?[20] The short answer is that not only is the Old Burmese on the Myazedi *not* the earliest evidence of written Old Burmese, but the evidence for written Old Burmese precedes that for written Old Mon in Burma by about a century. The sad truth is that most, if not all the evidence I use here was available to,[21] and indeed largely compiled by, the second generation of the Mon Paradigm advocates. For various reasons, including the belief that it contradicted the Mon Paradigm, however, they did not consider this evidence viable.

Depending on how one counts, I have found to date approximately thirty-six Old Burmese[22] inscriptions that precede the Myazedi, or thirty-seven, if one inscribed during the same year as the Myazedi is counted.[23] Approximately twenty-four of them have been published in a volume containing forty-two inscriptions, arranged chronologically and carefully edited.[24] Most of these are, however, recast stones ordered by King Bodawpaya in 1785 and now located in the Mahāmuni compound; they total approximately 719.[25]

The tradition of recasting old stone records was not new. Earlier kings had done what Bodawpaya did, having new stones cut of worn inscriptions, some now lost to us. The recasts summarize the contents of the originals; in most cases they include the donor's name, the day of the week and the year in which the original donation was made, and in a few cases duplicate the orthography of the original. Most important to the state and *saṅgha* in political and economic ways, the recast stones reaffirm the precise boundaries of the landed property that had been donated to the *saṅgha*. The main purpose of the recast stones was to verify the legal title to religious lands so that succeeding kings could, in the tradition of the kings named on the stones, redonate the lands as part of their own legitimation process. (It was also, of course, a way to keep track of the extent of tax-exempt *saṅgha* property.)[26]

Although I look with some skepticism on the historicity of events mentioned on these recast stones, so far no Burma scholar has provided any good reason to question the existence of the *originals* they represent. At some point *the originals from which these recasts were made did exist.* In the case of King Bodawpaya's recasts, not only have most of the originals survived, but a comparison between the stones he copied and their originals show that although mistakes were made—such as the interjection of modernized spelling in some cases and the miscopying of some dates—in the opinion of Duroiselle himself, the "percentage of inscriptions of which the date has . . . been misread is not on the whole very large. . . ."[27] Thus I use these twenty-four inscriptions here not for their information on historical events or orthography, but as representative of the general period in which their originals might have been written.

What is most important about these twenty-four stones is that eight of them belong to King Aniruddha's reign.[28] For a long time I wondered why there were so few inscriptions representing this most important reign for, apart from those in this group of twenty-four, there is only *one* surviving domestic original stone inscription attributed to Aniruddha, dated to 1058 AD. Yet Aniruddha was most likely the earliest, or at least one of the most effective consolidators of the Pagán kingdom. He was said to have been responsible for many of the technological and military achievements that allowed the expansion of the state and was probably the one who vigorously initiated, on a statewide level, the patronage of the *saṅgha* as a legitimating ideology of the state—the public expression of which are these very same donative stone inscriptions. Considering this, the extent of his patronage expressed on stone should have equaled if not surpassed that of many of his successors, and indeed that is how it is recorded in the chronicles.[29] Even the number of temples attributed to Aniruddha—each of which would ordinarily have had a stone record—far exceeds the number of inscriptions found during his reign if we discount these recast inscriptions.[30]

The scope and scale of temple construction by the king prior to any invasion of Lower Burma has convincing support from data analyzed by archaeologist Bob Hudson.[31] In his study, based on Pierre Pichard's *Inventory of Monuments at Pagán,* of eighty-six dated temples and monasteries constructed at Pagán, Hudson calculated the total volume (in cubic meters) of bricks, mortar, stone, and dirt used to build these edifices during the period 1050–1399 and then graphed this activity chronologically, with the dates divided into approximately ten-year segments. His work confirms an earlier study of mine, which used epigraphy only, that examined the amount of land, labor, and money that flowed to the *saṅgha* from state and society. His graph more precisely confirms my study regarding the general pattern, scale, scope, and chronology of temple-building in Pagán. Hudson's data show two large construction peaks beginning in 1050 AD, *before* the alleged conquest of Thatôn in 1057 and the alleged importation of Mon artisans and craftsmen, said to have been crucial to the temple-building program in Pagán. My study shows a similar, though less dramatic, development during the same time.[32]

This obvious development in temple-building during Aniruddha's reign is not consistent with the number of donative inscriptions conventionally attributed to his reign and earlier. Thus, although many of these recast inscriptions fill an important gap in the information about the Aniruddha period, as well as the chronology of religious donations made during it, they and the period they represent have been ignored or dismissed because they do not support the thesis that Old Mon precedes Old Burmese. Since these recast stones were inadmissible as evidence, the role of Old Burmese writing during Aniruddha's reign has also been dismissed. That, in turn, allowed the exaggeration of the role and period of his most notable successor, King Kyanzittha, who wrote mainly in Mon.

The dates on these twenty-four inscriptions *all precede* the Myazedi Inscriptions, in one case by over a century. This last date is recorded as *Sakarāj* 346 or 984 AD,[33] although a few internal contradictions cast some doubt on its reliability.[34] But the point I am trying to make is that it most likely had an original, dated to 984, well within the early decades of the Pagán Dynasty. This is when Saw Rahan (956–1001) and Kyaung Phyu Min (1001–1021), Aniruddha's grandfather and father, reigned, both of whom have been corroborated independently.[35] And as stated in an earlier chapter, new radiocarbon dates show that as early as 650 AD there was urban settlement at Pagán, while the foundations of the walls date to between 990 and 1030 AD. Also important, among the twenty-four recast inscriptions, eleven belong to the reigns of Aniruddha's two successors, Saw Lu and Kyanzittha, so they all predate the Myazedi.[36] Even if we discount the 984 AD stone, there is still ample evidence that Old Burmese was being written prior to the Myazedi Inscriptions of 1111/1112–1113.

However, lest these 24 stones be considered inadmissible as evidence for being recasts and not originals—which is after all my own criterion throughout this book for determining reliability—there is another, more recent compilation of inscriptions called *She Haung Myanma Kyauksa Mya* [Ancient Burmese stone inscriptions], volume I, which contains 225 original Old Burmese inscriptions dated from *Sakkarāj* 474 to 600, that is, 1112 to 1238 AD. (Note the starting date of the volume, 1112, the date for the Myazedi; so even the organization of a volume of inscriptions published in 1970 had assumed the Mon Paradigm to be correct.) Partly for that reason, volume I is divided into two sections, A and B (in Burmese *ka* and *kha*). Section A includes 187 Old Burmese inscriptions considered originals and presumably struck around the same time as the events they describe; section B contains 38 Old Burmese inscriptions considered less reliable, although nearly all still belong to the Pagán period. Some have been placed in the B section for reasons having more to do with the fact that they contradict assumptions of the Mon Paradigm than their intrinsic value. Of the 38 original Old Burmese inscriptions in section B that are dated, 7 precede the Myazedi.[37]

There is another original Old Burmese inscription that was not included in the *She Haung Myanma* that also precedes the Myazedi. It is found in a compilation called *Pagán Kyauksa Let Ywe Sin*[38] [Selected inscriptions of Pagán] by E Maung. The stone is apparently dated to 1082 AD, although I am not entirely clear how the editor arrived at that conclusion.[39] In a third compilation, this one by Luce and Pe Maung Tin, titled *Selections From the Inscriptions of Pagán,* that includes only what they considered to be originals, there are four Old Burmese inscriptions that predate the Myazedi stones,[40] three of which have already been included in the *She Haung* volume, thus adding a total of one more original Old Burmese inscription that preceded the Myazedi. In short, the Myazedi Inscriptions do not represent the earliest evidence of written Burmese. There are either eight or nine (if E Maung's 1082 inscription is counted) original Old Burmese inscriptions that precede the Myazedi *excluding* the twenty-four Bodawphaya recasts.

Old Burmese at the Mahābodhi Temple

In addition, two Old Burmese inscriptions were found at Bodhgayā at the Mahābodhi temple in the early part of the nineteenth century. They had been left there by envoys from at least three different missions sent from the kingdom of Pagán. The first left an Old Burmese inscription on a copper-gilt umbrella discovered eight feet under the modern ground level. It includes a line of text in Old Burmese under which is another line in what Sir Alexander Cunningham, noted India epigraphist and archaeologist, called mediaeval Nāgarī.

Although the first, most important digit on this Old Burmese text is not very clear and much damaged, the date given by the Nāgarī text is clear and reads "Sam 397." Cunningham assumes the Burmese used the Cūḷasakarāj dating system and wrote that the damaged numeral "ought to correspond with that in the Indian inscription below," and therefore dated it to 1035 AD.[41] The "Sam" preceding the numeric date is a bit puzzling, but it may be a misreading for "Sak," the abbreviation for *Sakarāj,* the era used in virtually all inscriptions of Pagán.[42]

As Cunningham was unable to read the entire date on the Burmese text because the copper has been crushed where the first digit was inscribed, he provided both a photograph of the copper text and a conjectural hand copy of it in his published work. But since the first digit on the copper is illegible, the hand copy had to be conjectural also, and that is what Luce stated he read. From that conjectural hand copy, he interpreted the date as *Sakarāj* [6]55, or 1293–1294 AD, placing the event in the thirteenth rather than the eleventh century. Luce made no comment on the *Nāgarī* text, the date of which was legible and confirmed Cunningham's conjectural reading of the Burmese date to 1035 AD.[43]

Unfortunately, even the two legible numerals of the date on the copper shown in the photograph provided by Cunningham are not accurately represented by the hand copy. On the hand copy, the two numerals do indeed look the way Pagán epigraphists would write "55," and therefore probably misled Luce into reading them as [6]55. On the photograph, however, they do *not* look like 55, but rather like 97. Nevertheless, misreading the last two numerals as 55 still does not justify reading the first illegible digit as a 6, especially when the *Nāgarī* text is clearly 3.

Cunningham's reading of the *Nāgarī* date as 397 would place the first Bodhgayā mission in the reign of one of Aniruddha's predecessors, Kyi-zo, whose historicity is confirmed by the most reliable and earliest of Burmese chronicles, the *Zatatawpon.*[44] More pertinent to the present topic, it demonstrates that written Old Burmese preceded the alleged conquest of Thatôn in 1057 by twenty-two years, the first dated Old Mon inscription in Burma (Kyanzittha's 1093 stone) by fifty-eight years, and the Myazedi Inscriptions of 1111/1112–1113 by more than seventy-seven years.

The second Old Burmese inscription at the Mahābodhi temple is more informative, and ultimately more important, for it has two legible, more precise dates on it and represents the last two missions. The stone was said to have been discovered in 1833 by Capt. George Burney, brother of Col. Henry Burney, British Resident at Ava and Amarapura, when the former was on a visit to Bodhgayā.[45] The narrative provided by this inscription describes the various dedications and repairs that had been made to the temple at different times, beginning with King Aśoka, who built the original temple. Subsequently, repairs were made by one Paṅsakū krī, a senior monk, after which additional repairs were said to have been made by a Siri Dharma Rājakuru (or Guna, depending on the reading), and finally repairs were made by the last two missions, at the completion of which this stone inscription was dated and erected.[46]

Cunningham's reading of the *Nāgarī* on the copper-gilt umbrella confirms at least the title "Sri Dharma Raja Guna" that is attached to an individual mentioned on both the umbrella and the inscription. Although Cunningham stated that he could not make out the rest of the Burmese on the umbrella, my reading of both the photograph and hand copy is "Sri Dharma Raja Guna Paṅsakū krī."[47] To me it appears as a single title (combining the Raja Guna and the Paṅsakū krī), not two different ones.[48] Whatever the case may be, the information given on the stone inscription not only confirms there was indeed an earlier, first mission, but also corroborates the title or part of a title of an individual involved in that mission, thereby lending much credibility to Cunningham's reading of the *Nāgarī* date as 1035 AD and not Luce's that places it in the thirteenth century.

Copies of the stone inscription were sent to Col. Henry Burney, who along with Burmese scholars at Ava read its dates as *Sakarāj* 467 and 468 (1105 and 1106 AD respectively). In 1862 Cunningham also saw the inscription, "fixed in a wall" he wrote, at the residency of the Mahant (a religious official). Cunningham's reading of the Burmese dates on it was *Sakarāj* 441 and 448 (AD 1079 and 1086 respectively). This agrees with the reading by Burney and the Ava scholars *in terms of the centenary numbers* but differs on the decade and one of the years. Three other scholars also tried their hand at reading these dates[49] and came to the conclusion that the first digit represents a 6 rather than a 4, thereby placing the missions in the thirteenth century. One last attempt to read the dates prior to this writing was made by Luce, who in 1976, not surprisingly, read the dates as 657 and 660, which also placed the second and third missions in the thirteen century, and coincided with his reading of the illegible first digit on the umbrella as a 6. In that 1976 article, Luce lamented the "failure of Ava scholars to read correctly" those dates, which "threw them [and also Cunningham] two centuries out in their reckoning."[50] But, as we shall see, it was Luce whose reckoning was wrong.

I have also read the microfilm[51] of the rubbing of the stone inscription and concur with Cunningham and Burney that *the centenary date* should be a 4, although the decades and years are not entirely clear. The most important factor in this controversy is, however, not the decade or year, important though they may be, but the century. At present, the issue ultimately boils down to interpretation: whether the first digit was a 6 or a 4, and, therefore, whether the missions occurred in the thirteenth or the eleventh centuries.

Fortunately, and even if the year is a matter of interpretation, the names of the week and month days were included in the stone inscription, and their readings are not contested. The first is recorded as Friday the 10th day of Pyatho (December/January), and the second as Sunday, the 8th day of Tazaungmôn (October/November). Realizing the importance of these details, Cunningham tested all conjectured years with the respective week and month days. He concluded that none matched any of the conjectured thirteenth-century years, but corresponded with the years *Sakarāj* 441 and 448 (1079 and 1086 AD).[52]

Since Cunningham's work preceded Luce's by almost a century, he obviously did not include Luce's readings in his tests. So I had Luce's dates cross-checked with J. C. Eade's invaluable reference work, *Southeast Asian Ephemeris,* with the indispensable help of my colleague Ken Breazeale from the University of Hawai'i's East-West Center who understands Eade's underlying mathematical principles and their tables which I do not.[53] It turns out that Cunningham was right. The week and month days in *Sakarāj* 657 and 660 (Luce's years) do not correspond with those on the Mahābodhi Inscription. Friday, the 10th waxing day of Pyatho in *Sakarāj* 657 AD falls on a Saturday, not a Friday, while Sunday, the 8th waxing of Tazaungmôn in *Sakarāj* 660 falls on a Tuesday, not a Sunday. I also had Cunningham's dates of *Sakarāj* 441 and 448 retested with Eade's work, and they are virtually right on the mark.[54]

There are, of course, a multitude of factors to consider when determining these dates, such as intercalary months, leap years, and things affecting the calculation of days of the week, and so on. But Eade's formulas take these factors into consideration, and even though his system is based on mathematical probability, those who have used it for the past decade have found it to be very accurate.[55] The only unknown that needs to be calculated here, in any case, is whether the *years* chosen by the different scholars corresponded with the week and month days already given by the Mahābodhi Inscription. In other words the known week and month days are the basis for calculating the unknown, conjectured years; there is no need to alter the week or month days, unless, of course, they do not correspond with one's preferred years.

This explains why the AD equivalents that Luce gave for his chosen years 657 and 660 were at first puzzling. As noted above, when Friday the 10th waxing of Pyatho is calculated according to Eade's tables using Luce's year 657, it falls on Saturday, December 17th. Yet Luce gave an AD equivalent of Friday, December 16th,[56] which is not the 10th, but the 9th waxing of Pyatho. Thus he appears to have deliberately chosen the wrong day of the month in order to get the correct day of the week (Friday), as given in the inscription. That this was not merely accidental is revealed by his doing the same thing with the second date. When Sunday, the 8th waxing of Tazaungmôn given on the inscription is calculated according to Eade's tables using Luce's year 660, it falls on Tuesday the 14th of October, not, as Luce has it, on Sunday the 12th of October.[57]

What Luce seems to have done in both cases was to make sure that the days of the week given on the Mahābodhi Inscription were matched by a Friday and Sunday during Pyatho and Tazaungmôn of his years 657 and 660. This implies that he had to have had in front of him a relevant Burmese calendar or had to have calculated the dates using known formulae, for it is not the kind of information that one carries in one's head. That Luce was familiar with the calendrical system and its implications is shown in volume III of his *Old Burma,* pages 327–337.[58] That means Luce must have been aware that Cunningham's years were virtually on the mark (and his own were not), for Cunningham's years would have shown up in his calculation process or in the tables he consulted. Of course it is also possible that Luce did not want to check Cunningham's dates. Therefore, despite chiding Burney, the Ava scholars, and Cunningham, it was Luce who was two centuries off in his reckoning. At least Cunningham, Burney, and the Ava scholars were intellectually honest and did not deliberately substitute bogus days to match those found on the inscription.

This calendrical evidence makes it fairly certain that all three missions occurred in the eleventh rather than the thirteenth century. That in turn means that the first mission which produced the copper-gilt umbrella dated to 1035 was indeed sent during King Kyi-zo's reign, while the missions of 1079 and 1086 occurred during King Saw Lu's and Kyanzittha's reigns respectively.

The evidence that these three missions occurred in the eleventh century needs no further corroboration, yet the case would certainly be enhanced if additional evidence was found, particularly if it was contemporary to the period of the missions. Fortunately—and this sort of corroboration rarely occurs—there are two inscriptions of the eleventh century that confirm one, and perhaps both missions, and in one case in terms of the exact date as well.

The first is an Old Burmese inscription, part of which dates to 1086 and part to 1105. It was erected by one "Matima Mahāthera" who, the context suggests, may have been the primate of at least two kings, Saw Lu and Kyanzittha, not entirely an uncommon practice in Burmese history.[59] He states explicitly that he went to worship at the Mahābodhi in *Sakarāj* 448

(1086 AD), the same date given by the Mahābodhi Inscription of the second mission, which also records that the *primate of the Burmese king* had come to Bodhgayā to oversee the Mahābodhi's restoration.[60]

But there might be a problem with the Mahāthera's statement, for it appears to suggest that his journey occurred around the time or shortly after King Aniruddha's successful campaign in Lower Burma, although Aniruddha's reign ended about a decade before 1086. At the same time, however, this discrepancy may be a misreading on our part, for there are four different readings of it.[61] In any case, the section regarding the date of the Mahāthera's trip to the Mahābodhi temple itself, 1086, is unambiguous, and it corresponds with Cunningham's reading of the second date on the Mahābodhi stone inscription.

The Mahāthera continues his narrative, stating that during Htilaing Shin's (Kyanzittha's) reign, in *Sakarāj* 467 (1105 AD), he donated some lands (in Burma).[62] As the 1105 portion of the stone follows the 1086 section rather smoothly, the Mahāthera may have inscribed the entire narrative in 1105 AD, and referred back to 1086, when he took the trip to Bodhgayā. But he could also have simply added the 1105 portion later to the original 1086 portion. Either way, it appears that the Mahāthera was a contemporary of Saw Lu and Kyanzittha, and perhaps even of Aniruddha.

Yet the Mahāthera's record—clearly a contemporary inscription and therefore the best evidence one is going to find to corroborate the Bodhgayā mission sent from the kingdom of Pagán—was relegated to the "B" section of the *She Haung* because, among other reasons, it contradicted the Mon Paradigm claim that the first evidence of written Old Burmese cannot precede the Myazedi Inscriptions.

The second source that corroborates the second mission is the Old Mon inscription of 1093 erected by King Kyanzittha at Prome. It states:

> Thereafter . . . the holy temple of Śrī Bajrās [the Mahābodhi] . . . (which had been) destroyed, . . . King [Kyanzittha] got (together) jewels of divers kinds (and) sent (them in) a ship with intent to build up the holy (temple) of Śrī Bajrās, to buy (land?) . . . (to dig a tank?) . . . to irrigate (?) arable land, to make dams, in order to burn tapers that should never be allowed to go out, to present drums, . . . xylophones, singing (and) dancing. . . . Thereafter, the great buildings which King Dharmāsok [Aśoka] built, which (were) old (and) in ruins, King [Kyanzittha] proceeded to build anew, (making them) finer than before. . . .[63]

We should note the emphasis on the funds that were acquired for the restoration of the Mahābodhi temple, for this is also recorded in the Mahābodhi Inscription as the expressed purpose of the second mission. In addition to the usual gold and silver offerings, the Mahābodhi Inscription notes the buying of land and cattle and the dedication of people to maintain the temple,[64] descriptions explicit or implied in the Prome Inscription.

The similarity of information in both the Mahābodhi and Prome inscriptions suggests that they were referring to the same mission. And since the Prome Inscription is dated to and erected in 1093 AD,[65] it is in a position to reaffirm both the first (1035) and second (1079 and 1086) Mahābodhi missions. Had the missions occurred in the thirteenth century, as Luce contended, how could this 1093 inscription know about them? All this, *prima facie,* verifies that the Old Burmese on the Mahābodhi preceded the first dated Old Mon inscription of Burma (1093) and that the missions took place in the eleventh and not the thirteenth century. Other missions were doubtless sent to Bodhgayā after the eleventh century; indeed, they remained a regular feature of the Burmese state well into the modern period. But as far as I know there are no thirteenth-century inscriptions in Burma that corroborate the information found on the Mahābodhi Inscription as explicitly as the two inscriptions just discussed do.

Luce's response to the above evidence (and he must have been thinking about it) was in the following manner. He rather arbitrarily divided the Old Prome Inscription of 1093 into two parts. The first part he acknowledged referred to a mission to Bodh Gaya, India, but does not offer any explanation for his own thirteenth-century readings of the Bodhgayā Inscriptions.[66] The second part, beginning with "Thereafter, the great buildings which King Dharmāsok built, which (were) old (and) in ruins, King [Kyanzittha] proceeded to build anew, (making them) finer than before, . . ." Luce argued, referred to "the cetī of Kyāk Talaṅ" and "the prāsāda of the great relic of *Satih,*" near Mt. Kelāsa north of Thatôn, . . ." *not* to Bodhgayā and the Mahābodhi temple.[67]

But nothing in the inscription even hints that the narrative of the mission had suddenly shifted from India to Lower Burma. The inscription states clearly that King Aśoka built these temples in India, not Burma, for which Luce had another answer, that this Dharmāsok was really an early Mon king of Thatôn, not Aśoka (thereby additionally "confirming" Thatôn's early existence).

The facts are that two independent sources, both contemporary to the events described in the Mahābodhi Inscription of Bodhgayā, not only corroborate precisely some of the narrative found in the Old Mon inscription of Prome, but confirm that the missions occurred in the eleventh century (and, therefore, that Old Burmese was being written at that time even in a foreign land). This is the kind of corroboration one can only pray for, particularly when dealing with stone epigraphs of a millennium ago. Yet their importance was ignored for a century and disingenuously deconstructed because it did not support a favorite thesis.

Of the Old Burmese inscriptions recovered in India, then, the 1035 copper-gilt umbrella inscription precedes the Myazedi Inscriptions by seventy-seven years and the alleged conquest of Thatôn by more than twenty-years. Indeed, it preceded King Aniruddha himself by about a decade. The first date on the second Mahābodhi Inscription (1079) demonstrates that written Old Burmese preceded the Myazedi Inscriptions by thirty-three years and the second date (1086) by twenty-six years. In short, the evidence shows that the first instance of written Old Burmese not only precedes that found on the Myazedi but also the first dated evidence of written Old Mon in Burma, effectively removing a major foundation stone of the Mon Paradigm.

Old Burmese in Votive Tablets

Original domestic lithic epigraphy *in situ* is perhaps the most informative and reliable in revealing the place of written Old Burmese in the history of Pagán and Burma. Such objects are heavy, cumbersome, essentially permanent legal records, not easily or meant to be moved. They inform us of provenance and most accurately represent the social and political context in which they are found.

In contrast, the votive tablet, which is easily carried in a bag, is not meant to be a fixed, dated, legal, or permanent record. It is therefore not as reliable in revealing either the context from which it was derived or its chronology, and its provenance is usually even more obscure. However, when the information on votive tablets reinforces that found on stone records, then their importance as a source appreciates. The evidence extracted from these votive tablets, therefore, should be seen as supplementary to the stone data, not the main source of information.

Hundreds ("thousands" according to Duroiselle) of votive tablets written in Old Burmese have been discovered.[68] Unfortunately, although none of these tablets is dated precisely, all Burma scholars knowledgeable about the subject attribute most of them to Aniruddha's reign—hence they are called "Aniruddha style votive tablets"—based mainly on paleography and style. If that stylistic and palaeographic assessment is correct, it once again places the writing on them to a period well before both the Myazedi Inscriptions and the first evidence of written Old Mon in Burma.

Of course, those subscribing to the Mon Paradigm could not allow this analytical concession, as we can see in this example from Ba Shin. He was studying the Lokahteikpan temple and attempting to date it by comparing ink inscriptions found on its walls with the script found on these votive tablets. He noticed that the ink inscriptions in Burmese were similar to the writing on the votive tablets, which he said represented some of the "oldest specimens of the Burmese written language extant. They record the names of trees, fruits, flowers, vegitables [sic], herbs, etc. offered to the Buddha."[69] But if we use Ba Shin's own chart and compare the written Burmese on the votive tablets and the ink inscriptions in the Lokahteikpan temple with the writing on the Myazedi Inscriptions and other Old Burmese samples from later periods, it is clear that the written Burmese on the votive tablets shows a remarkable *dissimilarity,* and far less congruence between it and all the rest, *including the writing found on the Lokahteikpan and the Myazedi.*[70]

For example, of the approximately thirty-eight words taken from the votive tablets, not a single one was similar to any word on the Myazedi in meaning or orthography. Comparing the words on the Lokahteikpan temple with those on the Myazedi produced only five words out of fifty-four that are similar in meaning and spelling. In other words, Ba Shin's own evidence does not support his contention that the Burmese on the temple or on the votive tablets was similar to that on the Myazedi.

Ordinarily that incongruity would have immediately suggested to someone not influenced by the Mon Paradigm that the writing on the votive tablets, as well as that in the Lokahteikpan, were possibly *older* than the writing on the Myazedi, particularly since most scholars familiar with the votive tablets place them in Aniruddha's reign, which preceded the Myazedi by over sixty-five years. But since Ba Shin, following Luce, had already stated that the Myazedi was the oldest dated Burmese inscription,[71] he was compelled to date the writing on the Lokahteikpan to a period close to the Myazedi;[72] indeed, he had to select a later date if he did not want to dislodge the entire Mon Paradigm. He therefore assigned the date of the temple itself, which does not have one, to a period after the Myazedi so that, in a circular fashion, the evidence in it of what he called "pre-Standard" Burmese automatically succeeded the earliest dated Mon inscription of 1093. And because, by association, he considered the Burmese writing on the votive tablets to be "pre-Standard" Burmese, the Burmese script on them was also placed later than the writing on the Myazedi.

Yet since his own comparative language chart showed a marked *dissimilarity* between the votive tablets and the writing on this temple with that on the Myazedi, he should have immediately noticed that something was amiss between his analysis and his evidence. But because Ba Shin was operating under the assumptions of the Mon Paradigm that the oldest written Burmese was represented by the Myazedi, the only conclusion he could have reasonably reached under the intellectual shackles he was in, was to date the Archaic Burmese in the Lokahteikpan and on the votive tablets to correspond with the Myazedi, rather than earlier, despite his data that showed otherwise. Had he not been under the theoretical constraints of the Mon Paradigm, I wonder where he would have placed the Burmese of the Lokahteikpan and the votive tablets? The latter never got a chance to be examined independently of the Mon Paradigm.[73]

"Aniruddha style" votive tablets were found all over the country, including at Pagán, Prome, Tagaung, Minbu, Sagaing, Arakan, Bassein, Thatôn, Tavoy, Pegu, Twanté (near Yangôn), and Mergui, on the tip of the Tenasserim Peninsular; in short, they cover the extent of the kingdom. Some even found their way to Bodhgayā and the Mahābodhi temple as we have seen.[74] Of the domestic votive tablets uncovered so far, approximately 108 were selected for their condition and typology, and described and analyzed by U Mya in 1961.[75] In 1969, in his *Old Burma-Early Pagán,* Luce also dealt with the subject, using a somewhat different typology.[76]

Many are recorded in Pali and Sanskrit, usually written in medieval *Nāgarī* and proto-Bengali script of the period between the ninth to the thirteenth centuries.[77] Most discovered so far, however, are written in "Archaic" Burmese, and a hoard of nearly a thousand was found at Pagán.[78] Of those that use the Mon *language* written in the then-current Pagán script,[79] we can count approximately thirty-one among the group chosen by Luce,[80] a far cry from the thousands found written in Old Burmese.

The function of votive tablets during Pagán times varied. They served as religious souvenirs for pilgrims visiting the capital, so that one scholar likened them to the postcards of today.[81] They also record donations made by commoners who could not afford to build expensive monuments such as *stupas* and monasteries. They were placed in edifices built by someone else at the time of consecration in order to accrue part of the merit that derived from the builder's donation. There must have also been other religious and secular functions of which we are not aware.

However, votive tablets made by or belonging to kings and officials of state, such as those issued and signed by Aniruddha himself, can be regarded as markers of a different sort. Since Aniruddha was not picking up souvenirs to show off to his friends that he had been to Pagán, his tablets were statements of his political influence and perhaps even control in the areas where they were found. Prince Saw Lu, probably Aniruddha's designated heir, was said to have issued at least one such votive tablet found at Mergui.[82] Two other "official" votive tablets, written in the Mon language, were also found near Tavoy. They belonged to two governors who had been appointed by King Kyanzittha to administer the province. Luce writes that the Mon on them is "of Kyanzittha's reign."[83]

On the one hand, then, we should not depend on votive tablets, particularly "commoner" ones, to give us precise, quantitative information regarding the ethnolinguistic makeup of the region in which they were found, simply from the languages found on them. To suggest that there may have been a sizeable population of those who spoke the same language as that found on the votive tablets could be just as misleading as to conclude, in today's world, that if one finds many Chicago Bulls T-shirts being worn in Bangkok, the *lingua franca* must have been English.

On the other hand, we *can* infer that the *proportion* of tablets containing a certain language, *when compared to the total number of tablets found,* provides a clue as to the relative size of the population that spoke that language vis-à-vis other languages. Because the Burmese language is represented by the largest number of records found during the Pagán Dynasty as a whole—well over 90 percent if one includes stone inscriptions—it is not unreasonable to assume that most of the population at the time the writing was produced and in the place where these records were found must have been Burmese speakers. This is especially true of the tablets inscribed by commoners, since royal languages can sometimes be minority languages, as is evident in Kyanzittha's case.

Perhaps more interesting, the large number of commoner votive tablets suggests that ordinary people, or those they paid to do so, were writing in Old Burmese as early as Aniruddha's reign, an unlikely situation had Aniruddha first obtained the script only in 1057. It further provides evidence regarding one of the known functions of the *saṅgha* throughout Burma's history, that is, the education of the general populace. That it performed a function during the Pagán period similar to what it has done in modern times is confirmed by other contemporary epigraphs.[84] Literacy among the general population is not something achieved in a few years, perhaps not even in a few decades, so that ordinary folk probably had knowledge of written Burmese well prior to 1057, conceivably well before Aniruddha's reign.[85]

In the final analysis, because the beginning of Aniruddha's reign precedes the beginning of Kyanzittha's by about forty years, the votive tablets made during Aniruddha's reign with Old Burmese written on them, even if undated and regardless of who wrote them, would still be earlier than the earliest Old Mon inscriptions of Burma first found during King Kyanzittha's reign, and would be over half a century earlier than the Myazedi Inscriptions. Not only do these votive tablets demonstrate that Old Burmese preceded Old Mon writing in Burma, but they also give additional credence to the presence of written Burmese on the original stones from which Bodawpaya had recast the twenty-four inscriptions discussed above, especially the one dated to 984 AD.

In summary, and contrary to the Mon Paradigm claim, written Old Burmese in lithic inscriptions and votive tablets was present in Pagán (and in India) well before the alleged conquest of Thatôn in 1057, before the first securely dated Old Mon inscription erected in Prome in 1093,[86] and before the Myazedi Inscriptions of Pagán in 1112–1113. It even precedes the Old Mon inscription of the Shwézigôn Pagoda Inscription, conjecturally assigned to 1086, a topic discussed in the following section.

The Place of Written Old Mon in Burma

As noted, the first dated Old Mon inscription to be erected in Burma was at Prome in 1093. The second oldest dated Old Mon inscription found so far appears five years later at Thatôn in the form of two, perhaps three duplicates, also products of King Kyanzittha. The rest of his Old Mon inscriptions are either undated or *assigned* dates by inference, not surprisingly, to fit the Myazedi declaration and therefore the Mon Paradigm. The most problematic among these is the Shwézigôn Pagoda Inscription, thought to be Kyanzittha's, and assigned by Luce to 1086 AD,[87] thus pushing the chronology of written Old Mon in Burma to over a decade before the securely dated 1093 Inscription.

There are serious problems with this conjecture. First, the inscription itself has only the following to say about its own date. Speaking in the Buddha's voice, it states: "A thousand six hundred (and) thirty years from my achievement of Nirvāṇa, at that time shall he [presumably Kyanzittha] become king of the Law in the city of Arimaddanpūr."[88] Nothing is said of when the Shwézigôn Pagoda itself was built or the date when the stone itself was erected, although the temple has generally been attributed to King Aniruddha much earlier. The inscription mentions only the year of King Kyanzittha's probable accession to the throne, which, if reckoned according to the Burmese tradition of the *parinibbānna* (544 BC), means this king named Śrī Tribhuvanāditya Dhammarāja shall be king of Pagán in 1086 AD. Only if one assumes that this accession occurred on the same date as the building of the Shwézigôn Pagoda—there is no such hint in the inscription itself—might 1086 AD be considered the date of the earliest Old Mon inscription in Burma.

Even granting that, written Old Burmese still precedes this inscription, for the original *Jātaka* plaques on the Shwéhsandaw temple, which belong to Aniruddha's reign, are written in Pagán Old Burmese,[89] and his reign precedes Kyanzittha's by approximately forty-two years. These plaques, then, are still earlier than the date given to the Shwézigôn Pagoda Inscription. Moreover, the *Jātaka* plaques found on the two Hpetleik temples (to be discussed in Chapter Nine), and written in Pali in the Pagán script, also date to before and during Aniruddha's reign.[90] In addition, four other dated Old Burmese inscriptions precede the date to which the Shwézigôn Pagoda Inscription has been assigned: one in 1058 (nearly thirty years earlier), one in 1081, two in 1082, and a fifth is contemporaneous with it, in 1086.[91]

Apart from these, the copper-gilt umbrella inscription of the Mahābodhi temple (1035) predates the Shwézigôn Pagoda Inscriptions by over three decades and precedes the first dated Old Mon inscription at the Prome Shwéhsandaw by fourteen years (and those of Thatôn in 1098 by nineteen years). The mission dated to 1079 on the second inscription of the Mahābodhi would fall ten years earlier than the conjectured date for the Shwézigôn, while the second mission (1086) would be contemporary with it.

And if the recast inscription dated to 984 is permitted as evidence—only for indicating the probable *presence* of its original and nothing more—it suggests that Old Burmese writing could have preceded both the Old Mon Shwézigôn Inscription assigned to 1086 and the securely dated Prome Inscription of 1093, the first by nearly a century and the second by more than a century. The 984 date also precedes Aniruddha himself, and his alleged conquest of Thatôn by seventy-three years.

After the Shwézigôn, Prome, and Thatôn Inscriptions, the Old Mon script appears on Kyanzittha's new palace inscription, assigned to 1102 AD, and the *Jātaka* plaques on the Ānanda temple, assigned to 1105. But once again, these are *given* dates designed to bolster the Mon Paradigm. In any case, they do not precede the Old Burmese inscriptions already discussed. Thereafter, Old Mon appears on the Myazedi Inscriptions of 1112–1113, by which time written Old Burmese had been around for decades, perhaps nearly a century. Finally, written Old Mon in the Pagán script can be found in numerous but undated ink inscriptions inside several temples, and appears at Haripuñjaya subsequently.

Not only does the earliest Old Mon writing in Burma *not* precede Old Burmese writing; it is also relatively late. This late appearance is supported by Mon scholar Gerard Diffloth who writes: "In the Mon heartland of Lower Burma, it is not until the XIth century, with one possible exception, that Old Mon inscriptions begin to appear. . . ."[92] And that one exception, Diffloth noted, is a tablet shown to him by Nai Pan Hla which was said to have been found at Winga in Lower Burma, a site *assumed* to have been pre-Pagán Mon. But the tablet is not dated; nor has it been shown to have been unearthed in a scientific excavation process that stratigraphically placed it in a pre-Pagán level. So its provenance and chronology are unclear and unknown. In fact, there is some question as to the date of Winga itself, since the most recent thermoluminescence analysis of two Winga shards date to the very late fifteenth and the seventeenth centuries, which were actually, not coincidentally, the glory days of the later Mon Kingdom of Pegu.

The lateness of Kyanzittha's Old Mon inscriptions, as compared to written Old Burmese, partly explains why Kyanzittha's inscriptions also show such high literary quality from the outset.[93] While there is no evidence that the Old Mon script of Pagán had gone through an earlier stage of development in Lower Burma, as one would expect if it had come from there, we can see such a sequence in Old Burmese.[94] By the time the Pagán script was used for writing the Old Mon language in Burma, the script was already a well-developed, polished eleventh-century product,[95] having gone through several centuries of evolution *in Old Burmese.*

To summarize, there are, in all, approximately thirty-six Old Burmese lithic inscriptions that precede the Myazedi Inscriptions, fifteen of which are original. About eleven are contemporary to the events they describe, while twenty-four are recasts. Of the total, approximately twenty-six Old Burmese inscriptions precede the first dated Old Mon inscription of Burma, twenty-seven if another erected on that same date is counted. Even if the twenty-four recast inscriptions of King Bodawpaya are inadmissible as evidence because they are not originals, only a *single* original contemporary inscription with a legible date is needed to prove that Old Burmese writing preceded both that found on the Myazedi and the earliest written Old Mon inscription in Burma. Among the corpus discussed, there are at least thirteen that meet the first requirement, and approximately six, the second. Written Old Mon, therefore, was preceded by written Old Burmese in the country, and moved from the Dry Zone, where the Pagán script originated, to Lower Burma and from there to Haripuñjaya in northern Thailand. It did not go the other way around as has been believed.

Conclusion

For over a century, written Old Mon was thought to have preceded written Old Burmese. That, in turn, has shaped the interpretation of Pagán (and Burma's) history in no small way. Yet, all analyses have been based on the same assumption with which the Mon Paradigm began: that for a millennium prior to the rise of Pagán there existed in Lower Burma a Mon civilization called Rāmaññadesa whose capital was Thatôn and whose culture (which included the Burma script) was transported to Pagán by the conquest of Aniruddha in 1057. This all-encompassing theme has been so thoroughly enmeshed in the historiography of early Burma that its extraction from the evidence has meant excising countless layers of historiography that most scholars have come to accept as history. It is my hope that my analysis and the evidence have put to rest a number of long-held beliefs.

First, the notion that the Old Burmese found on the Myazedi Inscriptions is the earliest example of written Burmese can no longer be sustained. Written Old Burmese is much older. Second, it has been demonstrated that written Old Burmese found in royal or elite stone inscriptions and commoner votive tablets also precedes the first dated evidence of written Old Mon in Burma by at least several decades, if not a century. Perhaps even more interesting, the widespread presence of commoner votive tablets written in Old Burmese probably shows that the vernacular was being written well before the first appearance of Kyanzittha's court Mon. This further augments the contention in Chapter Ten that Kyanzittha's reign was an anomaly, and not the starting point of a grand evolutionary scheme in which written Mon eventually begat written Burmese. It was the other way around: written Old Mon in Burma—the second phase of a process that actually began with written Old Burmese—was derived from the Old Burmese script, which in turn had been derived from the Pyū script. And finally, this evidence corresponds well with the best archaeological, epigraphic, and historical data and parallels the direction in which the earliest polities and urban civilization moved: from the agrarian interior to the commercial coasts.

9 The Mon Paradigm and the Evolution of the Pagán Temple

ONE OF THE most important assertions made by the Mon Paradigm, with a significant impact on the "knowledge" of the art and architecture of early Burma, concerned the evolution of the hollow Pagán temple called the *gu*,[1] a most ubiquitous style found there. Invariably the issue of the solid *stupa* or *cetiya* (*zedi* in Burmese) gets entangled in the analysis of the *gu*, but it will be part of the discussion only in so far as it is pertinent to the evolution of the *gu* and the Mon Paradigm interpretation of it. The critical question is one of origins and development: when, in what form, and from where did the Pagán *gu* emerge, and how did it develop? Is it, as the Paradigm claims, a Mon inspiration?

Although I would have preferred to leave this task to an art historian, because the hidden assumptions of the Mon Paradigm are not always apparent to art historical issues, the art historian therefore may not have had the occasion to seriously consider the implications of that thesis. I feel the Paradigm assumptions with regard to this field of study should be exposed first, after which art historians can reassess the established view independently of the Mon Paradigm, something that has been done only cautiously or not well at all.[2]

The overriding assumption, and hence the analytical framework, of the Mon Paradigm is the familiar one: that Mon Lower Burma civilized Burman Upper Burma. In terms of religious architecture this meant that the Pagán temple is said to have evolved first through a "Mon phase," then a "transitional phase," and finally, a "Burmese phase."[3] Not surprisingly the scheme resembles the Mon Paradigm's evolution of the writing system of Pagán, and like the other arguments, the development of temple style is used to support other Mon Paradigm claims.[4]

The Present State of the Subject

Whether one agrees with him or not, Luce's *Old Burma-Early Pagán* is the first important publication in English that attempted to provide a general theory regarding the evolution of the Pagán temple. As such, it is the starting point for any discussion of Pagán's "art historiography." It is also important for its factual data, which remain some of the most solid, detailed, and reliable, produced by one of the foremost scholars of Pagán. In recent years, however, a far more comprehensive, thorough, and neutral work on the architectural history of Pagán has appeared. This is Pierre Pichard's *Inventory of Monuments at Pagán,* published in seven volumes with an eighth that has just come out.[5] In cooperation with international and national organizations and individuals, Pichard has spent about a quarter of a century at Pagán on this work.

The *Inventory* focuses on the physical remains of largely religious buildings that were built on the approximately sixteen square miles of Pagán. The volumes are organized geographically, with every monument catalogued, numbered, measured, and provided with coordinates. Among other useful data, there are ground plans, cross sections, construction material, size, estimated date of construction, relevant and clear photographs, and a very helpful system of cross referencing throughout the corpus. It is, in my opinion, the most important compendium of architectural information on the archaeological site of Pagán published so far. The seven volumes I have seen include 2,064 monuments, more than three-quarters of which belong to the period between the eleventh and fourteenth centuries. Of these, approximately 810 are hollow temples or *gu*.[6]

Using more or less the same organizational scheme and covering part of the same ground as Pichard is the first volume of Myanmar Ministry of Culture's publication in Burmese called *Inventory of Ancient Monuments.*[7] This is a catalogue 150 buildings, based (as Pichard's complication is) on their geographic location (in this case around Nyaung-U), rather than on any predetermined, stylistic chronology. It includes the inventory number of each temple, ground plan, cross section, name of donor (when known), date or period to which each might belong (if known), basic measurements, and usually a color photograph of each edifice.

There were earlier works produced on Pagán,[8] most notably Henry Yule's,[9] which made important contributions to the study of its architecture, particularly some remarkable cross-sectional drawings of select Pagán temples. Yet such studies also imposed Eurocentric impressions consistent with the times, as we see here articulated by Mr. Oldham, a member of Yule's expedition.

> So strongly unlike all other Burman buildings, can these have owed their origin to the skill of a Western Christian or Missionary? . . . May not the true cross-like plan of the Ananda be thus symbolical, and may he not, in the long-trusting hope of a zealous worshipper of Christ, have looked forward to the time

> when this noble pile might be turned from the worship of an unknown god to the service of the Most High? I can't think any Burman ever designed or planned such buildings. . . .[10]

Of this Yule admitted, "such an impression, I know, was almost irresistible at times when on the spot. But, . . . I cannot think it [sic] probably founded in truth."[11]

In the early twentieth century, scholars like Taw Sein Ko and Duroiselle, both of whom worked for the Archaeological Survey, did much of the earliest spade work. They were followed by numerous scholars belonging to various disciplines, although none that I know of were art historians at the time. Art history was, at least in the field of Southeast Asia, a relatively new discipline. The late U Bo Kay, longtime resident and unassuming director of archaeology at Pagán, produced one of the first books in Burmese that systematically analyzed most of the important temples at Pagán, following a chronology based on early Burmese texts.[12] These were meticulous records of works of merit, mainly of royalty and the elite. And since building a religious edifice was probably the most important event in anyone's life in Burmese Buddhist society, these carefully preserved records are likely to be fairly reliable as sources. As director of archaeology, U Bo Kay had access to stone inscriptions as well, which he could use to cross check the texts. Unlike Luce, U Bo Kay avoided presenting any kind of broad conceptualization of temple styles or Pagán's art history. U Aung Kyaing, one of U Bo Kay's successors, who until recently held the same post of director of archaeology at Pagán, has been instrumental in maintaining the explosion of excavations and repairs and the building of a large, new museum.[13] His book, also in Burmese,[14] is even less concerned with the broader perspective of Pagán temple evolution and takes a much closer look at artistic details of select temples. It is rarely cited as a source in the works of current western art historians because few read Burmese well enough to make any credible assessment of it. Others, such as U Ba Shin, have focused on a single temple, while historian Than Tun has provided important insights into art history with his scholarship on epigraphy and history.

Among western aficionados of Pagán art, Paul Strachan's Kiscadale Press has provided valuable support for Pichard's *Inventory*. Although paying great deference to Luce, Strachan's own work has managed to wriggle free of the Mon Paradigm to a certain extent, even though it is still chained to it in many regards.[15] For the most part, however, his *Pagan* may be one of the first among western art books in English to criticize, albeit very gently and sparingly, some of the sacrosanctity of Luce's *Old Burma-Early Pagán*.[16] At the same time, Strachan's work is based less on rigorous scholarship than on personal experience and knowledge of popular culture, so his book is more a "coffee-table" treatment of the Pagán temples than a scholarly treatise. There are other art historians of Burma whom I have not discussed here, not because their works are unimportant, but mainly because they have focused on specialized subjects such as painting[17] or different regions of Burma, such as Arakan,[18] and do not directly address the issues being pursued here.[19]

It was Luce more than anyone else who formulated a thesis on the evolution of the Pagán temple, so it is his work that receives the closest scrutiny. This focus on Luce, as in the other chapters, is not meant to disparage him as a scholar of Pagán, but to reexamine the viability of *his ideas,* particularly his *interpretation* of the facts. For the most part, the facts themselves are not in dispute. But because Luce's "fingerprints" are all over Pagán studies, it is impossible not to mention his work every time an issue dealing with Pagán is raised.

Luce divided the evolution of the Pagán temple (both *zedi* and *gu*) into four periods or phases associated with the reigns of several notable kings. There was the pre-Aniruddha period, the reign of Aniruddha (1044–1077), the reigns of Saw Lu, Kyanzittha, and part of Alaungsithu's (1075–1105), and the "transitional period" (1113–1174). The first, he wrote, was a "period of widespread Paganism" and "peaceful co-existence between Buddhism and Vaishnavism . . . a common feature . . ." at Pagán. The second period, he claimed, saw the ascendancy of Buddhism, but in the absence of canonical texts (obtained only after the alleged conquest of Thatôn), it was "thinly spread" and therefore in balance between the Mahāyāna of East Bengal and Arakan and the Theravāda of Dvāravatī and Old Prome. Luce saw strong Pyū influence in architecture but "after the capture of Thatôn, Mon beauty of colour, ornament and design combines with Pāla Bengal strength to produce the typical art-forms of Early Pagán." The third period, he argued, followed the arrival of the full *Tipiṭakas* from Śrī Laṅka around 1075. It was characterized by the expansion of Theravāda Buddhism and the "splendid series . . . of 'Mon' temples. . . . The first masterpiece is Păhtothămyā, the climax Nanda temple. . . ." The last phase "witnessed the gradual passage from Old Mon dominance to Old Burmese. The first flowering is at Shwégugyi, . . . the first masterpiece Thatbyinnyu temple. . . ."[20] Because his *Old Burma-Early Pagán* does not go beyond 1165 and the alleged "capture of Pagán by Parākramabāhu's armada"—a thesis already demonstrated to be entirely without merit[21]—the work ends in the mid-twelfth century. Thus although the period to which he technically confines his evolutionary scheme begins with the "pre-Aniruddha period" and ends with King Kalagya, its implications go well beyond that date and also beyond mere chronology.

A second idea that shaped Luce's perspective on the evolution of the

Pagán temple was his belief that the hollow temple evolved from the solid *stupa*.[22] As he envisioned it, the temple began with the *stupa*, which was "essentially circular. . . . The big change comes with the squaring of the circle: not by tampering with its shape, but by building it up from below, placing the square under it, usually with an octagon in between. The lotus mat on which the *cetiya* rests . . . remains circular and topmost; but as the squareness below grows larger, the circle above gets less [sic]. The square terrace invited decoration: in Aniruddha's pagodas, usually *Jātaka* plaques, lining the plinth in pockets, . . . but 550 pockets were too many for the single terrace, and the unglazed plaques needed protection: so he added a low vaulted corridor, where the whole series could be fitted on both sides. . . ."[23] The vaulted corridors then became the roofs, so that interior space was created. And thus we have the evolution of the hollow Pagán temple directly from the solid *stupa*, a thesis that is highly problematic.

The third and last factor that Luce believed shaped the evolution of the Pagán temple, particularly in terms of a specific style, had to do with the temperament of certain ethnic groups. As he put it, "the Mon, like the Indian, is more of an Introvert";[24] that "taste for dim religious light . . . owed more, I suspect, to the romantic and poetic temperament of Old Mons, . . . [whereas] the Old Burman, a more earthy and prosaic person, as soon as he began to control the building, cleared the perforated windows, drove out the bats, opened large doorways on each face, and placed the main Shrine high above him on a platform. . . ."[25]

Luce elaborated by explaining what he meant by a Mon as opposed to a Burman temple. A Mon temple was "normally one storey, and in plan apparently asymmetric. It consists . . . of a square main block, the temple proper, containing a central Shrine or recess for images; a half-arched corridor (or corridors) surrounding it; and a vaulted Hall (with the only means of entrance) on one side. The main block is always dark, for the windows . . . are of perforated stone or brick. Even the Corridor is dim; and the Shrine containing the colossal image would often be pitch-dark, if it were not for . . . skylights casting mysterious rays on the face of the Buddha. Such temples, if not ruined, have nearly always Old Mon writing, never Old Burmese."[26] As we shall see, this elaboration was a self-fulfilling attempt that, wittingly or not, nevertheless reinforced the Mon Paradigm.

Problems of Analysis

Luce's four-phase evolutionary scheme poses some problems. Using the reigns of kings to organize historical periods in art implies that the pace and path of temple evolution is the same as that for political history, and the criterion and factors responsible for the evolution of temple style in Pagán is closely related to the personal reigns of kings and their particular historical circumstances. Yet the evidence shows that the stylistic development of the Pagán temple followed its own tempo and course, determined more by its own criteria—such as architectural and engineering concerns, the wealth accumulated by individuals and the state, occasionally personal preferences, and sometimes by the introduction of new or different religious ideas—than by political succession.

Luce's methodology also implies that the development of temple type was more an issue of time, for he adopted a standard western linear approach in which a direct cause-and-effect relationship existed between the passage of time, change, and progress,[27] thereby linking time with type as an irrevocable part of temple development.

Yet there was astounding continuity of the most dominant styles (or types), which suggests that "change" and "progress" in temple architecture were not inevitable consequences of the mere passage of time, even long periods of it. Rather, the evolutionary process not only at Pagán but in Burma in general is best represented by what the late Stephen J. Gould called in paleontological theory "punctuated equilibrium," where long periods of equilibrium—such as, in our case, the Pyū millennium—are punctuated by short periods of dramatic change—such as twelfth- and early thirteenth-century Pagán.

Indeed, the most dominant styles continued unchanged fundamentally; many temples built in the thirteenth century[28] retained all or most of their basic "prototype" forms without necessarily producing new "species." The Pagán temple did not evolve along an inevitable linear path from A to B, from prototype to its assumed offspring. Instead, many late temples remained very much like their earliest prototypes, retaining their original shapes, sizes, and designs, a pattern we shall examine in detail below.

Another problem with Luce's analysis is that he selected only 55 temples out of the 2,170 known at the time to represent his four-phase evolutionary scheme.[29] Of those 55, only 8 are securely dated by their own inscriptions, and 4 of them Luce rejected because they did not fit his criteria.[30] That means only 4 temples out of his chosen 55 (about 7 percent) have confirmed, epigraphic dates. Indeed, the original, epigraphic records of nearly 97 percent of the temples thought to be built during the Pagán period are missing,[31] so that their chronology is open to debate.

The reader may be surprised to learn, for example, that neither the famous Ānanda Temple attributed to King Kyanzittha nor the Shwéhsandaw attributed to Aniruddha has an original inscription that identifies the donor and date of construction; nor, for that matter, does the Shwézigôn, which is attributed to both. That attribution, though long thought to be true (and very possibly true), is nevertheless conjecture. Even the Thatbyinnyu, which has an *in situ* Pali inscription, does not explicitly say that it was

Alaungsithu who built it, even though it has long been attributed to him. In some cases a reasonable argument can be made that a certain temple belongs to a particular king's reign, usually because of identifiable votive tablets found inside or similar data, but even then the identity of the actual donor would still be uncertain.

Thus most of our current knowledge regarding donors and dates of Pagán temples is only accepted convention based on later texts and lists. But without these, there would hardly be a chronology of Pagán temples today, much like Burmese history itself.[32] These records include poems that celebrate the building of a temple, donative records kept on palm leaf, *thamaing* (histories) of specific temples, royal chronicles, and the stone and ink inscriptions found in the temples themselves.

Even if all the fifty-five temples selected by Luce were securely dated, the sample is too small to represent an evolutionary scheme for the entire Pagán period which stretched over several centuries and may have once included over 3,000 edifices.[33] It is true that Luce ended his study at 1165 AD, but he did so because from then on he considered most, if not all, temples to be "Burman" in style. In effect, he was dealing with the entire Pagán period.

In the absence of original epigraphy to confirm the chronology of temples, especially Luce's selected fifty-five, perhaps he should have taken a detailed look at style, other written texts that provide dates, construction methods, materials used, and, if financially feasible, scientific testing as a way of estimating the period to which the temples may have "belonged." Instead, Luce's selection was predetermined by the Aniruddha conquest story and his alleged acquisition of Theravāda Buddhist texts from Thatôn and Śrī Laṅka. Luce's choice, ultimately, was made under the assumption that an earlier Mon civilization existed in Lower Burma that had provided the necessary artistic and architectural models.

Let me cite just two specific examples. The dating of the Păhtothămyā temple[34] was determined by the historicity of the conquest of Thatôn story. This disallowed its being any earlier than Aniruddha's reign because the paintings found in the temple were said to have been based on texts belonging to the Sinhalese *Tipiṭakas,* and the Mon Paradigm could not concede that these texts existed in Pagán *before* Aniruddha's alleged raid of Thatôn.[35] And with no conquest of Thatôn, the mechanism for the importation of Śrī Laṅkan Buddhism to Pagán would have also been removed, thereby contradicting virtually every interpretation of Pagán's history, art history, and culture. Indeed, an entire generation of scholarship would have had to be reworked. However, if the temple were dated *later* than Aniruddha's reign —which is what Luce did[36]—then the Mon Paradigm would be upheld once more, and even "reconfirmed."

The other temple is the Lokahteikpan. U Ba Shin, whose contribution to the study of Pagán, particularly his seminal work on this temple is well recognized, and which Luce endorsed,[37] wrote that "no written evidence, inscriptional or otherwise, regarding its donor or its date has yet been discovered. . . ." The style of the Lokahteikpan, he continued, "differs from that of the typical 'Old Mon' type of temple, nor is it like that of the . . . Burmese type of temple."[38] The only indigenous alternative left, at least the most logical one to me, is that this was an earlier, Pyū-style temple. Indeed, Ba Shin himself admits that such "cave-temples" as the Lokahteikpan were first built by the Pyū, using the Léymyethna and the Bèbè of Śrī Kṣetra as models. "These two types of vaulted chapel[s] of the Pyūs," he wrote, "are probably the predecessors of the early *gus* or temples of Pagán."[39]

Why, then, not take the next logical step and suggest that the Lokahteikpan and other similar temples, being closer to Pyū-period styles, must be *earlier* rather than *later*, especially since Ba Shin and other Pagán scholars knew (or at least believed) that the Burmans were the immediate successors of the Pyū? But that could not be, for inside the temple were archaic Burmese ink inscriptions, and if dated to a period earlier than King Kyanzittha's reign, when the first evidence of Old Mon appears, that would have placed the temple, and the Burmese writing system, earlier than the Mon writing system, which the Paradigm could not allow. The sacrosanct belief that things perceived to be Burman must be later than things perceived to be Mon, even when the evidence points in the opposite direction, would not allow such an option.

Ba Shin went on to say that "the Old Burmese writing of this temple is archaic—and its juxtaposition with Old Mon shows that the temple is clearly of the "transitional period," comparable in date with the so called 'Myazedi' inscription, which, with the Kubyaukgyi Temple of Myinkaba village . . . dates from the very beginning of Alaungsithu's reign, say 1113 A.D."[40] Dating this temple according to a predetermined chronology—in which Old Mon predates Archaic Burmese, in which a "transitional period" bridges the "Mon" and "Burmese periods," and in which the Myazedi Inscriptions are used to establish the earliest date for written Burmese rather than the established stylistic methodologies of art historians—is yet another exercise in circular reasoning.[41] Ba Shin conveniently placed the Lokahteikpan temple in the early twelfth century by declaring that the Archaic Burmese in it was later than Kyanzittha's Mon inscriptions. All of this corroborated the erroneous linguistic and historical arguments of the Mon Paradigm, rather than providing a reliable art historical basis for dating the Lokahteikpan.

The second criterion Luce used to delineate the evolution of the Pagán temple—that the hollow temple evolved from the solid *stupa*—is very puzzling. Even undergraduate students of Asian art history would know better. Both the *stupa* and temple existed independently of each other in India as well as in Burma, at Pagán as well as at Śrī Kṣetra. They are a parallel, not a sequential development. A cursory glance at any art history text on the development of the *stupa* and temple in India would have dispelled this notion that temples evolved from *stupa*s.[42]

However, if by his statement Luce meant that *at Pagán* components of the temple and *stupa* were combined, then that poses no problems. Many of the temples in Pagán were, in fact, a synthesis of temple and *stupa* elements, where a miniaturized version of the bell-shaped *stupa* (or a variation of it, such as the *śikhara*) adorned the hollow temple underneath. It is true that art historians of Pagán such as Strachan might appear to agree with Luce's thesis,[43] but probably only in so far as the combination of elements in specific temples such as the East and West Hpetleik or Myinpyagu are concerned. Surely Strachan would not agree with the notion of a general evolution from the solid *stupa* to the hollow *gu*. These are clearly two different issues and historical processes.

Luce himself admitted that the "vaulted chapels of Śrī Kṣetra . . . are clear prototypes of Pagán architecture: the Bèbè . . . the Lémyet-hna . . . [and] the East Zegu, . . ."[44] while in the case of the *stupa,* he wrote that "it is as if the Burmans saw and copied a Pyū ruin."[45] This is, in fact, a recognition of parallel development of *gu* and *stupa,* so that Luce has contradictory theses being presented simultaneously, something that I cannot clarify for him. Figure 5 shows how the *stupa* evolved in Burma from the basic bulbous styles of the Pyū in the seventh and eighth centuries to those of tenth-century Pagán. From there (see Figure 6), it became a more distinctive form, with multiple plinths, during the Pagan period, until it arrived at today's highly elongated *anda* (literally "egg") as can be seen in the Shwédagôn at Yangôn. No *stupa* "became" a hollow temple.

The third and most serious problem in Luce's schema is the causal relationship he asserts between ethnicity and temple style, and style and chronology.[46] By interjecting a category of style called "Mon temples," he introduces the totally unprovable, even if relevant, factor of ethnicity into a historical analysis of art. He ascribed the genesis of this "Mon style" temple to the supposed arrival of the "full *Tipiṭakas*" from Śrī Laṅka and the resulting "expansion of Theravāda Buddhism." This, he claimed, inspired the crafting of the "full" 550 *Jātaka* plaques that were then placed on the sides of the plinths of two *stupa*s, the East and West Hpetleik, which he assigned to Aniruddha's reign.[47] For the protection of these plaques, he noted, roofs in the form of vaults were created, thereby producing hollow *gus*. Luce's evolution of the *gu* from the *stupa* was now completely entangled with the creation of a vague new category called the "Mon temple."

FIGURE 5: Evolution of the Burma *stupa:* Śrī Kṣetra to Pagán. *Top left:* Bawbawgyi, seventh century, Śrī Kṣetra; *Top right:* Payamā, seventh century, Śrī Kṣetra; *Middle left:* Būpayā, pre-eleventh century (?), Pagán; *Middle right:* Ngakywènadaung, pre-eleventh century (?), Pagán; *Bottom:* Lokananda, pre-eleventh century (?), Pagán

Again, this approach did not examine the evolution of temple style in terms of art history, but according to factors relating to the Mon Paradigm views on the historicity of particular cultures, events, and kings.

Luce then went a step farther. As already noted above, he defined the structure of a Mon-style temple as being one-storied, asymmetrical, with a main square block and central shrine or recess for images, a half-arched corridor (or corridors) surrounding it, a dark vaulted hall with perforated windows, and the presence of Mon writing. But the design he describes in fact delineates one of two actual (Śrī Kṣetra) *prototypes,* the basic structure from which most hollow temples of Pagán are, in fact, derived. By *labeling the prototype* of the most prevalent style of *gu* at Pagán "Mon," of course "Mon temples" will precede everything else! And since his evolutionary scheme had predetermined that Mon temples preceded Burman ones, Burman temples would now also come after Mon temples.

Then in direct contradiction to his own criterion of Mon temples being asymmetrical, the exemplary model he provided for his Mon-style temple was the Ānanda,[48] which is celebrated for its *perfect symmetry, not asymmetry.* He went on to explain that the essential reason he designated these prototype temples "Mon" was the presence in them of written Mon, usually in the form of ink inscriptions. Yet many of these Mon inscriptions, such as those in the Lokahteikpan, are much later additions, some as late as the seventeenth century, and therefore have nothing to do with the particular style of temple or its process of evolution, especially in the Pagán period, even if the ethnic argument were valid. Besides, there were many temples built in Pagán with the same or similar style that had no writing in them; what do we call these? In short, the reasons Luce gave for identifying these kinds of temples as "Mon" are spurious, selective, and contradictory.

After creating this elaborate if not confusing scheme, Luce finally added a disclaimer; saying that his use of the word "Mon" to describe these prototype temples was merely a matter of convenience.[49] But that convenient label had the effect of creating an inevitable link between ethnicity and style in the evolution of the Pagán temple that helped perpetuate the Mon Paradigm in the analysis of Pagán architecture for decades more to come.

The terms "Gothic" and "Baroque" serve as useful categories to identify certain European art styles, irrespective of the languages found within their contexts, the presence of such styles during the reigns of particular kings, or the ethnolinguistic group that created the artifacts. Italians as well as French and English, individuals as well as the state, could produce and recognize either style even if they changed them subtly. Why was it not possible to utilize a stylistic category derived from indigenous Burmese art vocabulary, rather than selecting an ethnic designation that did nothing to clarify or identify the artistic style one was attempting to describe? The rea-

FIGURE 6: Evolution of the Burma *stupa:* Pagán to Yangôn.

Top left: Shwéhsandaw, eleventh century; *Top right:* Shwézigôn, eleventh century; *Bottom:* Dhammayazika, twelfth century.

Opposite page, Top: Mingalazedi, thirteenth century; *Middle left:* Htupayôn, mid-fifteenth century, Sagaing; *Bottom left:* Shwémawdaw, fifteenth century, Pegu; *Right:* Shwédagôn, fifteenth century, Yangôn

son, I am convinced, was an overall desire to enhance the causal role of Mon civilization in the making of Pagán, the heart of the Mon Paradigm. In terms of temple architecture, this translated into using the ethnic term *mon* to represent a style that turns out to be, conveniently, the basic Pyū prototype.

Most unprovable of the criteria Luce used is the attribution of general human personality characteristics, such as introspection and prosaicness, to a particular ethnic group *because* of its ethnicity. Even more untenable is to then use such personality traits as a causal factor in the development of a particular temple style, so that Mons who were supposedly introspective were said to have built edifices that are dark and confining, while Burmans who were characterized as prosaic built ones that were "light and airy."[50] Automatically, then, dark and confining temples such as the Ānanda, said by the chronicles to have been built by King Kyanzittha, were defined as Mon (even though it was perfectly symmetrical). And temples such as the light and airy Thatbyinnyu were considered representative of Burman style, even though the temple was said to have been built by King Alaungsithu, Kyanzittha's own grandson, and has an *in situ* Pali inscription, which according to Luce's own criteria should be classified as North Indian. And what ethnic designation should be given to the Shwézigôn and Mingalazedi? They are neither gloomy nor airy, since they are solid *stupa*s with no interior space. Does that imply that neither Mon nor Burman built them? What happens if Tamil, Telegu, or Bengali craftsmen, confessed introverts as well as extraverts, built a temple in Pagán following a current and fashionable design? What ethnic designation would that temple have, and where in the four-phase evolutionary pattern would it fit stylistically?

And even if such essentialization of ethnicity, used as a causal factor in the development of style were accepted as a legitimate basis for argument, it still cannot explain the building of "gloomy" temples, such as the mid-twelfth-century Dhammayangyi or the thirteenth-century Payathonzu and Nandamanya, along with many others like them, throughout the so-called "transitional (i.e. Burman) period" and later, when they were supposed to have been "light and airy." And what about temples like the so-called Manuha, attributed to the eleventh century and an alleged Mon king, which is not all that "gloomy" nor early?[51]

Because a contrived relationship had been created between ethnicity and style and style and chronology, the Mon Paradigm was also compelled to attribute certain styles to certain prescribed "ethnic periods," even when many temples built at any one time were quite different stylistically and structurally, or, conversely, many were rather similar but built centuries apart.[52] The possibility that different donors might have expressed personal preferences in selecting styles, or that building hollow temples with interior space was far more complicated, and therefore more expensive, than building solid *stupas*, or that a temple's size was directly related to socioeconomic and political stature (not to mention engineering principles) were issues never considered seriously. Social, economic, and political factors, even personal tastes were ruled out, and ethnicity became the most important criterion for determining the categorization and evolution of temple styles at Pagán. But that proclivity to reify ethnicity was a marked feature of the colonial, not the Pagán period.

This twentieth-century projection backwards of what were alleged to have been Mon and Burman temperaments assumed to have been derived from ethnicity, probably stemmed from the sentiments of the age as well as Luce's own personal experiences with both ethnic groups (he was married to a Mon lady and his brother-in-law was the noted scholar of Pali and Burmese literature, Pe Maung Tin). It is perhaps the most problematic, even if one attributes it, charitably, to poetic license.

Apart from such mentalities of the age or personal experiences which affected his interpretation, Luce—and others who followed in his footsteps—were also self-taught art historians. They may not even have been aware of the conceptual issues and problems that were being discussed in the theoretical literature of the discipline that helps inform one in the analysis of data. A similar problem existed in the broader field of Burma Studies, which was also, by and large, unaccountable to scholars outside it. While foreign scholars may have ignored or been unaware of works published in Burmese such as U Bo Kay's, at the same time Burmese scholars did not seriously consider, if they were even aware of, progress being made in the relatively young discipline of art history outside Burma.

Problems of Evidence

Issues of evidence are, of course, closely intertwined with problems of analysis, and given that the primary weakness of the Mon Paradigm analysis of Pagán temple evolution rests with its treatment of evidence, it seems desirable to address that issue also.

Thatôn as Prototype?

The Mon Paradigm asserted that an earlier Mon civilization in Lower Burma brought about the later development of Pagán's architecture, despite the fact that, as an eminent archaeologist noted with some surprise, ". . . at Thatôn, not a single example of early temple architecture [of Burma] is to be found. . . ."[53] The belief regarding the antiquity of a Mon civilization in Lower Burma was so ingrained in the Mon Paradigm that the absence of evidence supporting that belief was more a cause for surprise than for questioning the assumption.

Another example of "evidence" used by the Mon Paradigm to demonstrate early Mon influence in Pagán art are the *Jātaka* plaques on many *stupas* and temples, sometimes appearing as glazed terracotta reliefs outside these buildings. Luce answers his own question regarding the source for the *Jātaka* plaques on the Hpetleik pagodas by attributing them to Aniruddha, saying: "It is seen in embryo in the Shwéhsandaw plaques at Pagán Museum . . . and is generally supposed (I think rightly) to have come with coastal Mon artists, after the capture of Thatôn."[54] Yet the most important part of that assertion—the evidence for it in coastal Thatôn itself at the time—was not provided.

As a result of Luce's assertions, however, the few remaining terracotta plaques illustrating *Jātaka* stories that line the Myatheindan Pagoda located outside the city walls of Thatôn were conveniently "assigned to the 11th and 12th centuries."[55] Why the eleventh and twelfth centuries? No explanation was given, except that the author apparently shared the Mon Paradigm view of Thatôn's earlier existence and the historicity of the Aniruddha conquest, so these plaques must have been earlier[56] and must have been the source for Pagán's *Jātaka* plaques. But in fact, neither the Thagya-paya nor the Shwézayan Pagodas at present-day Thatôn, on which a few plaques of these kinds appear, have been dated. The plaques could just as easily (and more likely) have come from Pagán. Similarly, although the terracotta panels found at the village of Kyôntu, near Pegu, are, according to another art historian, "reminiscent of the terra cottas and the bronze dancing figures at Srisketra," they are nevertheless given a Mon provenance and placed in the subsection of his work entitled "The Mons of Suvannabhumi."[57]

If one removes the assumptions about an earlier Thatôn—as has been shown again and again in this book—the entire Mon Paradigm falls apart. In India the *Jātaka* stories appear on stone relatively early (second century BC onwards), so that there is no reason why this artistic influence, like many other cultural items, could not have also come directly from India, or through a local intermediary like the Pyū, well before the first proven Burman-Mon contact in the late eleventh century.

The green glaze on many *Jātaka* plaques could easily have been another Pyū contribution, for the walls of one of its major cities were said by a ninth-century Chinese source to have used "green bricks."[58] In addition, one of the earliest bulbous *stupas* of Pagán, the Ngakywènadaung, was once covered with green glaze, parts of it still visible today.[59] (See Figure 5.) Although green glaze and *Jātaka* plaques are not necessarily connected, the plaques are most often found with green glaze on them, and both usages precede the first appearance of the Mon in Upper Burma.

As other examples, when seven undated Old Mon inscriptions were found within the Shwézayan Pagoda at Thatôn, five were summarily attributed to the eleventh century (the catch-all period), one to the "medieval period," while the last is illegible. A standing Buddha was also found which, unsurprisingly, was labeled a "prototype" of those in the Ānanda temple and conveniently dated to the tenth and eleventh centuries to precede them,[60] while Brahmanic and Indic sculptures found at Thatôn were not only provided a similar antiquity but also a Mon provenance.

With no solid evidence, only vague, incontestable, and also unprovable, statements remain to demonstrate Mon influence in Pagán art. To reiterate, Luce wrote that ". . . after the capture of Thatôn, Mon beauty of colour, ornament and design combines with Pāla Bengal strength to produce the typical art-forms of Early Pagán."[61] The statement implies that no "beauty of color" or "strength" (of what, we are not told), existed in Pagán art prior to the alleged conquest. That Mon "beauty of colour" and Bengali "strength" were ethnic traits, is, of course, impossible to affirm or deny, but became, nevertheless, part of the corpus of "evidence" for the Mon Paradigm.

It mattered little that no art and architectural remains even close to those left at Pagán in proven antiquity, quantity, and quality have been found at Thatôn. Even if the site is accepted as the Thatôn of legend and history for the sake of argument, it is barely 1,500 yards square, with at most three major *stupa*s and about seven undated Old and Middle Mon inscriptions.[62] This minuscule site was made to preempt Pagán, with its 2,800 monuments and nearly 1,200 surviving and mostly dated inscriptions, all produced several hundred years before Thatôn's first appearance in original epigraphy. And this is not to mention recent radiocarbon dates that show urban settlement at Pagán as early as the seventh century and the building of its palace by the tenth. Simply because Thatôn was assumed to have preceded Pagán, all remains of art and architecture found there and in Lower Burma in general were automatically considered to have been earlier, and made part of a scenario in which Pagán must have borrowed from Thatôn. The art of early Burma has not been analyzed independently of the Mon Paradigm, and it desperately needs to be.

The True Arch and the Mon

One of the most important and distinctive engineering features found in virtually all hollow temples of Pagán—the confident and ubiquitous use of the vault, which expressed knowledge of the true arch principle—points neither to Thatôn nor to the Mon in Burma or anywhere else.[63] The architects of Pagán used the cloistered vault, the barrel vault, the cupola, the 3/4 barrel, the 1/2 barrel, and the diaphragm vault.[64] (See Figure 7 for a good representative of this arching principle.) And whereas its use was dominant and pervasive at Pagán, it is not found at all in Thatôn or anywhere else in

Lower Burma,[65] or, for that matter, at Dvāravatī or any other Mon site in Southeast Asia.[66]

Leaving aside the controversial issue regarding the origins of the Pagán arch,[67] its absence in Lower Burma was attributed to the weather. As Luce put it: ". . . in view of the difference in yearly rainfall between Prome [this is equally applicable to Pagán as both lie in the Dry Zone] and the coast . . . may it not be an accident that vaulted temples survive at Prome [and Pagán] and not at Thatôn?"[68] In addition to explaining from the absence rather than the presence of evidence, Luce added that the Mon also rather "distrusted" the arch.[69] No reason, certainly no evidence, was given for this alleged distrust. It was clearly an attempt to explain why no evidence of the arch existed among the Mon.

Besides, Luce's argument would imply that all 1,501 religious edifices built at Pagán that used the vault were *not* built by the Mon, since, after all, they distrusted it, including what Luce considered the quintessential Mon temple, the Ānanda. He had contradicted virtually everything he had said previously with that assertion. The statement was also disingenuous, for by saying that the Mon distrusted the arch, he implied that they actually knew the engineering principle but consciously chose not to use it, as if that somehow ameliorated the absence of the true arch among the Mon.

In fact, having knowledge of this engineering principle is very important, for its use directly affects the style of the *gu:* its shape, size, interior

FIGURE 7: Pagán Arches

space, thickness of walls, weight of roofs, size of superstructures, number of windows, and the number of storeys. It is directly related to the structure of the hollow temple and is an indispensable component of its design, whether symmetrical or asymmetrical, dark or airy, with Mon, Burmese, or no writing in it, so that one could say with aplomb that without the knowledge and use of this principle, the styles of the hollow temples of Pagán would not have been what they were. And since there is no evidence of this engineering technique or the style of *gu* it invariably produced at any Mon site in Southeast Asia—Dvāravatī, Haripuñjaya, or Lower Burma—how can so structurally vital an engineering principle used in so prominent and ubiquitous a style at Pagán, be attributed to the Mon?

Although it has not been unequivocally established that the vaults in the seventh or eighth-century Bèbè, Lémyethna, and East Zegu of Śrī Kṣetra were original to the construction and not the result of later repairs by Pagán architects,[70] the point is that the principle of the true arch and its use in a variety of vaulting techniques during the Pagán period and earlier are found exclusively in Upper Burma. And if the traditional dating of the Păhtothămyā to the tenth century, and the Lokahteikpan to a time before the Myazedi Inscriptions are accepted as valid, then developed vaulting existed, at least at Pagán, well before evidence of first Burman-Mon contact and the documented presence of the Mon in Upper Burma by 1102.

The Vocabulary of Architecture and the Mon

Other details important to the vocabulary of temple construction are also pre- or non-Mon (or put in a nonethnic way, pre or non-Rāmaññadesa). Inside some of these smaller temples, for example, can be found paintings the themes of which are taken mainly from Indic cosmology. Many depict *Jātaka* stories along with well-known figures found in Brahmanic and Buddhist literature. The 108 auspicious signs on the sacred footprints of the Buddha are represented often. The many (particularly the 28) Buddhas of the previous dispensations are regularly painted on the walls, with the historical Buddha, Gotama, most prevalent. Buddhist texts, such as the rules contained in the *Vinaya* are also represented in graphic form. It is apparent that the *Dīpavaṃsa* or the *Mahāvaṃsa* were already known by the time of the Myinkaba Kubyaukgyi temple, the date of which is not certain, but in which can be found representations of certain important topics contained in those chronicles: the three Buddhist councils, the life of Aśoka, the coming of the religion to Śrī Laṅka, and even King Vijayabāhu, who in the myth and legend of Burma was an ally and friend of Aniruddha.[71] At Pagán, then, although the precise date of arrival is unknown, these Śrī Laṅkan texts were probably already known and likely preceded the first original references in Lower Burma by nearly five hundred years, for there they are found first in Dhammazedi's Kalyani Inscriptions of the late fifteenth century.

The word for hollow temples in Old Burmese is written as *ku* (pronounced *gu*), apparently taken from the Sanskrit *guhā* ("cave") which both the Pyū (as *go*) and Mon (as *guoh*) were said to have adopted as well.[72] The term *(put'uiw, păhto)* is also said to be Old Burmese and is used for the smaller hollow temples; the term is not, apparently, found in Old Mon.[73] The word is said to have come from the Pali *vatthu* (ground, site).[74] And as the *gu* or *put'uiw* was built at Śrī Kṣetra centuries before the first evidence of its presence at Pagán, and since it was found at Śrī Kṣetra well before the first documented appearance of the Lower Burma Mon there, it is likely that both the word and what it represents came via the Pyū. Here again, Luce admitted that "the large Pagán *ku,* 'temple,' evolved naturally from the vaulted chapels of Śrī Kṣetra."[75]

The word for the metal finial is *at'wat* (crown) a Tibeto-Burman term,[76] not an Austro-Asiatic one, the language family to which Mon belongs. The Burmese *hti* (Old Burmese *t'ī*), now used generally for the metal finial, apparently comes from the Sanskrit *(yaṣṭi,* Pali *yaṭṭhi),* and was once a reference to the "umbrella pole" that held the *at'wat.* The *aṇḍa,* the "egg" which forms the bulbous cylinder of the *stupa,* goes back to at least the Sanchi dome in India. It was lengthened by the Pyū of Śrī Kṣetra in the Payagyi, Payamā, and Bawbawgyi *stupa*s. As for the Pagán *aṇḍa,* one of the earliest is represented by the Būpaya, which, according to Luce, may "even go back to pre-Burmese times."[77] (See Figure 5.)

Many other words dealing with religious and related buildings owe nothing to the Mon language. One style of temple, called *umaṅ,* comes from the Pali for "cave" *(ummaṅgga),* and is most notably represented by the Kyaukku Ônhmin, an early cave temple dug into a hillside near Nyaung-U that may precede Aniruddha's reign. The Pali for tower, *prāsāda* (Burmese *pyathat*) is another term for the superstructure of the Pagán temple. The terms for the various parts of hollow temples, from the massive brick walls *(tantuiṅ)* that surround them to the plinth *(caṅkraṁ)* on which they stand, very likely derive from Sanskrit and then Old Burmese, not Old Mon. The word for ordination hall is also taken from the Pali *sīmā,* Old Burmese *sim.* The word for image *(puṁ)* comes from the Pyū *bo.*[78] The word for library *(cātuik)* is Old Burmese, as is the word for preaching hall *(tryā im).* Monastery is Old Burmese *kloṅ,* a term later used for all schools, which had previously been called *ca saṅtuik.* Buildings with a special roof normally built outside a monastery are still called *(tanchoṅ).* Rest houses *(carap)* were built as part of merit-making, meant for the use of pilgrims and others. Many practical nonreligious items were constructed to go along with religious donations, such as tanks or reservoirs *(kan),* wells *(riy twaṅ),* causeways *(tan-*

thaḥ), bronze bells *(kriy khoṅloṅ).* None of these owe anything to the Mon language. They are either Pali, Sanskrit, or Old Burmese, and the earliest appearance of these terms in original epigraphy are found not in Lower but in Upper Burma.

The earliest structures in Lower Burma appear to have been built mainly with laterite, while brick was the preferred material and used almost exclusively in Upper Burma in all the Pyū sites and Pagán. This is not to say that building material is an ethnic issue; rather, it has to do with geography—what is an easily obtainable natural resource—and the culture of technology. Laterite is abundant in the Chao Phya basin and southeastern Lower Burma, so it is well known and used, but it is not found in Upper or Central Burma. In Burma's history, the earliest use of well-burnt brick belongs to the Pyū and Burman, not the Mon; to put it in a nonethnic, geohistorical context, brick use belongs to early Śrī Kṣetra and Pagán, not to later Rāmaññadesa.

Accordingly, the Old Burmese word for brick, *ut,* is said to have been derived from the Pali *iṭṭhaka.*[79] *Ut-phuiw* (brick kiln) is also Old Burmese, and Luce makes no mention of any Mon equivalent. The word for stucco *(aṅkatiy),* often plastered on the brick at Pagán, is also said to be Indic and is mentioned as early as 1198.[80] It is the same word in Mon *(aṅkade),* but is first mentioned in original epigraphy *only in the late fifteenth century in Middle, not Old Mon,* about three centuries after appearing in Old Burmese.[81] This is not to suggest that Lower Burma did not have stucco until that time, but only that since the word and its use were much earlier in Upper Burma, the Burmese probably did not borrow it from the Mon.

Luce also declared that the Burmese word for mortar *(sarwat)* comes from Mon, but no evidence is provided except a citation to an inscription of 1236 AD.[82] Upon rereading the inscription, I found it has nothing to say about the etymology of *sarwat,* but just gives the cost of the mortar incurred in building an edifice.[83] Besides, I find it unconvincing that the two cultures that used brick earliest and almost exclusively in Burma—the Pyū and the Burman—had to borrow the word for mortar from a culture that originally did not, and whose contributions to brick monuments at Pagán was either nonexistent or late and minimal. Finally, the distinctive "finger-marked bricks," uncovered in many Pyū sites as well as in Pagán, have also been found in Lower Burma, as noted in Chapter Two, well before the first Mon kingdom appeared in the late thirteenth century.

The suffix added to the names of crafts to identify various skilled craftspeople who had a direct hand in building Pagán temples (*samā* "skilled person") is said to have been Mon in origin.[84] Once again, this is only an assertion without any evidence (or even argument) to suggest that it might be viable etymologically or historically. In fact, I know of no linguistic study independent of the Mon Paradigm that has been done on this topic to establish the theory as valid. Many of the terms for craftsmen and women start with the word *pan,* the root of which means "flower." A *pan pai,* for instance, is a blacksmith, while a *pan pu* is a carver in wood or stone, and a *pan tan* is a coppersmith. In all three cases, the particular craft is linked with the word for flower. Judson does not attribute *pan* to the Mon language, while Shorto has *pankhi,* "painter (in fresco)," dated at earliest to 1557.[85] All this suggests to me that the Mon of Lower Burma borrowed these words that were crucial to the art and crafts of Pagán from that culture, rather than the other way around. Simply because a large number of Indian loan-words said to have been derived directly from Sanskrit rather than Pali (although no chronology is provided) were supposedly found in Mon,[86] it was construed to imply that Burmese must therefore have obtained these words from the Mon, and not directly from the Sanskrit. Again, the assumption was that the Mon were early and the only intermediaries.

Yet centuries prior to Mon-Burman contact, there is evidence of written Sanskrit as well as Sanskrit Buddhism in Śrī Kṣetra and Pagán. And given the closeness of the Pyū and Burman language, culture, and history, there is no need to conclude that the Burmans obtained its Sanskrit words only via the Mon.[87] These terms could have been derived from Tamil or Tibeto-Burman, and especially from the Pyū, a people well known for their skills in gold and silversmithing.[88] The terms had probably become part of Burmese vocabulary centuries before the first Burman contact with the Mon.

Thus the etymology of Pagán's vocabulary of temple construction, comprising a whole compendium of words that are either references to or constitute different parts of temples and *stupa*s and their accouterments came from Pyū, Old Burmese, Sanskrit, and Pali, but rarely, if ever, from Mon.

In short, the inclusion of a "Mon phase" in Luce's four-phase evolutionary sequence is entirely spurious, made to coincide with the "Mon period" of King Kyanzittha's reign, the topic of Chapter Ten. It has more to do with reinforcing the thesis of an early Mon contribution to Pagán civilization than with constructing a viable theory from actual evidence regarding the origins and development of the temple at Pagán.

An Alternative Scheme

Without the intellectual shackles of the Mon Paradigm, how might the evolution of the Pagán temple (and peripherally, the *stupa*) look? First, once the evolution of the solid *stupa* in Burma is assessed independently not only of the *gu* but of a prior Lower Burma influence, the path becomes much clearer. Leaving aside for a moment those ruins at Beikthano the superstructure of which could well have been *stupa*s, as some scholars contend,[89] the more immediate prototypes of the Pagán *stupa* found within Burma itself seem to have been the Payagyi, Payamā, and Bawbawgyi temples of seventh-century Śrī Kṣetra (see Figure 5). In early Pagán, the style is reproduced by the Ngakywènadaung, the Būpaya, and the Lokananda, all of which are estimated to have been built prior to or during the eleventh century (see Figure 5). From another eleventh-century *stupa,* the Paunggu-paya of Myinkaba, several distinctly Pyū bronzes and stone sculptures have been excavated.[90] This establishes another fairly solid link between Pyū culture and early Pagán *stupa*s. Even the Aśokan method of "repairing" solid *stupa*s found in ancient India—encasing the old *stupa* with a new one—was used often in Pagán[91] and is still used today,[92] suggesting that some *stupa* repair traditions came early and directly from India.

The mid-eleventh-century Shwéhsandaw and the late eleventh-century Shwézigôn followed these earlier *stupa* styles, which were subsequently elaborated in the late twelfth-century Dhammayazika and culminated in the mid-thirteenth-century Hsutaungpyi Zedi[93] and the late-thirteenth-century Mingalazedi. There are, of course, hundreds of other *stupa*s of all sizes that are less well known, but which follow this path as well and can be found in Pichard's work. This essentially bell-shaped *stupa* is then elongated dramatically or subtly in the centuries that followed, finding brilliant expression in the mid-fifteenth-century Htupayôn of Sagaing, the Shwémawdaw of Pegu, and the Shwédagôn of Yangôn (see Figure 6); the epigraphic evidence for the latter two, notwithstanding their legends, does not precede the fifteenth century.

However, this path of development does not imply that no variations on the bell-shaped theme existed. Nor does it mean that one bell-shaped *stupa* necessarily produced another bell-shaped *stupa* that came later; the later *stupa* may have had its own immediate prototype. There is no reason to infer a linear, cause-and-effect relationship between earlier temples and later ones. Indeed, in some cases the bell shape reverted to the less elongated, pre-Śrī Kṣetra and pre-Pagán style of Śrī Laṅka's Anurādhapura. An example of this is the Kaungmhudaw of King Thalun, built in the seventeenth century (see Figure 8). Because the recreation of the purity of the past is central to the concept of religious reform in Theravāda Buddhism, one often finds ancient forms repeated or resurrected.

In contrast to the *stupa,* where the exterior shape is considered a major component of its style, it is the *gu* or hollow temple's internal structure that is more important, for that in large part determines form and shape, which in turn defines style. Analysis of its development is less an exterior visual assessment of changing or continuing shapes, and more an examination of changing or continuing internal structures. Of these the most important is the floor plan, the foundations upon which is built, in conjunction with vaulting principles, its total visual component.

And like the *stupa,* the prototype of the *gu* goes back to second-century BC Beikthano and its apparent contemporary, Binnaka, even to the extent to which the structure was apparently deliberately "misaligned."[94] In Beikthano we usually find the "one-face" design, which has an interior space that surrounds a solid central core that obviously supported a tower above it.[95] Although its use at Beikthano as a religious structure cannot be confirmed until perhaps the fourth century AD,[96] its design, especially the floor plans and superstructural support, clearly foreshadows the small one-face and "four-face" temples at Śrī Kṣetra. The basic difference among these early, small hollow temples, or between them and their larger, later counterparts at Pagán, is essentially one of variations on the same theme rather than something fundamentally new and different (see Figure 9).

At Śrī Kṣetra, another option was found for the central core: the vaulted chamber. This suggests that the principle of vaulting was still unknown at the earlier Pyū sites of Beikthano and Binnaka, but was known by the time of Śrī Kṣetra, although that remains to be seen, for the presence of a solid core does not necessarily mean the absence of the vault. Both can be found coterminously with Śrī Kṣetra's existence as a center of Pyū culture, whereas that cannot be proved to be the case earlier. To the

FIGURE 8: Devolution of the Burma *stupa:* The Kaungmhudaw

basic one-face plan of Beikthano and Binnaka, one or more vestibules were sometimes added by the time of Śrī Kṣetra. Their ground plans are asymmetrical, "looking" towards the single main entrance. As we can see in the "unnamed" temple in Figure 9, the single-entrance (one-face) temple had already developed a form—with a vestibule almost equal in size to the main chamber—that would be used in most single-face temples at Pagán. The best-known temples at Śrī Kṣetra in this one-face design are the Bèbè and the East Zegu, the *style* Luce had earlier labeled Mon.

By the seventh or eighth centuries, and the zenith of Pyū culture at Śrī Kṣetra, another design appears: the Léymyethna (literally "four-face") style, but with the solid, central core of Beikthano and Binnaka still intact (see Figure 10). As such, the Léymyethna design does not "favor" any particular direction (as its name—"four-face"—indicates) and may reflect the introduction of some new ideology or simply more confidence in the use of certain engineering techniques, or perhaps both.

These two basic *gu* styles[97] of Śrī Kṣetra and their variations and elaborations would, with very few exceptions, eventually dominate the *gu* of Pagán. Most are either of the one-face, single-main-entrance, asymmetric, long-axis style, usually but not always facing east, or the four-face, four-entrance, equal-axis, symmetric style, approximately facing the cardinal directions. Most Pagán *gu* are the one-face temple style. Neither design has anything to do with ethnicity. (See Figures 11 and 12 for the chronological pattern of *gu* built and for the percentages of the basic *gu* styles.).

At Pagán, one-face, single-entrance style temples found expression in the Nanpaya, Nagayôn, Thatbyinnyu, Sulamani, and Gawdawpalin. As Figure 9 demonstrates, the floor plans of the one-face temple remained essentially the same regardless of political chronology or size of the structure. Although one could argue that the larger temples actually had more than one doorway (which is true), they still possess only one *main entrance* towards which the central image and the ground plan are oriented. The other openings are quite obviously smaller and subordinate and have been added for light, balance, and other reasons; they are essentially elaborations on the overall one-entrance theme.

The prototype for the four-face plan, apparently appears first in the Léymyethna temple of Śrī Kṣetra.[98] At Pagán, this design finds magnificent fruition in what is probably the eleventh-century Ānanda and its "Greek cross" floor plan, and the monumental and equally majestic mid-twelfth-century Dhammayangyi. As with the single-entrance temples, there are dozens of smaller versions and variations on the four-face theme built later in the thirteenth century, as illustrated by the Léymyethna (at Wetkyi-in, temple no. 290 in Pichard). As Figure 10 shows, the floor plans of these four-face temples, like the one-face structures, continued to hold to that

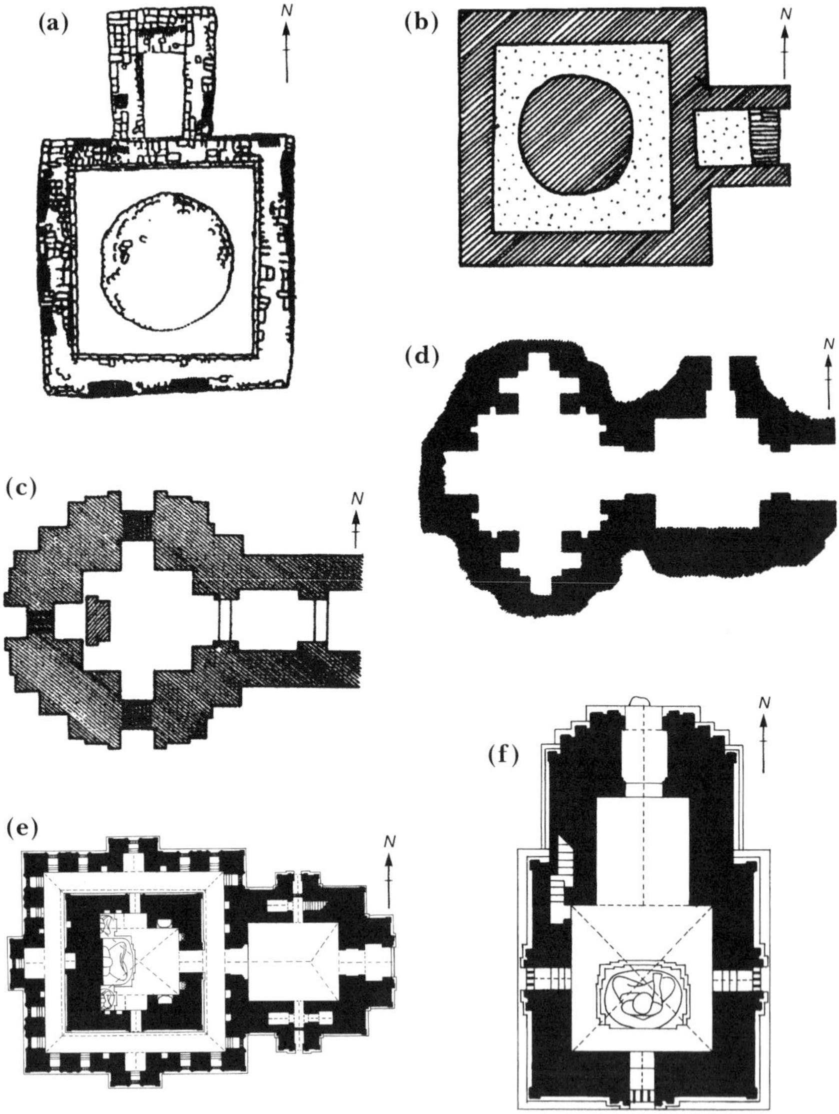

Figure 9: Ground Plans of "One-Face" Temples. *Sources:* G. H. Luce, *Phases of Pre-Pagan Burma,* Volume 2 (Oxford, 1985), and Pierre Pichard, *Inventory of Monuments at Pagan* (Mumbai, 1999). *(a)* Second–fourth-century Pyū structure at Beikthano; *(b)* Second–fourth-century Pyū structure at Binnaka; *(c)* East Zegu, seventh-century Pyū temple, Śrī Kṣetra; *(d)* Unnamed, seventh–ninth-century (?) temple, Śrī Kṣetra; *(e)* Păhtothămyā, mid-tenth century (?); *(f)* Lokahteikpan, early eleventh century (?); *(g)* Nanpaya, eleventh century (?); *(h)* Nagayôn, late eleventh century (?); *(i)* Kubyaukgyi, early twelfth century (?); *(j)* Shwégugyi, 1131 AD; *(k)* Thatbyinnyu, twelfth century (?); *(l)* Sulamani, 1183 AD; *(m)* Shinmahti, thirteenth century (?); *(n)* Hpayathonzu, thirteenth century

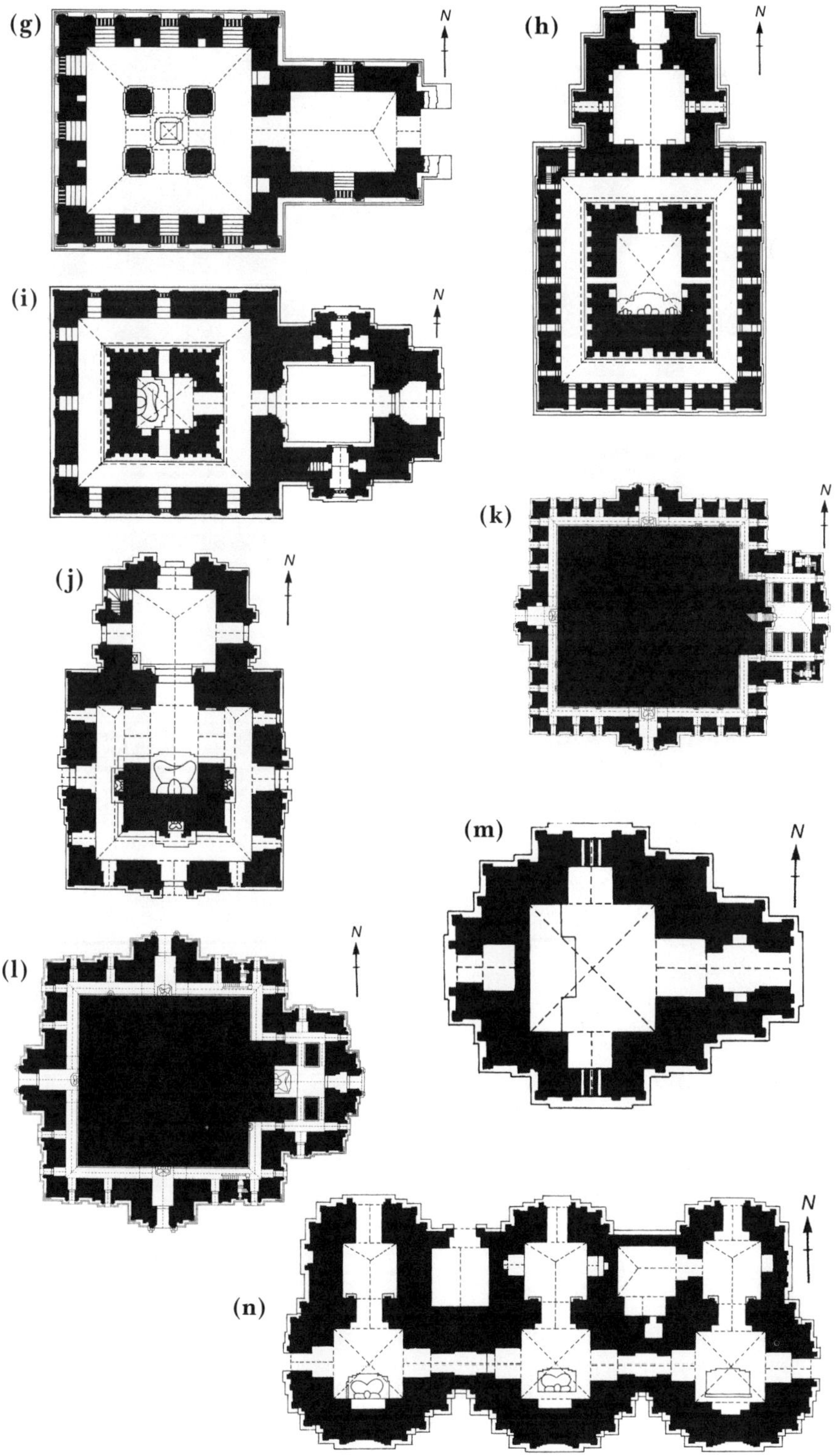

(g)
N
(h)
N
(i)
N
(k)
N
(j)
N
(m)
N
(l)
N
(n)
N

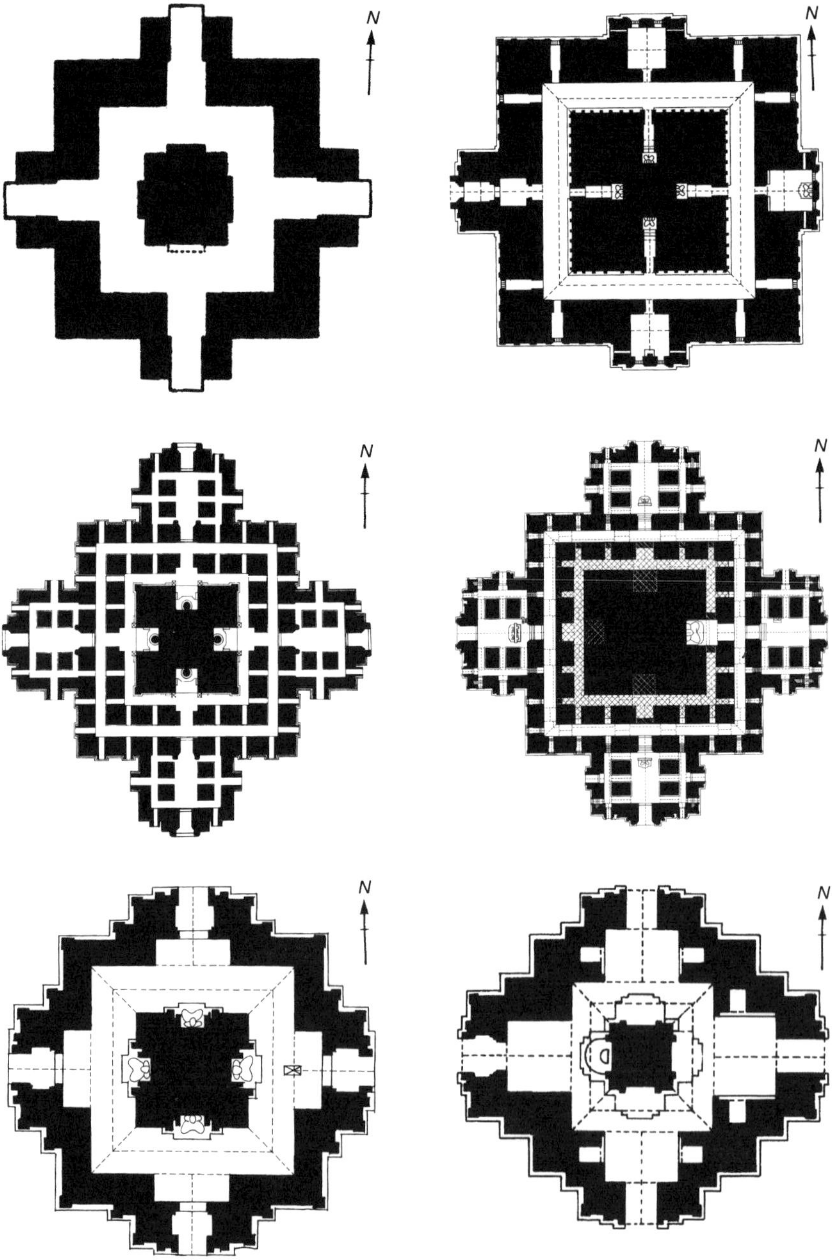

FIGURE 10: Ground Plans of "Four-Face" Temples. *Sources:* G. H. Luce, *Phases of Pre-Pagan Burma,* Volume 2 (Oxford, 1985), and Pierre Pichard, *Inventory of Monuments at Pagan* (Mumbai, 1999). *Top left:* Śrī Kṣetra Léymyethna, seventh century AD; *Top right:* Myinpyagu, eleventh century (?); *Middle left:* Ānanda, early twelfth century (?); *Middle right:* Dhammayangyi, 1165 AD; *Bottom left:* Kalakyaung, 1236 AD; *Bottom right:* Léymyethna, thirteenth century

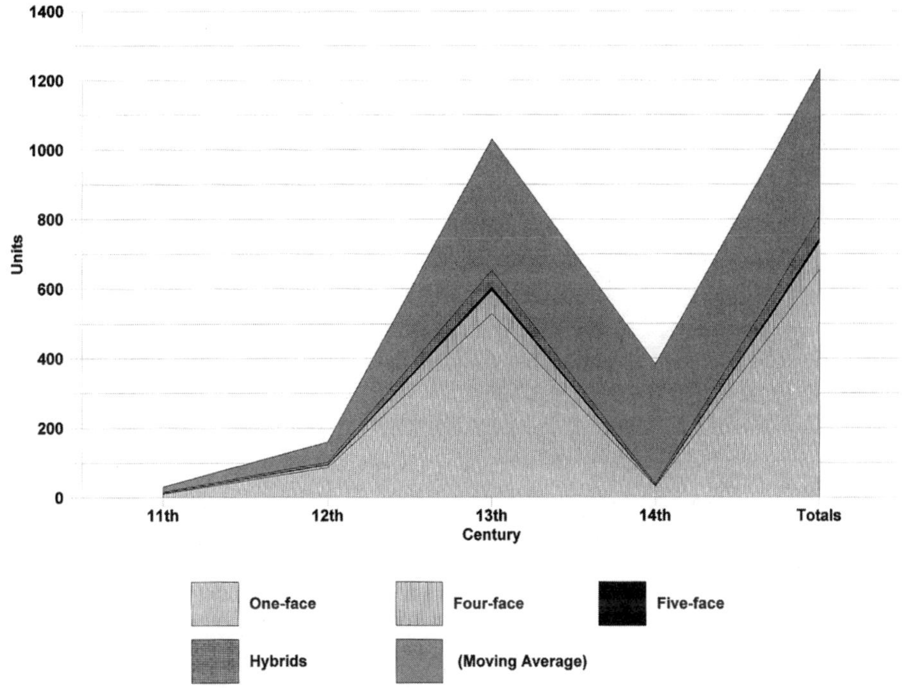

FIGURE 11: *Gu* Styles, Eleventh to Fourteenth Centuries

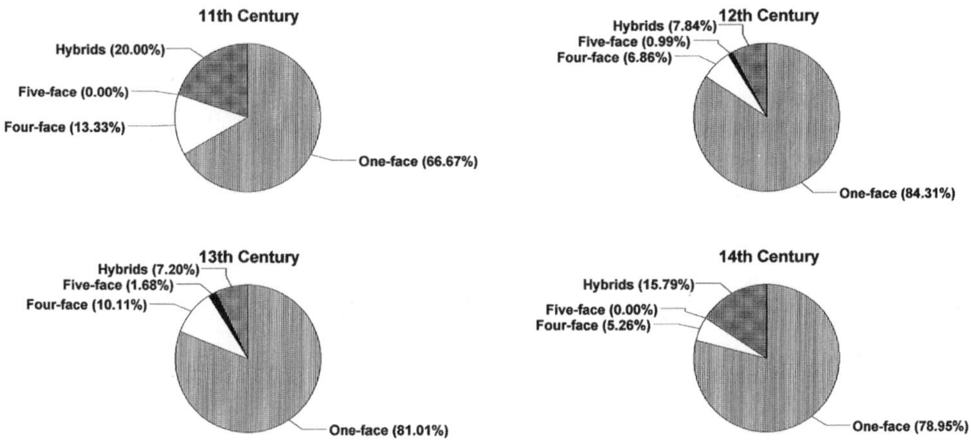

FIGURE 12: *Gu* Styles (Percentages), Eleventh to Fourteenth Centuries

principle throughout the centuries regardless of political fortunes, ethnicity, or size of the building.

Of all the hollow temples built at Pagán between the eleventh and fourteenth centuries, over 80 percent are of the asymmetrical, one-face design, while the four-face variety, the next largest in number, comprise a little more than 13 percent of total production (see Figure 12).[99] Most of the one-face temples were built in the twelfth century, which had clearly become the most popular design at the time—perhaps reflecting an appreciation of "classical" Pyū traditions.

Each of the two basic *gu* styles seems to have produced some hybrids that resulted in pentagonal and later, octagonal temples (as well as *stupas*).[100] The pentagonal—literally "Ngamyethna" or "five-face"—temples are sometimes five one-face-style temples placed more or less back to back, as in the Ngamyethna, shown in Figure 13, or a variation of the four-face temple made to produce a pentagonal structure.[101] In one case, the Hpayathonzu (literally, "group of three *payas*," here, temples), three one-face-style temples are strung side by side with connecting corridors (see Figure 9).

Often the one-face and four-face plans or their variations are combined so that, for instance, a temple is square and symmetrical but has only one main entrance and connected vestibule, with the central Buddha image facing that entrance. Or the temple is asymmetrical, but with four main entrances and four main Buddhas facing the four directions. Sometimes one of them comprises the first storey while the other becomes the second. Both the Minanthu Léymyethna and the Tonnekhya shown here in Figure 13, are clearly combinations of the two styles, where the asymmetrical one-face design and the symmetrical four-face style have been fused.

To these two basic styles and their variations, *stupa* components were added, resulting in a combination of *gu* and *stupa* which may have been the reason Luce concluded that the temple evolved from the *stupa*. One of the best examples of this synthesis is the Myinpyagu, which looks like a solid *stupa* from the outside, but is in fact a symmetrical, four-face hollow temple inside. Similarly, the Dhammayazika, although a solid *stupa,* has five smaller *gu* symmetrically arranged on each face of the pentagon. (Both are shown in Figure 13.) There are a number of pentagonal monuments at Pagán, of which the Dhammayazika is the example par excellence.[102] This pentagonal theme was extended to octagonal temples in later centuries, most built in the eighteenth and nineteenth. A very recent example is U Ne Win's Māhawizayā ("great victory") at the base of the Shwédagôn in Yangôn, which was built in the late 1970s or early 1980s.

In the same way that the solid *stupa*'s exterior could be refined and embellished—for instance, the *cetiya*'s *anda* might be bulbous or elongated—the *gu*'s interior also provided countless architectural possibilities, espe-

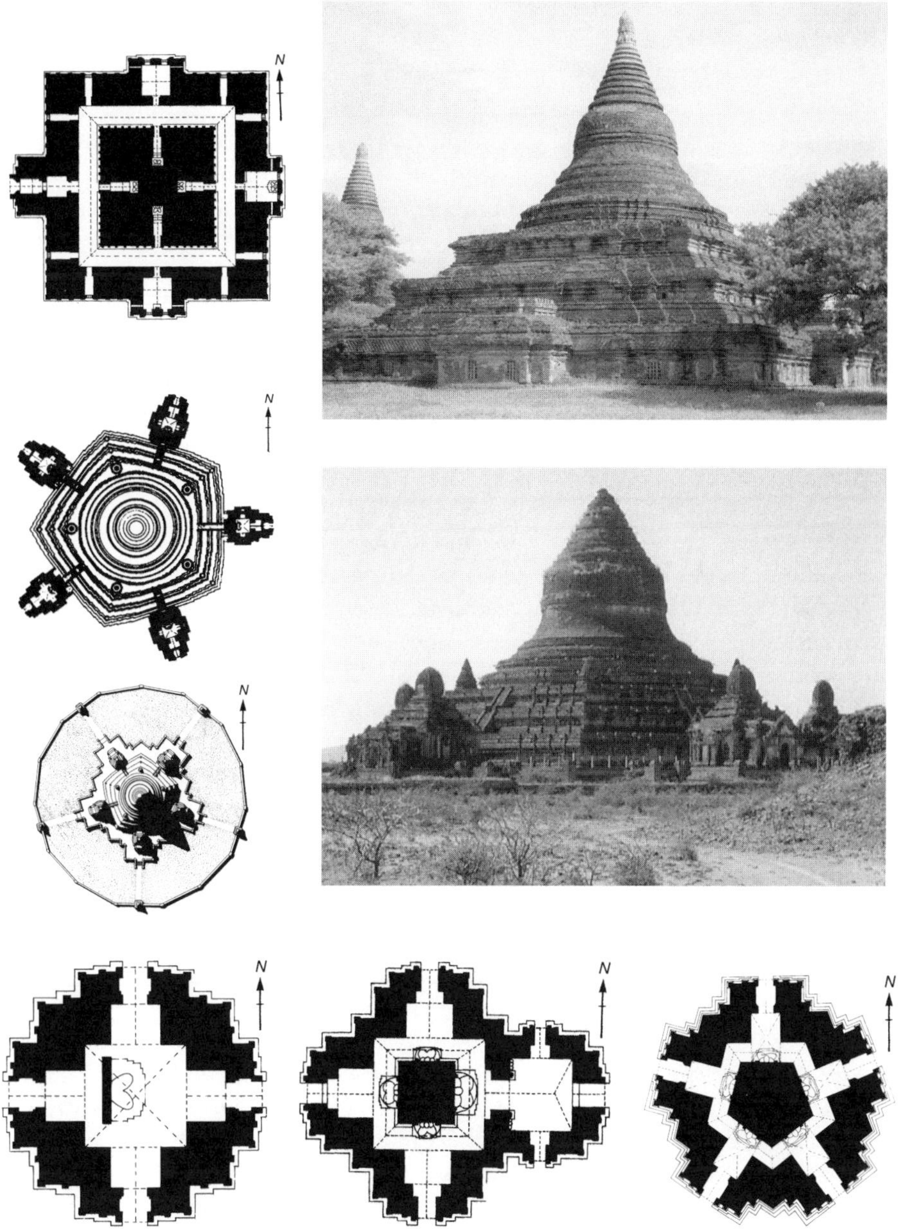

FIGURE 13: Ground Plans of Hybrids and Combinations. *Source:* Pierre Pichard, *Inventory of Monuments at Pagan* (Mumbai, 1999) and author's photographs. *Top left:* Myinpyagu, ground plan; *Top right:* Myinpyagu, exterior; *Second left:* Dhammayazika, exterior; *Third left:* Dhammayazika, aerial simulation; *Middle right:* Dhammayazika, with axial temples; *Bottom left:* Tonnekhya, thirteenth century, combination of one-face and four-face styles; *Bottom center:* Minanthu Léymyethna, thirteenth century, combination of one-face and four-face styles; *Bottom right:* Ngamyethna Hpaya, thirteenth century, combination of five one-face temples

cially with the use of true arches. There might be minor entrances on the sides of one-face, single-entrance temples, or vestibules added, or additional storeys built which would then need additional images and structural support such as hidden, relieving arches, corridors, and stairways, much of which did not necessarily affect the outside shape of the temple in any obvious way.[103] Thus although visually it may appear as if there were a very large variety of *gu* designs at Pagán, when the cross sections and particularly the ground plans are scrutinized, it is quite obvious that virtually all of them are variations on the one- or four-face theme, prototypes first found at Śrī Kṣetra, to which were added certain components of the solid *cetiya.* The rest, with very few exceptions, are sometimes simple, other times elaborate, syntheses of those two basic plans.

When we view the development of religious edifices in this way, as a parallel development of the *stupa* and temple with some crossing over, and when we base our analysis on architectural criteria, the Mon Paradigm becomes totally extraneous. Introverted Mons and extraverted Burmans, heavy rainfall, a conquering trope, the romanticized personalities of the kings in whose reign the temples were built, and so on are no longer needed. The chronology of temples can now be determined according to the available evidence or left undated, while style can be assessed by simply following the structural and technological development of the edifices themselves.

Nor do we need to assume that "prototypes" must change into or produce a new "species" in order to satisfy a fetish about linear change and "progress," although that can and does happen. With regard to temples in Burma, prototypes often continue unchanged over the centuries in their prototype form, alongside whatever "new species" they might have also spawned. Late thirteenth-century Pagán temples retained their basic seventh-century Śrī Kṣetra one-face design, an obvious continuity that does not, however, necessarily deny that processes of change were also taking place, producing branches and offshoots. This continuity of prototypes explains why *stupa*s, such as the Shwézedi of the thirteenth century,[104] is nearly identical in shape to the Shwéhsandaw (see Figure 6), thought to have been built nearly two hundred years earlier, or to the Myazedi, which is assigned to the early twelfth century.[105]

There is also no longer any need to force the chronology of the Păhtothămyā temple into a predetermined period of time in order to accommodate Aniruddha's alleged conquest of Thatôn and his bringing back certain texts in order to explain the presence of the textual themes painted in that temple. It means we can once again consider the viability of Burmese tradition regarding that temple, namely, that Saw Rahan, Aniruddha's grandfather was the one who built it in the mid-tenth century.[106] With recent radiocarbon dating of Pagán's foundations relatively close to his reign, that tradition once more becomes perfectly feasible. Similarly, there is no longer any reason to assign the Lokahteikpan to a period contemporary to or later than the Myazedi Inscriptions in order to accommodate the Mon Paradigm thesis that written Mon preceded written Burmese. Its chronology can be decided by style as well as the presence in it of very early Old Burmese ink inscriptions, the paleography of which best places it with Aniruddha's votive tablets, preceding King Kyanzittha's Old Mon inscriptions. In short, we can now examine style with art historical evidence, rather than forcing it into a preconceived thesis.

Conclusion

It is true that art historians studying Pagán in recent years have been regularly interpreting "outside" the context of the Mon Paradigm, but so far not one has explicitly and directly challenged it. Now that the Mon Paradigm is no longer viable, however, data on the art and architecture of Pagán can be interpreted even more freely, and will not have to address spurious issues that have linked ethnicity to temple style, and temple style to undated interior murals and ink inscriptions. Art historians can also disregard the conventional and conjectural dating schemes assigned to many Pagán temples that have for so long followed the Mon Paradigm's assumptions. And as several scholars of Southeast Asian and Pagán art have been doing,[107] more should now be inclined to acknowledge that influences from eastern or southern India or Śrī Laṅka came directly to Pagán without first going through a Lower Burma Mon "transitional phase."

Students of Pagán art may find that a great deal more is owed the Pyū and direct Indic influences than has been realized or admitted heretofore —in part, a reaction to the "Indianization" theory of George Coedes made earlier—and that Upper Burma's, especially Pagán's temple architecture, probably owed nothing to Lower Burma. This is particularly true of the bell-shaped *stupa*s of Yangôn and Pegu that stand out as exemplary models: they owed their symbolism, their form and design, their building techniques, and even their materials to early Pyū and Pagán *stupa*s. Their evolution probably began with the Bawbawgyi, Payamā, and Payagyi of Śrī Kṣetra; developed into the Būpaya, Ngakywènadaung, and Lokananda of the early Pagán period; crystallized in the Shwéhsandaw and Shwézigôn of the eleventh, the Dhammayazika of the twelfth, and the Mingalazedi of the thirteenth centuries; continued in the mid-fifteenth-century Htupayôn of Sagaing, eventually to flower in the Shwédagôn of Yangôn and the Shwémawdaw of Pegu of the late fifteenth century (see Figure 6).

As for the hollow temple, no genuine Pagán-style *gu* of similar size and structure, with its most important, unique, and invariable feature—the pointed, radiating arch and its vaults—has yet been found thereafter anywhere in Burma.[108] It appears that knowledge of the true arch may have been lost in Burma shortly after the Pagán Dynasty ended in the first half of the fourteenth century. Indeed, the vaulting of several small temples at Pinya, an early fourteenth-century city that briefly replaced Pagán as Upper Burma's center, shows clear signs of weak and crumbling arches, crudely buttressed by techniques we never see at Pagán, even as repair work (see Figure 14). Indeed, unrepaired arches at Pagán that were built centuries before the rise of Pinya still remain in much better condition than those built or repaired at later Pinya.[109]

FIGURE 14: Pinya Arch

Smaller hollow temples did continue to be built right up to the present, but none of these are even close in size or structure to the larger *gu* of Pagán such as the Ānanda, Sulamani, Dhammayangyi, and Htilominlo, which required true arch and vaulting principles to sustain their weight and size. In the late eighteenth century, when King Bodawpaya attempted to build the Mingun Pagoda—a structure he likely imagined to have been a Pagán-type Léymyethna-style *gu*—it was in fact a solid temple with no real interior, only small, token vestibules at each cardinal direction with crude, corbeled arches. The craftsmen and masons of the eighteenth century had clearly lost the knowledge of vaulting and keystone arching and could not reproduce the interior space so beautifully created by the magnificent vaulting at Pagán.

That loss had a direct effect on the style of future royal monuments, for they were all solid *stupa*s. Of these, the Shwédagôn of the Lower Burma Pegu Dynasty has become the exemplary model until today, so that in Burma the evolution of the temple did not *begin* with the solid *stupa* but *ends* with it. In much the same way that, and as part of the general historical processes in which peoples and cultures, languages and script, urbanism and state formation, religion and conceptual systems moved—from north to south, from Upper to Lower Burma rather than the other way around—so did art and architecture.

10 The Mon Paradigm and the Kyanzittha Legend

ONE OF THE most difficult obstacles to an untrammeled examination of the Mon Paradigm has been the legend of King Kyanzittha. By this I mean not only the story of the king as it is recorded in the Burmese chronicles and epigraphy, but also, and more importantly, the modern legend as it has been recreated by Luce.[1] It goes well beyond, and in many cases contradicts, what is contained in the chronicles and inscriptions, and therefore is very much a twentieth-century story. This chapter will assess Luce's interpretation of the evidence on Kyanzittha, and show how the legend is so thoroughly enmeshed in the Mon Paradigm's framework of analysis that one cannot address the latter without dealing with the former. Unfortunately, one consequence of this close entanglement is that we are virtually obliged to accept or reject *in toto* both the Mon Paradigm and the historiography of Kyanzittha so that the baby and the bath water are inseparable.

The chronicle account of the Kyanzittha story is clearly taken from a *Jātaka* tale or the legend of Aśoka as recorded in the *Mahāvaṃsa,* but it was adapted to the local Burma setting with familiar names and places. Kyanzittha was said to have been a young general under Aniruddha who betrayed the king by making love to a princess sent to the king from Vesali (or Pegu, depending on the version), who was being transported back to Pagán under Kyanzittha's guardianship.[2] That began the famous feud in Burmese history between king and general that continued with Aniruddha's successor, Saw Lu, until Kyanzittha ultimately triumphed. The feud, meant as Buddhist allegory of human frailties (in this case, desire), was taken by Luce as historical, and the reasons given for the story by the chronicles—rather straightforward and simple—were rejected and replaced with Luce's own twentieth-century value-ladened interpretations that helped serve the conclusions of the Mon Paradigm.

More serious in terms of methodology, by regarding a quarrel between king and favorite general over a woman—a standard trope found in many cultures, the most well-known western example being the competition of

Arthur and Lancelot over Guinevere—as historical rather than allegorical, Luce took what may have been a literary device used for legitimation purposes by the late chroniclers, and instead gave it historical (in)validity by analyzing it as an empirical problem, confusing (or at least intertwining) history with what was essentially hagiology.

More precisely, Luce extrapolated the simple story of Kyanzittha's betrayal of Aniruddha's personal trust well beyond its original narrative and intent and took it to represent a much larger geopolitical, ethnic, structural, and ideological divide that ultimately stemmed from Luce's own imagination and not the evidence. As a result, he turned a simple rift between king and general into a conflict between "monarchical" Pagán and the "old equal city-states" of Kyauksé, that is, between an egalitarian Kyauksé and an authoritarian Pagán,[3] or as Luce stated in a different article, between "feudal Kyauksé" and "imperial Pagán."[4] That allowed him to project onto Kyanzittha policies that were "based on consent rather than force," pointedly contrasting them to the "autocratic methods of Aniruddha,"[5] and pitting an "authoritarian" Aniruddha against a "democratic" Kyanzittha (all Luce's own words), a theme that recurred regularly in his work.[6] To that he added an ethnic component—and this is where the Mon Paradigm became entangled—the group that best represented "egalitarianism" and "democratic" values were the Mon. To Luce, ethnicity was as closely linked to political as it was to artistic predispositions.

All this Luce accomplished in the following ways. He declared Kyauksé to have been the first home of the Mon in Upper Burma. Then he placed Kyanzittha's birthplace there, which implied that he was brought up among the Mon, and that "explained" Kyanzittha's use of the Old Mon language in his royal edicts and works of merit. Furthermore, Kyanzittha, not Aniruddha, was given the credit for establishing "orthodox" Sinhalese Theravāda Buddhism in the kingdom of Pagán and hence ultimately in the entire country. Finally, Kyanzittha was said to have promoted what Luce considered "Mon culture" in such things as art and architecture, and this established the foundations for much of Pagán culture thereafter.[7] In short, what had been conventionally attributed to Aniruddha, Luce credited to Kyanzittha, so that Kyanzittha, not Aniruddha, became the champion of the people of the kingdom of Pagán.

Luce's transformation of King Kyanzittha turned a well-known historical figure into a well-liked historical figure. In the chronicles Aniruddha had been the epitome of legitimate and proper descent from royalty, the celebrated unifier of the kingdom of Pagán and *cakkavattī* par excellence. In contrast, Kyanzittha's legitimacy had been questioned, and his behavior portrayed as the sort exhibited by ordinary mortals, those subject to one of Buddhism's noble truths regarding desire. But since his political and military abilities were such that they could not be ignored, they ultimately justified his ascension to the throne. He became king as a result of his performance, rather than his birth, and that was precisely what appealed to both Luce and the new generation of modern Burmese.

This rather sentimental subtheme, clearly not found in the chronicles or the inscriptions, ultimately sprang from wishful thinking about certain, twentieth-century western values regarding representative government being celebrated during Luce's own day. These he projected backward onto his favorite king and the people whose modern representatives Luce had grown to love, who were showing all the signs of adopting those same values. Placed in the context of a mid-twentieth-century parliamentary Burma, Luce's portrayal of the two kings was almost an apology for the "authoritarianism" of the Burma's traditional hero, Aniruddha, whose behavior is atoned for by the more "democratic" Kyanzittha.

The Kyanzittha legend as we know it today is a modern invention, found only in twentieth-century Burma's historiography, not in any previous indigenous source. It thus needs to be reexamined by Burma scholars thinking outside the analytical and conceptual framework not only of the Mon Paradigm but also of a euphoric, newly independent, democratic Burma. It needs to be more accurately "relocated" within the context of Pagan's epigraphically confirmed history.

The Kyanzittha Legend and Old Kyauksé

The modern Kyanzittha legend depends on making two crucial, initial premises: first, that Kyauksé was the first home of the Mon in Upper Burma, and second, that Kyanzittha was born there. These two assertions, both intimately tied to the Mon Paradigm, in turn "explained" the "Mon period" in Pagán's history and Kyanzittha's supposed partiality for the language, religion, and culture of the Mon, which he was said to have promoted when he finally became king of Pagán.[8] That "Mon period" was used as "proof" that Pagán owed much of its culture to the Mon of Lower Burma. This is, of course, the heart of the Mon Paradigm.

But what does the evidence actually have to say of these two assertions? That Kyauksé was the first home of the Mon in Upper Burma has certainly no chronicle, and virtually no epigraphic, support. Of all the inscriptions found in Kyauksé that were produced during the entire Pagán period, only *one,* undated inscription with fifteenth-century orthography is in Old Mon. The rest, approximately 119 of them, are all written in Old Burmese.[9] This alone should have given pause to the Kyauksé thesis and raised some questions. Did the Mon, who were also erroneously credited with giving the Burmans their writing system, manage to produce only a *single* very late inscription during the entire 500-year Pagán period in the place said to have been their first home in Upper Burma?

That is not to say that no Mon ever lived in Kyauksé, but only that there is no epigraphic evidence for their dominant presence there, or at Pagán for that matter, *prior* to King Kyanzittha's reign. There certainly is no epigraphic evidence that they were in Upper Burma before the establishment of the walled city of Pagán sometime in the early eleventh century or during the reigns of the first several verifiable kings of the Pagán Dynasty in the late tenth and early eleventh centuries. The first epigraphic evidence to document the appearance of the Mon (as Rmeñ) in Pagán can be found only at the time of King Kyanzittha's new palace inscription, assigned to 1102 AD.

To be sure, a Tanluiṅ An (Talaing pond or lake, a presumed reference to the Mon) is mentioned in an Old Burmese inscription of 1082, and said to have been located in Kyauksé. The inscription was ostensibly erected during the reign of King Saw Lu that preceded Kyanzittha's ascension to the throne by a few years.[10] Yet Luce apparently did not accept its authenticity, for he wrote elsewhere that the word Tanluiṅ in domestic epigraphy does not appear until 1204.[11] Besides, during the Pagán and Ava periods the word Tanluiṅ was not an exclusive reference to the Mon, who were most commonly known as Rmeñ. Rather, Tanluiṅ was most often a reference to people living in Lower Burma in general, a topic to be discussed in detail in Chapter 11. Tanluiṅ An could have been an identifier of any Lower Burma ethnic or cultural group, or even a particular *design* or *type* of pond or lake that may have had Lower Burma affiliations. Certainly the phrase is hardly evidence for declaring that Kyauksé was the first "home of the Mon" in Upper Burma.

Finally, as Chapter Two has demonstrated, the archaeological data shows that two of the earliest urban sites in the Kyauksé plains, Binnaka and Mongmao, belonged to a different culture, the Pyū, with whom the Burmans, not the Mons, had the earliest and closest cultural, linguistic, and historical ties. The evidence also shows that Burmese, not Mon speakers were the very next group to occupy that region after the Pyū declined as a dominant force in Upper Burma.

Given the evidence, the most reasonable conclusion that should be drawn is that Kyauksé, in historic times at least, was first inhabited by the people called the Pyū, and they were followed by Burmese speakers sometime in the mid- to late ninth century. Thereafter, as the most important economic region of an expanding and ever-more-powerful Pagán kingdom, Kyauksé became the "home," not of the Mon, but of the ruling Burmese speakers, as the type, scope, and scale of the epigraphic evidence testifies.

Following the first erroneous connection, between Kyauksé and the

Mon, another had to be made between Kyanzittha and Kyauksé. Kyanzittha was said to have been known also as "Htilaing Shin" or "Lord of Htilaing," so a relationship was being created between Htilaing and Kyauksé. Although there were several Htilaings in Upper Burma, Luce found one in Kyauksé itself which he declared was Kyanzittha's birthplace, thereby providing the link that he needed between Kyanzittha's early upbringing and "Mon Kyauksé."[12] But a closer examination of the epigraphic details tells a much different and more complicated story.

The only contemporary Pagán record to mention the birthplace of a "Htilaing Shin" or "Lord of Htilaing" appears in an Old Burmese inscription of 1107 AD, originally found at Pareimma village,[13] a place which Luce himself located in the Chindwin River Valley,[14] north of the capital city of Pagán. It records the building of a temple by the Lord of Htilaing, whose birthplace, it said, was Parim Prañ (Parim city) *not* Kyauksé.[15] Parim or Pareimma is also the place where the first major Burmese chronicle places Kyanzittha's birth.[16]

Luce summarily dismissed the authenticity of this 1107 AD inscription, despite its being dated during Kyanzittha's reign and its inclusion of crucial information regarding the Lord of Htilaing's birthplace. The reason, Luce argued, was because its Old Burmese spelling and style belonged to the subsequent Ava period. He then chose three even *later* inscriptions as being more reliable. One is dated to the fourteenth century, the second is undated but assigned by Luce to the fifteenth century, and the third is also undated on the stone itself but given a date by the late nineteenth-century *Hmannan* chronicle that Luce accepts.[17] But none of the three inscriptions mentions King Kyanzittha or his birthplace. The only possibly relevant information they have is the word "Htilaing" and the phrase, the "Lord of Htilaing." Even then, the Htilaing in the fourteenth-century inscription simply refers to a monastery, not a place;[18] the second inscription records some rice fields east of Htilaing, so obviously that is a place name; and although the third mentions a "Lord of Htilaing," Luce himself admits that this person "is not Kyanzittha" but someone else of the Ava Dynasty.[19]

Thus the only source which had precisely the information Luce was seeking regarding the birthplace of "Lord of Htilaing"—the 1107 AD Inscription—was rejected as being too late, while three *even later* inscriptions were accepted. Why? It was because they happened to mention a Htilaing *in Kyauksé,* and this allowed Luce to link Kyanzittha (Lord of Htilaing) and Kyauksé. But since he admitted that the Lord of Htilaing in the third inscription was not Kyanzittha, and the Htilaing in the first was the name of a monastery, even those two links are spurious. The only evidence on which Luce's thesis rests, therefore, is the mention of a village named

Htilaing near some rice fields. That is the extent of the case supporting the assertion that Kyanzittha was born in Kyauksé.

Luce then rejected another perfectly good, Old Burmese inscription (the Taungbyôn Hlèdauk Inscription of 1111 AD) because part of the information it contained was directly contradictory to the legend of Kyanzittha as *he* (Luce) envisioned it.[20] In part, the Taungbyôn Hlèdauk inscription states that Kyanzittha was the "beloved son of king Noratha" [Aniruddha].[21] This, Luce countered, was "well-nigh incredible."[22] Why is it incredible? The reason he gave was actually a *non sequitur,* having nothing to do with the statement about Kyanzittha being Aniruddha's "beloved son" but with the inclusion of the names of two later kings on the *reverse side* of the stone.[23] But writing by later individuals on the reverse of a stone inscribed earlier is not at all uncommon and does not make the inscription *ipso facto* unreliable. In addition, it did not answer the question of why it was "well-nigh incredible" that Kyanzittha was the "beloved son of Noratha." It certainly is not reason enough to dismiss the information *on the obverse* as unreliable—unless, of course, it contradicts something else considered to be true.

And that "something else" is Luce's long-standing thesis of a rift between Aniruddha and Kyanzittha.[24] The statement that Kyanzittha was the "beloved son of Aniruddha," even as hyperbole, could not be accepted by Luce without retracting virtually everything he had written regarding the modern legend of Kyanzittha, including the false dichotomy he had created between Aniruddha's Burman, imperial, authoritarian Pagán and Kyanzittha's democratic, egalitarian, Mon Kyauksé.

Yet like the 1107 Inscription, the 1111 AD Taungbyôn Hlèdauk Inscription is the *only* contemporary, or almost contemporary, epigraphic evidence that actually links Kyanzittha (as Kalancacsa) with Htilaing Shin, or Lord of Htilaing. Without that link, there would be no contemporary evidence that he was indeed the Htilaing Shin of the chronicles, and the entire modern legend of Kyanzittha would cease to exist. It is a most important connection that Luce and all early Burma scholars have assumed to be correct, and on which virtually everything Luce wrote about Kyanzittha depends. This means that while Luce accepted as authentic the statement in it that Kyanzittha was Htilaing Shin, he simultaneously considered the same inscription as unreliable.

Thus two perfectly good Old Burmese inscriptions were rejected as late or unreliable for reasons *extrinsic* to them, namely, that they contradicted Luce's theory. Even *prima facie,* there are far better reasons for accepting them as authentic and reliable than for rejecting them. The important names, places, and dates they provide; their corroborative ability regarding other epigraphic and chronicle evidence; the contemporaneity of their orthography, style, and format—in short, just about everything suggests the inscriptions are genuine twelfth-century texts. As such, they really belong in section "A" of the *She Haung*, rather than the less credible section "B," but this placement too, probably following Luce, in turn helped perpetuate the modern legend of Kyanzittha and ultimately the Mon Paradigm.

Accepting both inscriptions as genuine would have brought up additional, uncomfortable issues for the Mon Paradigm. The 1111 AD inscription, particularly, raises questions regarding the end of Kyanzittha's reign, the beginning of Alaungsithu's, and the dates the Myazedi stones were inscribed.[25] The Myazedi simply states that 1,628 years after the Lord Buddha attained *parinirvāṇa* (that is, from Tuesday, 4 April AD 1083, first day of BE 1628, to Sunday, 21 April AD 1084, last day of BE 1628),[26] Śrī Tribhuvanāditya Dhammarāja (assumed to be King Kyanzittha) was lord of Pagán.[27] And as the Myazedi Inscriptions also state that this person ruled for twenty-eight years, they had to have been written after those years had elapsed.

If by BE 1628 is meant the earlier part of that year (April 1083 instead of April 1084), Kyanzittha could have actually relinquished the throne one year before convention has it; that is, in 1111 AD rather than 1112 AD. This would move up the accession of King Alaungsithu, his successor, by one year as well. That date is corroborated by an independent source, the most reliable of Burmese chronicles dealing with royal regnal years, the *Zatatawpon,* which gives 1111 AD as the beginning of Alaungsithu's reign.[28] And since the inscription was, in turn, erected by Alaungsithu himself, it strengthens the feasibility of 1111 AD as the date of his accession. This enhances the credibility of the statement on the stones regarding the kinship ties between Aniruddha and Kyanzittha, allowing us to seriously question the conjectured magnitude of the "rift" between the two men, which is at the heart of the modern legend of Kyanzittha.

The Kyanzittha Legend and a "Mon Period" at Pagán

From the erroneous assertions that Kyauksé was the first home of the Mon in Upper Burma and that Kyanzittha's birthplace was located there came the "explanation" regarding his partiality for their culture when he became king of Pagán.[29] As Luce put it: "The first half of the Pagán dynasty, for all its Burmese kings, was a Mon period, with Mon temples, Mon sculptures, Mon painting, and even the Mon language dominant at Pagán."[30] Yet his only evidence for this "Mon period" is Kyanzittha's use of Old Mon in his royal edicts. But such linkages between ethnicity and art (sculptures, painting, architecture) are not only tenuous but cannot be supported by the evidence of art history, as was demonstrated in Chapter Nine. Nor are the links regarding the writing system of Pagán, as was shown in Chapter Eight. Exactly what does the evidence show with regard to Kyanzittha's use of Old Mon in his edicts and its long-term, structural importance in the history and culture of the Pagán kingdom?

First, we should remember that at most there are about a dozen Old Mon stone inscriptions (including several duplicates) erected by Kyanzittha, and they represent less than one-half of one percent of the total surviving Pagán epigraphs. In contrast, there are approximately 700 Old Burmese inscriptions produced during the Pagán period, erected by royalty and commoners alike. The Old Mon language has been given an importance well out of proportion to its actual stature.

Second, the contents of the large majority of Kyanzittha's inscriptions are esoteric and redundant, reflecting the sentiments of a very small minority of people, or perhaps only Kyanzittha himself. This is suggested both by the high literary quality of his edicts and their abstruse themes that reflect hybrid Indic-indigenous conceptions of kingship involving arcane matters dealing with Indic deities and their role in the legitimation of the king. The inscriptions were obviously not meant for the edification of commoners, most of whom would have been Burmese speakers in any case, and probably without a knowledge of written Old Mon, but for that small group surrounding the king, who were literate in Old Mon. Indeed, the intended audience may have been even more selective. It is almost as if Kyanzittha were trying to convince *himself* that despite his disloyalty to Aniruddha and his banishment, and despite Saw Lu's position as heir apparent, he was nevertheless legitimate, for he actually won the throne. And to make sure that others understood this, he had the Lord Buddha prophesy that the Vedic deity Viṣṇu would be reborn as Kyanzittha in ten of his twelve Old Mon inscriptions.

In contrast, the majority of the Old Burmese inscriptions reflect what appears to have been the most common and cherished Buddhist values of the population at large, engraved on permanent and publicly displayed stone in a language meant for the bulk of society. They are anything but elite or esoteric, containing information about the ultimate desire for *nibbāna,* or a better rebirth on the path to it, of elite and commoner, peasant and prince, farmer and soldier, craftsman and scribe, monk and layman. The inscriptions record everything from the way plaster was made for temple walls, to the wages paid masons, the names of *kywan,*[31] litigations over land, the price of rice and elephants, and the fears and aspirations of ordinary people. It is these Old Burmese inscriptions, not Kyanzittha's royal edicts in Old Mon, that best represent the nature of state and society at Pagán.[32]

Third, one should also remember that Kyanzittha's reign lasted only about twenty-eight years. Although quite long by modern standards, it is just one of sixteen verifiable reigns (there could have been two more) that lasted nearly five hundred years, each averaging a little less than thirty years. Yet more is known of and written about Kyanzittha's reign, especially in English, than nearly all the other reigns combined, the result mainly of Luce's scholarship and influence. It is a skewed picture we have, for in the larger context of the Pagán Dynasty the quantity and quality of data taken from Kyanzittha's reign are minuscule, and not as extraordinary as scholars have made it out to be.

That, in part, explains some of the evidence that was at first puzzling: the Rmeñ as a distinct ethnic group cannot be found among any of the many ethnolinguistic groups mentioned in the Burmese language inscriptions of Pagán and Ava.[33] At first, this seemed incredible, for surely, I thought, the Rmeñ must have been more important than that in Pagán and Ava, revealing how much the Mon Paradigm has permeated Burma Studies, even to the extent that it was shaping the interpretation of a study questioning its viability. Once I recognized this, however, the import of the evidence became clearer: the Rmeñ was a small group of people arriving in Upper Burma in the twelfth century, and mentioned only in Kyanzittha's Old Mon language inscriptions, all (or most) confined to his twenty-eight-year reign. By the time of the Ava Dynasty, they had either integrated with the Burmese speakers to the extent that they were no longer as visible as the other ethnic groups, or they had never been as important as they were made out to be. Indeed, the sparseness of the evidence concerning the Rmeñ people, language, and culture at Pagán and Ava suggests a conclusion that is quite mind-boggling to western-trained Burma academics but totally consistent with the evidence and analysis presented so far in this book: the role of the Mon in Upper Burma's history, especially during the Pagán and even Ava periods, is negligible and has been much exaggerated. The modern legend of King Kyanzittha, closely tied to a "Mon period" at Pagán, is just one of many exaggerations that we have, unfortunately, come to accept as historical truth.

Finally, because Old Burmese inscriptions both *precede and succeed* King Kyanzittha's reign, one can legitimately regard the *lingua franca* of his reign as an interruption rather than a permanent trend or pattern, characteristic only of that specific period and portraying a one-time phenomenon in which one particular monarch happened to prefer written Old Mon. In other words, the importance of written Old Mon to the state and society of Pagán has been grossly exaggerated.

Soon after King Kyanzittha died, perhaps as early as 1111 AD, the Old Mon language disappeared as a medium for royal communication, and did not return to the heartland as such, except perhaps once, and then only in a marginally significant way.[34] If there were borrowing from the Mon into the Burmese language during Kyanzittha's reign, there is little evidence of it. But this is not surprising, given the elite nature of the edicts and the short period of time the language had to penetrate common usage effectively.[35] Without the Mon language, there is, of course, little else left that can be identified as Mon culture that might permit the term "Mon period." The mere use of the Old Mon language in royal edicts by one king did not have the kinds of consequences that have been attributed to it.

Old Burmese resumed its pre-Kyanzittha role under his successor and grandson, King Alaungsithu, regaining its position as the dominant language for both royalty and commoners until the present day. It would have been virtually impossible for any minority group to have gone against this strong current, particularly as the majority of the people in the kingdom were clearly Burmese speakers. The survival of approximately 814 Old Burmese stone inscriptions from Pagán and Ava, compared with only about 106 Old and Middle Mon stone inscriptions in both Upper and Lower Burma during the same approximate period of time, is testimony to that fact.[36]

But the question remains: why did Kyanzittha choose to write in the Mon language if he were not wholly or partly Mon or enamored of Mon culture? The short answer is that we do not know for certain. But that should not be construed to imply that the period therefore deserves the label "Mon." This is a subject fraught with myth and legend (both old and new), sentimentality, and other forms of emotionalism, as well as modern ethnic nationalism.[37] Kyanzittha's writing in Mon is a subject that has plagued Burma Studies from the start, and the only attempt made to explain it has been Luce's treatment. I do not expect to resolve the problem, but it should still be addressed as far as the evidence will allow.

We can begin by dispensing with Kyanzittha's putative Mon upbringing at Htilaing village in Kyauksé. We can also set aside the alleged feud between an authoritarian, imperial, and Burman Pagán and a democratic, egalitarian, and Mon Kyauksé. And we can lay to rest the idea that King Kyanzittha may have been Mon by birth and knew the language.[38] Tempting a thesis though that may be, there is no epigraphic or chronicle evidence to even hint that it is historically valid. We should remember, moreover, that the bulk of Kyanzittha's prophetic inscriptions were concerned with political rather than ethnolinguistic legitimacy. Thus there appears to have been a simple, practical reason for him to have used Old Mon. I think it had to do with the political realities of his reign, which emerged in consequence of his predecessor's accomplishments and policies.

Aniruddha had already conquered much of Burma, to Bhamo in the north, Inlé on the east, Arakan on the west, and also Lower Burma in the south, an expansion in which Kyanzittha, as Aniruddha's general, was very much involved. It is conceivable that Lower Burma had an influx of Mon speakers, perhaps fleeing the so-called cholera epidemic or the advance of Khmers into the Lower Burma region;[39] a late Mon history even records a Cambodian invasion of the Thatôn kingdom in the reign of one Udinna, alleged predecessor of the fictitious Manuha.[40] The Burmese chronicles also mention a battle in Lower Burma with the Khmers, even to the extent of naming the four generals that ostensibly led Pagán's forces.[41] And, as noted earlier, an inscription records Aniruddha's forces clashing with the Krom (presumably Khmers) in 1056, in whose armies there may have been Mon levies. Or there may have been other events about which we are unaware, that brought the Mon to Lower Burma by this time. It is possible, therefore, that in the decades between Aniruddha's first expansion into Lower Burma and Kyanzittha's continuation of that policy the Mon had become part of the kingdom of Pagán, as much the result of conquest as voluntary immigration.

Even if these campaigns in Lower Burma in the second half of the eleventh century did bring a Mon population back to Upper Burma—the transporting of labor from conquered territories has long been accepted as part of the early Southeast Asian historical scene, although that does not necessarily mean from a conquest of Thatôn per se—it is only later in King Kyanzittha's reign (1102 to be more exact) that the Rmeñ are first mentioned in Upper Burma. It is not until that time that a Mon population was possibly resident in the kingdom of Pagán. Kyanzittha's first use of Old Mon in his Old Prome Inscription of 1093 therefore probably addressed a *later* or post-Aniruddha, Lower Burma political concern, rather than an *earlier* pre-Aniruddha, Upper Burma cultural and ethnolinguistic situation.

On the other hand, because Kyanzittha also wrote in Old Mon in places that were not considered regions with large Mon populations (in Prome, a historically Pyū area and in Pagán, a predominantly Burmese speaking area),[42] it means the presence of Old Mon inscriptions in a particular region no more implies a large resident Mon population there than Aśoka's use of Sanskrit in his Kāliṅga Inscriptions suggests that the people there spoke an Indo-European rather than a Dravidian language. Moreover, King Kyanzittha also wrote in Pali and Old Burmese.[43] Thus the mere presence of royal edicts in Old Mon are not *ipso facto* evidence that all, most, or even a large number of the inhabitants living in the area were necessarily Mon speakers.

There also seems to have been personal reasons for Kyanzittha's use of Old Mon in his inscriptions. The Old Burmese inscription dated to 1107 AD[44] and attributed to Kyanzittha recalled one of his campaigns in the south where he was said to have destroyed "the Tanluiṅ region[45] called

Ussāla," the Pegu area of Lower Burma. This may or may not have been the event associated with the cholera epidemic mentioned in the Northern T'ai chronicle which spoke of the adversarial involvement of "the Pukam king," discussed in Chapter Six. Or it may have been a response to Pegu's appeal for help against the Khmer attacks mentioned in the chronicles. The 1107 inscription also states that from Lower Burma, King Kyanzittha obtained a "Tanluiṅ, replete with knowledge," a *sukhamaṅ* who became his advisor ("right hand man," wrote Luce).[46] This may have some support from the information found on the Shwézigôn Pagoda pillars that is assigned to King Kyanzittha,[47] where it also states that the king had "a Lord Mahāther, who possesses virtue, who is the charioteer of the Law, [who] King . . . [Kyanzittha] shall make . . . his spiritual teacher."[48]

This Talaing advisor may have been the historical figure behind the Shin Arahan legend of the chronicles. Perhaps, for some later hagiologic reason, he became more closely associated with King Aniruddha, but with the modern Kyanzittha legend, he reverted back to Kyanzittha.[49] The two statues facing each other in the West shrine in the Ānanda temple are supposed to represent Kyanzittha and Shin Arahan, but this is pure conjecture, based on twentieth-century assumptions about what Burmese racial features were *not* like during the Pagán period.[50]

In any case, the king's choice of this Tanluiṅ wise man as his advisor may help explain why Kyanzittha used Old Mon in his inscriptions, assuming of course, that the word Tanluiṅ did, at the time, refer to a Mon individual, since the term was used in general for all people who lived in Lower Burma, including the Rmeñ. And perhaps because Kyanzittha was probably not official heir to the throne and had spent much of his career on the battlefield, he may not have had the educational background that other princes would have had. He might therefore have depended a good deal on this advisor to compose his inscriptions. The advisor, in turn, may have preferred to use what he considered his mother tongue; there is no evidence to show that he had knowledge of Old Burmese.

In the final analysis, although King Kyanzittha's use of the Mon language in his "state memoranda" may imply a sizeable Mon population in Pagán which he was trying to welcome, appease, or inveigle politically, that in itself is not evidence or even corroboration of a conquest of Thatôn in 1057, or the removal of 30,000 people back to Pagán. Nor should it be construed to imply that Kyauksé was the first home of the Mon in Upper Burma, or that Kyanzittha's birthplace was there, or that, in an attempt to promote the culture of his supposed upbringing, he was responsible for a "Mon period" in Pagan's history. Kyanzittha's use of Old Mon during his reign does not need to suggest any larger significance beyond that use itself.

The Kyanzittha Legend and Sinhalese Orthodoxy

A third way in which the Kyanzittha legend is enmeshed in the Mon Paradigm is the role attributed to his reform of the religion at Pagán, conventionally credited to Aniruddha. Although this is not directly related to a history of Lower Burma "Mon culture" in the development of Pagán, reform of the religion is very much an issue in the growth and development of Pagán itself, and since King Kyanzittha was said to have been responsible for both the reform and establishment of Mon culture at Pagán during his reign, the two issues have become entangled. Underneath all these issues, however, is the "rift" between Aniruddha and Kyanzittha. Indeed, the entire Kyanzittha legend is ultimately based on this alleged rupture.

At the heart of Luce's thesis is the conclusion that Kyanzittha replaced the unorthodox "East Bengal, Tantric Mahayanist Pagán of Aniruddha's youth" with the orthodoxy of the Sinhalese Mahāvihāra tradition, bringing the kingdom of Pagán into that particular "Theravāda fold."[51] Aniruddha could not have done that, Luce argued, because he did not possess the full *Tipiṭakas* until the end of his reign. The "proof" of this, according to Luce, is that "nothing in all the temples of his reign suggests a knowledge of more than the *Jātaka* and the Eight Scenes of Gotama Buddha's life."[52] Thus the evidence for deciding orthodoxy and unorthodoxy at Pagán during Aniruddha's reign are the *Jātaka*s and the temples *assigned* to Aniruddha.

Orthodoxy and Bengal Tantric Mahāyāna Buddhism

This issue of Tantric Buddhism in Burma has long been debated, although not satisfactorily or in any depth.[53] I will leave the subject to a competent scholar of Tāntrism who is also knowledgeable about Pagán, but here, I wish only to examine the thrust of Luce's argument, that "the Pagán of Aniruddha's youth" was basically unorthodox because of the presence of Mahāyāna Buddhism, whether Bengal, Tantric, or both, and the evidence used as support for that contention.

No one would deny that Mahāyāna Buddhist ideas existed at Pagán, not only because both the Theravāda and Mahāyāna originally belonged to the same Old Wisdom school and therefore shared common doctrines, but since elements of both schools can be found among Pagán's predecessor, the Pyū, well before Pagán emerged. However, the conclusion that because there is evidence of Mahāyāna Buddhism at Pagán, it therefore implies that the mainstream ideology of society—and more specifically the state—could not have been Theravāda Buddhist simply does not follow.[54] In a multicultural society such as Pagán, which had been influenced by a variety of religions and religious traditions over centuries, it was not at all uncommon to find such a mixture. The presence of both religious schools is not mutually exclusive. Indeed, there were other, even more "contradictory" religious doctrines and ideas, such as supernaturalism, that coexisted with a central state ideology professing Theravāda Buddhism. This is no more strange than to have Jain and Brahmanic ideas flourishing in the quintessential model Buddhist state, Aśokan India.

That this kind of syncretism implied impurity or unorthodoxy is the judgment of both later chroniclers and twentieth-century scholars such as Luce who saw things in an "either-or" framework, a sentiment not necessarily shared, or at least not practiced, by the society of eleventh-century Pagán.

The actual history of Theravāda Buddhism in Burma suggests that "orthodoxy," however defined and by whomever, was not the result of a late, progressive, linear process, but was a cyclic, oscillating phenomenon found early *and* late, in different historical periods, and invariably shaped by Theravāda Buddhism's own doctrine of impermanence, hence the need for continuous reform.

More relevant to the present topic is the fact that by attributing these alleged Tantric Bengal Mahayanist elements to a period just prior to Kyanzittha's reign—that is, to "Aniruddha's youth"—it set up a straw man, so to speak, which was then easily demolished by another: the modern legend of Kyanzittha as the great reformer. In fact, both assertions were Luce's creations. The implication, of course, is that Kyanzittha was actually the one who purged the Ari "heretics" of the chronicles, thought of in historical terms by Duroiselle and Luce's generation as practitioners of Tantric Buddhism,[55] rather than in allegorical terms as representing unorthodoxy and therefore needing reform. In contrast to Duroiselle and the chronicles, Luce thought it was not Aniruddha who purged the Ari, but Kyanzittha, making him the real champion of orthodox Theravāda Buddhism at Pagán and hence of modern Burma as well.

Yet the art of Pagán during Kyanzittha's reign, which Luce used as evidence, does not support this scenario in even the most superficial way. Rather, the art of his reign displays as many, if not more, elements of Tantric and "ordinary" Mahāyāna Buddhism as Aniruddha's did. The epigraphic, artistic, and architectural evidence of several temples erected during Kyanzittha's reign suggests that Tantric Mahāyāna Buddhism was not only tolerated, but celebrated at the highest levels of society. Most notable in this regard is the art work found in the corridors of the Abèyadana, a temple that belonged to his own chief queen. Even Luce wrote of this art as being "not Theravādin."[56]

We also find in the art work and iconography of the so-called Nathlaung-gyaung, Hindu and Brahamanic themes that were most conspicuous during Kyanzittha's reign, not Aniruddha's. These are also more consistent with Kyanzittha's public persona as he, not Aniruddha, constructed it. Thus, for example, the central icon of the Nat-hlaung-gyaung is Viṣṇu seated on the world serpent, Ananta, with the Hindu trinity on lotus petals emanating from the body.[57] In this temple's ten arched niches are images in stone of the ten avatars of Viṣṇu. As a model of kingship, it is clearly Viṣṇu who is an integral part of Kyanzittha's legitimation ideology, not Aniruddha's, because Kyanzittha is said to be a reincarnation of Viṣṇu, as is amply documented in the king's many prophetic inscriptions. Although Luce *assigns* this temple to Aniruddha's reign or before, obviously to fit his thesis that unorthodoxy prevailed during Aniruddha's youth, in fact, the contents of this temple fit the conceptualization of Kyanzittha's kingship much better, and it was probably built during his reign.

The eclecticism of beliefs that had begun prior to both Aniruddha and Kyanzittha also continued long *after* their reforms. Even a cursory glance at any work on Pagán, including Luce's own,[58] shows that Mahayanist, Theravādin, Hindu, Brahmanic, and even non-Buddhist doctrines and motifs coexisted at Pagán well into the thirteen century in temples such as the Hpayathonzu, the Nandamanya, and the Viṣṇu temple of Nānādesi Vinnagar Alvār.[59] Mahāyāna Buddhism, Tantric or not, was therefore neither a unique phenomenon of "Aniruddha's youth" nor "reformed" so thoroughly during Kyanzittha's reign that it disappeared. Although justice cannot be done to this subject here, enough has been shown to conclude that Tantric and "ordinary" Mahāyāna Buddhism preceded, belonged to, and succeeded Kyanzittha's reign, so that there is no substance to the claim that Sinhalese orthodoxy began with his reign, and that it saw the end of these "undesirable" and "unorthodox" elements. Rather, this is Luce's familiar argument, that Kyanzittha's reign was a turning point, a watershed, where Mon culture, and now Theravāda orthodoxy, was first established. This deliberate focus on the presence of "unorthodoxy" during "the Pagán of Aniruddha's youth" has, for nearly half a century, created a conspicuous ideological, historical, and cultural break between the reigns of the two kings.

Orthodoxy and the *Jātakas*

Another category of evidence Luce used to demonstrate that Aniruddha's reign was generally less orthodox than Kyanzittha's was the corpus of *Jātaka* stories found in Pagán as terracotta plaques, many glazed and inserted in shallow niches usually on the plinths of *stupas* and temples. The gist of Luce's argument was that there were two *Jātaka* "recensions" (or types) in Burma. One was allegedly newer, Sinhalese, and more orthodox; it was composed of 547 *Jātaka*s. The other, allegedly "older" less orthodox group of 550 followed South Indian tradition. The two groups could be distinguished, he claimed, not only by their total number but also their unique *sequence* in the numbering of the *Jātaka*s from number 497 onward, which in the "Singhalese recension" is the "norm in Burma since 1100 A.D."[60]

But both traditional and current research on the *Jātaka*s shows that the picture is not as clear-cut or unambiguous as Luce painted it. Malalasekera, the noted Pali scholar, pointed out years ago that the history of the *Jātaka*s is anything but clear. "It is not possible to say when the *Jātaka*s in their present form came into existence nor how many of these were among the original number." At one time, he wrote, there were only five hundred *Jātaka*s.[61] T. W. Rhys-Davids, another noted Buddhist scholar who analyzed the content and structure of the *Jātaka*s, supports the likelihood of increasing numbers—from fable to *Jātaka* proper—in their development.[62] Oskar von Hinuber's recent research claims that the total number of *Jātaka*s was originally 550, with only 547 of them surviving, and hence the reason for the possible discrepancy, but he seems to accept the notion that there may have been more than one recension,[63] a notion for which, however, he cites as support Luce's statement. Ancient authors and works such as the *Thūpavaṃsa*[64] and the *Atthasālinī* cite 550.[65]

The point is not whether there were two distinct recensions of the *Jātaka*s, but that prevailing scholarly opinion during Duroiselle's and Luce's time held that one (the "550") was unorthodox and the other (the "547") was orthodox. The predominant, Sinhalese one was said to have been the orthodox version, which originated in Śrī Laṅka in the fifth century AD with the Buddhaghosa school.[66] Although the Sinhalese tradition was considered more orthodox in Burma, the *Jātaka*s were also referred to as the "550" (ostensibly representing the "older, less orthodox" South Indian tradition), so early Burma scholars rationalized this discrepancy in the following ways. Duroiselle wrote that although "the actual number . . . is 547 . . . the traditional number is 550." Luce himself stated that "even today, Burmans speak of the '550 *Jātaka*s,' never . . . of the '547 *Jātaka*s,'" and U Aung Thaw added that "the total number of *Jātaka* stories is 547 but these are traditionally called the 550 *Jātaka*s."[67]

Thus although scholarly opinion is still unclear with regard to the total number of *Jātaka*s, what was important to Luce's thesis was the link he then made between two imagined recensions and their putative orthodoxy, chronology, and ultimate origins. This allowed him to posit a false dichotomy that validated the differences he himself had created between the earlier "unorthodox" reign of Aniruddha and the later "orthodox" reign of Kyanzittha.

As evidence, Luce pointed to the series of *Jātaka* plaques on the East and West Hpetleik temples as representative of the 550 tradition. Apparently, he believed that the *Jātaka* series (actually only on the West Hpetleik temple, not both) were based on the addition of three extra *Jātaka*s from number 496 onward: the *Velāma,* the *Mahāgovinda,* and the *Sumedhapaṇḍita,* bringing the total to 550. This he contrasted to the alleged 547 in the Sinhalese series. Also, the West Hpetleik, according to Luce, "differs from normal Singhalese numbering, as found in Kyanzittha's series at the Nanda."[68] Thus both the total number of *Jātaka*s and their sequence on the Hpetleik and the Ānanda became the litmus test for the ultimate difference between orthodoxy and unorthodoxy. But there are several problems with this.

First, to whose reign did the *undated* Hpetleik temples belong? Why, to Aniruddha's, of course. Again Luce had made a self-serving assignment so that Aniruddha's reign was now linked to the allegedly "older" and less orthodox 550 recension of South India. He then claimed that "the present order of the *Jātaka* plaques on the west [Hpetleik] pagoda is chaotic," and blamed repair work done earlier by the archaeological department for that chaos. He felt that the sequence was "not so in Aniruddha's day,"[69] which, he believed, went in a counterclockwise direction deviating sharply with the Sinhalese sequence found on the Ānanda.[70] Yet according to Duroiselle, who first excavated the Hpetleik Pagodas in 1907, well before the supposedly sloppy repair work or Luce's analysis of it, the plaques "follow rigorously the order and numbers of the Singhalese recension. . . ."[71] Some of the earliest observers of the plaques found that most—over three-fifths of the present total of 240—were "firmly fixed in their original position."[72]

Moreover, of the 446 *Jātaka* plaques recovered from the two Hpetleik temples—out of a *presumed* total of 1,100, assuming each temple contained 550 to begin with—those that were found intact were in excellent condition, and the legends inscribed on each plaque were written on *top* of, not *below* the scene represented, as is the case with the rest of the *Jātaka* series at Pagán. This unique placement is found in only one other temple, the late nineteenth-century Pathodawgyi,[73] which suggests the Hpetleik temples may have been repaired much later and had their legends placed on top at that time.

We cannot know, therefore, if the Hpetleik *Jātaka* plaques, their total number, or their sequence (if that is even a significant issue) were original to the temple. We also do not know if this temple was repaired during the Pagán period itself before being obviously repaired subsequently. By the time of Luce's analysis, the evidence was both contaminated by repairs and too deeply influenced by his preconceived theoretical framework to have been of much objective value. Finally, Luce's thesis rests on evidence from a single temple, for only on the West Hpetleik can be found the three additional *Jātakas*; all others had 547.[74]

To single out an undated exception from nearly 3,000 religious structures built at Pagán (only nine of which used *Jātaka* plaques)[75] as evidence for determining the unorthodoxy of an entire reign is quite an extrapolation. That would be tantamount to concluding that if a certain version of the Bible depicted episodes in Jesus' life in a different order, and had three more or fewer stories in it, and this version were found in a single church in medieval Europe, that the difference was necessarily so vast an ideological divide that it defined what was orthodox Christianity for the entire period of the entire region in which that church was located.

A second problem with Luce's analysis was his contention regarding the Ānanda and its "normal Singhalese numbering" as an example par excellence of Sinhalese orthodoxy. According to recent research by U Aung Kyaing, director of archaeology for Upper Burma whose office is centered at Pagán, the Ānanda's upper plinths have 550 *Jātaka* plaques, not the "orthodox" 547.[76] In terms of the order in which they were placed, the last Ten Great *Jātakas* (or *Mahānipāta*) on the temple *do not* follow the alleged Sinhalese sequence as claimed.[77] The "absence" of "the Singhalese recension" on the West Hpetleik, therefore, no more suggests unorthodoxy than it does on the Ānanda, not to mention the "wrong" numbering of the *Mahānipāta* on the Ānanda. Either the Ānanda is not as orthodox as Luce has made it out to be, or the *Jātaka* recension and total number of *Jātaka*s on temples cannot be used as evidence for determining orthodoxy and unorthodoxy. In fact, the vast majority of temples built at Pagán did not have any *Jātaka* plaques on them. What does that suggest with regard to their (and Pagan's) orthodoxy or unorthodoxy? Probably nothing!

The notion that orthodoxy can be determined in this way is a twentieth-century idea based on at least one assumption, that there was an accepted "correct" version of the *Jātaka* series extant at the time on which any temple's series could be modeled. This has not been demonstrated, so assessments of the correctness or incorrectness of *Jātaka* numbers and numbering appears not to have been an eleventh-century Pagán concern, but rather a western, twentieth-century obsession with finding and "privileging" differences.

In addition, the analysis employed by Luce to make his case was anachronistic. The alleged "Singhalese recension" that he used as a basis for comparison with the Pagán *Jātaka* plaques cannot, as far as I can determine, be found in eleventh-century Śrī Laṅkan temples themselves.[78] That may be the reason Luce produced no evidence to demonstrate that Śrī Laṅka itself possessed and used the "547 series" on temples dated before those in eleventh-century Pagán. Instead, the comparison was made between actual eleventh-century Pagán *Jātaka* plaques and late Sinhalese *manuscripts,* using

Fausböll's nineteenth-century edition of the *Jātakas*. Even then, these were not the *Jātakas* themselves, but their *commentaries*.[79] In terms of actual chronology, Fausböll's *Jātakas* are nearly a millennium later than the *Jātaka* plaques on the temples of Pagán. How can much earlier plaques be derived from much later manuscripts, even if the latter were part of a presumed older Sinhalese tradition? That the tradition is said to go back to the fifth century and the Buddhaghosa school is not any assurance that Fausböll's manuscripts are necessarily fifth century.[80] This is not to say that these *Jātaka* stories were not of earlier Sinhalese or Indian origin, as Rhys Davids suggests;[81] only that the direct source of Fausböll's manuscripts is much later than the Pagán *Jātaka* plaques.

The *Jātakas* probably arrived well before the Pagán period. Duroiselle's archaeological report for Hmawza (Old Prome) described a terracotta plaque that resembles the *Mughapakkha Jātaka,* part of the so-called Sinhalese recension, among the Pyū remains several hundred years before Pagán emerged.[82] That may be one reason why subsequent borrowing of texts from Pagán posed no problems of orthodoxy to the Sinhalese. They could claim it was theirs to begin with, or equally acceptable because they belonged to Aśokan Buddhist India. The tradition was not exclusively Sinhalese but was part of a broader Indian Buddhist tradition, where the practice of using *Jātakas* as bas-reliefs on temples was already known during the Sunga period (185–72 BC) and best revealed on the railing medallions at Bharhut.[83] The tradition continued in the cave paintings at Ajanta, dated to the fifth century AD of the Gupta Age.[84] And the fact remains that the *Jātaka* plaques at Pagán precede the Fausböll manuscripts by nearly a millennium.

Orthodoxy and the Shwézigôn Pagoda

Luce used similar evidence found on the Shwézigôn Pagoda to support his thesis. All traditional sources attribute this temple to Aniruddha—although some state that it was begun by Aniruddha but completed by Kyanzittha[85]—and conventionally date it between 1059 and 1060.[86] Luce was the first (if not the only) scholar of Pagán to dispute this claim and ascribe the temple entirely to Kyanzittha. And why did he do this? He needed the temple to be Kyanzittha's if Aniruddha's reign were to be unorthodox.

He presented his case in the following way. First, he noticed that "both" the 550 and the 547 recensions of the *Jātakas* appear on the Shwézigôn Pagoda.[87] In order to address the issue that tradition assigned the temple to Aniruddha, Luce concluded that having both recensions on the Shwézigôn was a "muddle," containing "both and neither,"[88] caused, he said, by the ignorance of the canon at the time.[89]

Even working within a framework of analysis that posits two distinct series, we can still legitimately ask whether ignorance of the canon was the only reason for mixing (or "muddling") them. Could it not also have reflected the conceptual system in Pagán as it was practiced? Throughout Burma's history, particularly during the early years at Pagán, mixing doctrines from both schools of Buddhism and other ideological sources was the norm rather than the exception, as has already been demonstrated several times.

Luce's interpretation of the combined recensions as a muddle assumes that only the use of one kind, not both, can be considered legitimate. This seems a rather strict, "textually privileged" interpretation of human beliefs, and of Sinhalese orthodoxy, as well as a personal predisposition to see the world in an either-or mold. Perhaps there was even a third or a fourth way to represent the *Jātakas* in Pagán as part of orthodox doctrine, but such speculation is beyond the scope of this book.[90]

Luce then turned around and admitted that the Shwézigôn usually followed the Sinhalese recension of *Jātaka* plaques from number 497 onward.[91] But this admission placed him in a quandary, for it suggested that the Sinhalese recension must have existed at Pagán when the Shwézigôn was built because the plaques were found *in situ*. Ultimately, then, the issue boiled down to when and by whom was the Shwézigôn built. If it was Aniruddha, then Luce would have to explain the presence of the Sinhalese recension on the Shwézigôn this early, and that went against everything else he had written. It would also imply that the Sinhalese recension preceded both Kyanzittha's reign and his building of the Ānanda, which Luce assigns to 1105 AD, on which, Luce contends, is found the first evidence of the 547 series.[92] But if the Shwézigôn were Kyanzittha's temple, then nothing needed explaining and the Kyanzittha legend, the Mon period, and the Mon Paradigm would remain intact.

Not surprisingly, that is precisely the way Luce dealt with the issue. He simply disputed the conventional view that the Shwézigôn belonged to Aniruddha. "Improbable" he wrote,[93] and attributed the pagoda to King Kyanzittha instead. But why was it improbable? First, he argued, the Shwézigôn's terraces are different from the Shwéhsandaw's, which Aniruddha was said to have built; second, the *Jātaka* numbering differs from that in the West Hpetleik; and third, there is no mention of Aniruddha on two of the Shwézigôn's inscribed pillars.[94] Therefore, he concluded, the Shwézigôn could not have been built by Aniruddha! Luce then *reassigned* the conventional date given to the Shwézigôn Pagoda (1059–1060) to 1086 instead.[95] That automatically shifted the date of the Sinhalese recension on the *Jātakas* plaques there to a later period, and "proved" his assertion that Aniruddha could not have had the Sinhalese recension. Instead, Kyanzittha was to be regarded as the real reformer who brought Sinhalese Theravāda Buddhism to Pagán.

To validate this reassignment of the date of the temple, Luce cited the two Shwézigôn Pagoda pillar inscriptions at the eastern entrance, said to have been erected by King Kyanzittha. These Luce considered proof that the temple had been begun by Kyanzittha and completed around 1086.[96] In fact, however, the date on the pillar inscriptions alluded most likely to Kyanzittha's coronation; it has *nothing whatever to say about when the pagoda was begun, who its original donor was, or when it was completed.*[97] Rather, the subject matter concerns the now-familiar Kyanzittha prophecy.

That Kyanzittha invoked his coronation of nearly two decades earlier in these Shwézigôn pillar inscriptions is not difficult to understand. The temple was, after all, the palladium of the state and his father's greatest work of merit. It was therefore a most appropriate place for Kyanzittha (or any king, even Bayinnaung centuries later)[98] to commemorate the most important event of his reign—his accession. For Kyanzittha, it was both a personal and political act. Indeed, the bulk of the narrative on these pillars contains the most complete version of his prophecies, a perfectly suitable celebration of his achievements in his old age. And the fact that nothing was said on these pillars about Aniruddha specifically is surely not reason enough to conclude, as Luce did, that this demonstrates Kyanzittha was not Aniruddha's "beloved son," as recorded on the 1111 AD inscription.[99]

I would suggest, instead, that even though the two pillars were commemorating Kyanzittha's prophecy, the fact that they were placed at the Shwézigôn built by Aniurddha and not at one of Kyanzittha's own temples such as the Ānanda,[100] is even better reason not only for concluding that he (Kyanzittha) did not build the Shwézigôn, but that the 1111 AD inscription's statement itself (that he was the "beloved son of Aniruddha") is original, regardless of whether the kinship itself was empirically genealogical or fictive

In short, the building of the Shwézigôn Pagoda and the erecting of these pillars could have been and probably were *two separate events* years apart, a possibility never considered in Luce's analysis. He simply selected the only date on the pillars (probably Kyanzittha's coronation)[101] and concluded that construction of the pagoda must have occurred at the same time. The temple traditionally attributed to Aniruddha became Kyanzittha's, which eliminated the need to explain the Sinhalese recension of the *Jātakas* on it and bolstered his arguments about the "rift" between Aniruddha and Kyanzittha, the alleged "Mon period" in Pagán, and of course, the Mon Paradigm.

Orthodoxy and Possession of the Full *Tipiṭakas*

The last argument in the attempt to make Aniruddha's reign less orthodox than Kyanzittha's has to do with possession of the full *Tipiṭakas*. The Śrī Laṅkan chronicles tell a famous story about King Vijayabāhu I, who, because the religion there had been disrupted and its monks and texts corrupted by decades of Coḷa rule, requested from his "friend" and contemporary, Aniruddha of Pagán, monks who had been properly ordained (presumably in the Sinhalese *upasampadā* tradition) to reestablish orthodoxy in Śrī Laṅka by reordaining its monks. The process, to be legitimate, would include recitation of the full orthodox version of the *Tipiṭakas* that then would become sanctioned in Śrī Laṅka as the correct, purified texts. This story in the *Cūḷavaṃsa* is corroborated by the following Tamil inscription of 1137–1153, which suggests that the chronicle account may have been historical.

> As the number of the bhikkhus was not sufficient to make the chapter full for the (holding of the) ceremony of admission into the Order and other acts, the Ruler of men [Vijayabāhu I] who had at heart the continuance of the Order, sent to his friend, the Prince Anuruddha in the Rāmañña country[102] messengers with gifts and had fetched thence bhikkhus who had thoroughly studied the three Pitakas, who were a fount of moral discipline and other virtues, (and) acknowledged as theras. After distinguishing them by costly gifts, the King had the ceremonies of world-renunciation and of admission into the Order repeatedly performed by them and the three Pitakas together with the commentary frequently recited and saw to it that the Order of the Victor which had declined in Lanka again shone brightly.[103]

If Aniruddha had the full *Tipiṭakas* by the time of Vijayabāhu I's request—thought to have been early in his reign around 1055—it would have preceded his alleged conquest of Thatôn in 1057, during which, Luce argues, Aniruddha obtained his "trickle" of *Tipiṭakas*.[104] And if the Sinhalese account is accepted—which makes clear that Vijayabāhu is the one who is borrowing the orthodox texts from Aniruddha and not the other way around—it would suggest that Pagán *already had* the full *Tipiṭakas* before Vijayabāhu's request. Pagán was therefore quite "orthodox" well before Kyanzittha ascended the throne.

Very curiously, however, Luce cited this account to argue *just the opposite*. He wrote that "it seems unlikely... Aniruddha could have received from Ceylon more than a trickle of texts before Vijayabāhu ... [rather,] the main flood of the *Tipiṭaka* [could have] only reached Pagán in the closing years of Aniruddha's reign."[105] This assertion is quite puzzling, for it directly contradicts the narrative being used as evidence. Why would Luce use the *Cūḷavaṃsa* account at all when the chronicle clearly states that Aniruddha had the full *Tipiṭakas,* and Luce was trying to prove he did not? One reason, I think, was to preemptively disarm the account, the same *modus operandi* he used with regard to Kyanzittha's birthplace. It sounds as though he were responding to an actual query from another scholar who had asked him, "What about the *Cūḷavaṃsa* account?"

Luce's analysis was also not very well thought through. If Aniruddha did not have the full *Tipiṭakas* but only a "trickle of texts," it implies that Vijayabāhu accepted, and the *Cūḷavaṃsa* established as precedent in writing, what would obviously have been an illegitimate reformation. The absence of the full *Tipiṭakas* would have invalidated the reordination of Vijayabāhu's monks as well as the orthodoxy of their texts, when the need for orthodoxy was precisely the reason the Śrī Laṅkan king went to Aniruddha in the first place. Indeed, the authors of the *Cūḷavaṃsa* must have considered the monks from Pagán to have been properly ordained in the Mahāvihāra tradition with the necessary requisites to reordain Vijayabāhu's monks and reform the texts in Śrī Laṅka, otherwise such an event would never have been admitted in a "national" chronicle of the Sinhalese.[106] That in itself is of some assurance that the Sinhalese considered Pagán to have been orthodox at the time and in possession of the full *Tipiṭakas.*

And even if the account were an *ex post facto* legitimation statement regarding the purity of Pagan's *saṅgha* in order to claim the same purity for Vijayabāhu's *saṅgha,* it is still an admission of the orthodoxy of Pagan's monks and scriptures. The intention of the generation writing the *Cūḷavaṃsa* was obviously to contend that the original purity of the Sinhalese lineage had not been broken even under the "heretical" Coḷa rule, for that lineage had been retained and preserved at Pagán and with Vijayabāhu's initiative was once again reestablished. One must assume that the authors of the *Cūḷavaṃsa* believed that to have been true if the request by Vijayabāhu was to make any sense. All this is still perfectly viable even though we may not necessarily consider the *Cūḷavaṃsa* account to be empirical.

Yet because Luce challenged the narrative as if it were an empirical historical event, I am compelled to respond within the same analytical framework, without, however, necessarily endorsing the premise. And even if placed within that empirical historical framework, it *confirms, not denies,* the conclusion that Aniruddha's monks possessed the full *Tipiṭakas.* So whether allegorical or historical, symbolic or empirical, the *Cūḷavaṃsa* account supports the notion that Aniruddha had the full *Tipiṭakas.* In addition, the *Tipiṭakas* (as the "Three Gems") were known at Pagán and mentioned by name in an original epigraph prior to Kyanzittha's ascension.[107]

Luce's revisionist thesis that Aniruddha's reign was unorthodox while Kyanzittha's was orthodox fortified the notion with an ideological component that tensions existed between the two heroes of Burma's history and provided the Mon Paradigm with more "evidence" for the contrast it needed to distinguish their reigns. Most important in terms of Burma's historiography, Luce made Kyanzittha, not Aniruddha, the "true" champion of Sinhalese Theravāda Buddhism at Pagán, so that he "became" the founder of today's Burmese Buddhism. It was, wrote Luce, "Kyanzittha's main contribution to his country's history."[108] Yet this goes against all the evidence in the Burmese, Ceylonese, and Mon chronicles (historical as well as allegorical), in King Dhammazedi's Kalyani Inscriptions focused on this very issue of orthodoxy and reform, in the art and architecture of Pagán, and in the scholarship on this issue even of Luce's day.[109]

Conclusion

The three major components of the modern Kyanzittha legend cannot be supported by any primary evidence, epigraphic or chronicle. There is no evidence that Kyauksé was the first home of the Mon in Upper Burma or that Kyanzittha's birthplace was in Kyauksé instead of Parim. That means the explanation of the second component—a "Mon period" established in Pagán during Kyanzittha's reign because of his alleged upbringing among the Mon of Kyauksé—is also without merit. The only evidence for a "Mon period" at Pagán ultimately rests on a dozen redundant, esoteric, and clearly hagiographic Old Mon inscriptions that Kyanzittha erected.[110] And finally there is no evidence to support the assertion that only with King Kyanzittha was Theravāda Buddhism of the Sinhalese school finally established at Pagán.

All three claims are entangled in the so-called rift between Kyanzittha and Aniruddha. What began in the inscriptions as a cordial relationship between father and son, king and general, had become seven hundred years later in the chronicles a simple rift between the two concerning a woman. Then two hundred years later Luce turned this story of the pitfalls of desire into a geopolitical and structural contrast between a "feudal" Kyauksé and an "imperial" Pagán, between an "authoritarian" Aniruddha and a "democratic" Kyanzittha, between Bengal unorthodoxy and Sinhalese orthodoxy, and an ethnic conflict between Burman and Mon.

The implications of this alleged rift extended beyond the above issues to entangle itself even in the credibility of certain primary sources; in particular, two perfectly good, Old Burmese inscriptions, impugned because they contradicted the favored thesis, especially one that happened to confirm the account that Kyanzittha was the "beloved son" of Aniruddha.

(Indeed, much of the invented contrast between the reigns of Aniruddha and Kyanzittha seemed to have been intended to undermine that single sentence.) That 1111 AD inscription is probably the most damaging, contemporary epigraph to contradict the modern Kyanzittha legend as reconstructed.

Heretofore maligned for their contradiction of the favored Kyanzittha legend in the numerous ways discussed above, rather than for any intrinsic qualities of the stones, the renewed credibility of the two inscriptions in question should now be accepted, and once more regarded as reliable, primary data. That acceptance, in turn, should reopen the dates concerning King Kyanzittha's death, King Alaungsithu's accession, and the erection of the Myazedi Inscriptions, all very important to the interpretation of Pagán history.

Without the modern legend of Kyanzittha, the fictitious Mon period in Pagán history no longer need hinder any future reinterpretation of data. King Kyanzittha's actual historical role vis-à-vis Aniruddha, his contributions to Pagán society, his lineage, perhaps even his ethnic background are now open to reinterpretation, as are other important religious, artistic, and historiographic issues that have become entangled in the legend. Open to reassessment, too, are the chronology of certain temples, the arrival of certain Theravāda Buddhist texts, and the credibility of certain inscriptions, heretofore rejected for contradicting the Mon Paradigm.

Ultimately, the modern legend of Kyanzittha cannot sustain the viability of the Mon Paradigm or add anything to the theory concerning the existence of a Rāmaññadesa in Lower Burma prior to emergence of the Pagán kingdom. At best, it is irrelevant; at worst, it obfuscates Burma's early history. But why, then, was this modern legend so enthusiastically embraced by nearly everyone involved in the study of Pagán? Like much of the legend that was Lower Burma, it was embraced because it was commensurate with its *desired consequences.*

11 The Mon Paradigm and the Myth of the "Downtrodden Talaing"

One of the most important issues enmeshed in the historiography of early Burma is the notion of the "downtrodden Talaing." This is the belief that King Alaungpaya in the eighteenth century had conducted a war of extermination of the Mon people, enslaved them, and had deliberately created a derogatory Burmese term *(talaing)* to be used thenceforth for the Mon people. How tragic that these cultured people, the Mon, the "Greeks of Southeast Asia," who gave civilization to the more barbaric Burmese and T'ai speakers, were treated in this terrible way. This kind of commiseration made the Mon sentimental favorites of their colonial masters, both scholars and officials, and the myth became the basis for the conceptualization, organization, and reconstruction of nearly all of Burma's precolonial, and to an appreciable degree, also its colonial and postcolonial history. Not surprisingly, the theme of the "downtrodden Talaing" is thoroughly entangled in the Mon Paradigm, and although not entirely unambiguous, I suspect that sympathy for the Mon may have originally inspired the whole thesis; it certainly precedes it. This chapter describes the genesis, development, and perpetuation of one of the most egregious myths in colonial Burma's historiography.

Although I do not wish to debate the issue of whether the Mon as a people were in fact oppressed by Burmese speakers as claimed, it is, however, quite revealing that I have found nothing in the *precolonial* Mon histories that show any indication that they were, or felt themselves oppressed by any group, including the Burmese speakers, even when both parties were at war. Nor is this notion found in early Chinese, Arabic, or Burmese sources. Equally important, it is also *not found* in some of the earliest English-language reports about Burma, notably those of Michael Symes's missions to the court of Ava in 1759 and 1802.

In fact, the image of a victimized Mon people was not initially a *self*-image at all; it was a colonial construct, found originally *only in English* in the official memoranda just prior to and during the First Anglo-Burmese

War of 1824, and during the second half of the nineteenth century in western-language scholarship on Burma. Eventually this downtrodden image made its way into the colonial historiography of early Burma during the twentieth century, and from there to the next generation of Burma specialists, until today it is still being nurtured by our modern propensity to favor the underdog, celebrate minority ethnic autonomy, and show a general dislike for the authoritarian state, if not the state itself. It is as if colonial-period officials and scholars had produced a movie about early Burma in English unbeknownst to the indigenous, non-English-language-speaking society, which the following generations of Burma "experts" dealing with the subject of Mon-Burman relations largely accepted. And that "movie" rather than Burmese society itself, by and large informed today's understanding (actually misunderstanding) of Burma.

To reiterate, however, I am less concerned with the issue of alleged oppression, or even with the "real" etymology of the word *talaing,* than I am with showing *how* the notion of that supposed oppression was constructed and how colonial etymology of the word *talaing was made commensurate with its desired consequences.*

The First Anglo-Burmese War and the Downtrodden Talaing

So far, I have traced the notion of an oppressed Talaing peoples most explicitly to a proclamation made by Sir Archibald Campbell, commander of the British forces during the First Anglo-Burmese War of 1824, addressed to the Mons of the Delta.

> . . . Against you, inhabitants of the ancient kingdom of Pegue and the noble Talian race, we do not wish to wage war. We know the oppression and tyranny under which you have been labouring for a length of time, by the cruel and brutal conduct of the Burmese government towards you; they acknowledge you by no other title than the degrading and ignominious appelation [sic] of slaves; compare, therefore, your condition with the comfort and happiness of the four maritime provinces, . . . now under the protection of the British flag . . . choose from amongst yourselves a chief, and I will acknowledge him![1]

But how could Archibald Campbell, hitherto unknown in Burma affairs, have had such misinformation about the "Talian" people unless the information had been given to him? It suggests that prior to or during the First Anglo-Burmese War the notion of a downtrodden Talaing people was already present in the official discourse of the British Government of India. Yet I cannot find that notion earlier, even in one of the earliest British accounts of Burma: Michael Symes's journey to Ava in 1795 where, for the first time, he explains, in a footnote—suggesting that the use of the word "Taliens" among English speakers was new—that the people of Pegu, everywhere called Peguers, were actually called "Taliens" by the "Birmans."[2] Nearly all previous English-language accounts, such as that by Captain George Baker in 1755, referred to the people of Pegu as "Peguers," not Talaings. And importantly, neither Baker nor Symes had anything to say about any oppression or that the word *talaing* implied any sort of enslavement. Thus Campbell must have gotten that elsewhere or made it up as a contingency of war.

Symes's report was considered too "favourable" by the next envoy of the East India Company to Ava, Captain Hiram Cox, whose mission was from 1796 to 1798. According to Dorothy Woodman, Cox's *Journal* was "bad-tempered and misleading" and "provided the basis of one of the most hostile accounts of Burma ever written in time of peace."[3] Yet I did not find any reference in it that the word *talaing* implied enslavement, although Cox did write of the "tyranny," "impertinence," "dishonesty," "arrogance," "insolence," and "perversity" of "these [Burmese] people."[4] Cox's report was followed by G. T. Bayfield's *Historical Review of the Political Relations between the British Government in India and the Empire of Ava,* about which Hall wrote: it "is full of blemishes" [while his] "anti-Burmese prejudice has led him to be deliberately misleading, or even to falsify the record."[5] But he too apparently did not say anything about the downtrodden Talaing. Thus when and where precisely the notion of an enslaved Talaing people originated is not entirely clear, but it must have occurred after Symes (or Cox) but before or with Campbell.

Campbell's plea included another, related idea, called the "Pegu Project." Its objective was to take the Mon living in Burma and those who had fled to Siam during the previous several decades and recreate, at Pegu, "the ancient kingdom of the Mon" as a counterbalance to the court of Ava. The British Government of India, perhaps thinking that the Siamese might be eager to accept a strategy that would reduce the power of the Burmese while creating a buffer between them (the Siamese) and the Burmese, relayed the message to Siam to secure their help in the British War with the Burmese.

Captain Henry Burney, then envoy to the court of Siam, was to inform them of this strategy.[6] Apparently not Burney's own idea, he had obtained information from an intelligence report received from a Capt. Robert Fenwick, commanding officer at Martaban, and had presented it in a formal letter, signed by Burney, to the ministers of the king of Siam. In part, it stated that the British Government "has determined upon restoring the old Pegu Kingdom and establishing the Talliens as a barrier between the Burmese and English and Siamese. Such an arrangement will it is hoped be highly satisfactory to the Court of Siam, and urge it to the most prompt and decisive cooperation with the English."[7]

D. G. E. Hall in his biography of Burney made several attempts to convince the reader that Burney did not agree with the Pegu Project.[8] He even called it a "hare-brained" scheme and said that Burney bent over "backwards in an effort to treat the proposal seriously though quite obviously in his opinion it was impracticable and absurd."[9] These, however, were Hall's own conclusions made much later in hindsight; there is no evidence that Burney did not consider the project seriously at the time. Indeed Burney wrote that his concern was whether the British should keep "absolute pupillage" over the revived "Pegu Kingdom," not whether it was a viable idea, demonstrating that he did consider it seriously. The issue for Burney, it appears to me from his letters, was not so much *whether* the Pegu Project should be implemented, but *how* best to do it.

In any case, the *idea* of creating an independent Pegu kingdom ruled by the Mon, as well as the related notion that the word *talaing* conveyed notions of enslavement, had nonetheless become very much part of the official colonial discourse on Burma by the time the First Anglo-Burmese War had commenced. And although it may have originated as a political strategy—that was in fact discarded after Britain annexed the maritime provinces of Arakan and Lower Burma—it was likely the seed that later developed into the idea of the downtrodden Talaing. Virtually all the colonial scholars of Burma were also its officials, so that scholarship, like trade, followed the flag.

The Talaing Question and Scholarship of the Nineteenth Century

The policy that originally played the Mon minority of Burma against the Burman majority for immediate, wartime reasons, had direct consequences subsequently on colonial scholars and their Mon-speaking clients with regard to Mon-Burman relations. As wartime ideas led to a fuller, academic extrapolation of the downtrodden Talaing theme, scholars now searched for and "found" an etymology of the word *talaing* that fit those preconceptions. Unfortunately, the belief of the downtrodden Talaing (if not the etymology) is still with us today, much like the colonial period's projection backward into Burma's history of its prejudices regarding the myth of Rāmaññadesa.

The notion of the downtrodden Talaing appeared to have first surfaced among semischolarly publications in the mid-nineteenth century. Here the work of the Rev. Francis Mason was crucial. In the dedication of his book made to Phayre, on whom Mason depended heavily, he wrote:

> The golden age, when Pegu was *suvanna-bumme,* 'The land of gold,' and the Irrawaddy *suvanna nadee,* 'The river of gold,' has passed away, and the country degenerated into the land of paddy, and the stream into the river of teak. Yet its last days are its best days. If the gold has vanished,—so has oppression;—if the gems have fled,—so have the task-masters; if the palace of the 'Brama of Toungoo' is in ruins, who had 'twenty-six crowned heads at his command,'—the slave is free.[10]

Subsequently, the etymology of the word *talaing* became more seriously debated in semischolarly circles, albeit among a small group, beginning with Phayre in his 1873 article called "On the History of Pegu." There he suggested just the *opposite* of what most officials had been saying. He argued that the word *talaing* was likely derived from the word *talingana,*[11] a reference to the people from the Orissa region of South India by which (as Ussāla or Ussā) Lower Burma was also known. The word *talinga* is apparently a later variant of *kalinga.* As such it is found not just in Lower Burma but elsewhere in Island Southeast Asia, taking such forms as *keling, kaling, kling* in Malaya, Siam, Cambodia, and perhaps even the Philippines.[12]

The important point to note with Phayre's 1873 etymology is that *talaing* was considered an exogenous term with absolutely no ties to Alaungpaya's conquest of any downtrodden people. And even though Phayre's article is one of the earliest scholarly opinions on the subject without much linguistics theory to support it, it still receives acceptance among respected scholars today. As Wheatley stated rather emphatically in 1983, "there can be no doubt that the Burmese appellation 'Talaing' for the Mon people of the south is derived from Telingana. . . ."[13]

One year after Phayre's work was published, the Rev. James Madison Haswell published his *Grammatical Notes and Vocabulary of the Peguan Language,*[14] which ignored Phayre's opinion and continued the downtrodden thesis instead. He wrote that the etymology of the word Talaing stemmed from two Mon words, *ita luim* (or *ita lerm*), which he said meant "Father, we perish." Haswell conjectured that it was a "cry of distress doubtless . . . often heard in the wars of extermination waged by kings of the Alompran [Alaungpaya] Dynasty against the Peguans, whenever they raised the standard of revolt. From this was probably derived the word *talaing* the Burmese nickname for the Mons."[15] Absolutely no linguistic principles were presented to explain this conjectured etymology and link with Alaungpaya; it was simply asserted. But he had connected, perhaps for the first time the words *ita lerm, talaing,* and Alaungpaya.

In 1883 and 1884, about a decade after Haswell's work came out, Emil Forchhammer published the two parts of his *Notes on the Early History and*

Geography of British Burma. It was to become the most important source for perpetuating the theme of Burman oppression of the Mon. In part II Forchhammer took Haswell's statement about the plight of the Mon and made it part of the conclusions he had already reached regarding Mon-Burman relations and published in part I of his work in 1883. Like Haswell, Forchhammer ignored Phayre's thesis that the word *talaing* came from *talingana.* He offered instead the following explanation.

Prior to Alaungpaya's conquest of Pegu, he wrote, "the name *Talaing* was entirely unknown as an appellation of the Muns [Mon], and that it nowhere occurs in either inscriptions or older palm leaves and that by all nations of Further India the people in question is known by names related to either Mun or Pegu." He postulated that the "word '*Talaing*' is the term by which the Muns acknowledged their total defeat, their being vanquished and the slaves of their Burmese conqueror. They were no longer to bear the name of Muns or Peguans. Alompra stigmatized them with an appellation suggestive at once of their submission and disgrace." Therefore *talaing* meant "one who is trodden under foot, a slave. . . . Alompra could not have devised more effective means to extirpate the national consciousness of a people than by burning their books, forbidding the use of their languages, and by substituting a term of abject reproach for the name under which they had maintained themselves for nearly 2000 years in the marine provinces of Burma."[16] As we shall see, this was sheer nonsense.

Although the theme of the enslavement of the "Taliens" had appeared before both Haswell's and Forchhammer's works in Archibald Campbell's proclamation, it was Forchhammer who explicitly wrote that the word *talaing* meant, in the Mon language, being "trodden under foot," "a slave." That the word *talaing* was a reference only to the Mon may have come from Haswell, since the earliest version of what later became *Judson's Burmese-English Dictionary,* stated in 1826 that Talaing were Peguers;[17] that is, the many different people who happened to live in or were from Pegu. It was the way every other observer at the time and earlier had referred to them. And there is nothing in the 1826, the 1852, or the 1883 editions of *Judson's Dictionary* of Talaing being enslaved or downtrodden.[18] This notion appears only with the 1893 edition of *Judson's,* when Forchhammer's etymology of the word Talaing as "persons trodden upon" and Alaungpaya's alleged role were incorporated in it for the first time. Indeed, it was reproduced verbatim: "Alompra stigmatized them with an appellation suggestive at once of their submission and disgrace," exactly what Forchhammer had written in 1884.[19]

To be sure, Stevenson, the compiler of this edition did not agree with Forchhammer's etymology. He wrote in the preface that he had "inserted the extracts [from Forchhammer] because they are interesting. . . ." He then stated that he was "inclined to regard the derivation . . . [of Forchhammer] as somewhat fanciful . . . [and] think it is . . . highly probable that if Alaunghpara had wanted to leave a lasting stigma on the Mun, or *Talaing,* race, he would have used a Burmese epithet for the purpose," not a Mon one, since the word Talaing "is surely not a compound of any two *Burmese* words known to most persons. . . ."; it is derived from the Mon root *"lain,"* and the nominal particle *"ta."* Then he queried most revealingly whether *talaing* was even "a word now extant in the [Mon?] language?"[20] As we shall, see, it never was part of the Mon language![21]

As if to stress his point regarding fanciful attempts at etymology, Stevenson also noted that there were no linguistic grounds for another etymology provided by "the late Dr. Forchhammer" either. This had to do with the name of the town Bassein (Pathein in Burmese) which Forchhammer thought "was derived from the fact that in some bygone war a certain 'thein' (ordination hall) at the place had been the scene of much slaughter and therefore the Burmese called it Puthein, or 'hot thein.'"[22] Stevenson remarked that such a derivation was "very unusual" and very "unlikely."[23] We know, of course, that this was also sheer nonsense, as the word Bassein comes from the Old Burmese Pusiṁ, which had made its appearance at least by the mid-thirteen century in Old Burmese,[24] and only later appears in Middle Mon as Kusim in the Kalyani Inscriptions of the late fifteenth century.

Perhaps Forchhammer's views received attention because of his reputation as a scholar and his position as government archaeologist and professor of Pali at Rangoon College, and perhaps also because of his righteous indignation regarding the "plight" of the Mon, a sentiment which was clearly shared by others, such as Mason. However, when compared with Phayre's relatively neutral view of the same subject, Forchhammer's indignation is puzzling. It may have been the result of his personal experience among the Mon while conducting research for the publication of Part I in 1883. He focused on Lower Burma and particularly the Mon areas, and perhaps that shaped his views when Part II came out in 1884. Since it appeared a year after Phayre's *History of Burma,* it must have also been directed at Phayre's theory, still expressed in that *History,* that the word *talaing* was derived from *talingana.* It almost seems as if Forchhammer *wanted* to see the Mon as a "down trodden" group for some personal reason, the pursuit of which is beyond my competence and the subject of this book. Whatever the reason for Forchhammer's attitude, the discourse on the enslavement of the Mon that had appeared during the First Anglo-Burmese War of 1824–1826 had now not only permeated and shaped the works of both Haswell and Forchhammer but also found its way into *Judson's Dictionary* of 1893.

To reiterate, the definition of the word *talaing* as a downtrodden people was *new*. It was *not* found in the 1826, 1852, and 1883 editions of *Judson's*,[25] and the word itself might no longer have been widely used in indigenous society. The facts show, therefore, that only after 1884, and as a direct result of Forchhammer's definition, was the downtrodden definition of the word introduced into colonial-period scholarship for the first time. And its inclusion in the 1893 edition of *Judson's* was not the result of original and contemporary research, but of Stevenson's decision to include Forchhammer's "etymology" because it was "interesting." Thus the definition of the word *talaing*, in one of the most authoritative reservoirs of knowledge about Burma for westerners—*Judson's Burmese-English Dictionary*—on the eve of the twentieth century is actually a late nineteenth-century colonial-period construct.[26]

Forchhammer's definition had another important consequence: it also apparently changed the meaning of the word *myanmā* in *Judson's* subsequent editions. In the 1893 edition, *myanmā* had been defined as *both* "Talaings and Burmans collectively"[27]: that is, as an inchoate *national* term. Twinthintaikwun Mahasithu's *Myanma Yazawinthit* ["New history of the Myanma"], written about a hundred years before *Judson's* 1893 edition, also reveals a similar pattern in this development of the word *myanmā* from a more narrow, ethnolinguistic definition towards a more inclusive, collective, inchoate *national* term.[28] Indeed, as demonstrated in previous chapters, even the sixteenth-century sections of the *Zatatawpon* had begun to express similar sentiments. The process revealed a movement towards nationhood, in which the narrower, ethnic meaning of the word *talaing* had finally merged with the broader, more collective term *myanmā*, at least by the nineteenth century. This kind of evolution is not surprising because Burmese *(myanmā)* speakers were the dominant group that continued to rule the polity that became Burma, so that the name of the largest ethnic group and the name of the polity had become synonymous. The same happened to the Thai, Lao, Vietnamese, and Cambodian polities. However, in the 1953 and 1966 editions, the definition of the word *myanmā* had reverted to its more narrow, ethnolinguistic meaning to apply to Burmese speakers only, and the word *talaing* to Mon speakers only.[29] Forchhammer's ethnolinguistic definition had apparently influenced a change (at least in lexicography) in the direction towards which the word *myanmā* was naturally headed—a "national" meaning that included both groups.

It is true that the word *myanmā* (as *mranmā*) per se had appeared much earlier, in 1102 AD. At that time, though, it was an ethnonym for Burmese speakers, so that the term was used in adjectival phrases such as "Mranmā music" and the "kingdom" or "country of the Mranmā." This kind of usage was also applied to minority cultures and polities perceived to have been comprised of other ethnolinguistic groups, so that Pagán inscriptions mentioned "Rmeñ music," "Tircul music," and the "kingdom" or "country of the Tanluiṅ." By the late eighteenth and nineteenth centuries, however, Twinthin's chronicle and *Judson's Dictionary* were both using the word *myanmā* as if it referred to a national group (the Burmese), rather than just to an ethnolinguistic one (the Burmans).

But it did not remain that way, perhaps because of Forchhammer's ethnically loaded definition of *talaing* in the 1893 edition of *Judson's* that also changed the meaning of *myanmā* in its subsequent editions—after all the words had been combined—thereby helping to perpetuate that transformation. Forchhammer's retrogressive definition of *talaing* as a distinct, ethnolinguistic group had frozen in time both the definitions of *myanmā* and *talaing*, stopping their evolution towards the newer, collective, national meaning in the single term *myanmā* that they had already acquired by the late eighteenth and nineteenth centuries, reversing the trend backwards towards an eleventh-century definition instead.

Thus Forchhammer's views of reified ethnicity had prevailed. The manner in which people in positions of power and influence can and do change the path of language and history by the simplest of acts is rather amazing; in this case, a conjectural reconstruction of a single word based on not a shred of evidence. But in order to prevail, belief in that definition had to have also been part of a larger "consolidated vision," to use the late Edward Said's term, of others in power at the time.[30]

Notwithstanding the retrogressive definitions of the words *myanmā* and *talaing* as distinct ethnic terms in the 1953 and 1966 editions of *Judson's Dictionary*, the Constitution of 1947 deviated from that definition of *myanmā* in the political arena, and returned the term to the broader sociopolitical definition towards which it had been headed before colonial-period scholarship interfered. It became the word to represent all citizens of Burma.[31] Politics thawed what had been frozen in time by the pseudo linguists. J. S. Furnivall, with his usual vision, noted that the trend towards a "national consciousness" had been arrested by the British;[32] and I would argue, so was the word *myanmā* that expressed that national consciousness.

The Talaing Question in the Early Twentieth Century

By 1912 U May Oung had already proved Forchhammer's assertion—that the word *talaing* did not exist earlier than Alaungpaya—to be incorrect.[33] Duroiselle was more blunt: "the derivation offered by Forchhammer . . . followed later by J. Gray, is absolutely inadmissible, not only because it is fundamentally wrong, not to say absurd, but principally because it makes the word '*Talaing*' originate with Alompra in the 18th century." He then went on to cite the numerous texts that May Oung had presented earlier, extant prior to Alaungpaya, in which the word can be found.[34] They include Pagán and Ava period inscriptions, the literature of the Ava period, and the chronicles that followed both.[35] And as Wheatley showed later, the word was also found in Arabic and Chinese sources.[36]

In 1913 G. W. Cooper attempted to reconcile Phayre's etymology of *talaing* (that it came from *talingana*) and U May Oung's and Duroiselle's recent exposé of Forchhammer's erroneous assertion (that *talaing* was invented by and did not exist prior to Alaungpaya) with Haswell's etymology (that *talaing* was derived from *ita lerm*). That would preserve the all-important downtrodden thesis. Cooper therefore traced the origin of the word *talaing* not to Alaungpaya but to a class of people called Ita Lerm as described in two nineteenth-century Mon manuscripts.[37] These Ita Lerm were said to have been individuals born of exogamous marriages between Mon women of Lower Burma and South Indian fishermen of "Talingu." To verify the authenticity of the information contained in the two manuscripts, Cooper sought the testimony of five senior Mon monks.

He began by focusing on two questions. First, was the information about the Ita Lerm contained in the two manuscripts plausible?[38] In a written response, one of the priests, who was eighty-five years old, testified (in perfect Burmese), "I, . . . priest of the Thkekkaw Kyaung, . . . do certify that I have seen the *Weerng Dhat* manuscript [that is, the *Dhātuvaṃsa* or "Genealogy of the relics," originally a Sinhalese Buddhist text written in Pali] and that we, of the Mon race, accepted what is written in the manuscript as correct."[39] And what he verified was that "fishermen of Talingu, a Kala or foreign race, arrived in the Thatôn district and through their marriage with the women of that place (Mons) had children."[40] Of this Cooper wrote: "the *Talaings* therefore . . . were the offspring of a mixed marriage between the Indian fishermen . . . and the Mons. . . ."[41]

But neither the manuscripts nor the monk said any such thing. The translation of the manuscripts and the original Mon copies Cooper provided were *not* referring to the Talaing; they (and the monk) were both speaking of the Ita Lerm. Cooper, having assumed that the word *talaing* derived from the word *ita lerm* (following Haswell's etymology) had already concluded that the origin of the Ita Lerm people was the same as that of the Talaing. In effect, his research "results" only reiterated his original assumption.

Now that he had connected the Talaing and Ita Lerm via South India's "Talingu" (thereby accommodating Phayre's thesis), the next problem was to provide the Ita Lerm with some antiquity. He was compelled to do this by May Oung's and Duroiselle's articles that the word *talaing* preceded Alaungpaya. Cooper found the "answer" in the same two manuscripts.

They described a king named "Ajeen Neer Geerng Geer . . . [who] knowing that the race was destroyed or had [been] deteriorated by the father [this is probably where Haswell got his "Father, we perish" definition], offered them for that reason to the pagodas. . . . From that King's time, the year 300, up to now they are called *'Ita Lerm,'* and are well known by that name."[42] Cooper took this statement about the Ita Lerm being offered as pagoda servants and connected them to the Tanluiṅ people of the Pagán period by speculating that as pagoda servants the Ita Lerm had been taken to Pagán with their mythical king Manuha during King Aniruddha's equally mythical conquest of Thatôn in 1057.[43] (Once again the conquest of Thatôn served as the universal explanation for the history of the Mon in Lower Burma, and the downtrodden Talaing thereby became thoroughly entangled in the Mon Paradigm.) Needless to say, Cooper's analysis was an anachronistic quantum leap backward through time regarding terms and institutions not only separated by centuries of history but unproven to have been connected either linguistically or historically.

The second question Cooper asked the Mon monks was whether or not the Talaing and the Mon people were the same. Not only was the question misleading, it was also disingenuous, for it was deliberately designed to get a particular answer. Had he been genuinely interested in finding the origin of the Talaing, as suggested by the title of his article, he should have asked if *Ita Lerm* and *Talaing* were the same, not whether *Mon* and *Talaing* were. And by asking the question within the context of the manuscripts' description of the degraded Ita Lerm class, of course the Mon monks said no, not wishing to be associated with the Ita Lerm. Not surprisingly, the senior monk testified that "the Mons are not Talaings and should not be called thus for the reason that the Talaings are a degraded race and half castes," an obvious reference to the Ita Lerm, about whom he had just testified and therefore had every reason to believe was still the subject of discussion. The monk further stated that "this is also what is written in old manuscripts." That was *not* what was contained in the manuscripts the monk had been shown at all; the word *talaing* never once appears in them. Cooper's "methodology" had clearly misled the monk into assuming that Talaing and Ita Lerm were the same in order to get the answer he wanted. The monk then obliged Cooper by saying that "the Mons are not the same as *Talaings* but of a different class. . . ."[44] The testimony of the other four Mon priests followed suit, also written in perfect Burmese.

Cooper's entire approach was a self-serving process of subtly manipulating the contents of the texts and "leading the witnesses" to produce the results he wanted: namely, that the Ita Lerm were the origin of the Talaing and that present-day Mon did not consider themselves to be Talaing (alias Ita Lerm). Raising the second issue, which was quite irrelevant to the topic of his article, was clearly political, and led to his plea at the end, that "under these circumstances and out of some consideration for the Mon race as a whole, we should call them by their own name, Mon, and not Talaing as hitherto. . . . Why . . . should we continue to call them by a name which undoubtedly gives them pain?"[45]

But in fact Cooper never provided any evidence that the word *talaing* was ever used in precolonial Burma in such a derogatory manner. Indeed, as we shall see, the whole notion that the Talaing were a victimized, despised group belongs to twentieth-century colonial ethnography and found initially only in the English-language literature. It cannot be found in precolonial, indigenous texts. Thus for Cooper to entreat his readers to be more socially aware of the pain being called Talaing inflicted on the Mon (an invention of his own making) was a rather self-serving and self-righteous supplication. Nevertheless, it suggests that the issue had now shifted from shoddy historical linguistics and "methodology" to political correctness.

In 1914 Blagden wrote a devastating critique of Cooper's article and the sources on which he had depended. Probably the most balanced, clear-headed, and brilliant Burma scholar of this generation, Blagden showed that there is no good evidence that the word *talaing* was derived from *ita luim* (as he spelled it). "I am convinced," he wrote, "that [the Old Burmese form] *Tanluiṅ* . . . cannot by any of the ordinary principles of Mon word change be derived from *ita luim* . . ." or their old forms.[46] Moreover, Blagden argued, the word *ita* has not been found in the Pagán (and, I would add, Ava) inscriptions,[47] although *luim* might have been represented by the late (fifteenth century?) *rlum* or *rlim*. Therefore, Blagden concluded, he was not bound to admit that two Mon words were adopted into Burmese under the form *tanluiṅ*, before demonstrating instances of change of the *r* to *n* and *n* to *m*, either within the Mon language itself or between it and Burmese.[48] Besides, he wrote, it is not known whether *ita luim* is even Mon to begin with and whether it is two words or one.

Blagden's critique not only showed Haswell's original contention that the word *talaing* came from the word *ita lerm* to be linguistically untenable—on which Forchhammer's and Cooper's theses depended—it meant that the word and people called Tanluiṅ in Old Burmese are also unconnected to the word and people called Ita Lerm. In other words, although the account in the manuscripts Cooper presented as evidence on the origins of the Ita Lerm class per se may be entirely viable—that the class was perceived as a product of undesirable exogamous marriage patterns—that has no necessary bearing on the origins of the word and group of people known as Talaing or their assumed predecessors, the Tanluiṅ of the Pagán and Ava periods. There simply is no evidence that Ita Lerm and Talaing were ever connected historically, or (therefore also) etymologically. That notion also exists only in English-language scholarship, and, as far as I know, did not appear before Haswell's *Grammatical Notes* of 1874.

As to whether *ita lerm* was even a Mon expression presents an interesting case that needs more linguistic research. For our present purposes, the following will have to suffice. Because Halliday's *Mon-English Dictionary* published in 1922 includes the word *ita lerm* (as *italem*), at first glance it does appear to be a Mon word. But Halliday's definition of *italem* was taken verbatim from Haswell's *Grammatical Notes.* The entry in Halliday's dictionary said: "Italem, int. [interjection] Alas! (Literally: Father, we perish)."[49] Haswell's said: "int. Alas! Literally, Father [we] perish."[50] Therefore Halliday's definition is not independent confirmation of Haswell's, only reiteration, and nearly verbatim at that. In addition, Halliday's dictionary gave *apa* as the Mon word for "father," but stated that *ita* could be an obsolete form of "father," but only in combined form in the word *italem,* quite a tautology. In the end, neither Haswell nor Halliday provided any proof that *ita lerm* (or *italem*) existed prior to the mid-nineteenth-century manuscripts presented by Cooper or that the word (or words) were Mon to begin with.

I think it is quite possible that *ita lerm* might have been derived from the Pali and originally reflected Sinhalese social institutions, not Mon. If one looks at the Mon script in Cooper's manuscripts, rather than his awkward romanization into English, the spelling of *ita lerm* and the letters used to write it suggest a derivation from the Pali *itthi linga,* which means "female organ."[51] In the 1893 edition of *Judson's Dictionary* as well, the Pali word appears as *itthi liṁ* in the Burmese-Mon script, also meaning "the private parts of the female."[52]

This crucial term *ita lerm,* on which the entire theory of the downtrodden Talaing rests, with its heart-wrenching dramatic links to Alaungpaya's conquests and the alleged extermination of the Mon peoples and destruction of their culture, may actually be a reference to female sexual organs. Given the explanation in the Mon manuscripts presented by Cooper, where offspring degraded by their Mon mothers' sexual union with Indian fishermen became the Ita Lerm class, a Pali etymology for the expression actually makes more sense. The undesirability of certain exogamous marriage practices and their half-caste children, decried by the Mon, probably reflected what were originally Sinhalese caste rules. Remember that the two Mon manuscripts Cooper used were called the *Dhātuvaṃsa* (originally a Śrī Laṅkan text). The expression *ita lerm,* therefore, may have been a deliberate vulgar parody created by the Mon male, in which the woman (characterized by her sexual parts) was ultimately blamed for the degradation of "the race." Since Haswell and Halliday were both Christain missionaries, I suspect they would not have been particularly enamored of this definition, even had they known about or considered the Pali option. But because Judson seemed to have known his Pali well (and was also American Baptist), he probably had no such inhibitions.

All this only lends support to Phayre's position that the word *talaing* came from *talingana,* although not necessarily via *ita lerm.* Blagden supported Phayre by writing that the *talingana* derivation is more in accordance with "the ascertained rules of Mon word formation in the oldest known period of the language than the *ita luim* derivation."[53] Whatever the actual etymology of *ita lerm* or *talaing,* the evidence does not support Haswell's original thesis that *talaing* was derived from *ita lerm* and that the latter was a cry of distress caused by Alaungpaya.

But there is a caveat. Although clearly no precolonial linguistic or historical evidence has linked the words *talaing* and *ita lerm* with Alaungpaya's conquests, such an association may have developed subsequently among the Mon in the twentieth century. That would explain in part the colonial and early postcolonial ethnography regarding the status of people called Talaing. Blagden noted that "the Mon do use the term '*Talaing*' but apply it to a particular and somewhat despised class amongst themselves."[54] But, he concluded, it was likely an attempt "to shift on to the shoulders of a despised class the burden of a name which was unpopular because [it] was used by a foreign conqueror."[55] It is from this analysis by Blagden, apparently, that Wheatley nearly seventy years later obtained his information regarding the development of the word *talaing* as "presumably an attempt on the part of the [Mon] majority to shift the obloquy of a disparaging epithet on to the shoulders of the class least able to repudiate it."[56] These conclusions also seem to be confirmed by Christian Bauer, who states that the term *talaing* "is rejected nowadays by the Mons themselves who reconstruct it as a popular etymology of literary Mon . . . meaning *bastard.*"[57]

But since such usage by the Mon themselves is taken from twentieth-century testimonials, the derogatory connotation of the word appears to be a very late development. It may be that the word *talaing* replaced the despised *ita lerm* only during the colonial period, a phenomenon which Cooper and others then mistakenly projected back on Pagán times. As we shall see in the next section, prior to the twentieth-century the Mon never used the term *talaing* either for themselves or anyone else, and all earlier usage by others was neither derogatory, nor was it a term of subjugation and enslavement.

The Evidence on the Talaing (Tanluiṅ) people in Early Sources

The earliest possible reference to what may be the word *talaing* occurs in an external source: the *Hsin T'ang-Shu.*[58] Subsequently, an Arabic source dated to around 851 AD mentions the word *tanlwing* that some think may have been a reference to *talaing*.[59] It then appears in the late-thirteenth-century Yuan source discussed in earlier chapters regarding a "new Teng-lung kingdom." *Talaing* is found once again in an early-fifteenth-century Chinese account.[60] To date, I have not found it in any South Asian source.

Its first indigenous occurrence is in the Old Burmese inscriptions of Pagán. The two earliest are dated to 1082 and 1107, although Luce dates its first appearance to an inscription of 1204 AD instead.[61] Thereafter, it recurs in Ava period inscriptions[62] and the *Zatatawpon*, where the word *talaing* is found in what may be a fourteenth-century list of "one hundred and one people."[63] Subsequently, the word *talaing* is found in other sources,[64] including the early eighteenth-century chronicle of U Kala,[65] and Twinthin's, dated to the late eighteenth-century.[66] Around the same time that Twinthin wrote, *talaing* (as "Talien") appears in one of the earliest English-language sources to mention the subject, the first journal of Michael Symes, and by the beginning of the First Anglo-Burmese War of 1824–26, it is again mentioned in Archibald Campbell's proclamation as "Talian."

Moreover—and contrary to Stevenson's "etymology" discussed above that the word *talaing* was a combination of two Mon words—it has not been found in a single Old Mon inscription of the Pagán period so far recovered.[67] Nor is it found in a single Middle Mon inscription.[68] When King Dhammazedi wanted to celebrate the glory of his realm, he called it "this Rman kingdom of ours" not this "Talaing kingdom of ours." *Talaing* is also not found in any precolonial Mon chronicle discussed in the previous ten chapters. It is not found even in the manuscripts Cooper used to make his case, or in the early twentieth-century Mon chronicles published at Pak Lak, Thailand. And if Shorto's and Halliday's dictionaries, along with Bauer's works cited in this book, are, taken together, comprehensive, it means the word *talaing* cannot be found at all in the Mon language of Southeast Asia. It is truly a term used only in, or with reference to, Burma, and is clearly exogenous to Mon vocabulary itself.

In the earliest domestic sources written in both Old Burmese and Old Mon, the people called Talaing are also *not* connected to the people called Mon or Rmeñ, contradicting one of the most universally accepted conventions in the western study of Burma and considered to be "common knowledge." Indeed, if one were to ask anyone in Burma *not familiar with westernized Burma studies* what the word *talaing* means, they would invariably point to another ethnic group such as the Pwo Karen, or to a mixed group of some sort, but *not to the Mon.* That Talaing were not considered Mon is reinforced by a statement in the inscription of 1107 discussed in Chapter Ten, thought to have been erected by Kyanzittha, and written in Old Burmese. In it, the king stated that he had obtained a "Tanluiṅ wise man" on one of his Lower Burma campaigns when he destroyed the "Tanluiṅ kingdom" of Ussāla. Since he had already used the term Rmeñ five years earlier in his 1102 Old Mon inscription, why did the king not also say the "Rmeñ wise man," and the "Rmeñ kingdom of Ussāla," unless the word *talaing* was *not* a reference to the Mon people at the time?

It is possible that the Old Burmese did not yet have the word Rmeñ in its vocabulary at the time that Kyanzittha erected the inscription (1107), which is consistent with the late appearance of the Rmeñ people in Upper Burma, who are first mentioned in 1102. However, that would tend to confirm my contention that the Talaing and Rmeñ were indeed two distinct groups, as there already existed a word for the Talaing but not for the Rmeñ.

One could also argue, I suppose, that since the term *talaing* may have been a term of subjugation and an expression of hegemony on the part of the speaker, one would not expect to find an ethnonym such as Rmeñ, which reflects autonomy, in Old Burmese inscriptions, in much the same way Chinese texts used exogenous terms when referring to "inferior" Southeast Asians, or the way the United States government currently refuses to use the ethnonym Myanmā, obviously for political reasons but a statement of hegemony nevertheless. Yet nowhere in the Chinese, Arabic, Burmese, or the earliest of the English-language sources mentioned above was the word *talaing* ever used in a manner that suggested their subjugation or enslavement.

During the Pagán period, which provides some of the earliest and best evidence, people called Tanluiṅ enjoyed a variety of socioeconomic and political statuses, dominating no particular class or enjoying any special rank. One was a minister at court, others were well-to-do artisans and craftsmen, and still others were those called *kywan,* that is, people lower on the social scale and attached to institutions or individuals. *Kywan* were *not* slaves as we understand the term, even though twentieth-century convention continues to translate it that way, despite studies proving the contrary.[69] The largest number of Tanluiṅ mentioned during the Pagán period belonged to this *kywan* category.[70] So while some Tanluiṅ played important roles, many did not. Other ethnolinguistic groups were also present and performed similar varieties of functions, some more important, some less.[71] There is no reason to single out the Tanluiṅ in Pagán or Ava as being extraordinary, or having any more significance than any of the other minority cultural groups, unless, of course, one *wished* to emphasize that exemplary role *in retrospect,* so that their "plight" in the twentieth century as downtrodden people would appear even more tragic.

The word *talaing* was not used in a derogatory manner in later Burmese chronicles either; at least it is no different from the way "Mexican" and "Asian" are used in mainstream America today under noncontentious circumstances. Both U Kala and Twinthin used *talaing* in their eighteenth-century chronicles as a means of identification, not of disparagement, even though the latter's work was written only a few decades *after* the conquests of Lower Burma by Alaungpaya, when, according to Haswell and Forchhammer, the king allegedly invented this word of enslavement and subjugation for the Mon people. And that belief and definition of *talaing* can be found only in English-language sources, and only within the academic and official circles of colonial society. Neither its definition nor its use can be found elsewhere; that was not part of indigenous society or its sources, which existed outside that colonial enclave of "knowledge" and people. Eventually, however, that "knowledge" about the Talaing became part of colonial and postcolonial scholarship that fed what Steven Kemper calls western cognitive interests,[72] finally filtering down into Burmese society during the twentieth-century until it was applied to a despised group amongst the Mon by the Mon themselves. Only then were some of the Mon people of Burma persuaded (and rather easily too) by colonial officials and scholars that they were indeed "downtrodden" victims and that the word *talaing* was indeed a term of "enslavement." It is this latter "knowledge," begun by Haswell and Forchhammer, and perpetuated by Cooper, rather than Blagden's better-reasoned and more scholarly critique of it, that most scholars of Burma have chosen to inherit.

In the final analysis, the only thing we know for certain about who the Tanluiṅ people were during the Pagán and Ava periods is that they had come from, or were living in, Lower Burma at the time: that is all! It may be one of the reasons Luce wrote that the term *tanluiṅ* probably applied to the people of Lower Burma in a general way and not specifically to the Mon.[73] This was apparently still true by perhaps the fourteenth century when the *Zatatapon* listed Talaing and Rmañ as two distinct ethnic groups. By the time of U Kala's *Mahayazawingyi,* the word *talaing* was still being used for Lower Burma people, but a half-century later, those same people were being called both Talaing and Mon in Twinthin's chronicle. Apparently, then, what was once a general term for people in Lower Burma, had become, by the late eighteenth century, a more focused reference to the Mon people.[74] In short, the reconstruction of the word *talaing* stemmed not from sound linguistics or good history, but from the *desired political and social consequences* of that "etymology."

Conclusion

When colonial officials sought to recreate an independent Mon kingdom in Lower Burma as part of the British Government's 1824 war effort to counterbalance the Burmese monarchy in Upper Burma, it started a "discourse" on the "antiquity" of Mon civilization in Lower Burma and their alleged oppression by the Burmans ever since Aniruddha's eleventh-century "conquest of Thatôn." With Alaungpaya and his eighteenth-century unification of Burma fresh in the minds of early British writers—some of whom, like Baker, had actually met the king—it made the conquest story of Thatôn not only more believable, but current and relevant. This led some to create and endorse a popular etymology of the word that it meant downtrodden, derived from a deliberate policy on the part of Alaungpaya to degrade, enslave, and exterminate the Mon during his drive to unify Burma in the mid-eighteenth century.

But such conclusions cannot be found in non-western sources, including Mon-language texts. Nor can the derogatory use of the word *talaing* be found among the Mon people before the twentieth century, and even when it appears it was only after being pressed on them by colonial officials and scholars. The indignation eventually turned to sorrow and sympathy, as the plight of the Mon was compared with that of the Greeks, from which, of course, they would be rescued by those same colonial officials and scholars. By the early twentieth century both colonial masters and subjects were together lamenting and mourning the "loss" of the Mon's once-great culture of Burma.

With the help of their colonial "masters," the Mon[75] could now "reclaim their history and culture," but only with historiography, for it was something they could no longer do militarily or politically, in either Siam or Burma. In this endeavor, the conquest of Thatôn by Aniruddha became a rallying cry, the event that explained to the Mon how the Burmese speakers had oppressed them and taken away their ancient culture. As stated in an earlier chapter, the "fall of Thatôn" became their "Alamo," a symbol of their darkest tragedy, their loss of freedom, and the transference of their civilization to Pagán, along with their religion, spirit cults, monks, artists, sacred books, and of course, their *ita lerm* as pagoda servants. The notion of a "downtrodden" *Talaing* people could now be extended back to the eleventh century, while Pagán culture became the example par excellence of what Thatôn culture "must have" looked like earlier—exactly how early Burma archaeologists, in fact, interpreted their data!—in much the same way and perhaps for similar reasons that the Balinese, when their existence and culture was also being threatened by the Dutch, could point to Majapahit as the exemplar of their once-great culture.

However, this twentieth century portrayal of the relationship between Mon and Burmese speakers was not evident in earlier Mon texts concerning other contentious events. After all, it was only in the nineteenth and twentieth centuries when modern nations were in the making that the

Mon could consider the previous Upper Burma conquests of Lower Burma in a new, nationalistic category of thought.[76] Whereas the earlier Mon texts such as the *Yazadarit* had considered Upper Burma kings in much the same way that Siamese chronicles had regarded King Bayinnaung, even after two of his conquests of Ayudhyā in the sixteenth century: as a *cakkavattī* ("world conqueror") who belonged to a universal Buddhist world not composed of nations with marked boundaries and ascribed ethnicities. Only in a twentieth-century nation-state context, could Aniruddha be regarded as a Burman king who had conquered a Mon kingdom; these were categories, issues, and concerns not present before. Grieving Aniruddha's conquest of Thatôn while romanticizing Rāmaññadesa as the golden age of the Mon in Burma became important issues to the Mon only after colonial scholarship on the same subject had already appeared and molded it in that fashion. It was not only a late, colonially derived idea, but for the Mon of Burma, almost an afterthought, and mainly the perspective of those Mon who had not integrated well culturally or geographically into Burmese society but had retained their culture of exile in Siam.

This kind of "knowledge" and sentimentality regarding the Mon led to the interpretation of Burma's history by colonial scholarship mainly as an ethnic conflict, whereby one distinct ethnic group was depicted as being in a struggle for its life against another *because* of that imagined ethnicity. Forchhammer's words again best represent that view, despite its almost total historical *inaccuracy*.

> [The] maritime provinces of Burma have been for the last eight centuries the scene of struggle for supremacy between the Burmans and *Talaing*s. The victor destroyed the towns, fortifications, and religious buildings of the vanquished foe only to be served with a like measure of retribution when the latter again had found concert and strength under the cover of a feigned submission. It was the *Talaings* who suffered the last crushing defeat at the hands of the Burmans before the British conquered both. Alompra consigned the Talaing literature to the flames, defaced their inscriptions, prohibited the use of the Talaing language, and destroyed every town and village that ventured to oppose his progress. The *Talaings* today have nearly merged with the Burmans, their own vernacular is almost forgotten, their literature has not been rewritten, and their history and traditions are nearly effaced from their memory.[77]

Phayre also shared Forchhammer's views on the general picture of ethnic conflict, even if he disagreed with the etymology of the word *talaing* or Alaunghpaya's alleged role in it. Thus on several occasions, Phayre (among many other English writers) compared "Burma" with "Pegu," as if they were two different countries, and wrote of the people of Upper Burma from what he imagined was the true perspective that the Talaing had of them: namely, the "hated foreigners."[78] This binary model was perpetuated by Bode (and others), who, by the first decade of the twentieth century wrote in a similar vein when comparing Upper and Lower Burma as "two countries."[79] These views, incidentally, are astonishingly similar to those currently fashionable in the field of Southeast Asian studies, whereby differences *within* Burmese society are often regarded as profound and significant as those between it and those outside that culture, such as the West. The belief that ethnicity was a concrete, tangible entity rather than a relative, abstract perception shaped the periodizing of Burma's history into phases of ethnic dominance and decline, an organizational scheme not found in, or shared by earlier domestic chronicles.

Thus, despite the scholarly discrediting of Forchhammer's thesis of the downtrodden Talaing on several, crucial occasions by the first two decades of the twentieth century, the most important histories published on the country in English that followed him (as well as many that followed Phayre, Harvey, and Hall's works) nevertheless perpetuated the gist of Forchhammer's conclusions, so that the consensus of colonial scholarship on the nature and impact of ethnic relations on Burma's history by mid century had not changed but strengthened. In fact, it provided the ideological basis and vindication for implementing the colonial government's administrative policy of ethnic separation: divide and rule. It was, of course, rationalized as a process that equalized the races by eliminating the "traditional shackles" of hierarchy that had favored the majority ethnic group.

This late, colonially created image of "perpetual ethnic animosity" in the country was also projected backwards to a much earlier period, which additionally justified their policy as having "historical precedent." Then, when it was placed in a western methodological framework of linear progress, it indeed appeared to be a natural development "confirmed" by the rise of nation-states in Southeast Asia organized mainly around majority ethnic groups.

The myth of the "down trodden" *Talaing,* its *a posteriori* affirmation of the Mon Paradigm, and the role of ethnicity in the making of Burma's history were thereafter all institutionalized in colonial historiography and ethnography, in most cases by the same officials and scholars who had generated these ideas in the first place, to become the conceptual and empirical basis for Burma scholarship for at least another half-century, a process to be discussed in Chapter Twelve.

12 Colonial Officials and Scholars
The Institutionalization of the Mon Paradigm

THE PREVIOUS eleven chapters have shown how, for over one hundred years now, the Mon Paradigm has dominated virtually all interpretations regarding the early history of Burma and also influenced aspects of early Mainland Southeast Asian studies. The question that we might be asking by now is how and when was the Paradigm institutionalized? Who was involved, and why did these particular individuals at that particular time decide to interpret Burma's history in that particular way? The question of "how," "when," and "who" can be answered relatively satisfactorily even though not as precisely as desired. But the question of "why" must necessarily be a matter of interpretation. Certainly, all involved had their own prejudices, some clearly personal. But for most, a prevailing political, academic, social, and intellectual climate seemed to have shaped their perspectives.

At the same time we must remember that these individuals were pioneers: no one before them had seriously attempted to reconstruct Burma's history in a "scientific" way. And although the indigenous chroniclers were absolutely vital for the reconstruction of a coherent narrative with specific events and individuals—without whom no history of Burma could have been written in English—and often succeeded in reconstructing certain components that we might call "scientific history," the early colonial officials and scholars who wrote about Burma were in many ways the first to do so. This is particularly true of those who wrote during the nineteenth century, without the kinds of data, tools, or information that those who wrote at the turn of the twentieth century had. Thus although my critique may sound harsh at times, and is, admittedly, done in hindsight, it is not without an appreciation of the context in which these pioneers worked. The intent here is neither to rationalize nor condemn their scholarship, but to *explain* in greater detail how it was responsible for the genesis, development, and perpetuation of the Mon Paradigm.

This chapter will focus on the way the Mon Paradigm became institutionalized as a school of thought in the twentieth century, but built on the intellectual (and ideological) foundations laid in the nineteenth. As such, the chapter really has more to do with colonial historiography than with that of early Burma. Nonetheless, its colonial underpinnings are also an important component; indeed, some might say the *only* important component. Although I would not go that far, it is certainly true that the way the west has understood—and in many cases, misunderstood—precolonial Burma's history, has shaped our "knowledge" of Burma today.

The Origins and Development of the Mon Paradigm

The Mon Paradigm, as we have seen, was not created by any single individual. It began with King Dhammazedi attempting to legitimate his reign and programs, continued with U Kala for reasons still not entirely clear, and only sometime in the middle of the nineteenth century were both narratives combined by colonial officials and scholars to produce the thesis that the Lower Burma Mon were responsible for the culture and civilization of the Upper Burma Burmans. This colonial combination of the two indigenous parts and their establishment as "truth" is the subject of this chapter. It first describes the political, military, academic, and personal circumstances that resurrected Dhammazedi's "legend that was Lower Burma," and then addresses the institutionalization of the thesis that the Lower Burma Mon civilized the Upper Burma Burmans.

As demonstrated in Chapter Eleven, the seeds for resurrecting Dhammazedi's linking of Suvaṇṇabhūmi and Rāmaññadesa seemed to have been sown during the First Anglo-Burmese War of 1824–1826, when the British Government of India, desiring to establish a countervailing force against the Burmese monarchy and to legitimate their conquest of Lower Burma, proposed the Pegu Project. As colonial officials were also its scholars, this resulted in scholarly attempts to establish the antiquity of a Mon kingdom in Lower Burma. If only it could be shown that Suvaṇṇabhūmi was Rāmaññadesa, or was at least located in the Lower Burma region, it would provide a most important piece of evidence to justify the reestablishment of that ancient Mon kingdom. Although Dhammazedi had made that link in the fifteenth century, no one at this time knew about it, as the Kalyani Inscriptions had not yet been rediscovered.

But historical circumstances eventually overtook the Pegu Project. The British had won both the First and Second Anglo-Burmese Wars, which landlocked the Burmese monarchy in Upper Burma. It was only a matter of time before all of Burma was finally annexed (in 1885–1886), so that the Pegu Project was really no longer needed after the Second Anglo-Burmese War of 1852, and therefore never actually implemented. However, its concerns were already part of scholarly "discourse" by then, so that the search for an ancient Mon Kingdom in Lower Burma nonetheless continued unabated, and became an integral part of English-language scholarship on the early history of Burma.

Sometime before 1860 Bishop Paul Bigandet published the first edition of *The Life or Legend of Gaudama.* But only with the second edition, published in 1866, was the link made between Suvaṇṇabhūmi and Rāmaññadesa.[1] A Capt. H. Hopkinson, commissioner of the Martaban and Tenasserim Provinces, had convinced the American Mission Press, publishers of Bigandet's second edition, to include a supplementary section "on the names and situations of the principal towns and countries, mentioned in the *Legend,* with the view of identifying them with modern sites and places."[2] One of these was Suvaṇṇabhūmi, which appears in Bigandet's second edition as the "district of Thaton . . . in the country of Ramagnia. . . ."[3] Thus, and perhaps for the first time in the English-language scholarship of Burma, Suvaṇṇabhūmi was linked to Lower Burma via Rāmaññadesa.[4]

Arthur Phayre's article "On the History of Pegu" followed in 1873, where he made the same case, although in a more academic and scholarly manner.[5] He cited "as his chief authority" a narrative written in "the Talaing, or Mun, language by Tsha-ya-daw A-thwa, a Buddhist monk."[6] However, my research shows that this is the same work known as the *Slapat Rājawaṅ Datow Smin Roṅ,* discussed in earlier chapters. It was not an original composition written by the monk Phayre named, but a "collation, composition, and restoration" of another historical work.[7] Most important, it has nothing to say about Rāmaññadesa being Suvaṇṇabhūmi, at least not in the version Halliday translated. That explains Phayre's statement that he had obtained that particular information from another source:[8] namely, from "traditions current among the people of Pegu. . . ."[9] In other words, the belief that Rāmaññadesa was Suvaṇṇabhūmi has no better verification than "traditions current" at Pegu even by one of the foremost early colonial scholars of Burma. Perhaps for the above reasons, Phayre readily admitted that "the materials for a full history of the Mun people either do not exist, or are not now available in Pegu."[10] As we shall see, he was right on both counts, and such a full history would have to wait until 1910.

A Capt. C. J. F. S. Forbes, deputy commissioner of British Burma and Phayre's immediately subordinate, subsequently made the same connection between Suvaṇṇabhūmi and Rāmaññadesa in his *Legendary History of Burma and Arakan,* published posthumously in 1882.[11] Forbes had criticized Phayre's 1873 work on Pegu as "incomplete," while claiming that his own work had used "original Talaing" manuscripts along with U Kala's *Mahayazawingyi,* implying that Phayre had not.[12] It is a puzzling statement, and difficult to reconcile with what we know of Phayre's sources, which, more likely than not, Forbes had probably used freely with Phayre's knowledge and permission.[13]

In any case, the following year Phayre's *History of Burma* was published, in which he reiterated his 1873 position that "the identity of the Khryse of Ptolemy, of the Suvarna Bhumi of the Buddhist legends, and the city of Thahtun in Pegu . . . appears to be certain." But this time, he cited Bigandet's second edition, which now included Captain Hopkinson's supplement regarding Suvaṇṇabhūmi being Rāmaññadesa.[14] Thus, the "evidence" to support that most important connection being made between Suvaṇṇabhūmi and Rāmaññadesa in colonial sources was not only late, but the direct result of Captain Hopkinson's intervention that probably stemmed from the earlier concerns raised by the Pegu Project's attempts to justify the establishment of an ancient Mon kingdom in Lower Burma. Scholarship indeed followed the flag.

With regard to the second component of the Mon Paradigm—the "conquest of Thatôn"—Phayre's *History* was also one of the earliest publications in English to mention it, along with Forbes's *Legendary History* cited above.[15] But because Phayre admitted that in the "Talaing Chronicles, the conquest . . . is not to be found, . . ."[16] both he and Forbes must have obtained the story from U Kala's *Mahayazawingyi,* which Phayre reportedly had in his possession, and to which Forbes obviously had access as Phyare's immediate subordinate.[17] Only much later, in 1910 and 1912, were the *Pak Lat Chronicles* published, in which the complete version of the conquest as described in U Kala first appears in the Mon language, over two decades *after* Phayre's and Forbes' publications in the English language had also included the event.

Yet Michael Symes nearly eighty years earlier had already mentioned that event, along with the heart of the Mon Paradigm—the civilizing of Upper Burma by the Lower Burma Mon. Symes wrote in his *Journal* of his second trip to Ava in 1802 that "Much of Burmese civilization, including Hīnayāna Buddhism, had come to them from the Mons, whose independent kingdom with its capital at Thaton had been conquered by King Anawrahta in the middle of the eleventh century A.D. and incorporated in the empire of Pagan."[18] Until then, no English-language source that I know of had linked the conquest with its putative civilizing consequences.

It is curious that Phayre had nothing to say about that alleged civilizing process,[19] and this leads me to believe that he did not know of Symes's account, or it may not have been available at the time. The latter seems plausible, since we find no mention of this idea in the other early firsthand accounts that shortly followed Symes's, such as Hiram Cox's or John Crawfurd's.[20] Nor does it appear in 1833, when Father Vicentius Sangermano published *The Burmese Empire A Hundred Years Ago.* In fact, he had nothing to say even about Aniruddha.[21] It was also not part of Henry Yule's account of his mission to the court of Ava in 1855 (with Phayre), even though there was ample opportunity for the subject to come up, particularly as the two visited Pagán and made many drawings and notes about its temples.[22] Perhaps they were also not privy to Symes's second journal, which was not published until much later.

By 1860, however, the Rev. Francis Mason had expressed a similar idea, writing that "Anoratha is said to have built a series of pagodas and temples, in Pugan, on the model of those then existing in Thatung [Thaton]. . . ."[23] Although that idea may not have come from Symes—since he had nothing to say about Pagán temple styles being borrowed from Lower Burma—Mason's sentence sounds as if he had obtained the information from someone else ("Anoratha is said to have built . . ."). Finally, after twenty more years of simmering, a most explicit statement regarding this issue was made rather forcefully, by none other than Emil Forchhammer. He wrote that "there was no Burmese civilization to speak of till the Talaings conquered the upper country [sic],"[24] "nor did they [Burmans] prior to this event [the conquest of Thatôn] possess an alphabet, much less a literature," so that "the Burmans [must have] borrowed their alphabet from the Talaings."[25]

This claim, that Lower Burma Mon culture civilized Upper Burma Burman culture, the heart of the Mon Paradigm, originally made by Symes in 1802 nearly a hundred years earlier, had become, by the last quarter of the nineteenth century, the most dominating framework of analysis in the reconstruction of early Burma, which continued throughout the twentieth century in the work of seminal Burma scholars until today.[26]

In 1883 Forchhammer published a treatise on the ancient geography of Burma. There he attempted to link many of the toponyms in Buddhist Pali literature with those in Burma, as Bigandet's second edition had done, for by then Forchhammer was also convinced that Suvaṇṇabhūmi and Rāmaññadesa were indeed references to Mon Lower Burma. He even went so far as to state that "no reasonable objections can be raised in connecting the foundation of the Shwe Dagon Pagoda with Taphussa and Bhallika . . . in the 5th or 6th century before Christ as an accredited fact in the early history of British Burma."[27] And when Phayre's history appeared in the same year, it had the effect of confirming the antiquity of Rāmaññadesa, even though Phayre had said nothing about the Mon civilizing the Burman.

It must have been shortly after Phayre's *History of Burma* was published that the Kalyani Inscriptions were discovered.[28] Their narrative about Soṇa and Uttara, the Third Buddhist Council of Aśoka, and the arrival of orthodox Theravāda Buddhism in Southeast Asia clinched the issue for colonial scholarship and its view that the Suvaṇṇabhūmi of Aśokan India was indeed

Lower Burma's Rāmaññadesa. By then the conquest of Thatôn as described in U Kala's *Mahayazawingyi* (if not also Michael Symes's second journal) was already familiar to colonial scholars, and thus the three critical components of the Mon Paradigm had finally come together in colonial scholarship.

Then in the winter of 1886–1887 Forchhammer discovered the Myazedi Inscriptions. Often called the Rosetta Stone of Burma, these were absolutely crucial to the confirmation and expansion of the Mon Paradigm, particularly with regard to the writing system of Burma, as we have seen.[29] In the context of the recently consolidated concept that Suvaṇṇabhūmi was Rāmaññadesa, Forchhammer's assertion regarding Lower Burma's role in the civilizing of Upper Burma combined with his "downtrodden Talaing" notion to become the guiding framework of analysis for nearly every work on early Burma thereafter.

By 1909 Mabel Bode, in her *Pali Literature of Burma,* a seminal work in the understanding of the history of Theravāda Buddhism in Pagán and early Burma, not only continued the conquest story and its alleged civilizing consequences, but she took it for granted. She wrote: "The origin and history of the Mon or Talaing people, who were to be (unwillingly as it happened) the messengers of the purer Buddhism, need not be discussed here. The point from which we start is their acceptance of Buddhist teaching from India and the rise of a body of learned monks in Rāmañña who preserved the ancient Doctrine and Discipline and conveyed them to Upper Burma, where both had long been forgotten."[30] In other words, by the time her book appeared, the Mon Paradigm had already become the point of departure rather than a thesis under discussion. But because archaeological and epigraphic discoveries showed that Pali Buddhism already existed among the Pyū well before the alleged conquest of Thatôn, Bode had to quality her perspective on the Mon Paradigm. Whereas her predecessors regarded the Mon civilizing of Upper Burma as a novel event, she saw it as a resurrection of a long-forgotten tradition.

Then came the most revealing of colonial-era texts about the Mon, the two Pak Lat volumes written in the Mon language and published in 1910 and 1912. For the first time, a "comprehensive" history of the *Burma* Mon had been published in their own vernacular. Not only did the complete account of Aniruddha's conquest of Thatôn appear for the very first time in the Mon language, but so did the theme made popular by Forchhammer of its consequences—the Mon civilizing of Pagán. Heretofore, although the *Nidāna* may have mentioned the conquest story, the supposed consequences had hitherto not been found in any other dated Mon-language source concerning Burma. It is only in the *Pak Lat Chronicles* that we find, for the first time in Mon, the statement that as a result of Mon culture having been transported to Pagán, that kingdom thereafter "flourished like unto a heavenly city."[31]

This supports the contention that the Mons' realization of their plight as victims is also a late one, and was shaped, if not directly determined by turn-of-the-century colonial scholarship. Part of the reason the notion took so long to reach Mon sources is that this scholarship was published first in English, and only later was introduced to the Mon in both Burma and Siam. The Mon had had no way of knowing what was being written about them until colonial-period scholars finally told them.

Foremost among the disseminators of this information were scholars of the Mon language and culture who were in direct contact with Mon people. Especially important were the American missionary Robert Halliday, sometimes known as the "father of Mon studies in Burma"; Colonel Gerini, who knew the important Mon texts discussed in previous chapters, especially the "Gavaṁpati," and who had published treatises on Mon proverbs in the first issue of the Siam Society's journal; Professor Schmidt of Vienna, who wrote "A History of Pegu in the Mon Language" in German; and Dr. Frankfurter, chief librarian at the National Library in Bangkok, who, with his Mon assistant Phra Tepalok, pressed for the publication of the Pak Lat volumes.[32] In fact, the printer and publisher of these volumes, the superior of the Krun Cin Monastery in Thailand, at first had other priorities and had already begun publication of the *Tipiṭakas* in the Mon script. But after producing only twenty-one out of the thirty-nine anticipated volumes, he was persuaded by Frankfurter, who "urged the printing of . . . the historical books . . . [as] more likely to interest the outside world; and, as a result, . . . [the two volumes] . . . appeared."[33] Not coincidentally, they emerged at the beginning of the nationalistic period in Burma, when similar works were being produced by other regional ethnic groups. The *Dhanyawaddy Yazawinthit*[34] ("New history of *Dhanyawaddy*"), for example, which celebrated the kingdom considered by the Arakanese to have been their first, was also published in 1910.

It is also significant that the Pak Lat volumes were published not by the Burmanized Mon of Burma but by the Mon of Siam. These were the exiled descendants of those who had fled from the seventeenth-century wars between the two countries, the eighteenth-century reunification of Burma by Alaungpaya, and the First Anglo-Burmese War. The Mon in Siam were said to have retained much of their language, culture, and identity at their community at Pak Lak, south of Bangkok.[35] In contrast, the Mon who continued to live in Burma had become fairly well integrated into Burmese society. By the early twentieth century they had lost, or were rapidly losing, much of their language, culture, and identity.[36] This helps explain why even by 1913 the Burma Mon considered neither Thatôn nor its conquest by Aniruddha to have been the national disaster that the Siamese Mon thought it had been.[37]

Institutionalizing the Mon Paradigm

Early one evening in 1908 or 1909, when U Tun Nyein, then government translator, was taking a walk with J. S. Furnivall, he showed Furnivall an article published by a "Burman" in the new *Siam Society Journal.* On his way home, Furnivall reflected that "what we need in Burma is a Burma Society,"[38] and thus was born the idea of The Burma Research Society. Later he discussed his idea with Charles Duroiselle and U May Oung, and by 1910 the dream had become reality.[39]

The Society produced the first English-language academic journal in the country, the *Journal of the Burma Research Society.* It was devoted to scholarship focused on Burma, particularly its history, language, literature, ethnology, art, religion, archaeology, but on occasion, included subjects dealing with neighboring countries as well. Not surprisingly, of the first nineteen presidents (until 1959), thirteen were British colonial officials, one was an Indian, and five were Burmese. All the non-British presidents had been trained in England, or elsewhere in the English system, where they received higher degrees. Thus they were very much part of the westernized, elite class and shared, at least initially and in part, what the late Edward Said called a "consolidated vision."

Included in the very first issue of the *JBRS* was one article, "Some Anthropometric Data of the Talaings," which I have singled out as illustrative of the general sentiments at that time regarding ethnicity, a topic that underlay the premises of the Mon Paradigm. It was by a B. Houghton, who had measured the physical attributes of what he considered "the Talaing or Mon race." He wrote that "care was taken to avoid so far as possible any persons of Burmese or Indian blood—the Chaungzon township contains some of the purest strains of the old Talaing stock—but apart from this consideration, no attempt was made to discriminate in favour of specially good specimens, the men being measured just as they came."[40]

Much of the debate in that first decade regarding Mon history assumed its antiquity and pre-Pagán existence in Lower Burma. The main actors at the time were Blagden, Cooper, Furnivall, Duroiselle, Taw Sein Ko, and May Oung. Halliday became more prominent in the second decade, and finally Luce from the 1930s onward. From its start until 1977, with a brief hiatus just prior to World War II when the journal stopped publishing temporarily, virtually all the articles dealing with the Mon in Burma either accepted or advocated the Mon Paradigm.[41] Three of the last fourteen articles, in

1976 and 1977, were written by Luce,[42] who was still expounding the Mon Paradigm, and in the first volume of the last issue, Nai Pan Hla did much the same thing.[43] From the first to the last issue of the *JBRS*, then, the Mon Paradigm reigned supreme on subjects dealing with the Mon in early Burma.

However, there was, at the beginning of the twentieth century, at least one detractor. Taw Sein Ko was an official of the Archaeological Survey of Burma, and although very much part of the "consolidated vision" of the Mon Paradigm and its generation, he nevertheless had doubts that Burma's civilization owed everything to the Mon even though he accepted the conquest story as historical and the reasons Forchhammer had proposed for the alleged oppression of the Talaings.[44] But the social, academic, and administrative dominance of those advocating the Paradigm effectively isolated Taw Sein Ko's objections to a few short notes in the *Journal.* He eventually countered with his *Burmese Sketches,* two good-sized volumes published in 1913 and 1920.[45] Yet to no avail, for not only did Taw Sein Ko share many of its axioms, but the Mon Paradigm had grown much larger than any single individual.

In terms of Burma's archaeology, the numerous publications produced by the Archaeological Department of India, Burma Circle, were its main outlet of information. The most prominent were the *Archaeological Survey of India* (and later, of Burma), *Indian Antiquary,* and *Epigraphia Indica,* along with a whole series of Annual Reports and Memoirs under the Archaeological Department of India. Some of the same people from the Burma Research Society—particularly Forchhammer, Duroiselle, and Taw Sein Ko—were also responsible for submitting the Burma sections for these journals, as well as often being involved in the actual excavations and repair of monuments in Burma.

The Archaeological Department of Burma became independent between 1901 and 1902 and thereafter published the *Archaeological Survey of Burma* as a separate entity. Originally in English, by the late 1940s, however, it was produced only (or mainly) in Burmese. In terms of the Mon Paradigm, virtually everything excavated or discovered in Lower Burma and reported in this journal was assumed to have been Mon. But as most of these finds were Brahmanic or Hindu rather than Buddhist, their impact on the thesis is not clear. Indeed, the information in the *Archaeological Survey* ultimately helped kill the Mon Paradigm, for it contained much of the data on the Pyū civilization which would eventually contradict the favored thesis. That, however, would have to wait over a hundred years.

What the parent journal, the *Archaeological Survey of Burma,* could not do at the time, its offspring certainly did. That offspring was *Epigraphia Birmanica,* probably the most important journal to institutionalize the Mon

Paradigm, for it was virtually devoted from its inception to advancing the idea. In 1919 the first issue appeared under the directorship of Duroiselle, assistant archaeological superintendent for epigraphy. Both the conquest of Thatôn and its alleged consequences on Pagán were very much its focus. Although Forchhammer had popularized the theme earlier, Duroiselle presented an explicit articulation of the Mon Paradigm:

> The result of the conquest of Thatôn was momentous for Pagan; Anorata took Manuhā, the king of Thatôn, a captive to this capital, and with him, the most learned monks, the Pali scriptures and their commentaries, and all the best artisans and artists he could find. . . . Materially the conquerors, the Burmese became, to a great extent, intellectually the conquered; . . . The form of Mahāyānism then extant at Pagán gave way to the Hīnāyanism of Thatôn; magnificent temples were built under the supervision of Indian and *Talaing* architects; it is only soon after 1057 that inscriptions on stone and votive tablets in Burmese, *Talaing,* and Pali make their appearance at Pagán.[46]

With these words Duroiselle not only secured the antiquity of Mon civilization in Burma as historical, but provided a believable event in Burma's early history responsible for effecting the transportation of that culture. And it was backed by a "scientific" approach in a journal modeled after the respected *Epigraphia Indica.* The very fact that these statements appeared in the inaugural issues of the most prestigious scholarly publication in English that dealt with primary data on early Burma meant that what had been only a theory was now an established "truth."

Thereafter, virtually every piece of archaeological, epigraphic, art historical, numismatic, and other textual evidence discovered in Lower Burma was considered to be Mon and *earlier,* while virtually everything found at Pagán was Burman and *later.* Nondescript Brahmanic, Hindu, and Buddhist artifacts, even coins without any dates or Mon writing on them, were automatically considered to have been Mon so long as they were discovered in a location considered to have been a putative Mon center, such as Pegu, and were said to have belonged to "that" pre-Pagán Mon civilization, tautologically reconfirming the theory. Presumed antiquity was now linked to artifact, ethnicity, and geography in a static and irrevocable manner. Premise and proof had become synonymous.

In the very next issue of *Epigraphia Birmanica* Duroiselle's thoughts were further refined by Blagden,[47] who expressed them a bit more precisely and revealed the source of his inspiration.

> The conquest of the old Môn capital of Sadhuim (in Burmese pronounced Thatôn) was a critical moment in Burmese history in the same way that the

> Roman conquest of Greece was in the history of Rome. In each case the conquered nation imparted to the conqueror many things which he lacked and which he eagerly accepted. The Burmese took over from the Môns their form of Buddhism with its Pāli canon, their particular variety of the Southern Indian alphabet, and certain useful or ornamental arts and crafts. Monks, scholars, and skilled artisans were imported in considerable numbers from the Môn country to the Burmese capital, and it is largely due to the religious, scholarly and artistic impetus thus given that Burmese civilization, as illustrated for example in the temples and inscriptions of Pagan, took its particular line and form. That is not to say that the Burmese prior to this period were a mere race of savages any more than were the Romans before they fell under the glamour of Greek art and literature. But just as Rome became in a great measure Hellenized, so the Burmese adopted much from the Môns, and a great deal of what is now supposed to be distinctively and characteristically Burmese was in fact derived by them from the Môns. . . .[48]

The Mon Paradigm now had a comparative western model, Greece and Rome, which the western or westernized scholarly community could appreciate even better. What was new for Burma's history—it had already been suggested for India's—was the theme of the conquered having conquered the conqueror with its culture. In addition, Duroiselle, as superintendent of the Archaeological Survey, made what turns out to have been an extremely important *administrative* decision: the highest priority given to the *Epigraphia Birmanica* went to the translation of Mon inscriptions. By the time the journal was defunct—1934, for all practical purposes—no translation of Old Burmese had yet appeared in it, except for the Burmese face of the Myazedi Inscriptions. And that was done to highlight its Mon duplicate. Thus all the scholarly and financial resources for publishing this journal went to the translation of Mon only, even though Old Burmese inscriptions outnumbered Old Mon by a ratio of nearly fifteen to one.

With such privileging of Mon sources it was virtually inevitable that the Mon Paradigm would be passed on to, and perpetuated by, other scholars of Southeast Asia who were not in positions to seriously contest the decision that made Old Mon inscriptions the first and highest priority for translation. Old Mon inscriptions became the invariable, indeed only, choice of primary data for scholars of early Southeast Asia who required this kind of firsthand source material from Burma but did not have a reading knowledge of either Old Burmese or Old Mon.

As a consequence the Mon Paradigm found its way into works that were more widely read. A good illustration of this is John Jardine's introduction to the fourth edition of Father Sangermano's old *Burmese Empire*. This introduction clearly revealed that whereas the Mon Paradigm had *not* been part of Jardine's preface to the second edition in 1884, by the "Introduction" to the fourth edition in 1924, it certainly was. The 1884 text was little more than three pages without a word on Mon-Burman relations. The 1924 text was over twenty-two pages that essentially reiterated Forchhammer's claims, particularly of the Mon as victim and the Burman as oppressor. It is obvious that the perception with regard to Mon-Burman history had changed significantly between the late nineteenth century (and Jardine's preface) and the third decade of the twentieth (and his introduction) of the same book.

And here, once again, western history was used to illustrate this Mon-Burman relationship. Only this time, Jardine had likened it to that between the Romans and the Jews. He wrote: "Conquered at last, and ill-treated by the Burmese kings, the *trodden-down Talaings* [my emphasis] can apply to themselves what Seneca wrote of the Jews in the Roman Empire: '*Victoribus victi leges dederunt.*'"[49]

By the time the next major history of Burma written in English was published—G. E. Harvey's *History of Burma* in 1925—the Mon Paradigm had become gospel. It was now deeply embedded in the historiography of early Burma. It is in Harvey's work that the Aniruddha conquest story and its alleged consequences appeared in English in its fullest version for the first time.[50]

Harvey concluded that the conquest brought ". . . the end of Thaton as a royal city, and she could not recover her prosperity by sea trade because the receding coastline left her high and dry. Anawrahta rode back in triumph to Pagan. Like some great glittering snake the victorious host uncurled its long length and set out through the Delta creeks with a captive chief and court, all the monks, and an entire population, numbering 30,000; but the pride of the Burmese was Manuha's thirty-two white elephants, each laden with scriptures and relics. . . ."

He continued: "the influx of Thaton captives, many of them craftsmen, helped to civilise the north, and there were three immediate results. Firstly, Shin Arahan gained many helpers from the Thaton clergy, and got all the scriptures he wanted, housing them in the Tripitakataik library building which is still to be seen at Pagan. Secondly, Pali supersedes Sanskrit as the normal language of sacred books, and Hīnayāna teaching supersedes Northern Buddhism. Thirdly, the Burmese adopted the Talaing alphabet and for the first time wrote their language—the earliest inscription in Burmese is dated to 1058, the year after the conquest."[51]

Harvey's *History* was followed by the works of Luce and Pe Maung Tin, on whom many others have depended, particularly for the history of Pagán. Unlike Harvey's very human, and in many respects quite "autonomous" history, which relied heavily on the chronicles, Pe Maung Tin and Luce, for the most part, did not, even though Pe Maung Tin's translation of the Pagán sections of the *Hmannan,* published as *The Glass Palace Chronicle,*[52] was a major contribution to that "autonomous" genre of literature. Rather, both of them based much of their work on what *they* considered to be original inscriptions.

Dozens of publications by Pe Maung Tin in the first two decades of the *JBRS* hardly ever touched on the Mon Paradigm, even though, or perhaps because, he was self-conscious of his Mon cultural background.[53] For Luce, however, the reverse was true. As we have seen time and again, he accepted the chronicles' account of the conquest of Thatôn as historical, and rather than attempting to disprove it, as he normally did with other accounts in the chronicles, he sought to prove it instead.[54] He was convinced that the Mon Paradigm was correct, as is demonstrated by virtually everything he wrote. Luce subsequently passed the mantle on to his pupils and colleagues, mainly Burmese of Mon cultural background, virtually all of whom were instrumental in the reconstruction of state and society at Pagán. To be sure, not all accepted everything he wrote, but all operated *within the same analytical framework,* the consolidated vision that was the Mon Paradigm.

In 1939 B. R. Pearn published *A History of Rangoon.*[55] Basing much of his early account of Rangoon on Pe Maung Tin's translations of the Shwédagôn Pagoda Inscriptions and other local histories of religious buildings and places called *thamaing,* Pearn was one of the first to see through the Mon Paradigm and realize that the religious "history" of places like Rangoon and Lower Burma was actually hagiology and that its development was quite late. Although he also seemed to believe that the Mon were contemporaries with the Pyū, he ignored the thesis that the Mon had civilized Pagan, either because he was unaware of it, or, more likely, did not give it much credence. Thus he wrote, "while the rulers of Pagan had been erecting their magnificent temples, the Mons had produced nothing of comparable value, and even now in the days of their greatness their Kings had as yet aimed at no more than a stupa of sixty feet in height [a reference to the Shwédagôn Pagoda]. It is evident that the Delta had lagged far behind Upper Burma in civilisation. . . ."[56]

This contrary view was simply ignored by one of the most influential scholars of Southeast Asia at the time, who also happened to be a Burma specialist: D. G. E. Hall. As he did not read Burmese, he was dependent upon Phayre, Harvey, and Luce, particularly for the indigenous, narrative side of Burma's history. Not only did he perpetuate the Mon Paradigm, but he also took it to a much larger audience located outside the country. This is what he wrote in his *Burma,* first published in 1950.

> . . . the conquest of Thaton in 1057 was a decisive event in Burmese history. It brought the Burman into direct contact with the Indian civilizing influences in the south and opened the way for intercourse with Buddhist centres overseas, especially Ceylon. The possession of the Pali scriptures revolutionized his outlook: they supplied him 'ready-made, with a complete mental outfit.' . . . They introduced him to the Buddhist ethic, which, as monasteries and teachers multiplied throughout the land, began to exert its moral force, to restrain his more barbarous impulses, and to liberate him from the worst of his animistic practices.[57]

In 1955 an important organization was founded that became another conduit for the Mon Paradigm: the Burma Historical Commission, which is still active today. Its publication, *The Bulletin of the Burma Historical Commission,* was initially produced mainly in English. At least two of the Commission's first three publications were special studies that bolstered the Mon Paradigm. These were Ba Shin's *Lokahteikpan* and Luce and Ba Shin's *Pagán Myinkaba Kubyauk-Gyi Temple of Rajakumar,* which appeared as volume 2 (1961) of the *Bulletin.* The third volume of the Bulletin, in 1963, was the last largely English publication, but it was never officially distributed. Only a preliminary run of a few numbers occurred before it was stopped. The *Bulletin* continued to be published, however, in Burmese and is still in production.[58]

Then in 1959 Pierre Dupont published his *L'archéologie môme,* which should have raised some doubts about, if not temporarily arrested the Mon Paradigm. In it, as one might recall from Chapter One, he had questioned the entire notion of an early Rāmaññadesa and suggested that the Burma Mon of the fifteenth century had "recast aspects of their past . . ." by bestowing "the dignity of age on their newly purified faith."[59] But as Dupont did not go much farther than give his interpretation of the situation, Mon Paradigm scholars did not, and were not necessarily bound to accept it. Indeed, Luce knew about and cited Dupont's work[60] but did not address the issue (of an early Rāmaññadesa) raised by it. As often happened in Burma Studies in the country, the opinions of outside scholars, even if known, were sometimes simply ignored.

By the end of the first decade of the twentieth century, then, the Mon Paradigm had gained so much momentum that it had become a school of thought, and by the 1930s and 1940s it had become the only one. After World War II and into the 1950s it was no longer possible (as a practical matter) to even question it. Virtually everything that was written about early and even later Burma went towards verifying the Mon Paradigm rather than questioning it.

The Mon Paradigm in the Second Half of the Twentieth Century

During the 1960s and into the 1970s, another Burmese detractor appeared among the few who dared, or was simply competent enough in English, to challenge the dominant western scholars on the Mon Paradigm. This was Dr. Htin Aung, president of the Burma Research Society from 1954 to 1955. Typically his challenges revolved around the hidden assumptions buried in colonial issues, which were carried out in a most enthusiastic manner.[61] With regard to the Mon Paradigm, his *Burmese History Before 1287* is most relevant, for his earlier *History of Burma* had actually accepted the conventional view.[62] Some of his refutation, especially of Luce's arguments, is quite convincing. But since he seldom cited his sources or provided evidence to make his case, his work was simply a reasonable critique, not one that advanced the field in a substantive way with regard to hard data.

In contrast to Htin Aung, many more indigenous historians of Burma, including the Mon scholar Nai Pan Hla, blindly followed Luce's line of thinking. Most had formally or informally trained under Luce, and most published at least some of their works in English so that they reached a much broader and academically more influential audience than those who did not. Of these, the best known to western scholars is Dr. Than Tun.

Always the iconoclast, Than Tun was, nevertheless, very unlike Htin Aung. Whereas the latter had specialized in English literature, Than Tun was a trained historian who regularly cited his sources, and his research was ordinarily based on hard evidence, usually the original Old Burmese inscriptions. Yet he was very reluctant to criticize Luce, "his" *sayagyi* ("teacher"), either in public or in private. It was probably a matter of personal politeness. In his "History of Buddhism in Burma A.D. 1000–1300," originally written in 1956, Than Tun accepted the conventional version of Aniruddha's conquest of Thatôn and its consequences.[63] However, his *Khit Haung Myanma Yazawin* [Early history of Myanma], published in Burmese in 1969, questioned the historicity of the conquest as unproved by contemporary sources.[64] But he did not pursue the subject much beyond this.

In the mid-1970s Michael Mendelson's *Sangha and State in Burma* appeared, edited by John P. Ferguson. By then at least one aspect of the Mon Paradigm—the Theravāda Buddhist influence of Lower Burma on Upper Burma—was questioned, but no challenge was made concerning the antiquity of Mon civilization or the historicity of the conquest of Thatôn in 1057. Mendelson wrote: ". . . it is doubtful that any 'pure' form of Theravāda Buddhism existed in 1057 at Thaton [and] . . . equally difficult to accept [is] the concept of a purely Theravāda Thaton, since the available data suggest strong Hindu and Mahayanist presences at the time it reportedly 'civilized' the Upper Burmese conquerors."[65] (This thesis of a more Hindu and Brahmanic Thatôn had already been suggested as early as 1947 by Quaritch Wales.[66])

In other words, Mendelson was less concerned with the historicity of the conquest than with whether or not Thatôn (or even Ceylon at the time) had "pure" Theravāda Buddhism. The most important issue to him, as revealed in this and several other publications of his,[67] was the notion of "purity" in Buddhism itself. His work did not question the Mon Paradigm per se, but he did raise doubts about issues tangentially related to it.

In 1983 Paul Wheatley, using Pierre Dupont's earlier analysis and research on Dvāravatī, also challenged the Mon Paradigm. He invoked Dupont's earlier work and directly questioned the underlying basis for the Mon Paradigm: namely, the antiquity of Rāmaññadesa. But neither he nor Dupont questioned the conquest of Thatôn itself or the civilizing of Upper Burma by Lower Burma.[68]

In 1985 I published *Pagan: the Origins of Modern Burma.* Like my predecessors, I questioned neither the antiquity of Lower Burma Mon civilization, the historicity of the conquest of Thatôn, nor the civilizing of Burman Upper Burma by a Mon Lower Burma. Part of the reason was that each new study of early Burma sought new information, approaches, and theories rather than scrutinizing older ones. There were so many areas to investigate that one ordinarily did not have to find one's niche in someone else's thesis or footnote, as often happens in more crowded areas of study. Opportunities to conduct research on something new were far greater in the study of early Burma than in many other regions of Southeast Asia, provided one had the necessary language skills. Every new early Burma scholar had the potential to become a pioneer. Thus even if the Mon Paradigm had been identified this early as questionable, it probably would not have been a high priority for anyone's research agenda in any case.

As a result of this rather large consensus favoring the Mon Paradigm, even if partly by default, other scholars of Southeast Asia who were not necessarily Burma specialists understandably also accepted the thesis.[69] The Mon Paradigm had become "common knowledge" for anyone dealing with Mainland Southeast Asian history and culture.

This state of affairs continues today, so that the most recent scholarship on Burma as well as South and Southeast Asia still depends, in part, on the historicity of the Mon Paradigm. The latest PhD dissertation written on Pagán as of this writing, Tilman Frasch's work in German completed in 1996, preserves the Mon Paradigm. It endorses the alleged raid of Thatôn, its possession of the *Tipiṭakas,* and Shin Arahan's role, without questioning any of them. And for all of Frasch's proselytizing about having knowledge of Old Burmese being absolutely crucial to any study of Pagán, he cites Luce and *The Glass Palace Chronicles* as evidence for the above three "events."[70]

Emmanuel Guillon also continues to perpetuate the Mon Paradigm, although he does so with some skepticism and caution regarding certain issues.[71] In art history, recent works by Hiram Woodward, Claudine Bautze-Picron, and Donald Stadtner all acknowledge and perpetuate the Mon Paradigm although they appear to have distanced themselves, perhaps consciously, from Luce's theories.[72] Most obvious in this regard is art historian John Guy, who seems to have accepted the Paradigm only reluctantly. He focuses instead on the Pyū[73] and gives much more credence to the idea of direct influence from India than from the Lower Burma Mon.[74] Similarly, Andrew Huxley, whose work on Southeast Asian and Burma's legal history is extremely important to the field, did not question the Mon Paradigm in his earlier works. However, in a later one, he began to show some doubts, writing that ". . . if 10th century Rammanadesa was a flourishing base for legal inventiveness, it has left very few archaeological remains to testify to the fact." But later in the same article he wrote that "Mon chronicle traditions treat these centuries in a completely legendary fashion and only enter the realms of historical narration with king Manuha's defeat by Pagan in 1057, . . ."[75] thus suggesting that he still considers the latter event as historical.

Scholars of Buddhism, such as John Strong, understandably have also succumbed to the Mon Paradigm, particularly when writing on a subject like the Upagupta legend, which invariably included Burma.[76] I should quickly add, however, that he makes clear his purpose is not to separate fact from fiction, so is quite justified in reporting what that tradition says, without necessarily endorsing its historicity. And like John Guy, Strong seems uneasy with the historical claims made by the Mon Paradigm.

I cite these excellent scholars not to disparage their works, but to show the extent to which the Mon Paradigm remains a part of current scholarship on Burma as well as South and Southeast Asia. After all, it was challenged publicly for the first time only in 2001 in a paper I presented at an annual international conference in Burma,[77] and only as of this writing has it been reexamined in detail. It has taken nearly 125 years for this to happen.

Conclusion

By the early twentieth century colonial scholars had ordained as historical the three components of the Mon Paradigm: the antiquity of Rāmaññadesa, the conquest of Thatôn, and the civilizing consequences attributed to the Mon of Lower Burma. The thesis became the most important ideology in the historiography of early Burma. Although scholars knew that another Tibeto-Burman-speaking culture lived in and dominated Upper Burma and probably influenced Lower Burma for over a millennia, and knew that not a single contemporary source mentioned any kingdom or polity in Lower Burma prior to the late thirteenth century, that did nothing to change anyone's mind. Nor did the fact that approximately 900 inscriptions from both Upper and Lower Burma, in Burmese, Mon, and Pali failed to mention the conquest of Thatôn even once make any difference. The knowledge that not a single, dated Old Mon inscription written in the Dvāravatī Old Mon script was found in Burma, or that the Old Burmese script preceded the Old Mon script by several decades (if not more) in Burma, was cast aside as impossible. That not a trace of the true vault, the most fundamental engineering principle used at Pagán for the hollow temple, could be found at any Mon site in Southeast Asia did not seem to faze anyone. That Kyanzittha's reign was an anomaly, not a yardstick by which Pagán society and culture should have been measured, was simply inconceivable. And no one bothered to investigate whether or not the notion of the "downtrodden Talaing" had any credibility.

By the time the Mon Paradigm had become an essential part of Burma's historiography, the thesis had become larger than any single individual scholar. Too much time, energy, and material resources had gone into it, and too many personal reputations depended on its viability. Although that is not to deny that there were probably genuine convictions of its validity, those convictions were not based on original epigraphy and the kinds of sources the Mon Paradigm regularly touted as the only reliable kind; rather, they were based on the chronicles which it regularly disparaged as unreliable.

Not unlike the chroniclers, who had religious biases, colonial officials and scholars had their own concerns and prejudices that perpetuated the fiction nevertheless. One of these was that ethnicity was a tangible, concrete entity that could and did affect history, and this was particularly convincing in an age of ethnic nationalism. Another was a sentimental attachment to the *idea* of supporting a people thought to have been victimized by its neighbors. A third was the natural desire of scholars with an interest in antiquities to preserve what they thought was once an ancient culture that was rapidly being lost in the fast-paced modern world of the twentieth century. None of these concerns or biases are particularly impeachable, but they were, nonetheless, largely *responsible* for the way in which the Mon Paradigm was institutionalized.

13 Without the Mon Paradigm

IMAGINE, FOR A MOMENT, early Burma and Mainland Southeast Asian history without the Mon Paradigm. What would it look like? There would be no Soṇa and Uttara bringing the most orthodox version of the *Tipiṭakas* to Lower Burma, no ancient Rāmaññadesa or Thatôn there, no conquest by Aniruddha in 1057, and no Mon Lower Burma civilizing of Burman Upper Burma. Can Burma scholars live with the idea of a Burmese civilization that began without Mon Theravāda Buddhist influence and a "Mon" period in Pagán? Indeed, can we envision just the opposite, a history in which Lower Burma Mon culture was actually the much later beneficiary of Pagán civilization, including its script, its art and architecture, its physical infrastructure, its Buddhism and conceptual system? Can Southeast Asianists also reject the assumptions undergirding the Mon Paradigm that ethnic conflict was the overriding framework of analysis, organization, and periodization of Burma's history? Can we come to terms with a different view of the history of Dvāravatī and Theravāda Buddhism in the region that suddenly materializes when the Mon Paradigm is removed? Can scholars of Southeast Asia even consider the origins of the state in Burma and parts of Mainland Southeast Asia without maritime trade and commerce as its primary cause, as implied by the Mon Paradigm?

If the answer is yes, then a major paradigm shift in Burma Studies is required. Much will have to be qualified, reinterpreted, or discarded. If the answer is no, then *evidence,* not mere analysis or assertion, must be provided to show not only that an ancient Rāmaññadesa *did exist* in Lower Burma before the late thirteenth century, but that all the consequences attributed to it and its alleged conquest are equally viable. Given the preponderance of the evidence, the choice is clear.

Removal of the Mon Paradigm would free scholarship from the straitjacket confining our current "knowledge" about early Burma, and its consequent impact on understanding the larger region. It would eliminate the burden of having to account for the alleged presence and significance of a very early Theravāda Buddhist Mon state and culture in Lower Burma every time new data is found there. This would affect the study of Burma and early Mainland Southeast Asia in very specific ways, the focus of this concluding chapter. However, since the story is part of a much longer chronology and a much larger geopolitical, cultural, and economic context than just the history of the Mon speakers in Lower Burma, the analysis is also placed in a much longer and larger conceptual framework, beginning with the formation of the state in Burma.

State Formation, "Preclassical" Burma, and Indianization in the Early Urban Period

Although the subject of state formation is too complicated an issue to deal with properly here,[1] certain issues in it need to be raised because the Mon Paradigm has shaped conventional thought on the subject with regard to both Burma and Mainland Southeast Asia. By having made coastal Rāmaññadesa the earliest kingdom in both Burma and the region—dating it to before the first millennium AD—the Mon Paradigm has, in effect, credited the origins of the state in Burma with the Mon of Lower Burma rather than the Pyū of Upper Burma. This, in turn, implies that the state in Burma was ultimately based on the commerce and trade of the maritime world rather than the agriculture of the interior.

Yet, Rāmaññadesa does not appear until seventeen centuries *after* the earliest dated complex urban settlements (the basis for the state) had already emerged in Upper Burma's Dry Zone, the *foundations* of which—the prehistoric stone and metal cultures—are also located in the agrarian interior of the country, not on the commercial coast. The evidence from Upper Burma suggests a geopolitical, economic, and cultural connectedness between the stone and metal cultures of the interior and the subsequent urban settlements built nearby or in some cases over them, and ultimately also with the "classical" kingdom centered at the walled city of Pagán, which was built only yards from some of these earlier settlements.

In contrast, the few urban communities that have been discovered on or near the coast cannot be dated securely, but certainly not earlier than those found in the interior. Nor is there evidence of prehistoric cultures on the coast that can be said to predate those in the interior. Moreover, the consensus among today's Burma prehistorians is that even such Lower Burma cultural remains as there are resemble more the urban societies of the Tibeto-Burman-speaking Pyū culture of the interior than any other cultural group. The evidence suggests, therefore, that these coastal urban sites were the frontier appendages of a relatively similar, if not uniform, interior agrarian civilization, rather than the nuclei of an earlier and different, coastal one, whether Mon or otherwise, with the commercial wherewithal to have begun the process of urbanism and state formation in the area. The absence of any state infrastructure or its foundations in Lower Burma prior to the formation of the state in the interior allows us to challenge both the conventional view that maritime trade was the basis for state formation in western Mainland Southeast Asia in general,[2] and more specifically, its applicability to Burma, with the Mon as primary actors.

After the emergence of polities in the interior, the evidence for Dry Zone Paramountcy as the normative pattern in Burma's history thereafter is overwhelming: a densely populated, well-irrigated, highly predictable, and productive agrarian interior dominated a much later-developing, sparsely populated, monsoon-dependent trade and monocrop culture of Lower Burma for approximately two millennia. Although this does not mean that the coastal world played no significant role in the process of state development in Burma, it does suggest that this role came late and was irregular and marginal, comprising approximately 217 intermittent years out of a total 2,100 nearly unbroken years in the urban history of Burma.[3]

And because in Southeast Asia generally, domesticated agricultural production (especially of rice) also seems to have spread from north to south,[4] from the interior of the Mainland to its coasts, we have to wonder whether an initial pattern of agrarian-based state formation was not the norm rather than the exception. My guess is that the development, expansion, and regularizing of rice production itself was the ultimate basis for the subsequent growth of trade on a *statewide scale,* so perhaps a distinction needs to be made between what anthropologists call "primary" and "secondary" state formation, especially in Mainland Southeast Asia where agriculture was the basis for the former, and trade, for the latter. Of course, a third scenario is also possible, in which state formation was occurring in both locations: in the interior as well as on the coasts, either simultaneously or nearly so. But in Burma, the evidence for state formation in the agrarian interior clearly precedes that for the coasts by over a millenium.

Inasmuch as trade and commerce were unlikely candidates for the genesis of *primary* state formation in Burma, so also was the role of merchants and traders in it. This is not to say that traders and merchants had nothing to do with *secondary* state formation in Burma, but the earliest extant written texts suggest that a much more important role was played by a different class of people in primary state formation, particularly those well versed in the sometimes esoteric, certainly sophisticated literature of India. This was unlikely to have been within the normal expertise or self-interest of the ordinary trader and merchant. The earliest written evidence in Burma and the implications of other kinds of data such as iconography, *inter alia,* imply the influence of an established literate class of people whose professions were not likely to have been in trade and commerce but in the pursuit of "orthodox" ideology.

It could be countered that the environment of the coastal world, with its higher rate of rainfall, humidity, and so on, accelerated the deterioration of evidence. However, like the rest of the Mon Paradigm, this argument rests on the *absence,* rather than the *presence* of evidence, a flawed methodology that allows one to prove or disprove anything one wants. Besides, if the geographers are correct that the deltas of the major rivers of Mainland Southeast Asia have increased at the rate of several meters a year,[5] the material remains for that alleged coastal genesis should exist on land today, not submerged in water. And even if evidence of this kind of settlement is found between the coasts and the interior—for example, as at Angkor Borei recently[6]—the cause and effect relationship between such settlements and the formation of the (in this case, Angkorian) state, still needs to be demonstrated. It is not just a matter of presumed vanished evidence but one of not having shown the putative consequences of it.

There is no contemporary evidence on or near the coast of Lower Burma for anything remotely resembling a polity or even its foundations prior to the expansion of the interior cultures into that region. In the agrarian interior, to reiterate, Beikthano appeared nearly seventeen centuries before the first Lower Burma polity or kingdom, Śrī Kṣetra over eight centuries before, and Pagán more than six. The problem has been further obfuscated and complicated by linking the processes of state formation in Lower Burma to an ethnicity—the Mon. This is entirely spurious. Not only does the evidence show that Burma for nearly the entire first millennium AD is without a Mon-speaking population, but the coastal areas said to have been Rāmaññadesa were, at that time, an undeveloped, sparsely inhabited frontier region except for the few scattered urban settlements perhaps inhabited by a variety of different cultures. Can the currently dominant maritime, trade-centric, ethnic approach to state formation in Southeast Asian studies live with the paradigm shift I am proposing?

The subsequent *development* of complex urban centers—that is, the "preclassical" stage in Mainland Southeast Asia—is also pertinent. It has been chronologically, conceptually, and institutionally connected to the process of "Indianization," the first phase of which is usually dated to the first several centuries before and after the first millennium AD.[7] What this means is that Indianization has also been linked to mythical Rāmaññadesa, with numerous ramifications not only for Burma but for the rest of Southeast

Asia. Indic art forms, writing systems, literature, and conceptions of the state and leadership were thought to have gone through a coastal, Lower Burma Mon cultural prism *before* they went elsewhere inland.

In Burma the hard evidence does not support such a scenario; in fact, it is just the opposite. Indic influences infused with the kinds of ideologies and concepts likely to further stimulate state development moved in the same direction that state formation did: from north to south, from the interior to the coast, from agriculture to commerce, and from Tibeto-Burman to Austro-Asiatic speakers, not the other way around. Although later waves of Indian influence did come from the coast—perhaps as part of a secondary state-formation process—by that time the synthesis of indigenous foundations and direct Indic contributions among the Pyū of Burma were already well established.

The political and religious ideologies found in Buddhist texts attributed to Rāmaññadesa and Lower Burma—such as the *Tipiṭakas* and the *Jātakas*—should be returned to the places where they first appeared, Śrī Kṣetra and Pagán, which had acquired them directly from either India or Śrī Laṅka. So should other Indic traditions of patron-saints, especially those pertaining to Gavaṁpati, Upagupta, and Maitreya, along with indigenous conceptions framed in Indic formulae such as the Cult of the 37 Nats. There is no evidence that Indianization of the Pyū and Burmese cultures had anything at all to do with the Mon and certainly not with the nonexistent Rāmaññadesa.

The supposed Indianization of Rāmaññadesa in Lower Burma as early as the first century AD also raises serious problems for some of the history of early Southeast Asia. In particular, it affects Dvāravatī, and by so doing, affects several other polities and cultures of Mainland Southeast Asia said to have been build on, or at least influenced by that culture.[8] This first putative Old Mon center (kingdom, culture, polity, "imagined community") in Southeast Asia, thought to have arisen in the sixth century AD, appears to have "declined" by the end of the ninth when written Dvāravatī Old Mon disappears in epigraphy.[9] Because the corpus of Old Mon inscriptions found in Thailand and Laos shows that the oldest ones lay in Thailand's central plains, it is thought that Dvāravatī's center was also there. Wherever its exact location, the Mon Paradigm assumed that it was the source of Burma's Mon culture, which ostensibly makes its first appearance at Thatôn.[10]

However, the alleged connection between Lower Burma and Dvāravatī cannot stand up to scrutiny as shown in Chapter Seven. Besides, dating Rāmaññadesa to before the first millennium AD places it a good 600 years *prior to the beginning date given to Dvāravatī itself!* How could Dvāravatī be the source of Mon culture for Rāmaññadesa if it comes later? Moreover, this early dating of Rāmaññadesa implies that *it* was the source of Dvāravatī's Indianization, and, by extension, of subsequent western Mainland Southeast Asian polities as well. I seriously doubt any scholar of early Southeast Asia would agree that Lower Burma was the ultimate source of Indianization for the rest of Mainland Southeast Asia.

Pagán, the Development of Lower Burma, and the Birth of Rāmaññadesa in the "Classical" Period

During the first millennium AD, when Rāmaññadesa was said to have flourished, it is not even certain that the area where its center, Thatôn, was claimed to have been located was not under the ocean. The shoreline at the end of the first millennium was much farther inland, as studies on the Bay of Thailand attest.[11] And even if most of Rāmaññadesa were not under the ocean at the time, there still may not have been enough land on which to build the kind of major kingdom or center implied by the myth of Rāmaññadesa, since the west coast of the Tenasserim Peninsula is what Michel Jacq-Hergoualc'h calls a submergence coast. He writes that "the sea has penetrated deeply into the mountains, creating certain types of fjords or abers . . . limiting the coastal plains to a thin strip of earth somewhat enlarged over the centuries by alluvial deposits. . . ."[12] The relatively small hinterland of these coastal areas probably could not have sustained the population of a kingdom the size and scale of Rāmaññadesa implied by the Mon Paradigm. Thus, although Lower Burma may not have been a total wilderness, it was nonetheless not nearly as urbanized or populated as the Dry Zone was at the same time, and certainly not as economically, politically, or culturally advanced. If some Mon speakers and others had migrated into Lower Burma sometime before Pagán developed its infrastructure in the mid- to late eleventh century down there, it was probably involuntary: that is, "push" factors caused by one or more epidemics, along with the decline of their civilizations, and/or Khmer and T'ai expansion and pressure, rather than any particular attraction that Lower Burma had to offer.

At the end of the eleventh century, however, the situation had changed as Pagán expanded into and developed the frontier region of Lower Burma. Having already consolidated its power in the north, east, and west, King Aniruddha and King Kyanzittha advanced toward and took Lower Burma. Had there been any Old Mon speakers present already, it was probably during these campaigns, especially Kyanzittha's, that they were taken back to Pagán. Perhaps this is the historical basis for the myth of the conquest of Thatôn.

Subsequently, probably during the reign of Alaungsithu, Kyanzittha's successor, Old Burmese speakers from Upper Burma were being settled in Lower Burma as well; it was not just a one-way movement. They probably first occupied the urban sites left by the Pyū or the towns and villages that were already part of the local scene. The rest of them seem to have been created by the Pagán kingdom during the next two centuries, for their names are found written first in Old Burmese, centuries before they were duplicated in Middle Mon belonging to the fifteenth century.

This infrastructural development of Lower Burma probably occurred late in the eleventh century after the region had been conquered and placed under the authority of crown governors and local leaders appointed by the center, presumably enforced with garrisoned troops. It was the development that followed this "pacification," more than epidemics or battles, that stimulated Lower Burma's commercial, political, socioreligious, and demographic growth. The evidence seems to suggest, therefore, that it was Pagán's own growth and development in Upper Burma that was initially responsible for the subsequent establishment of a state infrastructure on the coasts of Lower Burma that finally culminated in the country's first Mon state in the late thirteenth century.

As the only exemplary center in Burma between the eleventh and the thirteenth centuries with the ability to attract and absorb an influx of people in economically and culturally meaningful ways, Pagán would have provided the "pull" factor that subsequently drew people to Upper Burma, including the Mon speakers. The magnificent capital and surrounding countryside offered cleared and irrigated fertile land to cultivate, a stable and peaceful society, and good employment opportunities in numerous sectors. The most economically attractive of these industries must have been the arts and crafts, part of the huge temple construction economy, with numerous related businesses and occupations. Brickmaking and masonry; gold, silver, and bronze craftsmanship; wood carving and carpentry; ceramics; animal husbandry; sugar palm extraction; bee and honey horticulture, were all industries and occupations directly related to temple-building. In addition to the actual construction of nearly 3,000 religious edifices during a span of approximately 300 years, all these buildings would have needed regular maintenance thereafter, providing a sustained demand for skilled and unskilled labor well beyond the Pagán period. Indeed, it still does today, as illustrated by the many businesses that depend on Pagán's existence, even if as a modern "pilgrimage" (tourist) site.

The need for skilled craftsmen is obvious in the repair of religious buildings. But unskilled labor was also needed as lay guardians of temples and monastic lands. These individuals would often be given land or its use and/or a share of its output, in return for services. Numerous other professions not directly related to construction benefited from temple-building and temple maintenance as well. These were the accountants, bankers, and scribes, who were indispensable for protecting and preserving the legal records of what amounted to perpetual tax-free religious property.

A similar demand could be found in the military sector, as Pagán expanded its hegemony. Crown soldiers were settled on premium irrigated crown land or in some instances in uncultivated areas that later became valuable crown land. They were given rights "to eat," "to live on," and "to work" these lands. Military service offered high status and political mobility upward all the way to the ministerial level at court, where the highest officers served the king. Both the religious and military sectors, therefore, had a direct affect on demographic growth, the expansion of agriculture production, and other components of the economy. And finally, Pagán financed and in other ways supported a regular, exciting social, religious, and state pageantry, based on a combined Indic and indigenous culture that was surely familiar and appreciated by all.[13]

Since Pagán paid its labor, especially the artisans and skilled craftsmen —in gold, silver, paddy, land, rights to land or produce, and other valuable items, such as elephants, boats, and horses—monumental temple-building was a major stimulus for economic development, creating opportunities not readily available elsewhere in the region at that time, perhaps with the exception of Angkor. But whether Angkor's artisans and unskilled labor were paid in cash (or convertible valuable commodities) to make it another nucleus of economic development during the same time is not entirely clear.[14]

It was economic growth in Upper Burma, therefore, that attracted people to and from Lower Burma, a *voluntary* movement that had little or nothing to do with wars or disease. Lower Burma's population probably consisted of Rmeñ, Tamil, and others collectively known by then as Tanluiṅ in the Old Burmese sources, including the people the Chinese called Kunlun, who supplied the steady demand for demographic resources important to the growth of the kingdom of Pagán, which, like most of the "classical" states in Southeast Asia, was short of labor.[15] The variety of influences found in the art and architecture of Pagán and the evidence in the Old Burmese inscriptions of this period demonstrate that people of many linguistic and cultural backgrounds lived and worked there, especially during the period of growth and efflorescence of the twelfth and thirteenth centuries.

Not only was Pagán's economy a tremendous socioeconomic magnet, the timing was also good. Pagán's temple construction occurred during a period of time when Dvāravatī, Śrī Vijaya, and the Coḷa empire had already experienced political and economic decline, so it would have attracted migration from such societies. Indeed, the economic situation at Pagán would have provided the kind of stability and employment opportunities that attracted most people, whether or not they were displaced and unemployed. To reiterate, it was Pagán's growth and development in Upper Burma that was in turn responsible for the growth and development of Lower Burma itself, on which the emergence of the first Mon state in Burma was based.

The lateness of this development of a Mon kingdom in Lower Burma frees Dvāravatī scholarship from having to explain an earlier Old Mon center in Lower Burma. Indeed, Dupont's doubts about the existence of an early Rāmaññadesa probably arose precisely because he was studying Dvāravatī. Now its data can be evaluated and interpreted without considering Lower Burma at all, and this will undoubtedly lead to new interpretations regarding Dvāravatī.

By the late thirteenth century, while the kingdom of Pagán was being harassed by the Mongols, Wareru (Magadu) of Martaban (1287–1296) seized the opportunity to establish the nucleus of an independent polity by attempting to take over the entire Lower Burma region. In the earliest Mon texts of Burma, Wareru is indeed featured as the founder of the Mon state in Lower Burma. But neither this endeavor nor another about ten years later succeeded totally, for a near-contemporary inscription at Pagán records the rewarding of one of its generals with land for "victory in the War at Dala" (near modern Yangôn) that occurred in the early 1290s. Despite the long-term effects of the drain of tax-exempt wealth to the *saṅgha* and pressure on its northern borders by one of the most powerful forces in history, the kingdom of Pagán still had enough power to assert its hegemony on the coast.

That, however, may have been its last hurrah. A decade earlier, in 1281, the kingdom of Haripuñjaya was taken by the forces of King Mangrai of Sukhodaya. This likely triggered a mass exodus of Mon speakers to Lower Burma, perhaps to Pegu. It might have been their best option, for Pegu was a city with whose culture and language the Old Mon speakers of Haripuñjaya were already familiar, and where kinship and other networks already existed, as is suggested by the later Northern Thai chronicles. For the first time, then, Lower Burma of the mid-1290s had the demographic resources to effect the rise of an independent kingdom led by Mon speakers. And it also had the physical and conceptual infrastructure, built by Pagán, on which to do so.

What is compelling about the "fall" of "Mon" Haripuñjaya in the development of a "Mon" Rāmaññadesa is that it occurred just two decades before a Chinese source for the first time in 1298 mentions an embassy sent from a "new Teng-lung kingdom" in Lower Burma. That act of independence coincides with several other events favorable to the establishment of a separate state in Lower Burma: the final weakening of Pagán caused by the continued drain of taxable wealth to the *saṅgha,* the resulting factionalism at the Pagán court (culminating in the ascendancy of the famous Three Brothers who began to carve the kingdom into three parts), and the pressure by the Mongols on the northern frontier.[16] All these factors contributed to the birth of historic Rāmaññadesa and occurred only towards the end of the thirteenth century, approximately thirteen hundred years *after* Rāmaññadesa was said to have first emerged.

Whether this Rāmaññadesa was composed entirely of Old Mon speakers is uncertain, for even Wareru himself is said in some western sources to have been a "Shan adventurer," or at least knowledgeable about the T'ai language.[17] His link to T'ai speakers explains, in part, why Haṁsavatī, the formal Pali name for Pegu, was considered a tributary of Sukhodaya in King Ram Kamhaeng's inscription of 1292, for, as we have seen, Wareru's mythology included his fleeing Sukhodaya to Lower Burma with a daughter of the king, whom he then made queen. Whatever historic Rāmaññadesa's main ethnic makeup, it was certainly Lower Burma's *first* independent kingdom.

The Crisis of the Thirteenth Century

Another important, long-held, and unresolved issue is known in the field as the "crisis of the thirteenth century." It was said to have been caused in part by the Mongols, who were thought to have sacked the capitals of the great "classical" kingdoms, thereby creating a new age with new centers of power significantly different from the old. And in part the crisis is also linked to the establishment of Theravāda Buddhism, a religion said to belong to the common people which therefore challenged the elitist Hindu-Buddhism of the "old Indian kingdoms," thus contributing to their decline. The Mon Paradigm is relevant here in numerous ways.

First, the role attributed to the Mongols in this "crisis," at least in terms of Pagán, has already been demonstrated elsewhere to be totally erroneous.[18] To be sure—although neither the proponents of the "crisis" nor of the Mon Paradigm saw it—the turmoil created by the Mongols in Upper Burma may have *accelerated* the emergence in Lower Burma of historic Rāmaññadesa; but it was not *caused* by the Mongol raids. Rather, as shown above, that process had begun much earlier and extended over a long period of time. A state infrastructure first had to be built in Lower Burma over a course of several centuries, beginning with the eleventh. That was what attracted the influx of labor into the region, which only by the late thirteenth century had a critical mass enabling it to create a polity independent of Pagán. Thus the Mongols' appearance on the scene around the same time helped destabilize the situation in Upper Burma that then provided the opportunity which the founders of historic Rāmaññadesa seized, establishing the first Mon kingdom in Burma.

Second, that Theravāda Buddhism was also responsible for creating this "crisis" is equally questionable. Theravāda Buddhism was not a thirteenth-century phenomenon, especially in Burma; it can be found as early as seventh-century Śrī Kṣetra for certain, if not even earlier at fourth-century Beikthano, and of course, it was present since the ninth century in Pagán. Pagán, in turn, had established Theravāda Buddhism in what became historic Rāmaññadesa in the eleventh-century. In Thailand, the establishment of "classical" Sukhodaya *preceded* the Mongol raids of the late thirteenth-century, and as far as we know, the kingdom began as a Theravāda Buddhist state; it did not replace any previous Hindu-Buddhist state. In all these places the kinds of "egalitarian" doctrines found in Theravāda Buddhism, and claimed to have caused the decline of the "classical" states in the thirteenth century, had long existed.

Besides, Theravāda Buddhism "belonged" as much to the elite as to the commoners, so it was not a matter of replacing the existing conceptual system of the old Hindu-Buddhist kingdoms by a process Lawrence Briggs has called "superbolshevism."[19] Although it is true that he was speaking mainly of Angkor, he still held Theravāda Buddhism *as an ideology* accountable for this class "revolution." But, as I have shown elsewhere, the long-term economic effects of the merit-path to salvation, found in Theravāda Buddhism and embraced by *both* elite and commoner, was what created the structural conditions for the decline of the Burmese state; it was not a class and ideological struggle between Hindu-Buddhist elite and Theravāda Buddhist commoner. Pagán's decline, and probably that of several other "classical" states had little or nothing to do with a grassroots movement of Theravāda Buddhist commoners fighting the tyranny of the elite class of Hindu-Buddhists. That was twentieth-century western egalitarian and revolutionary wishful thinking.

Indeed, the rise of post-Pagán Ava in Upper Burma and historic Rāmaññadesa in Lower Burma was less a revolutionary event that overthrew the old system and its principles than it was their *resurrection,* for structurally and ideologically both new polities were Pagán writ small.[20] Although they marked the beginning of a new era, they were not challenges to an old order.

But because *l'histoire événementielle,* often synonymous with linear change and progress, was very much a part of the western reconstruction of early Mainland Southeast Asian history, crises and upheavals became causal agents of that change and progress. If we remove this *crisis-seeking,* linear approach to structural change, however, the revolutionary character in the "decline" of the "classical" states of Mainland Southeast Asia takes on a more *evolutionary* quality, caused less by dramatic, externally generated events than by internal, structural contradictions.[21] It is more this evolutionary process, and less a revolutionary break with the "classical" past, that was instrumental in the making of the "postclassical" period. Both Ava and historic Rāmaññadesa were legacies of Pagán, not new products created by Mongol invasions or the superbolshevism of Theravāda Buddhism.

The "Postclassical" or "Early Modern" Period in Burma

By the beginning of the fourteenth century, the kingdom of Pagán had split into three centers—Pinya, Sagaing, and Myin Saing, ruled by the famous Three Brothers. Around the 1330s the last king of the Pagán dynasty had died, and in 1364 Ava emerged as the preeminent nucleus of power in Upper Burma, having reunited the dispersed human and material resources left there by the decline of Pagán. But as the center of gravity had shifted approximately ninety miles north of the old capital—in order to address what its new leaders perceived was a bigger threat, the Ming—Lower Burma became less of a priority and also less accessible than it had been under the Pagán Dynasty.

The weakening of Upper Burma's grip on Lower Burma enabled Binnya U, a successor of Wareru, to finally make Pegu the uncontested capital of Lower Burma. It was only during this First Ava Period—fourteenth to the early sixteenth centuries AD—that original dated evidence first appears in Lower Burma that documents the development of a sizeable, fairly well-integrated polity where the leadership and the center's *lingua franca* was now, and for the first time, clearly Mon. Ironically, then, the emergence of Ava and Rāmaññadesa was possible because of Pagán's decline in power on the one hand, but also, on the other, because of its legacy, built as they were on its demographic, physical, and institutional infrastructure.

Binnya U's famous descendant Yazadarit (1385–1423) kept Ava's ambitions confined to Upper Burma for several decades, despite many attempts by its kings to resurrect Pagán's hegemony on the coast. Occasionally Ava managed to conquer some of the port cities of Lower Burma, but Yazadarit always managed to take them back. Ultimately, a modus vivendi was reached between Ava and Pegu, and the two centers lived in peace for nearly a decade, a truce secured by the marriage to the king of Ava of one of Yazadarit's daughters, who was to become a famous queen in Lower Burma's history.

This was the celebrated Shin Saw Bu (1453–1474). After having spent several years of her life as a queen at Ava, part of the conditions for the truce, she ultimately escaped to Lower Burma with the help of two monks. Subsequently, she succeeded to the throne of Pegu after two successors of Yazadarit had reigned and became the second of only two women sovereigns in the history of the country.[22] After her long, peaceful, and prosperous reign in Pegu, she was followed by King Dhammazedi (1472–92), one of the monks who had helped her escape, who, by then, had shed his saffron robe. He was said to be her "son" in his Shwédagôn Pagoda Inscription but was actually her son-in-law, having married her daughter.

During his reign Pegu attained the pinnacle of its stature as the most powerful kingdom of the Mon in Lower Burma, and it was only then that Dhammazedi invented the tradition of an "earlier" Thatôn. In doing this, Dhammazedi established a fictive genealogical continuity between Thatôn and his own Pegu, replacing their actual historic and cultural ties to both Upper Burma and Thailand with a legendary, coastal Lower Burma Mon culture instead. It was this fifteenth-century reconstruction (and perspective) that was so enthusiastically embraced and perpetuated by colonial officials and scholars, in part because it was inscribed on sacrosanct stone, but also because they *desired* to see an ancient Mon kingdom in Lower Burma, which justified certain military objectives of the First Anglo-Burmese War. Once accepted by colonial scholars, "the legend that was Lower Burma" secured its place in the study and writing of Burma's history.

Unfortunately, the acceptance of an earlier, mythical Rāmaññadesa has minimized the contribution made by the Burma Mon of historic Rāmaññadesa to the history of "postclassical" Southeast Asia. Partly because the legendary stature of mythical Rāmaññadesa has weighed so heavily on the assessment of historic Rāmaññadesa, the latter, invariably, has been found wanting. As a result, scholars have tended to favor the importance of mythical Rāmaññadesa and have given far less time and effort to the reconstruction of historic Rāmaññadesa. Now, however, without the Mon Paradigm, historic Rāmaññadesa's significance to Burma and Southeast Asian history can be more insightfully and freely assessed.

Already one such assessment can be made: the contribution by the Lower Burma Mon to the history and culture of Burma during the Ava period (1364–1527) is clearly more important than heretofore thought. It had more than five hundred years (even if intermittent) with which to work. Both linguistics and history should bear me out on this. Similarly, the Lower Burma Mon contribution during the "postclassical" period to coastal activities in the Bay of Bengal, the Gulf of Martaban, and the Straits of Malacca —particularly vis-à-vis Vijayanagara, Ayudhyā, Arakan, and Malacca and their maritime satellites elsewhere in Southeast Asia—is likely to be far more important than any attributed to them during any other period of time, historic or legendary.

Thus in the history of early maritime Southeast Asia, the significance and impact of the Burma Mon lies not during the "classical" period when Śrī Vijaya, the Coḷas, and the Śrī Laṅkans were the premier powers, but during the "postclassical" period when the Ming, the Spanish, the Malays, the Indians, and the Portuguese were the dominant players. In the history of early Mainland Southeast Asia as well, the Burma Mon contributed most to the period when Ayudhyā and Ava were dominant, not when Pagán and Angkor were the main centers of power. This totally different picture, made possible only by removing the Mon Paradigm, should be the basis for any future assessment of the Mon people and culture of Lower Burma.

In 1539 this relatively new and short-lived Mon kingdom of Rāmaññadesa was conquered by an Upper Burma power initially centered at Toungoo, a city on the edge of the Dry Zone and once a provincial seat of Ava. The Toungoo leaders saw Pegu's strategic potential as a commercial center and moved their capital there, rebuilding and enlarging it so that it later became the capital of the entire country. Under the Toungoo rulers,[23] Pegu was even more involved in the trade and commerce of the "long sixteenth century,"[24] particularly in the region around the Gulfs of Martaban and Thailand, the Kra Isthmus, the Bay of Bengal, and the waters of Island Southeast Asia, not to mention the Gulf of Mexico and the Pacific coast of California.[25] Pegu became the premier center of all western Mainland Southeast Asia for the next sixty years, when it conquered Chiang Mai, Ayudhyā, and Vientiane, at the time the major regional centers of power.

But this empire was no longer the Rāmaññadesa of Shin Saw Bu and Dhammazedi, but of Tabinshwehti and Bayinnaung, Burmese speakers from the Dry Zone of Upper Burma. Like others before and after them, these new rulers invited local Mon talent to their court, such as Bannya Dala who wrote the *Yazadarit.* Thus Mon-led Rāmaññadesa had already ceased to exist by the first quarter of the sixteenth century. Its "golden age" had amounted to only some 200 years out of a total 1,500 years dominated by agrarian, inland, Dry Zone Burma. It was the new, sixteenth-century *Burmese-Mon* Rāmaññadesa (although it was not called that) that western scholarship remembers best, partly because this was the entity described in many of the earliest firsthand western-language accounts.

In 1599, just sixty years after Pegu was taken by the Toungoo rulers, the once-preeminent center of western Mainland Southeast Asia was burnt to the ground by the new coastal power of Arakan, centered at Mrauk-U, a destruction completed by the later arriving forces of another coastal power, Ayudhyā.[26] Well before that event, however, by 1555, Pegu's leaders had already regained control of the demographic and agrarian resources of Upper Burma, so that the destruction of 1599 only accelerated their anticipated move back to Upper Burma and to a way of life with which they had always been more comfortable. They returned to a familiar human and physical landscape where the heart of Burmese culture lay, with its myriad temples and monasteries, monks and lay supporters, its artists and their crafts. This was where most of the history of Burma had been made. The old city of Ava was rebuilt to serve as the capital of Upper Burma under the Second Ava Dynasty (also called the restored Toungoo Dynasty by western historians).

Shortly after the Second Ava Dynasty had begun to successfully exert its authority over Lower Burma, Lower Burma reconstituted itself as a viable center of power. Pegu was rebuilt as its seat of power and authority, so that by the first quarter of the eighteenth century the situation was not unlike that from the late thirteenth to the mid-fifteenth century, where two more or less equal centers of power faced each other, one inland and the other coastal. By the middle of the eighteenth century, Lower Burma had regained much of its old wealth and power, having once again become involved in the maritime trade and commerce of the seventeenth and eighteenth centuries, which was in part stimulated by the arrival of more Western powers in Southeast Asia. Pegu's location was still ideal, and it grew into a power that could now contest that of Ava. Lower Burma once more became independent of Upper Burma, and it seemed as if the glory days of Yazadarit, Shin Saw Bu, and Dhammazedi had returned, although this time English, French, Italian, Portuguese, Armenian, and other Europeans were also involved in Pegu's reemergence.

In 1752, for the first time in Burma's 2,000-year history, an independent, coastal Burma power defeated its agrarian counterpart when Pegu took Ava. But Pegu was not seriously interested in unifying the country—it wanted mainly to preserve its economic way of life untrammeled by the Dry Zone powers. Its real competitor was now maritime commercial Ayudhyā, not interior agrarian Ava, so it neither established Ava as its capital, nor did it move the bulk of its population and other resources there. Instead, it left a governor to administer Upper Burma and returned to the coast with Ava's entire court, its ministers, books, and treasures, in effect, its regalia for legitimacy.[27] Uncomfortable in the Dry Zone and its conservative agrarian way of life in any case, the coastal invaders wanted to return to the more exciting "international" environment of the maritime world.

That decision was crucial, for it allowed Upper Burma to once more reconstitute itself and set the stage for the last Dry Zone dynasty, the Kônbaung, which rose from the ashes of Ava to reunify the country for the last time under the Burmese monarchy. Whereas the agrarian world seemed to need and want to control the revenues of the coastal world, the reverse, for the most part, was not true. The coast was satisfied with trading for the interior's food supplies and other commodities. It had no desire to live there, farm the land, and produce the crops needed. When in 1757 Upper Burma under Alaungpaya took Pegu and reunified the country for the last time, Lower Burma once again became part of a unified kingdom centered in Upper Burma, thus returning to the pattern begun by the Pyū in the first millennium AD. The political and cultural center of the country remained in the Dry Zone for nearly 130 more years until the British finally annexed it. As trade and commerce grew during the nineteenth and twentieth centuries, the epicenter of the country once more returned to Lower Burma, where it remains to this day.[28]

The Reification of Ethnicity and Colonial Historiography

For all these known events in the precolonial history of Burma, one cannot find indigenous, contemporary evidence that any of them were *caused* by ethnicity; most, if not all, were the result of power struggles among the elite and their clients, sometimes complicated by external invasion and interference, but based mainly on geopolitical, religious, and economic concerns. Indigenous texts such as the *Yazadarit Ayedawpon* characterize the tension between the First Ava Dynasty and Pegu (exemplified by their respective kings Mingaung I and Yazadarit), not as an ethnic conflict between a Burman and Mon king, but between two strong, equally Buddhist, equally legitimate leaders who ruled two different geopolitical regions of the country. More than anything else, the chronicles were concerned with who was purer in terms of promoting Sinhalese Buddhism. And in the romanticized story of Minguang I and Yazdarit, when one died, the other was said not only to have shed tears but to have died very shortly thereafter, with the clear suggestion that although they may have been contestants they were also soul mates.[29] Even if allegorical, the story hardly suggests a worldview centered on reified ethnicity, or if empirical, of a history depicted as a perpetual struggle between Burmese and Mon speakers.[30]

The same can be said of Alaungpaya and his major adversary, the king of Pegu, Binnya Dala. The history surrounding Alaungpaya's conquest of Lower Burma and reunification of the country—which colonial scholars claimed was perfect evidence of ethnic conflict for it was allegedly intended to exterminate the Talaing—was anything but that. A closer examination even of Alaungpaya's edicts directed specifically at the people of Pegu and their king as part of his campaign against them does not support any such interpretation.[31]

Out of the ninety-nine edicts of Alaungpaya that have survived, fewer than ten were directed at Pegu during his campaign.[32] Of these, only *one,* and composed in Pali verse at that, was a direct reference to the Pegu king and his followers whose character was impugned *because* they were Talaing.[33] Even in this case, most of the people would not have understood the Pali verse. This single instance, whose target audience was either the court and king or its monks, surely cannot be construed as evidence that Alaungpaya was waging a campaign of extermination against the Talaing people of Lower Burma.

The other nine edicts, written in Burmese and presumably meant to be comprehensible to the majority of the people, focused on Alaungpaya's role as a great Buddhist king, a *cakkavattī,* who would conquer the world by spinning his disk, the *cakra,* not because of his superiority as a Burman king. Nor did Alaungpaya state that the Pegu king was weak *because* he was Talaing; rather, he was weak because of his *karma,* while Alaungpaya was strong because of his. Alaungpaya also claimed to have Sakka's support,[34] wielded his weapons, and was about to achieve a *dhammavijaya* or righteous victory.[35] He thus attempted to persuade the people of Pegu to surrender because of such Buddhist principles. If the issue were ethnicity, why were such religious principles even invoked?

Apart from this negative campaign waged via palm-leaf dispatches, Alaungpaya's actual behavior also contradicts the conventional colonial view that ethnicity was the main reason for this war. The band of soldiers that Alaungpaya selected to secretly penetrate Pegu, mix with the population and remain apart from each other until the given signal, when they were to attack the palace,[36] surely would not have been even considered, much less deployed, had there been a general sense that a noticeable physical difference existed between Talaing and Burman, the ultimate basis for reified ethnicity. Indeed, it tells us that ethnicity was never an issue.[37]

Furthermore, the Pegu monarch was always addressed in Alaungpaya's edicts as "the king of Hanthawaddy," not the "Talaing king," while the latter's replies were always addressed to "Alaungmintaya, king of Ratanasingha [Shwebo]," not "the Burman king."[38] This was public, formal recognition of a geopolitical contest between coastal Hanthawaddy and interior Shwebo, not an ethnic one between Burman and Talaing.

Alaungpaya also refrained from using the word Talaing in a disparaging manner, even in situations most suited for doing so. Replying to a Captain Baker, who had told him that an alliance with the East India Company would benefit the king in all future rebellions, Alaungpaya retorted:

> ". . . have I asked? or, do I want any Assistance to reduce my Enemies to subjection? let none conceive such an opinion? have I not, in three Years time,

> extended my Conquest three Months journey on every Quarter, without the help of Cannon, or Muskets? Nay, I have with Bludgeons only, opposed and defeated those Peguers, who destroyed the Capital of this Kingdom; and took the Prince prisoner; . . . don't talk of Assistance, I require none, the Peguers I can wipe away as thus"[39] [drawing the palm of one hand over the other].

Then he added that he could "crush 100 such as the King of Pegu," without any reference to his ethnicity.[40]

It is true, however, that Alaungpaya played the *Burman* ethnic card,[41] but that was because most of the population were Burmese speakers and thus was to his military and political advantage. It does not mean that his goal was one of ethnic cleansing or that the cause of the conflict was ethnicity. He also did not target any other ethnic group, such as the Chin, Shan, or Arakanese, who were loyal to him, but only those who opposed him, which happened to be the Lower Burma Talaing. This suggests a power struggle in which patron-client ties were also very much part of the picture. Playing the Burman ethnic card, then, was an immediate strategy of psychological warfare meant to help accomplish the king's long-term *political* goal: the unification of Burma.

Thus the history of Burma, especially between the sixteenth and eighteenth century, cannot be depicted as an endemic ethnic battle between Lower Burma Talaing and Upper Burma Burman. Much like the fourteenth and fifteenth centuries, the former period witnessed a struggle for hegemony between the agrarian interior and the commercial coast in which *several* ethnic groups, in patron-client relationships to the dominant elite, were involved, with religious purity and legitimacy as the ultimate ideological rationale.

But colonial historiography nevertheless conceptualized Alaungpaya's (and also Aniruddha's and Bayinnaung's) reunification of Burma as mainly an ethnic issue. In Alaungpaya's case at least, that led to the erroneous myth of the "downtrodden Talaing," which was then projected backwards on nearly a millennium of Burma's earlier history. An invariable cause-and-effect relationship was created between ethnicity and major historical events since antiquity, so that all of Burma's history indeed looked like a continuous ethnic struggle that had endured until modern times. This ethnic interpretation of Burma's history—central to the Mon Paradigm—remains the dominant historiographic framework for the analysis of precolonial, colonial, and postcolonial Burma. Today's belief in the presence of *inherent,* and enduring ethnic animosities in Burma stems from this colonial construction, a topic that certainly needs to be reassessed. As a start, the following alternative should be considered.

Upstream-Downstream: A Geopolitical and Economic Approach

This twentieth-century ethnic framework of Burma's history conceptually divided the country into static ethnic zones, in which were placed discrete ethnic groups with seemingly impregnable physical, mental, social, and cultural boundaries. Thus as abstract and intangible a concept as ethnicity was used to reconstruct something as concrete and physical as a map, as if that twentieth-century prejudice somehow represented a twelfth-century geophysical reality (see Figure 1). Notwithstanding this great leap that attempted to reconstruct historical reality from modern "imagined communities," the epigraphic and archeological evidence suggests, instead, that indigenous conceptions of the actual physical space at issue were based on geopolitical and economic, rather than ethnic, concerns.

Lower Burma, the Wet Zone, is and was known at least from Pagán times as *akriy,* that is, "downstream," the "lower part of a river" (in this case, the Irrawaddy).[42] "Downstream in Tala" is a phrase found in several inscriptions of the Pagán period and other literary sources for defining Lower Burma.[43] Even in a *sittan* of 1581, Lower Burma is still called "the place downriver."[44] It was the region south of Prome that was considered to be the end of the Dry Zone and the gateway to both Lower Burma and Arakan province.[45] Upper Burma, in contrast, was and is generally called *anya,* a reference to the "upstream" regions of the Irrawaddy, but mainly indicating the Dry Zone.[46] Consequently, an individual from Upper Burma would be known as *anyatha,* or "son of the *anya* region," and hence the term "Anyathian Man" given to Palaeolithic man of Upper Burma by western anthropologists in the 1930s, while someone from Lower Burma would be *akriytha,* or "son of the *akriy* region."

The principle that the Irrawaddy defined cultural and geopolitical space was also true for places east and west of it: Sunārparanta was the name given by early Burmese sources to the region north and west of the river, while Tambadīpa, the region south and east of it.[47] Thus the Irrawaddy River, the constant, the fixed marker, defined these geopolitical and cultural regions; little hint of *ethnic regions* was attached to any of these terms except in the general, ambiguous word *tanluiṅ* used for everyone in Ussā Paikū. And this geopolitical and economic perspective of Upper and Lower Burma was a genuinely indigenous, early, historical one, not one derived from external observers using their own criteria for measuring and categorizing "the Other." The view Burmese culture had of its homeland, therefore, consisted of two *environmentally* distinct areas: those living upriver and those living downriver,[48] those in Dry Zone agriculture and those dealing with Wet Zone maritime trade and commerce.

By the middle of the Pagán period both regions shared common religious traditions, a common writing system that had become the standard for center and provincial administration, a common vocabulary of political ideology and symbolic dimensions of the state derived from a common Indic and indigenous conceptual system, a common structure of state and society, common principles in a coded civil and criminal law, common styles in religious art, and probably even similar tastes in dress and food.

Of course there would be tension and conflict, particularly of the kind one finds when people live in such close proximity and are dependent on each other economically. And of course there were regional, cultural, and linguistic differences and perceptions of such differences between the people of Upper and Lower Burma, of the capital and the outlying villages, and of those living in the plains and those in the hills. The same is true in any multicultural state or polity with many subparts.

But too often we in the West "privilege" categories of difference, while "deprivileging" categories of similarity. We tend to base our construction of "the Other" on our own historical experiences and parochial views of what we think is a universal truth about humanity, rather than on a closer scrutiny of the primary and preferably indigenous evidence. It is true that differences are expressed in that evidence. But they are infrequent and appear in inchoate form. Perhaps the first example occurs in King Kyanzittha's description of Lower Burma as the "Tanluiṅ kingdom," and another occurs in a more developed form in King Dhammazedi's Kalyani Inscriptions, when he coined the term Rāmaññadesa, the "realm of the Rman."

Yet even these early views of a general regional ethnocultural distinction between Upper and Lower Burma superimposed on the more prevalent geopolitical one do not necessarily imply the kind of absolute ethnic rupture that modern scholars have inferred. Rather, the distinctions were very much concerned with each side's claims to earlier, purer Buddhist origins, and hence to orthodoxy and cultural antiquity. The reason for making these ethnocultural distinctions of what were really geopolitical regions had more to do with religious one-upmanship, legitimacy, and political power than with ethnicity.

Moreover, even if certain regions came to generally represent the habitat of particular ethnic groups, surely such "ethnic space" must have had considerable flexibility and movement. These were not static, unchanging territories with impregnable boundaries forever fixed on a map, for we know Austro-Asiatic speakers settled in Upper Burma, while Tibeto-Burman-speaking peoples from Upper Burma moved into Lower Burma, and many areas were mixed. The best example of this was Tavoy, a major town located in the midst of the Mon of Lower Burma, whose inhabitants were Burmese, not Mon speakers.

And because there seemed to have been few strict rules against exogamy in Burma, especially of the kind one might expect in a "caste" society, these different ethnolinguistic groups very likely also intermarried. In elite society as well, political alliances were established between royalty and provincial "aristocracy" belonging to different ethnolinguistic groups and cemented by political appointments and marriage. Shin Saw Bu's case would have been just one of many. The image of an impenetrable block of Mon speakers occupying Lower Burma from time immemorial, which buttressed itself against another block of Burmese speakers in Upper Burma, never or seldom intermingling and therefore experiencing centuries of ethnic conflict, is a twentieth-century, imagined and desired portrait; it is not supported by the evidence.

Encouraged by segments of the colonial establishment, Mon nationalism in the early twentieth century shifted what had been a genuinely academic topic (that should have been resolved academically) into an ethnic one that became entangled in colonial politics and missionary concerns. What had been basically a linguistic and historiographic issue had become a politically charged crusade for ethnic minority rights. In this struggle, a presumably "victimized" Mon population of Lower Burma was depicted as having struggled against an oppressive Burman Upper Burma for centuries. Not only did the prevailing political view effectively disarm any potential *academic* challenges to it, but the most important scholars in the forefront of early Burma Studies at the time were also of Mon cultural background and seemed rather enamored of the whole thesis.

Thus the political and administrative policies of colonial officials and scholars and the sentiments of their native proteges had reformulated "ethnic relations" into a form that the protagonists themselves had seldom, if ever, experienced in their early history. This external view of ethnic relations in precolonial Burma is truly one seen from the "deck of a Dutch ship," to use C. Van Leur's famous phrase, not one derived from Burma's Dry Zone rivers and paddy fields or its Wet Zone port cities and bazaars.

Then what had been a worldwide call for "national self-determinism" vis-à-vis colonialism between the two World Wars was reinterpreted much more narrowly. The issue was no longer one of indigenous people fighting foreign colonialists but of minority ethnic groups fighting the majority ethnic group *within* the same nation. The oppressor had been deftly switched from an external, usually western, colonial power to an internal majority ethnic group. And because reified ethnicity was not a viable category of argument, it was replaced with the phrase "local autonomy," a much more credible (and fashionable) concept to advocate than reified ethnicity. Yet much of the "evidence" garnered from history and linguistics to legitimate the colonial legacy of reifying ethnicity and the postcolonial rhetoric of privileging "local autonomy" turns out to be exogenous, late, and legendary.

In sum, the historiography of the past century and a quarter has placed a millennium of Upper and Lower Burma relations in a largely *binary*, dichotomous ethnic framework of Burman versus Mon,[49] center versus periphery, and majority versus minority, rather than situating these relations in a larger, longer, more encompassing, mainly unified, geopolitical, religious, social, cultural, and economic *dualism*. It is a major distortion in which the Mon Paradigm has played a crucial part that needs to be rectified.

Conclusion

If, without the Mon Paradigm then, the history and historiography of the entire precolonial period in Burma can be *this* different from the conventional one affecting not just esoteric and narrower Burma issues but those as broad as state formation and Indianization in the region, one wonders how different the early histories of the rest of Southeast Asia might also be without their own "Mon Paradigms." For surely, there must be comparable, still undisclosed conventions infecting their historiographies as well, especially as they too were reconstructed largely during the colonial period by officials and scholars who shared similar values and mentalities with those in Burma. That I am not alone in questioning a possible early "Southeast Asia Paradigm" is attested by doubts raised recently with regard to the early existence of Champa in Southern Vietnam, suggesting that there may not have been a unitary state there as well.[50] And Champa, like Rāmaññadesa, Funan, and Dvāravatī of the "preclassical" period, was thought to have played a similarly fundamental, foundational role in the making of the "classical" states of Southeast Asia. Might not, then, our conventional views regarding the origins of the "classical" period itself, and of the nature of its states, also be wrong?

If so, do we have the time and resolve—some of us are in our twilight years after all—to rectify this and see it all through? If not us, who? Although the next generation of Southeast Asia historians may not be as enamored of these early issues as some of us of the earlier generation are, the intellectual and academic problems of the Mon Paradigm are very pertinent to those current in colonial studies today. Indeed, in many cases, these kinds of issues have been raised and addressed much better by the younger generation—as their education has been thoroughly immersed in them—than by the older generation. The former can probably explain much better the colonial period constructs responsible for some of these "inventions of tradition" than we can.

But—to ask the question one more time—can we live without the Mon Paradigm? The answer is we can and we must. For the historical reality is that the Mon Paradigm is a myth: Soṇa and Uttara had nothing to do with the origins of Theravāda Buddhism in Burma, and perhaps even in the rest of Southeast Asia; there was no Mon kingdom in Lower Burma called Rāmaññadesa that preceded Pagán; there was no conquest of Thatôn by Aniruddha in 1057; and as a consequence Lower Burma did not "civilize" Upper Burma. It was the other way around: Pagán settled, developed, and "civilized" Lower Burma. It was Pagán's economic, political, and cultural development of the interior and its agrarian sector that enabled the subsequent rise of coastal, trade-centered Rāmaññadesa. Like it or not—and notwithstanding my Mon father—the making of "classical" Burma has little or nothing to do with the Mon of Lower Burma. We must come to terms with this old and erroneous sentiment no matter how undesirable this dualistic interpretation of early Burma may seem in today's political world of binary constructs, lest we perpetuate for yet another generation a myth that has been allowed to continue far too long.

Notes

Abbreviations used in the Notes after first mention

ASB	Archaeological Survey of Burma
ASI	Archaeological Survey of India
BBHC	*Bulletin of the Burma Historical Commission*
BEFEO	Bulletin l'École française d'Extrême-Orient
BSOAS	*Bulletin of the School of Oriental and African Studies*
DPPN	*Dictionary of Pali Proper Names*
EB	Archaeological Survey of Burma. *Epigraphica Birmanica*
IB	*Inscriptions of Burma*
JAS	*Journal of Asian Studies*
JBRS	*Journal of the Burma Research Society*
JRAS	*Journal of the Royal Asiatic Society*
JSEAS	*Journal of Southeast Asian Studies*
JSS	*Journal of the Siam Society*
List	*Epigraphia Birmanica: A List of Inscriptions Found in Burma*
MKPC	*Mon Kyauksa Paung Chyok*
MM	*Mandalay Mahamuni Tantuin Atwinshi Kyauksa Mya*
MSSK	*Myanma Cway Cum Kyam*
SMK	*She Haung Myanma Kyauksa Mya*

Chapter 1: Introduction

1. Documentation in this introductory chapter will be minimal, as subsequent chapters regarding the assertions made here will include complete citations. The Kalyani Inscriptions, often dated to 1476, were in fact not actually inscribed until 1479.

2. My use of the term "Burma" (or for that matter "Myanmar") should not be construed as a political statement, but a matter of habit, although for official references I would no more refuse to use "Kampuchea" or "Mumbai" than I would "Myanmar." Besides, for a Burmese speaker, using the term "Myanmar" as a noun by itself is awkward, as it is really an adjective and needs another word, like *pyi* (country), after it.

3. This title derives from a paper I presented in December 2001 in Yangôn, Myanmar, at the annual meeting of the Universities Historical Research Centre, December 12–14.

4. Knowledge about the Third Buddhist Council, and hence Soṇa and Uttara's journey to Suvaṇṇabhūmi, was not unknown earlier in Pagán. Indeed, their story is represented as a mural on the Myinkaba Kubyaukgyi temple, thought to have been

built in the eleventh century. My point, however, is the connection suggested between Suvaṇṇabhūmi, Lower Burma, and the Third Council, a link I have not found in any of the standard Mon language texts of the precolonial era written between the Kalyani Inscriptions and the twentieth century. The first Burmese source to connect Suvaṇṇabhūmi and Mon Lower Burma after Dhammazedi appears to have been U Kala's work, written in Burmese, in which he displays an obvious uncertainty about even that claim (*Mahayazawingyi* [Great royal chronicle], ed. Saya Pwa [Yangon: Hanthawaddy Press, 1960], vol. 1, p. 100). Half a century later, another Burmese-language palm-leaf manuscript entitled "Thatôn Yazawin" (Chronicle of Thatôn) was said to have been copied, probably verbatim, from a Mon chronicle *(yazawin)* around 1789. It mentions a Suvaṇṇabhūmi Myo (that is, "city of Suvaṇṇabhūmi"), which is curious since the Suvaṇṇabhūmi of Buddhist legend is a much larger entity, in fact, a whole region. At the end of the manuscript, the copyist wrote that the original was the old Mon-language *yazawin* "written by Gunawuddhi and others," which he had "corrected." This Burmese version can be found as microfilm Reel 74 of the Toyo Bunko microfilm project on Burma under "Thatôn Yazawin." The catalogue of the Toyo Bunko project itself is in English and published as *List of Microfilms Deposited in The Centre for East Asian Cultural Studies,* Part 8. Burma (Tokyo, The Toyo Bunko, 1976), p. 22.

5. U Kala, *Mahawazawingyi,* pp. 174–184. The subsequent *Hmannan Mahayazawindawgyi* [Great royal chronicle of the Palace of Mirrors], vol. 1, ed. U San Tun (Yangon: Pyi Gyi Man Taing Press, 1967), pp. 240–249, has the same account. Note that when Bayinnaung took Ayudhyā in the mid-sixteenth century, he was also said to have brought back exactly 30,000 people to Pegu. For English-language versions of the story, see Sir Arthur Phayre, *History of Burma* (New York: Augustus M. Kelley, 1969), pp. 34–35; G. E. Harvey, *A History of Burma: From the earliest times to 10 March 1824: The beginning of the English Conquest* (London: Frank Cass, 1925), p. 28; and D. G. E. Hall, *Burma* (London: Hutchinson University Library, 1960). pp. 15–16.

6. Quoted in Harvey's *History,* p. 28.

7. Michael Symes's 1802 account of Ava may be the first by an English-language author to accept the Mon Paradigm. He wrote, "Much of Burmese civilization, including Hinayana Buddhism, had come to them from the Mons, whose independent kingdom with its capital at Thaton had been conquered by King Anawrahta in the middle of the eleventh century AD and incorporated in the empire of Pagan." Michael Symes, *Journal of his Second Embassy to the Court of Ava in 1802* (London, George Allen & Unwin Ltd, 1955), p. xix.

8. H. L. Shorto, "The *dewatau sotāpan:* A Mon Prototype of the 37 Nats," *Bulletin of the School of Oriental and African Studies* [hereafter cited as *BSOAS*], 30 (1967): 138–139, and "The 32 *Myos* in the Medieval Mon Kingdom," *BSOAS,* 36 (1963): 572–591, went beyond most by suggesting that even the 37 Nat Cult originated with the Mon. He also claimed, in "The Gavampati Tradition in Burma," in *R. C. Majumdar Felicitation Volume,* ed. Himansu Bhusan Sarkar (Calcutta: Firma K. L. Mukhopadhyay, 1970), p. 26 and passim, that this tradition was borrowed from the Mon of Lower Burma as well, a topic to be discussed in greater detail in Chapter Four.

9. D. G. E. Hall, *A History of South-East Asia* (New York: St. Martin's Press, 1968), p. 143.

10. The most recent and comprehensive view of the Mon Paradigm is that of

G. H. Luce, found in numerous works, but most completely developed in his three-volume *Old Burma, Early Pagan* (New York: J.J. Augustin, 1969), p. 31 especially, and passim. But Luce was merely perpetuating, albeit with much extrapolation, a perspective begun much earlier. Even non-Burma scholars of Southeast Asia, such as George Coedes, managed to get involved in this thesis regarding an early Mon Theravāda Buddhist state when he suggested that Theravāda Buddhism was introduced in the eleventh century to Lower Burma by refugees fleeing a cholera epidemic in Haripuñjaya; see Coedes, *The Indianized States of Southeast Asia,* ed. Walter F. Vella and trans. Susan Brown Cowing (Honolulu: East-West Center Press, 1968), p. 149. There are many recent works that are steeped in the Mon Paradigm, as the subsequent chapters and citations will demonstrate.

11. The most important and earliest generation of scholars involved in the reconstruction of early Burma at the time, such as Professor Pe Maung Tin, U Lu Pe Win, U Tun Nyein, and a little later, Mon Bokay were of Mon cultural background. G. H. Luce of course was not, but he married Pe Maung Tin's sister and thus was intimately connected to that culture. In a country dominated by those whose cultural background was Burman, it is understandable why these scholars may have embraced the Mon Paradigm.

12. Quoted in Paul Wheatley's *Nāgara and Commandery,* University of Chicago Department of Geography Research Papers, nos. 207–208 (Chicago, 1983), p. 200. For the French, see Pierre Dupont, *L'archéologie mône de Dvaravati* (Paris: École française D'Extrême-Orient, 1959), pp. 8–9. My thanks to Ken Breazeale for the correct translation.

13. A recent, stimulating review article by David Ludden puts such bias in a revealing context; see his "Modern Inequality and Early Modernity: A Comment for the *AHR* on Articles by R. Bin Wong and Kenneth Pomeranz," *American Historical Review* 107 (April 2002): 470–480.

14. G. H. Luce, "Note on the Peoples of Burma in the 12th–13th Century A.D.," *Census of India* 11, 1 (1931), p. 299.

15. One Burma scholar of the post-Luce generation who has managed to escape the Mon Paradigm, but without directly questioning it, is Janice Stargardt, as demonstrated in *The Ancient Pyu of Burma,* Volume One: *Early Pyu Cities in a Man-Made Landscape* (Cambridge and Singapore: Publications on Ancient Civilization in South Asia and Institute of South East Asian Studies, 1990).

16. This re-creation can be found in G. H. Luce's *Old Burma-Early Pagan,* vol. 1, opposite the Foreword.

17. Wheatley, *Nāgara,* p. 199.

18. Chapter Twelve is devoted to the origins and development of the Mon Paradigm where I discuss the issue in detail.

19. To name just two, Tilman Frasch's *Pagan: Stadt und Staat* (Stuttgart: Steinger Verlag, 1996) and Emmanuel Guillon's *The Mons: A Civilization of Southeast Asia,* trans. James V. Di Crocco (Bangkok: The Siam Society, 1999), still accept the Mon Paradigm. My thanks to Lily Handlin for translating the pertinent sections of Frasch's work for me.

20. As I stated in the Preface, one of the best indications of this was the subsequent creation of a historical committee in Burma to investigate whether the paper I delivered in Yangon was sound.

21. See Charles Backus, *The Nan-chao kingdom and T'ang China's southwestern frontier* (London: Cambridge University Press, 1981), pp. 46–50; Michael Blackmore, "The Rise of Nan-chao in Yunnan," *Journal of Southeast Asian History* 1 (1960): 47–61. Luce admitted in *Phases of Pre-Pagan Burma: Languages and History,* vol. 1 (Oxford: Oxford University Press, 1985), p. 100, that he pleads guilty "to having long regarded them [the Lolo] as basically Dai."

22. Postmodernists might retort that this is impossible, but it is the best I can do at this time without getting into my subconscious.

23. I do not pretend to know the Mon language, but as of this writing, nearly all Mon inscriptions found in Burma have been translated either into Burmese or English. The former version is more important because the scripts for both languages are virtually identical in Burma. This means one can read the actual words of the Mon version while obtaining meanings from translations.

24. Donald K. Swearer in "Myth, Legend and History in the Northern Thai Chronicles," *Journal of the Siam Society* [hereafter cited as *JSS*] 62, 1 (January 1974): 67–88, has shown the complexities of this kind of issue.

Chapter Two: The Pyū Millennium

1. He wrote that "the name 'Pyū' has merely been attached to it as a convenient label . . . but by no means to be accepted as final." Archaeological Survey of Burma, *Epigraphia Birmanica: Being Lithic and Other Inscriptions of Burma* [hereafter cited as *EB*] (Rangoon: Government Printing, 1919), 1:61.

2. Stargardt, in her *Ancient Pyu,* had summarized and analyzed the many disparate pieces of scholarship that had hitherto contributed to the understanding of the Pyū. The latest scholarship on the Pyū is Hudson's dissertation (see bibliography).

3. Taw Sein Ko, *Burmese Sketches,* vol. 1 (Rangoon: British Burma Press, 1913), p. 19.

4. G. H. Luce, "The Ancient Pyu," *Burma Research Society Fiftieth Anniversary Publications No. 2* (Rangoon: Burma Research Society, 1960), pp. 308–309. Unfortunately, Luce used the term "dacoit" rather than "rebel" for translating the Chinese word, which obfuscates the issue since dacoit is a Hindi or Hindustani term. See also Chen Yi-sein, "The Chinese in Upper Burma Before A.D. 1700," *Silver Jubilee Publication* (Yangon: Ministry of Culture and Burma Historical Researches, 1982), and *Man Shu (Book of the Southern Barbarians),* trans. Gordon H. Luce and ed. G. P. Oey, Cornell Southeast Asia Program Data Paper no. 44 (Ithaca 1961), pp. 90–91. The Chinese words are represented, respectively, by 驃 and 剽.

5. Edward Harper Parker, *Burma: With Special Reference to her Relations with China* (Rangoon: Rangoon Gazette Press, 1893), p. 12; Luce, "The Ancient Pyu," p. 309.

6. Luce, "Ancient Pyu," pp. 309–310.

7. Chen Yi-Sein, "Lin-Yang (Visnu City) 1st–5th Centuries AD," *Studies in Myanma History,* vol. 1 (Yangon: Innwa Publishing House, 1999), p. 78.

8. John Guy, "A Warrior-Ruler Stele from Śrī Kṣetra, Pyū, Burma," *JSS* 85, 1 and 2 (1997): 85–94; and Aung Thaw, *Historical Sites in Burma* (Rangoon: Ministry of Union Culture, 1972), pp. 6–8, passim.

9. Apart from the possible links to Southwest India with regard to the Pyū writing system (this is contested, as we shall see below), there are other intriguing com-

mercial and religious ties between the two, as demonstrated by Jan Christie Wisseman in "Medieval Tamil-language Inscriptions in Southeast Asia and China," *Journal of Southeast Asian Studies* [hereafter cited as *JSEAS*] 29, 2 (September 1998): 239–268.

10. *EB* 3, 1 (1923): 42. But Blagden, who translated this inscription, states (in note 9) that its meaning "has not been determined."

11. Myanmar, Archaeological Department, *She Haung Myanma Kyauksa Mya* (Ancient Burmese stone inscriptions) [hereafter cited as *SMK*], 5 vols. (Yangon: Sape Beikman, 1972–present). The first known mention of "Pyū" as an ethnic term appears to be in 1200 AD, when a "Mr. Pyū" is mentioned, although the spelling could mean "Mr. White" as well. (*SMK* 1:71). However, in 1207, when the word is spelled correctly as "Pyū," a "Pyū mound" was mentioned (*SMK* 1:83).

12. I should add a word of caution that not all students of the pre-Pagán millennium see its culture as necessarily uniform or continuous. To me, however, the evidence seems convincing enough.

13. Currently there are even two graduate students in western academia working on the Pyū.

14. Aung Thaw, *Historical Sites,* p. 6, and Stargardt, *Ancient Pyu,* chapter 4, both using radiocarbon results, date the beginnings of Beikthano Myo, the first putative Pyū city, to about 180 BC. The most recent research that generally supports the above works, is an article by Bob Hudson, Nyein Lwin, and Win Maung on "The Origins of Bagan: New Dates and Old Inhabitants" published in *Asian Perspectives Special Issue: The Archaeology of Myanma Pyay (Burma),* eds. Miriam T. Stark and Michael A. Aung-Thwin (Honolulu: University of Hawai'i Press, 2002) pp. 48–74. There is also a palm-leaf "History of Taundwingyi," the town nearest to the ancient site, that might throw some light on it. The text of the palm leaf is included in reel 78 of *List of Microfilms,* p. 22. Finally, U Myint Aung writes that the *Zambu Kungya Kyan,* a text believed to come from fourteenth-century records that Pyū culture had spread their settlements to "every nook and corner of the country." See "The Development of Myanmar Archaeology," *Myanmar Historical Research Journal* 9 (June 2002), p. 23.

15. King Kyanzittha's palace inscription, assigned to 1102, is the first time that the term Rmeñ (Mon) appears in original, domestic epigraphy, with the inference that the Mon were contemporaneous with the Pyū (*EB* 3, 1:1–68). Luce's conjectural map in *Old Burma* (see this book, Chapter One, Figure 1) suggests that the country was divided into three large ethnic blocks—the Mranmā on the north, the Pyū in the middle, and the Rmeñ in the south. In other words, Luce used conjecture as "evidence" to prove itself.

16. To be demonstrated below.

17. The Chinese sources mention nine walled cities (the latest count is a little more than a dozen, depending on what one counts) and 298 districts. See, for example, Parker, *Burma,* p. 12. For their locations, see my *Making of Modern Burma* on CD-ROM (Honolulu: Center for Southeast Asian Studies, 2001) under "Maps," and Bob Hudson et al., "Origins of Bagan," p. 64.

18. Michael Aung-Thwin, *Irrigation in the Heartland of Burma: Foundations of the Pre-Colonial Burmese State* (DeKalb, IL: Center for Southeast Asian Studies, 1990). These large Pyū cities were strategically placed to control the same three major areas

of agricultural production well before Pagán reestablished them for its use. Hudson's map in "Origins of Bagan," p. 64, shows their location, as does my cruder map in "Burma Before Pagán: The Status of Archaeology Today," *Asian Perspectives* 25, 2 (1982–1983): 1–21.

19. U Aung Myint's *Kaung Kin Dat Pon Mya Hma Myanma She Haung Myo Taw Mya* (Ancient royal cities of Myanmar from aerial photographs [hereafter *Aerial Photographs*]), Yangon: Ministry of Culture, 1998, is a most useful publication that sheds much light on the subject.

20. See Thiripyanchi U Tha Myat, *Pyū Phat Ca* (Pyū reader) (Rangoon: U Hla Din, 1963), p. 78, and Luce, *Phases,* 1, p. 150, for the inscription. For the coins, see U Shwe Zan, *The Golden Mrauk-U* (Yangon: U Shwe Zan, 1995), p. 53.

21. Aung Thaw, *Historical Sites,* p. 14; Robert S. Wicks, *Money, Markets, and Trade in Early Southeast Asia: The Development of Indigenous Monetary Systems to AD 1400* (Ithaca: Southeast Asia Program, 1992), p. 114.

22. Taw Sein Ko, *Burmese Sketches,* 1:83.

23. Wheatley, *Nāgara,* Chapter I, "The City and Its Origins." A partially dissenting view can be found in Richard O'Connor, *A Theory of Indigenous Southeast Asian Urbanism* (Singapore: Institute for Southeast Asian Studies, 1983) where he addresses Southeast Asian urbanism as an issue but not necessarily its link to state formation. See also the latter's "A Regional Explanation of the Tai *Muang* as a City-State" in Mogens Herman Hansen's edition of *A Comparative Study of Thirty City-State Cultures* (Copenhagen: The Royal Danish Academy of Sciences and Letters, 2000), pp. 431–443.

24. As far as I can tell, the city of Beikthano is not mentioned in the chronicles.

25. Aung Thaw, *Historical Sites,* p. 6; Stargardt, *Ancient Pyu,* p. 408; Hudson et al., "Origins of Bagan," p. 65.

26. Neither Mongmao nor Binnaka is mentioned as a Pyū city in the chronicles, but Bhinnakaraja, the "king of Bhinnaka" is, in *The Glass Palace Chronicle of the Kings of Burma,* trans. Pe Maung Tin and G. H. Luce (Rangoon: Burma Research Society, 1960), p. 3. Interestingly, he is linked to the fall of Tagaung, the city long considered by Burmese speakers to be the origins of their culture.

27. Maung Win Maung (Tampawady), "Binnaka Myo Haung" (Ancient city of Binnaka), MSS, 1981. For a summary in English, see my "Burma Before Pagán," p. 16–17.

28. The city is listed as "Bhinnaka-mrui kui kro kui con cactam 'Sittan of Beinnaka'" [sic] in *List of Microfilms,* p. 29. The copy of the palm-leaf manuscript is on reel number 95, item no. 8, dated to 1833 AD.

29. J. C. Eade, *The Calendrical Systems of Mainland South-East Asia* (Leiden: E.J. Brill, 1995), pp. 13, 78.

30. Michael Aung-Thwin, "Heaven, Earth and the Supernatural World: Dimensions of the Exemplary Center in Burmese History," In *The City As a Sacred Center: Essays on Six Asian Contexts. International Studies in Sociology and Social Anthropology,* eds. Bardwell Smith and Holy Baker Reynolds (Leiden: E.J. Brill, 1987), pp. 88–102.

31. Stargardt, *Ancient Pyu,* p. 177–190. All the information contained here on Mongmao has been derived from U Sein Maung's reports titled "Mongmao: A forgotten city," in *The Working Peoples Daily,* January 21, 23, and February 3, 1981. See also Aung-Thwin, "Burma Before Pagán," pp. 17–18.

32. Luce, *Phases,* 1:72, 78.

33. *Man Shu,* p. 90.

34. *Man Shu,* p. 90.

35. *Man Shu,* pp. 90–91.

36. Aung Thaw, *Historical Sites,* pp. 11–15; U Myint Aung, "The Excavations at Halin," *Journal of the Burma Research Society* [hereafter cited as *JBRS*] 53, 2 (December 1970): 55–62.

37. Hudson et al., "Origins of Bagan." See also, Bob Hudson, U Nyein Lwin, and U Win Maung (Tanpawady), "Digging for myths: archaeological excavations and surveys of the legendary nineteen founding villages of Pagán," in *Burma: Art and Archaeology,* eds. Alexandra Green and T. Richard Blurton (New York: Art Media Resources, Ltd., 2002), pp. 9–21.

38. Taw Sein Ko, *Burmese Sketches,* 2:278–282, Aung Thaw, *Historical Sites,* pp. 11–15, and Thiripyanchi U Tha Myat, *Pyū Phat Ca,* pp. 21–22.

39. Bob Hudson, "Halin—Recalibrating the Radiocarbon Dates," 2001, MSS.

40. G. H. Luce, "Sources of Early Burma History," in *Southeast Asian history and historiography: Essays presented to D. G. E. Hall,* eds. C. D. Cowan and O. W. Wolters, with a foreword by John M. Echols (Ithaca: Cornell University Press, 1976), p. 35.

41. Aung Thaw, "Bronze culture and tradition in Myanmar," *The Working People's Daily,* September 2, 1990, p. 9; September 9, 1990, p. 9. "Expert team conducting research on ancient objects unearthed in Budalin Township," *Myanmar Alin* (New light of Myanmar), February 25, 1999, p. 5, 12. Another report by a Dr. Tin Thein also appeared in Burmese in the *Kyehmon* (The mirror), on April 29, 1998, p. 5, on the same subject. An analysis of these finds, with their implications, can be found in English in *Proceedings of the Workshop on Bronze Age Culture in Myanmar* (Yangon: Universities Historical Research Centre, 1999) and Elizabeth Moore and Pauk Pauk's "Nyaung-gan: A Preliminary Note on a Bronze Age Cemetery Near Mandalay, Myanmar (Burma)," in *Asian Perspectives Special Issue* 40, 1 (2002): 35–47. See also Moore's more recent work on this subject entitled "Bronze and Iron Age sites in Myanmar: Chindwin, Samon, and Pyu," *SOAS Bulletin of Burma Research* 1, 1 (Spring 2003): 24–39.

42. Aung-Thwin, *Irrigation,* pp. 68, 72, 73.

43. Luce, "Old Kyauksé and the Coming of the Burmans," *JBRS* 42, 1 (1959): 75–112.

44. The present excavated city may have been a later construction, so that there could have been more than one Halin period, with an older one underneath that is more circular like its contemporaries in Arakan, Thailand, and Cambodia.

45. Myint Aung, "Excavations at Halin" p. 55, states that it is about two square miles. The hectare figure comes from Bob Hudson, personal communication.

46. Aung-Thwin, "Heaven, Earth and the Supernatural World," pp. 88–102.

47. See Harvey's *History,* p. 320–321, for a description of this practice in the nineteenth century.

48. The miniature site plans of these two cities at the provincial museum of Arakan clearly show this. For the early history and culture of Arakan, see U Shwe Zan, *Golden Mrauk-U.* For a recent work on Arakan of this period meant for the general public, one should consult Pamela Gutman's *Burma's Lost Kingdoms: Splendours of Arakan* (Trumbull, CT: Weatherhill Inc., 2001). For a scholarly treatment of Arakan, see her Ph.D. dissertation entitled "Ancient Arakan: With Special Reference

to its Cultural History between the 5th and 11th Centuries," Australian National University, 1976.

49. The miniature site plan displayed at Sukhodaya archaeological park reveals a similar design and use of water.

50. U Tha Myat, *Pyū Phat Ca,* 22.

51. U Myint Aung, "Excavations at Halin," pp. 55–64; and Aung Thaw, *Historical Sites,* pp. 11–15.

52. Aung Myint, *Aerial Photographs,* p. 113–116; Hudson et al., "Origins of Bagan," and Moore, "Bronze and Iron Age." Moore, E., and U Aung Myint, "Finger-marked designs on ancient bricks in Myanmar," *JSS* 79, 2 (1991), pp. 81–102.

53. As noted above, G. H. Luce considered Halin the latest Pyū city.

54. *Zatatawpon Yazawin* (Chronicle of royal horoscopes), ed. U Hla Tin (Rangoon: Ministry of Culture, 1960), p. 36. Dwattabaung, however, is preceded by two brothers from Tagaung, the place to which the Burmese trace their origins. His story is similar to a much later (1825) Mon tale called the *Lik Smin Asah,* to be discussed fully in Chapter Six. It concerns Samala and Wimala, the two founding brothers of Pegu, who came from India to live as hermits in Lower Burma. Thus, this "quintessential" Mon tale may actually have been derived from the *Zatatawpon* or an even earlier Pyū tradition, since Śrī Kṣetra is also known as Yathe Myo or "City of the Hermit(s)." See *Glass Palace Chronicles,* p. 19. Moreover, it does not seem to be just a coincidence that of the seven auspicious individuals who founded Śrī Kṣetra, one was Rishi the Hermit (*Zatatawpon,* p. 36).

55. Indeed, the *Zatatawpon,* p. 35–37, explicitly states, and has a chart that illustrates, two distinct dynasties of Śrī Kṣetra.

56. The well-known phrase belongs to the late Stephen J. Gould, renowned paleontologist.

57. Luce, *Phases,* p. 17. Chinese sources describe Śrī Kṣetra as being circular. (Parker, *Burma,* p. 12). See Hudson et al., "Origins of Bagan," for Śrī Kṣetra's hectares.

58. *Man Shu,* p. 90.

59. Parker *Burma,* p. 13. *Man Shu,* p. 90.

60. *Man Shu,* p. 90. Also, Parker, *Burma,* pp. 12–13, where the Chinese source states that the city "is built of greenish glazed tiles . . ." and elsewhere in the narrative, "with bricks of vitreous ware . . . ." (p. 13). Chen Yi-sein, in his article "The Location of the Pyu Capital in the 800–832 Period," *Proceedings of the Myanmar Two Millennia Conference 15–17 December 1999* (Yangôn, Universities Historical Research Centre, 2000), pp. 1–12, writes that the word *ch'ing-p'i* in the *Man-shu* and *Hsin T'ang shu* are references to "ordinary bricks" (p. 10). Yet he translated the word *ch'ing* as "blue," "black" or "green," with the implication that they were glazed. I am not certain how the apparent contradiction is reconciled.

Geok Yian Goh, a PhD student studying early Burma at the University of Hawai'i, with reading knowledge of classical Chinese, has also read the relevant passage in the *Man-shu* for me. She confirms Chen's translation that the word *ch'ing* is "blue, "black," or "green" and suggests that most probably *ch'ing* refers to a greenish-blue hue in the color of the glazed bricks. If true, it appears that the bricks used to construct the walls of the P'iao capital were indeed glazed with a blue or greenish color, a technique which was used quite regularly later during the Pagan period, particularly on *Jātaka* plaques of temples, and, in one case at least, the entire stupa: the Ngakywènadaung.

61. Kyaw Nyein, "The Ceramic Industry of the Pagán Period," *Bulletin of the Burma Historical Commission* [hereafter cited as *BBHC*] 3 (1963): 180–184; see also *Ceramic Traditions in Myanmar* (Yangon: SEAMEO Regional Centre for History and Tradition, 2003), and Paul Strachan, *Pagán: Art and Architecture of Old Burma* (Arran: Kiscadale Publications, 1989), p. 38. One of the earliest reports on the Ngakywènadaung was made by a Rev. H. I. Marshall of the American Baptist Mission, who mentioned in 1904 that this bulbous-shaped *stupa* was "covered with green glazed tiles" (Taw Sein Ko, *Burmese Sketches,* 2:259).

62. Hudson et al., "Origins of Bagan," p. 64, is one of the few, and most recent, to include Wati.

63. Maung Win Maung, "Binnaka."

64. Luce, *Phases,* 1:68.

65. Parker, *Burma,* p. 11 and Chen Yi-Sein, "Lin-Yang," p. 73. The number thirty-two is curious for it is often symbolic of the thirty-two deities of Tāvatiṁsa ruled by Sakka, as well as the "Thirty Myos" (cities or towns) of Lower Burma, a tradition hastily attributed to the Mon by Shorto.

66. The classic study is O. W. Wolters' *Early Indonesian Commerce: A Study of the Origins of Srivijaya* (Ithaca: Cornell University Press, 1967).

67. Aung-Thwin, "Burma Before Pagán"

68. Parker, *Burma,* p. 14.

69. The Japonica variety had fewer grains on each stalk, while the Indica variety, with more grains on each stalk, provided a much larger yield, which has implications for population growth, and therefore also for socioeconomic and political development. See Aung-Thwin, *Irrigation,* p. 33; Tadayo Watabe, Koji Tanaka, and Koung [sic] Nyunt. "Ancient Rice Grains Recovered from Ruins in Burma–A study of the Alteration of Cultivated Rice." *Preliminary Report of the Kyoto University Scientific Survey to Burma 1974.* Kyoto: Kyoto University, 1976.

70. Stargardt's *Ancient Pyu,* chapter 2, argues that the Pyū may have been the ones responsible for the kinds of irrigation technology known in Burma by the nineteenth century. A review of her book by Peter Bellwood in *The Review of Archaeology* 13, 2 (Fall 1992): 1–7, and Stargardt's response in the same journal, 14, 2 (Fall 1993): 2–32, and a response to the response by Bellwood in the latter issue, pp. 33–35, are instructive.

71. Michael Aung-Thwin, *Pagán: The Origins of Modern Burma* (Honolulu: University of Hawai'i Press, 1985), and *Irrigation.*

72. Michael Aung-Thwin, "Principles and Patterns of the Precolonial Burmese State," in *Tradition and Modernity in Myanmar: Proceedings of an International Conference held in Berlin from May 7th to May 9th, 1993,* eds. Uta Gärtner and Jens Lorenz. (Berlin: Humboldt-Universität Fakultätsinstitut für Asien-und Afrikawissenschaften, 1994), pp. 15–44.

73. Craig Reynolds, "A New Look at Old Southeast Asia," *JAS* 54, 2 (1995): 419–446.

74. As contrast, see Michael Aung-Thwin's "Lower Burma and Bago in the History of Burma," in *The Maritime Frontier of Burma: Exploring Political, Cultural and Commercial Interaction in the Indian Ocean World, 1200–1800,* eds. Jos Gommans and

Jacques Leider, (Leiden, Koninklijke Nederlandse Akademie van Wetenschappen, 2002), pp. 25–57.

75. Aung Thaw, "The 'Neolithic' Culture of the Padah-lin Caves," *Asian Perspectives* 14 (1971): 123–133; Michael Aung-Thwin, "Origins and Development of the Field of Prehistory in Burma." To be sure, some "neolithic" implements have been found in Lower Burma as well, but compared with the quantity, proliferation, distribution, and chronology of their counterparts in Upper Burma, the Lower Burma findings, at least to date, are hardly contenders for an alternative approach.

76. Aung-Thwin, "Principles and Patterns."

77. I owe the phrase to W. Donald MacTaggart of Arizona State University. Personal communication, July 21, 1992.

78. The Chinese sources state that "gold and silver are used as money, the shape of which is crescent-like . . . ." (Parker, *Burma,* p. 14). See also Robert Wicks, *Money, Markets, and Trade,* p. 112–114; Robert S. Wicks, "The Ancient Coinage of Mainland Southeast Asia," *JSEAS* 16, 2 (1985): 195–225.

79. Myint Aung, "The Capital of Suvannabhumi unearthed?" *Shiroku* 10 (1977): 41–53, here p. 42; and Aung Myint's *Aerial Photographs,* p. 116.

80. Wicks, *Money, Markets, and Trade,* p. 115–116; Aung Thaw, *Excavations at Beikthano* (Rangoon: Ministry of Union Culture, 1968) and *Historical Sites.* The horde of coins found at Pegu almost surely belonged to the Pyū period and are quite distinctly Pyū, not Mon, and will be discussed in Chapter Three.

81. Wicks, *Money, Markets, and Trade,* 112–114.

82. Stargardt, *Ancient Pyu,* p. 282.

83. Aung Thaw, *Excavations;* Stargardt, *Ancient Pyu;* Aung-Thwin, "Burma Before Pagán."

84. Aung Thaw, *Excavations.* I do not want to get into a debate on whether this was "true" Roman or Indian rouletted blackware as per Bellwood. The point is that this kind of pottery seems to have been quite common to other areas of Southeast Asia around this time.

85. Luce, *Phases,* 1:72–73. For accounts of the musicians, see also Dr. Khin Maung Nyunt, "The Myanmar Performing Arts of the Pyū Period," *Myanmar Perspectives* 4, 1 (1999): 31–36; and also D. E. Twitchett and A.H. Christie, "A Medieval Burmese Orchestra," *Asia Major* (New Series) 7, 1–2 (1959): 171–195.

86. Luce, *Phases,* 1:68, 73.

87. Wheatley, *Nāgara,* p. 270.

88. Parker, *Burma,* p. 15.

89. See Aung Thaw, *Historical Sites,* p. 31 and Stargardt, *Ancient Pyu,* plate 28a, for their photographic representation.

90. Aung Thaw, *Historical Sites.* Among others, the stone beads and sprinkler vessels found at Winga are identical, or nearly so, to those found at Beikthano.

91. Hudson et al., "Origins of Bagan."

92. Stargardt, *Ancient Pyu,* p. 200.

93. Stargardt, *Ancient Pyu,* p. 200

94. Both Stargardt, *Ancient Pyu,* p. 192, and Richard M. Cooler, *The Karen bronze drums of Burma: types, iconography, manufacture, and use* (Leiden and New York: E.J. Brill, 1994), suggests a pre-Indic culture that was based on fertility, the seasons, rain, and other such natural phenomena.

95. Stargardt, *Ancient Pyu,* chapter 5.

96. Aung Thaw, *Historical Sites,* p. 10; Stargardt, *Ancient Pyu,* p. 193–194.

97. Aung Thaw, *Excavations,* p. 172.

98. Stargardt, *Ancient Pyu,* 195; Aung Thaw, *Excavations,* p. 172.

99. Both Stargardt, *Ancient Pyu,* p. 192, and Aung Thaw, *Excavations,* p. 64, are agreed on this link.

100. Aung Thaw, *Historical Sites,* p. 20–21.

101. Aung Thaw, *Historical Sites,* p. 16–33.

102. Ray, Nihar-Ranjan, *Sanskrit Buddhism in Burma* (Amsterdam: H.J. Paris, 1936), chapter 3, pp. 40–61, 81. Also, U Tin, "Mahayan gaing Myanma naingnan tho sheuswa yauk thi akyaung," [The earliest arrival of the Mahayan Sect to Pagán, Burma], *JBRS* 19, 2 (1929): 36–42. According to Taranatha, the famous Tibetan monk who traveled in Southeast Asia during the sixteenth century, when Magadha was captured by the Turks *(Turuskas)* in the tenth century, many monks and scholars fled to "Pukham," among other places in Southeast Asia. Some of these included the Mantrayanas.

103. Aung Thaw, *Historical Sites,* p. 28; Luce, "Ancient Pyu," p. 247.

104. G. H. Luce, "Mons of the Pagán Dynasty," *JBRS* 36, 1 (1953): 4–5.

105. Aung Thaw, *Historical Sites,* p. 38; Luce, *Phases,* 1:175.

106. Guy, "Stele."

107. *EB* 1, 2:114.

108. Guy, "Stele."

109. Aung Thaw, *Historical Sites,* p. 2.

110. U Tha Myat, *Pyū Phat Ca,* p. 25. Luce, *Phases,* 1, p. 139 thinks it was "Gupta script." See also Daw Than Swe, *Pyusa Khinbha Shwe Pechat Dat Pon Mya* [Photographs of Pyū writing on Khin Bha's gold palm leaves], (Yangon: Directorate of Burmese, 1991).

111. Duroiselle, "Excavations at Hmawza," *Archaeological Survey of India,* 1927, pp. 171–181. He was one of the pioneers in Burma history and director of the Archaeological Department, Burma.

112. U Tha Myat has deciphered and translated into Burmese the entire twenty leaves. See his *Pyū Phat Ca,* pp. 23–33.

113. Aung Thaw, *Historical Sites,* p. 32; Tun Aung Chain, "The Value of Myanmar Traditional Texts," in *Myanma Thamaing Thutethana Sasaung* (Myanmar historical research journal) 1 (November 1995), p. 279; and Maung Tun Nyein, "Maunggun Gold Plates," *Epigraphia Indica* 5, 4 (1898): 101.

114. *EB* 1, 2:77, note 1.

115. Aung Thaw, *Historical Sites,* p. 111.

116. Aung Thaw, *Historical Sites,* p. 116; Luce, *Phases,* 1, p. 165.

117. Luce, *Phases,* 1, p. 164; Aung Thaw, *Historical Sites,* p. 116.

118. Luce, *Phases,* 1, p. 163.

119. Luce, *Phases,* 1, p. 162.

120. Ray, *Sanskrit Buddhism,* p. 4. John S. Strong, in *The Legend and Cult of Upagupta: Sanskrit Buddhism in North India and Southeast Asia* (Princeton: Princeton University Press, 1992), p. 3, places the Upagupta tradition in Northern India.

121. All three can be found in Burma today, although the Soṇa and Uttara tradition eventually became the dominant one for the whole culture, but probably not

until after the Pegu Dynasty of the fourteenth century AD emerged and pushed that tradition, a topic to be discussed in greater detail in subsequent chapters.

122. Ray, *Sanskrit Buddhism,* p. 21 and Aung Thaw, *Historical Sites,* p. 32.

123. Ray, *Sanskrit Buddhism.* The issue here is not so much "the many faces of Maitreya," as Kitagawa aptly puts it in *Maitreya, the Future Buddha,* eds. Alan Sponberg and Helen Hardacre (New York: Cambridge University Press, 1988), pp. 7–22, but the presence of his "ideology" among the Pyū and centrality among the Burmese speakers in Pagán, all found well before evidence of Mon presence in Burma and certainly before proven Mon-Burman contact.

124. On this subject, see Pamela Gutman's, "The Pyu Maitreyas," in *Traditions in Current Perspective* (Yangon: 1996), pp. 165–178, especially page 167, and G. H. Luce, *Phases,* 1:53.

125. Aung-Thwin, *Pagán,* pp. 19, 31, 40.

126. U Tha Myat, *Pyū Phat Ca,* p. 77, line 5 and 6 of Pyū inscription.

127. Aung-Thwin, *Pagán,* passim; Melford Spiro, *Buddhism and Society: A Great Tradition and Its Burmese Vicissitudes* (Berkeley: University of California Press, 1982), second edition, pp. 168–169.

128. Ray, *Sanskrit Buddhism,* p. 43; Aung Thaw, *Historical Sites,* p. 28.

129. Hence, the word *hpaya* in Burmese is used for both the Buddha and the temple.

130. To be sure, of the few found, cited in Luce, *Phases,* 1:125–177, none is dated.

131. Shorto, "32 *Myos*" and *"dewatau sotāpan."*

132. It is possible to argue that it may have existed then, but there is no clear evidence of it. My earlier views in *Pagán* (p. 54) had concurred with Shorto's, but I now have reservations about them.

133. Luce, "Ancient Pyu," p. 243.

134. Aung-Thwin, "Heaven, Earth and the Supernatural World."

135. *EB* 1, 2:114.

136. *Glass Palace Chronicles,* p. 14.

137. *The Sheaf of Garlands of the Epochs of the Conqueror: Being a Translation of Jinakālamālīpakaraṇaṁ of Ratanapañña Thera of Thailand,* trans. N. A. Jayawickrama (London: Pali Text Society, 1968), xii. Probably the most detailed and accurate study of the Southeast Asian calendar is J. C. Eade's *The Calendrical Systems.*

138. Taw Sein Ko, *Burmese Sketches,* 2:277–278.

139. Luce, "Ancient Pyu," p. 243.

140. The best, concise work on the Pyū language is U Tha Myat's *Pyū Pha Ca.* It contains comparisons of relevant Indic scripts of various periods in terms of all consonants and vowels with actual samples from the epigraphy found at the Pyū sites of Halin and Śrī Kṣetra.

141. Ray, *Sanskrit Buddhism,* p. 19.

142. See Stargardt's *Ancient Pyu,* pp. 192, and 290–295, on the presence of Brāhmī script at Beikthano.

143. C. O. Blagden, "The Pyū Inscriptions," *Epigraphia Indica* 12 (1913–1914): 127–132; U That Myat, *Pyū Pha Ca,* pp. 50–51; Luce, "Ancient Pyu," p. 310. The entire dating system on which the Pyū kingdom of Śrī Kṣetra has hitherto been based may now have to be revised, or at least reconsidered. In 1993 a team of Burma

scholars discovered a stone inscription written in Pyū. From the information contained in that inscription, and a reassessment of other Pyū inscriptions, they concluded that the earlier dating scheme should be changed. Instead of 638 years added to Pyū dates to arrive at the AD dates, as has been customary, we now need to add only 319 or 320 years, which makes everything approximately 300 years earlier. The city and kingdom of Śrī Kṣetra may therefore have emerged as early as the fourth century rather than the seventh (see Tun Aung Chain, "The Kings of the Hpayahtaung Urn Inscription," *Myanmar Historical Journal,* no. 11 (June 2003): 1–15; and San Win, "Dating the Hpayahtaung Pyu Urn Inscription," *Myanmar Historical Journal,* no. 11 (June 2003): 15–22).

To be sure, the ultimate basis for this new dating system is interpretive. The team assumes that the fourth-century Gupta Calendar rather than the seventh-century Pyū calendar was used, since the script in the above Pyū inscription is thought to have been fourth-century Gupta, hence the reduction by 300 years. Yet as I show elsewhere in this book, paleography is hardly foolproof when precise dates are required, and unfortunately the stone itself does not state what era was used; only the numerical dates are given. Therefore it is still not clear what the AD equivalent of the Pyū years are. This is an issue that will be debated for many more years to come.

144. Aung Thaw, *Historical Sites,* p. 31. However, Luce, *Phases,* 1:139, considers the script to be "Gupta" although I am not certain what that means.

145. Aung Thaw, *Historical Sites,* p. 28. For a reproduction of the upper part of the inscription in Pyū identifying the Four Buddhas, see U Tha Myat, *Pyū Pha Ca,* page 34. However, he does not include the lines inscribed below that identify the disciples and the donors.

146. Aung Thaw, *Historical Sites,* p. 31. Janice Stargardt, *Tracing Thought Through Things: The Oldest Pali Texts and the Early Buddhist Archaeology of India and Burma* (Amsterdam: Royal Netherlands Academy of Arts and Sciences, 2000) seems to disagree. My thanks to Shah Alam-Zalini, a graduate student at the University of Hawai'i working on the Pyū, for alerting me to this source. Stargardt mentions the two reliquary deposits from Khin Ba mound and criticizes the Kadamba hypothesis. Her analysis is based on Harry Falk's "Die Goldblätter aus Śrī Kṣetra," *Wiener Zeitshrift für die Kunde Sudasiens* 41 (1997): 53–92. The origins of the Pyū script is eagerly awaiting exploration.

147. Harvey, *History,* p. 307; Luce, in *Phases,* 1:74, note 16, cites others: *ASB* (1937–1938):11; ASI (1936–1937): 80; and Louis Finot, "Un nouveau document sur le bouddhisme birman," *Journal Asiatique* 20 (July–August 1912): 132. See also U Tha Myat, *Pyū Pha Ca,* 1–18.

148. Aung Thaw, *Excavations.*

149. *EB* 1, 1:60.

150. Luce, *Phases,* 1:63.

151. *Man Shu,* p. 91.

152. Parker, *Burma,* p. 15. The problem may be in Parker's translation or it may be in the Chinese texts themselves.

153. Personal communication, Sun Laichen, University of California, Fullerton, September 7, 2002, suggests it is not.

154. In *Phases,* 1:103, Luce writes that the "Mranma longed to escape the Nan-

chao yoke [and p. 106, the "Nan-chao tyranny"] so that they took their first opportunity to do so, in or after 835, by descending to the hot malarious plains of Central Burma, where Nanchao armies, used to the cold plateaux of Yunnan, durst not follow them except on a cold-weather raid."

155. Bob Hudson, personal communication.

156. Information regarding the last item can be found in Moe Kyaw Aung, "Excursions to the Thuyethamein-Kuseik Area," *Forward* 8, 21 (June 1970), 12–17, cite on p. 15, which revealed a passage from the "Paticcasamuppada," or the "Law of Cause and Effect."

157. *SMK* 1:83; 2:40; 3:202, 262, 235; 4:175. See also U Tha Myat, *Pyū Pha Ca,* p. 77, and Luce, *Phases,* 1:66–67. The word *lin* is usually reserved for "husband," but sometimes used as "spouse" as well during the Pagán period.

158. The "coming of the Burmans" in the ninth century is a long-held conclusion that needs to be more thoroughly examined. I have provisionally accepted it here as it is, for at the moment, it is beside the point. For a recent analysis of this thesis, see Luce, *Phases* 1:98–108.

159. The issue here is not whether this Indic culture was borrowed directly from India—some of it certainly was—but whether the Burmese speakers obtained it from Lower Burma Mon speakers, as claimed by the Mon Paradigm.

160. *Zatatawpon,* p. 54.

161. Peter Grave and Mike Barbetti, "Dating the City Wall, Fortifications, and the Palace Site at Pagán," in *Asian Perspectives Special Issue: The Archaeology of Myamna Pyay (Burma),* ed. Miriam T. Stark and Michael A. Aung-Thwin (Honolulu: University of Hawai'i Press, 2002), p. 81. Thus, only a 131-year discrepancy exists between the *Zatatawpon* date of 849 AD and the 980 AD radiocarbon date.

162. However, this assumption may not be valid, as the *Zatatawpon* recalled that both the walls of the city and the palace within were built at the same time.

163. Grave and Barbetti, "Dating . . . ," p. 81.

164. Aung-Thwin, *Pagán,* p. 22.

165. *Mandalay Mahamuni Tantuin Atwinshi Kyauksa Mya* (Inscriptions within the compound of the Mandalay Mahamuni Pagoda) [hereafter MM], vol. 1 (Yangon: University of Yangon Department of History, 1989), pp. 1–7.

166. *Zatatawpon,* pp. 36–37.

167. *Zatatawpon,* pp. 37–38. His title is sometimes recorded as "Pyūsawhti" (Princely Ruler of the Pyū). See the *Hmannan Mahayazawindawgyi,* 1:201–202, and Taw Sein Ko, *Burmese Sketches,* 2:337.

168. Shorto, "Gavampati Tradition," p.25.

169. Thus, Pyumin*hti*'s successor was *Hti*minyin, then *Yin*minpaik, followed by *Paik*thelay and so on [all my emphases]. See Charles Backus, *Nan-chao kingdom,* p. 51, regarding this "patronymic linkage system" that seems to be Tibeto-Burman, not Austro-Asiatic. We can be assured, of course, that even the late chroniclers had no way of knowing they were documenting what we have come to recognize *only in modern times* as a patronymic system.

170. Hudson et al., "Origins of Bagan," pp. 62–65.

171. *Man Shu,* p. 90 states that "the common people all live within the city-wall." Other Chinese sources state that "the people all live inside it" (Parker, *Burma,* p. 13).

172. Aung Thaw, *Historical Sites* and *Excavations;* also Myint Aung, "Excavations at Halin." Subsequently, Stargardt in *Ancient Pyu* synthesized the best-known published works in English on this culture under one cover. See also Aung-Thwin, "Burma Before Pagán."

173. Bob Hudson thinks it reveals the development of an elite core, most of whom lived inside the walled section (Hudson et al., "Origins of Bagan," p. 66).

174. Aung-Thwin, *Irrigation.*

175. Aung-Thwin, *Pagán;* and "The Role of *Sāsana* Reform in Burmese History: Economic Dimensions of a Religious Purification," *JAS* 38, 4 (August 1979): 671–688. There are many examples of this: donations made in the mid-eleventh century were still valid and considered glebe in the fourteenth century (*SMK* 3:285, 287). Indeed, during my several visits to Pagán during the 1970s and 1990s, I found lands still held today as religious property that had been donated during the mid- to late eleventh century AD.

176. Mabel Haynes Bode, *The Pali Literature of Burma* (London: The Royal Asiatic Society of Great Britain and Ireland, 1909), reprint 1966, chapter 2.

177. U Myint Aung, "Suvannabhumi"; and his "The Excavations of Ayethama and Winka (?Suvannabhumi)," in *Essays Given to Than Tun on his 75th Birthday: Studies in Myanma History,* 1 (Yangon: Innwa Publishing House, 1999), p. 53. However, I have since discussed the issue at length with U Myint Aung and should point out that he is now also rather skeptical of the Mon Paradigm.

Chapter 3: Rāmaññadesa, an Imagined Polity

1. Wheatley, *Nāgara,* p. 203.

2. Wheatley, *Nāgara,* p. 222.

3. Wheatley, *Nāgara,* p. 203.

4. C. O. Blagden, "Etymological Notes: II. Mon and Rāmaññadesa," *JBRS* vol. 4, pt. 1 (1914), pp. 59–60; "Etymological Notes: VII. Mon, Rman, Rāmañña," 5, 1 (1915), p. 27. Note that the word is not *rmañ* but *rman.* Although this might be baffling when reproduced in English, it is quite obvious in the Burma script with which the Mon language was written in the country. Nai Pan Hla's reproduction in *The Significant Role of The Mon Language and Culture in Southeast Asia: Part I* (Tokyo: Institute for the Study of Languages and Cultures of Asia and Africa, 1992), p. 3 makes this clear.

5. Wheatley, *Nāgara,* p. 221.

6. Luce, *Old Burma* 1:68.

7. Christian Bauer, *A Guide to Mon Studies* (*Monash University Centre of southeast Asian Studies Working Paper, no. 32* Clayton, Australia: 1984), p. 2. See also Jan Wisseman Christie, "The Medieval Tamil-language Inscriptions." Both inscriptions that she cites, one dated to 883 and the other to 1021 AD, mixed place names and ethnonyms. For example, Champa (the place name) is followed by *Kmira, Kling,* and *Singhala,* all ethnonyms. Similarly, neither *Remman* nor *Remen* is a place name, and neither tells us where these people lived or came from. Blagden also refers to J. M. Krom's article of 1914 in the *JRAS* (October 1914), p. 1026, regarding the two Javanese inscriptions that mentioned the forms *remen* or *rmeñ.* Michael Vickery has also helped me by citing four cases where *rmeñ* and its equivalents were mentioned in Khmer inscriptions of the relevant period (personal communication, Feb. 9, 2004).

Hiram Woodward, in *The Art and Architecture of Thailand: From Prehistoric Times through the Thirteenth Century* (Leiden: E.J. Brill, 2003), p. 137, cites a work by Bernard Groslier which was said to have referred to a Khmer (Prasat Ben Vien) inscription dated sometime between 944 and 946 that mentions victories by Rājendravarman over Champa and a Rāmaṇya, which Groslier places in Khorat. The spelling of Rāmaṇya is curious, for usually it is not spelled with *both* the *nya* (reflecting the tilde) and the dot under the "n." Whatever the reason, the evidence as it stands still does not place either the people or their place in Lower Burma.

8. Bauer, *A Guide,* p. 3. For a more recent and complete study of the Mon language in Southeast Asia by Bauer, see his "Notes on Mon Epigraphy," *JSS* 79, 1–2 (1991): 31–83; 61–79; also H. L. Shorto's *Dictionary of Mon Inscriptions: From the Sixth to the Sixteenth Centuries* (London: Oxford University Press, 1971), p. 325, for both the words *rmeñ* and *rman.*

9. Blagden cites the work Krom published in *Verhandelingen of the Batavia Society,* 60 (1913): 120–128, in his own article in the *JBRS* 5, 1 (1915): 27.

10. There is no date on it.

11. Luce, "Note on the Peoples" p. 298, mentioned 126 "Rmeñ chiefs." However, when one reads the original inscription translated by Blagden (*EB* 3, 1:40), there is nothing about "chiefs," just 126 Rmeñ.

12. That is, if Tircul refers to the P'iao of the Chinese sources and the Pyū of Burmese inscriptions. There is a problem here, however. Why are the Burmese using a Chinese term (P'iao) and not the ethnonym Tircul? It would be equivalent to the Burmese today using the anglicized term "Karen," rather than "Kayin," or "Rangoon" rather than "Yangôn." And why does the term Pyū appear for the first time only in the thirteenth century if it were synonymous with the Chinese P'iao?

13. However, the fact that King Kyanzittha in one of his Mon inscriptions erected in Lower Burma in the late eleventh century mentions repairing the "pagoda of Kyāk Talaṅ" (*kyāk* being a Mon term for "temple" here), it appears that Mon speakers were probably already present there by then. *EB* 2, 2:146.

14. Bauer, *Guide,* p. 3.

15. Blagden, "Notes on Talaing Epigraphy," *JBRS* 2, 1 (1912): 39.

16. Luce, "Note on the Peoples," p. 304, referring to *EB* 3, 1:5. Shorto confirms that *rman* is Medieval (Middle), not Old Mon. (*Dictionary of Mon Inscriptions,* p. 325)

17. Blagden, "Etymological Notes," *JBRS* 5, 1 (1915): 27.

18. Blagden, "Etymological Notes," *JBRS* 4, 1 (1914): 59.

19. Bauer, *Guide,* p. 3. Nai Pan Hla, *Significant Role,* p. 3.

20. The word apparently appears earlier in a tenth-century Khmer inscription. See Woodward, *Art and Architecture of Thailand,* p. 137.

21. It is far easier to see this in native script than in transcribed English.

22. See Nai Pan Hla, *Significant Role,* p. 3. He uses *rāmaṇya* as an ethnonym, not a place name.

23. Luce, "Note on the Peoples, p. 298.

24. See *Old Burma,* 2, "attachment."

25. *EB* 1,2:90–168.

26. *SMK* I, no. 41, pp. 65–69.

27. *SMK* 3:274–275, dated to 1316, and *SMK* 3:30. Highway signs today that refer to Pegu still use the term.

28. For the 1105 and 1107 inscriptions, see *SMK* 1:326–329.

29. Wheatley, *Nāgara,* p. 221. However, it was Sir Arthur Phayre in his *History,* p. 28 who first proposed this idea, followed by Luce, in *Old Burma* 1:21.

30. Basically, these are found in volumes 4 and 5 of *SMK.*

31. Tin Hla Thaw, "History of Burma: A.D. 1400–1500." *JBRS* 42, 2 (December 1959): 135–151; see specifically pp. 146–147.

32. *SMK* 5:59.

33. *SMK* 5:35.

34. *SMK* 5:47, line 29.

35. Luce, *Old Burma,* 2, "attachment."

36. In the English *translation* of the Kalyani Inscriptions, of course, the term "Mon" is used, but in the original it is *Rman.*

37. *SMK* 5:69.

38. Hiram Woodward, *Art and Architecture of Thailand,* p. 137.

39. That is, those published and translated into English as of this writing. In several places Prasert inserts the word "Rāmaññadesa" in parentheses, indicating that it is not part of the original. See *Epigraphic and Historical Studies,* ed. and trans. Prasert Na Nagara and A. B. Griswold (Bangkok: The Historical Society, 1992).

40. *Epigraphic and Historical Studies,* p. 281. All this assumes that this Haṁsavatī was not a place within Thailand itself, "near the present Sukhothai" according to Shorto's translation of "Gavampati," p. 2, a section of the Mon text called the "Uppanna Sudhammawatī-rājāwaṁsa-kathā," still in unpublished typescript. My sincere thanks to Professor Victor Lieberman for providing me with a copy. This manuscript is *not* the same as Shorto's article, the "The Gavampati Tradition in Burma."

41. Paul Wheatley, *The Golden Khersonese* (Westport, CN: Greenwood Press, 1973), p. 202. The *Mahāvaṃsa* referred to this place called Mâppapâḷam as Papphālama instead.

42. Rhys Davids, T. W. "The Conquest of South India in the Twelfth Century by Parakrama Bahu," *Journal of the Asiatic Society of Bengal* 51 (1872): 197–201. See also Michael Aung-Thwin, *Myth and History in the Historiography of Early Burma: Paradigms, Primary Sources, and Prejudices (Athens: Ohio University Press, 1988),* p. 10.

43. Archaeological Survey of Ceylon, *Epigraphia Zeylanica,* ed. and trans. Don Martino de Zilva Wickremasinghe, 2 (London: Oxford University Press, 1928), pp. 152–156.

44. Archaeological Survey of Ceylon, *Epigraphia Zeylanica* 2, 40:242–255.

45. Luce, *Old Burma,* 1:40.

46. This is the belief that Vijayabāhu I of Anurādhapura requested monks from Aniruddha to start a new order in Śrī Laṅka.

47. Senarat Paranavitana, *Ceylon and Malaysia* (Colombo: Lake House Investments Ltd., 1966), p. 84.

48. Wheatley, *Golden Khersonese,* p. 210.

49. Gabriel Ferrand, *Relations de voyages et de textes géographiques arabes, persans, et turcs relatifs á l'extrême orient du VIII au XVIII siècles,* 2 vols. (Paris: Leroux, 1913).

50. Harvey, *History,* p. 10.

51. As quoted in Harvey, *History,* p. 10.

52. Harvey, *History,* p. 10.

53. *Dictionary of Pali Proper Names* [hereafter cited as *DPPN*], comp. G. P. Malalasekera, (London: The Pali Text Society, 1960), 2:717.

54. U Shwe San, *Golden Mrauk-U,* p. 150.

55. Phayre, *History*, p. 42.

56. *Dīpavaṃsa: An Ancient Buddhist Historical Record*, trans. Hermann Oldenberg. Reprint. (New Delhi: Asian Educational Services, 1982), p. 8.

57. One of the more recent scholarly treatments of Pali literature is Steven Collins's "What is Literature in Pali?" in *Literary Cultures in History: Reconstructions from South Asia*, ed. Sheldon Pollock (Berkeley: University of California Press, 2003), pp. 649–688. In it (p. 681), Collins apparently does not consider "early" Rāmañña-desa to be historical, as he makes no mention of it and begins with the thirteenth-century Mon state of Pegu instead.

58. *Cūḷavaṃsa: Being the More Recent Part of the Mahāvaṃsa*, trans. Wilhelm Geiger (and from the German into English) by Mrs. C. Mabel Rickmers (Colombo: The Ceylon Government Information Department, 1953), Part I, chapter 50, p. 214. This is confirmed by S. Paranavitana, who states that it is the first reference to Burma in the Sinhalese chronicle (*Ceylon and Malaysia*, p. 63).

59. Sirima Wickramasinghe, "The Sources for a study of the Reign of King Parākramabāhu I," in *The Polonnaruva Period*, ed. by S. D. Saparamadu. Third edition. (Dehiwala, Sri Lanka, Tisara Prakasakayo, 1973); and O. H. De A. Wijesekera, "Pali and Sanskrit in the Polonnaruva Period," in *The Polonnaruva Period* p. 191 and 105, respectively. Malalasekera in *DPPN* 1:1136, confirms that Dhammakitti was not from Ceylon, but Tambarattha, normally thought to be a reference to Pagán, but was not identified here.

60. For these and other kinds of "locating" the present in the past in the Sinhalese chronicles, one should consult Steven Kemper's *The Presence of the Past: Chronicles, Politics, and Culture in Sinhala Life* (Ithaca: Cornell University Press, 1991).

61. Chen Yu-jing, *Chen Yu-jing Dong-nan-ya Gu-shi yan-jiu he-ji* (Collected works on early Southeast Asian history), Vol. 2, (Hong Kong: Commercial Press, 1992), p. 748; and Li Fang, et al., *Tai-ping Yu-lan*, vol. 4, *juan* 787 (Beijing: Zhong-hua shu-ju, 1985), p. 3485. My thanks to China historian Geoff Wade for the information as well as the translation.

62. Personal communication (January, 2004) with Geoff Wade, who wrote that "Lin-yang" is the modern Mandarin pronunciation. In Cantonese, it is "Lum-yeung," and the *l/r* distinction is not clear. In Vietnamese, it is "Lam-du'o'ng." Also, an eminent Southeast Asia linguist, F. K. Lehman, tells me that he has grave doubts that Lin-yang is "Rammanya," as reproduced in the above mentioned Chinese sources, or as it should be, Rāmañña (personal communication, January 28, 2004).

63. Again, my thanks to China historian Geoff Wade for providing me with both the text and its translation.

64. Also, "Nan-zhou yi-wu-zhi" (An account of the strange things in the South), included in Li Fang, *Tai-ping Yu-lan*.

65. Chen Yi-Sein, "Lin-Yang," p. 79.

66. Zhu Zhi, *Fu-nan-ji*, cited in Chen Yu-jing, *Chen Yu-jing*, pp. 748–749. My thanks again to China historian Geoff Wade for both the source and the information regarding the "Heng River" extract (personal communication, March 4, 2004).

67. G. H. Luce, "Countries Neighbouring Burma: Parts 1 & 2." *JBRS* 14, 2 (1924): 137–205. Also reprinted in *Burma Research Society Fiftieth Anniversary Publications No. 2* (Rangoon: Burma Research Society, 1960), p. 255. See also Chen Yi-Sein, "Lin-Yang."

68. Luce, *Phases,* 1:68–71.

69. The location of this place is not at all certain, but some China historians think it might be somewhere near the Gulf of Thailand (personal communication, Geoff Wade, March 8, 2004).

70. Wheatley, *Golden Khersonese,* pp. 41–42 cites J. Takakusu's *A Record of the Buddhist Religion as practiced in India and the Malay Archipelago (671–695 A.D.) by I-Tsing,* (Oxford: Oxford University Press, 1896); and I-Ching, *Chinese Monks in India,* trans. Latika Lahiri (Delhi: Motilal Banarsidass, 1986).

71. G. H. Luce, "Countries Neighbouring Burma: Parts 1 & 2," *Journal of the Burma Research Society* 14, 2 (1924), p. 260.

72. Wheatley, *Golden Khersonese,* p. 258, identifies this as Lang-hsi-chia on the Malay Peninsula.

73. For a translation of his work by Samuel Beal, see *Si-Yu-Ki: Buddhist Records of the Western World, Translated from the Chinese of Hiuen Tsiang (A.D. 629),* vol. 2, reprint (New York: Paragon Book Reprint Corp., 1968). pp. 199–200 (in Wheatley, *Golden Khersonese,* p. 256).

74. See his "Wen Dan and Its Neighbours: The Central Mekong Valley in the Seventh and Eighth Centuries," in Mayoury Ngaosrivathana and Kennon Breazeale, eds., *Breaking New Ground in Lao History: Essays on the Seventh to Twentieth Centuries* (Chiang Mai, Thailand: Silkworm Books, 2002), pp. 25–72.

75. *Man Shu,* p.90–91. See also Parker, *Burma,* p. 12–15, and Backus, *Nan-chao kingdom,* passim.

76. Parker, *Burma,* p. 15.

77. Luce, *Phases,* 1:68.

78. Wheatley, *Golden Khersonese,* p. 285.

79. Sun Laichen, "Chinese Historical Sources on Burma: A Bibliography of Primary and Secondary Works," *The Journal of Burma Studies: Special Issue* 2 (1997): 1–116.

80. Luce, *Phases,* 1:71–72.

81. *Man Shu,* p. 90.

82. *Man Shu,* p. 90.

83. *Chau Ju-Kua: His Work on the Chinese and Arab Trade in the twelfth and thirteenth Centuries, entitled Chu-fan-chi,* translated from the Chinese and annotated by Friedrich Hirth and W. W. Rockhill, reprint (Taipei: Ch'eng-Wen Publishing Company, 1970), pp. 58–59; see also Chou Ta-Kuan, *The Customs of Cambodia,* trans. J. Gilan d'Arcy Paul, 3rd ed. (Bangkok: The Siam Society, 1993).

84. Chen Yi-Sein, "The Chinese in Upper Burma," p. 1. Although Chen's article focuses on Upper Burma, he does mention Pegu, but (most appropriately) not until the Ming Dynasty.

85. This is supported by Wheatley's statement in his exhaustive study, *Nāgara,* p. 222.

86. My sincere thanks to Professor Sun Laichen of the University of California, Fullerton, who translated the text for me. Moreover, Chen Yi-Sein, in "Lin Yang," p. 77, writes: "In the Pyū chapter of the New History of T'ang Dynasty, the name T'eng-ling . . . is used both as an ethnic name and a place name," which he assumes to be Talaing. In the very next page, he writes that "Teng-ling . . . is the sinicised Telinga . . . ," thereby acknowledging the old theory that the word came from South India.

87. See *Yüan-ch'ao-cheng-mien-lu* as translated by Edouard Huber and summarized in English by Luce in his "Note on the Peoples," p. 300. However, Sun Laichen (personal communication) states that the word "new" does not appear in the original Chinese text used by Huber.

88. *The Legend of Queen Cāma: Bodhiraṃsi's Camādevīvaṃsa, a Translation and Commentary,* tr. by Donald K. Swearer and Sommai Premchit (Albany, NY: State University of New York Press, 1998), pp. 18, 20, 43, 64. Swearer, in "Myth, Legend, and History, " p. 79, appears to agree.

89. *Sheaf of Garlands,* pp. 117, 156.

90. U Tet Htoot, "The Nature of the Burmese Chronicles," in *Historians of Southeast Asia,* ed. D. G. E. Hall, (London: Oxford University Press, 1961), p. 53. See also U Maung Maung, *The Story of Wunzin Min Yaza* (Yangôn: Tain Lon Zambu Press, 1912?), and Charles Duroiselle's reference to it in "The story of Wunzin Min Yaza," *JBRS* 2, 1 (1912): 117–119. The *Myanma Cway Cum Kyam* (Encyclopedia Myanmar) [hereafter cited as *MSSK*] on CD-ROM (Yangôn: Forever Group, 1998–1999) also has a brief account of Min Yaza.

91. U Kala, *Mahayazawingyi,* 1:180–184.

92. Sithu Gamani Thingyan, *Zimme Yazawin: Chronicle of Chiang Mai,* ed. Tun Aung Chain and trans. Thaw Kaung and Ni Ni Myint (Yangôn: Universities Historical Research Centre, 2003), pp. 5, 6, 7, 10, 12, 35.

93. *Zambudipa Okhsaung Kyan* (Treatise adorning the head of Zambudipa), compiled by J. F. Furnivall and Pe Maung Tin (Yangôn: Burma Research Society, 1960), p. 8.

94. David K. Wyatt and Aroonrut Wichienkeeo, *The Chiang Mai Chronicle* (Chiang Mai: Thailand, Silkworm Books, 1995). p. xxx. But Wyatt thinks (p. xxxi) the manuscript they translated and published—the one I am using here—was written only in 1827. However, the editor of U Kala's *Mahayazawingyi* listed a *"Zimme Yazawin"* (Burmese for "Chiang Mai Chronicle") as one of U Kala's sources. But because the former was written over a century earlier than the *Chiang Mai Chronicle* translated by Wyatt and Wichienkeeo, they could not have been the same. Besides, the earliest extant *Zimme Yazawin* found in Burma is dated later than U Kala's, cited above and recently published. Nor is it a Burmese translation of a Thai chronicle, but one written in Burmese. U Kala used several of these kinds of sources, including the *Putage Yazawin* (Portuguese chronicle), the *Siho Yazawin* (Sihala chronicle), and the *Tarup Yazawin* (Chinese chronicle), all written in Burmese; see U Kala, p. *"nga."* In short, the *Zimme Yazawin* said to have been used by U Kala must have been an earlier version than that cited above, or another name used by the Burmese for the *Jinakālamāli.*

95. Wyatt and Aroonrut, *Chiang Mai Chronicle,* pp. 35–36.

96. This trope regarding Aniruddha is nicely brought out by Geok Yian Goh in a graduate paper she wrote for Asian Studies at the University of Hawai'i, entitled "Tracing the Buddha's Footsteps through the Chronicles of the Three Regions of the Loka Buddha," Fall 2002.

97. Wyatt and Aroonrut, *Chiang Mai Chronicle,* pp. 37–38.

98. *The Crystal Sands: The Chronicles of Nagara Sri Dharrmaraja,* trans. David K. Wyatt (Ithaca: Cornell Southeast Asia Program, 1975).

99. *Crystal Sands,* pp. 72–73.

100. Amatgyi Bannya Dala, *Yazadarit Ayedawpon* (The royal crisis account of *Yazadarit*). (Yangôn: Swesa Press, 1974), p. 3.

101. *Crystal Sands,* pp. 22, 24, 26.

102. *The Royal Chronicles of Ayutthaya,* trans. Richard D. Cushman and ed. David K. Wyatt (Bangkok: The Siam Society, 2000).

103. Luce, *Old Burma,* 2, "attachment," which is a list mainly of place names in Lower Burma.

104. See *SMK* 1:66 for Tavoy (Taway), among others. For Saṅthut (Thandôk) southeast of Mergui, see either Luce, *Old Burma,* 1:27, or the original Old Burmese in *Inscriptions of Burma* [hereafter cited as *IB*], comps. and eds. G. H. Luce and Pe Maung Tin, 5 vols., Rangoon: Rangoon University Press, 1933–1956, Plate 3:225. The latter is reproduced in *SMK* 3:53–54. An Aniruddha seal was also discovered at Mergui itself, while ten miles southeast of Mergui at a place called Maunglaw, a Pali inscription thought to belong to Aniruddha's son, Saw Lu, was also found. Two governors of Kyanzittha have left two votive tablets at the Môkti Pagoda, six miles south of Tavoy (Luce, *Old Burma,* 1:26–27).

105. See Luce, *Old Burma,* 2, "attachment," for the majority of these names.

106. E Maung, "Some Place-Names in Burma," *JBRS* 39, 2 (1956): 7. Shorto's *Dictionary of Mon Inscriptions,* p. 234, confirms the late appearance of the word Bago (Pugo, Pago) and categorizes it as Medieval (Middle), not Old Mon.

107. Guillon is surely wrong in saying that the Burmese *phaikhu* [Paykū] is derived from the Bago of Mon (*The Mons,* p. 17). It is the other way around.

108. Luce, *Old Burma,* 2, "attachment." Shorto's *Dictionary of Mon Inscriptions,* p. 50, also has Kusim as Medieval (Middle) Mon.

109. *SMK* 1:345. Luce, however, in *Old Burma,* 1:84, note 12, thinks the stone may date from the early Ava period, although I see no intrinsic reason the date given on the stone (equivalent to 1176 AD) is not original. Either way, the Old Burmese Muttama still precedes the Old Mon Mattma.

110. Luce, *Old Burma,* 2, "attachment."

111. Most of the information given in this paragraph can be found in Luce, *Old Burma,* 2, "attachment."

112. For Tavoy, see *SMK* 1:66, line 7, among other sources. Luce, *Old Burma* 1:100, note 10, and p. 101, states that Dawāy was the Old Mon term for the Old Burmese Taway, but did not cite any source or provide any date. Yet Dawāy (Tavoy) as a place name does not appear in Shorto's *Dictionary of Mon Inscriptions.*

113. Luce wrote that Takun (Dagôn, Yangôn) may have been the Old Burmese Henbuiw dated to 1113 AD, originally taken from a Pyū word (*Old Burma* 1:20, 74, 107–108). The word "Takun" itself apparently did not appear until 1400, although King Narapatisithu's Old Burmese inscription of 1196–1198 mentions a "Takaṁ village" in the same context with other Lower Burma place names such as Tavoy and Tenasserim. It looks like a misspelling for "Takun." See *SMK* 1:66.

114. Luce, *Old Burma,* 2, "attachment."

115. In Luce's list, six "places" are categorized as Old Mon, when, in fact, Ayethèma is a town, Kyāk Talaṅ is a pagoda, and Rakṣa Pura belongs to the realm of mythology. In fact, there is really only one that is a town (*Old Burma,* 2, "attach-

ment" and 1:56). One can also discount Robert Halliday's article entitled "Dictionary Jottings: Talaing place-names in Burmese," in the *JBRS* 20, 1 (1930): 22–23, as he was dealing with post-fifteenth-century names which have no bearing here.

116. Luce, *Old Burma,* 2, "attachment."

117. Luce, "Mons of the Pagán Dynasty," *JBRS* 36, 1 (1953): 5.

118. Luce, *Old Burma,* 2, "attachment," gives that late date to Muttama. Shorto's *Dictionary of the Mon Inscriptions,* p. 285, categorizes Mattma, Muttama's equivalent in Mon, as Medieval (Middle), not Old Mon, hence later in the fifteenth century.

119. *Epigraphic and Historical Studies,* p. 281, note 131. In the Rāma Gāṁhèṅ inscription, a "Moan..n" is mentioned, followed by "Hansabati" (Haṁsavatī or Pegu). Prasert and Griswold take "Moan..n" to be Martaban.

120. Luce, *Old Burma,* 2, "attachment," also his *Phases,* 1:72. In *SMK* 1:345, Muttama is mentioned as early as 1176 AD, although this inscription may be a later recast.

121. Luce, *Old Burma,* 2, "attachment."

122. Material excavated at Ayetthèma and Winga has been dated recently by the thermoluminescence method to approximately the sixteenth century AD.

123. *EB* 1, 2:144.

124. Pe Maung Tin, "A Mon Inscription by Kyanzittha at Ayetthema Hill," *JBRS* 28, 1 (1938): 92–94. Pe Maung Tin guessed that the inscription belonged to Mt. Kelāsa in Lower Burma, therefore its provenance is really unknown. See also Luce, *Old Burma,* 1:56.

125. *EB* 1, 2:146.

126. *EB* 1, 2:139.

127. *EB* 1, 2:139.

128. Luce, *Old Burma* 1:63.

129. There is yet another duplicate stone that represents two of the above two stones, found lying under a banyan tree and later moved to the Shwézayan Pagoda in Thatôn, that is not in Luce's list but included in a later compilation of Mon inscriptions; see *Mon Kyauksa Paung Chyok* (Collection of Mon stone inscriptions) [hereafter cited as *MKPC*], 2 parts, comp. and ed. U Chit Thein (Yangôn: Ministry of Culture, 1965), part 2:54–55.

130. *MKPC* 2:50–54.

131. *EB* 1, 2:73.

132. Luce, *Old Burma,* 2, "attachment." They are Kun-gyan-gôn, Sittang (the place, not the river), Winga, Zingyaik, and Kawliya. Indeed, all five are found on King Dhammazedi's Kalyani Inscriptions of 1479, as are most of the other medieval Mon sites found in Lower Burma.

133. Even these have not been dated scientifically.

134. *SMK* 1:65–69. Chen Yi-Sein, in "Lin-Yang," claims that the Tun-sun of the Chinese sources can be found in Tenasserim. Wheatley, the most reliable of historical geographers of Southeast Asia, however, placed Tun-sun in what is now Thailand, which he wrote superceded Dvāravatī (*Golden Khersonese,* p. 292; *Nāgara,* pp. 212–213).

135. Aung-Thwin, *Pagán,* chapter 9 and passim.

136. See *SMK* 1:66, and *SMK* 3:53, as illustrative.

137. Ray, *Sanskrit,* p. 80.

138. Even by the early to mid-nineteenth century, the Delta still had to be cleared and drained before it could be cultivated. See Michael Adas, *The Burma Delta* (Madison, University of Wisconsin Press, 1974), introduction, especially page 4.

139. Michel Jacq-Hergoualc'h, "The Mergui-Tenasserim Region in the Context of the Maritime Silk Road: From the Beginning of the Christian Era to the End of the Thirteenth Century AD," in *The Maritime Frontier of Burma: Exploring Political, Cultural and Commercial Interaction in the Indian Ocean World, 1200–1800,* eds. Jos Gommans and Jacques Leider, (Leiden: Koninklijke Nederlandse Akademie van Wetenschappen, 2002), pp. 79–92. Also, *Burma Gazetteer: Thaton District,* vol. A (Rangoon: Government Printing, 1931), p. 8, states that "there is no doubt that many years ago Thaton was a sea-port; the sea then covered the present fertile plain west of the Muttama range. The sea also touched the foot of the Kelatha hills where Ayetthema (Taikkala) is situated."

140. Luce, *Old Burma,* 2, map of "Rāmañña Desa," attachment, and in this book, Figure 1.

141. *EB* 3:188.

142. *EB* 3 is the version I use here. But Taw Sein Ko had much earlier published a translation of the Pali text in 1892 (*ASI,* "The Kalyānī Inscriptions erected by King Dhammacetī at Pegu in 1476 A.D." [Rangoon, Government Printing, 1892], pp, 1–105). It was later reprinted as "A Preliminary Study of the Kalyani Inscriptions of Dhammacheti," *Indian Antiquary* 22 (1893), p. 7.

143. Bauer, *Guide,* p. 13. If Bauer is correct, Blagden's physical isolation from the rest of the early Burma scholars in Burma may have been what made his interpretations more objective and neutral, as he was for the most part unencumbered by the intellectual baggage of the Mon Paradigm as proved again and again in his analyses. However, from a note in his paper called "Notes on Talaing Epigraphy," it appears he delivered it in Burma "before the Annual Meeting of the Society held on the 8th February, 1912." Of course, someone else could have read the paper.

144. *EB* 4, 1:19.

145. *Dīpavaṃsa,* p. 160. An analysis of such missions can be found in "Rethinking Buddhist Missions," a Ph.D. dissertation by Jonathan Walters for the University of Chicago, 1992.

146. The *Mahāvaṃsa or The Great Chronicle of Ceylon,* translated into English by Wilhelm Geiger, assisted by Mabel Haynes Bode, reprint (Colombo: Ceylon Government Information Department, 1960), p. 86.

147. Wheatley, *Nāgara,* p. 200.

148. *Mahāvaṃsa,* pp. 86–87.

149. *EB* 3:185–187.

150. *EB* 3, 2:185 and passim, where he writes: "in Suvaṇṇabhūmi, which is the Mon country."

151. *Mahāvaṃsa,* p. 86.

152. *EB* 3:185. The translator in a note (no. 5) to this section states: "So far as can be conjectured from the fragmentary remains of the Mon text, it probably expressed itself in this way: 'in Suvaṇṇabhūmi, which is the Mon country.'"

153. *EB* 3:185.

154. *EB* 3:185.

155. Phayre, *History,* p. 288.

156. Luce's "attachment" also fixes the first mention of Suvaṇṇabhūmi to King Dhammazedi's Kalyani Inscriptions of 1476–1479.

157. The Rāma Gāṁhèṅ Inscription of 1292 also claimed that Sukhodaya had a "Surbarnnabhum" under its control, but that place is located within Thailand itself. *Epigraphic and Historical Studies,* p 281.

158. *DPPN* 1:991. In fact, Pe Maung Tin, in "The Shwé-dagôn Pagoda; Part I," *JBRS* 24, 1(1934): 8, shows that the story about the two brothers does not appear until Buddhaghosa's commentaries of the fifth century AD and that "[h]e [Buddhaghosa] gives no hint that he is thinking of Lower Burma." It appears, then, that as early as 1934 Pe Maung Tin may have had doubts about this myth, although he never pursued the topic further.

159. *DPPN* 1:330.

160. *DPPN* 1:991.

161. *EB* 4, 1:40–42.

162. Shorto, "Gavamapati Tradition," p. 26.

163. The Burmese version of this inscription's last few lines are flaked off and therefore, the name of the donor is missing, but the Mon version is not: it was erected by King Dhammazedi. See Pe Maung Tin's three-part series on this inscription called "The Shwé-dagôn Pagoda; Part I," 24, 1 (1934): 1–91.

164. There are actually two inscriptions, one Burmese and one with two faces, in Mon and Pali. I have used the Burmese version where the Mon is flaked off and the Mon version in translation where the Burmese is not well preserved. The Burmese is in *SMK* 5:80, while the Mon is translated in *EB* 4, 1:35–43. On the Mon version the particular part about Rāmañña is flaked off (p. 36), while on the Burmese it is clearly legible.

165. *EB* 4, 1:21.

166. Paranavitana, *Ceylon and Malaysia,* p. 2.

167. *Epigraphic and Historical Studies,* p 281.

168. J. G. de Casparis, *Indonesian palaeography: a history of writing in Indonesia from the beginnings to c. A.D. 1500* (Leiden: E.J. Brill, 1975) and Dr. N. J. Krom's *Hindoe-Javaansche Geschiednis* ('s-Gravenhage, Martinus Nijhoff, 1931), p. 248. My thanks to Uli Kozok for these references.

169. *Zambudipa Okhsaung Kyan,* pp. 8, 14.

170. U Tet Htoot, "The Nature of the Burmese Chronicles," p. 54, note 5. U Kala, *Mahayazawingyi,* 3:175, addressed Chiang Mai as "Suvaṇṇabhūmi Chiang Mai." Indeed, the *Zimme Yazawin* states that "Chiang Mai . . . is Suvaṇṇabhūmi." (p. 1)

171. Wyatt and Aroonrut, *Chiang Mai Chronicle,* pp. 3–5.

172. U Kala, *Mahayazawingyi,* 1:100.

173. Pāññāsāmi, *Sāsanavaṃsa* (History of the religion), trans. Bimala Churn Law (London: Pali Text Society, 1952), p. 40.

174. U Kala mentions it in the context of Aśoka's Third Buddhist Council and the sending of missionaries to Lower Burma (U Kala, *Mahayazawingyi,* 1:100).

175. Pāññāsāmi, *Sāsanavaṃsa,* p. 42.

176. Pāññāsāmi, *Sāsanavaṃsa,* p. 61.

177. As late as King Mindon's reign and his holding of the Fifth Buddhist Council, the first since Parākramabāhu I's in the twelfth century, Upper Burma likely

retained the prestige of being the center of Orthodox Theravāda Buddhism in the Buddhist world. It was only after annexation and the elimination of the monarchy—hence, also the legitimacy of the *saṅgha*—that this prestige declined and shifted to Lower Burma (and the Shwédagôn Pagoda), which until then had not enjoyed such status.

178. The one exception was Pe Maung Tin, as we have observed above.

179. Luce, *Old Burma* 1:21.

180. U Myint Aung, "Excavations," and "Suvannabhumi," 41–53. See also Sao Saimong Mangrai, "Did Soṇa and Uttara Come to Lower Burma" *JBRS* 59, 1–2 (December 1976): 155–164. In this article, it was assumed Suvaṇṇabhūmi was Burma and thus taken as self-evident, so the questions he posed sought answers about the historicity of Soṇa and Uttara instead.

181. Wheatley, *Golden Khersonese,* pp. 144–147.

182. Paranavitana (in *Ceylon and Malaysia,* p. 2) wrote that the Sinhalese literature of the twelfth or thirteenth century knew Lower Burma as Aramaṇa (Pali Rāmañña). There are other references to an Aramaṇa in earlier inscriptions, but these are either clearly in South India, not Lower Burma, or too late to be of relevance here.

183. *DPPN* 2:1263.

184. J. F. Fleet "Mahishamandala and Mahishmati," *JRAS* (1910): 428.

185. The Burma Karen experience in this regard is excellently described in Jessica Harriden's "'Making a Name for Themselves': Karen Identity and the Politicization of Ethnicity in Burma," *The Journal of Burma Studies,* 7 (2002): 84–144.

186. I acknowledge that shared knowledge is, ultimately, a *dual* rather than a *binary* process.

187. As noted earlier, Tilman Frasch's 1996 dissertation on Pagán, Emmanuel Guillon's 1999 study, *The Mons,* and even the careful work of Hiram Woodward in *The Art and Architecture of Thailand,* published as recently as 2003, all continue to accept, thereby perpetuate, the "legend that was Lower Burma."

Chapter Four: Thatôn (Sudhuim), an Imagined Center

1. I use the terms Thatôn and Sudhuim interchangeably, depending on the most accurate context.

2. *DPPN* 2:1202–1203.

3. Blagden, "Etymological Notes. VI. Thaton," *JBRS* 5, 1 (1915): 26. [Hereafter Blagden, "Thaton."]

4. Blagden, "Thaton," p. 26. He wrote: "The Mons do not turn *s* into the sound of the English *th* as the Burmans do, and the Mon name of the town in modern times is properly... *Sadhuim,* though Haswell... has the forms... *Kadhuim* and... *Satuim.* In the 15th century inscriptions we find an older form... *Sudhuim,* which of course supports the modern form first mentioned and seems to dispose of Haswell's variants. Further back than that I have not, as yet, succeeded in tracing the name in its Mon form.... The probability, however, is that it is not really a Mon word at all."

5. Blagden, "Thaton," p. 26.

6. Blagden, "Thaton," 27.

7. R. Halliday's *A Mon-English Dictionary* (Rangoon: Ministry of Union Culture,

1955) does not contain the word, where (on pages 429–463) it should be. It is also not found in H. L. Shorto's *A Dictionary of Modern Spoken Mon* (London: Oxford University Press, 1962), where it should have been placed between pages 189 and 197. However, Shorto's *Dictionary of Mon Inscriptions* does have the word *Sudhuim* (p. 380), but it is identified as Middle, not Old Mon.

8. Blagden, "Thaton," p. 26.

9. Aung Thaw, *Historical Sites,* pp. 34–40. Note that Aung Thaw has placed the chapter on Thatôn *later* than those on Halin and Śrī Kṣetra of the Pyū. See also Luce's map of Thatôn in *Old Burma,* 1, facing p. 25.

10. Aung Thaw, *Historical Sites,* p. 35. The plan of Thatôn that Aung Thaw examined was probably taken from *Burma Gazetteer: Thaton District,* comp. U Tin Gyi, Volume A (Rangoon: SGP, 1931), p. 23. The latest report on Thatôn as of this writing is Daw Baby, *Thaton Myohaung* (The ancient city of Thatôn) (Yangôn: Department of Archaeology, 2000), and it is devoid of virtually any evidence for dating the place. The wall has been excavated in two places, which has revealed a habitation layer under part of the wall. The building material was brick with laterite.

11. *Burma Gazetteer, Thaton District,* p. 23.

12. Wheatley, *Nāgara,* chapter 3; U Shwe Zan, *Golden Mrauk-U,* pp. 153, 164; U Aung Myint, *Aerial Photographs,* passim; Srisakra Vallibhotama, "The Ancient Settlements of Sukhothai," in *Papers from a Conference on Thai Studies in Honor of William J. Gedney,* eds. Robert J. Bickner, et al. (Ann Arbor: Center for Southeast Asian Studies, 1986), pp. 231–238; Miriam T. Stark, et al., "Results of the 1995–1996 Archaeological Field Investigations at Angkor Borei, Cambodia," *Asian Perspectives* 38, 1 (Spring 1999): 7–36, are all examples. Michael Francis Dega's "Prehistoric Circular Earthworks of Cambodia," Ph.D. dissertation, University of Hawai'i at Manoa, 2001, suggests a prehistoric tradition for this circular design.

13. Aung Myint and Moore, "Finger-mark Designs," pp. 91–101.

14. The archaeologist who performed the excavations was U Myint Aung, who writes: " . . . the bricks used in this building and its architectural style [are] . . . no later than the Pagan period . . . ." See p. 165 of his "Editor's Note on Excavation of Old Thaton," *JBRS* 59, 1–2 (December 1976): 165–166.

15. Luce, *Phases,* 1:159–162; Aung Thaw, *Historical Sites,* pp. 34–40.

16. Aung Thaw, *Historical Sites,* pp. 34–40.

17. Luce, *Old Burma,* 2 "attachment."

18. *MKPC.*

19. One inscription, the authenticity of which is questioned but is dated to 1067, will be discussed in Chapter Five.

20. *SMK* 1:66 and p. 345. No one appears to have noticed it, but this inscription, attributed by everyone to Narapatisithu, may actually have belonged to his son and successor, King Natonmya.

21. *SMK* 3:22, 53, 150.

22. Tin Hla Thaw, "History of Burma," p. 138.

23. See *MKPC* 2:60–61 for the Burmese translation. For the Mon, see 1:114–117.

24.Tin Hla Thaw, "History of Burma," p. 143.

25. Luce's list of place names in *Old Burma,* 2, "attachment," cites Dhammazedi's 1476 Kalyani Inscriptions as the earliest source as well.

26. *EB* 3, 2:276.

27. For an English translation of one of these, see Shorto's "Gavampati Tradition," pp. 16–17. For the Burmese translated from the Mon, see *MKPC* inscription no. 87, pp. 98–90, and no. 89, pp. 91–92.

28. Shorto, "Gavampati Tradition."

29. Guillon, *The Mons,* p. 44 has a short paragraph on Gavaṁpati, in which he claims that some twelfth-century inscriptions mentioned the deity. I presume these are the same Old Mon inscriptions of Kyanzittha cited by Shorto and under discussion here, none of which is linked to the Mon or to Thatôn; the association is an anachronistic recreation on the part of Shorto.

30. Shorto, "Gavampati Tradition," pp. 19–20; Luce, *Phases,* 1:49. There is an Old Burmese inscription of 1058 that mentions a dedication by King Aniruddha to a "Lord Gavam" which can be found in *Selections From the Inscriptions of Pagan,* comps. G. H. Luce and Pe Maung Tin (Rangoon: British Burma Press, 1928), pp. 1–2. It mentions a statue being carved of the Buddhist saint called "Lord Gavam." However, "Lord Gavam" here is more likely to have been the monk being honored on the inscription, and to whom a royal monastery, a horse, lands, and an elephant were being donated. And even if one concedes that the reference were to the statue of the saint and not the monk, it is still not evidence to support Shorto's claims that Gavaṁpati in the eleventh century was tutelary deity of Thatôn and patron saint of the Mon.

31. *EB* 1, 2:114.

32. *EB* 3:185.

33. Shorto, "Gavampati Tradition," p. 19. However, Shorto has him as the founder of the dynasty, perhaps a mistake for Sīrimāsoka.

34. Shorto, "Gavampati."

35. Shorto also projected other, later Mon beliefs concerning concepts surrounding the 32 Myos and the Cult of the 37 Nats backward onto an earlier era in his "32 *Myos*" and *"dewatau sotāpan"* articles. In my *Pagan* (p. 56, note 21, and page 221), I had concurred with Shorto's assessment, and with the Mon Paradigm in general, as did all Burma historians.

36. Luce, *Old Burma,* 1:21, 24.

37. Luce, *Old Burma,* 1:24.

38. In 1959 Pierre Dupont raised doubts about the existence of Thatôn: ". . . it should be stated also that the titling [of the king] contains no mention either of Thatôn (Sudhammavati) or of the land of the Mon (Rāmaññadesa)." My thanks to Ken Breazeale for his translation of this sentence from Pierre Dupont's *L'Achéologie mône de Dvāravatī,* pp. 8–9.

39. Phayre, *History,* p. 27; Robert Halliday, *The Talaings* (Rangoon: Government Printing, 1917), pp. 6–7. On p. 3 in Amatgyi Bannya Dala's *Yazadarit,* it states that when Narapatisithu came down to Lower Burma, Muttama was inhabited by *bilu,* the Burmese equivalent to *rakṣa.* Thus, even in the Mon tradition, it was not Thatôn but Muttama that was linked to these *rakṣa.*

40. For the resurgence of Śrī Vijaya in Malacca, see O. W. Wolters, *The Fall of Srivijaya in Malay History* (Ithaca: Cornell University Press, 1970).

41. Chris Baker's interesting article describes this look seaward and southward by Ayudhyā. See his "Ayutthaya Rising: From Land or Sea?" *JSEAS* 34, 1 (February 2003): 41–62.

42. Amatgyi Bannya Dala, *Yazadarit,* p. 7. It is a Mon history translated into

Burmese by the Mon minister Bannya Dala who served Hanthawaddy Hsinphyushin (Bayinnaung) during the mid-sixteenth century. It was retranslated (also into Burmese) by Nai Pan Hla in 1977 as *Yazadarit Ayedawpon Kyan* [The treatise of the royal crisis account of Yazadarit], (Yangôn: Min Hlaing Daw Press, 1977). Chen Yi-Sein in "Lin-Yang," p. 73, thinks that the "Sea *Jakun* or *Orang Laut,*" based in "Jahor and Sumatra" which both Burmese and Chinese sources apparently considered pirates and called "Salon," were called *rakṣa* by the Indians.

43. Bilu Kyun or Ogre Island lies off Muttama and Maulamyaing where the Thanlyin (Salween) empties into the Gulf of Muttama. It makes a far better candidate for this Rakṣapura than Thatôn does..

44. Wheatley, *Golden Khersonese,* p. 202.

45. Aung-Thwin, *Myth and History,* chapter 1, p. 9.

46. Wheatley, *Golden Khersonese,* p. 256. For a translation by Samuel Beal, see *Si-Yu-Ki,* pp. 199–200.

47. U Tet Htoot, "Nature," p. 53.

48. The date 1825 comes from the last leaf on the microfilm copy which is in the India Office Library where it is known as Chevilliot 3447.

49. *Legend of Queen Cāma,* p. xxvi, note 2.

50. *Legend of Queen Cāma,* p. 106.

51. *Legend of Queen Cāma,* pp. 105–106.

52. *Sheaf of Garlands,* p. 157.

53. The editors of the *Legend of Queen Cāma* write (p. xxv) that the text noted earlier by Coedes is identical to the story of Cāmadevī as translated by Auguste Pavie in *Mission Pavie* (Paris, 1898), based on a Luang Prabang manuscript dated 1646.

54. Coedes, *Indianized,* p. 149, dates it to the "first half of the 11th century" but fails to cite his source other than the *Cāmadevīvaṃsa.*

55. *Legend of Queen Cāma,* p. 20.

56.Coedes, *Indianized,* p. 140, note 57.

57. Noted below.

58. It is true that another inscription (*SMK* 1, section *"kha,"* pp. 326–327) with a date of 1086 mentions King Aniruddha, who, it said, "displaying his might," marched to "Ussa Paykū," as Pegu and its region was known, and is still today. But the editors do not think this is an original inscription. Indeed, on line 16 of the inscription a date of 1105 is encountered, so the inscription cannot be dated earlier than that.

59. *Sheaf of Garlands,* xxix.

60. *Sheaf of Garlands,* 104.

61. *Sheaf of Garlands,* p. 104.

62. Shorto, "Gavampati Tradition," p.25.

63. Luce, *Old Burma,* 1:22, had also assumed the same.

64. In U Kala, *Mahayazawingyi,* 1:115, Śrī Kṣetra is called *Yathe Pyi* (the "hermit kingdom").

65. *Sheaf of Garlands,* p. 104, note 2, quotes Coedes, p. 80. Coedes may have confused Puṇṇagāma with Pugarāma, by which Pagán is known. For example, see U Kala, *Mahayazawingyi.* 1:184, 249. The late eighteenth-century *Myanma Yazawinthit* (p. 85) also states that Aniruddha named Pagán Paukarama (i.e. Pugarāma). The early sixteenth-century *Yazawingyaw* (p. 77) uses the term Pukaṁ as do the *Zatataw-*

pon (p. 37) and the *Maniyadanabon* (p. 5), and *not* Puṇṇagāma. The Kalayani Inscriptions recalled a Pugama. Unfortunately, Luce also confused the two. See his *Old Burma,* 2:273.

66. H. L. Shorto, "A Mon Genealogy of Kings: Observations on *The Nidāna Árambhakathā,*" in *Historians of Southeast Asia,* ed. D. G. E. Hall (London: Oxford University Press, 1961) [hereafter cited as Shorto, *Nidāna*], p. 64.

67. It was compiled and published only in 1910.

68. Shorto, "*Nidāna,*" p. 66.

69. Shorto, "*Nidāna,*" p. 65.

70. It is on pages 9–34 and 45–61 of the *Nidāna Rāmādhipati-kathā,* which, upon binding, was named *Rājāwaṅsa Dhammacetī Mahāpiṭakadhara,* ed. Phra Candakanto (Pak Lat: Siam, 1912).

71. I am thinking mainly of the scholarship of Nai Pan Hla, a Mon scholar of Burma, who has not discussed this problem in any of his published works that I have seen.

72. *Lik Smin Asah: The Story of the Founding of Pegu and a Subsequent Invasion from South India with English Translation, Notes, and vocabulary of Undefined Words,* trans. by Robert Halliday (Rangoon: American Baptist Mission Press, 1923), p. vi.

73. Halliday, *The Talaings,* p. 5. See also Phayre, *History,* pp. 29–30.

74. Amatgyi Bannya Dala, *Yazadarit,* p. 3.

75. Some of the contents in the *Nidāna* suggest that it is later than it is made out to be. It includes the story of Prince Asah's fight with the Indian, which is not found until the *Lik Smin Asah,* and that work was not composed until 1825. See Halliday's introduction to *Lik Smin Asah,* p. vi.

76. The author must have forgotten that they were *not* supposed to go back to India but to Lower Burma, since the story had already been shifted from India to Burma!

77. Amatgyi Bannya Dala, *Yazadarit,* pp. 3–4.

78. This story is in Amatgyi Bannya Dala, *Yazadarit,* pp. 3–4. In *SMK* 1:355, an inscription of Pagán mentions that King Sithu (obviously Narapatisithu here), descended to Lower Burma in 1192 AD.

79. This tradition is also found in the Thai chronicles. See Mom Chao Chand Chirayu Rajani, *Guide through the Inscriptions of Sukhothai,* University of Hawai'i Southeast Asian Studies Program Working Paper, no. 9, (Honolulu: 1976), p. 15. Baker, "Ayutthaya," (p. 50), also mentions this son-in-law relationship between the "kings" of Ayutthaya and the Chinese emperors.

80. Emil Forchhammer, *The Jardine Prize: An essay on the sources and development of Burmese Law from the era of the first introduction of the Indian Law to the time of the British occupation of Pegu with Text and Translation of King Wagaru's Manu Dhammasattham* (Rangoon: Government Press, 1885), 4–10 of "Preface."

81. Amatgyi Bannya Dala, *Yazadarit,* p. 12.

82. *SMK* 1:355; *SMK* 3:196, 199.

83. *Epigraphic Studies,* p. 320. Indeed, both the *Mūlasāsanā* and the *Jinakālamālī* attribute the origins of Sinhalese Buddhism in Sukhodaya to Muttama.

84. *Epigraphic Studies,* 281 and passim.

85. Amatgyi Bannya Dala, *Yazadarit,* pp. 1–3. See also "Yazadarit Ayedawpon,"

Myanma Swe Son Kyan (Encyclopedia Myanmar) on CD-ROM by Yangôn: Forever Group, 1998–1999.

86. U Kala, *Mahayazawingyi,* 1:178–180. I am assuming that the two "Indian Brothers" refer to Samala and Wimala and not another pair of brothers, even though founding brothers are a common motif in the origin stories of every major city in Burma.

87. Twinthintaikwun Mahasithu, *Twinthin Myanma Yazawinthit* (Twinthin's new chronicle of the Myanma), (Yangôn: Mingala Pon Hneit Press, 1968), vol. I, pp. 84–85.

88. *Slapat Rājawaṅ Datow Smin Roṅ: A History of Kings With Text, Translation, and Notes,* trans. R. Halliday (Rangoon: Burma Research Society, 1923), p. 10. It was published as a special issue in the *JBRS* as volume 13, 1–2 (1923).

89. There is some confusion on this issue as well. In *The Talaings* (p. 129), Halliday stated that Schmidt's title was *A History of Pegu in the Mon Language,* but on pp. 9–10 of the preface to his translation of the *Slapat,* Halliday calls it "Slapat Rājāwaṅ Datow Smin roṅ."

90. For a description and analysis of this manuscript, see C. O. Blagden's "The Chronicles of Pegu: A Text in the Mon Language," *JRAS* (1907): 367–374.

91. Richard M. Eaton, "Locating Arakan in Time, Space, and Historical Scholarship," in *The Maritime Frontier of Burma: Exploring Political, Cultural and Commercial Interaction in the Indian Ocean World, 1200–1800,* eds. Jos Gommans and Jacques Leider, (Amsterdam and Leiden: Koninklijke Nederlandse Akademie van Wetenschapen and KITLV Press, 2002), p. 225–231.

92. Quotes by Jesuits visiting Lower Burma at the time can be found in Harvey, *History of Burma,* pp. 183–184.

93. Phayre, p. 30. However, I have not been able to find them among the dynastic lists provided by Nilakanta Sastri's *A History of South India,* Third Edition (London: Oxford University Press, 1966).

94. By the very end of the sixteenth century, Pegu had rapidly declined in power, but its rulers had already developed plans for returning to the agrarian Dry Zone well in advance of its destruction. One might notice that much like the Mon texts themselves, I have deliberately collapsed two dynasties into one at Pegu in order to focus on the city itself: Yazadarit's fourteenth-to-fifteenth-century dynasty, of which Dhammazedi was a part, and Bayinnaung's Toungoo Dynasty, that established Pegu as its center in the mid-sixteenth century.

95. U Kala, *Mahayazawingyi,* 1:246–247.

96. *Lik Smin Asah,* 175–181.

97. It appears that a general of Vijayanagara got confused with the notorious Portuguese adventurer de Brito, who had set out to carve a kingdom for himself in Lower Burma during the first half of the seventeenth century. *Lik Smin Asah,* p. 178. If this is indeed de Brito in the story, it would confirm the lateness of these legends.

98. He does not name them, but they are obviously Wimala and Samala.

99. Phayre, *History,* pp. 27–28.

100. Phayre, *History,* p. 29. In fact, all fifty-nine names on this list are given the title *"rāja"* except Manuha, who is tacked on at the end with the Burmese equivalent, *"min,"* instead. The names seem to have been randomly picked from the *Mahāvaṃsa.*

101. Phayre, *History,* pp. 29–30.

102. Phayre's list of the Thatôn and Pegu kings can be found in his *History* on pp. 288–289, while those of the *Cūḷavaṃsa,* volume 2, can be found on pages ix–xv.

103. John W. Spellman, "The Symbolic Significance of the Number Twelve in Ancient India," *Journal of Asian Studies,* 22, 1 (November 1962): 79–88.

104. Nai Pan Hla, "Mon Literature and Culture over Thailand and Burma," *JBRS* 41, 1 (1958): 66. The Gavaṁpati legend, of course, is most eruditely presented by H. L.Shorto in his "Gavampati Tradition."

105. Pāññāsāmi, *Sāsanavaṃsa,* p. 41.

106. I have deliberately not used the phrase "contested narratives," popular though it may be today, precisely because I feel that differences or "contradictions" do not necessarily imply competition or adversarial relationships in all contexts, however true that may be in the United States today. We certainly cannot impose that model onto either the premodern or the modern Asian world, especially while accusing colonial historians of doing the same thing. There is also often an assumption that *differences* imply *changes,* particularly when placed in a framework of linear time, which is not necessarily the case.

107. Pāññāsāmi, *Sāsanavaṃsa,* p. 41.

108. U Kala, *Mahayazawingyi,* 1:178. It should be added, however, that the two brothers were not named but referred to as the two "Indian brothers" of Thatôn. That this account was written in the context of a conquest suggests one cannot get a more "contested" situation than that, yet the narrative was inclusive rather than exclusive. Note that the stories of Soṇa and Uttara and of Tapussa and Bhallika going to Lower Burma are also included in the *Sāsanavaṃsa,* an Upper Burma text espousing a different tradition.

109. It is interesting to note that the mythical founding fathers of Rome, Romulus and Remus were also said to have been brothers suckled by a she-wolf.

110. Shorto, perhaps mistakenly, states that Sūriyakumā was *founder* of the Thatôn Dynasty ("Gavampati Tradition," p. 27), whereas in the Kalyani Inscriptions he was the last of that dynasty. Sūriyakumā was Manohor's formal title. (*EB* 3, 2:187).

111. Halliday, *The Talaings,* p. 5.

112. D. G. E. Hall, *Henry Burney: A Political Biography* (London: Oxford University Press, 1974), 92, suggests that Burney and other British officials were already speaking of a "Doorawuddee" (Dvāravatī) as early as 1824, nearly a hundred years before the subject appeared in Burma scholarship. One of the first was probably Halliday's "The Mon Inscriptions of Siam," *JBRS* 22, 3 (1932): 107–119. Robert Brown in *The Dvāravatī Wheels of the Law and the Indianization of South East Asia* (Leiden: E. J. Brill, 1996), p. xxii, attributes to M. Stanislas Julien, in 1857, the earliest modern scholarship to have identified Dvāravatī (in Dvarapati and Darapati).

Chapter Five: The Conquest of Thatôn, an Imagined Event

1. The one exception, an inscription dated to 1067, is actually a late sixteenth- or seventeenth-century copy or recast, to be discussed below.

2. Luce, *Old Burma,* 1:24, note 89. For the inscription itself, see *SMK* 1:322–323. Although Luce gives the date as 1068, the inscription itself gives *Sakarāj* 429, i.e. 1067. But he is referring to the same inscription being discussed.

3. Luce, "Mons of the Pagán Dynasty," p. 10. Manuha per se is not even a Mon

name and therefore does not appear in Shorto's *Dictionary of Mon Inscriptions.* Manohor, of course, is Middle Mon, but does not occur until 1476. As for "Makuta," it is unclear where Luce got it since it is on neither of the two inscriptions, as we shall see. H. G. Quaritch Wales did mention it before Luce did, in his article called "Anuruddha and the Thaton Tradition," *JRAS* 3–4 (1947): 155.

4. Htin Aung's earlier response to Luce on this issue was mainly a good argument against Luce's thesis. However, Htin Aung did not use any primary sources to demonstrate his point. Essentially, he also accepted the historicity of the conquest of Thatôn and of the existence of King Manuha and/or "Makuta," although he does not consider them the same persons. See Maung Htin Aung, *Burmese History Before 1287: A Defence of the Chronicles* (Oxford: The Asoka Society, 1970), chapter V.

5. It is not, as I will demonstrate below, found on the Kalyani Inscriptions, as Luce claimed.

6. Luce, "Mons of the Pagán Dynasty," p. 1.

7. Luce, *Old Burma,* 1:24.

8. Luce, *Old Burma,* 1:24 himself wrote that "neither has a legible date . . . ."

9. Shorto, *Dictionary of Mon Inscriptions,* x. Shorto does not explain this linguistic continuity, but I guess that early written Old Mon was relatively isolated, and that only later in the sixteenth century, when Pegu became the capital of the Upper Burma Toungoo Dynasty, did Old Mon make the kinds of contact with the dominant language in the country, Burmese, which may have produced the first noticeable changes.

10. To be sure, Nai Pan Hla has assigned 4 terracotta tablets inscribed in Mon, out of 131 pieces recovered from a place called Winga near Thatôn, to the sixth century AD on paleographic grounds. However, the only scientific dating of objects from Winga are late—fifteenth and seventeenth century—as already demonstrated in earlier chapters.

11. For the photograph of their rubbings, see *IB,* Portfolio IV, numbers 358 and 359, although the rubbing is scarcely legible.

12. *MKPC* part 2:1,3.

13. Luce, *Old Burma,* 1:24.

14. *Slapat,* p.52; Halliday, *The Talaings,* p. 11.

15. Shorto, *Dictionary of Mon Inscriptions,* p. x.

16. Shorto, *Nidāna,* p. 67.

17. *Epigraphic Studies,* p. 311.

18. The *Yazadarit* does not begin with King Yazadarit, as one might expect, but with Magadu, probably the real founder of the first Mon Dynasty of Burma. All the Mon histories in translation I have consulted, after the usual two-brothers legends, begin with Magadu as well.

19. Amatgyi Bannya Dala, *Yazadarit,* p. 10 onward.

20. Luce, *Old Burma,* 1:26, note 98.

21. *SMK* 3:274.

22. U Saw Tun, personal communication.

23. *SMK* 3:322–323. This is one of the reasons I think that the stone may be a late record, and its author may have been one of Bodawpaya's ministers who was in charge of recasting, collecting, and cataloguing Old Burmese donative inscriptions in the eighteenth century.

24. Shorto, *Nidāna,* p. 64.

25. *SMK* 1:322.

26. *EB* 3:187.

27. Shorto, *Nidāna,* p. 66. Also, *Lik Smin Asah,* p. 73.

28. That in itself is puzzling for the average annual rainfall at Pagán is only forty-five inches.

29. Htin Aung, *Burmese History,* page 17, quotes the "reverse" of the stone. I do not know where he got that information since he does not cite his source, but the original reverse, which I have seen, has nothing to do with the subject on the obverse. I think he may have been using a Bodawpaya copy that was recast in 1785. It can be found in *MM* no. 34, p. 306. It does say some of the things Htin Aung claims it says.

30. Luce, *Old Burma,* 1:24, note 89.

31. *MM* no. 34, p. 306

32. Luce, *Old Burma,* 1:18–28.

33. *SMK* 1:326–327.

34. Luce, *Old Burma,* 2:246.

35. Indeed, as we shall see below, a major story in the Pali chronicles of Northern Thailand records a clash between Aniruddha and the Khmers, which, in important ways, sounds very much like the story surrounding the alleged conquest of Thatôn and Manuha.

36. Luce, *Old Burma,* 1:8, quotes E. Aymonier, *Journal Asiatique,* (jan-fev 1891): pp. 29, 53; and (mars-avril, 1903): 194, 201. He also cites Louis Finot, *BEFEO,* 3 (1903): 634, and Coedes, *États Hinuouise* (1964 edition), p. 257.

37. Luce, *Old Burma,* 1:27.

38. Thiripyanchi U Mya, *She Haung Ok Khwek Yokpwa Sintutaw Mya: Votive Tablets of Burma,* part I, (Yangon: Archaeological Survey of Burma, 1961). p. 78. Only one votive tablet has been found in the present township of Thatôn, while one other was discovered at the Shwézayan Pagoda at Thatôn. Neither has been identified as having belonged to Aniruddha.

39. U Mya, *Votive Tablets,* part 1, where he lists and describes over one hundred such tablets, twenty-three of which belonged specifically to Aniruddha.

40. By the Burma script I mean the script the Burmese, Mon, Shan, and Arakanese used in Burma, starting at least by the Pagán period, to write their own languages.

41. Nai Pan Hla discovered two of "Aniruddha's tablets" written in Mon; one at Momeit in Upper Burma and the other at Kalamyo, on the Chindwin River northwest of Pagán. See his "Old Terracotta Votive Tablets & New Theories on History of Old Burma," *Traditions in Current Perspective: Proceedings of the Conference on Myanmar and Southeast Asian Studies 15–17 November 1995, Yangon* (Yangon: Universities Historical Research Centre, 1996), pp. 145–155. One wonders about their original provenance, as neither is dated. If they are Aniruddha-period tablets that Aniruddha inscribed personally, his conquest of the south—the Thatôn issue notwithstanding—is even better documented. As labor was in short supply throughout early Southeast Asia, he likely brought Mon speakers back with him and settled them in Upper Burma.

42. Luce, *Old Burma,* 1:26.

43. Luce, *Old Burma,* 1:27.

44. Pe Maung Tin, "The Dialect of Tavoy," *JBRS* 23, 1 (1933): 32–46. What is also very interesting about this subject is that the "Phongsawadan Môn Phama," (Annal of the Mon of Burma) in *Prachum Phongsawadan* [Collection of historical papers], vol. 2, part 1 (Bangkok: Khurusapha 1963), p. 19–20, gives the same account that people at Inlé *today* still give about their Tavoy origins and how they were settled at Inlé by King Alaungsithu. The Thai source, translated from Mon to Thai in 1857, the compilation of which may have been as early as 1793, reads: "The king [A-lang-kha-cho] . . . rounded up the Raman people of Sittang and resettled them in Pagan. Pegu and Sittang thus became depopulated, and few people remained. He sent Burmese people to live at Tavoy, and thus the Tavoyans speak Burmese. Even though their dialect of Burmese has changed over a long period, the Burmese can still understand the Tavoyans. The Tavoyan language even today is not like the Raman language." My thanks to Ken Breazeale for both the translation and the source.

45. King Kyanzittha's Prome Inscription of 1093 is the earliest *dated* Mon epigraphic text found in Burma. See *MKPC* parts 1 and 2, and *Old Burma,* 1:55.

46. The latest and most complete collection of Old Burmese inscriptions of the Ava period can be found in volume 4 (and most of 5) of *SMK* if we date the Ava period as covering the years 1364–1527.

47. *EB* 3, 2:188, note 4.

48. It could well have been from Śrī Laṅka, as recorded in the Pali chronicles to be discussed in the next chapter.

49. *EB* 3, 2:187–188.

50. *EB* 3, 2:188.

51. Luce, *Old Burma,* 1:23; 2:286.

52. Most of the ten Kalyani Inscriptions are inscribed on both faces and each face contains about 70 lines of text, which comes to a total of approximately 1,400 lines of text.

53. *EB* 3, 2:188–192.

54. Aung-Thwin, "*Sāsana* Reform."

55. Ray, *Sanskrit,* p. 4. For what is probably the best analysis of the Upagupta tradition, lineage, and Theravāda Orthodoxy, see Strong, *Legend and Cult of Upagupta.*

56. Aung-Thwin, "Sāsana Reform."

57. Bode, *Pali Literature,* p. 8. See also Taw Sein Ko, *Burmese Sketches,* 1:89. The issue here is less about the "correctness" of the Buddhaghosa and Upagupta traditions than it is about Dhammazedi's use of the *upasampadā* tradition to effect his goals. Complicating the issue is the Mon jurist of the sixteenth century, also named Buddhaghosa, who translated the *Wagaru Dhammathat* into Pali (Bode, *Pali Literature,* p. 86).

58. Taw Sein Ko, *Burmese Sketches,* 1:89.

59. Ray, *Sanskrit,* p. 83.

Chapter Six: The Conquest of Thatôn as Allegory

1. Many such issues are raised in Kemper's, *Presence of the Past,* an indispensable work for understanding the *vaṁsa* tradition. Similarly, Jonathan S. Walters's "Buddhist History: The Śrī Laṅkan Pāli Vaṃsas and Their Community," in *Query-*

ing the Medieval: Texts and the History of Practices in South Asia, ed. by Ronald Inden, Jonathan Walters, and Daud Ali (Oxford: Oxford University Press, 2000), pp. 99–164, deals with what he calls the connectedness of calculable and incalculable time, precisely what Dhammazedi was doing in his conflation of time. See also Michael Aung-Thwin, "Spirals in Burmese and Early Southeast Asian History," *Journal of Interdisciplinary History* 21, 4 (Spring 1991): 575–602, for a discussion of some relevant issues with regard to time. In this chapter, however, I am concerned mainly with the historicity of the Mon Paradigm and the relationship of Southeast Asian chronicles to it.

2. *Zatatawpon,* p. 41, is the location where the story should appear.

3. *Zatatawpon,* p. 36. Tayôk Pye Min is the late thirteenth-century Pagán king who came to be known as the "king who fled the Chinese," while Thihathu (Sīhasū) is one of the famous "Three Brothers" who repelled the Mongols. See Michael Aung-Thwin, "The Myth of the 'Three Shan Brothers' and the Ava Period in Burmese History," *JAS* 55, 4 (November 1996): 881–901.

4. It could have been Pinya, founded in 1312.

5. Michael Aung-Thwin, *Myth and History,* chapter 2.

6. The other mention occurs in the *Zambu Kungya Po Yaza Mu Haung,* as is noted by Tet Htoot, "Nature," p. 53. The *Zambu* survives as a copy dated to 1825 and can be found in E. Chevilliot, comp., "Catalogue of Burmese Mss," manuscript no. 3447 of The India Office, n.d. Tet Htoot states on p. 53 that the *Zambu* is the only chronicle that mentions Disāpramok, which is not accurate.

7. *Zatatawpon,* p. 35.

8. The *Zatatawpon*'s criterion for "periodization" is the rise and fall of dynasties, and its criterion for their labeling is the capital city. Thus the Tagaung, Śrī Kṣetra, Pagán, Pinya, Sagaing, and Ava Dynasties are named for the cities which the dynasty occupied. The reason the scheme does not include either the Toungoo or Pegu Dynasties is probably that the author was writing earlier than either, and later additions to the chronicle were mainly horoscopes, not data of a historiographic nature.

9. *Zatatawpon,* p. 37.

10. Archaeologist Bob Hudson and his colleagues are on a quest to locate some if not all of these villages. See Hudson et al., "Digging for myths," pp. 9–21.

11. Bob Hudson et al., "Origins of Bagan."

12. *Zatatawpon,* p. 40.

13. *Zatatawpon,* p. 41.

14. *Zatatawpon,* p. 41. This sentence, apparently by the original author, suggests he had other texts, which he called "ancient," that are now lost to us as originals.

15. Tet Htoot, "Nature," p. 53. See also U Maung Maung, *Story of Wunzin Min Yaza* and Duroiselle's reference to it in "The story of Wunzin Min Yaza." *MSSK* also has a brief account of Min Yaza.

16. The quote is taken from *The Maniyadanabon of Shin Sandalinka,* trans. by L. E. Bagshawe, Cornell University Southeast Asia Program Data Papers, no. 115 (Ithaca: 1981), p. 8, because the *Zambu* manuscript in the India Office is incomplete and does not contain this particular section. Bagshawe adds in a note that "the author does not mention that this was a military looting," revealing both a current bias being projected onto the Ava period as well as his acceptance of the conventional Aniruddha story as historical.

17. At least the first part of the *Yazawinkyaw* was said to have been finished on Sakarāj 864, or AD 1502. See Shin Thilawuntha *Yazawinkyaw* (Celebrated chronicle), ed. Pe Maung Tin (Yangôn: Burma Research Society, n.d.) p. 75, and Pe Maung Tin, *Myanma Sape Thamaing* (History of Burmese literature) (Yangôn: Khettara Press, 1977), p. 97.

18. The author wrote that the first part of the chronicle, which deals with the kings of Śrī Laṅka was completed in 1502. But the second part, dealing with Burma's kings was finished only by 1520. See Shin Thilawuntha, *Yazawinkyaw,* p. 75.

19. Shin Thilawuntha, *Yazawinkyaw,* p. 77.

20. The long inscription can be found in *SMK* 5:21–33.

21. Another point to be noted is that the information contained in these stories do not necessarily appear in linear fashion, so that whereas Aniruddha is mentioned in the late thirteen-century *Zatatawpon,* the king is not found in the early sixteenth-century *Yazawinkyaw,* but then does reappear subsequently.

22. *Sheaf of Garlands,* xxix.

23. *Sheaf of Garlands,* p. 186.

24. *Sheaf of Garlands,* xxxii–xlvi.

25. *Sheaf of Garlands,* p. xxxv.

26. *Sheaf of Garlands,* xxxii–xlvi.

27. There are other "functions," of course. For example, Anne Blackburn sees the text as evidence of "successful localization of an imported lineage" in her "Localizing Lineage: Importing Higher Ordination in Theravādin South and Southeast Asia," in *Constituting Communities: Theravāda Buddhism and the Religious Cultures of South and Southeast Asia,* ed. John Clifford Holt et al. (Albany, NY: State University of New York Press, 2003), pp. 131–149.

28. A Thai poem, adapted from a Sanskrit work, deals with the love affair between Aniruddha, grandson of Krishna, and Usha, daughter of the demon King Bana with 1,000 arms. In the battle brought about because of the affair, Anirut (Aniruddha) wins, and he and Usha live happily ever after. It is curious that the demon is called Bana (Baña)—a Mon title of royalty—and that the story is reminiscent of Magadu's eloping with the daughter of the Sukhodaya king. There may be some conflation, if not confusion, between the Anriuddha in Sanskrit and Thai literature with the Pali and Burmese Aniruddhas. The Thai poem can be found in *Saranukrom wattanatham thai phak klang* (Thai cultural encyclopaedia, central region), vol. 15, (Bangkok: Thai Cultural Encyclopaedia Foundation, 1999), pp. 7, 304–307. My thanks to Ken Breazeale for this valuable reference and translation.

29. *Sheaf of Garlands,* xxvi.

30. *Sheaf of Garlands,* p. 143.

31. *Sheaf of Garlands,* pp. 142–144.

32. *Sheaf of Garlands,* p. 144.

33. *Sheaf of Garlands,* p. 145.

34. *Sheaf of Garlands,* p. 156.

35. *Sheaf of Garlands,* p. 156.

36. Woodward, p. 137, notes a tenth-century Khmer inscription that recorded Angkorian king Rajendravarman's conquest of a Ramaṇya, thought to be within Thailand itself. Moreover, as noted in Chapter Three, a Rāmaññanagara appears to

have also existed in Northern Thailand, which was mentioned in the context of Haripuñjaya in the *Cāmadevīvaṃsa*.

37. *Sheaf of Garlands,* pp. 156–157.

38. *Legend of Cāmadevī,* p. 164.

39. Shorto, "Gavampati Tradition," p. 25.

40. Coedes, *Indianized,* p. 180.

41. *Sheaf of Garlands,* pp. 100, 142, 156. The word is spelled differently from Rāmañña, something Pali authors would immediately notice, so it is unlikely to be inadvertent.

42. Amatgyi Bannya Dala, *Yazadarit,* p. 8.

43. Constance M. Wilson, "The Holy Man in Thailand and Laos," *JSEAS* 28, 2 (September 1997): 349, n. 16.

44. Mabel Haynes Bode, *The Pali Literature of Burma* (London: The Royal Asiatic Society of Great Britain and Ireland, 1909; reprint London, 1966), chapter 2, shows the stature and image Pagán had during these centuries.

45. An interesting note here is that the *Jinakālamālī* was written around the same time as the supposed "1067" inscription (the sixteenth century), which also contains the story of Manuha of Thatôn building his colossal statue. Perhaps there is a connection between this late inscription and the *Jinakālamālī*.

46. *Old Burma,* 1:42–43. Luce had compared dry, donative inscriptions meant as legal records with the allegorical tales in U Kala's *Mahayazawingyi* to arrive at this conclusion. Why, then, not compare Kyanzittha's prophetic and allegorical inscriptions with those accounts in U Kala that are historically factual? That would turn the conclusion around, making Kyanzittha's original, primary, inscriptions the "sham" and U Kala's words "true historiography."

47. Harvey's translation of this event in *History of Burma,* p. 27, said to have been taken from the 1910 version of the *Uppanna,* does not mention the crucial details. "Manuhaw," incidentally, is spelled the way it is in the "1067" inscription.

48. *Lik Smin Asah,* p. vi.

49. "Ayedawpon" literally means "a royal story of great importance," usually of famous kings. Some Burmese authors writing in English use the term "memoir" for "Ayedawpon."

50. Amatgyi Bannya Dala, *Yazadarit,* page *hsa.*

51. Amatgyi Bannya Dala, *Yazadarit,* page *sa.*

52. See Nai Pan Hla, "Yazadarit Ayedawpon Kyan nhin Mon Thichin mya" and his *Yazadarit,* p. 9. However, Tet Htoot, "The Nature of Burmese Chronicles," p. 58, suggests that the version we have is in fact a translation from the Mon.

53. It is difficult to tell whether this is actually the same one mentioned in Harvey's with a slightly different title.

54. Nai Pan Hla, *Yazadarit,* p. 9. Shorto, however, states that "the history of Thatôn is almost entirely legendary . . . ." p. 66.

55. Duroiselle, in an article in the *JBRS* lists the Hanthawaddy chronicle as a publication only of 1910. See his "Talaing Nissayas," *JBRS* 3, 2 (1913): 104.

56. Twinthintaikwun Mahasithu, *Mahayazawinthit (Nyaung Yan Set)* [Great new chronicle of kings (Nyaung Yan Dynasty)], vol. III (Yangon: U Kyi Aye Publications, 1997), page *khaw.*

57. One palm-leaf version of the *Yazadarit* is in the National Library (no. 2290).

58. Nai Pan Hla, *Yazadarit,* pp. 9–10.

59. Amatgyi Bannya Dala, *Yazadarit,* p. 175. Aniruddha's inability to obtain relics in Burma, according to the Mon texts, contrasts sharply with his successful exploits in Śrī Laṅka and Thailand according to the Pali texts of Northern Thailand.

60. Shorto, "Gavampati," p. 18. One should not confuse this unpublished text that Shorto translated with his article called the "Gavampati Tradition."

61. Shorto, "Gavampati," pp. 1, 2–3, 9–10.

62. *Reprint from Dalrymple's Oriental Repertory, 1791–7 of Portions Relating to Burma* (Rangoon: Government Printing, 1926), p. 12.

63. Shorto, "Gavampati," p. 3. The statement that Tavoy is the "boundary of the Mon country" strengthens my contention that the first Mon polity in Lower Burma emerged only after the expansion of Pagán into this area, as suggested by the Burmese dialect spoken at Tavoy. The Pagán word for cross-legged, *thaway,* is Burmese, not Mon, and is found much earlier in the inscriptions of Pagán (see *SMK* 1:345 among others). In short, Mon sources themselves help verify the lateness of their own emergence in the region.

64. U Kala, *Mahayazawingyi,* p. *kha.* See also Victor Lieberman's assessment of U Kala's chronicle in "How Reliable is U Kala's Burmese Chronicle? Some New Comparisons," *JSEAS* 17, 2 (1986): 236–255.

65. U Kala, *Mahayazawingyi,* 1:180–184.

66. U Kala, *Mahayazawingyi,* 1:174–184.

67. U Kala, *Mahayazawingyi,* I, pp. 363–440; 2:1–47.

68. U Kala did mention Manuha's exile in Pagán and his building of the colossal Buddha image there as found in the *Jinakālamālī.* See U Kala, *Mahayazawingyi,* 1:184.

69. U Kala, *Mahayazawingyi,* 1:*nga.*

70. The Burmese palm-leaf manuscript called the "Thaton Yazawin" is basically the story of Gavaṁpati and his arrival at Suvaṇṇabhūmi Myo (or "city of Suvaṇṇabhūmi"), and about King Tissa Raja. Its copyist stated that the copying was completed in *Sakarāj* 1160 (AD 1789) on *Tawthalin Lasan,* 5th day (the fifth waxing day of the moon in the month of *Tawthalin,* about September). At the end, the copyist wrote that this was the old Mon language *yazawin* written by Gunawuddhi and others which he "corrected," but he gave no further details. Until a more thorough comparison can be made with other original Mon manuscripts dealing with Thatôn, it is difficult to know what text was actually copied by whom and whether this was the one U Kala used. Reel 74 of the Toyo Bunko microfilm project on Burma is a copy of this "Thaton Yazawin," (*List of Microfilms,* p. 22).

71. *The Royal Chronicles of Ayutthaya,* translated by Richard D. Cushman and edited by David K. Wyatt (Bangkok: The Siam Society, 2000).

72. Wyatt and Aroonrut, *Chiang Mai Chronicle,* xxvii–xxx, state that there are many versions of the *Chiang Mai Chronicle,* but that they chose the one which they considered the best. It is that version to which I refer.

73. This chronicle has been recently published in English. See Sithu Gamani Thingyan, *Zimme Yazawin.*

74. Than Tun, "Administration Under King Thalun (1629–1648)," *JBRS* 51, 2 (1968): 173–188.

75. Guides today will tell tourists that the style of the pagoda was taken from the shape of one of the queen's breasts, a totally unfounded local tradition.

76. Victor Lieberman, *Burmese Administrative Cycles: Anarchy and Conquest, c. 1580–1760* (Princeton: Princeton University Press, 1984).

77. U Kala, *Mahayazawingyi,* 1:174.

78. DPPN, 2:67.

79. The author confuses Mahāsamata with Mahāsamanta, p. 34.

80. *Slapat,* p. 48.

81. Shorto, *Nidāna,* p. 64.

82. *Slapat,* p. 66.

83. *Slapat,* p. 55. She was said to have given her weight in gold, which, with her crown on, was twenty-five *viss,* not quite ninety lbs., making her a slight woman indeed.

84. Shorto, "Gavampati," pp. 14–15. This is very interesting as the Trāp and paṇḍit inscriptions, probably erected by Yazadarit, are the only ones to mention a Rakṣapura.

85. *Maniyadanabon,* p. ix.

86. *Maniyadanabon,* p. x.

87. Actually Min Yaza died about the same time.

88. The manuscript of the old version, according to Tet Htoot, is in the India Office Library. But the microfilm copy I obtained from them, using the catalogue number given by Tet Htoot, is actually dated to 1825 and has "pt. VI" written on the cover. The other parts (I–V), presumed to have been related to this manuscript, are actually not.

89. *Maniyadanabon,* p. viii.

90. Twinthintaikwun, *Myanma Yazawinthit,* 1:85.

91. Bodawpaya could not have known at the time that later, under King Mindon, the author of the *Sāsanavaṃsa* found another direct link to the Third Council for Upper Burma's *saṅgha.*

92. Twinthintaikwun, *Myanma Yazawinthit,* 1:90. I checked the manuscript on palm leaf and it has the phrase *"lup kram"* in there as well. See *List of Microfilms,* reel 70, on leaf *(gu).* The statement about the white elephants with which to bring back the *Tipiṭakas* is also here.

93. *MM* I:34, p. 306. Since Twinthin would have been very familiar with Old Burmese, and was in charge of recasting the Old Burmese donative inscriptions, I wonder what role he had, if any, with regard to the now infamous "1067" recast inscription.

94. "Mahayazawinthit," palm-leaf MSS, leaf *"gu"* as reproduced in *List of Microfilms.*

95. For a brief synopsis of these issues, see Michael Aung-Thwin, "Burmese Historiography—Chronicles *(Yazawin),*" in *Making History: A Global Encyclopedia of Historical Writing,* ed. D. R. Woolf, (New York: Garland Publishing, 1997). There are some serious problems with regard to the title of the second volume of Twinthin's chronicle published in 1997. It appears as *Maha Yazawinthit* rather than *Myanma Yazawinthit,* which is the title of the first volume published in 1968. The difference is crucial and profound. The problem may lie with either the title of or the palm-leaf manuscript itself that was used for the 1997 publication. There are four versions of Twinthin's work in the National Archives: two are handwritten copies of palm-leaf manuscripts, and two are actual palm-leaf manuscripts, one is numbered 1472, and the other, in two parts, is numbered 2089 and 2090. The 1997 publica-

tion, subtitled as volumes 2 and 3, which includes the Nyaung Yan or Second Ava Dynasty, used manuscript no. 2090. I have scrutinized that manuscript on microfilm and it is indeed titled "Mahayazawinthit." But its colophon at the end states that it was "copied" in the year 1164 (1802 AD) on such and such a day, after three o'clock in the afternoon. It is therefore a copy and was completed during Twinthin's lifetime since he lived until 1809. The copyist may have absentmindedly reverted to the common title of *Maha Yazawin* instead of using the new *Myanma Yazawin*. Since Myint Swe, editor of the first volume does not provide the number of the palm-leaf manuscript he used, I am not certain which of the four his work represented. It is unlikely, however, that he used no. 2089, for the Myint Swe publication goes up to the end of King Tabinshwethi's reign in 1550, as does the palm-leaf manuscript numbered 1472, whereas manuscript 2089 goes up to the end of the First Ava Dynasty in 1527. However, because the second part of that manuscript (no. 1472) is missing, we still do not know when it was actually written. In any case, it is *not* the same as the first part of the *Maha Yazawinthit* (that is, no. 2089) for the reasons given. The only way to settle this is to check the original title of no. 1472, said to be located in the National Library. The Toyo Bunko's reel, no. 77, is listed as NL 1472 (National Library, 1472), but the palm leaf itself does not have an original title page, only the label put there by the microfilmers at the time of filming.

96. Sunait Chutintaranond, "King Bayinaung as Historical Hero in Thai Perspective," *Comparative Studies on Literature and History of Thailand and Myanmar* (Bangkok and Yangon: Chulalongkorn University Institute of Asian Studies and Yangon Universities' Historical Research Centre, 1997), pp. 9–15.

97. The other is the much earlier *Zatatawpon Yazawin*. However, as stated above, I do not wish to evaluate this chronicle on this particular issue unless I have the original or a microfilm copy of it. Its original organization may not be represented accurately in the published version.

98. Harvey, *Burma,* xxiii and p. 219.

99. Twinthintaikwun, *Myanma Yazawinthit, "Matika"* (table of contents) and the text itself, passim. In the copy of the manuscript at the National Archives from which the 1997 publication was derived, Twinthin begins each dynasty with a clearly demarcated introduction, indented and set apart from the rest by using only half the palm leaf and centering it, so that his intent for organizing his text according to centers of power is quite clear. This intent is reflected in the published version, even though it followed modern publishing protocols such as chapters, titles, and subtitles. In other words the published version seems to have faithfully reproduced the original in terms of organization into periods determined by capital cities, as far as it could with modern formatting and binding considerations. However, the original still needs to be scrutinized to be certain.

100. Twinthintaikwun, *Myanma Yazawinthit,* 1:89–91, describes the account.

101. The conventional translation of *Mahayazawingyi* is "great chronicle." But the "*maha*" (great in Sanskrit) is the qualifier of "*yaza*" (king) not of "*win*" (chronicle, from the Sanskrit "*vaṃsa*" or genealogy). The literal translation should be "history (or genealogy) of great kings" not "great history of kings." If the word "*gyi*" (great in Burmese) is also included in the translation, although here it is redundant, then the whole title should be "the great history of great kings."

102. *Hmannan,* 1:240.

103. *Hmannan,* 1:230–274.

104. Bode, Pali Literature, xi.

105. Shorto, "Gavampati Tradition," p. 20.

106. Paññāsāmi, *Sāsanavaṃsa,* p. 41.

107. Shorto, "Gavampati Tradition," pp. 16–17 for the translation of those inscriptions.

108. Paññāsāmi, *Sāsanavaṃsa,* p. 41.

109. Paññāsāmi, *Sāsanavaṃsa,* p. 44.

110. Paññāsāmi, *Sāsanavaṃsa,* pp. 69–71.

111. Most colonial authors considered Mindon a "good" king in contrast to Thibaw, his successor, in particular. Their criterion for his success and "goodness" was his willingness to accommodate the West and adopt western ways, such as developing the telegraph, Morse code, railways, a "modern" tax system, salaries, and so on. However, neither Mindon nor his subjects saw his success or failure in that way.

112. Bode, *Pali Literature,* p. 93.

113. Ludu Daw Ahmar, *The World's Biggest Book* (Mandalay: Kyipwayay Press, 1974).

114. The Sixth Synod was also convened by a Burmese leader, U Nu in 1954. See U Nu, *Saturday's Son* (New Haven: Yale University Press, 1975), p. 273.

115. Of course, if Nai Pan Hla is correct, Aniruddha's conquest was not mentioned because Bannya Dala allegedly skipped the first part where, presumably, it would have been included, although the provenance and date of that first part was not provided and remains unknown, and may even have been compiled only later, perhaps only in these volumes.

116. It was edited by Phra Candakanto (Pak La: Thailand, 1910). Harvey calls it the *Paklat Talaing Chronicle* in his *History,* p. 383. One should also be aware that this same volume has another title, *Pathama Sudhammavati Gavampati, Rajadhiraj* (see Charles Duroiselle, "Talaing Nissayas," *JBRS* 3, 2 (1913): 103–145).

117. Shorto translated this work, which he said was located on pages 26–99 of the first volume of chronicles issued from Pak Lat. In "The Gavampati Tradition," he stated that the manuscript from which this "Gavampati" text comes may go back to 1710 (p. 18).

118. Upon binding, it was titled the *Rājāwaṅsa Dhammacetī Mahāpiṭakadhara.* Shorto translated this work, but it remains unpublished. My thanks again to Victor Lieberman for sending me a copy.

119. Halliday, *The Talaings,* p. 130, and *Lik Smin Asah,* vii, note.

120. Halliday, in assessing the *Lik Smin Asah,* describes how this happened, and I suspect it happened in many other cases as well. It was not only a matter of people not knowing the older vocabulary, so that new words were substituted for the old ones without a secure knowledge of the former's meaning, or of making careless "typos," but it was also a deliberate attempt to rewrite what was currently thought to be the "truth" or an attempt to "improve" on the prose or verse of the older version. Sometimes, Halliday writes, long insertions were made, obscure words omitted with better-known ones taking their place, and a "manifest desire on the whole to make the text plainer" (p. v).

121. Duroiselle, "Talaing Nissayas," p. 105.

122. W. G. Cooper, "A Note on Talaing Nissaya and Vocabulary," *JBRS* 4, 2 (1914): 126.

123. Harvey, *History*, p. 27.

124. It is true that the *Nidāna* is said to have mentioned the conquest also, but there is no way of knowing whether that portion of the text can also be dated to 1538.

125. *Lik Smin Asah*, "Introduction."

126. Luce, *Old Burma*, 1:42.

127. Indeed, that Aniruddha "belonged" to other Theravāda Buddhist traditions is demonstrated by the many publications of the king by the Thai, such as "Anurut kham chan" (Anuruddha in Chan verse), published in BE 2502, and "Bot lakhon anurut roi rueang khong khun suwan" (The play "A hundred accounts of Anuruddha" by Khun Suwan), published in BE 2503. My thanks to Ken Breazeale for this information. See also Maneepin Phromsuthirak, "Thai Interpolations in the Story of Aniruddha," *JSS* 67, 1 (January 1979): 46–53.

128. Bayinnaung is regarded in the same manner by the Mon histories. He is called *Jamnah Duik Cah*, the conqueror of ten directions. Halliday, *The Talaings*, p. 132.

129. Luce explicitly cited the Kalyani Inscriptions in his *Old Burma*, 1:23; 2:286, as containing the conquest story.

Chapter Seven: The Mon Paradigm and the Origins of the Burma Script

1. By "the Burma script" I mean the written form of both the Mon and Burmese languages found during the Pagán period, which I also refer to as the "Pagán script" when the occasion warrants it. However, it is often disingenuously called the "Mon script" in early Burma scholarship so that its putative Mon origins are continuously underscored, even though those using the term know full well that the script was used more often to write Burmese (Luce, *Old Burma*, 1:52).

2. *EB* 1, 1:6. Also Halliday, in *The Talaings*, p. 120, writes that the alphabet "is practically the same as the Burmese, but it has two additional consonants and there are differences in the vowels."

3. I do not want to get involved in the Dvāravatī controversy per se, summarized recently by Robert L. Brown in his *Dvāravatī;* I simply want to say that Luce attributes the Burma script to that kingdom, polity, state, or whatever it may have been. According to David Wyatt, in his "Relics, oaths and politics in thirteenth-century Siam," *JSEAS* 32, 1 (February 2001): 3–65, here p. 6, notes 1 and 2, a stimulating synthesis of Dvāravatī's history can be found in Dhida Saraya's, *(Si) Thawarawadi* (Bangkok: Muang Boran, 1989). He also cites apparently the same work in English: Dhida Saraya, *(Sri) Dvaravati: The Initial Phase of Siam's History* (Bangkok: Muang Boran, 1999).

4. Luce, *Old Burma*, 1:97; ASB, *A List of Inscriptions Found in Burma*, comp. and ed. Charles Duroiselle (Rangoon: Government Printing, 1921), iv. Hereafter cited as *List*.

5. Harvey, p. 307; *List*, p. iv; Emmanuel Guillon, *The Mons*, p. 80; and Tha Myat, *Pyū Reader*. Duroiselle, in *List*, p. iv, wrote that although the Pyū script comes from Kadamba, the "Talaing" script comes from "the Pallavas of Kāñcipura." Aung Thaw,

Historical Sites, p. 31; Harvey, *History,* p. 307, both concurred but did not provide any supporting arguments.

6. Luce, *Old Burma,* 1:97, and with Ba Shin, "Pagan Myinkaba Kubyauk-Gyi Temple of Rajakumar (1113 A.D.) and the Old Mon Writings on Its Walls," *Bulletin of the Burma Historical Commission,* 2 (1961), p. 309. Yet Tha Myat, in his *Mun Myanma Ekaya Thamaing* [History of Mon-Myanma alphabet] (Yangon: Ministry of Culture (?), 1956), p. 40, states that the Śrī Kṣetra and Dvāravatī scripts are "similar" even if one did not derive from the other.

7. Luce, *Phases,* 1:162. See U Mya's *Votive Tablets,* plate no. 87, which shows the script.

8. The Pyū script of seventh- and eighth-century Śrī Kṣetra remained basically the same as that found on the early twelfth-century Myazedi Inscriptions, while the Old Mon script of Pagán showed no detectable changes until the mid-fifteenth-century inscriptions of Shin Saw Bu. This issue will be discussed below.

9. The two letters, according to Duroiselle, are the *"b"* and *"mha."* He wrote that the Talaing invented them "to represent sounds in their language which no Indian letters could do adequately . . . ." (*EB* 1, 1:6).

10. *EB* 1, 1:6–7.

11. *List,* pp. 2–4.

12. By "alphabet" I presume Duroiselle meant script, for the alphabet itself ultimately comes from Sanskrit.

13. *List,* iv.

14. Luce, *Phases,* 1:74, note 16.

15. Sastri, *History of South India,* p. 15, and chapter VIII.

16. Louis Finot, "Un nouveau document sur le bouddhisme birman," *Journal Asiatique,* 10th Series, 20 (July–August 1912), pp. 121–136; Tun Nyein, "Maunggun Gold Plates," pp. 101–102. Stargardt thinks Finot's thesis is erroneous (citing Falk's "Die Goldblätter"), and that the "real affinities . . . of both the golden Pali Text and lid rim inscription of the Great Silver reliquary lie with Andhra scripts of the 5th century. . . ." Her arguments are found in *Tracing Thought Through Things,* pp. 19–20; 24.

17. Much of the archaeological work done during the second and third decade of the twentieth century provided considerable new information on the so-called Pyū culture, a thrust led by Duroiselle, and published in the issues of the *Archaeological Survey of India* of the 1920s–1930s.

18. Blagden had begun to decipher the Pyū language almost immediately after the so-called Myazedi Inscriptions were found, and his results were published in the first issue of the *Epigraphia Birmanica,* although he had earlier published "A Preliminary Study of the Fourth Text of the Myazedi Inscriptions," *JRAS* (1911): 365–388.

19. Indeed, the Mon Paradigm was difficult to let go. Thus Luce wrote: " . . . the unlettered Burmans, even from the first, had adopted Mon script in spite of their linguistic, and very likely racial, closeness to the Pyū" ("The Ancient Pyū," p. 253).

20. *EB* 1, 1:7.

21. The Burmese alphabet is taken directly from the Pali/Sanskrit alphabet.

22. *Chau Ju-Kua,* pp. 58–59. It is true that there is some ambiguity regarding the word Pagán (note 10), but the translators seem to think it was a reference to

that kingdom. Missions were sent again in 1007, 1020, 1030, 1042, 1050, 1053, 1056, and 1061. Luce, in *Old Burma,* 1:58, reading the *Sung-shih* of T'o-t'o places another diplomatic mission in 1106 AD.

23. *Chau Ju-Kua,* p. 59, note 25.

24. Alexander Cunningham, *Mahâbodhi, or the great Buddhist temple under the Bodhi tree at Buddha-Gaya,* (Varanasi: Indological Book House, 1961), pp. 25–29, and plate XXIX. These dates are not without controversy (see Chapter Eight).

25. Shorto, *Dictionary of Mon Inscriptions,* p. x.

26. *MKPC* part 2:50–54.

27. Luce, "Countries Neighbouring Burma: Part 2," 170–205.

28. Luce, *Old Burma,* 1:97, where he wrote that the Burma script came via Dvāravatī from perhaps the Kāñcipura script of South India. Emmanuel Guillon seems to agree, saying that the Dvāravatī script belongs to the Old Tamil of the Pallavas as well as other scripts used in South India around the lower river valley of the Krisna (Guillon, *The Mons,* p. 79).

29. Luce and Ba Shin, "Pagan Myinkaba," 307–312.

30. Although I would have preferred to examine his theory on the basis either of his latest scholarship or an analysis specifically designed to address the issue at hand, as he left us none, this article is the best option we have.

31. Luce and Ba Shin, "Pagan Myinkaba," 309–312.

32. Shorto, *Dictionary of Mon Inscriptions,* xxviii.

33. Note that I am not speaking here of language evolution but of script evolution, which, in the writing of Old Mon in Burma spans a period from the late eleventh century to the mid-fifteenth century. It was only then that inscriptions written in Middle Mon proper appear. Even then, it differs from Old Mon "chiefly in certain archaic features of orthography." Shorto, *Dictionary of Mon Inscriptions,* p. x.

34. Luce and Ba Shin, "Pagan Myinkaba," 307.

35. This is dealt with in detail below. But a quick glance at Tha Myat's *Mun Myanma* makes the link between Śrī Kṣetra Pyū and Myazedi Pyū clear, and that between Kadamba and Śrī Kṣetra highly probable.

36. Luce and Ba Shin, "Pagan Myinkaba," 307.

37. Luce and Ba Shin, for example, accept the date for Dvāravatī from Coedes's paleographic assessment of the Lopburi pillar (see "Pagan Myinkaba," 307).

38. Wheatley, *Nāgara,* p. 203. among others.

39. H. Krishna Sastri, then assistant archaeological superintendent for epigraphy, Southern Circle, examined several inscribed terracotta tablets found at Pagán and concluded that on one, he recognized characters that were "partly Grantha" (Taw Sein Ko, *Burmese Sketches,* 2:284).

40. Gerald Diffloth, *The Dvaravatii Old Mon Language and Nyah Kur* (Bangkok: Chulalongkorn University Printing House, 1984).

41. This sixteenth-century dating may, however, be debatable, because back in the 1930s Coedes dated two Haripuñjaya inscriptions very tentatively to the thirteenth century: 1218 and 1219 AD (*Epigraphic Studies,* p. 187). In contrast, the most thorough and recent research that supports the statement that there is only one dated Mon inscription (to 1504) comes from "Charuk nai prathet thai lem 2 akson panlawa akson mon phuttha sattawat thi 12–21" (Inscriptions in Thailand, volume 2, Pallava and Mon Scripts, Buddhist Centuries 12–21), in *Charuk nai prathet thai*

[Inscriptions in Thailand], 5 volumes (Bangkok: National Library and Fine Arts Department, B.E. 2529 [1986]), ed. Kongkaeo Wiraprachak. My thanks to Ken Breazeale for providing me with both this information and a synopsis of each inscription.

42. Diffloth, *Nyah Kur,* pp. 11–13.

43. Diffloth, *Nyah Kur,* p. 27.

44. Diffloth, *Nyah Kur,* pp. 5–11. However, the Old Mon inscription of Ban Thalar, about sixty-five kilometers north of Vientiane, is a puzzle, with an early date conjecturally and tentatively assigned to it by Guillon.

45. Diffloth assigns the Old Mon inscriptions of Haripuñjaya, Mokhei near the Kra, and Nakhon Sri Thammarat to the twelfth or thirteenth centuries. *Nyah Kur,* page 6.

46. Diffloth, *Nyah Kur,* p. 11. Notice that I am not referring to the language but to the script.

47. See Luce, *Phases,* 1:162–167, 175; U Mya, *Votive Tablets,* passim.

48. The first dated evidence of Old Mon in Burma is found in Kyanzittha's Old Prome Inscription of 1093, to be documented more fully below.

49. *MKPC* includes all known, dated and undated, Old Mon inscriptions of Burma discovered up to 1965. This includes three cited by Luce, in *Phases,* 1:172–177, found in Lower Burma, two of which he implied may be pre-Pagán. All are undated and written in the Pagán script. One is a votive tablet found in the Bingyi Cave at Thatôn (and not included in *MKPC*), which U Mya, the scholar most renowned for his work with Burma's votive tablets, assigns to a much later period. He thinks it postdates the reigns of both Aniruddha and Kyanzittha and resembles the script found during King Narapatisithu's reign, in the very late twelfth century. It may have actually belonged to the thirteenth century. (U Mya, *Votive Tablets,* pp. 54–55.) On the whole, he writes that the tablets found at Thatôn are very much like Pagán votive tablets with some small differences. I include in this corpus of Old Mon inscriptions three additional votive tablets discovered after *MKPC* was published: one found in 1971 at Momeit, another at Kalaymyo in 1983, and a third, whose provenance was not given but is likely to be Pagán. These are described by Nai Pan Hla in "Old Terracotta Votive Tablets," pp. 156–157. They are also undated and written in the already evolved Pagán script so they do not provide any new information on the present issue. And finally, two terracotta tablets written in Mon have been found at Winga, a Lower Burma urban site. U Myint Aung describes this site in his "Excavations," pp. 52–53. He writes that Nai Pan Hla assigned their paleography to the sixth century since they were said to resemble those of Pharapathom in Thailand. If by Pharapathom he means Nakhon Pathom, where there is an inscription that Diffloth also assigns to the sixth century AD (p. 7), it has several problems. First, it is undated, and since, as stated above, Old Mon spans a long period of time, it is difficult to say to which century it belongs. Second, someone could have carried these votive tablets to Winga since there is no proof that they were made there. Third, Thai Mon scholars have assigned the date of the script on those tablets to the twelfth century. (Diffloth, p. 7). Finally, even if the script is sixth century and even if the tablets were produced at Winga, it still says nothing about the presence of a Mon kingdom or state there. Besides, as shown elsewhere, the earliest TL dates of Winga potsherds are late fifteenth to seventeenth century.

50. Guillon, *The Mons,* p. 80.

51. Indeed, no link between the script found at the pagoda and the Mon ethnic group has been established, just assumed, especially in Luce's *Phases,* 1:162; Aung Thaw, *Historical Sites,* pp. 111, 116; and U Mya's, *Votive Tablets,* pp. 61–62. Besides, as noted, there are only seven fragmentary Old Mon inscriptions of the alleged kingdom of Dvāravatī, even if one counts each separately. They are the two fragments from Nakhon Pathom on one stone, which Shorto dates to the sixth century, and four votive inscriptions on an octagonal pillar from San Sung, Lopburi, which he guesses may have belonged to the seventh century (Shorto, *Dictionary of Mon Inscriptions,* p. xxviii, and Diffloth, *Nyah Kur,* pp. 4–11.) Since Shorto's publication, Guillon updates the number with five more fragments. (See Guillon, *The Mons,* p. 81.) All are written on terracotta tablets, also without dates. This means that not only are they too small in number to be of much use as a standard, their chronology is not certain. And, they could have been made at any time during the five-century span when Old Mon existed or could have been carried to or from anywhere.

52. Although this may put a damper on the 1067 Old Burmese inscription that has been declared late because of its cursive style, it is the Tamil with which we are here concerned.

53. Sastri, *History of South India,* p. 15.

54. Luce, "Pagan Myinkaba," p. 308.

55. Shorto, *Dictionary of Mon Inscriptions,* p. xxviii; Guillon, p. 81.

56. As demonstrated earlier, there were, until very recently, a total of only about twenty-five Mon inscriptions found in Thailand. Of these, only one has a date, of 1504. Shorto's *Dictionary of Mon Inscriptions* also has a short paragraph on discoveries of Mon inscriptions too late to be incorporated in it (p. xxxiii). But it has been supplemented by Diffloth's, *Nyah Kur,* pages 4–11, and Bauer's *Guide to Mon Studies* and his newer "Notes On Mon Epigraphy." None of these has materially affected my analysis.

57. One of the coins appears to be a Pyū issue (Skilling, "Dvaravati," p. 94, illustration 24). If true, it suggests some contact between the Pyū of Śrī Kṣetra and Dvāravatī. They were contemporaries, and the possibility raises some interesting questions.

58. Robert Brown in his *Dvāravatī,* p. xxi, said it best: ". . . it is almost totally without a history. Not one monument or art object is dated. There are no indigenous texts associated with Dvāravatī. While there are a few Dvāravatī inscriptions, these are almost exclusively religious, consisting mostly of quotations from standard Indian texts. The only other written information regarding the culture comes from some brief references in Chinese histories."

59. See *MKPC "Matika"* (table of contents), pages sa to ta.

60. Diffloth, *Nyah Kur,* p. 10.

61. The number depends on how and what one counts.

62. Diffloth, *Nyah Kur,* pp. 4–11. Indeed, there is even a difference between Dvāravatī Old Mon and Haripuñjaya Old Mon, which raises some very interesting issues to be addressed below.

63. Woodward, *The Art and Architecture of Thailand,* p. 137.

64. Indeed, the Wieng Mano Inscription of Lampun, the capital of Haripuñjaya, said to be the earliest Old Mon Haripuñjaya inscription is not dated, although

the dates *assigned* to it differ from individual to individual depending on their theoretical proclivities. Whereas Shorto assigns it to around 1100, Luce, not surprisingly, prefers a tenth-century date. But their grounds for dating it this early are based on the Mon Paradigm's premises (see *Epigraphic Studies,* p. 186, for a discussion of this inscription.)

65. *Sheaf of Garlands,* p. 104, note 1.

66. Luce, "Pagan Myinkaba," 309.

67. Diffloth, *Nyah Kur,* p. 10. For its translation, see *Epigraphic Studies,* pp. 185–189.

68. As for the language, unlike Dvāravatī Old Mon, Haripuñjaya Old Mon not only represents a late phase of Old Mon which was just starting to show some characteristics of Middle Mon, but scholars are beginning to find linguistic differences between Burma Old Mon and Dvāravatī Old Mon as well (Diffloth, *Nyah Kur,* pp. 10–11), suggesting that the journey taken by Old Mon may need even further reconsideration.

69. To be cited below.

70. Tha Myat, *Mun-Myanma,* p. 8.

71. He is listed, although rarely, as a "reference," but one wonders whether his work was actually read. Shorto lists him in his *Dictionary of Mon Inscriptions,* p. xxxvi and puts him in the bibliography. Luce properly credits him also, but cites his work only in a footnote, without any attempt to summarize his contrary thesis. Luce, *Phases,* 1:74, note 21.

72. U Tha Myat, who has studied the Pyū script carefully, comparing it with the major Indian scripts of the time, concludes that the Pyū writing on the Myazedi Inscriptions did not use Indian scripts of the same era (eighth to twelfth century AD) but of an earlier era without changing them, even when changes had occurred in India itself. See his *Myazedi Khaw Gubyauk Kyi Pyū Kyauksa* [The Pyū Inscription of the so-called Myazedi] (Rangoon: Democracy Publishing Co., Ltd, 1958?), pp. 7–8, and also his *Mun-Myanma,* p. 8.

73. Tun Nyein, "Maunggun Gold Plates," pp. 101–102.

74. Finot, "Un nouveau document," pp. 121–136.

75. See Luce, *Phases,* 1:61 for these details.

76. Luce, *Phases,* 1, p. 74. See also ASB, *Exploration and Research: Report of the Superintendent for the Year 1937–38* (Rangoon: Government Printing, 1938), pp. 10–11; and ASI, *Annual Report* (Calcutta: Government Printing, 1936–1937), p. 80.

77. Even if Stargardt's opinion of Falk's article, "Die goldblätter" is correct, and the Pyū script came from Andhra instead of Vanavasi, it still does not mean that the Pagán script came from Dvāravatī. Unfortunately Stargardt does not provide the necessary details in her *Tracing Thoughts* for me to determine whether Falk's thesis is viable. The point being made here, in any case, is that the Pagán script did not come from the Dvāravatī script.

78. Aung Thaw, *Historical Sites,* p. 4.

79. Stargardt, *Ancient Pyū,* p. 291.

80. Tha Myat, *Pyū Phat Ca,* pp. 19–78. I have counted an inscription as distinct when the donor, place, occasion, or date are different.

81. Tha Myat, *Pyū Phat Ca,* p. 37.

82. Tha Myat, *Pyū Phat Ca,* p. 22.

83. Luce, *Phases,* 1:62. The reason for Luce's date is complicated but clearly has to do with his thesis that Halin was the last capital of the Pyū, the one he said was raided by Nanchao forces. His identification that it was Halin is based on the notion that the Mi-no of the *Man Shu* was Halin, which makes it impossible for Halin to be earlier than Śrī Kṣetra.

84. This assignment is not altogether uncontested. Guillon does not agree with the date of at least one of those inscriptions in *The Mons,* p. 80. But the originally assigned date may have been the reason Luce wrote that "we need to remember that the earliest extant (Tircul) writing dates from the seventh century AD . . . ," which then places it later than sixth-century Dvāravatī Mon, a convenient date. *Phases,* 1:62.

85. Shorto, *Dictionary of Mon Inscriptions,* p. xxviii; Coedes, *Indianized,* pp. 76–77. Guillon also disputes some of this in *The Mons,* p. 79. Diffloth thinks the oldest may be the Phu Krang Inscription, which may be datable to the sixth century AD, while others (Thoem, Champa) think it may be twelfth century (Diffloth, p. 7).

86. Stargardt, *Tracing Thought Through Things,* p. 25.

87. U Tha Myat, *Pyū Phat Ca,* p. 21.

88. Luce, *Phases,* 1:65–66.

89. U Tha Myat, *Pyū Phat Ca,* p. 22; Luce, *Phases,* 1:66.

90. U Tha Myat, *Pyū Phat Ca,* pp. 21–22.

91. Sastri, *History of South India,* p. 15.

92. Part of the confusion stems from scholars using dynastic names such as Kadamba and Pallava for the scripts they used.

93. Most early and recent scholars consider these to be from about 500 AD onward. See Tun Nyein, "Maunggun Gold Plates," p. 101; Finot, "Un nouveau document . . . ," p. 131, as cited in Coedes, *Indianized,* p. 287; and Stargardt, *Tracing Thought Through Things,* p. 20.

94. On this manuscript, see Duroiselle, *ASI* (1927): 179–180; 200–201, and U Lu Pe Win, *ASB* (1939):12–22. Luce thinks it is in Gupta script. See his *Phases,* 1:139.

95. Tha Myat, *Pyū Phat Ca,* pp. 38–39.

96. Tha Myat, *Pyū Phat Ca,* pp. 50–51.

97. Aung Thaw, *Historical Sites,* p. 116.

98. Luce, *Phases,* 1:164.

99. *ASI* (1937): 80–81; Luce, *Phases,* 1:167.

100. Tha Myat, *Pyū Phat Ca,* p. 77. Although neither this votive tablet nor the Shwéhsandaw is dated, the latter is thought to belong to Aniruddha's reign.

101. Tha Myat, *Pyū Phat Ca,* p. 78.

102. Bob Hudson et al., "Origins of Bagan."

103. Sastri had reason to think that the Burmese numerals of the early Pagán period, Aniruddha's time, were "more allied to Telugu and Kannada than to Tamil." (Cited in Taw Sein Ko, *Burmese Sketches,* 2, p. 317).

104. Finot assigns the script on these gold plates of Maung Kan to the sixth century on paleographic grounds and also thinks the script is Kadama. ("Un nouveau document," pp. 121–136) as recalled by Luce, in *Phases* 1:175.

105. Tha Myat, *Mun Myanma,* charts, passim.

106. That one numeral found on the gold-leaf manuscript discovered at Śrī

Kṣetra and assigned to the seventh century "looks more like Old Burmese" to Luce (*Phases,* 1:140) seems to confirm that suggestion.

107. Tha Myat, *Mun Myanma,* p. 15. For a large (approximately 4' x 5') comprehensive chart on the writing system of Burma, see Burma, *Report of the Director, Archaeological Survey, Burma for the year ending 30th September 1958* (Yangon: Archaeological Survey, nd), back cover inset. This volume is actually in Burmese, although the English title cited herein also appears on the cover; the Burmese title actually has: "for the years 1957–58."

108. Tha Myat, *Mun Myanma,* p. 15.

109. Robert Shafer, "Further Analysis of the Pyu Inscriptions," *Harvard Journal of Asiatic Studies* 8, 4 (September 1943): 313–366.

110. Tha Myat, *Pyū Phat Ca* and *Myazedi* make clear this link between the Burmese and Pyū scripts. See also Blagden's discussion on this issue in *EB* 1, 1:60.

111. This is common knowledge, but see Halliday, *The Talaings* p. 119.

112. *EB* 1, 1:60; Luce, *Phases,* 1:63;

113. Luce, *Phases,* 1:140.

114. Luce, *Phases,* 1:63. Indeed, if we scrutinize the glossary provided by Blagden in *EB* 1, 1:64–68, the closeness of the two languages is astonishing. Taw Sein Ko had suggested prior to Blagden's work not only that Pyū might be related to Lolo and Lisu, but that its living representative might well be Kadu. See Taw Sein Ko, "The Linguistic Affinities of the Pyū Language," *JBRS* 5, 2 (1915): 102–110.

115. *EB* 1, 1:61.

116. *EB* 1, 1:59–68. Also Blagden, "A Preliminary Study." The Pyū words for "wife" and "son" (or offspring), are not only exactly the same as in Burmese but are spelled in almost exactly the same way on the Myazedi, the only difference being the "*yecha*" (long vowel marker) used in the Burmese and left out in the Pyū. Even the tone markers for both are identical.

117. Luce, *Phases,* 1:64.

118. Hla Pe, "A Tentative List of Mon Loan Words in Burmese," *JBRS* 50, 1 (June, 1967): 70–94.

119. Luce, "Mons of the Pagán Dynasty," p. 3.

120. Blagden, "Etymological Notes—Thaton," p. 28.

121. Luce's favored criterion is phonetics. See his *Phases,* 2, charts, passim.

122. U Tha Myat, *Myazedi,* pp. 7–8. See also A. H. Dani, *Indian Paleography* (Oxford: Clarendon Press, 1963), pp. 241–247.

123. Luce, *Phases,* 1:62.

124. Shafer, "Further Analysis," found some changes in grammar and phonetics.

125. *EB* 1, 1:61.

126. Tha Myat, *Pyū Phat Ca,* p. 21.

127. Luce, *Phases,* 1:62.

128. The last mention of a Pyū king, Sīhavikrama, dates to 718 AD (Luce, "Ancient Pyū," p. 248).

129. Backus, *Nan-chao,* p. 98.

130. Backus, *Nan-chao,* p. 102. However, Luce disputes this in "Sources," pp. 37–39.

131. *Man Shu,* p. 91.

132. Hall, *Burma,* p. 10.

133. The patronymic linkage system of most of the people of the Nanchao kingdom, whereby the name of a son always contains an element from that of his father, is also a feature in the Burmese chronicles' account of the early part of the Pagán Dynasty going back to a Pyūminhti (Umbrella of the Pyū King) (U Kala, *Mahayazawingyi,* 1:140–145.) For a discussion of the issues and myths concerning Nanchao, see Backus's treatment in *Nan-chao kingdom,* chapter 3. See also Blackmore, "The Rise of Nan-chao in Yunnan."

134. After the "decline" of Śrī Kṣetra as the center of political power in Burma, only three Pyū inscriptions are found in the next five centuries, only one of which can be considered a script of any stature: the Pyū face on the Myazedi.

135. Aung-Thwin, *Pagán,* p. 21.

136. Luce, "Ancient Pyu."

137. Tha Myat, *Pyū Phat Ca,* p. 77. This is a very interesting Pyū inscription, for it was a donation by a person with the title of *"Samben Srī Bañano,"* which Mon Paradigm scholars say is a Mon title. Yet the word *"Srī"* in the title does not use the unique Mon form of a dot in the middle of a nearly complete circle, but uses the form one finds in Burmese. The word in Pyū clearly predates any found in Mon. See also Luce, *Phases,* 1:66.

138. Chen Yi-Sein, "The Chinese Inscription at Pagán," *BBHC* 1, 2 (December 1960): 153–157.

139. *SMK* 1:83; 2:40; 3:202, 262; 4:175. In English, see Luce, *Phases,* 1:66–67. What is also interesting is the association made (in an Ava inscription, *SMK* 5:105) between "daughters of Brahmins and Pyū daughters" as if the two were synonymous.

Chapter Eight: The Place of Written Burmese and Mon in Burma's Early History

1. Although there are two stones, they are not exact duplicates so that early epigraphists labeled them "A" and "B." If parts of one were illegible, the other was used and vice versa. Although the presence of two originals in itself may seem curious, Taw Sein Ko in 1913 offered an explanation for it. He suggested that one was a copy, since it was struck on lower-grade (soft-grained) stone, used large letters that were not carefully struck, and was found near the Library. The other was inscribed on fine-grained stone, with precise, small, clear letters; it was obviously well made and was recovered near the assumed place of donation (Taw Sein Ko, *Burmese Sketches,* 1:65). If he is correct, that opens up the whole issue of whether copies in general are necessarily late and therefore unreliable. They could be contemporaneous to the original and should therefore be treated as primary, rather than secondary evidence.

2. I say "conventionally dated" because it is not entirely clear to what the dates on the stones refer. That they were erected between 1111 and 1113 (an issue to be discussed below), seems reasonably clear. But the date could be referring to the time Arimaddanapūra (Pagán) was founded, the accession of King Kyanzittha, or the time the donation recorded on the inscriptions was made. There are at least two different readings and translations of this first, important sentence on the Pyū face of the inscriptions. U Tha Myat, in his *Myazedi Pyu Kyauksa,* pp. 28 and 30, gives one. Blagden, the first to decipher the Pyū face of the inscriptions—he published

his findings nearly half a century earlier as "A Preliminary Study of the Fourth Text of the Myazedi Inscriptions"—gives the other reading on pp. 365–388. See also C. O. Blagden, "The Talaing Inscription of the Myazedi Pagoda at Pagan, With a Few Remarks on the Other Versions," *JRAS* 25 (1909): 1017–1051.

3. Shorto, *Dictionary of Mon Inscriptions* (ix–x, xxviii), considers this to be the first dated Old Mon inscription of Burma. U Chit Thein's comprehensive collection of Old Mon lithic inscriptions supports Shorto's assessment by showing that there is no dated Old Mon inscription of Burma before 1093. Luce, of course, could not concede this, as he had already assigned the Trāp and Paṇḍit inscriptions to "c. 1050," even though they have no legible dates on them. Similarly, he assigns another Old Mon inscription, found thirty miles north of Maulamyaing (Moulmein) in the Kawgun Cave, also not dated, to "shortly before Aniruddha's capture of Thatôn (c. 1057 AD)" (Luce and Ba Shin, "Pagan Myinkaba," p. 308). Such self-serving conjectures aside, there is not a single original, *dated* Old Mon inscription of Burma that predates Kyanzittha's Old Prome Inscription of 1093. Indeed, even Luce admitted that this inscription was "the earliest version of his [Kyanzittha's] legend" (see *Old Burma,* 1:55).

4. One of the first to say this, back in 1912, was Taw Sein Ko in his *Burmese Sketches,* p. 271. Ba Shin, in his *Lokahteikpan: Early Burmese Culture in a Pagán Temple* (Rangoon: Burma Historical Commission, 1962), reiterates it on pp. 20–43. Also Ba Shin and Luce, in "Pagán Myinkaba," p. 277, wrote that the Burmese on the Myazedi was "the first known dated inscription in Burmese." This statement has been repeated time and again until it has become "common knowledge" in Burma Studies. It is still being repeated by scholars of Southeast Asia, few of whom had actually done original research on the issue using primary sources. See, for example, David Bradley's *Proto-Loloish* (Copenhagen: Scandinavian Institute of Asian Studies, 1979), p. 17; Guillon, *The Mons,* p. 53; and George Van Driem, *Languages of the Himalayas,* 1 (Leiden: E.J. Brill, 2001): 270, 438, 439. My thanks to Lily Handlin for the Van Driem citation.

5. The first serious, scholarly study, by Duroiselle and Blagden, to compare Old Mon and Old Burmese from epigraphic sources used only the data on the Myazedi Inscriptions, whose Old Burmese was already assumed to be the earliest evidence of Burmese and later than Old Mon, so theirs was a foregone conclusion (EB 1, 1:1–67).

6. Even this information is not unambiguous. U Tha Myat's translation of the same Pyū face states that the "1,628 years after the *parinibbānna*" was a reference to the official naming of Pagán as Arimaddanapūra, not Kyanzittha's accession (Tha Myat, *Myazedi,* p. 30).

7. Ba Shin, *Lokahteikpan,* p. 25.

8. Most Burma scholars assume cursive Burmese to be *late,* not early. The issue of whether cursiveness indicates earliness or lateness is inconsistently applied by scholars of Old Burmese throughout the literature.

9. Ba Shin, *Lokahteikpan,* p. 25.

10. Luce and Ba Shin, "Pagan Myinkaba," p. 315.

11. Shorto, *Dictionary of Mon Inscriptions,* p. xi.

12. Shorto, *Dictionary of Mon Inscriptions,* p. ix.

13. Queen Ajāwlat stated that she herself, not her mother, had the stone

inscribed, by several persons of stature, which would explain the fine quality of "Queen's Burmese." See *SMK* 1:29–31. Luce, who trained in English literature, probably knew the significance of "Queen's English" in English history, and this may have informed his ideas about Queen Ajāwlat's inscription and its "standardization" of Burmese.

14. For example, see *SMK* 3:1, 2, 122–123, passim.

15. The inscription can be found in *SMK* 2:33–50, but the published version will not reveal those characteristics; one has to observe the actual stone or its rubbing. It appears that the scribe even had different size vowel circles for different consonants (which written Burmese is cognizant of today) in order not to obfuscate the text. I measured each letter of the rubbing hanging on my wall. The stretching of the rice paper on which the rubbing was made sometimes adds a millimeter to the letters in that stretched area, but otherwise, the letters are exactly the same size.

16. Compare, for instance, the inscriptions of any of the kings, queens, ministers, daughters of ministers, and so on, with any commissioned by commoners, of which there are many. The discrepancy is quite obvious. See *SMK* 1, 2, 3, 4, and 5, passim.

17. For one example, see *A Comparative Word-List of Old Burmese, Chinese and Tibetan,* (London: School of Oriental and African Studies), 1981, published posthumously.

18. Luce, *Phases,* 2:1–130.

19. There are many who have claimed this, but I cite only one: Ba Shin, *Lokahteikpan,* p. 25.

20. Although not surprising, it is revealing, that three Old Mon inscriptions in Burma dated by Shorto to the thirteenth and fourteenth centuries were dated by Luce to the eleventh and early twelfth centuries, clearly to support the Mon Paradigm (see Shorto, *Dictionary of Mon Inscriptions,* p. xxxiii).

21. I am referring to both the so-called "Bodawpaya" volumes of inscriptions that were published in the late nineteenth and early twentieth centuries, around the time Blagden published his theories in *Epigraphia Birmanica. List,* edited by Duroiselle, was also available shortly thereafter. Later, of course, the huge five-volume *Inscriptions of Burma* was published, which included a selection of inscriptions that Luce and Pe Maung Tin considered to be "original."

22. Since I contend that the Mon Paradigm's evolutionary sequence is flawed, I do not follow its sequence of Archaic, Standard Old, and Modern and will refer to all Pagán Burmese as Old Burmese.

23. In the extremely valuable *List,* Duroiselle counted fifty Burmese inscriptions that precede the Myazedi, both copies and originals. I take my count from *SMK; Selections from the Inscriptions of Pagán; Pagan Kyauksa Let Ywe Sin* [Selected inscriptions of Pagán], comp. E Maung (Rangoon: Pannya Nanda Press, 1958), volume 1; and *MM,* none of which is entirely comprehensive by itself, but taken together are nearly so.

24. *MM.*

25. *MM, ka.*

26. Aung-Thwin, "Sāsana Reform."

27. Duroiselle, *List,* p. v.

28. *MM,* pp. 1–133.

29. U Kala, *Mahayazawingyi,* 1:188–196, 201; *The Glass Palace Chronicle,* pp. 91–92.

30. Luce, *Old Burma* 1:285–298.

31. Bob Hudson, "Pagán and Its Monasteries: Time, Space and Structure in Burma's Medieval Buddhist City," B.A. (Honors) thesis, Archaeology Department, University of Sydney, 1997. For a recent synopsis, see Hudson et al., "Origins of Bagan," pp. 49–53.

32. Aung-Thwin, *Pagan,* chapter 8, pages 188–189 (graphs).

33. See, *MM* 1:1–216, inscription numbers 1–24. The one in question is a late copy, but it is clear, particularly the date. There are others as well. For example, see *Selections from the Inscriptions of Pagán,* nos. 1–4; *Pagan Kyauksa Let Ywe Sin,* 1; and *SMK* 1:321–329.

34. See *MM,* p. 1.

35. Aung-Thwin, *Pagan,* p. 22.

36. *MM,* pp. 1–216.

37. I have excluded the 1067 Inscription in this count for reasons discussed in Chapter Five. Besides, the Mon Paradigm scholars themselves date it to the sixteenth century.

38. *Pagán Kyauksa Let Ywe Sin,* p. 1. It is also found in *Selections from the Inscriptions of Pagán,* pp. 1–2.

39. There is a reference to 444 at the very end of the inscription but one cannot be certain it is a date since the term *"Sakarāj"* does not precede the number as it should. It is possible that the mason forgot to place the date at the beginning of the stone, where it is usually placed, and by the time he reached the end had no space left.

40. *Selections from the Inscriptions of Pagán,* nos. 1 to 4, pp. 1–8. I have not counted the obverse of the Hlèdauk Inscription since it includes thirteenth-century information.

41. Cunningham, *Mahâbodhi,* p. 27.

42. See J. S. Furnivall's "The Cycle of Burmese Year-Names," *JBRS* 12, 2 (August 1922): 80–95.

43. See his "Sources of Early Burma History," p. 39, where Luce said he read the "hand copy of his [Cunningham's] plate XXIX rather than the photograph and came up with "[sa]karac [6]55 khu // siridhammarajakuru . . . (kusil//)."

44. *Zatatawpon,* p. 39.

45. Cunningham, *Mahâbodhi,* p. 27, gives a different account of it, attributing the "discovery" to Col. Henry Burney rather than his brother, although Colonel Burney himself attributes it to his brother; see Henry Burney, "Translation of an Inscription in the Burmese Language, discovered at Buddha Gaya, in 1833," *Asiatic Researches* 20, 1 (1836): 161–189.

46. Cunningham, *Mahâbodhi,* pp. 75–77.

47. See Cunningham, *Mahâbodhi,* plate XXIX.

48. See Cunningham, *Mahâbodhi,* plate XXIX.

49. See note 31 in Luce, "Sources of Early Burma," p. 37.

50. Luce, "Sources of Early Burma," p. 38. On pages 40–42, Luce was rather critical of Cunningham for "misreading" the date on the umbrella, but not those on the stone inscription. The reason Luce gave for criticizing Cunningham had to

do, ostensibly, with Cunningham's being misled by the Ava scholars in reading the dates on the stone, not on the umbrella. It was another in a series of Luce non sequiturs.

51. *Inscriptions of Burma,* plate 299, Portfolio III.

52. Cunningham, *Mahâbodhi,* p. 28.

53. J. C. Eade's *Southeast Asian Ephemeris: Solar and Planetary Positions A.D. 368–2000* (Ithaca, NY: Cornell University Southeast Asia Program, 1989) confirms Cunningham's findings. Luce, in "Sources of Early Burma," cites Cunningham's work in note 32, p. 39, which means he knew of Cunningham's results regarding the impossible thirteenth-century dates, yet he is silent about this matter.

54. However, the inscription's Friday, the 10th of *Pyatho* in Cunningham's date of *Sakarāja* 441 actually falls on a Thursday. Eade's mathematical calculations have taken into account the various intercalary months and leap years that allow a discrepancy of perhaps one "off" day. The off day can be affected by whether the following or preceding month is an intercalary one or the next month is the beginning of a new year, which in the case of Cunningham's date, it is (Eade, *Southeast Asian Ephemeris,* p. 83).

55. Again, my thanks to Ken Breazeale for this information.

56. Luce, "Sources of Early Burma," p. 41.

57. These have been calculated by Ken Breazeale from Eade's work.

58. The calendar in the jacket pocket of the book belonged to U Ka whose help Luce acknowledged but the calendar is in Luce's handwriting. He also cited Sir Alfred M. B. Irwin's *The Burmese Calendar* (Bombay: British India Press, 1910) and Irwin's *The Burmese and Arakanese Calendars* (Rangoon: 1909).

59. Disāpramok was minister to three successive kings of Pagán, Min Yaza to three at Ava, and Kin Wun Mingyi to at least two during the Kônbaung Dynasty.

60. Cunningham, *Mahâbodhi,* p. 27. There are several translations of the entire inscription, but Luce's "Sources of Early Burma," pp. 40–42, represents the most contested.

61. *SMK* 1:326–327. To make sure my reading was correct, I asked a noted expert in Old Burmese, U Saw Tun of Northern Illinois University, for his opinion. He, in turn, corresponded with another expert, U Tin Htwe of Heidelberg University. U Tin Htwe's response amounted to seventeen pages of closely written Burmese regarding approximately four lines of this inscription, which shows the kinds of difficulties we sometimes encounter.

62. This date could be identical to Burney's reading, depending on the day of the week and the month involved.

63. *EB* 1, 2:163–164.

64. Luce, "Sources of Early Burma," pp. 41–42.

65. *EB* 1, 2:148, 150.

66. Luce, *Old Burma,* 1:62.

67. Luce, *Old Burma,* 1:63.

68. Duroiselle, "Excavations at Pagán," *Annual Report of the Archaeological Survey of India, 1926–27* (Calcutta: Government of India, 1930), pp. 167–168.

69. Ba Shin, *Lokahteikpan,* pp. 24–25.

70. Ba Shin, *Lokahteikpan,* pp. 36–39.

71. Ba Shin, *Lokahteikpan,* p. 35. Luce also stated this. See his and Ba Shin's "Pagan Myinkaba," p. 277.

72. Ba Shin, *Lokahteikpan,* p. 35.

73. The dating of many undated Pagán temples has also been determined by the assumptions of the Mon Paradigm (discussed in Chapter Nine), so that one could make a case that the entire field of the art and architectural history of Pagán is open to reexamination. It will be interesting to see what kind of art historical sequence emerges from such a reexamination.

74. Cunningham, *Mahâbodhi,* plate XXIV.

75. U Mya, *Votive Tablets.*

76. Luce, *Old Burma,* 2:2–43.

77. Ray, *Sanskrit,* pp. 31–32.

78. Luce, *Old Burma,* 2:31.

79. Nai Pan Hla, "Old Terracotta Votive Tablets," pp. 145–164, writes that two tablets thought to have been inscribed by Aniruddha were discovered in the 1970s and 1980s, both in the Dry Zone of Burma, written in the Mon language. Although it is difficult to make any conclusions about them, the fact that Aniruddha also wrote in Mon on his tablets should not be surprising, given his conquest of Lower Burma and his efforts at unification. The problem here lies with identifying these particular tablets with Aniruddha.

80. Luce, *Old Burma,* 2:2–31. Note that since Mon and Burmese scripts were the same, I have counted only those that had the actual Mon language represented, not those that are in Pali written in what is labeled as "Mon script," for that assumes the Mon Paradigm is correct, therefore making the conclusion circular.

81. Gutman, *Burma's Lost Kingdoms.*

82. U Mya, *Votive Tablets,* plate no. 39, description on page 76. But it is not certain these belonged to Saw Lu because the title on them could have represented another Pagán king, such as Kyanzittha.

83. Luce, *Old Burma,* 1:100.

84. Aung-Thwin, *Pagan.*

85. The literacy rate in Pagán is, of course, not known. But the majority of the Old Burmese inscriptions of the Pagán period were erected by commoners and non-royalty (see Aung-Thwin's *Pagan,* chart on p. 240), which suggests that such activity was not an elite monopoly. The first census after annexation of Upper Burma, according to J. S. Furnivall, *Colonial Policy and Practice: A Comparative Study of Burma and Netherlands India* (New York: New York University Press, 1956), pp. 13, 122, 208, reveals a male literacy rate in Upper Burma of 46.2 percent as opposed to that in British Burma of 44.3 percent. D. G. E. Hall, in *Burma* (p. 137), wrote that there was a "high degree of literacy throughout the country" when the British arrived, but he failed to cite his source.

86. *MKPC.* One original Old Burmese inscription that precedes King Kyanzittha's 1093 inscription by nearly four decades is the Gavam Kyaung Inscription of 1058, also called the Let-the-she Paya Inscription. In addition, *SMK* 1, section *kha;* pages 321–322, 324, 325, has four inscriptions that precede 1093, not counting the controversial inscription dated to 1067 which most attribute to the sixteenth century or later. If we include one inscription contained in *Pagán Kyauksa Let Ywe Sin,* p. 1, dated to s444/1082, and the two at Bodhgayā, altogether there are eight Old Burmese inscriptions that precede 1093. Luce and Pe Maung Tin's *Selections from the Inscriptions of Pagán,* pp. 1–3, also shows some that predate 1093, but these have already been counted in the above computation.

87. Luce, *Old Burma,* 1:77, rightly places a "?" next to the date.

88. *EB* 1, 1:4; 1, 2:141.

89. During a visit in July 2002 to the Pagán museum, I read tablet no. "*ca* 500" from the Shwéhsandaw Pagoda with U Myint Aung and the assistant curator regarding the *Wutaka Jātaka.* The script *and the language* is Old Burmese, with the museum caption stating that the "*purā loṅ* [the Buddha] was a quail." This means that if the date of the Shwéhsandaw given by Luce (the 1060s) is correct, it precedes the Myazedi Burmese by nearly half a century.

90. Luce, *Old Burma,* 1:44, 262–264, where they are dated either before or during Aniruddha's reign. The *Jātaka* plaques are in the Pali language, but written in the Pagán script. However, Luce contends that they were written in the early Mon script, which is not wrong, as both Old Mon and Old Burmese were written in the Pagán script. But by saying the writing is in the Mon script is a bit disingenuous, for it "privileges" the Mon Paradigm.

91. *SMK* 1:321–322; 324–327. Also, *Selections from the Inscriptions of Pagán,* pp. 1–3; and *Pagán Kyauksa Let Ywe Sin,* pp. 1–2.

92. Diffloth, *Nyah Kur,* p. 10. Diffloth's contention is partially supported by Duroiselle, who earlier wrote that "no original inscriptions whatsoever were found in Pagán or elsewhere in Burma, written either in Burmese or in Mon, antedating the middle of the eleventh century, that is, the fall of Thatôn in 1057." See *List,* p. vi. He is correct about the Mon, but, as shown here, not the Burmese.

93. Luce, *Old Burma,* 1:54, himself calls Kyanzittha's Mon inscriptions "literature" of a high order. But, of course, it is meant to support a different perspective.

94. The data in Tha Myat's *Pyū Phat Ca* seems to suggest this evolution even if the author did not explicitly state it. However, he does caution us to be critical of accepting the notion that the Burma script derived from the Thatôn conquest. I owe this information to U Saw Tun of Northern Illinois University, who had studied under U Tha Myat.

95. Shorto notes that the "writing [the Burma script] was in use long before the floraison . . . ." See his *Dictionary of Mon Inscriptions,* p. xi.

Chapter Nine: The Mon Paradigm and the Evolution of the Pagán Temple

1. The origins of the solid *stupa* at Pagán is not, for the most part, relevant to the thesis of the Mon Paradigm, whereas the *gu* is. I have, therefore, separated discussion of the two as much as possible.

2. Although a few art historians of Burma have viewed certain of Luce's interpretations with some gentle skepticism, as we shall see below, not a single one has questioned the existence of an earlier Mon polity in Lower Burma. That means they have not questioned the consequences of this assumption for art history either. Probably the most explicit statement regarding Mon influence in Pagán art was made by Quaritch Wales, who wrote: "The Mons . . . were primarily responsible for the constructions at Pagán . . ." ("Dvāravatī in South-East Asian Cultural History," *JRAS* 1–2 [1966]: p. 50).

3. Luce, *Old Burma,* 1:282–283.

4. Admittedly, Luce gives credit to the Pyū in several cases, but then it is almost immediately forgotten and the analysis returns to the assumptions held by the Mon Paradigm.

5. Pierre Pichard, *Inventory of Monuments at Pagán,* vols. 1–7 (Kiscadale: EFEO and UNESCO, Gartmore, Scotland and Paris, 1992–2000). Volume 8 is supposedly published, but I have not yet seen a copy.

6. My analysis and assessment, represented by Figures 11 and 12, are based entirely on data taken from Pichard's first seven volumes, although he states in "A Distinctive Technical Achievement: The Vaults and Arches of Pagan," in *The Art of Burma: New Studies,* ed. Donald M. Stadtner (Mumbai, India: Marg Publications, 1999) that there are altogether over 2,800 monuments built at Pagán, of which 974 temples and 523 monasteries were constructed between the eleventh and fourteenth centuries. Pichard's work will be well used and appreciated by scholars for many more decades to come. Among other reasons, the most important is that he makes little or no attempt to impose an assumed chronology of style or any other theory on the data. Rather, it is an inventory, as the title states, that scholars can treat as raw material with which they can then construct whatever broad patterns and theses they might envision, hopefully, as dictated by the evidence rather than by the political or art historical sentiments of the age in which they happen to write. My only reservation about Pichard's work is his use of anachronisms, such as the term "slave," when that term has been clearly demonstrated, for some time now, to be a late, perhaps nineteenth-century misnomer of an entirely different situation during Pagán times; see Aung-Thwin, "*Athi, Kyun Taw, Hpaya Kyun:* Varieties of Commendation and Dependence in Pre-Colonial Burma," in *Slavery, Bondage and Dependency in Southeast Asia,*" edited by Anthony Reid (New York: University of Queensland Press, 1983), pp. 64–89.

7. Myanmar, Ministry of Culture, *Inventory of Ancient Monuments in Bagan,* vol. 1 (Yangon: Ministry of Culture, 1998). Another useful work, more focused and with greater detail but more limited, is the Myanmar Department of Higher Education's *Architectural Drawings of Temples in Pagán* (Yangon: Ministry of Education, 1989).

8. The introductory section to Strachan's *Pagan* provides a brief summary of the first westerners who encountered Pagán.

9. *A narrative of the mission to the court of Ava in 1855 compiled by Henry Yule together with the journal of Arthur Phayre, envoy to the court of Ava, and additional illustrations by Colesworthy Grant and Linnaeus Tripe with an introduction by Hugh Tinker* (Kuala Lumpur: Oxford University Press, 1968).

10. *Narrative of the mission,* p. 43.

11. *Narrative of the mission,* p. 44.

12. Bo Kay, *Pagan Thutethana Lan Nyun* [Research guide to Pagán] (Yangôn: Sape Beikman Press, 1981).

13. Allegations have been launched by individuals and groups with obvious political agendas that many of the recent repairs, especially of the finials of *stupas* at Pagán, have been dictated by the military government. This could not be farther from the truth. I have personally quizzed U Aung Kyaing, currently director of archaeology for Upper Burma and previously of Pagán, and his assistants regarding this issue. The decisions were made at the local level and carried out by the Pagán Archaeological Department; the design of the repairs had nothing whatsoever to do with central policy. What U Aung Kyaing and his assistants did was scour all the wall paintings of Pagán temples to determine the period design of finials. The early Myinpyagu and the Lokahteikpan wall paintings both contain examples of period *stupa* shapes and finials. (My thanks, again, to Lily Handlin for her excellent photo-

graphs taken from the Lokahteikpan.) U Aung Kyaing's team also studied original stone finials that had fallen off during the earthquake of 1975, from the Mingalazedi, for example, and now preserved in the new museum to provide plaster molds or models of actual finials. Aung Kyaing and his crew also scrutinized the thirty-three encased *stupa*s of Pagán whose outer layers had, for a variety of reasons, been fully or partially destroyed, thereby exposing the inner, Pagán-period *stupa*s and revealing the original design of the finials. For this topic, see Kyawt Hmu Aung, "The Encased *stupa*s of Bagan," *Myanma Thamaing Thutethana Sasaung* [Myanmar historical research journal], 10 (December 2002), pp. 31–52. This information was then used to make the repairs we see today. The common metal finial, which we are so used to in modern times (such as that on the Shwédagôn at Yangôn), and the type that is being "lamented" by students of Burma in general, is actually a late design and not a Pagán period style at all. The righteous indignation of these political groups to the events of 1988 and afterwards have placed even the daily routines of the Archaeology Department at Pagán and its restoration activities into an authoritarian verses democratic framework which has no basis of fact. This sentiment is surely one reason why Pagán has not received World Heritage Site status, which it deserves far more than many other places that have it, such as Sukhodaya and Chiang Mai.

14. Minbu Aung Kyaing, *Bithuka Letkyamya* [Architectural features] (Yangon: Capebiman Press, 1985).

15. This is most evident in his following Luce's chronology and the Mon Paradigm with regard to the Thatôn conquest. However, Strachan does seem a bit wary of Thatôn's role (even if for the wrong reasons), for he did write that "there is no substantive evidence to suggest that the Mons originated the type of brick temple found at Pagán" (*Pagan,* p. 9).

16. His assessment of Luce is actually confined largely to a few notes, so that it is more a case of "no, it isn't so" rather than an in-depth analysis and critique. For example, note 26, p. 144, which, along with the statement in note 15, is virtually his entire critique of Luce on Pagán architecture.

17. Myanmar, Ministry of Culture, *Sheyo Myanma Pagyi* [Traditional Myanma paintings] (Yangon: Ministry of Culture, n.d.).

18. Although Gutman's recent *Burma's Lost Kingdoms* focuses on Arakan and discusses issues and problems in Burma's art history, it is not concerned with the Mon Paradigm, nor with Pagán's architecture per se, which is the focus of this chapter. For her latest work on some of these issues, see "A Burma origin for the Sukhothai walking Buddha," in *Burma Art and Archaeology,* eds. Alexander Green and T. Richard Blurton (Chicago: Art Media Resources, 2002), pp. 35–43.

19. I am thinking particularly of works such as the following: *The Art of Burma: New Studies,* edited by Donald M. Stadtner (Mumbai: Marg Publications, 1999); Richard M. Cooler's, "Sacred Buildings for an Arid Climate: Architectural Evidence for Low Rainfall in Ancient Pagán," *The Journal of Burma Studies,* 1 (1997): 19–44; Nina Oshegowa, *Kunst in Burma* (Leipzig: E.A. Seemann, 1988); U Kan Hla [pseud. Sergey S. Ozhegov] "Pagán: Development and Town Planning," *Journal of the Society of Architectural Historians,* 36, 1 (March 1977): 15–29; and Philip Rawson, *The Art of Southeast Asia* (London: Thames and Hudson, 1967), pp. 161–202.

20. Luce, *Old Burma,* 1:282–283.

21. Michael Aung-Thwin, "The Problem of Ceylonese-Burmese Relations in the 12th Century and the Question of an Interregnum in Pagán: 1165–1174 A.D., *JSS* 64, 1 (January 1976): 53–74. A more recent version of this appeared again in Aung-Thwin, *Myth and History,* chapter 1.

22. Luce, *Old Burma,* 1:299.

23. Luce, *Old Burma,* 1:299.

24. Luce, *Old Burma,* 1:299.

25. Luce, *Old Burma,* 1:300.

26. Luce, *Old Burma,* 1:300.

27. For a more elaborated discussion of this topic, see Aung-Thwin, "Spirals in Burmese and Early Southeast Asian History."

28. The Nandamanya, Winido, Thetkyamuni, Zulain, and Kondawgyi, to name a few.

29. Pichard's work through volume 7 lists 2,064 temples, but his volume 8 brings the total now to about 2,800.

30. In Chapters 13 to 20, from pages 257–422 of *Old Burma,* 1, Luce discusses all the temples and *stupas* that he had decided to include and date.

31. Of the 2,170 religious buildings of Pagán in the list noted above, only 77 of their original, donative stone inscriptions survive (Tun Nwe, "Pagán Paya Sayin Kyai Shadawpon" [Search for the broad list of Pagán temples] in *Pagán Letthit nhin Achya Satan Mya* [Fashionable Pagán and other essays] (Mandalay: Kyi Pwa Yei Press, 1996), pp. 61–105, and Appendix *"kha,"* pp. 78–81.) A more accurate and recent list paints a similar picture. Of the 2,064 mainly religious buildings erected in Pagán according to Pichard's *Inventory* (up to volume 7), 1,627 are estimated to have been constructed during the early Pagán period (to 1300 AD). Of these, only 61 can be confirmed by epigraphy regarding their donors and dates. That is only about 3 percent.

32. Ironically, and significantly, they are precisely the kinds of sources Luce had throughout his career disparaged.

33. Bo Kay, *Pagan,* pp. 11–16.

34. Luce, in *Old Burma,* 1:302–303, proposes a date of 1080. But, as shown, the first dated evidence of written Mon in the Pagán script is Kyanzittha's 1093 inscription at Prome, so that the dating of the Păhtothămyā is once again based on a prior assumption that the Mon gave the script to the Burmese at Pagán. He also translates the word Păhtothămyā as "Pagoda with many children" (p. 304) which is quite wrong, mixing up the object with the subject. It should be "many sons of the *pahto.*"

35. Luce, *Old Burma,* 1:302.

36. Luce, *Old Burma,* 1:302–303.

37. Luce, *Old Burma,* 1:384–388.

38. Ba Shin, *Lokahteikpan,* p. 4. Lily Handlin of Harvard has been working on the Lokahteikpan Temple for the past several years, the only non-art historian of Southeast Asia that I know of in the West currently dealing with this topic. And although a professor of American history, her work has shown more depth and detail than that of many art historians of Pagán.

39. Ba Shin, *Lokahteikpan,* p. 2.

40. Ba Shin, *Lokahteikpan,* pp. 1 and 2.

41. Ba Shin, *Lokahteikpan,* p. 23.

42. Just as one example, see Benjamin Rowland's chapter on Southeast Asia in *The art and architecture of India: Buddhist, Hindu, Jain* (Baltimore: Penguin, 1977); Heinrich Zimmer, *The Art of Indian Asia,* 1 (Princeton: Princeton University Press, 1955), pp. 5–6; and Rawson's chapter on Pagán in his *Art of Southeast Asia.*

43. Strachan, *Pagan,* pp. 41–42.

44. Luce, *Old Burma,* 1:301. Sir John Marshall had written earlier that the sculptured stone found at East Zegu "plainly derives its style from the familiar Gupta work of Northern India. It can hardly be assigned to a later date than the seventh century A.D., and may be earlier" (cited in Taw Sein Ko, *Burmese Sketches,* 2:265).

45. Luce, *Old Burma,* 1:238–239.

46. Claudine Bautze-Picron, *The Buddhist Murals of Pagan: Timeless Vistas of the Cosmos* (Trumbull, CT: Weatherhill, 2003), p. 2, recognized this problem as well.

47. The construction dates of these two temples have been estimated to be the eleventh century for reasons that I discuss in Chapter Ten.

48. Luce, *Old Burma,* 1:282–283.

49. Luce, *Old Burma,* 1:300.

50. Luce, *Old Burma,* 1:299.

51. See Luce, *Old Burma,* 1:286 and passim. "Its" inscription, of course, is the now notorious, late sixteenth-century stone dated to 1067. Pierre Pichard, in "A Distinctive Technical Achievement: The Vaults and Arches of Pagán," in *Art of Burma,* cited above, pp. 72–73, concurs that the temple "could have been renovated, if not rebuilt, at a later time."

52. The overall treatment of architecture can be found in Luce's *Old Burma,* 1, chapters 12–20. For a Burmese (although ethnically Mon) perspective, see Bo Kay's *Pagan.* One need only glance at the illustrations in any major work of art history on Pagán to see that style does not reveal date.

53. Aung Thaw, *Historical Sites,* p. 42.

54. Luce, *Old Burma,* 1:267.

55. Aung Thaw, *Historical Sites,* p. 37.

56. Aung Thaw, *Historical Sites,* pp. 34–35.

57. Donald M. Stadtner, "The Art of Burma," in *Art of Southeast Asia* (New York: Harry N. Abrams, Inc., 1998), p. 48. However, I cannot fault Stadtner entirely for placing these in the "Mon Suvannabhumi" section, since at the time he published, no one had yet challenged the Mon Paradigm. Besides, as he states, these are more reminiscent of the Pyū in any case, and, he wrote, these "terra cottas . . . differed sharply from their nearest neighbors, the Dvaravati."[sic] (p. 48) This suggests he had doubts about their Mon provenance.

58. *Man Shu,* pp. 90–91.

59. Luce, *Old Burma,* 1:258–259. See also Kyaw Nyein, "The Ceramic Industry of the Pagán Period," pp. 182–183.

60. Aung Thaw, *Historical Sites,* p. 37.

61. Luce, *Old Burma,* 1:283.

62. Aung Thaw, *Historical Sites,* p.37.

63. The most authoritative scholarship on the subject to date is unquestionably Pierre Pichard's article on the "Vaults and Arches of Pagán."

64. Pichard, *Inventory,* 1:44–47.

65. The vaulted shrine found during excavations in Old Pegu by J. A. Stewart

(who was not an archaeologist) is not only late, but does not resemble Pagán arches. See his "Excavation and Exploration in Pegu," *JBRS* 7, 1 (1917): 17–18. As Pegu itself did not appear in original epigraphy until 1266 AD, this may well have been a late construction.

66. Dupont in his study of Dvāravatī did not find a single radiating arch there (*L'archéologie mône,* p. 125).

67. Unlike the case in Burma, most of the arches used in Southeast Asia that are contemporary or prior to the Pagán period are corbeled, not keystone, such as those in Angkor and Java, while those in India are late. Pichard mentions Debala Mitra's work which suggests that the Buddhist site of Ratnagiri in Orissa used arches thought to have been built between the seventh and tenth centuries that show a strong technical similarity with the vaults of Pagán (see Pichard, "Vaults and Arches of Pagán," p. 66). However, not only did the Ratnagiri vault span a small distance (some three meters), it also appears to be an isolated case and not securely dated. Like the Bodhgayā Temple, it also could have been repaired later by engineers from Pagán. Of the Mahābodhi, even Luce wrote that "the brick work, voussoir and relieving voussoir there . . . , have all the marks of Early Pagán workmanship" (*Old Burma,* 1:347). Cunningham, whose work focused specifically on the Mahābodhi Temple, agreed and stated: "This work [repairs of the west entrance] I believe to have been done by the Burmese, between A.D. 1035 and 1086" (Cunningham, *Mahâbodhi,* p. 25). But even if the Pagán arches came from Ratnagiri, where did the arches of Śrī Kṣetra come from, as they are earlier than those *estimated* for Ratnagiri? Indeed, Heinrich Zimmer in *The Art of Indian Asia,* 2, plate 99, dates the Mahābodhi repairs to the seventh and eighth centuries AD, which suggests the Pyū may have been responsible for them. To use one small isolated example in India as evidence to conclude that it was responsible for 974 temples built at Pagán with the true arch is not very convincing. See also Helmut Loofs-Wissowa, "The True and the Corbel Arch in Mainland Southeast Asian Monumental Architecture," in *Southeast Asia in the 9th to 14th Centuries,* edited by David G. Marr and A.C. Milner, (Singapore: Institute for Southeast Asia Studies, 1986), pp. 239–253.

68. Luce, *Old Burma,* 1:302.

69. Luce, "Mons of the Pagán Dynasty," p. 7. In *Old Burma,* 1:406, he wrote: "Their [Mon] strange reluctance to trust the radiating arch."

70. But Luce contradictorily concedes to their being "clear prototypes of Pagán architecture . . . " Luce, *Old Burma,* 1:301; *Department of Higher Education,* p. 2; Luce, *Phases,* 1:133.

71. Luce, *Old Burma,* 1:246. Also Pichard, *Inventory,* passim.

72. *EB* 1, 1:65; Luce, *Old Burma,* 1:243.

73. Shorto, *Dictionary of Mon Inscriptions,* between pages 234–240, where it should have been.

74. Luce, *Old Burma,* 1:235.

75. Luce, *Old Burma,* 1:243.

76. Luce, *Old Burma,* 1:236.

77. Luce, *Old Burma,* 1:238–239.

78. *EB* 1, 1:67.

79. Luce, *Old Burma,* 1:232, note 28.

80. Luce, *Old Burma,* 1:232.

81. *SMK* 1:63, line 3; also p. 300, lines 5, 9, for the Old Burmese, while the earliest evidence for the Mon is found during King Dhammazedi's reign, in the late fifteenth century. Luce cites *EB* 4, 1:33, Inscription IV B, line 32, which is the Mon transliteration. The English translation is on page 42 of *EB*. Shorto, in his *Dictionary of Mon Inscriptions*, p. 2, also shows it to be Middle Mon.

82. Luce, *Old Burma*, 1:232, note 31, writes that *srot* in Old Mon is *sarwat* in Old Burmese. Yet Shorto does not include the word *srot* in his *Dictionary of Mon Inscriptions*. The closest he has is *saray*, which he defines as "(part of the name of?) material used in building of a pagoda (?)" (see p. 367). The source for *saray* is "late Old Mon of Lamphun," which is later than the first appearance at Pagán.

83. See *SMK* 1:300, line 8.

84. Luce, in his "Economic Life of the Early Burman," *Burma Research Society Fiftieth Anniversary Publications No. 2* (Rangoon: Burma Research Society, 1960), p. 327, states that the word for "expert," the suffix used for craftsmen, *samā*, was said to have come from Mon. It is only an assertion; there is no proof provided.

85. *Judson's Burmese-English Dictionary* (Rangoon: Baptist Board of Publications, 1852, 1883, 1893), pp. 671–675 of the 1893 edition; Shorto, *Dictionary of Mon Inscriptions*, p. 230.

86. Blagden, "Notes on Talaing Epigraphy," p. 43.

87. Luce suggests this. See his "Mons of the Pagán Dynasty," p. 3.

88. The Pagán and National Museums have ample examples of gold and silver work excavated from Śrī Kṣetra. See also Luce, "Ancient Pyū," p. 313.

89. Stargardt, *Ancient Pyu*, pp. 202–206; Aung Thaw, *Beikthano*, p. 65.

90. Pichard, *Inventory*, 5:269, inventory no. 1339.

91. Luce, *Old Burma*, 1:257, 280–281. Pichard's *Inventory* shows numerous cases of this practice.

92. I saw this method in 1978 when I visited Sagaing.

93. Pichard, *Inventory*, 4:114–115, no. 906.

94. Almost invariably the Pagán *gu* are several degrees off due north, either eastwards or westwards, as were the fourth-century Pyū temples.

95. Stargardt, *Ancient Pyu*, pp. 200–206.

96. Stargardt, *Ancient Pyu*, p. 191.

97. Unless, of course, someone uncovers a four-faced style earlier than that at Śrī Kṣetra.

98. Léon-Marie-Eugène de Beylié, *Prome et Samara: voyage archéologique en Birmanie et en Mésopotamie* (Paris: E. Leroux, 1907), p. 101; Luce, *Phases*, 2: plate no. 22; Aung Thaw, *Historical Sites*, p. 20. Incidentally, the term Léymyethna itself is Old Burmese and found throughout the Pagán period, whereas its Mon equivalent of *kyak pan*, is Middle Mon, and cannot be found earlier in epigraphy. See Luce, *Old Burma*, 1:245, note 160, where no citation is provided for this Mon term. Shorto has a long entry for the word *kyak* itself, pp. 59–60. As *kyek*, meaning Buddha or Buddha image, it appears in the Myazedi Inscriptions.

99. My analysis has included all the data contained in the seven volumes published by Pichard, and with a very few exceptions, I have tentatively accepted his estimated dates of construction.

100. There may have been earlier pentagonal and octagonal monuments elsewhere in South and Southeast Asia, but at Pagán, and in terms of the hollow tem-

ples, these appear to have been products of the earlier one-face and four-face designs.

101. For a detailed study of these, see Pierre Pichard's *The Pentagonal Monuments of Pagán* (Bangkok: White Lotus, 1991).

102. Pichard, *The Pentagonal Monuments.*

103. The Sulamani and Gawdawpalin, one-entrance temples with two storeys, did have hidden vaulted corridors which were recently revealed by the earthquake of 1975 as well as with geophysical sounding devices. See Myanmar, Department of Higher Education, *Architectural Drawings,* p. 2.

104. Pichard, *Inventory,* 5:234, no. 1316 of the inventory.

105. Pichard, *Inventory,* 5:239, no. 1320 of the inventory.

106. Myanmar, Department of Higher Education, *Architectural Drawings,* p. 3.

107. Illustrative of this trend are Claudine Bautze-Picron, in "Between India and Burma: The 'Andagu' Stelae," in *Art of Burma,* pp. 37–52; and John Guy, "Offering up a rare jewel: Buddhist merit-making and votive tablets in early Burma," in *Burma: Art and Archaeology,* eds. Alexandra Green and T. Richard Blurton (Chicago: Art Media Resources, 2002), pp. 23–33.

108. As Pichard notes in "Vaults and Arches of Pagán," p. 78, although some monasteries and temples were built in the fourteenth century with the Pagán vault, by the First Ava Dynasty it would have been rare to find one, and it certainly would not be of the same quality, size, and scale as those found at Pagán.

109. There is no literature on this topic, but I visited Pinya precisely to observe this phenomenon first hand. Of course, this conclusion is only preliminary.

Chapter Ten: The Mon Paradigm and the Kyanzittha Legend

1. G. H. Luce, "The career of Htilaing Min (Kyanzittha)," *JRAS* 1–2 (1966): 53–68.

2. Luce actually wrote that Kyanzittha was "highly sexed" ("The Career," p. 56).

3. Luce, *Old Burma,* 1:41, 52.

4. Luce, "The career," p. 55.

5. Luce, *Old Burma,* 1:52.

6. Luce used those very words, that "Kyanzittha was more democratic . . . ." (*Old Burma,* 1:273).

7. Luce, *Old Burma,* 1:56, 61.

8. Luce, "The career," pp. 53–68. Luce also wrote of Kyanzittha's "unmistakable attachment to Mon culture and religion . . . ." (*Old Burma,* 1:51)

9. Although in *List,* pp. 208–213, edited by Duroiselle and published in 1921, no Old Mon inscription was listed under Kyauksé, two years later, in *EB* 3, 1 (1923): 70–73, also edited by Duroiselle, one short inscription appears, described and translated by Blagden. He wrote that the inscription "reminds one more of fifteenth-century orthography than of the eleventh-century . . ." (p. 70). Luce, in his "Old Kyauksé," pp. 80–81, while admitting that there were more than 119 Old Burmese inscriptions found at Kyauksé, states that there may have been one in Old Mon. He was likely referring to Blagden's. In U Chit Thein's newer *MKPC,* p. 58, there is also only one listed.

10. This inscription can be found in *Selections from the Inscriptions,* pp. 2–3, line 3.

11. Luce, "Note on the Peoples of Burma," Appendix F. I cannot account for

the contradiction between Luce's date of 1204, said to be the first appearance of the word *tanluiṅ,* and his own footnote in *Selections from the Inscriptions.*

12. Luce, *Old Burma,* 1:50–52.

13. *SMK* 1:329–330.

14. Luce, *Old Burma,* 1:50.

15. The lineage and story of Kyanzittha's birth saw lively debate in the early decades of the twentieth century, summarized in Taw Sein Ko's *Burmese Sketches,* 2:376–380.

16. U Kala states that during Kyanzittha's battle for the throne, the headman of Htilaing, north of the capital, gave the king his daughter in marriage and thereby became his client, from which Kyanzittha received the name "Lord of Htilaing." For the story's first appearance in the chronicles, see *Mahayazawingyi,* 1:208–209.

17. Luce, *Old Burma,* 1:50–51, makes it appear that the third stone is actually dated. It is not. In *List,* p. 139, Duroiselle states in a footnote regarding this inscription that "this is the date given in the *Hmannan Yazawin.* The inscription bears no date."

18. The inscription is reproduced in *SMK* 3:304–305.

19. Luce, *Old Burma,* 1:51.

20. *SMK* 1:331–332.

21. That the Taungbyôn Hlèdauk Inscription is dated to 1111 AD and written in King Alaungsithu's voice raises some extremely important issues in Pagán studies: the dating of the Myazedi Inscriptions, the regnal years of Kyanzittha, and the ascension of Alaungsithu. The most reliable and oldest extant portions of the *Zatatawpon* chronicle (p. 40) also gives Kyanzittha's death as 1111 AD. So Alaungsithu's accession that same year is quite possible, giving credence to the date and reliability of this inscription.

22. Luce, *Old Burma,* 1:51.

23. Luce, *Old Burma,* 1:51. However, the compiler of *SMK* 1:332, states that he does not know if the base had any lines of text.

24. Luce, *Old Burma,* 1:41, 52. The thesis goes back to his "Old Kyauksé," p. 112, published in 1959.

25. As noted in earlier chapters, the Myazedi Inscriptions did not say that the king mentioned on the stones, Śrī Tribhuvanāditya Dhammarāja, was Kyanzittha; that is only an assumption.

26. Personal communication from Ken Breazeale, who figured these dates out using Eade's computations.

27. Even this is disputed. U Tha Myat translates the Pyū face as saying "one thousand six hundred and twenty-eight years after Lord Buddha had attained Nibbana, this city was named Arimaddanapur," *not* that Śrī Tribhuvanāditya Dhammarāja was king. In other words, we do not know if the 1,628 years brought us to the reign of the king or the date when Pagán was given its formal name (see *Pyū Phat Ca,* p. 76).

28. *Zatatawpon,* p. 40.

29. Luce, in his "The career," p. 55, stated that Kyanzittha, "though a Burman, loved the Mons."

30. Luce, "A Century of Progress in Burmese History and Archaeology," *JBRS* 32, 1 (1968): 88.

31. *Kywan* were people attached to either the crown or the *saṅgha.*

32. Aung-Thwin, *Pagan.*

33. Tin Hla Thaw, "History of Burma," p. 138, demonstrates that the entire corpus of Ava inscriptions did not once mention Rmeñ, but did refer to people known as Tanluiṅ.

34. I am thinking of King Bayinnaung's trilingual inscription on a small bell at the Shwézigôn Pagoda at Pagán where he recorded his donation in Mon, Pali, and Burmese.

35. The issue of Mon loan words in Burmese is a major topic in itself and cannot be dealt with here in any thorough way, except to reiterate what has been said above. There is no proof that if such borrowing occurred, it happened during Kyanzittha's reign, that it did not go from Burmese to Mon instead, that a third source was not responsible for the common words in both languages, or that any borrowing did not occur during the Ava/Pegu period of Burma's history when Mon and Burman had experienced 700 years of continuous contact. That neither Old Mon nor Old Burmese saw much significant change between the eleventh and fifteenth centuries seems to confirm that most of the borrowing occurred later.

36. These numbers reflect only stone inscriptions. I have not included ink glosses on temple walls, captions under *Jātaka* plaques, and other such smaller items. Of the stones, the number also depends on how one counts. Shorto, in his *Dictionary of Mon Inscriptions,* xxviii–xxxiii, counts each stone separately, although he does not do the same with votive tablets and ink glosses. U Chit Thein, in *MKPC,* also counts each stone as a separate inscription (hence, his number of 106), even if the text continues to another stone. Thus, for example, the Kalyani Inscriptions comprise ten stones, but it is one continuous narrative that can be counted either as ten inscriptions or one.

37. I have had threatening emails from Mon exiles in Thailand or their advocates who claim to have read drafts of the paper I presented in Yangôn in 2001. They consider this study to be another case of Burman hegemonism and a threat to their political agenda.

38. Luce wrote that King Kyanzittha wrote Old Mon "like a master," although there is no evidence that he personally wrote the inscriptions ("The career," p. 55).

39. U Kala, *Mahayazawingyi,* 1:196–197.

40. G. H. Luce, "A Cambodian (?) Invasion of Lower Burma—A Comparison of Burmese and Talaing Chronicles, *JBRS* 12, 1 (1922): 39–45.

41. U Kala, *Mahayazawingyi,* 1:196.

42. The Prome Inscription has been discussed at length. Kyanzittha also erected the Shwézigôn, Myakan, and Alanpagán Inscriptions at Pagán, all in Old Mon (*EB* 1, 2:90–143).

43. *List,* pp. 4–7, has seven inscriptions in Burmese and Pali attributed to Kyanzittha.

44. For the 1107 inscription, see *SMK* 1:329–330.

45. The word used on the inscription was *prañ,* which can have different meanings—city, capital, country, region, abode, and so on—depending on the context. I chose "region" because there is no independent evidence of any city or capital at Pegu until 1266. See *SMK* 1:329. Some consider this inscription to be a late copy, but that does not vitiate the point.

46. *EB* 1, 2:117; Luce, *Old Burma,* 1:57, 72.

47. *EB* 1, 2:129, where it says that 1,628 years after the *parinirvāṇa* (1083/4 AD), Viṣṇu will become king in Pagán as Kyanzittha.

48. *EB* 1, 2:117.

49. I think the switch of the Tanluiṅ wise man from Kyanzittha to Aniruddha has to do with the myth concerning Aniruddha's conquest of Thatôn. It provides Aniruddha with a good reason to search for the holy scriptures. The motif of Shin Arahan and Aniruddha is, of course, taken from the story of Aśoka and Nigrodha in the *Mahāvaṃsa,* Chapter V, p. 31, and repeated in the *Glass Palace Chronicle,* p. 72–73, where the comparison is made explicit.

50. It may have been Duroiselle who began this convention as early as 1918, and is quoted in Taw Sein Ko's *Burmese Sketches,* 2:379. Harvey, in *Burma,* p. 40, picked it up, with the assumption that Kyanzittha was either Indian or Arakanese, rather than Burman, simply from the way the statue looked to him. Luce continued the assertion (in *Old Burma,* 1:54, 57), stating that the statues did indeed represent Shin Arahan and Kyanzittha.

51. Luce, *Old Burma,* 1:61.

52. Luce, *Old Burma,* 1:38.

53. See Ray, *Sanskrit Buddhism,* and Duroiselle, "The Arī of Burma and Tāntric Buddhism," *Archaeological Survey of India, Annual Report: 1915–16* (Delhi: Indological Book House, Reprint, 1972): 79–93; and "The Derivation of 'Ari,' *JBRS* 10, 1 (1920): 28–30; 1, 3:158–159. However, Than Tun is skeptical of the Tantric elements and their alleged relationship to the legendary Aris, as is Strachan. Than Tun's views are expressed in his PhD dissertation, written in 1956 at the University of London, entitled "History of Buddhism in Burma: A.D. 1000–1300." It was enlarged and published under the same title in *JBRS* 61 (December 1978). Strachan's view can be found in his *Pagan,* pp. 129–134, and passim. But I do not think any Burma scholar denies that there were several ideologies present at the same time at Pagán.

54. Charlotte Galloway, "Relationships between Buddhist texts and images of the Enlightenment during the early Pagan Period," in *Burma: Art and Archaeology,* ed. Alexandra Green and T. Richard Blurton (Chicago: Art Media Resources, 2002).

55. Whether or not these "Aris" necessarily represent Tantric Mahāyāna sects rather than simply a name given to forest monks is difficult to tell. I am not endorsing the view that they were Tantric, but since Luce took the chronicle account of them as historically valid and saw them as Tantric, I am compelled to address this issue within that context. In any case, Duroiselle preceded Luce in this thesis in his "The Arī of Burma."

56. Luce, *Old Burma,* 1:61. See also U Mya, *Abeyadana Lainggu Paya* [Abeyadana nitched-cave temple] (Rangoon: The Archaeological Survey of Burma, 1968), especially pp. 59–66; and Bautze-Picron's *The Buddhist Murals of Pagan,* particularly pp. 170–179.

57. Aung Thaw, *Historical Sites,* pp. 41–98, especially p. 73. The issue here is not whether Viṣṇu can also be considered a Buddhist deity, as he was in Śrī Laṅka; he may well have been. Rather, my objection is that Luce used his iconography as evidence to date the temple to Aniruddha's reign so that it fit his thesis, whereas everything in Kyanzittha's reign makes him a far more likely candidate to have used the

Viṣṇu ideology. John Clifford Holt's "Minister of Defense? The Viṣṇu Controversy in Contemporary Sri Lanka," in *Constituting Communities: Theravāda Buddhism and the Religious Cultures of South and Southeast Asia,* edited by John Clifford Holt et al., (Albany, NY: State University of New York Press, 2003), pp. 107–130, shows how the deity has numerous historical "functions."

58. Luce, *Old Burma,* 1:268, 275–276; 288.

59. The Hpayathonzu and Nandamanya have had ample treatment in most of the works I have cited. The Viṣṇu temple is less well known, but its inscription can be found in Archaeological Survey of India, "A Vaishnava Inscription at Pagan," *Epigraphia Indica,* 7, 27 (1902–1903): 197–198. In addition, I have personally observed a rather large stone *lingam* and *yoni* in one of the five shrines surrounding one of the most "orthodox" temples at Pagán: the Dhammayazika of King Narapatisithu built in 1196–1198. Although the *lingam-yoni* stone appears to be *in situ,* it is not certain, of course, whether it was part of the original dedication.

60. Luce, *Old Burma,* 1:262.

61. *DPPN* 1:951–952. *The Dīpavaṃsa,* p. 141, does mention the *Jātakas* as comprising part of the canon but says nothing further.

62. T. W. Rhys-Davids, *Buddhist India,* reprint (New Delhi: Indological Book House, 1970): 85–88.

63. Oscar von Hinuber, *A Handbook of Pali Literature* (Berlin: Walter de Gruyter, 1996), p. 54.

64. *The Chronicle of the Thūpa and the Thūpavaṃsa: Being a Translation and Edition of Vācissaratthera's Thūpavaṃsa,* translated by N. A. Jayawickrama (London: Luzac & Company Ltd., 1971): 31. My thanks to Lily Handlin for alerting me to this reference.

65. *The Expositor (Atthasālinī),* trans. Maung Tin, 2 vols. (London: Pali Text Society, 1921–1923), p. 40.

66. Charles Duroiselle, "Pictorial Representations of Jātakas in Burma," *Archaeological Survey of India, Annual Report 1912–13,* reprint (Delhi: Indological Book House, 1972), p. 88.

67. *EB* 2, 1:iv. See also Luce, *Old Burma,* 1:262, and Aung Thaw, *Historical Sites,* p. 84.

68. Luce, *Old Burma,*1:262, note 33. Although Luce makes it appear that both temples had the 550 *Jātakas*, Aung Thaw, in *Historical Sites,* p. 84, states that only the West Hpetleik had evidence of it.

69. Luce, *Old Burma,* 1:262–263.

70. Luce, *Old Burma,* 1:264, note 45.

71. Duroiselle, "Pictorial Representations," p. 88.

72. Taw Sein Ko, *Burmese Sketches,* 1:68–69. For the most recent data, see Pierre Pichard's *Inventory,* 4:263–266.

73. Duroiselle, "Pictorial Representations," p. 91.

74. Duroiselle, "Pictorial Representations," p. 89. Aung Thaw, *Historical Sites,* p. 84.

75. Duroiselle, "Pictorial Representations," pp. 89–90. There may, of course, be painted representations in the interior of other temples.

76. Aung Kyaing, *Ananda* [in Burmese] (Yangon: Sape Beikman Press, 1984), p. 41.

77. *EB* 2, 1:v.

78. Benjamin Rowland in *Art and architecture of India,* chapter 20 on Ceylon, mentions no such use of the *Jātaka* plaques on temples, although they are found early in Bharhut (pp. 83–84) and the Borobudur (p. 453). Neither did S. Paranavitana in "The Art and Architecture of the Polonnaruva Period," in *The Polonnaruva Period,* ed. S. D. Saparamadu, third edition, (Dehiwala: Sri Lanka, Tisara Prakasakayo, 1973). Duroiselle, "Pictorial Representations," p. 89, is also of the opinion that Pagán is the only place where the complete collection of the *Jātakas* were made on terracotta and placed on temples.

79. Rhys-Davids, *Buddhist India,* pp. 90–91.

80. Luce, *Old Burma,* 1:262. For Fausböll, see *The Jātaka together with its commentary Jātakatthavaṇṇanā for the first time edited in the original Pali,* 6 vols., reprint (London: Pali Text Society, 1962–1964). Fausböll did not say that the *Jātakas* in his manuscripts preceded those on the Pagán temples. See also Oscar von Hinuber, *Die Sprachgeschichte des Pali im Spiegel der sudostasiatischen Handschriffenumberlieferung* (Stuttgart: Akademie der Wissenshaften und der Literatur, 1988), p. 7, note 8. My thanks to Lily Handlin for this information.

81. Rhys-Davids, *Buddhist India,* p. 93, states that the commentaries of the *Jātakas* were compiled in the fifth century AD in Śrī Laṅka.

82. There is some evidence that the Pyū used *Jātaka* plaques of the Sinhalese series. See Duroiselle's "Excavations at Pagán," p. 173.

83. Rowland, *Art and architecture of India,* pp. 83–84.

84. C. Roy Craven, *A Concise History of Indian Art* (New York: Oxford University Press, 1976), p. 125.

85. For instance, see U Kala, *Mahayazawingyi,* 1:190–195, and *Zatatawpon,* p. 89.

86. Duroiselle, "Pictorial Representations," p. 89.

87. I am not addressing the issue of whether there were, in fact, two distinct recensions, but since Luce believed there were and based his argument on that belief, my analysis must also work within that framework.

88. Luce, *Old Burma,* 1:269–272.

89. Luce, *Old Burma,* 1:273. That may have given some reprieve in *his* mind, although I am not certain how "both and neither" recensions can exist simultaneously.

90. According to Pichard's *Inventory,* there are 420 plaques left *in situ* on the Shwézigôn, with 597 pockets for them. This suggests that a different "recension" might have existed, an idea that has not been taken into account in Luce's analysis (Pichard, *Inventory,* 1:66). Similarly, there were originally 601 *Jātaka* plaques on the Dhammyazika Pagoda (Pichard, *Inventory,* 4:172), which suggests still another "recension." If nothing else, these various numbers suggest duplication or redundancy, which would tend to alter the sequence, on which the Luce thesis depends.

91. Luce *Old Burma,* 1:269. This admission reveals that what he really meant by the term "muddle" was that the Shwézigôn plaques were a "mixture" of the "two" recensions, not "both and neither."

92. Luce, *Old Burma,* 1:62.

93. Luce, *Old Burma,* 1:60.

94. Luce, *Old Burma,* 1:60–61.

95. Luce, *Old Burma,* 1:61.

96. Luce, *Old Burma,* 1:57.

97. *EB* 1, 2:93. As Duroiselle put it: "There is no evidence as to the date when the inscription itself was engraved . . . ."

98. King Bayinnaung in the sixteenth century erected a bell at the Shwézigôn which he inscribed with three languages: Pali, Burmese, and Mon, symbolic of cultures of his kingdom.

99. Luce, *Old Burma,* 1:268.

100. Although Luce dates the Ānanda to 1105, which serves the modern Kyanzittha legend, Duroiselle however, dates it to 1090. See his "Talaing Plaques," *EB,* 2, 1:iii; and "Stone Sculptures in the Ananda Temple at Pagán," *Archaeological Survey of India: Annual Report, 1913–1914,* pp. 64–65. This, of course, could be used to argue that written Old Mon in the Pagán script might have been a bit earlier than I have contended in this book, but since the temple is not dated by an original epigraph, the 1093 Old Mon inscription of Kyanzittha is still the first dated evidence for written Old Mon in Burma.

101. Luce, *Old Burma,* 1:61.

102. Since the *Cūḷavaṃsa* was not written before the second half of the thirteenth and continued to be written into the nineteenth century, this reference to the "Rāmañña country" is not evidence that it was contemporary to Vijayabāhu I. Rather, it reinforces my contention that Rāmaññadesa did not appear until the late thirteen century.

103. *Cūḷavaṃsa,* pp. 214–215.

104. Luce, *Old Burma,* 1:40

105. Luce, *Old Burma,* 1:40.

106. I am aware that Kemper in *Presence of the Past* (p. 3) is reluctant to call the *Mahāvaṃsa* Ceylon's "national" chronicle. I am saying only that no other text probably represented Ceylon as well as the *Mahāvaṃsa* did, particularly in the past, and in that important text, borrowing orthodox Buddhism and its texts from Burma is freely admitted.

107. *SMK* 1:325. The inscription is dated to 1082, prior to Kyanzittha's ascension either in 1084 or 1086. In part it reads: "This is a good deed done for the benefit of the Three Gems." One could argue, I suppose, that this was not a specific reference to the *Tipiṭakas,* but a general reference to the Buddha, *Saṅgha,* and *Dhamma.*

108. Luce, "The career," p. 64.

109. To name but one, see Bode's *Pali Literature.* As the citations above have shown, there is much recent scholarship that does not support Luce's contentions.

110. There are ink inscriptions written in Mon in various temples, but to my knowledge, none has been securely dated to the Pagán period. Even if the temple in which such inscriptions appear is securely dated, there is still no guarantee that the ink writings were contemporary to the building of the temple.

Chapter Eleven: The Mon Paradigm and the Myth of the "Downtrodden Talaing"

1. Quoted in Dorothy Woodman, *The Making of Burma* (London: The Cresset Press, 1962), p. 75. This proclamation was made late in 1824, after the British had taken the maritime provinces in Lower Burma.

2. Michael Symes, *An account of an embassy to the kingdom of Ava in the year 1795. . . ,* vol. 1 (Edinburgh: Constable and Co., 1827), p. 39.

3. Woodman, *Making of Burma,* p. 44.

4. Capt. Hiram Cox, *Journal of a residence in the Burmham empire: and more particularly at the court of Amarapoorah,* (London: J. Warren, 1821), pp. 112, 262, 304, 327.

5. Quoted in Woodman, *Making of Burma,* p. 45.

6. *The Burney Papers,* 1: sections 1–4 (Westmead, England: Gregg International Publishers Ltd., 1971 edition), pp. 129, 132–133. Halliday also reported that one of Burney's letters stated: ". . . the British Government has resolved upon establishing the old kingdom of Pegu . . . ." (see his "The Mons in Siam," *JBRS* 12, 2 (1922): 69–70.

7. *Burney Papers,* 1, 1–4:125–126. Burney wrote and signed this letter, which was dated 27th December 1825, and delivered it personally.

8. Hall, *Henry Burney,* pp. 24, 50, 92–93, defends Burney and suggests that he actually rejected the idea. Burney's own letters (*Burney Papers,* p. 61) are less unequivocal.

9. Hall, *Henry Burney,* pp. 50, 92–93.

10. F. Mason, *Burmah, Its People and Natural Productions . . .* (Rangoon: Thos. Stowe Ranney, 1860), p. iii.

11. Arthur Phayre, "History of Pegu," *JRAS* 42, 1 (1873): 23–57, 120–159; 43, 1 (1874): 6–21. (Here, pp. 32–33).

12. Luce, "Note on the Peoples," pp. 299–300, for the first three countries mentioned.

13. Wheatley, *Golden Khersonese,* p. 192.

14. James M. Haswell, *Grammatical notes and vocabulary of the Peguan Language* (Rangoon: American Baptist Mission Press, 1874).

15. Haswell, *Grammatical notes,* p. 79. Taw Sein Ko much later picked up Haswell's belief, stating that Alaungpaya had "stamped out the Talaing tongue" in the eighteenth century. (*Burmese Sketches,* 1:83).

16. E. Forchhammer, *Notes on the Early History and Geography of British Burma, Part II.* (Rangoon: Government Press, 1884), pp. 11–12. See also *Hobson-Jobson: A Glossary of Colloquial Anglo-Indian Words and Phrases, and of Kindred Terms, Etymological, Historical, Geographical and discursive,* compiled by Henry Yule and A. C. Burnell (New York: Humanities Press, 1968), pp. 889–890. It is curious that Hall used the same word ("extirpate") that Forchhammer used when conveying the same message: "The Burmese kings had done their utmost to extirpate" the royal family of Pegu (see his *Henry Burney,* p. 92).

17. *A Dictionary of the Burman Language; with explanations in English. Compiled from the Manuscripts of A. Judson . . . and of other Missionaries in Burmah,* ed. J. Wade (Calcutta: 1826), p. 175.

18. *Judson's Dictionary,* (1852), p. 335, and (1883), p. 289. My thanks to John Okell of London for checking these rare sources for me.

19. *Judson's Dictionary,* (1893), p. 507. Hereafter, all references to *Judson's,* unless otherwise specified, are to the 1893 edition.

20. *Judson's Dictionary,* p. iii.

21. Neither Shorto, in his *Dictionary of Mon Inscriptions* and *Dictionary of Modern Spoken Mon,* nor Halliday in his *Mon-English Dictionary,* has an entry for it. It is only in the twentieth century that the Mon began to use it.

22. *Judson's Dictionary,* p. iii.

23. *Judson's Dictionary,* p. iii.

24. Aung-Thwin, *Myth and History,* chapter 1; Luce, *Old Burma,* 1:122–123.

25. E. A. Stevens had compiled what appears to be the second *Judson's Burmese-English Dictionary,* which was produced in 1852 after Judson died in 1850 without completing it.

26. By the time the 1952 Centenary edition of *Judson's* was published belatedly in 1953, and although the editors had finally expunged Forchhammer's note found in the 1893 edition about Alaungpaya and his alleged oppression of the *Talaing,* they had nevertheless retained his ethnic focus on the word *talaing* by defining it as "Peguan or Talaing, Mun." The first edition of what became *Judson's,* the 1826 version, had not linked the word *talaing* with the Mun ethnic group, but with the peoples of Pegu, so that it was more a geosocial term. Hence, it read: "[talaing], adj. pertaining to the Peguese. [Talaing-pyay], n. Pegu." (*A Dictionary of the Burman Language,* p. 175.)

27. *Judson's Dictionary,* (1893), p. 507.

28. Twinthintaikwun, *Myanmayazawinthit,* I, p. 14.

29. *Judson's,* (1953) and (1966), p. 789.

30. Said's phrase means that whether subconsciously or deliberately a particular world view is shared by numerous people benefiting from, in this case, colonialism. Thus even Blagden, whose work is objective in many ways, succumbed to Forchhammer's views of the oppressed Mon (see Blagden, "The Chronicles of Pegu," p. 372).

31. For an analysis of the Constitution, see Josef Silverstein, *Burma: Military Rule and Politics of Stagnation* (Ithaca: Cornell University Press, 1977), chapter 3. A more detailed assessment from primary sources and personal experience as an official of the Burma government, is Maung Maung's *Burma's Constitution* (The Hague: Martinus Nijhoff, 1959).

32. Furnivall, *Colonial Policy and Practice,* p. 17.

33. U May Oung, "Origin of the Word 'Talaing,'" *JBRS* 2, 1 (1912): 73–74.

34. Charles Duroiselle, "Note on the word "Talaing," *JBRS* 2, 1 (1912): 100–101.

35. In addition to the Pagán and Ava inscriptions in which the word is found as *tanluiṅ* (to be documented below), U Kala's chronicle preceded Alaungpaya, as did several other works written in the fifteenth and sixteenth centuries, all of which used the word *talaing.*

36. Wheatley, *Nāgara,* p. 221.

37. W. G. Cooper, "The Origins of the 'Talaings,'" *JBRS* 3, 1 (1913): 1–11.

38. The manuscripts he was using, written by a Meerm Htaw Tu (in Burmese, Maung Shwe Tu), are dated to *Sakarāj* 1203 or 1841 AD (Cooper, "Origins," p. 4).

39. It is interesting that a Mon monk would accept a Sinhalese manuscript about themselves as representative of the Mon of Lower Burma.

40. Cooper, "Origins," p. 2.

41. Cooper, "Origins," p. 2.

42. Cooper, "Origins," p. 2.

43. Cooper, "Origins," p. 8.

44. Cooper, "Origins," p. 5.

45. Cooper, "Origins," p. 3.

46. Blagden, "Etymological Notes: I. *Talaing,*" *JBRS* 4, 1 (1914), p. 58. This is

confirmed by modern linguists as well. F. K. Lehman wrote me that *ita lerm* "cannot . . . (even imaginably) have given rise to 'talaing' in Burmese or any other language" (personal communication, June 6, 2003). Christian Bauer's "Notes to Mon Epigraphy," p. 75, includes the word *ita,* but it is defined as a Middle Mon term of respect. Shorto's *Dictionary of Mon Inscriptions,* p. 17, has two meanings for *ita:* one is a female personal name and the other, a title of respect.

47. *SMK* 4 and 5 approximately.

48. Blagden, "Etymological Notes: I. *Talaing,*" p. 58.

49. Halliday, *Mon-English Dictionary,* p. 23.

50. Halliday, *Mon-English Dictionary,* p. 23. Shorto's *Dictionary of Modern Spoken Mon,* pp. 8–9, does not have it at all.

51. Mahathera A. P. Buddhadatta, *Concise Pali-English Dictionary* (Colombo: The Colombo Apothecaries' Co., Ltd., 1968), p. 50.

52. *Judson's Dictionary,* p. 149. I do have one reservation about the word being derived from Pali. Six other words in Halliday's *Mon-English Dictionary* beginning with the same letter are associated with females and all are kinship terms, hence unlikely to have been borrowed. They include "grandmother," "younger sister," "older aunt," "midwife," "an aunt younger than one's parents," and "elder sister" (p. 79). If these are indigenous Mon words current at the time of Halliday's work, then probably *italem,* beginning with the same letter *i,* is neither related to "father" nor likely to be obsolete.

53. Blagden, "Etymological Notes: I. *Talaing,*" p. 59.

54. Blagden, "Etymological Notes: I. *Talaing,*" p. 57.

55. Blagden, "Etymological Notes: I. *Talaing.*" p. 58. I am not certain to what "chronicle" he was referring, but I presume it was the Mon manuscripts presented as evidence by Cooper.

56. Wheatley, *Nāgara,* p. 221, note 1.

57. Bauer, *Guide to Mon Studies,* p. 3. Among others, Nai Pan Hla, *Significant Role of the Mon Language,* p. 3, considers the term *talaing* to be "vulgar."

58. Wheatley, p. 225, note 28, refers to this Chinese text in the narrative which mentions a T'an-laing island thought to be a dependency of Dvāravatī. It is highly conjectural.

59. Wheatley, *Nāgara,* p. 221, note 1.

60. J. S. Furnivall, "Notes on the History of Hanthawaddy, Part II—The First Talaing Dynasty," *JBRS* 3, 2 (1913), p. 166.

61. Both the 1082 and 1107 inscriptions are discussed in Chapter 10. For the 1204 evidence, see Luce, "Note on the Peoples."

62. See also Tin Hla Thaw, "History of Burma," p. 147.

63. *Zatatawpon,* pp. 99–100. What is curious in this text is that while Talaing was listed as one of the "101 Races," so is Rman, suggesting that they were two different ethnic groups.

64. U May Oung, "Origin of the Word 'Talaing."

65. U Kala, *Mahayazawingyi,* II, passim.

66. Twinthintaikwun, *Myanmayazawinthit,* I, passim.

67. See *MKPC* cited earlier, which contains all the Old Mon inscriptions of Burma up to its publication.

68. Shorto's *Dictionary of Mon Inscriptions* does not have it.

69. *Kywan* were clients in a patron-client relationship. The term is wrongly translated as "slave," which has a modern meaning not applicable to their situation at Pagán. See Aung-Thwin, *"Athi, Kyun Taw, Hpaya Kyun."*

70. Luce, "Note on the Peoples," p. 300.

71. Luce, *Old Burma,* 1:28.

72. Kemper, *Presence of the Past,* p. 169.

73. Luce, *Old Burma,* 1:21.

74. This would explain why, in the 1826 edition of *Judson's,* the entry for *talaing* reads (the brackets in the entry represent the Burmese text): "[talaing], adj. pertaining to the Peguese. [Talaing-pyay], n. Pegu" where there is no mention of Talaing being Mon (or Mun). (See, *A Dictionary of the Burman Language,* p. 175. In the next edition, in 1852, p. 335, the entry has added the word Mun (Mon) to the definition: "[talaing], n. a Peguan or Talaing, [mun]." That continues with the 1883 edition, p. 289, where the entry states: "[talaing], n. a Peguan or Talaing, [mun] [– kayin], n. a Pwo Karen . . . ." And as we have seen, only by the 1893 edition, revised and enlarged by Robert C Stevenson do we have Forchhammer's "etymology" of the "enslavement" of the Talaing added because Stevenson found it "interesting."

75. One can trace the beginnings of this sentiment to Forchhammer in his *Notes on the Early History,* 1883, p. 2. Even Blagden was swayed by it and appealed to the British Government to right the wrongs allegedly perpetrated by the Burmans against the Mons in his "Chronicles of Pegu," (p. 374). Bode also sympathized, particularly in terms of the Mon being the preservers of the Sinhalese tradition of Theravāda Buddhism in her *Pali,* p. 9. Most sympathetic about the loss of Mon civilization was Robert Halliday, who wrote in his *Talaings* that the "*Talaings* . . . [are] a people without a country . . . [and] as a separate people with laws and government of their own, no longer exist . . . [hence] one wishes that their own race characteristics could be preserved . . . . (pp. 16–18). See also his "Mon Inscriptions of Siam."

76. Sunait Chutintaranond, "Cakravartin: Ideology, Reason and Manifestation of Siamese and Burmese Kings in Traditional Warfare (1538–1854), in *On Both Sides of the Tenasserim Range: History of Siamese-Burmese Relations* (Bangkok: Chulalongkorn University, 1995), pp. 55–93.

77. Forchhammer, *Notes on the Early History,* Part I (1883): 1–2.

78. Phayre, *History,* p. 35.

79. Bode, *Pali Literature,* p. 9, n. 2.

Chapter Twelve: Colonial Officials and Colonial Scholars

1. Paul Ambrose Bigandet, *The Life, or Legend of Gaudama, the Budha of the Burmese with Annotations, the ways to Neibban, and Notice of the Phongyies, or Burmese monks,* second edition (Rangoon: American Mission Press, 1866), pp. 389–390.

2. Bigandet, *Legend,* pp. 423–430.

3. Bigandet, *Legend,* p. x, p. 389

4. As shown in Chapter Eleven, the Rev. Francis Mason had implied such a link in 1860, but he did not explicitly tie it to Rāmaññadesa.

5. Phayre, "On the History of Pegu," p. 24.

6. Phayre, "On the History of Pegu," p. 23; *History,* p. vii.

7. *Slapat,* p. 34.

8. Phayre, "On the History of Pegu," pp. 27–28.

9. Phayre, *History,* p. 24.

10. Phayre, *History,* p. vii.

11. C. J. F. S. Forbes, *Legendary History of Burma and Arakan* (Rangoon: Government Press, 1882), p. 10.

12. Forbes, *Legendary History,* preface.

13. These colonial officials, scholars, and missionaries knew each other, read each other's works, sometimes dedicated their publications to each other, in some cases worked in the same offices, and likely discussed many of these issues at length with each other. So precisely where information originated and to whom it was dispersed at what particular time, is difficult to determine.

14. Phayre, *History,* p. 24. However, Phayre cites the wrong page number (101) in Bigandet's work, which has nothing to say about Suvaṇṇabhūmi or Soṇa and Uttara, but discusses the Shwédagôn Pagoda and the two other merchant brothers, Tapussa and Bhallika. Apparently Phayre had confused the two. Forbes, in *Legendary History,* p. 10, stated that "Talaing legends" mention the Soṇa and Uttara story, but he does not document any source and may have obtained his information from Phayre's articles of 1873–1874. Phayre, similarly refers to "traditions current among the people of Pegu" as noted above, as well as "Talaing chronicles" (p. 26), in making his case. However, Blagden wrote in "The Chronicles of Pegu," p. 372, that Phayre did not have access to Mon sources, a curious statement.

15. Forbes, *Legendary History* p. 23. He quotes an inscription of Arakan that allegedly records Aniruddha's bringing back of monks well versed in the scriptures from Thatôn, although without a conquest. Unfortunately, Forbes provides no documentation for the quote.

16. Phayre, *History,* p. 31. He had used the manuscript version of the *Yazadarit* and the *Slapat,* neither of which mentioned the alleged conquest (see Phayre, *History,* p. 58). Halliday also states that Phayre "evidently followed this work [*Yazadarit*] for that period of Talaing history, except that he has read it in a Burmese translation . . ." (see his *Talaings,* p. 130).

17. Phayre, *History,* p. vii.

18. Michael Symes, *Journal of his Second Embassy to the Court of Ava in 1802* (London, George Allen & Unwin Ltd, 1955), p. xix.

19. Phayre, *History,* p. 26.

20. Cox, *Journal;* and John Crawfurd, *Journal of an Embassy from the Governor General of India to the Court of Ava in the year 1827* (London: Henry Colburn, 1829).

21. Vicentius Sangermano, *The Burmese Empire a Hundred Years Ago* (New York: Augustus M. Kelley, 1969).

22. *Narrative of the Mission to the court of Ava,* especially chapter 2, pages 30–54, where Yule gives a detailed description of some major temples of Pagán which the Mon Paradigm later claimed were built in "Mon style" or by Mon architects.

23. Mason, *Burmah,* p. 44. He must have been referring to the *stupa* rather than the *gu,* for the latter, particularly in terms of Pagán scale and style, has not been found in Lower Burma.

24. The only time the Mon conquered Upper Burma was in the eighteenth-century, so obviously this statement is an error, but not uncharacteristic of Forchhammer's treatment of Burma's history.

25. Forchhammer, *The Jardine Prize,* p. 4–5. See also his "Introductory Remarks" in John Jardine's *Notes on Buddhist Law: III Marriage,* (Rangoon: Government Printing, 1882), pp. ix, where he claims that prior to "Anawratha's conquest (10th century A.D.) [sic] of the Talaing dominions, . . . they [Burmans] possessed no written books in their idiom before this event took place." Forchhammer continues to express similar sentiments in his "Remarks" until p. xv, and in his *Notes on the Early History and Geography, Part I,* pp. 11, 13, 14, where he speaks of the antiquity of the Mon.

26. By the twentieth century, as we shall see, we find, among many others, Harvey, *History,* pp. 3–11, 29, and 236, who stated unequivocally that "the Burmese owed their civilisation to the Talaings . . ." Luce, in *Old Burma,* 1:20–27 was more emphatic while even those outside Burma Studies with a much broader audience, like George Coedes in his *Making of Southeast Asia,* p. 113, relayed the same message. All had accepted the notion that Mon civilization in Lower Burma preceded Pagán, and that it was carried to the latter kingdom after the conquest of Aniruddha in 1057.

27. *Notes on the Early History and Geography Part I,* p. 16.

28. Forchhammer, *Notes on the Early History and Geography, Part I,* p. 6, mentioned them for the first time in this publication. Phayre never mentioned them when he discussed Dhammazedi in his *History* (pp. 85–86), which leads me to believe they were discovered after the latter went to press.

29. Blagden, "Notes on Talaing Epigraphy."

30. Bode, *Pali Literature,* pp. 9–10; 13–14.

31. Harvey, *History,* p. 383.

32. Halliday, *The Talaings,* pp. v, 129–130.

33. Halliday, *The Talaings,* p. 130.

34. Harvey, *History,* p. 376.

35. Hall, *Burma,* chapter 8, deals with the flight of the Mon to Siam. Halliday, in *The Talaings,* p. 2, suggests they had retained their culture in Siam.

36. Halliday, *The Talaings,* p. 16. See also Crawfurd's *Journal,* p. 29.

37. Halliday, *The Talaings,* p. 5.

38. J. S. Furnivall, "Twenty Five Years: A Retrospect and Prospect," *JBRS* 25, 1 (1935): 40.

39. J. S. Furnivall, "The Dawn of Nationalism in Burma," *JBRS* 33, 1 (1950): 1–7.

40. B. Houghton, "Some Anthropometric Data of the Talaings," *JBRS* 1, 1 (1911): 70. This kind of physical measurement of people (and criminals) during the nineteenth-century was rather standard in both the academic and juridical world, something we call the "criminalization of ethnicity" in the field.

41. Today the easiest way to peruse the *JBRS* is to use the CD-ROM produced by the Myanmar Book Centre & Book Promotion & Service Ltd. (Bangkok: Thailand, 1998).

42. See the *JBRS,* volumes 58 and 59, published in 1976 and 1977.

43. Nai Pan Hla, "Editor's Note on Excavation of Old Thaton," *JBRS* 59, 1–2 (December 1976): 165–166.

44. Taw Sein Ko, *Burmese Sketches,* 2, p. 365

45. The first volume was reviewed in a short note by May Oung, "Review of '*Burmese Sketches*' by Taw Sein Ko," in *JBRS* 3, 2 (1913): 191–192, in which this mar-

ginalization of Taw Sein Ko was actually mentioned. Part of the reason seems to be that Taw Sein Ko, who was of Chinese descent, preferred to see some of Burmese civilization as having originated in China. Many objected, as they were convinced of the correctness of the Mon Paradigm.

46. *EB* 1, 1:7.

47. Although the editor of this volume is noted as Duroiselle and no name is given for the authorship of the text being quoted herein, it is clear from the remarks in the text that Blagden was its author. Among other things, he thanks Duroiselle in the footnotes for certain information (p. 85).

48. *EB* 1, 2:73.

49. Sangermano, *Burmese Empire,* p. x. Literally translated, the phrase means: "the vanquished have given laws to the victors." My thanks to Stephen O'Harrow of the University of Hawai'i for the proper English rendition of the Latin.

50. Harvey, *History,* 383.

51. Harvey, *History,* pp. 28–29.

52. Although most commonly thought of as a joint product by both Luce and Pe Maung Tin, it was in fact the latter's translation and thesis at Oxford. For its publication, Luce helped with regard to English style (*Glass Palace Chronicle,* p. xxiii). For a recent analysis of this work, see Tun Aung Chain's "Pe Maung Tin and Luce's *Glass Palace* Revisited," in *U Pe Maung Tin—A Tribute* (Yangôn: Universities Historical Research Centre, 1999), pp. 46–60.

53. Many of the works by Pe Maung Tin focused on Pali literature, his forte. Despite his Mon background, Pe Maung Tin may have been skeptical of the early Lower Burma theme, which is hinted at in an article of his called "A Note on the Development of the Burmese Language," *JBRS* 24, 1 (1934): 58–59. Perhaps he also did not want to criticize his brother-in-law, Luce, in public.

54. Luce, *Old Burma,* 1:20–24.

55. Corporation of Rangoon, *A History of Rangoon,* comp. B. R. Pearn (Rangoon: American Baptist Mission Press, 1929).

56. Corporation of Rangoon, *History of Rangoon,* p. 17.

57. Hall, *Burma,* p. 16.

58. Thus, for example, in 1964 it published *Pagan Minsasu Thutethana Lokngan* [Research project on the collection of Pagán ink inscriptions], comp. Bohmu Ba Shin (Yangôn: Ministry of Culture, 1964).

59. Quoted in Wheatley, *Nāgara,* p. 200. For the French, see Dupont, *L'archéologie mône de Dvaravati* pp. 13–15.

60. Luce, "Dvāravatī and Old Burma," p. 11.

61. Maung Htin Aung, *The Stricken Peacock: Anglo-Burmese Relations 1752–1948* (The Hague: Martinus Nijhoff, 1965).

62. Maung Htin Aung, *A History of Burma* (New York: Columbia University Press, 1967), pp. 32–33; and *Burmese History Before 1287,* particularly chapters 5–7.

63. Than Tun, "History of Buddhism," introduction (p. iii). Note that this was not part of the regular issues of the *Journal,* which terminated in 1977.

64. Than Tun, *Khit Haung Myanma Yazawin* [Early history of Myanma] (Yangôn: Maha Dagon Publishers, 1969), p. 119. My thanks to U Saw Tun of Northern Illinois University for reminding me of this.

65. E. Michael Mendelson, *Sangha and State in Burma: A Study of Monastic Sectar-*

ianism and Leadership, ed. John P. Ferguson (Ithaca: Cornell University Press, 1975), p. 35.

66. H. G. Quaritch Wales, "Anuruddha and the Thaton Tradition."

67. Michael Mendelson, "The King of the Weaving Mountain," *Royal Central Asian Journal* 48 (1961): 229–237; "A Messianic Buddhist Association in Upper Burma," *BSOAS* 24 (1961): 560–580; and "Observations on a Tour in the Region of Mount Popa, Central Burma," *France-Asie* 19 (1963): 786–807.

68. Wheatley, *Nāgara,* p. 200.

69. An influential art historian in Southeast Asian studies, Quaritch Wales had as early as 1947 in "Anuruddha and the Thaton Tradition" accepted the historicity of the conquest. However, in his 1973 *Early Burma-Old Siam* (London: Bernard Quaritch, Ltd.), a play-on-words of Luce's *Old Burma-Early Pagan,* he was less than enthusiastic about what he called Luce's "Burma-centric" perspective (p. xiii). Nevertheless he continued to accept the conquest of Thatôn and at least parts of the Mon Paradigm.

70. Tilman Frasch, *Pagan: Stadt und Staat,* pp. 287–288. My thanks again to Lily Handlin for her reading of the German.

71. As late as 1999, Emmanuel Guillon, in *The Mons,* has continued to accept the conquest of Thatôn as probably historical, although he considers many of the other stories about Aniruddha as likely to be myth (pp. 112–113).

72. Both Woodward, *The Art and Architecture of Thailand,* p. 137, and Stadtner, "The Art of Burma," p. 48, perpetuate the myth. And although Bautze-Picron, in *The Buddhist Murals of Pagan,* pp. 3–4, seems willing to reject the Mon Paradigm in terms of Pagán's frescos and to accept direct Indic influences, she still considers the conquest of Thatôn and its "Mon" influences credible, so she, too, perpetuates the myth.

73. John Guy, "The Art of the Pyu and Mon," in *The Art of Burma: New Studies,* ed. Donald M. Stadtner. Mumbai: India, Marg Publications, 1999, pp. 13–28.

74. John Guy, "Offering up a rare jewel," pp. 23–33.

75. Andrew Huxley, "Sanction in the Theravada Buddhist Kingdoms of S.E. Asia," *Transactions of the Jean Bodin Society for Comparative Institutional History* 58, 4 (Brussels: De Boeck Université, 1991), p. 336, and another he edited entitled "Thai, Mon, and Burmese Dhammathats, who influenced whom?" in *Thai law: Buddhist Law, Essays on the Legal History of Thailand, Laos and Burma* (Bangkok: White Orchid, 1996), pp. 81–131.

76. Strong, *The Legend and Cult of Upagupta,* pp. 174–175, accepts the Mon Paradigm. But on p. 3 and chapter 8, he made some important reservations.

77. Michael Aung-Thwin, "The Legend That Was Lower Burma," paper presented at the International Conference on Texts and Contexts, Universities Historical Research Centre, Yangon, Myanmar, December 12–14, 2001.

Chapter Thirteen: Without the Mon Paradigm

1. As of this writing, the most recent treatment of state formation in Southeast Asia is Tony Day's *Fluid Iron: State Formation in Southeast Asia* (Honolulu: University of Hawai'i Press, 2002).

2. There are several Southeast Asianists who hold such views, perhaps best represented by Kenneth R. Hall's *Maritime Trade and State Development in Early Southeast*

Asia (Honolulu: University of Hawaii Press, 1985). But Chris Baker's "Ayutthaya Rising: From Land or Sea?" *JSEAS* 34,1 (February 2001): 41–62, puts a different perspective on what the "conventional" view is.

3. Aung-Thwin, *Lower Burma and Bago,* pp. 25–28. Note that the urban history I speak of here extends to the end of the monarchy in 1886 (hence, the 2,100 years), whereas my calculation of fifteen centuries in the article cited reaches only to the end of the sixteenth century.

4. Peter Bellwood, "Southeast Asia before History," in *The Cambridge History of Southeast Asia.* Volume One: *From Early Times to c. 1800,* ed. Nicholas Tarling (Cambridge: Cambridge University Press, 1992), pp. 93–94. See also Tadayo Watabe's much earlier English-language draft of a paper entitled "Origin and Dispersal of Cultivated Rice in Asia," originally published in Japanese. His thesis is that both Indica and Japonica varieties of rice originated in Yunnan and moved from there southwest and southeast to the coasts of the Asian landmass.

5. The late Paul Wheatley puts the rate of deposition of silt by the Irrawaddy at more than 60 yards a year, that of the Mekong at between 60 and 80 yards, and the Ci Manuk and Solo deltas at as much as 100 yards. See *Nāgara,* p. 274.

6. Stark, et al., "Results of the 1995–1996 Archaeological Field Investigations."

7. I do not wish to debate this often controversial large issue except where mythical Rāmaññadesa has affected its analysis and understanding.

8. As I do not want, nor am I competent, to debate the Dvāravatī issue here, I refer readers to Wyatt's thoughtful article, "Relics, oaths and politics in thirteenth-century Siam." In it, he refers to Dhida Saraya's *(Sri) Dvaravati: The Initial Phase of Siam's History* (Bangkok: Muang Boran, 1999). However, I should add that Saraya has virtually nothing to say about Rāmaññadesa and Lower Burma during the first millennium, which is unfortunate, as it ignores rather than addresses the problem. She does state, correctly, that the appearance of Rāmaññadesa was late (pp. 141–142). As of this writing, the latest publication on "Dvāravatī" is Peter Skilling's, "Dvāravatī: Recent Revelations and Research," *Dedications to Her Royal Highness, Princess Galyani* . . . (Bangkok: Siam Society, 2003), pp. 87–112, and Woodward, *Art and Architecture of Thailand.*

9. Diffloth, *Nyah Kur,* p. 11.

10. The most explicit connections made between the two in terms of art history was G. H. Luce, in his "Dvāravatī and Old Burma," *JSS* 53, 1 (January, 1965): 9–26. In terms of Theravāda Buddhism and script, see his "Rice and Religion: A Study of Old Mon-Khmer Evolution and Culture," *JSS* 53 (1965), p. 140.

11. Wyatt, "Relics, oaths and politics," p. 7; and P. Pramojanee and T. Jarupongskul, "Evolution of Landforms and the Sites of Ancient Cities and Communities in Lower Chao Phraya Plain," in Kajit Jittasevi, ed., "Proceedings for the International Workshop Ayudhya and Asia," Bangkok: Core University Program between Thammasat University and Kyoto University, BE 2540 [AD 1997]), pp. 15–35.

12. Jacq-Hergoualc'h, "The Mergui-Tenasserim Region," p. 83. Forbes, in his *Legendary History,* p. 6, wrote that "the sea once . . . reached to the walls of the city of Thatone instead of being as now twelve miles distant."

13. Aung Thwin, *Pagan,* chapters 4–8.

14. Merle C. Ricklefs, many years ago, published a seminal article called "Land and the Law in the Epigraphy of Tenth-Century Cambodia," *JAS* 26, 3 (1967):

411–420, that threw some light on this subject. More recently, Michael Vickery, in *Society, Economics, and Politics in Pre-Angkor Cambodia: The 7th–8th Centuries* (Tokyo: The Centre for East Asian Cultural Studies for UNESCO, 1998), has given us a more comprehensive, detailed look at Angkor in those centuries. But whether Angkor paid their artisans in ways that made it attractive for such people to migrate to that center is not as well known.

15. There were thus sound economic, social, and religious reasons for immigrating to Pagán, not at all related to twentieth-century biases that seem to envision only escape from authoritarian rule as valid causes for such movement.

16. Aung-Thwin, *Myth and History,* chapters 2–5.

17. Halliday, in *The Talaings,* pp. 10–11, 130, disputes this, saying Phayre was using the Burmese version of the story. Wareru, from the T'ai Hwarow, a title given to him by Pra Ruang of Sukhodaya, was called Magadu (his Mon name), and his links with Sukhodaya may be the reason Phayre considered him Shan (or T'ai). This is consistent with Phayre's erroneous "Shan Period" thesis in Burma's history.

18. Aung-Thwin, *Myth and History,* chapter 3.

19. Lawrence Palmer Briggs, "The Ancient Khmer Empire," *Transactions of the American Philosophical Society,* New Series, 41, 1 (February, 1951): 259.

20. My current research on the kingdom of Ava between 1364–1527 demonstrates this point in greater detail.

21. For Pagán especially, see Aung-Thwin, *Pagan,* chapter 9.

22. The other was reportedly Kuvera of Arakan, who reigned for seven years during the Candra Dynasty. She may have been the "woman ruler" mentioned in one of the Arabic sources discussed earlier.

23. With regard to the Toungoo rulers and their dynasty, see Lieberman, *Burmese Administrative Cycles,* and also his newest work, *Strange Parallels: Southeast Asia in Global Context, c. 800–1830* (Cambridge: Cambridge University Press, 2003), chapter 2, which places it in a broader "global" context.

24. The phrase, of course, is from Anthony Reid's *Southeast Asia in the Age of Commerce 1450–1680* (New Haven: Yale University Press, 1993), p. 1.

25. Aung-Thwin, "Lower Burma and Bago . . ." p. 51, note 35.

26. It is interesting that most coastal powers regarded other coastal powers, not the agrarian ones, as their main competitors, and agrarian powers seem to have regarded their real competitors as other agrarian powers. As a result, we rarely find an agrarian kingdom or polity destroying, rather than attempting to control, a coastal kingdom or polity and vice versa. Each needed the other: the coasts needed food and other products from the interior, and the interior needed luxury goods and a window onto the outside world from the coasts.

27. This account may have been the basis for the Thatôn story.

28. I would not be surprised, however, if the next capital returned to the interior.

29. Amatgyi Bannya Dala, *Yazadarit,* p. 357.

30. As Jonathan Walters shows in "Buddhist History," p. 148, this misinterpretation of texts by modern scholars plays out in similar ways in the present conflict between Tamils and Sinhalese.

31. U May Oung, "Origin," p. 74, confirms this by writing that "the *Alaung-min-*

dayagyi Ayedawpon, a detailed account of the great king's exploits, does not mention the alleged re-naming of the Mons" [to Talaing].

32. *The Royal Orders of Burma, A.D. 1598–1885: Part Three, A.D. 1751–1781,* vol. 3, ed. Than Tun (Kyoto: The Centre for Southeast Asian Studies, Kyoto University, 1985).

33. *Royal Orders,* 3:23–24.

34. *Royal Orders,* 3:22–23.

35. *Royal Orders,* 3:36–37.

36. Phayre, *History,* p. 165

37. Crawfurd wrote in his *Journal,* p. 29, that "The Peguans, or Talains, do not differ materially from the Burmans, except in dialect; and even this distinction, in a great measure, ceases as we approach the northern confines of their ancient domain; for here the Burmese language prevails, even with the Peguans."

38. *Royal Orders,* 3:30–31.

39. *Reprint from Dalrymple's Oriental Repertory,* p. 151.

40. *Reprint from Dalrymple's Oriental Repertory,* pp. 151–152.

41. Lieberman, *Burmese Administrative Cycles,* especially pp. 236–247, shows how Alaungpaya used reified ethnicity for his political goals.

42. *SMK* 1:355; 3:60, 150, 158. Aung-Thwin, "Lower Burma . . . ," pp. 30–31. The "upstream-downstream" concept is, of course, well known and used in Southeast Asian Studies; it is not my own. But it has not been applied to Burma heretofore, particularly as it is being done in this book.

43. Aung-Thwin, *Pagan,* p. 105.

44. *Zambudipa Okhsaung Kyan,* pp. 41–47.

45. The Anh Pass through the Arakan Yomas lay across the river from Prome (Prañ).

46. *SMK* 3:121, 158, and passim.

47. Aung-Thwin, *Myth and History,* p, 57.

48. Conceivably we might add the hills as a third genuine category. But even this is still an environmental, not an ethnic, distinction, expressed in the term *taungthu,* meaning "mountain person."

49. The exceptions are Bob Taylor and Victor Lieberman, who have argued against such views. See Robert H. Taylor, "Perceptions of Ethnicity in the Politics of Burma," *Southeast Asian Journal of Social Sciences,* 10, 1 (1982): 7–22, and Victor B. Lieberman, "Ethnic Politics in Eighteenth-Century Burma," *Modern Asian Studies,* 12, 3 (1978): 455–482. Of course, they were influenced by the earlier works of Burma anthropologist F. K. Lehman, particularly his "Ethnic Categories in Burma and the Theory of Social Systems," in *Southeast Asian Tribes, Minorities, and Nations,* ed. Peter Kunstadter (Princeton: Princeton University Press, 1967), pp. 93–124.

50. This view was presented by Michael Vickery in a recent paper delivered at the National University of Singapore in July of 2004 entitled "Champa Revised."

Bibliography

Adas, Michael. *The Burma Delta.* Madison: University of Wisconsin Press, 1974.

Amatgyi Bannya Dala, *Yazadarit Ayedawpon* [The royal crisis account of *Yazadarit*]. Yangôn: Swesa Press, 1974.

Archaeological Survey of Burma. *Epigraphia Birmanica: Being Lithic and Other Inscriptions of Burma.* Volume I, part I. Edited by Taw Sein Ko and Charles Duroiselle. Rangoon: Government Printing, 1919.

———. *Epigraphia Birmanica: Being Lithic and Other Inscriptions of Burma.* Volume I, part II. Edited by Charles Duroiselle. Rangoon: Government Printing, 1920? Reprint, Rangoon, 1961.

———. *Epigraphia Birmanica: Being Lithic and Other Inscriptions of Burma.* Volume II, part I. Edited by Charles Duroiselle. Rangoon: Government Printing, 1921. Reprint, Rangoon, 1961.

———. *Epigraphia Birmanica: Being Lithic and Other Inscriptions of Burma.* Volume II, part II. Edited by Charles Duroiselle. Rangoon: Government Printing, 1921.

———. *Epigraphia Birmanica: Being Lithic and Other Inscriptions of Burma.* Volume III, part I. Edited by Charles Duroiselle. Rangoon: Government Printing, 1923.

———. *Epigraphia Birmanica: Being Lithic and Other Inscriptions of Burma.* Volume III, part II. Edited by Charles Duroiselle. Rangoon: Government Printing, 1928.

———. *Epigraphia Birmanica: Being Lithic and Other Inscriptions of Burma.* Volume IV, part I. Edited by U Mya. Rangoon: Government Printing, 1934.

———. *Exploration and Research: Report of the Superintendent for the Year 1937–38.* Rangoon: Government Printing, 1938.

———. *A List of Inscriptions Found in Burma.* Compiled by Charles Duroiselle. Rangoon: Government Printing, 1921.

Archaeological Survey of Ceylon. *Epigraphia Zeylanica.* 2 volumes. Edited and translated by Don Martino de Zilva Wickremasinghe. London: Oxford University Press, 1928.

Archaeological Survey of India. *Annual Report.* Calcutta: Government Printing, 1936–1937.

———. "The Kalyānī inscriptions erected by King Dhammacetī at Pegu in 1476 AD Rangoon, Government Printing, 1892.

———. "A Vaishnava Inscription at Pagan." *Epigraphia Indica* 7, 27 (1902–1903): 197–198.

The Art of Burma: New Studies. Edited by Donald M. Stadtner. Mumbai: India, Marg Publications, 1999.

Aung Myint. Editor's Note on "Excavation of Old Thaton," *Journal of the Burma Research Society* 59, 1–2 (December 1976): 165–166.

———. *Kaung Kin Dat Pon Mya Hma Myanma She Haung Myo Taw Mya* [Ancient royal cities of Myanmar from aerial photographs]. Yangôn: Ministry of Culture, 1998.

Aung Thaw. *Excavations at Beikthano.* Rangoon: Ministry of Union Culture, 1968.

———. "Expert team conducting research on ancient objects unearthed in Budalin Township." *Myanmar Alin* (February 25, 1999): 5, 12.

———. *Historical Sites in Burma.* Rangoon: Ministry of Union Culture, 1972.

———. "The 'Neolithic' culture of the Padah-lin Caves." *Asian Perspectives* 14 (1971): 123–133.

Aung-Thwin, Michael. "*Athi, Kyun Taw, Hpaya Kyun:* Varieties of Commendation and Dependence in Pre-Colonial Burma." In *Slavery, Bondage and Dependency in Southeast Asia.* Edited by Anthony Reid. New York: University of Queensland Press, 1983.

———. "Burma Before Pagan: The Status of Archaeology Today." *Asian Perspectives* 25, 2, (1982–1983): 1–21.

———. "Burmese Historiography—Chronicles (Yazawin)." In *Making History: A Global Encyclopedia of Historical Writing.* Edited by D. R. Woolf. New York: Garland Publishing, 1997.

———. "Heaven, Earth and the Supernatural World: Dimensions of the Exemplary Center in Burmese History." In *The City As a Sacred Center: Essays on Six Asian Contexts. International Studies in Sociology and Social Anthropology.* Edited by Bardwell Smith and Holy Baker Reynolds. Leiden: E. J. Brill, 1987.

———. *Irrigation in the Heartland of Burma: Foundations of the Pre-Colonial Burmese State.* DeKalb, IL: Center for Southeast Asian Studies, 1990.

———. "The Legend That Was Lower Burma." Paper presented at the International Conference on Texts and Contexts, Universities Historical Research Centre, Yangôn, Myanmar, December 12–14, 2001.

———. "Lower Burma and Bago in the History of Burma." In *The Maritime Frontier of Burma: Exploring Political, Cultural and Commercial Interaction in the Indian Ocean World, 1200–1800.* Edited by Jos Gommans and Jacques Leider. Leiden: Koninklijke Nederlandse Akademie van Wetenschappen, 2002.

———. *Making of Modern Burma* [CD-ROM]. Honolulu: The University of Hawai'i Center for Southeast Asian Studies, 2001.

———. *Myth and History in the Historiography of Early Burma: Paradigms, Primary Sources, and Prejudices.* Athens: Ohio University Press, 1998.

———. "The Myth of the 'Three Shan Brothers' and the Ava Period in Burmese History." *Journal of Asian Studies* 55, 4 (November 1996): 881–901

———. "Origins and Development of the Field of Prehistory in Burma." In *Asian Perspectives Special Issue: The Archaeology of Myanma Pyay (Burma).* Edited by Miriam T. Stark and Michael A. Aung-Thwin. 40, 1 (2002): 6–34.

———. *Pagan: The Origins of Modern Burma.* Honolulu: University of Hawai'i Press, 1985.

———. "Principles and Patterns of the Precolonial Burmese State." In *Tradition and Modernity in Myanmar: Proceedings of an International Conference held in Berlin from May 7th to May 9th, 1993.* Edited by Uta Gartner and Jens Lorenz. Berlin: Humboldt-Universität Fakultätsinstitut für Asien- und Afrikawissenschaften, 1994.

———. "The Problem of Ceylonese-Burmese Relations in the 12th Century and the Question of an Interregnum in Pagán: 1165–1174 A.D." *Journal of the Siam Society* 64, 1 (January 1976): 53–74.

———. "The Role of *Sāsana* Reform in Burmese History, Economic Dimensions of a Religious Purification." *Journal of Asian Studies* 38, 4 (August 1979): 671–688.

———. "Spirals in Burmese and Early Southeast Asian History." *Journal of Interdisciplinary History* 21, 4 (Spring 1991): 575–602.

Ba Shin. *Lokahteikpan: Early Burmese Culture in a Pagan Temple.* Rangoon: Burma Historical Commission, 1962.

Baby, Daw. *Thaton Myohaung* [The ancient city of Thatôn]. Yangôn: Department of Archaeology, 2000.

Backus, Charles. *The Nan-chao kingdom and T'ang China's southwestern frontier.* London: Cambridge University Press, 1981.

Baker, Chris. "Ayutthaya Rising: From Land or Sea?" *Journal of Southeast Asian Studies* 34, 1 (February 2003): 41–62.

Bauer, Christian. *A Guide to Mon Studies.* Monash University Centre of Southeast Asian Studies Working Paper, no. 32. Clayton, Australia: 1984.

———. "Notes on Mon Epigraphy." *Journal of the Siam Society* 79, 1 and 2 (1991): 31–83 and 61–79.

Bautze-Picron, Claudine. "Between India and Burma: The 'Andagu' Stelae." In *The Art of Burma: New Studies.* Edited by Donald M. Stadtner. Mumbai: India, Marg Publications, 1999.

———. *The Buddhist Murals of Pagan: Timeless Vistas of the Cosmos.* Trumbull, CT: Weatherhill, 2003.

Bellwood, Peter. "Reply to Stargardt." *The Review of Archaeology* 14, 2 (Fall 1993): 33–35.

———. "Review of Stargardt, *The Ancient Pyu of Burma.*" *The Review of Archaeology* 13, 2 (Fall 1992): 1–7.

———. "Southeast Asia before History." In *The Cambridge History of Southeast Asia.* Volume One: *From Early Times to c. 1800.* Edited by Nicholas Tarling. Cambridge: Cambridge University Press, 1992.

Bennett, Paul J. "The 'Fall of Pagan': Continuity and change in 14th Century Burma." In *Conference Under the Tamarind Tree: Three Essays in Burmese History.* Yale University Southeast Asia Monograph Series, no. 15. New Haven: Yale University Press, 1971.

Beylié, Léon-Marie-Eugène de. *Prome et Samara: voyage archéologique en Birmanie et en Mésopotamie.* Paris: E. Leroux, 1907.

Bigandet, Rev. Paul Ambrose. *The Life, or Legend of Gaudama, the Budha of the Burmese with Annotations, the ways to Neibban, and Notice of the Phongyies, or Burmese monks.* Second Edition. Rangoon: American Mission Press, 1866.

Blackburn, Anne M. "Localizing Lineage: Importing Higher Ordination in Theravādin South and Southeast Asia." In *Constituting Communities: Theravāda Buddhism and the Religious Cultures of South and Southeast Asia.* Edited by John Clifford Holt et al. Albany, NY: State University of New York Press, 2003.

Blackmore, Michael. "The Rise of Nan-chao in Yunnan." *Journal of Southeast Asian History* 1 (1960): 47–61.

Blagden, Charles Otto. "The Chronicles of Pegu: A Text in the Mon Language." *Journal of The Royal Asiatic Society* (1907): 367–374.

———. "Etymological Notes: I. *Talaing*." *Journal of the Burma Research Society* 4, 1 (1914): 57–60.

———. "Etymological Notes: II. *Mon and Ramaññadesa*." *Journal of the Burma Research Society* 4, 1 (1914): 59–60.

———. "Etymological Notes: VI. Thaton." *Journal of the Burma Research Society* 5, 1 (1915): 26–27.

———. "Etymological Notes: VII. Mon, Rman, Rāmañña." *Journal of the Burma Research Society* 5, 1 (1915): 26–27.

———. "A Further Note on the Inscriptions of the Myazedi Pagoda, Pagan, and other Inscriptions throwing light on them." *Journal of The Royal Asiatic Society* (1910): 797–812.

———. "Môn Inscriptions Nos. IX–XI." *Epigraphia Birmanica* 3, 1 (1923): 1–73.

———. "The Môn or Talaing Face of the Myazedi Inscription at Pagan." *Epigraphia Birmanica*. Volume I, part I. Rangoon: Government Printing, 1919.

———. "Notes on Talaing Epigraphy." *Journal of the Burma Research Society* 2, 1 (1912): 38–42.

———. "A Preliminary Study of the Fourth Text of the Myazedi Inscriptions." *Journal of The Royal Asiatic Society* (April 1911): 365–388.

———. "The Pyu Face of the Myazedi Inscription at Pagan." *Epigraphia Birmanica*. Volume I, part I. Rangoon: Government Printing, 1919.

———. "The Pyū Inscriptions." *Epigraphia Indica,* 12 (1913–14): 127–132.

———. "The Pyu Inscriptions." *Journal of the Burma Research Society* 7, 1 (April, 1917): 37–44.

———. "The Talaing Inscription of the Myazedi Pagoda at Pagan, With a Few Remarks on the Other Versions." *Journal of The Royal Asiatic Society* 25 (1909): 1017–1051.

Bo Kay, U. *Pagan Thutethana Lan Hnyun* [Research guide to Pagán]. Yangôn: Sape Beikman Press, 1981.

Bode, Mabel Haynes. *The Pali Literature of Burma*. London: The Royal Asiatic Society of Great Britain and Ireland, 1909. Reprint, London, 1966.

Bradley, David. *Proto-Loloish*. Copenhagen: Scandinavian Institute of Asian Studies, 1979.

Briggs, Lawrence Palmer. "The Ancient Khmer Empire." *Transactions of the American Philosophical Society*. New Series, 41, 1 (February, 1951): 1–295.

Brown, Robert L. *Dvāravatī: Wheels of the Law and the Indianization of South East Asia*. Leiden: E. J. Brill, 1996.

Buddhadatta, Mahathera A. P. *Concise Pali-English Dictionary*. Colombo: The Colombo Apothecaries' Co. Ltd., 1968.

Burma. *Report of the Director, Archaeological Survey, Burma for the year ending 30th September 1958*. Yangon: Archaeological Survey, nd.

Burma: Art and Archaeology. Edited by Alexandra Green and T. Richard Blurton. Chicago: Art Media Resources, 2002.

Burma Gazetteer: Thatôn District. Volume A. Compiled by U Tin Gyi. Rangoon: Government. Printing, Burma, 1931.

Burma Historical Commission. *Pagán Minsasu Thutethana Lokngan* [Research project on the collection of Pagán ink inscriptions]. Yangôn: Ministry of Culture, 1964.

Burney, Henry. "Translation of an Inscription in the Burmese Language, discovered at Buddha Gaya, in 1833." *Asiatic Researches* 20, 1 (1836): 161–189.

The Burney Papers. 5 volumes. Westmead, England: Gregg International Publishers Ltd., 1971.

Casparis, J. G. de. *Indonesian palaeography: a history of writing in Indonesia from the beginnings to c. A.D. 1500.* Leiden: E. J. Brill, 1975.

Ceramic Traditions in Myanmar. Yangôn: SEAMEO Regional Centre for History and Tradition, 2003.

"Charuk nai prathet thai lem 2 akson panlawa akson mon phuttha sattawat thi 12–21" [Inscriptions in Thailand, volume 2: Pallava and Mon Scripts, Buddhist Centuries 12–21]. In *Charuk nai prathet thai* [Inscriptions in Thailand]. 5 volumes. Edited by Kongkaeo Wiraprachak. Bangkok: National Library and Fine Arts Department, BE 2529 [1986].

Chau Ju-Kua: His Work on the Chinese and Arab Trade in the twelfth and thirteenth centuries, entitled Chu-fan-chi. Translated from the Chinese and Annotated by Friedrich Hirth and W. W. Rockhill. Taipei: Ch'eng-Wen Publishing Company, 1970.

Chen Yi-Sein. "The Chinese in Upper Burma Before A.D. 1700." In *Silver Jubilee Publication.* Yangôn: Ministry of Culture and Burma Historical Researches, 1982.

———. "The Chinese Inscription at Pagán," *Bulletin of the Burma Historical Commission* 1, 2 (December 1960): 153–157.

———. "Lin-Yang (Viṣṇu City) 1st–5th Centuries AD." In *Studies in Myanma History,* volume 1. Yangôn: Innwa Publishing House, 1999.

———. "The Location of the Pyu Capital in the 800–833 Period." In *Proceedings of the Myanmar Two Millennia Conference 15–17 December 1999.* Yangôn: Universities Historical Research Centre, 2000.

———. "Pyu Khit Myanma Naingnan e Naingnan Khya Set San Ye" [International relations of Myanmar during the Pyu period]. In *Researches in Burmese History,* no. 4, Yangôn: Ministry of Culture, 1979.

Chen Yu-jing. *Chen Yu-jing Dong-nan-ya Gu-shi yan-jiu he-ji* [Collected works on early Southeast Asian history by Chen Yu-jing]. Volume 2. Hong Kong: Commercial Press, 1992.

Chevilliot, E., compiler. "Catalogue of Burmese Mss." Manuscript #3447 of The India Office, n.d.

Chou Ta-Kuan. *The Customs of Cambodia.* Translated by J. Gilan d'Arcy Paul. Third Edition. Bangkok: The Siam Society, 1993.

Chutintaranond, Sunait. "Cakravartin: Ideology, Reason and Manifestation of Siamese and Burmese Kings in Traditional Warfare (1538–1854)." In *On Both Sides of the Tenasserim Range: History of Siamese-Burmese Relations.* Edited by Sunait Chutintaranond and Than Tun. Bangkok: Chulalongkorn University, 1995.

———. "King Bayinnaung as Historical Hero in Thai Perspective." *Comparative Studies on Literature and History of Thailand and Myanmar.* Bangkok and Yangôn: Institute of Asian Studies Chulalongkorn University and Universities' Historical Research Centre, 1997.

Coedes, George. *The Indianized States of Southeast Asia.* Edited by Walter F. Vella and translated by Susan Brown Cowing. Third Edition. Honolulu: East-West Center Press, 1968.

Collins, Steven. "What is Literature in Pali?" In *Literary Cultures in History: Reconstruc-*

tions from South Asia. Edited by Sheldon Pollock. Berkeley: University of California Press, 2003.

Constituting Communities: Theravāda Buddhism and the Religious Cultures of South and Southeast Asia. Edited by John Clifford Holt et al. Albany: NY: State University of New York Press, 2003.

Cooler, Richard M. *The Karen bronze drums of Burma: types, iconography, manufacture, and use.* Leiden and New York: E. J. Brill, 1994.

———. "Sacred Buildings for an Arid Climate: Architectural Evidence for Low Rainfall in Ancient Pagan." *Journal of Burma Studies* 1 (1997): 19–44.

Cooper, W. G. "A Note on Talaing Nissaya and Vocabulary." *Journal of the Burma Research Society* 4, 2 (1914):125–135.

———. "The Origins of the 'Talaings.'" *Journal of the Burma Research Society* 3, 1 (1913): 1–11.

Corporation of Rangoon. *A History of Rangoon.* Compiled by B. R. Pearn. Rangoon: American Baptist Mission Press, 1929.

Cox, Capt. Hiram. *Journal of a residence in the Burmham empire: and more particularly at the court of Amarapoorah.* London: J. Warren, 1821.

Craven, Roy C. *A Concise History of Indian Art.* New York: Oxford University Press, 1976.

Crawfurd, John. *Journal of an Embassy from the Governor General of India to the Court of Ava in the year 1827.* London: Henry Colburn, 1829.

The Crystal Sands: The Chronicles of Nagara Sri Dharrmaraja. Translated by David K. Wyatt, Ithaca: Cornell University Southeast Asia Program, 1975.

Cūḷavaṃsa: Being the More Recent Part of the Mahāvaṃsa. Part II. Translated by Wilhelm Geiger and from the German into English by Mrs. C. Mabel Rickmers. Colombo: The Ceylon Government Information Department, 1953.

Cunningham, Alexander. *Mahâbodhi, or the great Buddhist temple under the Bodhi tree at Buddha-Gaya.* Varanasi: Indological Book House 1961.

Dani, A. H. *Indian Paleography.* Oxford: Clarendon Press, 1963.

Day, Tony. *Fluid Iron: State Formation in Southeast Asia.* Honolulu: University of Hawai'i Press, 2002.

Dega, Michael Francis. "Prehistoric Circular Earthworks of Cambodia." Ph.D. dissertation, University of Hawai'i at Manoa, 2001.

Dictionary of Pali Proper Names. 2 volumes. Compiled by G. P. Malalasekera. London: The Pali Text Society, 1960.

A Dictionary of the Burman Language, with explanations in English. Compiled from the Manuscripts of A. Judson, D.D. and of other Missionaries in Burmah. Profits devoted to the support of the Burman Mission. Edited by J. Wade. Calcutta: Baptist Mission Press, 1826.

Diffloth, Gerald. *The Dvaravati Old Mon Language and Nyah Kur.* Bangkok: Chulalongkorn University Printing House, 1984.

Dīpavaṃsa: An Ancient Buddhist Historical Record. Translated by Hermann Oldenberg. Reprint. New Delhi: Asian Educational Services, 1982.

Dupont, Pierre. *L'archéologie mône de Dvaravati.* Paris: École française D'Extrême-Orient, 1959.

Duroiselle, Charles. "The Arī of Burma and Tāntric Buddhism." *Archaeological Survey of India, Annual Report: 1915–16.* Delhi: Indological Book House, Reprint, 1972: 79–93.

———. "The Burmese Face of the Myazedi Inscription at Pagan." *Epigraphica Birmanica* 1, 1 (1919): 1–52.

———. "The Derivation of 'Ari.' *Journal of the Burma Research Society* 10, 1 (1920): 28–30; 1, 3: 158–159.

———. "Excavations at Hmawza," *Archaeological Survey of India,* 1927, pp. 171–181.

———. "Excavations at Pagán," *Annual Report of the Archaeological Survey of India, 1926–27.* Calcutta: Government of India, 1930.

———. "Note on the word "Talaing." *Journal of the Burma Research Society* 2, 1 (1912): 100–101.

———. "Pictorial Representations of Jātakas in Burma." In *Archaeological Survey of India, Annual Report 1912–13.* Reprint. Delhi: Indological Book House, 1972: 87–119.

———. "Stone Sculptures in the Ananda Temple at Pagán." *Archaeological Survey of India: Annual Report, 1913–1914.* Delhi: Indological Book House, Reprint, 1972.

———. "The story of Wunzin Min Yaza." *Journal of the Burma Research Society* 2, 2 (1912): 117–119.

———. "Talaing Nissayas." *Journal of the Burma Research Society* 3, 2 (1913: 103–143.

———. "The Talaing Plaques on the Ananda, Plates." *Epigraphica Birmanica* 2, 2 (1921): 1–175.

———. "The Talaing Plaques on the Ananda, Text." *Epigraphica Birmanica* 2, 1 (1921): 1–210.

Eade, J. C. *The Calendrical Systems of Mainland South-East Asia.* Leiden: E. J. Brill, 1995.

———. *Southeast Asian Ephemeris: Solar and Planetary Positions A.D. 368–2000.* Ithaca: Cornell University Southeast Asia Program, 1989.

Eaton, Richard M. "Locating Arakan in Time, Space, and Historical Scholarship." In *The Maritime Frontier of Burma: Exploring Political, Cultural and Commercial Interaction in the Indian Ocean World, 1200–1800.* Edited by Jos Gommans and Jacques Leider. Amsterdam and Leiden: Koninklijke Nederlandse Akademie van Wetenschapen and KITLV Press, 2002.

Epigraphic and Historical Studies. Edited and translated by Prasert Na Nagara and A. B. Griswold. Bangkok: The Historical Society, 1992.

Essays offered to G. H. Luce by his colleagues and friends in honour of his seventy-fifth birthday. Edited by Ba Shin, Jean Boisselier and A. B. Griswold. Ascona, Switzerland: Artibus Asiae, 1966.

The Expositor [Atthasālinī]. Translated by Maung Tin. 2 volumes. London: Pali Text Society, 1921–1923.

Falk, Harry. "Die Goldblätter aus Śrī Kṣetra." *Wiener Zeitshrift für die Kunde Sudasiens.* 41 (1997): 53–92.

Fausböll, V. *The Jātaka together with its commentary Jātakatthavannana for the first time edited in the original Pali.* 6 volumes. London: Trubner, 1877–1897. Reprint, Pali Text Society, London, 1962–1964.

Ferrand, Gabriel. *Relations de voyages et de textes géographiques arabes, persans, et turcs relatifs á l'extrême orient du VIII au XVIII siècles.* 2 volumes. Paris: Leroux, 1913.

Finot, Louis. "Un nouveau document sur le bouddhisme birman." *Journal Asiatique* 10th Series, 20 (July–August 1912): 121–136.

Fleet, J. F. "Mahishamandala and Mahishmati." *Journal of The Royal Asiatic Society.* (1910): 425–447.

Forbes, Captain C. J. F. S. *British Burma and its people: being sketches of native manners, customs, and religion.* London: J. Murray, 1878.

———. *Legendary History of Burma and Arakan.* Rangoon, Government Press, 1882.

Forchhammer, Emil. *The Jardine Prize: An essay on the sources and development of Burmese Law from the era of the first introduction of the Indian Law to the time of the British occupation of Pegu. With Text and Translation of King Wagaru's Manu Dhammasattham.* Rangoon: Government Press, 1885.

———. *Notes on the Early History and Geography of British Burma.* Part I. Rangoon: Government Press, 1883.

———. *Notes on the Early History and Geography of British Burma.* Part II, Rangoon: Government Press, 1884.

Frasch, Tilman. *Pagan: Stadt und Staat.* Stuttgart: Steinger Verlag, 1996.

Furnivall, J. S. *Colonial Policy and Practice: A Comparative Study of Burma and Netherlands India.* New York: New York University Press, 1956.

———. "The Cycle of Burmese Year-Names," *Journal of the Burmese Research Society* 12, 2 (August 1922): 80–95.

———. "The Dawn of Nationalism in Burma." *Journal of the Burma Research Society* 33, 1 (1950): 1–7.

———. "Notes on the History of Hanthawaddy. Part II—the First Talaing Dynasty." *Journal of the Burma Research Society* 3, 2 (1913): 165–169.

———. "Twenty Five Years: A Retrospect and Prospect." *Journal of the Burma Research Society* 25, 1 (1935): 40–47.

Galloway, Charlotte. "Relationships between Buddhist texts and images of the Enlightenment during the early Pagan Period." In *Burma: Art and Archaeology.* Edited by Alexandra Green and T. Richard Blurton. Chicago: Art Media Resources, 2002.

The Glass Palace Chronicle of the Kings of Burma. Translated by Pe Maung Tin and G. H. Luce. Rangoon: Burma Research Society, 1960.

Goh, Geok Yian. "Tracing the Buddha's Footsteps through the Chronicles of the Three Regions of the Loka Buddha." Asian Studies graduate paper, University of Hawai'i. Fall 2002.

Grave, Peter, and Mike Barbetti. "Dating the City Wall, Fortifications, and the Palace Site at Pagan." In *Asian Perspectives Special Issue: The Archaeology of Myanma Pyay (Burma).* Edited by Miriam T. Stark and Michael A. Aung-Thwin. Honolulu: University of Hawai'i Press, 2002.

Guillon, Emmanuel. *The Mons: A Civilization of Southeast Asia.* Translated by James V. Di Crocco. Bangkok: The Siam Society, 1999.

Gutman, Pamela. "Ancient Arakan: With Special Reference to its cultural History between the 5th and 11th Centuries." Ph.D. dissertation. Australian National University, 1976.

———. "A Burma origin for the Sukhothai walking Buddha." In *Burma: Art and Archaeology.* Edited by Alexander Green and T. Richard Blurton. Chicago: Art Media Resources, 2002.

———. *Burma's Lost Kingdoms: Splendours of Arakan.* Trumbull, CT: Weatherhill Inc., 2001.

———. "The Pyu Maitreyas." In *Traditions in Current Perspective.* Yangôn: 1996.

Guy, John. "The Art of the Pyu and Mon." In *The Art of Burma: New Studies.* Edited by Donald M. Stadtner. Mumbai: India, Marg Publications, 1999.

———. "Offering up a rare jewel: Buddhist merit-making and votive tablets in early Burma." In *Burma: Art and Archaeology.* Edited by Alexandra Green and T. Richard Blurton. New York: Art Media Resources, 2002.

———. "A Warrior-Rule Stele from Śrī Kṣetra, Pyū, Burma." *Journal of the Siam Society* 85, 1 and 2 (1997): 85–94.

Hall, D. G. E. *Burma.* Third Edition. London: Hutchinson University Library, 1960.

———. *Henry Burney: A Political Biography.* London: Oxford University Press, 1974.

———. *A History of South-East Asia.* NY: St. Martin's Press, 1968.

Hall, Kenneth R. *Maritime Trade and State Development in Early Southeast Asia.* Honolulu: University of Hawai'i Press, 1985.

Halliday, Robert. "Dictionary Jottings: Talaing place-names in Burmese." *Journal of the Burma Research Society* 20, 1 (1930): 22–23.

———. *A Mon-English Dictionary.* Bangkok: The Siam Society, 1922. Reprint, Rangoon, Ministry of Union Culture, 1955.

———. "The Mon Inscriptions of Siam." *Journal of the Burma Research Society* 22, 3 (1932): 107–119.

———. "The Mons in Siam," *Journal of the Burma Research Society* 12, 2 (1922): 69–70.

———. *The Talaings.* Rangoon: Government Printing, 1917.

Harriden, Jessica. "'Making a Name for Themselves': Karen Identity and the Politicization of Ethnicity in Burma." *Journal of Burma Studies* 7 (2002): 84–144.

Harvey, G. E. *A History of Burma: From the earliest times to 10 March 1824: The beginning of the English Conquest.* London, Frank Cass: 1925.

Haswell, Rev. James M. *Grammatical notes and vocabulary of the Peguan language. To which are added a few pages of phrases, &c.* Rangoon: American Mission Press, 1874.

Herbert, Patricia. *The Hsaya San Rebellion 1930–1932 Reappraised.* Melbourne: Monash University Centre of Southeast Asian Studies, 1982.

Hinuber, Oskar von. *A Handbook of Pali Literature.* Berlin: Walter de Gruyter, 1996.

———. *Die Sprachgeschichte des Pali im Spiegel der sudostasiatischen Handschriffenumberlieferung.* Stuttgart: Akademie der Wissenshaften und der Literatur, 1988.

Hla Pe, Dr. "A Tentative List of Mon Loan Words in Burmese." *Journal of the Burma Research Society* 50, 1 (1967): 71–94.

Hmannan Mahayazawindawgyi [Great royal chronicle of the Palace of Mirrors]. 3 volumes. Edited by San Tun. Yangôn: Pyi Gyi Man Taing Press, 1967.

Hobson-Jobson: A Glossary of Colloquial Anglo-Indian Words and Phrases, and of Kindred Terms, Etymological, Historical, Geographical and discursive. Compiled by Henry Yule and A. C. Burnell. New York, Humanities Press, 1968.

Holt, John Clifford. "Minister of Defense? The Viṣṇu Controversy in Contemporary Sri Lanka." In *Constituting Communities: Theravāda Buddhism and the Religious Cultures of South and Southeast Asia.* Edited by John Clifford Holt et al. Albany, NY: State University of New York Press, 2003.

Hoshino, Tatsuo. "Wen Dan and Its Neighbours: The Central Mekong Valley in the Seventh and Eighth Centuries." In *Breaking New Ground in Lao History: Essays on the Seventh to Twentieth Centuries.* Edited by Mayoury Ngaosrivathana and Kennon Breazeale. Chiang Mai, Thailand: Silkworm Books, 2002.

Houghton, B. "Some Anthropometric Data of the Talaings." *Journal of the Burma Research Society* 1, 1 (1911): 70–74.

Htin Aung, Maung. *Burmese History Before 1287: A Defence of the Chronicles*. Oxford: The Asoka Society, 1970.

———. *A History of Burma*. New York: Columbia University Press, 1967.

———. *The Stricken Peacock: Anglo-Burmese Relations 1752–1948*. The Hague: Martinus Nijhoff, 1965.

Hudson, Bob. "Pagán and Its Monasteries: Time, Space and Structure in Burma's Medieval Buddhist City." B.A. (honors) thesis. University of Sydney, Archaeology Department, 1997.

Hudson, Bob, U Nyein Lwin and U Win Maung (Tanpawady). "Digging for myths: archaeological excavations and surveys of the legendary nineteen founding villages of Pagan." *Asian Perspectives Special Issue: The Archaeology of Myanma Pyay (Burma)*. Edited by Miriam T. Stark and Michael A. Aung-Thwin. Honolulu: University of Hawai'i Press, 2002.

———. "The Origins of Bagan: New Dates and Old Inhabitants." In *Asian Perspectives Special Issue: The Archaeology of Myanma Pyay (Burma)*. Edited by Miriam T. Stark and Michael A. Aung-Thwin. Honolulu: University of Hawai'i Press, 2002.

———. "The Origins of Bagan: The Archaeological Landscape of Upper Burma to AD 1300." Ph.D. dissertation, University of Sydney, 2004.

Huxley, Andrew. "Sanction in the Theravada Buddhist Kingdoms of S.E. Asia," *Transactions of the Jean Bodin Society for Comparative Institutional History* 58, 4 (1991): 335–370.

———, Editor. "Thai, Mon, and Burmese Dhammathats—who influenced whom?" In *Thai law, Buddhist law: Essays on the legal history of Thailand, Laos, and Burma*. Bangkok: White Orchid Press, 1996.

I-Ching. *Chinese Monks in India: Biography of Eminent Monks Who Went to the Western World in Search of the Law During the Great T'ang Dynasty*. Translated by Latika Lahiri. Delhi: Motilal Banarsidass, 1986.

Inscriptions of Burma. 5 volumes. Compiled and edited by G. H. Luce and Pe Maung Tin. Rangoon: Rangoon University Press, 1933–1956.

Irwin, Sir Alfred M. B. *The Burmese and Arakanese Calendars*. Rangoon: Hanthawaddy Printing Works,1909.

———. *The Elements of the Burmese Calendar from A.D. 638 to 1752*. Bombay: British India Press, 1910.

Jacq-Hergoualc'h, Michel. "The Mergui-Tenasserim Region in the Context of the Maritime Silk Road: From the Beginning of the Christian Era to the End of the Thirteenth Century AD." In *The Maritime Frontier of Burma: Exploring Political, Cultural and Commercial Interaction in the Indian Ocean World, 1200–1800*. Edited by Jos Gommans and Jacques Leider. Leiden: Koninklijke Nederlandse Akademie van Wetenschappen, 2002.

Jardine, John. *Notes on Buddhist Law: III Marriage*. Rangoon: Government Printing, 1882.

The Journal of Henry Burney in the capital of Burma 1830–1832. Edited by Nicholas Tarling. Auckland, New Zealand: The University of Auckland, 1995.

Judson's Burmese-English Dictionary. Maulmain: American Mission Press, 1852.

———. Rangoon: American Baptist Mission Press, 1883

———. Rangoon, Government Printing 1893.

———. Rangoon, Baptist Board of Publications, 1953, 1966.

Kala, U. *Mahayazawingyi* [Great royal chronicle]. Edited by Saya Pwa. Yangôn: Hanthawaddy Press, 1960.

Kan Hla, U, [pseud. Sergey S. Oshegov]. "Pagan: Development and Town Planning." *Journal of the Society of Architectural Historians* 36, 1 (March 1977): 15–29.

Kemper, Steven. *The Presence of the Past: Chronicles, Politics, and Culture in Sinhala Life.* Ithaca: Cornell University Press, 1991.

Khin Maung Nyunt. "The Myanmar Performing Arts of the Pyu Period." *Myanmar Perspectives* 4, 1 (1999): 31–36.

Krom, N. J. *Hindoe-Javaansche Geschiednis.* 's-Gravenhage, Martinus Nijhoff, 1931.

Kyaw Nyein. "The Ceramic Industry of the Pagan Period." *Bulletin of the Burma Historical Commission* 3 (1963): 180–184.

Kyawt Hmu Aung. "The Encased Stupas of Bagan." *Myanma Thamaing Thutethana Sasaung* [Myanmar historical research journal]. 10 (December 2002): 31–52.

Laichen, Sun. "Chinese Historical Sources on Burma: A Bibliography of Primary and Secondary Works." *Journal of Burma Studies* 2 (1997): 1–116.

The Legend of Queen Cāma: Bodhiraṃsi's Cāmadevīvaṃsa, a Translation and Commentary. Translated by Donald K. Swearer and Sommai Premchit. Albany, NY: State University of New York Press, 1998.

Lehman, F. K. "Ethnic Categories in Burma and the Theory of Social Systems." In *Southeast Asian Tribes, Minorities, and Nations.* Volume I. Edited by Peter Kunstadter. Princeton: Princeton University Press, 1967.

Li Fang, et al. *Tai-ping Yu-lan.* Volume 4. Bei-jing: Zhong-hua shu-ju, 1985.

Lieberman, Victor B. *Burmese Administrative Cycles: Anarchy and Conquest, c. 1580–1760.* Princeton: Princeton University Press, 1984.

———. "Ethnic Politics in Eighteenth-Century Burma." *Modern Asian Studies* 12, 3 (1978): 455–482.

———. "How Reliable is U Kala's Burmese Chronicle? Some New Comparisons." *Journal of Southeast Asian Studies* 17, 2 (1986): 236–255.

———. *Strange Parallels: Southeast Asia in Global Context, c. 800–1830.* Cambridge: Cambridge University Press, 2003.

Lik Smin Asah: The Story of the Founding of Pegu and a Subsequent Invasion from South India with English Translation, Notes, and Vocabulary of Undefined Words. Translated by Robert Halliday. Rangoon: American Baptist Mission Press, 1923.

List of Microfilms Deposited in The Centre for East Asian Cultural Studies Part 8. Burma. Tokyo: The Toyo Bunko, 1976.

Loofs-Wissowa, Helmut. "The True and the Corbel Arch in Mainland Southeast Asian Monumental Architecture." In *Southeast Asia in the 9th to 14th Centuries.* Edited by David G. Marr and A. C. Milner. Singapore: Institute for Southeast Asian Studies, 1986.

Luce, G. H. "The Ancient Pyu," *Burma Research Society Fiftieth Anniversary Publications No. 2* (Rangoon: Burma Research Society, 1960): 307–321.

———. "The Ancient Pyu," *Journal of the Burma Research Society* 27, 3 (1937): 239–253.

———. "A Cambodian (?) Invasion of Lower Burma—A Comparison of Burmese and Talaing Chronicles. *Journal of the Burma Research Society* 12, 1 (1922): 39–45.

———. "The career of Htilaing Min (Kyanzittha)." *Journal of The Royal Asiatic Society* 1–2 (April 1966): 53–68.

———. "A Century of Progress in Burmese History and Archaeology." *Journal of the Burma Research Society* 32, 1 (1968): 79–94.

———. *A Comparative Word-List of Old Burmese, Chinese and Tibetan.* London: School of Oriental and African Studies, 1981.

———. "Countries Neighbouring Burma: Parts 1 & 2." *Journal of the Burma Research Society* 14, 2 (1924): 137–205.

———. "Dvāravatī and Old Burma." *Journal of the Siam Society* 53, 1 (1965): 9–26.

———. "Economic Life of the Early Burman." *Burma Research Society Fiftieth Anniversary Publications No. 2.* Rangoon: Burma Research Society, 1960.

———. "Mons of the Pagan Dynasty." *Journal of the Burma Research Society* 36, 1 (1953): 1–19.

———. "Note on the Peoples of Burma in the 12th–13th Century A.D." *Census of India.* 11, 1 (1931): 296–306.

———. *Old Burma-Early Pagan,* 3 volumes. New York: J. J. Augustin, 1969–1970.

———. "Old Kyaukse and the Coming of the Burmans." *Journal of the Burma Research Society* 42, 1 (1959: 75–109.

———. *Phases of Pre-Pagan Burma: Languages and History.* 2 volumes. Oxford: Oxford University Press, 1985.

———. "Rice and Religion: A Study of Old Mon-Khmer Evolution and Culture." *Journal of the Siam Society* 53 (1965): 139–152.

———. "Sources of Early Burma History." In *Southeast Asian history and historiography: Essays presented to D. G. E. Hall.* Edited by C. D. Cowan and O. W. Wolters with a foreword by John M. Echols. Ithaca: Cornell University Press, 1976.

Luce, G. H. and Ba Shin. "Pagan Myinkaba Kubyauk-Gyi Temple of Rajakumar (1113 A.D.) and the Old Mon Writings on Its Walls." *Bulletin of the Burma Historical Commission* 2 (1961): 277–416.

Ludden, David. "Modern Inequality and Early Modernity: A Comment for the *AHR* on Articles by R. Bin Wong and Kenneth Pomeranz." *American Historical Review.* 107 (April 2002): 470–480.

Ludu Daw Ahmar. *The World's Biggest Book.* Mandalay: Kyipwayay Press, 1974.

The Mahāvaṃsa or The Great Chronicle of Ceylon. Translated into English by Wilhelm Geiger, assisted by Mabel Haynes Bode. Colombo: Ceylon Government Information Department, 1960.

Maitreya, the Future Buddha. Edited by Alan Sponberg and Helen Hardacre. New York: Cambridge University Press, 1988.

Man Shu [Book of the southern barbarians]. Translated by Gordon H. Luce and Edited by G. P. Oey. Cornell Southeast Asia Program Data Papers. no. 44. Ithaca: Cornell University Center for Southeast Asian Studies, 1961.

Mandalay Mahamuni Tantuin Atwinshi Kyauksa Mya [Inscriptions within the compound of the Mandalay Mahamuni pagoda]. Volume I. Yangôn: University of Yangôn Department of History, 1989.

The Maniyadanabon of Shin Sandalinka. Translated by L. E. Bagshawe. Cornell University Southeast Asia Program Data Papers, no. 115. Ithaca: Cornell University Center for Southeast Asian Studies, 1981.

Mason, Rev. F. *Burmah, Its People and Natural Productions, or Notes on the Nations, Fauna, and Minerals of Tenasserim, Pegu and Burmah, with Systematic Catalogues of the known Mammals, Birds, Fish, Reptiles, Insects, Mullusks, Crustaceans, Annalids, Raidates, Plants and Minerals, with Vernacular Names.* Rangoon: Thos. Stowe Ranney, 1860.

Maung, E. "Some Place-Names in Burma," *Journal of the Burma Research Society* 39, 2 (1956): 182–192.

Maung Maung, U. *Burma's Constitution.* The Hague: Martinus Nijhoff, 1959.

———. *The Story of Wunzin Min Yaza.* Yangôn: Tain Lon Zambu Press, 1912?

May Oung. "Origin of the Word 'Talaing'." *Journal of the Burma Research Society* 2, 1 (1912): 73–74.

———. "Review of *'Burmese Sketches'* by Taw Sein Ko," *Journal of the Burma Research Society* 3, 2 (1913): 191–192.

Mendelson, E. Michael. "The King of the Weaving Mountain." *Royal Central Asian Journal* 48 (1961): 229–237.

———. "A Messianic Buddhist Association in Upper Burma." *Bulletin of the School of Oriental and Asian Studies* 24 (1961): 560–580.

———. "Observations on a Tour in the Region of Mount Popa, Central Burma." *France-Asie.* 19 (1963): 786–807.

———. *Sangha and State in Burma: A Study of Monastic Sectarianism and Leadership.* Edited by John P. Ferguson. Ithaca: Cornell University Press, 1975.

Minbu Aung Kyaing. *Ananda* [in Burmese]. Yangôn: Sape Beikman Press, 1984.

———. *Bithuka Lakyamya* [Architectural features]. Yangôn: Sape Beikman Press, 1985.

Moe Kyaw Aung. "Excursions to the Thuyethamein-Kuseik Area." *Forward* 8, 21 (June 1970): 12–17.

Mon Kyauksa Paung Chok [Collection of Mon stone inscriptions]. Compiled and edited by U Chit Thein. Yangôn: Ministry of Culture, 1965.

Moore, Elizabeth. "Bronze and Iron Age sites in Myanmar: Chindwin, Samon, and Pyu." *SOAS Bulletin of Burma Research.* 1, 1 (Spring 2003): 24–39.

Moore, Elizabeth, and U Aung Myint, "Finger-marked designs on ancient bricks in Myanmar." *Journal of the Siam Society* 79, part 2 (1991), pp. 81–102.

Moore, Elizabeth and Pauk Pauk. "Nyaung-gan: A Preliminary Note on a Bronze Age Cemetery Near Mandalay, Myanmar (Burma)." In *Asian Perspectives Special Issue: The Archaeology of Myanma Pyay (Burma).* Edited by Miriam T. Stark and Michael A. Aung-Thwin. (Honolulu, University of Hawai'i Press, 2002.

Mya, Thiripyanchi U. *Abeyadana Lainggu Paya* [The Abeyadana temple]. Rangoon: Archaeological Survey of Burma, 1968.

———. *She Haung Ok Khwek Yokpwa Sintutaw Mya: Votive Tablets of Burma.* Part I. Yangôn: Archaeological Survey of Burma, 1961.

Myanma Cway Cum Kyam [Encyclopedia Myanmar]. CD-ROM. Yangôn: Forever Group, 1998–1999.

Myanmar. Archaeological Department. *She Haung Myanma Kyauksa Mya* [Ancient Burmese stone inscriptions]. 5 volumes. Yangôn: Sape Beikman, 1972–present.

Myanmar. Department of Higher Education. *Architectural Drawings of Temples in Pagan.* Rangoon: Ministry of Education, 1989.

Myanmar. Ministry of Culture. *Inventory of Ancient Monuments in Bagan.* Volume I. Yangôn: Ministry of Culture, 1998.

———. *Sheyo Myanma Pagyi* [Ancient Myanma paintings]. Yangôn: Ministry of Culture, n.d.

Myint Aung, U. "The Capital of Suvannabhumi unearthed?" *Shiroku.* 10 (1977): 41–53.

———. "The Development of Myanmar Archaeology." *Myanmar Historical Research Journal* 9 (June 2002): 11–29.

———. "Editor's Note on Excavation of Old Thaton," *Journal of the Burma Research Society* 59, 1–2 (December 1976): 165–166.

———. "The Excavations of Ayethama and Winka (?Suvannabhumi)." In *Essays Given to Than Tun on his 75th Birthday: Studies in Myanma History.* Volume I. Yangôn: Innwa Publishing House, 1999.

———. "The Excavations at Halin." *Journal of the Burma Research Society* 53, 2 (December 1970): 55–64.

Nai Pan Hla. "Editor's Note on Excavation of Old Thaton." *Journal of the Burma Research Society* 59, 1 and 2 (December 1976): 165–166.

———. "Mon Literature and Culture over Thailand and Burma." *Journal of the Burma Research Society* 41, 1 (1958): 64–75.

———. "Old Terracotta Votive Tablets & New Theories on History of Old Burma." In *Traditions in Current Perspective: Proceedings of the Conference on Myanmar and Southeast Asian Studies 15–17 November 1995, Yangôn.* Yangôn: Universities Historical Research Centre, 1996.

———. *The Significant Role of The Mon Language and Culture on Southeast Asia, Part I.* Tokyo: Institute for the Study of Languages and Cultures of Asian and Africa, 1992.

———. "Yazadarit Ayedawpon Kyan nhin Mon Thichin Mya [The Yazadarit Ayedawpon treatise and Mon songs." *Journal of the Burma Research Society* 56, 1 (1973): 99–126.

A narrative of the mission to the court of Ava in 1855 compiled by Henry Yule together with the journal of Arthur Phayre, envoy to the court of Ava, and additional illustrations by Colesworthy Grant and Linnaeus Tripe with an introduction by Hugh Tinker. New York: Oxford University Press, 1968.

Nu, U. *U Nu—Saturday's Son.* New Haven: Yale University Press, 1975.

Nyunt Han, U, U Win Maung (Tanpawady) and Elizabeth Moore. "Prehistoric grave goods from the Chindwin and Samon river regions." In *Burma: Art and Archaeology.* Edited by Alexander Green and T. Richard Blurton. Chicago: Art Media Resources, 2002.

O'Connor, Richard. "A Regional Explanation of the Tai *Muang* as a City-State." In *A Comparative Study of Thirty City-State Cultures.* Edited by Mogens Herman Hansen. Copenhagen: The Royal Danish Academy of Sciences and Letters, 2000.

———. *A Theory of Indigenous Southeast Asian Urbanism.* Singapore: Institute for Southeast Asian Studies, 1983.

Oshegowa, Nina, *Kunst in Burma.* Leipzig: E.A. Seemann, 1988.

The Padaeng chronicle and the Jengtung State Chronicle Translated. Translated by Sao Saimong Mangrai. Ann Arbor: Center for South and Southeast Asian Studies, 1981.

Pagan Kyauksa Let Ywe Sin [Selected inscriptions of Pagán]. Compiled by Professor E Maung. Yangôn: Panna Nanda Ponhneik Press, 1958.

Paññāsāmi, *Sāsanavaṃsa* [History of the religion]. Translated by Bimala Churn Law. London: Pali Text Society, 1952.

Paranavitana, Senarat. "The Art and Architecture of the Polonnaruva Period." In *The Polonnaruva Period.* Edited by S. D. Saparamadu. Dehiwala, Sri Lanka: Tisara Prakasakayo, third edition, 1973.

———. *Ceylon and Malaysia.* Colombo: Lake House Investments Ltd., 1966.

Parker, Edward Harper. *Burma: With Special Reference to her Relations with China.* Rangoon: Rangoon Gazette Press, 1893.

Pe Maung Tin. "The Dialect of Tavoy." *Journal of the Burma Research Society* 23, 1 (1933): 32–46.

———. "A Mon Inscription by Kyanzittha at Ayetthema Hill." *Journal of the Burma Research Society* 28, 1 (1938): 92–94.

———. *Myanma Sape Thamaing* [History of Burmese literature]. Yangôn: Khettara Press, 1977.

———. "A Note on the Development of the Burmese Language," *Journal of the Burma Research Society* 24, 1 (1934): 58–59.

———. "Report of the Superintendent, Archaeological Survey, Burma 1917." *Journal of the Burma Research Society* 6, 3 (1916): 285–286.

———. "The Shwé-dagôn Pagoda; Part I," *Journal of the Burma Research Society* 24, 1 (1934): 1–26; 26–57; and 24, 3 (1935): 58–91.

Phayre, Sir Arthur. *History of Burma.* Reprint. New York: Augustus M. Kelley, 1969.

———. "History of Pegu." *Journal of the Asiatic Society of Bengal* 42, 1 (1873): 23–57.

———. "On the History of Pegu." *Journal of the Asiatic Society of Bengal* 42, 2 (1873): 121–159.

"Phongsawadan Môn Phama," [Annal of the Mon of Burma]. In *Prachum Phongsawadan* [Collection of historical papers]. Volume 2, part 1. Bangkok: Khurusapha 1963.

Phromsuthirak, Maneepin. "Thai Interpolations in the Story of Aniruddha." *Journal of the Siam Society* 67, 1 (January 1979): 46–53.

Pichard, Pierre. "A Distinctive Technical Achievement: The Vaults and Arches of Pagan." In *The Art of Burma: New Studies.* Edited by Donald M. Stadtner. Mumbai, India: Marg Publications, 1999.

———. *Inventory of Monuments at Pagan.* 8 volumes. Gartmore, Scotland: Kiscadale and Paris: UNESCO, 1992–2000.

———. *The Pentagonal Monuments of Pagan.* Bangkok: White Lotus, 1991.

Pramojanee, P. and T. Jarupongskul. "Evolution of Landforms and the Sites of Ancient Cities and Communities in Lower Chao Phraya Plain." In *Proceedings for the International Workshop Ayudhya and Asia.* Edited by Kajit Jittasevi. Bangkok: Core University Program between Thammasat University and Kyoto University, BE 2540 [AD 1997].

Proceedings of the Workshop on Bronze Age Culture in Myanmar. Yangôn: Universities Historical Research Centre, 1999.

Rajani, Mom Chao Chand Chirayu. "Guide through the Inscriptions of Sukhothai." University of Hawai'i Southeast Asian Studies Program Working Paper, no. 9. Honolulu: 1976.

Rājāwaṅsa Dhammacetī Mahāpiṭakadhara. Edited by Phra Candakanto. Pak Lat: Siam, 1912.

Rawson, Philip. *The Art of Southeast Asia.* London: Thames and Hudson, 1967.

Ray, Himanshu Prabha. "Early maritime contacts between South and Southeast Asia." *Journal of Southeast Asian Studies* 20 (1989): 42–54.

———. "In Search of Suvarnabhumi: Early Sailing Networks in the Bay of Bengal." In Indo-Pacific Prehistory 1990: Proceedings of the 14th Congress of the Indo-Pacific Prehistory Association. Canberra: Indo-Pacific Prehistory Association and Jakarta: Associasi Prehistorisi Indonesia, 1991.

Ray, Nihar-Ranjan. *Sanskrit Buddhism in Burma.* Amsterdam: H. J. Paris, 1936.

Reid, Anthony, "Economic and Social Change, c. 1400–1800." In *The Cambridge History of Southeast Asia.* Volume I: *From Early Times to c. 1800.* Edited by Nicholas Tarling. Cambridge: Cambridge University Press, 1992.

———. *Southeast Asia in the Age of Commerce 1450–1680.* New Haven: Yale University Press, 1993.

Reprint from Dalrymple's Oriental Repertory, 1791–7 of Portions Relating to Burma. Rangoon: Government Printing, 1926.

Reynolds, Craig. "A New Look at Old Southeast Asia." *Journal of Asian Studies* 54, 2 (1995): 419–446.

Rhys-Davids, T. W. *Buddhist India.* Reprint. New Delhi: Indological Book House, 1970.

———. "The Conquest of South India in the Twelfth Century by Parakrama Bahu." *Journal of the Asiatic Society of Bengal.* 41 (1872): 197–201.

Ricklefs, Merle C. "Land and the Law in the Epigraphy of Tenth-Century Cambodia." *Journal of Asian Studies* 26, 3 (1967): 411–420.

Rowland, Benjamin. *The art and architecture of India: Buddhist, Hindu, Jain.* Baltimore: Penguin Books, 1977.

The Royal Chronicles of Ayutthaya. Translated by Richard D. Cushman and edited by David K. Wyatt. Bangkok: The Siam Society, 2000.

The Royal Orders of Burma, A.D. 1598–1885. Part Three: *A.D. 1751–1781.* 10 volumes. Edited by Than Tun. Kyoto: The Centre for Southeast Asian Studies, Kyoto University, 1983–1990.

San Win. "Dating the Hpayahtaung Pyu Urn Inscription." *Myanmar Historical Journal* 11 (June 2003): 15–22.

Sangermano, Vicentius. *The Burmese Empire a Hundred Years Ago.* New York: Augustus M. Kelley, 1969.

Sao Saimong Mangrai. "Did Soṇa and Uttara Come to Lower Burma?" *Journal of the Burma Research Society* 59, 1–2 (December 1976):155–164.

Saranukrom wattanatham thai phak klang [Thai cultural encyclopaedia, central region]. Volume 15. Bangkok: Thai Cultural Encyclopaedia Foundation, 1999.

Saraya, Dhida. *(Sri) Dvaravati: The Initial Phase of Siam's History.* Bangkok: Muang Boran, 1999.

Sastri, Nilakanta. *A History of South India.* 3rd edition. London: Oxford University Press, 1966.

Sein Maung U. "Mongmao: a forgotten city." *The Working Peoples Daily.* January 21, 23, and February 3, 1981.

Selections From the Inscriptions of Pagan. Compiled by G. H. Luce and Pe Maung Tin. Rangoon: British Burma Press, 1928.

Shafer, Robert. "Further Analysis of the Pyu Inscriptions." *Harvard Journal of Asiatic Studies* 7, 4 (September 1943): 313–366.

The Sheaf of Garlands of the Epochs of the Conqueror: Being a Translation of Jinakālamālīpakaraṇaṁ of Ratanapañña Thera of Thailand. Translated by N. A. Jayawickrama. London: Pali Text Society, 1968.

Shorto, H. L. "*The dewatau sotāpan:* A Mon Prototype of the 37 Nats." *Bulletin of the School of Oriental and Asian Studies.* 30 (1967): 132–133.

———. *A Dictionary of Modern Spoken Mon.* London: Oxford University Press, 1962.

———. *A Dictionary of the Mon Inscriptions from the Sixth to the Sixteenth Centuries.* London: Oxford University Press, 1971.

———. "Gavampati." Typescript translation in the possession of Professor Victor Lieberman, University of Michigan.

———. "The Gavampati Tradition in Burma." In *R. C. Majumdar Felicitation Volume.* Edited by Himansu Bhusan Sarkar. Calcutta: Firma K. L. Mukhopadhyay, 1970.

———. "A Mon Genealogy of Kings: Observations on The *Nidāna Árambhakathā.*" In *Historians of South East Asia.* Edited by D. G. E. Hall. London: Oxford University Press, 1961.

———. "The 32 *Myos* in the Medieval Mon Kingdom." *Bulletin of the School of Oriental and Asian Studies* 36 (1963): 572–591.

Shwe Zan, U. *The Golden Mrauk-U.* Yangôn: U Shwe Zan, 1995.

Silverstein, Josef. *Burma: Military Rule and Politics of Stagnation.* Ithaca: Cornell University Press, 1977.

Sirisena, W. M. *Sri Lanka and South-East Asia.* Leiden: E. J. Brill, 1978.

Sithu Gamani Thingyan. *Zimme Yazawin* [Chronicle of Chiang Mai]. Translated by Thaw Kaung and Ni Ni Myint. Edited by Tun Aung Chain. Yangôn: Universities Historical Research Centre, 2003.

Si-Yu-Ki Buddhist Records of the Western World Translated from the Chinese of Hiuen Tsiang (A.D. 629). Volume I. Translated by Samuel Beal. New York: Paragon Book Reprint Corp., 1968.

Skilling, Peter. "Dvāravatī: Recent Revelations and Research." *Dedications to Her Royal Highness Princess Galyani Vadhana Krom Luang Naradhiwas Rajanagarindra on her 80th birthday.* Bangkok: The Siam Society, 2003.

Slapat Rājawaṅ Datow Smin Roṅ [History of kings]. Translated by R. Halliday. *Journal of the Burma Research Society* 13, 1 and 2 (1923): 9–31; 33–67.

Spellman, John W. "The Symbolic Significance of the Number Twelve in Ancient India." *Journal of Asian Studies* 22, 1 (November 1962): 79–88.

Spiro, Melford. *Buddhism and Society: A Great Tradition and Its Burmese Vicissitudes.* Berkeley: University of California Press, 1982.

Stadtner, Donald M. "The Art of Burma." In *Art of Southeast Asia.* New York: Harry N. Abrams, Inc., 1998).

Stargardt, Janice. *The Ancient Pyu of Burma.* Volume One: *Early Pyu cities in a Man-Made Landscape.* Cambridge and Singapore: Publications on Ancient Civilization in South Asia and Institute of South East Asian Studies, 1990.

———. "Reply to Bellwood's review." *The Review of Archaeology* 14, 2 (Fall 1993): 2–32.

———. *Tracing Thought Through Things: The Oldest Pali Texts and the Early Buddhist*

Archaeology of India and Burma. Amsterdam: Royal Netherlands Academy of Arts and Sciences, 2000.

Stark, Miriam T., et al. "Results of the 1995–1996 Archaeological Field Investigations at Angkor Borei, Cambodia." *Asian Perspectives,* 38, 1 (Spring 1999): 7–36.

Stewart, J. A. "Excavation and Exploration in Pegu." *Journal of the Burma Research Society* 7, 1 (1917): 14–25.

Strachan, Paul. *Pagan: Art and Architecture of Old Burma.* Arran, Scotland: Kiscadale Publications, 1989.

Strong, John S. *The Legend and Cult of Upagupta: Sanskrit Buddhism in North India and Southeast Asia.* Princeton: New Jersey, 1992.

Swearer, Donald K. "Myth, Legend and History in the Northern Thai Chronicles." *The Journal of the Siam Society* 62, 1 (January 1974): 67–88.

Symes, Michael. *An account of an embassy to the kingdom of Ava, in the year 1795... to which is now added, A narrative of the late military and political operations in the Birmese Empire; with some account of the present condition of the country, its manners, customs, and inhabitants.* Edinburgh: Constable & Co., 1827.

———. *Journal of his Second Embassy to the Court of Ava in 1802.* London, George Allen & Unwin Ltd, 1955.

Takakusu, J. *A Record of the Buddhist Religion as practiced in India and the Malay Archipelago (671–695 A.D.) By I-Tsing.* Oxford: Oxford University Press, 1896.

Taw Sein Ko. *Burmese Sketches.* 2 volumes. Rangoon: British Burma Press, 1913–1920.

———. "The Linguistic Affinities of the Pyu Language." *Journal of the Burma Research Society* 5, 2 (1915): 102–110.

———. "A Preliminary Study of the Kalyani Inscriptions of Dhammacheti, 1476 A.D." *Indian Antiquary* 22 (1893): 29–53; 85–89; 150–159; 206–218; 236–243.

Taylor, Robert H. "Perceptions of Ethnicity in the Politics of Burma." *Southeast Asian Journal of Social Sciences* 10, 1 (1982): 7–22.

Tet Htoot, U. "The Nature of the Burmese Chronicles." In *Historians of South East Asia.* Edited by D. G. E. Hall. London: Oxford University Press, 1961.

Tha Myat, Thiripyanchi U. *Mon Myanma Ekaya Thamaing* [History of Mon-Myanma alphabet]. Yangôn, 1956.

———. *Myazedi Khaw Gubyauk Kyi Pyū Kyauksa* [The Pyū Inscription of the so-called Myazedi]. Rangoon: Democracy Publishing Co., Ltd, 1958?

———. *Pyū Phat Ca* [Pyū reader]. Rangoon: U Hla Din, 1963.

Than Swe, Daw. *Pyusa Khinbha Shwe Pechat Dat Pon Mya* [Photographs of Pyū writing on Khin Bha's gold palm leaves]. Yangôn: Directorate of Burmese, 1991.

Than Tun. "Administration Under King Thalun (1629–1648). *Journal of the Burma Research Society* 51, 2 (1968): 173–188.

———. "History of Buddhism in Burma: A.D. 1000–1300." Ph.D. dissertation. University of London, 1956.

———. "History of Buddhism in Burma A.D. 1000–1300." *Journal of the Burma Research Society* 61, 2 & 3 (December 1978): 1–265.

———. *Khit Haung Myanma Yazawin* [History of Ancient Myanma]. Yangôn: Maha Dagon Publishers, 1969.

———. *Myanma Thamaing Lik Kwet Mya: Missing Links in Myanma Chronicle* [Burmese and English]. Yangôn: U Win Kyaw Htun, 2003.

Thilawuntha, Shin. *Yazawinkyaw* [Celebrated chronicle]. Edited by Professor Pe Maung Tin. Yangôn: Burma Research Society, n.d.

Tibbetts, G. R. "Arabic works relating to South-East Asia." *Malay Library Group.* I, 4 (1956): 79–86.

———. "Early Muslim traders in South-East Asia." *Journal of the Malay Branch of the Royal Asiatic Society.* 30, 1 (1957): 1–44.

———. "Pre-Islamic Arabia and South-East Asia." *Journal of the Malay Branch of the Royal Asiatic Society.* 29, 3 (1956): 182–208.

———. *A study of the Arabic texts containing material on South-East Asia.* Leiden: Brill, 1979.

Tin, U. "Mahayan gaing Myanma naingnan tho sheuswa yauk thi akyaung," [The earliest arrival of the Mahayan sect to Pagán, Burma]. *Journal of the Burma Research Society* 19, 2 (1929): 36–42.

Tin Hla Thaw. "History of Burma: A.D. 1400–1500." *Journal of the Burma Research Society* 42, 2 (December 1959): 135–151.

Tun Aung Chain. "The Kings of the Hpayahtaung Urn Inscription." *Myanmar Historical Journal* 11 (June 2003: 1–15.

———. "Pe Maung Tin and Luce's *Glass Palace* Revisited." In *U Pe Maung Tin—A Tribute.* Yangôn: Universities Historical Research Centre, 1999.

———. "The Value of Myanmar Traditional Texts." *Myanma Thamaing Thutethana Sasaung* [Myanmar historical research journal]. No. 1 (November 1995): 275–290.

Tun Nwe. "Pagán Paya Sayin Kyai Shatawpon" [Search for the large list of Pagán temples]. In *Pagán Letthit nhin Achya Satan Mya.* [Fashionable Pagán and other essays]. Mandalay: Kyi Pwa Yei Press, 1996.

Tun Nyein, Maung. "Maunggun Gold Plates." *Epigraphia Indica.* 5, 4 (1889–1899): 101–102.

Twinthintaikwun Mahasithu. *Mahayazawinthit (Nyaung Yan Set)* [Great new chronicle (Nyaung Yan Dynasty)]. Volume 3. Yangôn: U Kyi Aye Publications, 1997.

———. *Twinthin Myanma Yazawinthit* [Twinthin's new chronicle of the Myanma]. Volume 1. Yangôn: Mingala Pon Hneik Press, 1968.

Twitchett D. E. and A. H. Christie. "A Medieval Burmese Orchestra." *Asia Major* New Series 7, 1 and 2 (1959): 171–195.

Vallibhotama, Srisakra. "The Ancient Settlements of Sukhothai." In *Papers from a Conference on Thai Studies in Honor of William J. Gedney.* Edited by Robert J. Bickner, et al. Ann Arbor: Center for Southeast Asian Studies, 1986.

Van Driem, George. *Languages of the Himalayas.* Volume 1. Leiden: E. J. Brill, 2001.

Vickery, Michael. "Champa Revised." Paper delivered at the National University of Singapore. July 2004.

———. *Society, Economics, and Politics in Pre-Angkor Cambodia: The 7th–8th Centuries.* Tokyo: The Centre for East Asian Cultural Studies for UNESCO, 1998.

Wales, H. G. Quaritch. "Anuruddha and the Thaton Tradition." *Journal of The Royal Asiatic Society* 3–4 (1947): 152–156.

———. "Dvāravatī in South-East Asian Cultural History." *Journal of The Royal Asiatic Society* 1–2 (1966): 40–52.

———. *Early Burma-Old Siam.* London: Bernard Quaritch, Ltd., 1973.

Walters, Jonathan S. "Buddhist History: The Śrī Laṅkan Pāli Vaṃsas and Their Community." In *Querying the Medieval: Texts and the History of Practices in South Asia.* Edited by Ronald Inden, Jonathan Walters, and Daud Ali. Oxford: Oxford University Press, 2000.

———. "Rethinking Buddhist Missions," Ph.D. dissertation, University of Chicago, 1992.

Watabe, Tadayo. "Origin and Dispersal of Cultivated Rice in Asia." Typescript in author's possession.

Watabe, Tadayo, Koji Tanaka, and Koung [sic] Nyunt. "Ancient Rice Grains Recovered from Ruins in Burma–A study of the Alteration of Cultivated Rice." *Preliminary Report of the Kyoto University Scientific Survey to Burma 1974.* Kyoto: Kyoto University, 1976.

Wheatley, Paul. *The Golden Khersonese.* Westport, CN: Greenwood Press, 1973.

———. *Nāgara and Commandery.* University of Chicago Department of Geography Research Papers, nos. 207–208. Chicago: 1983.

Wickramasinghe, Sirima. "The Sources for a Study of the Reign of King Parākramabāhu I." In *The Polonnaruva Period.* Edited by S. D. Saparamadu. Third Edition. Dehiwala, Sri Lanka, Tisara Prakasakayo, 1973.

Wicks, Robert S. "The Ancient Coinage of Mainland Southeast Asia." *Journal of Southeast Asian Studies* 16, 2 (1985): 195–225.

———. *Money, Markets, and Trade in Early Southeast Asia: The Development of Indigenous Monetary Systems to AD 1400.* Ithaca: Cornell University Southeast Asia Program, 1992.

Wijesekera, O. H. De A. "Pali and Sanskrit in the Polonnaruva Period." In *The Polonnaruva Period.* Edited by S. D. Saparamadu. Third Edition. Dehiwala: Sri Lanka, Tisara Prakasakayo, 1973.

Wilson, Constance M. "The Holy Man in Thailand and Laos." *Journal of Southeast Asian Studies* 28, 2 (September 1997): 345–364.

Win Maung (Tanpawady). "Binnaka Myo Haung" [Ancient city of Binnaka]. Typescript. 1981.

Wisseman Christie, Jan. "The Medieval Tamil-language Inscriptions in Southeast Asia and China." *Journal of Southeast Asian Studies* 29, 2 (September 1998): 239–268.

Wolters, O. W. *Early Indonesian Commerce: A Study of the Origins of Srivijaya.* Ithaca: Cornell University Press, 1967.

———. *The Fall of Srivijaya in Malay History.* Ithaca: Cornell University Press, 1970.

Woodman, Dorothy. *The Making of Burma.* London: The Cresset Press, 1962.

Woodward, Hiram. *The Art and Architecture of Thailand: From Prehistoric Times through the Thirteenth Century.* Leiden: E. J. Brill, 2003.

Wyatt, David K. "Relics, oaths and politics in thirteenth-century Siam." *Journal of Southeast Asian Studies* 32, 1 (February 2001): 3–65.

Wyatt, David K. and Aroonrut Wichienkeeo. *The Chiang Mai Chronicle.* Chiang Mai, Thailand: Silkworm Books, 1995.

"Yazadarit Ayedawpon." *Myanma Swe Son Kyan* [Encyclopedia Myanmar on CD-ROM]. Yangôn: Forever Group, 1998–1999.

Yazadarit Ayedawpon Kyan [The treatise of the royal crisis account of *Yazadarit*]. Translated by Nai Pan Hla. Yangôn: Thein Than Oo Press, 1977.

Yuan-ch'ao-cheng-mien-lu. In *Census of India.* 11, 1 (1931): Appendix F.

Zambudipa Okhsaung Kyan [Treatise adorning the head of Zambudipa]. Compiled by J. S. Furnivall and Pe Maung Tin. Yangôn: Burma Research Society, 1960.

Zatatawpon Yazawin [Chronicle of royal horoscopes]. Edited by Hla Tin. Yangôn: Ministry of Culture, 1960.

Zhi-yuan Zhengmian Lu [Records of the expeditions against Mian during the reign of the Zhi-yuan]. Translated by Sun Laichen. MSS.

Zhu Zhi, "Shui-jing-zhu." In *Chen Yu-jing Dong-nan-ya Gu-shi yan-jiu he-ji* [Collected works on early Southeast Asian history by Chen Yu-jing]. Volume 2. Hong Kong: Commercial Press, 1992.

Zimmer, Heinrich. *The Art of Indian Asia.* Volume 1. Princeton: Princeton University Press, 1955.

Index

Abhidhamma, 32, 169
Abu Dulaf, 50
Alaungpaya, 11, 141–142, 261–278, 314–316
Alaungsithu, 139, 181, 204, 207–208, 214, 242, 245, 260, 304
Amarāvatī, 25, 31
Amarapura, 81, 187
Ānanda, 198, 206, 211, 214, 217–218, 225, 235, 247, 252–256
Anaukpetlun, 138
Angkor, 44, 55, 81, 126, 129, 131, 167, 302, 306, 309, 312
Angkor Thom, 126
Aniruddha: allegories concerning, 105; and Angkor, 129; and Bodawpaya, 143; and Cāmadevi, 152; in chronicles, 123, 136, 138, 139, 140–144, 150, 151, 236; clash with Khmers, 246; conquests of, 1, 41, 65, 83, 112–113, 129; contemporaries of, 118; conversion of, 117; donations of, 111; general of, 236; grandfather and father of, 176; grandfather of, 159, 232; as great Buddhist king, 115, 126, 129, 132, 142, 144, 147, 150; heir of, 195; inscriptions of, 183; in Kalyani Inscriptions, 68, 99, 113–115, 124, 143, 151; king of Pagan, 1, 124, 126, 151, 170, 247, 279; and Kyanzittha, 49, 65, 237, 241, 242–249, 255, 259, 260, 304; legend of, 123–124, 145, 150, 237; and Manuha, 2, 57, 110, 117, 126, 132, 148, 271; miraculous powers of, 126, 129; and orthodoxy, 257–259; period before, 203; predecessors of, 122, 186; primate of, 191; reform of, 90, 111, 114, 117–118, 143, 152; as reformer, 117; reign of, 38, 184, 193, 196, 204, 247, 251, 257; search for relics, 126, 129, 135, 151; and Shin Arahan, 138–139; son of, 112; spelling of name, 109; story of, 105, 118, 120, 123–124, 143, 145, 147; successors of, 184, 234; temples of, 37, 111, 184, 197, 204–206, 248–249, 251–256; unifier of Pagan, 41, 131, 184, 316; and Vijayabāhu, 146, 218; votive tablets of, 112, 193–194, 233
Anurādhapura, 31, 138, 223
Arakan, 16, 18, 20, 23, 27, 51, 83, 111, 170, 311
Arakanese, 10, 18, 35, 51, 87, 98–99, 101, 287, 316
Aramaṇa, 49, 74
Ari, 1, 87, 136, 249
Arimaddanā, 122
Arimaddana, 124, 126, 128–129, 146, 149
Arimaddanapūra, 151
Arimaddanapura, 113–114, 149
asañ, 40
Aśoka: conversion by Nigrodha, 138–139; as great reformer, 115–119; and the Kāliṅga Inscrip-

tions, 63, 245; and Lower Burma, 70–75; and the Mahābodhi Temple, 187; in the *Mahāvaṃsa,* 234; as quintessential model Buddhist king, 151–152; and the Third Buddhist Council, 1, 117, 142, 151, 152
Assam, 20
Ava: chronicles of, 90–93, 121, 124; city of, 57; decline of, 131; and Dhammazedi, 67, 116; first dynasty, 13, 56, 122, 239; Htupayôn temple of, 232; inscriptions of, 37, 48, 75, 109, 113, 243–244, 270–275; kingdom of, 72–73, 116; Mingaung I of, 96, 141; Narapati I of, 83; period, 16, 48; the Pyū at, 175; the Rmeñ at, 243; second dynasty and period of, 137, 142, 186–187, 261–263, 284–285; Wun Zin Min Yaza of, 89
Avalokiteśvara, 31
Ayetthèma, 63, 70
Ayudhyā, 87–88, 131–137, 279, 311–313
Ayuthaya, chronicles of, 58

Bago. *See* Pegu
Bannya Dala, 94, 100, 134, 137, 141, 148, 312
Bassein, 57, 60, 83, 89, 195, 267
Bawbawgyi, 31, 168, 220, 223, 233
Bayinnaung, 74, 94–97, 133–134, 136, 138, 144, 150, 256, 279, 312
Bèbè, 31, 208, 219, 225
Beikthano, 18, 22, 27, 29–31, 36, 169, 302, 309
Bhallika, 71–73, 77, 95, 99, 101, 285
Binnaka, 18–19, 22, 25–28, 30, 224–225, 239
Bodawpaya, 98, 110, 114, 141–142, 183, 194, 199, 235
Bodhgayā, 158, 171, 185–187, 190–191, 195
Brāhmī, 22–23, 35–36, 169–172
Brahmā, 32
Buddhaghosa, 33, 116–117, 251, 254
Buddhism: as allegory, 87–88; Aniruddha's introduction and reform of, 117; Hīnayāna, 284; introduction to Southeast Asia, 1, 68, 131, 152; and King Kyanzittha, 236–259; under King Mindon, 46; Mahāyāna, 31, 247; modern scholars of, 297; and the Pyū, 23–33; Śrī Laṅkan, 96, 206, 314; Tantric, 247–249
Buddhist Council, 1, 69, 74–75, 117, 147, 151, 285
Burman: anglicized term for Mranmā, 44; culture, 88, 103, 150, 177, 179, 207, 220; people, 2, 3, 11, 77, 86, 172, 200; and the Pyū, 39–40, 175–177, 221; relations with the Mon, 3, 33–34, 40, 103, 218, 259, 262, 266, 292, 314, 315
Burmese speakers: domination of Burma by, 22, 34, 60–65, 174–175, 244, 261, 305–319; and Indic culture, 37–38; and Mon speakers, 41, 58, 243, 278; at Pagán, 31, 37, 40, 112, 151, 157, 195, 238, 242; and the Pyū, 9–21, 26–28, 35–39, 85, 175–177

Cāmadevī, 125, 128–131
Cāmadevīvaṃsa, 56, 90–93, 127
cakkavattī, 1, 144, 237, 279, 315
Cambodian, 45, 125, 129, 246, 268
Canāśapura, 162
Ceylon, 29, 51, 68, 71, 73, 123, 257, 294, 296
Ceylonese, 31, 33, 35, 69, 259
Cham, 91, 112
Champa, 26, 76, 320
Chau-Ju-Kua, 55
Chiang Mai, 56, 74, 125, 128, 136–137, 152, 312
Chindwin River, 42, 240
Coḷa, 49, 88, 257–258
colonial: period and rule, 117, 147, 214, 274, 287, 320; scholarship, scholars, and officials, 2–13, 74–77, 102–115, 141–150, 261–169, 272–274, 278–288, 297–320

Cūḷasakarāj, 35, 186
Cūḷavaṃsa, 51–52, 100, 121, 257–258
Cult of the 37 Nats, 2, 34, 303

Dagôn, 60, 135, 140
Dala, 61, 307
Daway, 135
de Brito, 99, 133, 138
devanāgarī, 28, 112
Dhammavijaya, 151
Dhammazedi: and the chronicles, 87–94, 140; as great reformer, 115–117, 142, 151, 219, 259; King of Pegu, 1, 67, 121, 275, 311; and the Legend that was Lower Burma, 2, 42, 46, 69–77, 99–100, 130, 282, 311; and the Mucalinda Inscription, 60
Dhātuvaṃsa, 270
Dīpavaṃsa, 51, 69–70, 87, 121–122, 138, 152, 219
Disāpramok, 121
Du'wop, 61
Dvāravatī: and Burma culture, 10, 26, 39, 82, 153, 166, 175, 217–218; history of, 299, 303; "home" of the Mon, 102, 176; "kingdom" of, 3, 296, 306, 320; study of, 307; writing system of, 156, 160–161, 163–170, 178, 298
Dwattabaung, 24, 139

East Zegu, 31, 209, 219, 225

Gavaṁpati, 2, 84–86, 100–102, 135, 140, 145–146, 149, 287, 303
Gotama, 36, 219, 248

Halin, 19–25, 27, 33, 35, 169, 178
Haṁsavatī, 49, 57, 74, 76, 80, 90–92, 308
Hanthawaddy, 48, 134, 315. *See also* Haṁsavatī
Haripuñjaya: conquest of, 307; epidemic at, 128; founding of, 125, 131; "kingdom" of, 3, 56, 82, 90, 130, 159, 198; Old Mon inscriptions of, 164–166; Pagán script at, 166, 197–198; as Rammanṇa, 128
Hīnayāna, 33, 284
Hmannan, 101, 144–145, 240, 293
Hmawbi, 61
Hsüan-tsang, 53–54, 89

Ibn al Fakih, 50
Ibn Battutah, 50
Ibn Khordazbeh, 50
India: under Aśoka, 72, 77, 129, 248, 285; under Buddhism, 1, 73, 101, 134; cultural influences from, 30–31, 99, 232, 297, 303; Old Burmese inscriptions in, 192, 195; Red-Polished Ware of, 29; scripts derived from, 33, 36, 157, 163, 166, 291; Telegu people of, 14
Indra, 35, 79, 98, 138
ita lerm, 265, 270–274, 278
ita luim, 265, 272, 274
I-tsing, 53, 89

Jambudīpa, 123, 138
Jātaka, 82, 197, 216, 219, 236, 250, 253–254
Javanese, 14, 44–45, 74, 87–88
Jinakālamālī: as allegory, 131–132; and the conquest of Thatôn narrative, 126–129, 138, 147, 149

Kakusandha, 36
Kalyani Inscriptions: date of, 1, 68, 94; discovery of, 75, 282, 285–286; and King Aniruddha, 115, 151; Lower Burma place-names in, 267; regarding *rāmañña,* Rāmaññadesa, *rman,* Sudhuim, and Suvaṇṇabhūmi, 46, 48, 51, 56, 65, 68–76, 83, 318
Kalyani Sima, 68
Kāñcipuram, 155
Kassapa, 36, 63
Kawgun Cave, 32, 61
Khăbin, 61
Khmers, 111, 246
Koṇāgamana, 36

Kônbaung, 123, 144, 313
Krapañ, 61
K'un-lun, 29
Kusim. *See* Kusumīya
Kusumīya, 89
Kyaik Talan, 159
Kyaik Tè, 64, 158
Kyāk Bār, 61
Kyāk Talañ, 61, 63, 192
Kyanzittha: accession of, 196, 259; Alaungsithu, successor of, 304; art during reign of, 248–249; birthplace of, 237–242, 247; champion of Mon culture, 2, 85, 237–238; in the chronicles, 236–237; conquest of Lower Burma, 49, 65, 112, 125, 246, 304; death of, 244; epigraphic evidence concerning, 241; first inscription of, 32; as general of Aniruddha, 246; governors under, 195; grandfather of Alaungsithu, 214; historiography of, 236; as Htilaing Shin, 191, 240–241; image of, 247; king of Pagan, 2, 123, 236–256, 318; legend of, 61, 63–64, 85, 123, 249, 255; modern legend of, 11, 234–260; Old Burmese inscriptions of, 246, 275; Old Mon inscriptions of, 47, 84, 86, 161, 163, 165, 187, 198, 243–246; Old Mon language of, 199–200, 237, 244–246; and orthodoxy, 236, 247–256; primate of, 190, 247; as Rājakumār's father, 180; reign of, 32, 41, 83, 190, 195, 199, 244–245, 298; rift with Aniruddha, 237, 241–242, 248, 256, 259; as son of Aniruddha, 241–242; as successor of Aniruddha, 185; temples built by, 214, 254–256; temples repaired by, 63; unifier of Pagan, 131
Kyauksé, 18, 22, 27, 237, 239, 259
Kyaung Phyu, 38, 159, 176, 185
kywan-tō, 40

Lakṣmī, 31
Lémyethna, 31, 219
Léymyethna, 208, 225, 230, 235
Lin-yang, 52, 53
Lokahteikpan, 193–195, 208, 211, 219, 233, 294

Magadu, 73, 95–96, 98, 108, 130–131, 134, 307
Mahābodhi, 159, 185–193, 198
Mahāmuni, 183
Mahānagara, 126–129
Mahāsamatta, 139
Mahāvagga, 33
Mahāvaṃsa, 51, 69–70, 121, 122, 124, 138, 146, 150, 152, 219, 235
Mahāvihāra, 2, 68, 74, 115–117, 125, 138, 248, 258
Mahāyāna, 31, 117, 204, 248–250
Mahayazawingyi, 1, 10, 56, 74, 97–98, 133, 136–138, 277, 283–286
Mahayazawinthit, 134
Maitreya, 2, 33–34, 151, 303
Majapahit, 87, 278
Makuta, 4, 106–109
Malacca, 87, 311
Malay, 26, 87
Man Shu, 19–21, 25, 36, 37, 40, 54–55
Mandalay, 19, 23, 35, 81, 141, 146–147
Maniyadanabon, 124, 141–143
Manohāra, 126, 128–132, 149, 152
Manuhā, 290
Manuha: in the chronicles, 136, 140; and the Kalyani Inscriptions, 115–117; legendary king of Thatôn 2, 84–85, 93, 117, 149, 151, 245, 271; as Makuta, 106–108; as Sūriyakumā, 100, 102; as a trope, 126, 148
Mergui, 60, 65, 83, 112, 195
Mi-ch'ên, 19–21, 55
Min Yaza, 56, 89, 123, 141, 143
Minbu, 18, 22, 40, 195
Mindon, 28, 74, 141–146
Mi-no, 19–21
Mirmā, 45. *See also* Mranmā
Mongmao, 18–19, 22–23, 25–27, 30–31, 81, 239

Mopī, 61
Mranmā, 4, 44–45, 268
Muttama, 30, 43, 54, 60, 74, 80, 83, 87–88, 95–97, 99, 130
Myanmā, 122, 143, 268–269, 276
Myanma Yazawinthit, 97, 142–143, 268
Myanmar, 16, 202
Myazedi: inscriptions, 12, 36–37, 160–179, 184–198, 207–291; Temple, 231

Nagarjunakonda, 14, 25, 31, 169
Nakhon Pathom, 169
Nakhon Sri Thammarat, 57–58
Nanchao kingdom, 7, 20, 175
Narapatisithu, 47, 58, 65, 83, 95–96, 115–116, 131, 183
nats, 138
nibbāna, 243
Nidāna, 93–95, 97, 99, 102, 110, 133, 136, 148–149, 286
Nidāna Árambhakathā, 93, 133, 149. See also *Nidāna*
Nigrodha, 138–139
nirvana, 34
Nyah Kur, 163, 167

Pagán: arch, origins of, 217–219; architects of, 217, 219; architectural history, 202; architecture of, 10–11, 23, 25, 30–31, 34, 219, 233; Aris of, 87; art history, 202; art of, 216; arts and crafts vocabulary of, 221–222; Buddhism at, 31; Burmese language at, 170–171; Burmese speakers at, 31, 112; city of, 39, 72, 81, 85, 93, 117, 124, 128, 176, 217; city walls of, 91–92; civilization of, 2, 86, 89, 154, 157, 217, 222; court, 159; craftsmen of, 221; culture of, 18, 37–38, 40, 42, 103; decline of, 11, 55, 91–92, 131; development of, 9, 12, 14, 80; director of archaeology, 203; dynasty of, 13, 38–39, 56, 91, 102, 121, 144, 185, 196; early temple style, 223; education at, 196; foundations of, 26; founding of, 22, 122; gates of, 122; genesis of, 14; golden age, 2; historiography, 11, 201–202; history of, 2, 192, 199; hollow temples of, 219, 230; inscriptions of, 34, 35, 37, 44, 47, 75, 83, 96, 105, 111, 186–187; irrigation at, 27; kingdom of, 9, 11, 13, 39–41, 47, 58, 65, 67, 154, 179, 186, 191; kings of, 122–123, 164; Kyanzittha of, 15, 32; language at, 112, 135, 165, 172–174, 178; language usage at, 109, 113; lecture on, 106; millennium before, 12–13, 15; Mon culture in, 41; "Mon period" at, 11; monarchy of, 39; Narapatisithu of, 58, 95, 96; Old Burmese at, 176, 197; Old Mon language at, 164–165; Old Mon script at, 165–166, 198; Old Mon speakers at, 165; origins of, 10, 34, 46, 122; orthodoxy of, 2; orthography, 160; pentagonal temples at, 229–230; period, 3, 27, 46, 58, 123, 143, 157, 175, 206; period architecture, 10; period site, 11; Pyu at, 16; rainfall at, 218; records, 159; recumbent image at, 132; religious buildings at, 217; rise of, 12; royal donations of, 83; royal titles at, 110; scholars, 202–204, 207; script, 10, 35, 60–61, 83, 155–156, 158, 161–165, 178–199; settlement at, 185, 217; settlement of Lower Burma, 112; site of, 202, 221; society at, 159, 176; studies of, 203, 208; temple chronology of, 206; temple dates and donors, 207; temple evolution, 202–208, 215, 222; temple style at, 218–219; temples of, 109, 202–203, 216; term for, 93; tourist guides at, 132; troops of, 96, 167; tutelary deity of, 85; vaulting at, 218–219; Viṣṇu at, 32; votive tablets of, 195; word, 91, 111; works on, 201–202; writing

system of, 110, 166, 169–171, 176, 201; written Burmese at, 179–180
Paikū. *See* Pegu
Paññasāmī, 145, 147
Parākramabāhu, 49, 51, 99, 115–116, 151, 204
Pareimma, 240
Parinirvāṇa, 113–114
Pathein, 60. *See also* Bassein
Payamā, 29, 31, 220, 223, 233
Paykū. *See* Ussā Paikū
Pegu: city of, 33, 68, 92, 134, 169; destruction of, 95, 99, 312; dynasty/kingdom of 1, 83, 94, 107–108, 197; as Haṁsavatī, 49, 74, 80, 308; in legend, 29, 85, 94, 98–101, 117, 148; as Mon center, 48, 67, 74, 83, 96, 102, 307, 311; origins of, 29, 92, 97; as place-name, 29, 57, 60, 194; Project, 263–266, 282, 284; as regional center, 27, 73, 88, 137, 310, 312–314; as Ussā or Ukkala, 47, 71, 246
P'iao, 14–15, 20–21, 26, 28–29, 36, 44, 54, 175
Pinya, 121–123, 234, 310
Poḷonnaruva, 49
Prāsāt Mahādhāt Satih, 61, 64
Prome, 16, 168, 170, 179, 191–198, 204, 218, 246, 254, 317
Pugaṁ, 122
purā kywan, 40
Pusiṁ. *See* Bassein
Pyū: alphabet, 173; artifacts, 19, 23, 25, 28, 30, 32; Buddhism, 30; carpenter, 37; cities, 18–19, 21, 23, 25, 28–29, 35, 37, 40, 53, 81; city walls, 25; civilization, 289; coins, 24, 28; conceptual system, 30, 32; concubine, 37; connection to Burmese writing system, 167; culture, 14, 16, 18, 26, 27, 30–42, 155, 169, 222, 224, 233; dancers, 29; decline of, 27, 36, 58, 131; designs on coins, 24; dominance, 39; domination, 39; Era, 35; fingermarked bricks, 81; firewood dealer, 37; funerary practices, 30; heartland, 27; historical pattern, 27; history, 35, 40; iconography, 31, 222; inscriptions, 34, 36, 168–169; king, 39; kingdom, 24, 30, 37, 42, 175; language, 16, 23, 34, 36, 175, 178, 222; linguistic affinity to Burmese, 171, 172; millennium, 206; musical troupe, 54; paleography, 170; people, 3, 4, 13, 15, 27, 30, 155, 157, 175, 248; period, 14, 18, 22, 26, 34, 40–41, 65, 92; polity, 15–16, 20, 25, 40; population, 39; region, 39, 246; rice lands, 37; script, 32–33, 35–36, 154, 157, 160–162, 168–176, 200; sculpture, 32; singers, 44; sites, 18–19, 24, 27, 35, 65, 70, 169, 221, 224; society, 37; spouse, 37; state, 27, 41, 67; temple style, 208, 214; toddy palms, 37; tradition, 230; village, 37; vocabulary, 171, 220; word, 13–15, 18

Rājakumār, 173, 179, 180
Rakṣapura, 4, 60, 86–88, 108
Rāma Gāṁheṅ, 61, 92, 308
Rāmādhipati, 67
Rāmañña, 2, 46, 48–49, 51, 54, 57, 72, 74, 127–129, 257, 286
Rāmaññadesa: in Chinese sources, 26, 52–56; and the "Classical States of Southeast Asia," 320; in epigraphy, 9, 44, 47–50, 58–61, 64; etymology of, 44–46, 68; as historic kingdom, 9, 12, 92, 131, 300, 308–312; and "Indianization," 303–304; as legend, 1, 2, 7, 9, 42, 73, 75, 78, 103, 145, 260, 282; as Mon center, 10, 279; origins and development of, 42, 67, 304–307; in regional chronicles, 50–51, 56–58; as Suvaṇṇabhūmi, 282–286
Ratanapañña Thera, 92, 125, 151
Rman, 44, 48, 275, 318

Rmeñ, 7, 44–48, 54–55, 244, 246–247, 269, 306
Roṅmla, 61

Sadhuim, 7, 290
Sagaing, 122, 195, 223, 310
Sakrā, 24, 35
Śākyamuni, 64
Salween River, 61
Samala, 94–95, 97–101
saṅgha, 40, 68, 74, 115, 142, 145, 147, 184, 196, 258, 307, 308
Sanlyaṅ. *See* Syriam
Sanskrit, 29, 33, 49, 54, 79, 107–110, 159, 166, 172, 174, 220–222, 246
Sarvāstivāda, 33
sāsana, 115–116
Sāsana Council, 146
Sāsanavaṃsa, 74–75, 101, 145–147
Shin Arahan, 1, 117, 123, 136, 138–144, 247, 292, 296
Shin Saw Bu, 61, 67, 72, 83, 98–99, 131, 140, 148, 310, 312– 313, 319
Shwédagôn, 57, 71–77, 95, 141, 152, 233, 235, 293, 311
Sīhala, 125, 145
Śiva, 32, 82
Sūriyakumā, 84–85, 100, 110, 114, 117
Sūriyakumāra, 114, 129
Sôkkaté, 122
Soṇa and Uttara: and the Ceylonese Theravāda school, 33, 117, 146, 321; in the Kalyani Inscriptions, 70–71; in the *Mahāvaṃsa,* 69; and their mission to Suvaṇṇabhūmi, 68–69, 102, 152, 285; as part of the legend that was Lower Burma, 72–77, 85, 99, 101; and the Third Buddhist Council, 1, 117, 142, 151, 285
Śrī Bajrās, 191
Śrī Canāśa, 163
Śrī Kṣetra: archaeological evidence concerning, 25, 29–31, 34, 169; in Chinese sources, 25; in chronicles, 35; city of, 13, 19, 21, 24, 32, 37, 54, 85, 93; dynasty/kingdom of, 13, 24, 29, 32, 92, 129, 131, 302; and the Gavaṁpati legend, 85; Indic culture at, 31–32, 33–34, 221, 309; inscriptions found at, 30, 32, 35–36; kings of, 122, 129, 131; as a major Pyū center, 27, 33, 54, 81, 93, 129 and its script, 22, 154–156, 160–177; temples at, 207–220, 222–232
Śrī Laṅka: Buddhist texts of, 99, 150, 203, 250, 303; and Burma's Buddhist tradition, 68, 96, 102, 115, 125–126, 131, 147, 150, 152, 218; inscriptions of, 49; kings of, 115–122, 124, 131; literature of, 51, 121, 256, 273; and Rāmaññadesa, 57; relations with Burma, 256–257; temple styles of, 222, 232
Śrī Tribhuwanādityadhammarāja, 84
Śrī Vijaya, 26, 49, 87–88, 306, 312
Sudhamma, 79, 80, 88, 90–93, 127, 129, 152
Sukhodaya, 23, 74, 81, 96–97, 130–131, 307–309
Sulaymān, 50
Suvaṇṇabhūmi: in Buddhist literature, 42; in Burma's epigraphy, 68, 70, 75; in Chiang Mai, 74; in the domestic chronicles, 74–76, 140; as eastern India, 69, 76; in Java, 74; as the legendary "land of gold," 68; as Lower Burma's Rāmaññadesa, 1, 2, 68, 70, 72, 75, 85, 95, 145, 282–286; as maritime Southeast Asia, 76; in modern historiography, 75–76; and the Shan, 74
Syriam, 61

Tabinshwehti, 94, 312
T'ai, 3, 7, 46, 49, 61, 96–97, 130–131, 166, 261, 304, 308
Talaing: in Arabic sources, 275; in Chinese sources, 55, 274–275; in domestic sources, 57, 238, 275, 277; as a "downtrodden" people, 11, 260–268, 271–280, 286, 292,

315–316; etymology of, 47, 262–269, 270–274; as *Ita Lerm,* 271–278; as Mon, 155, 267, 271, 276; script, 157, 285, 292
Tamil: craftsmen, 214; inscription, 257; language, 89, 222; people, 306; Sangam Literature, 35; script, 155
Tamils, 164
Tanluiṅ, 47–48, 239, 246–247, 269, 271–272, 274, 275–277, 306, 318
Tāntrism, 248
Tanu-Phlū, 61
Tāvatiṁsa, 35, 138, 151
Tapussa, 71–73, 77, 95, 99, 101
Tavoy, 28, 60, 81, 83, 112, 135, 195, 318
Tayôk Pye Min, 121
Telegu: craftsmen, 214; influence, 14; Kannada script, 170; people, 14; script, 157; speakers, 15
Tenasserim, 47, 49, 58, 65, 83, 88, 111, 112, 195, 283, 304
Thailand: Buddhist Era of, 179; chronicles of, 56; country of, 23, 26, 56, 76; Gulf/Bay of, 53, 304, 312; kingdom of, 98; spread of Ceylonese Buddhism in, 125–126; central plains of, 131, 162, 303; Mon center in, 148; Mon chronicles published in, 275–287; Mon inscriptions of, 161–162, 303; Mon speakers of, 89, 165; Mon text from, 98; Sukhodaya of, 81, 309
Thalun, 138, 142, 223
Thatôn: architecture at, 216; as center of the Mon, 91, 95, 98, 101, 103, 199, 217, 304, 311; chronicle of, 134, 137; city of, 6, 9, 47, 58, 60, 67, 70, 79–90, 92, 94, 112, 114, 129, 144; conquest of, 1, 2, 9–10, 34, 74, 87, 91, 103–153, 154–159, 271, 278–279, 284, 297–298, 304; as "country of the Talaing", 56; decay of, 143; deity of, 86; dynasty of, 70, 85; historicity of, 9, 88–89, 92, 119; historiography of, 103, 110, 115, 134, 140, 145, 159–160, 215, 278, 296; history of, 93–94, 97, 102, 148; iconography at, 217; inscriptions of, 86, 159, 161, 165, 198; king of, 85, 100, 105, 110, 117, 192, 290; kingdom of, 245; language of, 164; legend of, 82; Manuha, king of, 74; mythology of, 89, 97, 99, 109, 159–160; name, 81; as national tragedy, 102; origins stories of, 94, 97, 100–101, 134; pagodas at, 215; plan of, 81; region of, 32, 63, 67, 74, 97, 108, 159, 216; remains of, 81; script of, 159, 161; site of, 42, 80, 82–83, 86–88, 94, 102–103, 112, 194, 216; as Sudhamma, 88; as Sudhammapura, 47, 145; as Sudhuim, 64, 79, 87, 114; texts from, 207; tradition of, 74, 117, 151, 299, 311; use of the arch at, 216; word, 79–80, 87–88, 93, 290
Theravāda Buddhism: and the "Crisis of the Thirteenth Century," 308–309; and early Southeast Asian history, 299, 308–310, 321; and its historiography in Burma, 152, 285–286; history of, 248; and King Aniruddha, 1, 236; and King Kyanzittha, 248–255, 259; in Lower Burma, 140; and "orthodoxy," 115, 131, 147, 295–296; among the Pyū, 15, 32–33; and supernaturalism, 248; and temple style, 203–222
Theravāda Buddhist: center, 88; commoner, 309; countries, 147, 150; culture, 2, 12; formula, 32; heaven, 151; iconography, 31; influence, 295, 299; king, 150; kingdom, 83, 89, 91; orthodoxy, 11, 75, 152; polity, 42, 44; state, 73, 248, 300, 309; texts, 82, 206, 260; theme, 126; tradition, 150; world, 146
Theravāda Buddhists, 1, 68, 84, 146
Thilawuntha, 56, 124, 125
Thūpavaṃsa, 251
Tipiṭakas, 2, 126, 143, 146, 151, 203, 257–259, 287, 296, 299, 303

Tircul, 14, 15, 44–45, 269
Trāp and Paṇḍit Inscriptions, 86, 105–108, 159
Twanté, 111, 195
Twinthin, 97, 99, 101, 142–144, 151, 268–269, 275, 277

U Kala: chronicle written by, 1, 56, 97, 133–136, 143–144, 283; and the conquest of Thatôn narrative, 2, 10, 99, 136, 142, 150–153, 284–286; and Lower Burma as Suvaṇṇabhūmi, 74–75, 144; parents of, 136; political context of, 138; as private historian, 1; sources used by, 136–138, 144
Upagupta, 2, 33, 115, 297, 303
upasampadā, 73, 116, 125, 257
Ussā Paikū, 48, 111, 317
Ussāla, 47, 95, 247, 265, 276
Uttara. *See* Soṇ and Uttara

Vesāli, 81
Vijayabāhu, 116, 131, 146, 152, 219, 257, 258
Vinaya, 32–33, 71, 170, 219
Viṣṇu, 18, 31–32, 61, 63–64, 82, 243, 250

Wimala, 85, 94–95, 97–101
Winga, 30, 42, 82, 198

Yang-chü-mieh, 26
Yangôn, 33, 57, 60, 65, 75, 140, 170, 233, 307
Yazadarit, 83, 88, 96, 107–108, 134–136, 141, 311, 313–314
Yazadarit Ayedawpon, 94–97, 99, 133–135, 137, 140, 149, 279, 312, 314
Yazawinkyaw, 124–125, 145
Yüan, 55, 275
Yunnan, 7, 20, 38, 45, 55

Zatatawpon Yazawin, 24, 38, 56, 90, 121–124, 186, 241, 268, 275
Zimme Yazawin, 57, 137

About the Author

Born and raised in Burma, MICHAEL AUNG-THWIN attended high school in South India before pursuing undergraduate and graduate studies in the United States. He received a Ph.D. from the University of Michigan, Ann Arbor, in 1976. He is presently professor of Asian studies at the University of Hawai'i at Mānoa. Over the last decade his research has taken him to England, Sri Lanka, and Thailand, and he has made annual trips to Myanmar. He is the author of *Myth and History in the Historiography of Early Burma: Paradigms, Primary Sources, and Prejudices* (1998) and *Pagan: The Origins of Modern Burma* (1985).

HAWAI'I

Production Notes for
Aung-Thwin / THE MISTS OF RĀMAÑÑA

Cover and interior designed by University of Hawai'i Press production staff with text set in New Baskerville and display in Esprit

Composition by Josie Herr

Printing and binding by The Maple-Vail Book Manufacturing Group

Printed on 60# Sebago Eggshell, 420 ppi